A
DICTIONARY
OF
BALLET

G. B. L. Wilson

★

A
DICTIONARY
OF
BALLET

THIRD EDITION

WITH EIGHT PAGES OF PHOTOGRAPHS
AND TWENTY LINE DRAWINGS

THEATRE ARTS BOOKS
New York

Third edition, revised, enlarged and entirely re-set, 1974
Theatre Arts Books
333 Sixth Avenue, New York 10014
First published 1957 by Penguin Books
Second edition 1961 by Cassell & Co

ISBN 0-87830-039-2

Library of Congress Catalog Card No. 73-88212

Printed in Great Britain by
Hazell Watson & Viney Ltd
Aylesbury, Bucks

Dedicated to
Beryl Grey and Arnold Haskell
who encouraged me and first opened the doors for me

Illustrations

vi

LINE DRAWINGS

The line drawings by Peter Revitt illustrate the entries on Arabesque (p. 21), Attitude (p. 28), Cou-de-pied (p. 129), Croisé (p. 133), Dégagé (p. 152), Directions (p. 164), Écarté (p. 175), Effacé (p. 178), Five Positions (p. 203), Hands (p. 244), Mime (p. 336), Pointe (p. 395) and Seconde (p. 448). There are several examples of dance notation within the entry under that heading (pp. 141–143).

Abbreviations

Am.	American	Ind.	Indian
app.	appeared	It.	Italian
arr.	arranged	l.	left
Ass.	Association	lit.	literally
Austral.	Australian	m.	music
B.	Ballet	mar.	married
b.	born	Met. Op.	Metropolitan Opera House
bibl.	bibliography		
c.	*circa* (about)	Mus.	Museum
Canad.	Canadian	Nat.	National
cent.	century	N.Y.	New York
C. Garden	Royal Opera House, Covent Garden	opp.	opposite
		Orig.	Original
ch.	choreography	pf.	pianoforte
Ch. Élysées	Champs Élysées	Prof.	Professor
chor.	choreographer, choreographed	q.v.	*quod vide* (which see)
		r.	right
Co.	Company	R.	Royal
Col.	College	R.A.D.	Royal Academy of Dancing
comp.	composed		
cont.	contemporary	R.S.F.S.R.	Russian Socialist Federated Soviet Republic
cost.	costumes		
cr.	created		
d.	died	Russ.	Russian
Dan.	Danish	sc.	scene
dec.	décor	Sch.	School
educ.	educated	schol.	scholarship
Eng.	English	Soc.	Society
fl.	*floruit* (flourished)	Sp.	Spanish
f.p.	first produced	Swed.	Swedish
Fr.	French	S. Wells	Sadler's Wells
Ger.	German	Th.	Theatre
Gr.	Greek	Univ.	University
Hon.	Honorary	U.S.	United States of America
illus.	illustration.		
Imp.	Imperial	vid. inf.	*vide infra* (see below)
incl.	including	vid. sup.	*vide supra* (see above)

Preface to the Third Edition

In 1957 the Penguin Press published my *Dictionary of Ballet* as a paperback and in 1960, after I had made a number of corrections and additions, it was translated into Italian and published by U. Mursia and Co. in Milan. It was rewritten and considerably enlarged for Cassells, who published it as a hardback book in 1961—the first time a paperback book had subsequently appeared as a hardback volume. After that edition had been unavailable for a number of years, A. & C. Black, who in the 1950s had published a number of important books on ballet (thanks to the initiative of their late director Cyril Swinson and of Arnold Haskell), offered to publish this new edition of *A Dictionary of Ballet* on which I had been working for several years.

This time I have cast my net much wider than before into an art which in the previous decade has enormously increased in its styles, its variety and in its participants and audiences. Whereas before one had thought of ballet as a compact, esoteric art confined to a comparatively few opera houses throughout the world, one now sees it as a much more diverse entertainment which can best be described in the form of a simile. I picture it as a large country house with a long continuous history. The earliest part, like a château in style, is built by French architects in the seventeenth century. At the beginning of the nineteenth century a large mock-Gothic wing is added and the furniture (the ballets) change from classical to romantic pieces. Russian princes, employing foreign architects, embellish it at the end of the nineteenth century, and in the twentieth century English and American architects renovate it and erect a new façade.

This Dictionary is a guide to this rambling edifice. As the reader passes through the corridors, it can tell him about the rooms and their previous inhabitants—and, indeed, of its present occupants in even more detail, for a new book is most valued for its new facts. However, if this were all, the book might still convey the impression that this was nothing more than an historic monument. So to breathe life into the scene I have occasionally left the drugget and stepped over the velvet cord—and opened some of the doors and cupboards. Then the reader can look into the living quarters of these artist-inhabitants and learn something of how they live, their schools, their teachers, their talk and also about those who give them immortality—their writers, their delineators and their critics. If the reader detects what appears to him to be an occasional flippancy, he should recall the entry 'σῦκοφάντης' in that most austere of all dictionaries, Liddell and Scott's *Greek-English Lexicon*, and remember the pleasure it gave him during his construes.

Standing in the grounds of this conglomeration of buildings is also a new construction, still unfinished and without a roof. It is the Modern Dance and it is so diverse that it is shapeless, yet with occasional angles of beauty which light up and relieve a general prospect of ugliness and despair. It is typical of the world today, perhaps, and this Dictionary guides the reader up to it, but without attempting completeness in a subject which is itself so incomplete and uncertain of its destination.

The entries in this work are, then, chiefly concerned with the Classical Ballet, the ballet of the Opera House, but touch also on the Modern Dance, Spanish and Indian Dancing, and the other entertainments which a serious lover of the dance is likely to encounter in the course of his ballet-going or his reading and writing.

I have attempted to describe in simple words the various steps and technical terms of the *danse d'école*. Of the contemporary dancers mentioned, most will be found to be the soloists and leading dancers of the ballet companies existing at the moment, as listed in their programmes. I have included a few of the many writers on the dance, and some teachers, but I am conscious that the list is very incomplete and I hope that those whom I have omitted will forgive me.

The ballets chosen are chiefly those of special or historical interest, or are to be found in the recent or present-day repertoires. The only composers and designers I have included are those who appear to have made a special contribution to the art of ballet.

In listing the ballets, a system has been followed which gives first the choreographer, then the composer, and then the artist responsible for the décor (which includes the costumes unless otherwise stated). The name of the company first producing the ballet is then given, with the theatre and date of first performance. In brackets are given the names of the chief dancers on that occasion.

In the spelling of Russian names I have not been consistent: I have used the spelling which is already most familiar in this country.

Cross-references are not specifically indicated except by an occasional 'q.v.'. For the most part, all words, names and titles (of a ballet connotation, of course) will be found elsewhere in the book under their own entries.

Every country must produce its own distinctive reference book even though each is dealing with a world-wide art. Chujoy's and Manchester's *Dance Encyclopedia* (New York 1967) gave a vivid picture of the American scene, Suriz's *Vse o Balete* (Moscow-Leningrad 1966) concentrated largely on ballet behind the Iron Curtain, whilst Horst Koegler's *Ballettlexikon*, which he has been writing at exactly the same time as I have been engaged on this book, gives a remarkably complete picture of ballet in Germany. That is as it should be, and this *Dictionary of Ballet*, while attempting to cover ballet throughout the world, is most sharply focused on the English-speaking nations.

In compiling the Dictionary I have drawn on all sources available to me, and as well as the books mentioned above, the *Enciclopedia dello Spettacolo* (Rome 1954–66) and Natalia Roslavleva's scholarly *Era of the Russian Ballet* (London 1966) have been extremely valuable. Especially important have been the journals *The Dancing Times* and *Dance and Dancers* of London, the American *Dance News* and *Dance Magazine* and Friedrich's annual *Ballett* (edited by Horst Koegler).

For French affairs I am indebted to Marie-Françoise Christout and to Martine Kahane, Keeper of the Paris Opéra Library and Museum. For the Scandinavian entries Anna Greta Ståhle has been my guide and for ballet in Italy, Freda Pitt. Jennie Walton, Rosemary Winckley and Natalia Roslavleva kept me in touch with the Russian scene. My correspondent in Austria has been Christl Himmelbauer and in the United States Miss P. W. Manchester. Dame Peggy van Praagh has helped me with the Australian ballet, and Dulcie Howes and Marjorie Sturman with South Africa. Metin And helped me with Turkey, and Gedeon Dienes and Geza Körtvélyes with Hungary.

I owe a great debt to Mary Clarke and Friderica Derra de Moroda, both of whom read through my manuscript and gave me advice, and I spent several days in the latter's vast library in Salzburg. My greatest single helper throughout has been my friend Ivor Guest, who eagerly put at my disposal all his researches on the history of ballet, on which he is without peer. The Press Officers of The Royal Ballet (Sheila Porter), Festival Ballet (Vivian Wallace) and Ballet Rambert (Valerie Bourne) fed me with all the information I asked for, and on matters of technique I have had the benefit of the advice of Anna Northcote, Audrey Harman and Edward Espinosa.

For assistance in assembling and typing the entries I have had an army of volunteers and I am especially grateful to Maria Calderon, Selina Molteno, Anne Carter and Ann Nugent for their sterling work in my house.

There must be omissions in the text of the Dictionary—some through lack of space and some from unintentional oversights on my part. There are doubtless errors also, and I should be glad to be told of these so that they can be put right in later editions.

Kew Gardens,   *G. B. L. Wilson*
Surrey

A

ABRAXAS, ballet, ch. Luipart, m. Werner Egk, dec. Znamenacek, f.p. Prinzregenten Th., Munich 6 June 1948 (Luipart, Solange Schwarz, Kladivova, Nilanova-Sanftleben). Ballet based on Heine's poem *Doktor Faustus* whose score has been used by many chors., notably by Charrat (Berlin Städtische Oper, 8 Oct 1949, Charrat, Gabor Orban.).

ABSOLUTE BALLET, or ABSTRACT BALLET, a composition of abstract or pure dance-movement, untrammelled by a plot or association of ideas. There is no more reason why ballet has to be programmatic than music. Examples of absolute ballets are Ashton's *Symphonic Variations* and Balanchine's *Concerto Barocco* and *Agon*.

ABSTRACT DANCE, dance form originating in the work of the German painter, Oskar Schlemmer (q.v.), at the Bauhaus, Weimar, in the mid-1920s, in which the danced movement was entirely subordinated to the geometrical figures and planes created by the costumes in colours and varying textures.

ABYSS, THE, ballet, ch. Stuart Hodes, m. Richter, cost. Delfau, f.p. Harkness B., Casino, Cannes 21 Feb 1965 (Lone Isaksen, Bruhn). The rape of a girl, and her saviour.

ACADEMIC BALLET, see CLASSICAL BALLET.

ACADÉMIE ROYALE DE DANSE, L', was founded in Paris in 1661 by Louis XIV, on the advice of Cardinal Mazarin, with the object of re-establishing the art of dance in its perfection. It consisted of a council of thirteen dancing-masters and met in a tavern L'Épée de Bois in the Rue de Venise (in preference to the room in the Louvre placed at its disposal). They were Galand du Désert (dancing master to the Queen), Prévost (dancing master to the King), Jean Renaut (dancing master to the Dauphin), Guillaume Raynal (dancing master to Monsieur, the King's brother), Guillaume Guéru, Hilaire d'Olivet, Bernard du Manthe, Jean Raynal, Nicolas de Lorges, Guillaume Renaut, Jean Picquet, Florent Galand du Désert and Jean de Grigny. The Académie codified the court dances and character dances. It was attacked by Noverre in his *Letters* and ceased to function in 1780. In 1856 an Académie Impériale de Danse was founded as a private institution but it was torn by intrigues and came to an end in 1861. No known records of its deliberations exist. The year 1661 can conveniently be taken to be the starting date of the art of ballet as we know it today.

ACADÉMIE ROYALE DE MUSIQUE, L', the name of the Paris Opéra from 1671. The Académie d'Opéra had been founded by the Abbé Perrin and

I

the Marquis de Sourdéac in 1669 and produced its first opera-ballet, *Pomone* (ch. Beauchamp, m. Cambert), in 1671 when it changed its name to the above. An earlier academy, l'Académie de Musique et de Poésie, founded by the poet de Baïf and the musician J. T. de Courville and granted a royal charter by Charles IX in 1570, disappeared in the political strife consequent on the massacre of St Bartholomew's Eve in 1572, but not before it had inspired the ideas which led to the *Ballet Comique de la Reine* (q.v.) of Beaujoyeux. According to the politics of the time, the Académie Royale has changed its name to Académie Nationale and Académie Impériale de Musique, and from 1871 it has been the Théâtre National de l'Opéra—see under PARIS OPÉRA BALLET.

ACROBATS OF GOD, ballet 1 act, ch. Martha Graham, m. Surinach, cost. Graham, dec. Noguchi. f.p. Martha Graham Dance Co., Adelphi Th. N.Y., 27 Apr 1960 (Graham, McGehee, Hodes, Winter, Paul Taylor, Bertram Ross). Has three mandoline players on stage. A celebration of the tribulations and glories of a dancer's world.

ACT, THE, ballet, ch. Linda Hodes, m. Page and Johnson, f.p. Batsheva Dance Company, Ohel-Shem Th., Tel-Aviv 19 Oct 1967. Taken into repertory of B. Rambert, Arts Th., Cambridge 15 July 1968 (Mac-Sween, Curtis, Bruce). A ventriloquist and his dummy (which takes over his act).

ADABACHE, Olga, b. St Petersburg 1918. Fr.-Russ. dancer. Pupil of Mme d'Alessandri. Danced with Nouveau B. de Monte Carlo 1947–48 and cr. rôle of *Salome* (ch. Lifar). In Cuevas B. 1952–62.

ADAGE or ADAGIO, It. *ad agio*, at ease. (1) A series of exercises executed to a slow tempo in the centre of the class-room to develop line and balance. (2) Name given to that part of the classical pas de deux in which the ballerina, supported by her partner, executes steps and achieves positions calculated to display her line and technique. The adagio is frequently the supreme moment in a classical ballet, and demands as much from the danseur as from the ballerina. (3) By extension, a dance sequence executed to slow tempo as contrasted with Allegro. (4) Adagio Dancers are frequently an ingredient of Music Hall or Cabaret. Their movements are usually acrobatic rather than classical.

ADAM, Adolphe C., b. Paris 1803, d. there 1856. Fr. operatic composer whose name is best known today because of the popularity of his ballet *Giselle*. He composed some thirty-nine operas and fourteen ballets including *Le Corsaire*, *La Fille du Danube*, *La Jolie Fille de Gand*, and *Le Diable à Quatre*. The area of London known as Swiss Cottage derives from the public house built and named after the success of his opera *Le Chalet* in London 1834.

ADAMA, Richard (Holt), b. Long Beach, Calif. 1928. Am. dancer and chor. Pupil of Nijinska 1946–48, Nora Kiss 1950–55, Georgia Hiden 1957–61. Joined Orig. B. Russe 1948, de Cuevas 1949–55 as soloist, Vienna Staatsoper 1955 becoming principal dancer 1957. To Hanover as assistant b. master 1961. Director of Ballet at Bremen 1963–68, mounting *La Sylphide* (m. Schneitzhoeffer) 1964, *Giselle* 1966 (using complete orig. score). Mounted Rameau's *Platée* for Gärtnerplatz Th., Munich 1969 and Gluck's *Don Juan* for Vienna Staatsoper 1969. Director of Hanover B. 1970–72.

'ADAME MIROIR, ballet 1 act. Book J. Genet, ch. Janine Charrat, m. Milhaud, dec. P. Delvaux, f.p. Ballets de Paris, Th. Marigny, Paris 31 May 1948 (Petit, Skouratoff, Perrault, Hamilton).

ADAMS, David, b. Winnipeg 1928. Canadian dancer. Pupil of Gweneth Lloyd, S. Wells Sch., and Volkova in London 1946–47. Danced with R. Winnipeg B. 1939–46, S. Wells Th. B. 1946–47, Metropolitan B. 1947–48, Canadian Nat. B. 1951–61. A principal dancer of Festival Ballet 1961–69. Has chor. several ballets. In 1970 joined Royal B. as soloist.

ADAMS, Diana, b. Staunton, Va. 1926. Am. dancer. Pupil of Emily Hadley, Caton, de Mille, and Tudor. First appeared in *Oklahoma!* 1943. Joined Ballet Theatre 1944 and N.Y. City Ballet 1950, becoming a principal. Cr. rôles in *Fall River Legend, Agon, Liebeslieder Walzer*. Danced in Gene Kelley's film *Invitation to the Dance* and Danny Kaye's film *Knock on Wood* 1954. Teaches at Sch. of Am. B. in N.Y.

ADAMS, Lawrence, b. Winnipeg 1936. Brother of David Adams. Canadian dancer. Studied under Volkoff and Betty Oliphant in Toronto and Mara McBirney in Vancouver. Entered Canad. Nat. B. 1956. Joined Les Grands B. Canadiens 1958–59, Robert Joffrey B. 1960–61 and re-joined Canad. Nat. B. 1963 as soloist.

ADAMS, Valerie, b. Bournemouth 1935. Eng. dancer and teacher. Pupil of Elizabeth Collins (Wessex Sch.) and S. Wells Sch. Joined S. Wells B. at C. Garden 1953. Joined teaching staff of S. Wells Sch. 1955. In 1956 to The Hague to found the ballet sch. at the Koninklijk Conservatorium voor Musik and was ballet principal until 1961. Re-joined Royal B. Sch. 1962, becoming assistant to Craftsman Course 1968 and director of Teachers Training Course 1971.

ADAM ZERO, ballet 1 act. Book Michael Benthall, ch. Helpmann, m. Bliss, dec. Furse, f.p. S. Wells B., C. Garden, London 10 Apr 1946 (Helpmann, June Brae, Gillian Lynne, Paltenghi). The life cycle of Man symbolized in the creation of a ballet.

ADDISON, Errol (Addison Smith), b. Heaton 1901. Eng. dancer and

3

teacher. Début at age of 4. Principal dancer *Prince Igor*, C. Garden 1918. Joined Diaghileff's Co. 1918. Danced in musicals 1923–47. Joined International B. 1947 as principal dancer. Taught at S. Wells Sch. 1954–62 and was ballet-master S. Wells Th. B. in 1955. Pupil of Cecchetti and took over his sch. in 1923 when his master left England. From 1963, teaches privately in London.

ADÉLAÏDE. (1) Dance to Ravel's *Valses Nobles et Sentimentales* and his libretto, ch. I. Clustine for Mlle Truhanova, f.p. Châtelet Th., Paris 22 Apr 1912. (2) Ballet to same score but Lifar's libretto, ch. Lifar, dec. Brianchon, f.p. Paris Opéra 21 Dec 1938 (Lifar, Chauviré, Darsonval).

ADIRKHAEVA, Svetlana, b. 1938. Russ. dancer. Trained in Leningrad. From 1955–60 soloist N. Ossetian Lyric Th., from 1960 soloist of Bolshoi B. Honoured Artist R.S.F.S.R.

ADRET, Françoise, b. Versailles 1920. Fr. dancer and chor. Pupil of Rousanne, Kiss, Lifar. Worked with Lifar in 1948, ballet-mistress Petit's Ballets de Paris. From 1951–58 ballet-mistress of Nederlands Opera, Amsterdam. Director of ballet at Nice 1960–65 (co. also danced in Lisbon). Chor. *Sleeping Beauty* in Zagreb, *Cinderella* in Johannesburg (1966), *Phèdre* in Warsaw (1967). Ballet mistress Bordeaux 1967–68. In 1969 appointed Director of the Ballet-Théâtre Contemporain at the Maison de la Culture, Amiens. Among her ballets are *Conjuration* (1948), *Billard* (1951), *La Porte Ouverte* (1956), *Les Amants de Meyerling* (1961).

AFTER EDEN, ballet, ch. John Butler, m. Lee Hoiby, dec. Carzou. f.p. Harkness B., Monte Carlo 15 Mar 1965 (Lawrence Rhodes, Lone Isaksen).

AFTERNOON OF A FAUN, ballet 1 act, ch. Robbins, m. Debussy, dec. J. Rosenthal, f.p. N.Y. City B., City Center, N.Y. 14 May 1953 (Le-Clerq, Moncion). A strange ballet of mood for two dancers, set in ballet studio. Also in the repertoire of Robbins' co., Ballets: U.S.A. (Curley, Norman) 1958, and of R. Danish B. Revived for Royal B. by Robbins, f.p. C. Garden 14 Dec 1971 (Sibley, Dowell). Also see *Après-midi d'un Faune, L'*.

AGE OF ANXIETY, ballet based on W. H. Auden's poem, ch. Robbins, m. Bernstein (2nd Symphony), dec. O. Smith, f.p. N.Y. City B., City Center, N.Y. 26 Feb 1950 (LeClerq, Bolender, Robbins, Moncion).

AGITANADO, in Sp. dancing, danced with a gypsy style or feeling.

AGLAË, ou L'ÉLÈVE DE L'AMOUR, ballet 1 act. Book and ch. Filippo Taglioni, m. Keller, f.p. St Petersburg 22 Jan 1841 for Marie Taglioni. This inspired Dolin's ballet *Romantic Age* (1942). Cupid, a young nymph (*l'élève de l'amour*), a faun, and a youth.

AGON, ballet, ch. Balanchine, m. Stravinsky, f.p. N.Y. City B., City Center, N.Y., 1 Dec 1957 (Diana Adams, Melissa Hayden, B. Walczak, B. Milberg, T. Bolender, R. Tobias, J. Watts, A. Mitchell, R. Lubell, F. Russell, Dido Sayers, R. Sobotka). Danced by Royal B., C. Garden, 25 Jan 1973 (Derman, Connor, Dowell, Wall). An abstract ballet, also chor. in many Continental opera houses by various chors. With ch. by MacMillan, dec. Georgiadis, f.p. Royal B., C. Garden, London, 20 Aug 1958 (Linden, Blair).

AGRIONIA, ballet, ch. Jack Carter, m. Salzedo, dec. and cost. Peter Farmer, f.p. London Dance Theatre, Theatre Royal, Newcastle, 22 June 1964 (Joyce Graeme, Yvonne Meyer, Kay Elise, McDowell, Etheridge). Three sisters who murder the eldest sister's son.

AHONEN, Leo, b. Viipuri 1939. Finnish dancer. Studied with the Kirov B. and the Scandinavian Sch. of B. Joined Finnish Nat. Opera B. 1954 and became a principal dancer. Toured Canada and America with Bolshoi group 1966 and became teacher of the Dutch National B. Joined R. Winnipeg B. 1966 as dancer and teacher. Re-joined Finnish B. 1967 as assistant ballet master. Joined San Francisco B. 1968, Houston B. 1972.

A.I.D., see ARCHIVES INTERNATIONALES.

AILES DE PIGEON, Fr. pigeon's wings, a difficult step in which the dancer leaps off one leg, throwing the other leg forward. The legs beat, change, and beat again, and the dancer lands on the leg he jumped from (also called Pistolet).

AILEY, Alvin, b. Rogers, Texas 1931. Am. mod. dancer and chor. Studied under Lester Horton and was a member of Lester Horton Dancers. Formed his own company, the Alvin Ailey Dance Theatre, in 1957, now considered to be the best modern Negro dance group. They danced in the Far East (1962) and toured Europe in 1964, visiting Paris and London (Shaftesbury Theatre). Returned to London 1965 and paid subsequent visits with success. Chor. *Mourning, Mourning* for Horton Dancers 1953. For Robt. Joffrey Ballet *Feast of Ashes* (1962), for Harkness Ballet *Ariadne* (1964) and *Macumba* (1966). Among his ballets for his own group are *Blues Suite* (1958), *Revelations* (1960), *Roots of the Blues* (1961), *Been Here and Gone* (1962). The repertoire of his group also includes Horton's *The Beloved* and Talley Beatty's *The Road of the Phoebe Snow* (1959). Among the dancers have been Joyce Trisler, Hope Clarke, Joan Peters, James Truitte, William Louther. Ailey also chor. the dances in Barber's opera *Antony and Cleopatra* which opened the new Metropolitan Opera at Lincoln Center, N.Y. 1966. His Co. danced at the Edinburgh Festival 1968, toured Russia with great success in 1970 and also had a triumphant season at S. Wells

Th. that year. Their dancers then included Judith Jamison, Dudley Williams, Miguel Godreau, Kelvin Rotardier. In 1972 the co. was renamed Alvin Ailey City Center Dance Co.

AIMEZ-VOUS BACH?, ballet, ch. B. Macdonald, m. Bach, cost. practice dress, f.p. Banff School Festival B., Banff Sch. of Fine Arts, Univ. of Alberta, Canada 6 Aug 1962 (Jennifer Penney, Stephanie Finch, John Stanzel). A classical class and rehearsal, subsequently 'jazzed up'. When this ballet was first given it was called *Pointe Counterpoint*, and also at the Banff Festival 1964. It was taken into the R. Winnipeg B. repertoire (and subsequently into companies all over the world) as *Aimez-vous Bach?*

AIR DE CARACTÈRE, in the Fr. Court B., a piece of music affected to the entry of a given character, e.g. entry of the beggars, of the winds, etc.

AIR, EN L', lit. 'in the air', is said of a movement in the air (e.g. a turn in the air or tour en l'air) and of the open position of the working leg raised off the ground, at 90° (position en l'air) or 45° (demi-position en l'air) to the supporting leg, to the front (fourth front), side (second position) or back (fourth back). Opposite, à terre.

AITKEN, Valerie, b. Dundee 1945. Scottish dancer. Pupil of Ebdon, P. Bedells, R. Ballet Sch. Joined Festival B. 1965 becoming soloist 1970.

ÅKESSON, Birgit, b. Malmö 1908. Swed. dancer and chor. with very personal modern style. Studied under Wigman and joined her group in Dresden 1931. Debut in Paris 1934 and toured Europe and America with her. Spent the War in Sweden and toured Europe and America again after it. Chor. her first ballet *Sisyphus* (q.v.) for R. Swed. B. 1957. Ch. *Rites* (1960), *Play for Eight* (1962), *Icaros* (1963). From 1963–66 she joined Tudor and Cullberg as joint artistic directors of R. Swedish B. Co-founder with Bengt Hager in 1964 of the Choreographic Institute, Stockholm. Headed the choreographic department until 1968, then took leave of absence to pursue dance studies in Africa.

AKYÜZ, Jale, b. Istanbul 1941. Turkish dancer. Studied under B. Appleyard and Molly Lake in Turkey and at Royal B. Sch. Entered Turkish State B. and became a principal dancer.

ALBAN, Jean-Pierre, b. Cairo 1932, d. London 1973. German dancer. Studied in Berlin and made debut at Berlin Opera. Danced in Charrat's Co. Joined Festival B. 1956 as soloist, becoming a principal.

ALBERT (François Decombe), b. Bordeaux 1789, d. Fontainebleau 1865. Fr. dancer and chor. Inspired by seeing Vestris dance at Bordeaux, he studied under Coulon. Joined Paris Opéra in 1803, premier danseur 1817, maître de ballet 1829. Created and danced in *La Jolie Fille de*

Gand (1842), also *Cinderella* (1822) and *Le Séducteur au Village* (1818). Ballet master at Her Majesty's Th. London in 1832 and later in Naples and Marseilles. He was a very handsome man and virile dancer.

ALBERTIERI, Luigi, b. Italy c. 1860, d. N.Y. 1930. It. ballet-master, dancer, and teacher. Foster-son of Cecchetti. Danced Moscow and Italy and appeared in Empire Ballets in London. Became ballet-master Chicago Opera 1910 and of Met. Op. N.Y. 1913. Author *The Art of Terpsichore* (1923). Also, from 1915, had his own school in N.Y.

ALBRECHT, Angèle, b. Freiburg-Breisgau 1942. German dancer. Studied in Munich under van Sachnowski and at Royal B. Sch. 1959–60. Joined Mannheim B. 1960 and to Hamburg B. 1961 becoming soloist. Guest artist Wuppertal B. 1963. Soloist of B. du XXme Siècle from 1968.

ALDAR KOSE, ballet, ch. Kholphen, m. Korchmarev, f.p. Turkmenian Ballet, Ashkhabad 31 Oct 1942 (K. Ismailov, Akhunov).

ALDER, Alan, b. Canberra 1939. Australian dancer. Pupil of Todd and Campbell-Smith. To Royal B. Sch. 1957, danced with C. Garden Opera B. 1957–58. Joined Royal B. 1958–63. Returned to Australia and joined Australian B. 1963 as soloist, principal dancer 1969. Mar. Lucette Aldous.

ALDOUS, Lucette, b. Auckland, New Zealand, 1939. New Zealand dancer. Studied in Sydney and at Royal Ballet School 1955–57. Joined Ballet Rambert 1957 becoming soloist and in 1958 ballerina. Ballerina Festival B. from 1963 to 1967 when she joined the Touring Royal B. as a principal. Guest artist Australian B. 1970 partnered by Nureyev in his *Don Quixote*. Danced in Teheran and Johannesburg 1970. From 1971 ballerina of Australian B. Mar. Alan Alder.

ALDRIDGE, Robert, b. c. 1738 in Ireland, d. Edinburgh 1793. Irish dancer and teacher. He had a famous sch. in Dublin in the middle of the eighteenth century. He composed ballets (chiefly of the Irish reel and jig variety) in London and finally opened a successful dancing sch. in Edinburgh. He was the teacher of Slingsby (q.v.).

ALEGRIAS, Sp. flamenco dance in 3/4 or 6/8 time.

ALEKO, ballets based on Pushkin's poem *The Gypsies* (1823–24). (1) In 1937, m. Vassilenko for the Soviet B. (2) By Ballet Theatre to Tchaikovsky's Trio in A minor, ch. Massine, dec. Chagall, f.p. Palacio de Bellas Artes, Mexico City 8 Sept 1942 (Markova, Skibine).

ALEKSANDROVA, Natasha, b. Leningrad 1936. Russ. dancer. Trained at the Vaganova Sch. Leningrad. Joined Kirov B. 1953 and promoted to prima ballerina of the Novosibirsk B. 1960. Returned to Kirov B. 1968.

ALEXANDER, Dorothy, b. Atlanta, Ga. 1904. Am. dancer and teacher.

7

Studied under many teachers in America and opened her own school in Atlanta 1921. Formed concert group 1929 which in 1941 became the Atlanta Civic B. In 1956 the first Regional Ballet Festival was held in Atlanta with herself as first President and she subsequently became the leading figure in the movement and in 1963 permanent director of the National Regional Ballet Association.

ALEXANDER, Rolf, German dancer. Studied under Jooss at Essen and principal dancer of B. Jooss until 1947. Danced in films and musicals 1947–51 when he re-joined Jooss.

ALEXANDRE LE GRAND, ballet, prologue, 3 sc. and epilogue, ch. Lifar, m. Gaubert's symphonic suite *Inscriptions pour les Portes de la Ville*, dec. P. R. Larthe, f.p. Paris Opéra 21 June 1937 (Lorcia, Chauviré, Schwarz, Lifar).

ALGAROFF, Youly, b. Simferopol 1918. Russ. dancer. Studied under Edouardova in Berlin, and under Kniaseff in Paris. Joined B. des Ch. Élysées 1945 as soloist and Nouveau B. de Monte Carlo 1946. Engaged as étoile by Paris Opéra 1953. Partnered Chauviré in Russian tour 1960. From 1965, an impresario, in Paris.

ALGERANOFF, Harcourt (Essex), b. London 1903, d. Robinvale, Australia 1967. Eng. dancer. Toured with Pavlova 1921–31, member of Markova-Dolin Co. and de Basil's Co. From 1943 soloist and teacher with International B. for whom he chor. *For Love or Money* (1951). To Australia 1954, where he worked with Borovansky B. and for the Austr. Children's Theatre. Author of *My Years with Pavlova* (1957). Mar. Algeranova.

ALGERANOVA, Claudie (Leonard), b. Paris 1924. Eng. dancer. Studied Cone-Ripman Sch. Joined International B. 1941 becoming joint ballerina. Joined Borovansky B. in Australia 1954 as ballerina. Ballerina in Lucerne 1959 and in Munich. Retired 1967 to become secretary of Munich B. Mar. Algeranoff.

ALGO, Julian, b. Ulm 1899, d. Stockholm 1955. German dancer and chor. Pupil of Edouardova, Volinin, Kroller, and of Laban in Stuttgart. Principal dancer at Berlin Opera 1922–25. Ballet-master at Duisburg-Bochum 1925–31. Appointed principal dancer and chor. of Royal Swed. B. in 1931. Won 1945 A.I.D. Competition in Stockholm with *Visions* (m. Moussorgski, dec. Algo) and mounted it in 1950 for the International B. in England. Chor. over twenty ballets in Stockholm, notably *Prima Ballerina* (1935), *Casanova* (1937), and *Orpheus in Town* (1938) (in the modern style, m. Rosenberg, dec. Jon-And).

ALGUES, LES, ballet 4 sc., ch. Charrat, m. Bernard, book and dec. Castelli, f.p. Charrat's Co., Th. des Ch. Élysées, Paris 20 Apr 1953

(Charrat, Fris, Chazot, van Dijk). This powerful ballet of a lunatic asylum makes use of *musique concrète*, one of the first to do so.

ALHAMBRA BALLETS, ballets given at the Alhambra Th., London, from 1871 to 1914, remarkable for the long series of successes by the composer, Georges Jacobi, and for the appearance of such famous dancers as Pierina Legnani, Judith Espinosa, Ekaterina Geltzer, and Tikhomiroff. See I. Guest's article in *Dance Perspectives* (1959).

ALHANKO, Anneli, b. Bogota, Colombia 1953. Finnish dancer. Pupil of B. of Geijerstam, N. Kozlovsky, and R. Swed. B. Sch. from 1963. Also of Franchetti, Northcote, von Bahr. Joined R. Swed. B. 1971 and danced solos. Won Varna silver medal 1972. Danced with R. Swed. B. in Brighton 1972.

ALICE IN WONDERLAND, ballet 2 acts, ch. Charnley, m. Horovitz, dec. Rowell, f.p. Festival B., Pavilion, Bournemouth 9 July 1953 (Belinda Wright, Gilpin, Beckett). With chor. by A. Mitterhuber, same music, mounted at the Theater an der Wien, Vienna 1970 (Anne Paulle).

ALLAN, Maude, b. Toronto 1883, d. Los Angeles 1956. Canadian dancer and teacher. Début in Vienna 1903 in *The Vision of Salome* (m. Richard Strauss). Her dances were usually barefoot and wearing the loose gown associated with the original Greek Dance. She toured the world and lived and taught in England from 1928 to 1940. Author of *My Life and Dancing* (1908).

ALLARD, Marie, b. Marseilles 1742, d. Paris 1802. Fr. ballerina. A popular dancer in her day, her greatest claim to fame is, perhaps, as the mistress of her teacher and partner, Gaetano Vestris, to have given the world Auguste Vestris. In 1782 she retired having become very fat. Made her début at Opéra 1760. Danced in *Les Petits Riens* (Mozart-Noverre 1779), *Les Indes Galantes*, *Devin du Village*, *Medée et Jason* (Noverre).

ALLEGRO, a dance sequence executed to fast time. Also, the last part of a ballet class, which contains the turns, jumps, and other quick steps.

ALLEGRO BRILLANTE, ballet 1 act, ch. Balanchine, m. Tchaikovsky 3rd piano concerto, f.p. N.Y. City B., City Center N.Y., 1 Mar 1956 (Maria Tallchief, Magallanes). In repertoire of many cos., f.p. Royal B., Stratford-on-Avon 27 Feb 1973.

ALLENBY, Jean, b. Bulawayo 1945. S. African dancer. Pupil of Ainscough and Poole. Principal dancer in CAPAB B., Cape Town from 1969.

ALLEMANDE or ALMAN, dance in 4/4 time known in Germany in the sixteenth century, adopted at the Fr. Court where it was retained in modified form until the end of the reign of Louis XIV. The Allemande still danced in country districts of Germany and Switzerland (where it is variously known as the Alewander, Allemandler, or Schwobli) is a lively composition in 3/4 time, which has no apparent connexion with the former and is regarded by some authorities as having heralded the waltz.

ALLONGÉ, lit. extended, usually referring to the stretched-out line of an arabesque.

ALMA, OU LA FILLE DE FEU, ballet 4 sc. Book Deshayes, ch. Fanny Cerrito and Jules Perrot, m. G. Costa, scenery W. Grieve, f.p. Her Majesty's Th., London 23 June 1842 (Cerrito, Perrot). Cerrito scored one of her greatest triumphs in this story of a marble statue which comes to life, especially for her execution of the *Pas de Fascination* (a tambourine dance) and in the *Pas de Trois*.

ALONSO, Alberto, b. Havana 1917. Cuban dancer and chor. Brother of Fernando A. Trained in Havana. In B. Russe de Monte Carlo 1935–40, Am. Ballet Th. 1943–45, B. Alicia Alonso 1948. Member of Cuban Nat. B. Chor. *Carmen Suite* 1967 for Bolshoi B., Moscow.

ALONSO, Alicia (Martinez), b. Havana 1917. Cuban dancer. Studied Fedorova and Vilzak. Started her career in musicals, joined B. Caravan 1939, B. Th. 1941, rejoined in 1943, and was their ballerina until 1948 when she formed her own Co. (Ballet Alicia Alonso) in Cuba, having been decorated by the Cuban Government in 1947. Cr. rôle of Lizzie Borden in *Fall River Legend*. Has chor. several ballets. In 1951 became prima ballerina of B. Th. Mar. Fernando Alonso. Danced in Russia 1957–58 and 1960. Her own Co. became the Ballet de Cuba in 1955 and has toured extensively with her as ballerina. Her school in Havana has produced many fine dancers. In 1972 staged *Giselle* at Paris Opéra and danced it.

ALONSO, Fernando, b. Havana 1914. Cuban dancer and chor. Studied with Mordkin and Vilzak. Début with Mordkin B. Soloist in B. Th. and in his wife's B. de Cuba of which he is Director, and teacher in her school.

AMATI, Olga, b. Milan 1924. It. dancer. Entered Scala, Milan, Sch. 1934, studied under Giussani, Volkova, Bulnes, and became prima ballerina 1942, dancing all the leading rôles at the Scala until 1956. Then danced in Naples and from 1961 has taught in the Rome Opera.

AMAYA, Carmen, b. Barcelona 1913, d. Bagur 1963. Sp. dancer. Danced in revues in Paris and in Spain. Her Co., consisting largely of members of her family, toured Europe and U.S. with great success. In Buenos Aires the Amaya Th. was built for her. First app. in N.Y. 1941 and in London 1948 (Princes Th.). Her gypsy flamenco dancing was remarkable.

AMBERG, George, b. Halle, Germany 1901. Am. Citizen 1946. Writer on art and ballet. Curator of Dance Archives, Mus. of Modern Arts, N.Y. 1943. Edited *Art in Modern Ballet* (1946) and wrote *Ballet in America* (1948) and many important articles.

AMBROSE, Kay, b. Woking 1914, d. London 1971. Eng. artist and writer on ballet. Illustrated Haskell's Pelican *Ballet* (1938). Wrote and illustrated *Ballet Lover's Pocket-Book* (1943), *Ballet Lover's Companion* (1948), *Classical Dances and Costumes of India* (1950), *Beginners, Please* (1953). Travelled widely with Ram Gopal and his Company, as art-director, lecturer and dancer. Artistic Director and publicist of National B. of Canada 1952–61.

AMERICA, BALLET IN. When the story of the emergence of an Am. ballet comes to be written, it may well be found that the main stream stems from the meeting in London, in 1933, of Lincoln Kirstein and George Balanchine. As a result of this meeting, Balanchine was invited to the U.S. and, with Kirstein and E. M. M. Warburg, formed at Hartford, Conn. the Sch. of Am. B. (1934) which was to be the foundation of a professional teaching body along the lines of the Russ. Imperial schools. In Dec. 1934 the Am. B. Co. made its début at Hartford, followed in March 1935 by its first N.Y. season with a repertoire of ballets by Balanchine (*Alma Mater, Dreams, Reminiscences, Serenade, Trans-cendence, Errante,* and *Mozartiana*) and a company of dancers incl. Ruthanna Boris, Annabelle Lyon, William Dollar, and Eugene Loring. After a tour in the Eastern States, the Co. was engaged by the Met. Op. Ass. to provide the ballets at the Op. House, and strengthened by the engagement of a number of dancers incl. Anatole Vilzak and Lew Christensen. The highlights of their seasons at the Met. Op. were the production (1936) by Balanchine of Gluck's *Orpheus* and the creation in 1937 of Balanchine's *The Card Party* and *Le Baiser de la Fée.* Early in 1938, as a result of differences in artistic policy the collaboration of the Am. B. Co. and the Met. Op. Ass. came to an end. In the meantime Kirstein had formed, early in 1936, B. Caravan to give performances of works by younger Am. chors. with dancers drawn, in the main, from the Am. B. Co. In their first three seasons they presented a number of works incl. *Pocahontas, Filling Station* by Lew Christensen, and Eugene Loring's *Billy the Kid.* In the autumn of 1938, as Am. B. Caravan, they undertook their first extended tour. In March 1941 the Am. B. and B. Caravan merged for a good-will tour of S. America under the direction of Balanchine, with a company incl. Marie-Jeanne, Todd Bolender, Lew Christensen, William Dollar, John Kriza, Nicolas Magellanes, and John Taras. At the end of the tour, in October, the company ceased as a performing unit. The next major creative venture was the staging by Balanchine at the Met. Op. in 1943 of Bach's *St Matthew Passion* with forty-six dancers drawn from the Sch. of Am. B. In July 1946 Balanchine and Kirstein founded the B. Society (q.v.) which succeeded Am. B. Caravan and the Am. B. and became the N.Y. City B. (q.v.) The part that AMERICAN BALLET THEATRE (q.v.) played in the development of American ballet is no less important. See also CATHERINE LITTLEFIELD, B. RUSSE DE MONTE CARLO, SAN FRANCISCO B., AMERICAN B., AMERICAN B. CO., AMERICAN DANCE TH., AMERICAN FESTIVAL B., PITTSBURGH B. TH., PHILA-DELPHIA B., PENNSYLVANIA B., BOSTON B., JOFFREY B., WASHING-TON NAT. B. etc., and under various directors names, e.g. CUNNING-HAM, GRAHAM, AILEY, TAYLOR, NIKOLAIS etc. There are also Cos. which give intermittent seasons in particular cities or regions, e.g. Kansas City B. (founded 1957 by Dorothy Perkins), Houston B., Wisconsin B., San Diego B., Milwaukee B., Tulsa Civic B. etc. and the many REGIONAL BALLETS (q.v.).

AMERICAN BALLET, a company formed in 1924 by Fokine and his wife, composed of many of their pupils. Its first performance was at the Met. Op., N.Y. 26 Feb 1924 with the ballets *Les Elfes* (m. Mendelssohn, it later was danced by the Théâtre d'Art du Ballet, q.v.), *Medusa* (m. Tchaikovsky) and *Olé Toro* (m. Rimsky Korsakov). After a tour the Co. broke up the same year.

AMERICAN BALLET COMPANY, founded and directed by Eliot Feld, first performed at the Spoleto Festival, Italy, 27 June 1969, giving *At Midnight, Harbinger, Meadow Lark* (all chor. Feld), *Caprichos* (ch. Ross), and first performance of *Cortège Burlesque* and *Intermezzo* (both chor. Feld), during the season. It gave its first N.Y. performance at Brooklyn Academy of Music 21 October 1969, with the same works and also *Carnaval* (ch. Fokine), *Games* (ch. McKayle) and *The Maids* (ch. Ross). Among the dancers were Christine Sarry, Elizabeth Lee, Cristina Stirling, Christine Kono, Olga Janke, John Sowinski, Alfonso Figueras, with Bruce Marks and Edward Verso as guests. It disbanded in April 1971.

AMERICAN BALLET, SCHOOL OF, the official school of the New York City Ballet (in New York). Founded in 1934 by Lincoln Kirstein and Balanchine who are its directors. Among its teachers are Danilova, Doubrovska, Eglevsky, Muriel Stuart, Stanley Williams. It is a part of the Juilliard School.

AMERICAN BALLET THEATRE, the official name since 1957 of the great American company hitherto known as Ballet Theatre. The first appearance of Ballet Theatre was at the Center Th., N.Y., on 11 Jan 1940 with over 100 dancers (incl. a Negro group of 14). Founded by Lucia Chase and Richard Pleasant, its first directors, it was from the start essentially Am. in composition and included amongst its dancing members most of the dancers of the Mordkin B. as well as Alicia Alonso, Nora Kaye, and Eugene Loring. If it could not be equally Am. in its repertoire, every opportunity was given to as yet little known Am. chors. such as Agnes de Mille (*Obeah, Tally-Ho, Three Virgins and a Devil*), Jerome Robbins (*Fancy Free, Interplay, Facsimile*), Eugene Loring (*The Great American Goof*), and Michael Kidd (*On Stage!*). The presence of Fokine, who restaged *Les Sylphides, Carnaval, Le Spectre de la Rose, Petrouchka,* and *Russian Soldier* (besides creating *Bluebird*), ensured an impeccable production of these works. His death in the summer of 1942, whilst working on *Helen of Troy* (later staged by Lichine), was a great loss to the Co. Anton Dolin restaged a number of the classical ballets, incl. *Giselle* and *Swan Lake,* Act II, and chor. three new ballets. Antony Tudor has been associated with Am. B. Th. from its inception, reviving *Dark Elegies, Jardin aux Lilas,* and other early works, and creating *Dim Lustre, Pillar of Fire, Undertow,* etc., in which he explored a psychological approach in an almost 'Proustian' style which has undoubtedly enlarged the range of choreographic expression. Markova joined B. Th. for their second season. Massine came to Am. B. Th. as chor. in 1942, and created *Aleko, Don Domingo,* and *Mlle Angot.* Richard Pleasant resigned as director at the conclusion of the second season, and Germaine Sevastianov took over the general direction and, in November 1941, concluded an arrangement with the impresario, S. Hurok, to present the Co. In 1943, Sevastianov joined the U.S. Army and was succeeded by J. Alden Talbot as general director, a post which he held until the end of 1945. The conclusion of 1945 marked an important change in policy of the company. The contract with Hurok was not renewed; Massine, Markova, and Dolin, amongst others, did not rejoin for the 1946 season; Lucia Chase and Oliver Smith became joint directors, with Tudor as Artistic Administrator, and it was made known that, breaking with its past history of commercial successes based on the guest star system, Am. B. Th. would aim at a consolidation of its artistic principles. In this year it revisited Covent Garden, the first Am. Co. to do so, and made a tremendous impression with such ballets as *Fancy Free* and *Pillar of Fire,* and with its ballerina Nora Kaye. Later B. Th. changed its name to Am. National B. Th. (for foreign tours) and in 1957 to American Ballet Th. They have steered a course less *avant-garde* than the N.Y. City B. and its predecessors, and less conservative than the B. Russe de Monte Carlo, and have succeeded in creating a definitely Am. style which defies precise definition, but may perhaps be said to be marked by the Am. urge for self-expression and vitality, curbed by a strict classical training. In 1956, leading dancers

13

were Nora Kaye, Rosella Hightower, Lupe Serrano, Ruth Ann Koesun, J. Kriza, H. Lang, Scott Douglas, Erik Bruhn. The company ceased to dance in 1958 but was re-formed by Lucia Chase in 1960. After a N.Y. season it made a European tour and was the first Am. company to dance in Russia (Moscow, Leningrad and Tiflis, 1960). The principal dancers in 1960 were Kaye, Bruhn, Serrano, Kriza, Douglas, Koesun, Fernandez, Addor, Rall, Sallie Wilson, Glen Tetley, Christine Mayer. Regisseur, Dimitri Romanoff. From 1962 to 1964 Am. Ballet Theatre combined with the Washington B. Guild but in 1964 it moved to N.Y. In 1965 it celebrated its 25th anniversary at the N.Y. State Th., Lincoln Center, and having found its old form was a great success. Robbins created his *Les Noces* (Stravinsky) for it, and *Dark Elegies* and *Fancy Free* were revived. The National Council on the Arts gave it a large grant in 1965 and the company resumed its tours and gave its N.Y. season at the State Th. In 1968 its principal dancers were Toni Lander, Sallie Wilson, Eleanor d'Antuono, Ruth Ann Koesun, Gayle Young, Cynthia Gregory, Royes Fernandez, Bruce Marks, Ted Kivitt. In 1966 it made its second visit to Russia and in 1970 came to Covent Garden for the third time and, on its return to America, Makarova joined as ballerina.

AMERICAN BALLET THEATRE SCHOOL, the official school of the American Ballet Theatre, in New York, founded by Lucia Chase. Leon Danielian is director, it has among its teachers Lazowski, Maule, Orloff, Pereyaslavec, Swoboda, Patricia Wilde.

AMERICAN DANCE THEATRE, the name of Alvin Ailey's company (see AILEY).

AMERICAN FESTIVAL BALLET, founded in 1957 in Bremen by Renzo Raiss, based in Europe and toured there and in Israel, S. America etc. It first appeared in New York (Fashion Inst. of Technology) in 1964, sponsored by the Harkness Foundation. Its principal dancer was Christine Hennessy and its ballets were chor. by Raiss, Gore, Sanders and included classical excerpts. It no longer exists.

AMIEL, Josette, b. Vanves 1930. Fr. dancer. Trained by Jeanne Schwarz and Volinine. Became principal dancer at the Opéra Comique but entered the Paris Opéra corps de ballet in 1952. Became première danseuse 1955 and étoile in 1958. Danced Odette-Odile in Bourmeister's *Swan Lake* at the Opéra 1961. Guest artist in many countries, partnered by Flemming Flindt.

AMODIO, Amedeo, b. Milan 1940. It. dancer. Studied at Scala Sch. Milan and became a member of the Scala B. To Rome Opera 1966 as primo ballerino. Chor. many ballets.

AMOR, ballet 2 acts, 17 sc., ch. Manzotti, m. R. Marenco, dec. Edel. f.p. Scala, Milan 17 Feb 1886 (Antonietta Bella, Ernestina Operti, Cecchetti). A typical spectacular ballet by Manzotti (q.v.) in which there appeared 72 girls, 36 boys, 64 mimes, 48 children, 48 coryphées, 350 figurants, 1 elephant and horses, cows etc.

AMOR BRUJO, EL (*L'Amour Sorcier, Love the Magician*) score for a ballet by Manuel de Falla, of which the first chor. was Pastora Imperio (Teatro Lara, Madrid 15 Apr 1915). Others who have used it have been Bériza (Paris 1925), A. Bolm (1925), Argentina (Trianon Lyrique, Paris 1925), Boris Romanoff (Monte Carlo 1931), Woizikovsky (1935), Lifar (Paris Opéra 26 Jan 1943, dec. Brayer, danced by Teresina, Darsonval, Petit, Lifar), Mariemma (Opéra Comique, Paris 1947), Pilar Lopez (Comedy Th., Madrid, March 1955), Antonio (Saville Th., London 5 Apr 1955, danced by Antonio, Segovia; dec. Caballero), Ruth Page (South Bend, Indiana, 13 Jan 1958).

AMOUR ET SON AMOUR, L', ballet 1 act, ch. Babilée, m. Franck (*Psyche*), dec. Cocteau, f.p. B. des Ch. Élysées, Th. des Ch. Élysées, Paris 13 Dec 1948 (Babilée, Philippart). This was Babilée's first ballet.

AMOURS DE JUPITER, LES, ballet 5 sc. by Boris Kochno, to themes from the *Metamorphoses* of Ovid, ch. Roland Petit, m. Jacques Ibert, dec. Jean Hugo, f.p. B. des Ch. Élysées, Th. des Ch. Élysées, Paris 5 Mar 1946 (Petit, Babilée, Ethery Pagava, Ana Nevada, Skorik, Philippart).

ANASTASIA, ballet, ch. MacMillan, m. Martinu, dec. Barry Kay. f.p. Deutsche Oper B. Berlin 25 June 1967 (Lynn Seymour, Vergie Derman, Holz, Bohner). About the claim of a woman, Anna Anderson, to be Anastasia, youngest daughter of Tzar Nicholas. Films and electronic music are also used. When MacMillan returned to London as Director of the Royal B., he mounted a new *Anastasia* in three acts, of which the above was the third. It was f.p. Royal B., Covent Garden 22 July 1971 with dec. Barry Kay (Seymour, Beriosova, Trounson, Rencher, Grater). The first act was set in a forest in 1914 to Tchaikovsky's First Symphony, the second, a ball in Petrograd 1917 to his Third Symphony.

ANATOMY. Weaver, in his *Anatomical & Mechanical Lectures upon Dancing* (1721) was the first to insist on a sound anatomical basis for the teaching of ballet (as did Noverre after him), although to this day the importance of taking into account the anatomical structure of the would-be dancer is not always fully appreciated. A few of the leading schools insist on examination by a suitably qualified medical practitioner before accepting a student for training, or have a consulting physiotherapist on their staff. Where this is not the case, parents are well advised to seek qualified advice before their children start ballet classes.

15

It is a fallacy that ballet exercises necessarily remedy faulty carriage. Mild deviations in growth (which are not immediately apparent to the layman and should be dealt with by the orthopaedic surgeon) can become permanent deformities in the space of a few months' training in a strenuous and essentially adult art. Bibl. E. M. Agnew, *Anatomical Studies*, C. Sparger, *Anatomy and Ballet* and *Beginning Ballet* and Joan Lawson *The Teaching of Classical Ballet*.

ANATOMY LESSON, THE, ballet, ch. Tetley, m. Landowsky, dec. Wijnberg. f.p. Nederlands Dans Th., The Hague 28 Jan 1964 (J. Flier). The Rembrandt painting.

ANAYA, Dulce, b. Havana 1933. Cuban dancer. Studied under Milenov, Alonso, Oboukhoff, and Vladimiroff. Joined Ballet Theatre (as Dulce Wöhner). Became ballerina of Alonso's Ballet de Cuba 1949. Joined Ballet Theatre 1951. In 1957 became ballerina of Stuttgart Staatsoper, and of Munich Staatsoper 1958-63. Ballerina Hamburg 1963. Returned to Munich 1964-65. Dancing in America from 1968.

ANCIENT RUSSIA, ballet to Tchaikovsky's Concerto No. 1 in B Flat minor, ch. Nijinska, dec. Goncharova (originally used for *Bogatyri*), B. Russe de Monte Carlo, f.p. Cleveland, Ohio 11 Oct 1943.

AND, Metin, b. Istanbul 1927. Turkish writer on drama and ballet. Educ. Istanbul Univ. Teacher in Dance Dept. of Ankara Univ. Author of several books on theatre and ballet in Turkish, and in English *Dances of Anatolian Turkey* (Dance Perspectives No. 3) (1959), *History of Theatre and Popular Entertainment in Turkey* (1964) and articles in the British and American dance periodicals.

ANDERSEN, Ib, b. Copenhagen 1954. Dan. dancer. Pupil of R. Dan. B. Sch. Joined R. Dan. B. 1973 dancing solo roles.

ANDERSEN, Ruth, b. Randers 1931. Dan. dancer. Entered Royal Dan. B. Sch. 1941, joined the Co. 1949 and promoted solodancer 1956.

ANDERSSON, Gerd. b. Stockholm 1932. Swed. dancer. Pupil Royal Swed. B. Sch. Joined R. Swed. B. 1948 becoming solodancer in 1953 and prima ballerina 1958. Made a film with Gene Kelly in Hollywood in 1959 and also danced in *Where the Rainbow Ends* in England. Cr. main rôle in *Echoing of Trumpets* (Tudor 1963). Guest artist in Ruth Page Ballet, Chicago 1967, Canadian Nat. B. 1968, Festival B. 1973.

ANDERTON, Elizabeth, b. London 1938. Eng. dancer. Trained by Nesta Brooking, won first Beaumont Scholarship to R. Ballet Sch. 1952. Joined S. Wells Opera B. 1955. Entered Touring Royal Ballet 1957 and became soloist 1958, then principal.

ANDRADE, Adolfo, b. Buenos Aires 1925. Argentinian dancer and chor. Studied under Borowsky, Bulnes, Lambrinos, Peretti, and Kiss. In de

Cuevas Ballet 1955–56, Ballet Théâtre de Béjart 1956–57, in *Le Rendezvous Manqué* 1957–58, and in the companies of Charrat, Babilée, and Miskovitch 1958–59. A principal dancer in Massine's Balletto Europeo, Nervi and Edinburgh, 1960, and in Munich B. 1961. Now works in Paris producing operettas etc.

ANDREANI, Jean-Paul, b. Rouen 1930. Fr. dancer. Studied at Paris Opéra becoming étoile 1954. In 1950 tradition at the Opéra was broken by his dancing the rôle of Frantz in *Coppélia*, but the *travesti* dancing of the rôle was resumed the same year.

ANDREEV, Alexei, b. Leningrad 1920. Russ. dancer and chor. A principal male dancer at Kirov Th., Leningrad. Chor. *Native Fields* (1954).

ANDREYANOVA, Yelena I., b. St Petersburg 1819, d. Paris 1857. Russ. dancer. Graduated from Imp. Sch. St Petersburg 1837 and became ballerina. She was one of the first Russian dancers to appear outside Russia—she made her début at the Paris Opéra 1845 and danced in Milan. She had modelled herself on Taglioni, whom she succeeded in St Petersburg and she was the first to dance *Giselle* in Russia (Bolshoi Th., St Petersburg 18 Dec 1842). Her protector was Gedeonov the Director of the Imperial Ths., St Petersburg.

ANGE GRIS, L', ballet, ch. Skibine, m. Debussy, dec. Sébire, f.p. de Cuevas Co., Deauville 20 Oct 1953 (Marjorie Tallchief, Skibine, Jean Quick).

ANGIOLINI, Gasparo, b. Florence 1731, d. Milan 1803. It. dancer, composer, and chor. Settled in Vienna 1757 when Gluck was Kapellmeister for the Court Th. Chor. *Don Juan* with Gluck's music 1761. Claimed this as first ballet in the form of a dance drama. In 1765 chor. *Semiramis* also to Gluck's music—and several other ballets for this composer. Succeeded Hilferding as maître de ballet at St Petersburg 1760. Returned to Vienna 1763. Chiefly remembered for his bitter controversies with Noverre, deprecating Noverre's practice of giving the stories of his ballets in the programme and his disregard of the unities and the laws of drama. These were in the form of letters 'from G.A.' and were written in 1773–75. He also worked in Italy (Venice, Milan, Turin) and in Moscow. Another member of the family, Fortunata A., was prima ballerina in Vienna 1793–1808 and danced at King's Th. London, 1809–12 and 1814. See FLORE ET ZÉPHIRE.

ANGLO-POLISH BALLET, a company formed in London in 1940 by the dancers Czeslow Konarski and Alicja Halama. A Pole, Jan Cobel, took the Co. over in 1941 and it toured England with success, in London in 1942, 1943, and 1947. Its chief ballet was *Cracow Wedding*, a divertissement of Polish national dances, and in the repertoire were *Swan Lake*, *Sylphides*, *Pan Twardowski*. It toured Italy for ENSA (a service for the

17

entertainment of troops) in 1944 and India in 1945. Eventually it came to an end, but it did valuable service during the War and provided refuge for many good dancers, incl. Sally Gilmour, Leo Kersley, Alexis Rassine and Gordon Hamilton.

ANIMAUX MODÈLES, LES, ballet in 6 entrées (based on 6 of La Fontaine's fables), ch. Lifar, m. Poulenc, dec. Brianchon, f.p. Paris Opéra 8 Aug 1942 (Lorcia, Schwarz, Chauviré, Lifar).

ANISIMOVA, Nina A., b. St Petersburg 1909. Russ. dancer and chor. Entered Leningrad Sch. 1919, studied under Vaganova, graduated 1926. To Azerbaijan, Ukraine, where she distinguished herself as a character dancer. Returned to Kirov Th., Leningrad in 1933, where she became a prima ballerina. In 1936 she chor. her first ballet, *The Andalusian Wedding* (m. Chabrier), for the pupils of the Leningrad Sch. In 1942 chor. *Gayané* (m. Khatchaturian, dec. Altman) and danced in it at Perm, partnered by Sergeyev. In 1944 she chor. *Song of the Crane* in Ufa. In 1945 staged *Fountain of Bakhchisarai* in Sofia, in 1946 chor. *The Fairy Veil* at Maly Th., Leningrad. Stalin Prize 1949. Mounted *Cinderella*, Belgrade 1963, *Swan Lake*, Copenhagen 1964. Since 1963 teacher at Leningrad.

ANNABEL LEE, ballet with sung words (Edgar Allan Poe), ch. Skibine, m. Schiffmann, dec. Delfau, f.p. de Cuevas Co., Deauville 26 Aug 1951 (Marjorie Tallchief, Skibine).

ANNA KARENINA, ballet 3 acts, ch. Plisetskaya, with Natalia Ryshenko and Victor Smirnov, m. Schedrin (on Tchaikovsky themes), dec. V. Levental (Plisetskaya's cost. by Cardin), f.p. Bolshoi Th. Moscow 10 June 1972 (Plisetskaya, Liepa, Fadeyechev). An adaptation of Tolstoy.

ANSERMET, Ernest, b. Vevey 1883, d. Geneva 1969. Swiss conductor for Diaghileff B. at the first perfs. of *Parade* (1917), *Three-cornered Hat* (1919), *Chant du Rossignol* (1920), *Pulcinella* (1920), *Chout* (1921), *Renard* (1922), *Les Noces* (1923).

ANTHONY, Gordon, b. 1902. Eng. photographer, brother of Ninette de Valois. Educ. St Paul's. One of the leading photographers of the ballet, specializing in studio portraits showing the dancers in the characters of their ballets, often with ingenious use of shadow-motifs in background. Much of the popularity of ballet in the de Basil Co. and early Sadler's Wells periods is due to his work which appeared regularly in the *Tatler*, the ballet journals, and his books. His first book *Markova* appeared in 1935, and his publications incl. *Margot Fonteyn, Beryl Grey, Massine, Sadler's Wells Ballet*, etc. Gave up photography in 1953.

ANTIGONE, ballet, ch. Cranko, m. Theodorakis, dec. Tamayo. f.p. Royal

APPARITIONS

Ballet, Covent Garden, 19 Oct 1959 (Beriosova, Blair, Burne, Farron, Somes).

ANTONIA, ballet, ch. Gore, m. Sibelius, dec. Cordwell, f.p. B. Rambert, King's Th., Hammersmith 17 Oct 1949 (Hinton, Paltenghi, Gore). A powerful ballet on the theme of jealousy.

ANTONIO (Antonio Ruiz Soler), b. Seville 1921. Sp. dancer. Studied under Realito (b. c. 1880). With his cousin, Rosario, as his partner made début in Liège, 1928. Since then the pair danced with enormous success all over the world. Début America 1940, at Edinburgh Festival 1950, London 1951. Formed a ballet company in 1953, without Rosario but with Rosita Segovia and Carmen Rojas. Rosario re-joined him in 1964 for their London and N.Y. seasons. His most remarkable dance is his *Zapateado*.

APLOMB, best defined by Despréaux in *L'Art de la Danse* 1806. '. . . *se dit lorsque la tête et les reins sont en ligne perpendiculaire audessus de la partie du pied sur laquelle tout le corps est porté. On peut être en équilibre sans être d'aplomb; mais il n'y a pas d'aplomb sans équilibre.*' (When the head and the small of the back are in a straight line and held directly above the supporting foot. One can be in equilibrium without *aplomb*—but not the reverse.)

APOLLON-MUSAGÈTE (APOLLO). (1) Ballet 2 sc., book and m. Stravinsky, ch. Adolph Bolm, dec. N. Remisoff, f.p. Library of Congress, Washington 27 Apr 1928 (Bolm, Ruth Page, Berenice Holmes, Elise Reiman). (2) Ballet 2 sc., m. Stravinsky, ch. Balanchine, dec. Bauchant, f.p. Diaghileff's Co., Th. Sarah Bernhardt, Paris 12 June 1928 (Lifar, Nikitina, Tchernicheva, Doubrovska), and subsequently by the Am. B., dec. S. Chaney, Met. Op., N.Y. 27 Apr 1937, and, as *Apollo*, by Ballet Theatre, dec. Tchelitchev, f.p. Met. Op. 25 Apr 1943 (Eglevsky, Zorina, Kaye, Hightower), and again for the Paris Opéra 21 May 1947, dec. A. Delfau (Kalioujny, Maria Tallchief, Jacqueline Moreau, Denise Bourgeois). Also in the repertoire of the R. Danish B. (Copenhagen, 9 Jan 1957 Kronstam, Mollerup, Simone, Petersen) and, as *Apollon-Musagète*, of the Royal Ballet (C. Garden 15 Nov 1966, MacLeary, Beriosova, Parkinson, Mason) and many other Cos.

APPALACHIAN SPRING, ballet, ch. Martha Graham, m. Copland, dec. Noguchi, cost. Gilfond, f.p. Library of Congress, Washington 30 Oct 1944 (Graham, Cunningham, Hawkins). A group dance.

APPARITIONS, ballet in prologue, 3 sc., and epilogue. Book C. Lambert (from the theme of Berlioz's *Symphonie Fantastique*), ch. Ashton, m. Liszt (orch. G. Jacob), dec. C. Beaton, f.p. S. Wells Th., London 11 Feb 1936 (Helpmann, Fonteyn, Turner). It was partly paid for by

19

the money handed over on the winding up of the Camargo Society. Revived in 1947 by S. Wells Th. B. (Heaton, Field).

APPEL, Peter, b. Surabaya 1933. Dutch dancer, teacher and ballet master. Studied in Holland under Kumysnikov and Karel Shook. Joined Dutch National B. 1954, soloist 1957. To Basel as first soloist 1962. Ballet master Larrain's *Cendrillon* Co., Paris 1963, of Festival B., Verona 1964. Teacher and soloist Hamburg 1966, teacher and asst. ballet master Cologne 1966 and Director 1969–71. From 1971 director of Cologne Dance Academy.

APPLEYARD, Beatrice, b. Maidenhead 1918. Eng. dancer and chor. Studied under de Valois, Karsavina, and Nijinska. An original member of the Vic-Wells B., becoming a soloist. Joined Markova-Dolin 1935. Principal dancer and chor. at Windmill Th., London. Chor. dances for several London musicals. Teacher in Turkey from 1951.

APRÈS-MIDI D'UN FAUNE, L', ballet 1 act, ch. Nijinsky, m. Debussy, dec. Bakst. f.p. Diaghileff's Co., Th. du Châtelet, Paris 29 May 1912. There is some doubt as to who was the author of the idea for this ballet. Nijinsky himself is generally credited with having conceived both book and choreography, but Stravinsky has stated that the theme was Diaghileff's but was later modified by Bakst. Nijinsky's interpretation of Debussy's music (a setting for Mallarmé's poem), a two-dimensional frieze-like tableau in the style of the figure on antique Greek vases, and his use of heavy, angular movement and turned-in positions came as a shock to an audience accustomed to the light extended movement, turned-out positions, and rounded form of the classical ballet. At the first performance, the final scene of the ballet, in which the Faun (Nijinsky) having failed to catch the fleeing nymphs, found consolation in the scarf dropped by one of them (Nelidova), caused something of a scandal. After much ink had been spilled for and against it, this episode was somewhat amended. A version by Lifar omits the nymphs. See AFTERNOON OF A FAUN.

ARABESQUE, a pose, probably inspired from the flowing leaf-like ornament of the Renaissance (said to be of Moorish origin), in which the body is supported on one leg, which may be straight or half bent (fondu), whilst the other is fully extended with the arms disposed in harmony, usually so as to give the longest possible line from fingertips to toe. There are a number of arabesque positions, the nomenclature of which varies with the system of teaching. The arabesque, giving as it does an impression of arrested flight or of poise for flight, is one of the most beautiful of dancing poses. Cecchetti system gives the following names to them, *First Arabesque* (raised arm is opposite to the raised working leg), *Second Arabesque* (raised arm and working leg the same side), *Third Arabesque* (both arms forward, the raised one opposite side to working leg), *Fourth Arabesque* (like First but on a fondu), *Fifth Arabesque* (like Third but on a fondu). The Russian (Vaganova) system is different.

An Arabesque

ARAIZ, Oscar, b. Bahia Blanca 1940. Argentinian dancer and chor. Pupil of Elide Locardi, Renate Schottelius and Dore Hoyer. Joined the ballet of the Teatro Argentino in La Plata and became a principal dancer. Member of Dore Hoyer's group. In 1968 founded the San Martin Ballet at the Teatro San Martin in Buenos Aires and was Director and principal dancer (see SAN MARTIN). Chor. *Halo* (m. Albinoni) for La Plata Th. 1965 (also in repertoire of Nederlands Dans Th. as *Auriole*), *Rite of Spring* (m. Stravinsky) for Colon Th. Buenos Aires 1966 and many ballets for San Martin B. e.g. *Symphonia* (m. Berio, Cage etc.), *Presentaçion* (m. Lopez), *Ebony Concerto* (m. Stravinsky) 1968, *Miraculous Mandarin* (m. Bartok), *Romeo and Juliet* (m. Proko-fieff) 1969 etc.

ARAUJO, Loipa, b. Havana. Cuban dancer. Pupil of Alicia and Fernando Alonso and Fokine. Principal dancer of the Nat. B. of Cuba. Won Varna Gold Medal in 1965. To B. de Marseille 1973.

ARBEAU, Thoinot, b. Dijon 1519, d. Langres 1596, pen-name of Jehan Tabourot, Canon of Langres, who in 1588 published his *Orchéso-graphie*, a detailed and witty study of the social dances of his time. This remarkable book, which provides one of the principal sources of our knowledge of fifteenth- and sixteenth-century dances, has been made available in an English translation by C. W. Beaumont, with the airs transposed into modern musical notation by Peter Warlock. These airs are used in Ashton's *Capriol Suite*.

ARCADE, ballet, ch. A. Labis (his first), m. Berlioz (overtures), f.p. Paris Opéra 9 Dec 1964 (Vlassi, Thibon, Labis, Parmaine, Bonnefous). Pure dancing.

ARCHIVES INTERNATIONALES DE LA DANSE (A.I.D.), a dance archive founded and endowed by Rolf de Maré in Paris in 1931, in memory of the Swedish Ballet and its choreographer Jean Börlin, with Dr Pierre Tugal as curator. Housed in the Rue Vital, Paris, it contained a complete record, with models, of the Swedish Ballet, relics of Pavlova and Argentina, a fine library of books, lithographs, and press-cuttings of the Dance. Dissolved in 1950, the greater part of the collection was transferred to the Musée de l'Opéra, Paris, and the remainder went to Stockholm, forming the Dance Museum at the Opera House now transferred to the Dance Museum. See GREEN TABLE, THE.

ARENA (Antoine des Arens, Antonius de Arena), b. Soullies (Toulon), d. there 1544. Fr. writer on theory of the dance. His book in macaronic Latin on *Bassas Dansas*, 1529, contains descriptions of branles, basses danses etc. His real name was Antoine de la Sablé.

ARGENTINA, LA (Antonia Mercé), b. Buenos Aires 1888, d. Bayonne 1936. Sp. dancer who was largely responsible for the revived interest in the Sp. dance of which she is considered by many as having been the greatest exponent. Studied under her father and début at age of 9 at Royal Th., Madrid. Début N.Y. at Park Th. 1919, in London 1924. Her first appearance in Paris was in 1905 at the Jardin de Paris music hall. Last appeared in London 1935 and Paris 1936. Of her Ritual Fire Dance in *El Amor Brujo* (Opéra Comique, Paris, 1929) Levinson wrote: '*Elle porte en elle l'enivrant poison, mais aussi l'antidote, le vertige et l'équilibre, la folie et la sagesse, la Ménade et la Muse.*'

ARGENTINITA, LA (Encarnaçion Lopez), b. Buenos Aires 1895, d. N.Y. 1945. Sp. dancer and chor. Went to Spain when she was four and first danced in gypsy ensembles in Madrid. She had a triumph in Paris 1924 and in 1927 founded, with the poet F. G. Lorca, her Ballet of Madrid. In 1938 toured Central and S. America with her troupe (with her sister Pilar Lopez). Fled Spain in Civil War and danced in Paris, London, Switzerland etc. In 1939 collaborated with Massine at Monte Carlo in *Capriccio Espagnol*. Guest artist with Ballet Theatre in *Goyescas* and *Bolero* in 1945. One of the greatest Sp. classical dancers.

ARGYLE, Pearl (Pearl Wellman), b. Johannesburg 1910, d. Hollywood 1947. Eng. dancer, début 1926 with Rambert dancers. She danced many leading rôles for the Ballet Rambert. Also danced for Les Ballets 1933, Camargo Soc., and S. Wells B. Will be specially remembered for her great personal beauty and the creations of *Fille au Bar* (*Bar aux Folies-Bergère*, de Valois) and the *Mermaid* (Howard). When Markova left the Wells (Vic-Wells B.) in 1935, she became its first entirely Eng.-trained ballerina, dancing *Swan Lake* and (her finest rôle) the Fairy in *Le Baiser de la Fée*. When Paul Valéry saw her in *Mermaid* he was ecstatic in his praise of her poetic charm, and J. L. Vaudoyer wrote: '*Sa rare beauté, qui a encore le charme indéterminé de l'enfance, irradie ce halo poétique, fait de mystère et de pureté, grâce auquel un être vivant propose momentanément de croire à l'existence des êtres rêvés.*' She lived in America from 1938 and appeared in several films and musicals.

ARI, Carina (Jansson), b. Stockholm 1897, d. Buenos Aires 1970. Swed. dancer and chor. Studied at sch. of R. Swed. B. and under Fokine in Copenhagen. Prima ballerina of Börlin's B. Suedois 1920–24. She cr. the chief rôle in *Le Cantique de Cantiques* at Paris Opéra 2 Feb 1938 (ch. Lifar, m. Honegger, dec. Colin). At Paris Opéra she chor. *Rayon de Lune* (m. Fauré 1928), and at Opéra Comique *Valses de Brahms* and *Jeux de Couleurs* (m. Ingelbrecht). Mar. the owner of Bols (Dutch liqueur). There is an annual Carina Ari Prize in Stockholm for ballet, and a £1,000,000 foundation for training dancers etc.

ARMS, see PORT DE BRAS.

AROVA, Sonia (Errio), b. Sofia 1927. Bulgarian-Eng. dancer. Family moved to Paris 1936 where she studied under Preobrajenska. She came to England in 1940 and entered the Cone-Ripman Sch. Joined International B. 1942, Ballet Rambert 1946, Metropolitan B. 1947. Returned to Paris to study. Guest artist B. des Ch. Élysées 1951, Orig. B. Russe (London) 1952, Festival B. as ballerina 1952, Guest artist Komaki Ballet Co. (Japan) 1952, de Cuevas Co. 1954, Ballet Theatre 1955. Danced in Europe 1958–60 in American Festival B., was Nureyev's partner for his début in America (Chicago 1962) in Ruth Page's Co. (of which she has been guest artist since 1955). Guest artist with Royal B. at C. Garden 1962 (dancing *Swan Lake* with Nureyev). Guest ballerina Australian B. 1962–63, Washington Nat. B. 1963–65, Ballet Theatre 1965. From 1966 ballerina and director of Norwegian B., Oslo. Appointed director of Hamburg B. 1970. To America 1971 as director of San Diego B. Mar. Sutowski.

ARPINO, Gerald, b. Staten Island, N.Y. 1928. Am. dancer and chor. Studied under Mary Ann Wells, Seattle and modern dancing with May O'Donnell. Joined Joffrey Co. 1956 as principal dancer. Co-director and teacher at Joffrey Sch. and assistant director in 1965 of the Robert Joffrey Ballet on its re-formation. Chor. first ballets *Partita for Four* and *Ropes* in 1961. Then *Sea Shadow* and *Incubus* 1962, *Palace* 1963, *Viva Vivaldi!* 1965, *Olympics* (m. Mayuzumi) 1966, *Nightwings* (m. La

23

Montaine) 1966, *Elegy* (m. Panufnik) 1967, *Cello Concerto* (m. Vivaldi) 1967, *The Clowns* (m. Hershy Kay) 1968, *Fanfarita* 1968, *A Light Fantastic* (m. Britten) 1968, *Secret Places* (m. Mozart) 1968, *Chabriesque* 1972.

ARQUÉ, Fr. bow-legged (opp. jarreté). The term 'danseur clos' is also used.

ARRIÈRE, EN, Fr. backwards.

ART ET DANSE, Fr. journal devoted to the dance (ballet, modern, and folk), published in Rouen. It appears every two months (first number was Nov.–Dec. 1953) and was edited by Matias Desève, now by Girette Chabetay.

ARTS COUNCIL OF GREAT BRITAIN, THE, the body which distributes public money for the development of the arts. It started as C.E.M.A. (Council for the Encouragement of Music and the Arts) in 1939 as a wartime committee to keep the arts alive and it financed exhibitions, concerts, drama and ballet for factories, towns and troops. Among other things it guaranteed the Sadlers' Wells Ballet against loss. In 1945 it was re-named the Arts Council, under the chairmanship of Lord Keynes, and subsidizes the Royal Ballet, the Royal Opera, the B. Rambert, Scottish Th. B., S. Wells Opera etc. and innumerable groups of artists, dancers, actors, writers, and painters. In 1970–71 it distributed over £9,000,000.

ARTS EDUCATIONAL SCHOOLS, a leading English ballet and drama school with a co-educational day school in London of 400 pupils and a residential establishment at Tring Park, Hertfordshire with 275 girls. Before 1962 it was called the Cone-Ripman School. This was formed in 1944 when the Cone Sisters School of Dancing (founded in London 1919) amalgamated with the Ripman School (founded in London 1922). The school was administered by Grace Cone and Olive Ripman (b. 1886) from 1944 until 1966 when Beryl Grey became director, succeeded in 1968 by Mrs M. I. Jack. Among the actors and dancers produced by the school are Julie Andrews, Claire Bloom, Anton Dolin, John Gilpin, Evelyn Laye, Gillian Lynne, Julia Farron, Pauline Clayden, Margaret and Julia Lockwood, Antoinette Sibley. Alicia Markova has always been closely associated with it and presents an annual Markova Award to the best dancer. It is now situated in the City of London and called Arts Educational Trust. See CONE, Grace.

ARVIDSSON, Lillemor, b. Göteborg 1942. Swed. dancer. Studied under Emy Agren, Nina Kozlowsky and entered R. Swed. B. Sch. 1956. Joined R. Swed. B. 1961 becoming soloist 1966.

ASAFIEV, Boris V., b. St Petersburg 1884, d. Moscow 1949. Russ. composer of ballets. Studied at St Petersburg Conservatoire under Rimsky-Korsakov and Liadov. Among his ballets are *The Flames of Paris, The Fairy's Gift, The Fountain of Bakhchisarai, Prisoner of the Caucasus, Christmas Eve, Peasant Lady*. He was a vigorous Soviet writer on music. In his twenties he was ballet pianist at the Maryinsky Th., later he became a conductor there and then at the Bolshoi Th., Moscow. He wrote as a musicologist under the name Igor Glebov.

ÅSBERG, Margaretha, b. 1939. Swed. dancer and chor. Trained in R. Swed. B. Sch. from 1952, entered R. Swed. B. 1957 and left in 1962 to study modern dance at Juilliard and Graham schools in N.Y. Entered the Choreographic Institute, Stockholm 1967 and engaged by R. Swed. B. in 1968 to teach modern techniques. Chor. '... *from one point to any other point* ...' 1968.

ASEL, ballet, ch. Vinogradov, m. V. Vlasov, dec. Levental. f.p. Bolshoi B., Moscow 7 Feb 1967 (Timofeyeva, Fadeyechev, Sekh). About present-day Kirghizia—a truck-driver and a demobilized soldier.

ASHBRIDGE, Bryan, b. Wellington, New Zealand, 1926. New Zealand dancer. Studied in Wellington and from 1939 in Sydney under Kirsova and Borovansky. To S. Wells Sch. 1947 and joined S. Wells B. 1948, becoming soloist. Returned to N.Z. 1965 to teach. Assistant to Director Austral. B. 1969. Played cricket for N.Z.

ASHMOLE, David, b. Cottingham, Yorks 1949. Eng. dancer. Studied at Kilburn Sch., Wellingborough and Royal B. Sch. Joined Royal B. 1969 becoming soloist 1972.

ASHTON, Sir Frederick W. M., b. Guyaquil, Ecuador 1904. Eng. dancer and chor. Studied under Massine and Rambert. Danced Ida Rubinstein Co. 1928, B. Rambert 1926 and 1928–35. Joined S. Wells B. 1935, becoming principal chor., one of the artistic directors in 1938, Associate Director 1952, and in 1963 he succeeded de Valois as Director. Created C.B.E. in 1950, knighted 1962. Danish Order of Dannebrog 1964, D.Litt. (Durham) 1962. Ballets include: for Marie Rambert, *Tragedy of Fashion* (1926) (in revue *Riverside Nights*, his first ballet), *Capriol Suite* (1930), *Les Masques* (1933). For Camargo Society, *Façade* (1931). For S. Wells B., *Les Rendezvous* (1933), *Apparitions, Nocturne* (1936), *Les Patineurs, A Wedding Bouquet* (1937), *Horoscope* (1938), *Dante Sonata* (1940), *The Wanderer* (1941), *Symphonic Variations* (1946), *Scènes de Ballet, Don Juan, Cinderella* (1948), *Daphnis and Chloë, Tiresias* (1951), *Sylvia* (1952), *Homage to the Queen* (1953), *Rinaldo and Armida, Madame Chrysanthème* (1955), *Birthday Offering* (1956), *Ondine* (1958), *La Fille Mal Gardée* (1960), *Les Deux Pigeons* (1961), *Persephone* (1962), *Marguerite and Armand* (1963), *The Dream* (1964), *Monotones* (1965 and 1966), *Sinfonietta* (1967), *Enigma Variations* (1968).

For S. Wells Th. B., *Valses Nobles et Sentimentales* (1947). For Festival B., *Vision of Marguerite* (1952). For B. Russe de Monte Carlo, *Devil's Holiday* (1939). For N.Y. City B., *Illuminations* (1950), *Picnic at Tintagel* (1952). For R. Danish B., *Romeo and Juliet* (1955). Also made the ballet for film *Tales of Hoffmann* (1950). In 1970 he chor. *Lament of the Waves* and *The Creatures of Prometheus*, was appointed Companion of Honour and retired at the end of the season with the title of Founder-Choreographer of the Royal B. Awarded Carina Ari Medal 1972. For Royal B. chor. *Siesta* (m. Walton, 1972), and *Walk to the Paradise Garden* (m. Delius, 1972) and the film *Tales of Beatrix Potter* (1971). Mounted his *Fille Mal Gardée* for the Australian, R. Swedish and Hungarian Nat. Bs. and continued to dance one of the Ugly Sisters in his *Cinderella* during 1972. To mark his retirement a gala was given at C. Garden 24 July 1970 *A Tribute to Sir Frederick Ashton*, at which extracts from 36 of his ballets were danced by the Royal B. (incl. *Symphonic Variations* in full). It was devised by John Hart, Michael Somes and Leslie Edwards, with a narration by Robert Helpmann (written by William Chappell) and (as it was a secret from Ashton himself) programmes were not distributed until the audience filed out.

ASSEMBLÉ or PAS ASSEMBLÉ, lit. a uniting step. A leap in which the dancer brings the feet together in the fifth position before alighting. There are six basic assemblés (over, under, devant, derrière, en avant, en arrière) and they can be executed en place or élancé.

ASSEMBLY BALL, ballet 1 act to Bizet's Symphony in C, ch. and dec. Andrée Howard, f.p. S. Wells Th., London, for the first appearance of the newly-formed S. Wells Opera B. 8 Apr 1946 (Brae, Kersley, Newman).

ASSOCIATION DES ÉCRIVAINS ET CRITIQUES DE LA DANSE, L', a Fr. society of ballet-writers founded in 1935 with Rolf de Maré as president. After the war it was re-formed with Pierre Michaut as president, Irène Lidova as secretary. It awards the René Blum Prize annually (q.v.), and judged the prizes in the Paris International Festival (q.v.).

ASSOCIATION PHILANTHROPIQUE DE SECOURS MUTUELS DES ARTISTES (HOMMES) DE L'OPÉRA, founded in 1835 by Filippo Taglioni and Jean Coralli, the maîtres de ballet at the Paris Opéra. One of the first benevolent societies in France, it was dissolved in 1947 when it was absorbed into the Société des Artistes et Amis de l'Opéra (q.v.), which served a similar purpose but for both sexes.

ASTAFIEVA, Seraphine, b. 1876, d. London 1934. Russ. dancer and teacher. Graduated from the Imperial Sch., St Petersburg to the

Maryinsky Th. in 1895, in Diaghileff's Co. 1909–11. Opened Sch. in 1916 at 152 King's Road, Chelsea, London, which was attended by, among others, Alicia Markova, Anton Dolin, and Margot Fonteyn. In 1968 a plaque was fixed to the house in Chelsea where she lived and taught.

ASTAIRE, Fred (Austerlitz), b. Omaha 1899. Am. tap dancer on stage and film. With his sister Adèle danced in N.Y. and London in many successful shows (*Over the Top*, 1917, *Lady be Good*, etc.). Dancing with Ginger Rogers, he appeared in films (*Flying Down to Rio*, 1933, *Top Hat, Follow the Fleet, Swing Time*, etc.) until the partnership broke up in 1939. Later partners were Eleanor Powell (*Broadway Melody of 1940*), Rita Hayworth (*You were never Lovelier*, 1942), and Judy Garland (*Easter Parade*, 1948), Leslie Caron (*Long Legs*, 1954), Audrey Hepburn (*Funny Face*, 1956).

ASTARTE, ballet, ch. Joffrey, m. the Crome Syrcus, dec. Skelton, cost. Sherrer, f.p. Joffrey B., City Center Th., N.Y. 20 Sept 1967 (Trinette Singleton, M. Zomosa). Mixed media, with films, and searchlights playing on the audience.

ASTROLOGUE, L', ballet 3 sc., ch. Lifar, m. Barraud, dec. Roland-Manuel, f.p. Paris Opéra 24 Apr 1951 (Bardin, Ritz).

ATANASSOF, Cyril, b. Puteaux-Seine 1941. Fr. dancer (Bulgarian father). Studied at Paris Opéra Sch. from 1953. Entered Paris Opéra 1957, becoming premier danseur 1962 and étoile 1964.

À TERRE—see PAR TERRE.

ATLAS, Helen, b. N.Y. 1931. Am. writer and editor. Studied ballet with Mordkin. Graduated in Political Science 1953. Became interpreter at United Nations, N.Y. (speaking Russian and French). From 1963 to 1968 assistant and interpreter for Sol Hurok. In 1969 took over *Dance News* in New York as Editor and Publisher, after Chujoy's death.

AT MIDNIGHT, ballet, ch. Feld, m. Mahler (the 5 Rückert songs), dec. Baskin, f.p. Ballet Th., City Center, N.Y. 1 Dec 1967 (Bruce Marks, Christina Sarry, Cynthia Gregory, Orr).

ATTACK, the sharp and decisive interpretation of a movement or variation.

ATTITUDE, position derived from the statue of Mercury by Giovanni da Bologna (1524–1608), said to have been introduced by Carlo Blasis, in which the body, which may be in various positions, is supported on one leg (bent or straight) with the corresponding arm opened to the side or back (or front) whilst the other leg is extended to the back at an angle of 90° with the knee bent and the corresponding arm raised above the head (fifth position en haut or fourth en haut, Cecchetti).

27

*An Attitude (arm position sometimes known as
attitude ordinaire)*

ATTITUDE GREQUE, a different form of attitude in which the heel of the
working foot touches the back of the supporting leg, either à terre or
en l'air. The same arm as the supporting leg is held above the head
(as in en couronne) and the other arm is held in the 'gateway' position
(see PORT DE BRAS). The head is in profile looking towards the working
leg and the body leans over towards the working leg. It can be taken en
face, croisée, or ouverte. Pirouettes can be done in this position (but
without the normal use of the head).

AUBADE, ballet, book and m. Poulenc, ch. Nijinska, f.p. soirée of Vicomte
de Noailles, Paris 19 June 1929. Revived with book and ch. Balanchine,
dec. Ortiz, by Nemchinova Co. Th. des Ch. Élysées, Paris, 22 Jan.
1930 (Nemchinova, Dolin). This version, with dec. Cassandre (his first
work for the theatre), was adopted by Blum's Co., f.p. Monte Carlo
11 Apr 1936 (Nemchinova). A version by Lifar was given by the
Nouveau B. de Monte Carlo, Monte Carlo, December 1946 (Jeanmaire,
Skouratoff), and was later danced by Charrat's Co. The story of Diana
and Actaeon.

AUBER, Daniel F. E., b. Caen 1782, d. Paris 1871. Fr. composer whose
ballet scores include: *Le Dieu et la Bayadère* (1830), *Masaniello* (or *La
Muette de Portici*) (1828), and *Marco Spada* (1857). His music has also
been used by Ashton for *Les Rendezvous*, by Gsovsky for *Grand Pas
Classique* and by Ruthanna Boris for *Quelques Fleurs*.

AUBRI (Santina ZANUZZI), b. Venice 1738, d. there. It. dancer. Casanova records that she danced in Vienna but was expelled for misconduct. She went to Russia with Hilferding and danced there, leaving St Petersburg 1764 when she married the Fr. dancer Pierre Aubri. In 1766 Angiolini took her back to Russia with great success. Catharine the Great honoured her and gave her many presents in 1783 when she returned to Venice. She was one of the first of the It. dancers to make her career in Russia.

AUBRY, Julie, Fr. dancer who at the *Fêtes Civiques* of the Revolution impersonated *Liberté*, while her colleagues Mlles Duchamp and Florigny were *Égalité* and *Fraternité*. In 1807, when descending in a *gloire* at the Paris Opéra, she fell and broke her arm. The Empress Josephine organized a ball for her and she retired on the proceeds.

AUDEOUD, Susana (Janssen), b. Bern 1919. Swiss dancer. Studied with Garraux in Bern, Sartorio in Florence and with Preobrajenska, Volinine etc. Learned Spanish dancing from La Quica and Estampio and became prima ballerina of the Madrid Opera in 1947. There she met José Udaeta and in 1948 they gave their first recital of Spanish dancing, in Geneva. As *Susana and José* they toured the world giving recitals until 1970.

AUGUSTA, LA PETITE, see MAYWOOD.

AUGUSTA, Mlle (Caroline Augusta Josephine Thérèse Fuchs, Comtesse de Saint-James), b. 1806, d. 1901. Fr. dancer. Danced *La Muette de Portici*, Brussels, and *La Sylphide*, 1843. She was a very popular dancer in America, making her début there in *Les Naiades*, and danced *La Bayadère* 1836. She was the first to dance *Giselle* in N.Y. 1846—a month later than Mary Anne Lee danced it in Boston.

AUGUSTE, d. 1844. 'King of the Claque' at the Paris Opéra during the administration of Dr Véron. He was paid in tickets given to him, with instructions for the evening, by the Opéra, which he distributed to his lieutenants and resold, keeping the money. In addition he received a regular fee from the dancers and singers (Taglioni and Elssler entrusted their applause to him, Lise Noblet paid him 50 francs a performance). He was strictly honest in his dealings and his judgement was respected by the management. He left a large fortune.

AUGUSTYN, Frank, b. Hamilton, Ont. 1953. Canad. dancer. Pupil of Oliphant and Seillier at Canad. Nat. B. Sch. Joined Co. 1970, soloist 1971.

AULD, John, b. Melbourne 1930. Austr. dancer. Studied with Borovansky and joined his Co. 1951. Danced in London (musicals) 1952 and rejoined Borovansky B. 1954 as soloist. To Festival B. 1961, later becoming asst. artistic director. Appointed asst. ballet-master of Gulbenkian Ballet, Lisbon 1965. In 1971 became manager of the Touring Royal B. and assistant to the Directors.

AUMER, Jean, b. Strasbourg 1774, d. St Martin 1833. Fr. dancer and chor. Pupil of Dauberval at Bordeaux. Engaged by the Paris Opéra 1798. His first ballet was *Jenny or the Secret Marriage* (1806), followed by *Les Deux Créoles* (1806). Ballet-master at Lyon 1807. From 1808 to 1815 ballet-master at the court of King Jerome at Kassel. From 1815–20 at Vienna. Returned to Paris 1820 and produced *La Fête Hongroise* (1821), *Alfred the Great* (1822), *Aline* (1823), *Le Page Inconstant* (1823), *La Somnambule* (1827), *Manon Lescaut* (1830). He also chor. a ballet *La Belle au Bois Dormant* (m. Herold, with Noblet as the Princess, f.p. Paris Opéra 27 Apr 1829) and was probably the first to do so. From 1823–25 ballet-master at Her Majesty's Th., London.

AUREOLE, ballet, ch. Paul Taylor, m. Handel, cost. white practice. f.p. P. Taylor Dance Co., Connecticut Coll., New London, U.S.A., 4 Aug 1962 (Taylor, Walton, Wagoner, Kinney, Kimball). Abstract, modern style.

AURIC, Georges, b. Lodève, Hérault 1899. Fr. composer (one of 'Les Six'). Ballets include *Les Fâcheux* (1924), *Les Matelots* (1924), *La Concurrence* (1924), *Le Peintre et son Modèle* (Massine 1949), *Phèdre* (1950). His *Bal des Voleurs* (Massine) for the Nervi Fest. 1960 was danced by the Royal B. in 1963. Director of the Paris Opéra 1962–67.

AURIOL, Francisca, d. 1862. Fr. dancer, daughter of the famous Fr. clown J. B. Auriol. London début 1847 at R. It. Opera. Joined Flexmore's ballet troupe and married him 1849. The Auriol-Flexmores were a famous pair, dancing serious ballets and extravaganzas in England and on the Continent.

AURORA'S WEDDING, suite of dances from the last act of *The Sleeping Beauty*, with some additions. Ch. Petipa, m. Tchaikovsky, cost. from Benois's *Pavillon d'Armide*, dec. Bakst, f.p. Diaghileff's Co., Paris Opéra 18 May 1922 (Trefilova, Vladimiroff). This divertissement was all that remained from the 1921 production of *The Sleeping Princess*. It is in the repertoire of several companies. In the 1921 version Nijinska chor. the *Chinese Dance*, the *Three Ivans* and the *Florestan and his Sisters* variations.

AUSTRALIA, BALLET IN, the principal ballet is the Australian Ballet (q.v.), based on Melbourne. However there are many other, smaller Cos., among them the *West Australian Ballet Co.* (directed by Rex Reid, at North Fremantle), *Ballet Victoria* (at Melbourne), *Queensland Ballet Co.* (directed by Charles Lisner at Brisbane). Among the principal schools are the Australian Ballet Sch. (in Melbourne, directed by Margaret Scott), the Scully-Borovansky Sch. (in Sydney, Kathleen Danetree, Nellie Potts), Lorraine Norton Sch. (in Sydney), Kathleen Gorham Ballet Academy (in Melbourne), Paul Hammond Ballet Sch. (in Melbourne), Bodenweiser Dance Centre (in Sydney) etc. The Royal Academy of Dancing, the Cecchetti Society and the British Ballet Organization are all strongly represented.

AUSTRALIAN BALLET, THE, for its beginnings see BOROVANSKY. On the disbanding of his company in 1960 an Australian Ballet Foundation was formed by directors of the Australian Elizabethan Trust and J. C. Williamson Theatres Ltd, and in 1962 a new company, The Australian Ballet, was instituted using most of the old dancers of the Borovansky B. and with Peggy van Praagh as Director (and Ray Powell as ballet-master). The first performance was in Sydney 2 Nov. 1962—the guest artists were Sonia Arova, Erik Bruhn, Tatiana Zimina, Nikita Dolgush-in and Jonathan Watts. The principal dancers were Kathleen Gorham, Marilyn Jones, Garth Welch, Algeranoff and Caj Selling. They performed *Swan Lake* (in full), *Coppelia*, *Les Sylphides*, *Lady and the Fool*, *Les Rendezvous*, Powell's *One in Five* and Rex Reid's *Melbourne Cup*. In 1965 the company performed at the Baalbeck Festival, the Paris International Festival and then in London, Birmingham, Liverpool, Glasgow and Cardiff (Commonwealth Arts Festival). Robert Helpmann became co-director with van Praagh in 1965 and chor. for them *The Display* (1964), *Yugen* (1965) and *Sun Music* (1968). In 1965 Nureyev mounted *Raymonda* for them, and *Don Quixote* in 1970, dancing in them himself. They toured the Far East in 1968, and N.Y. and America in 1971. In 1970 among their dancers were Marilyn Jones, Kathleen Geldard, Barbara Chambers, Alida Belair, Patricia Cox, Garth Welch, Warren de Maria, Alan Alder, Karl Welander, Kelvin Coe, Robert Olup, and in 1972 Lucette Aldous, Marilyn Rowe, Kathleen Geldard, Patricia Cox, Garth Welch, Alan Alder, Kelvin Coe, R. Olup, G. Norman. The Australian B. Sch. was established 1964 in Melbourne with Margaret Scott director. To Russia, Poland, London 1973.

AUSTRIA, BALLET IN, the principal Co. is the Vienna Staatsoper Ballet (q.v.). The *Theater an de Wien* also has a resident Co. directed (1972) by Alois Mitterhuber. It has 30 dancers and besides performing in the operas and operettas has ballet-evenings and also special matinees for children (chor. by Mitterhauber, *Peter Pan*, *Alice in Wonderland* etc.). The *Volksoper Ballet* at the Volksoper in Vienna has 38 dancers, directed by Madam Dia Luca and Gerhard Senft. They performed (mostly folk dances and waltzes) at the Festival Hall in London in 1970. There is also a ballet attached to the Raimund-Theater (28 dancers) dancing in

31

the operettas. There are also ballets attached to the opera houses in Graz (director Eva Bernhofer), Linz (director Anna Vaughan), Salzburg (director Armin Wild), Klagenfurt (director Ioan Farcas), Innsbruck, St Polten and Baden.

AUTUMN LEAVES, the only ballet chor. by Pavlova, m. Chopin, dec. Korovine, f.p. Rio de Janeiro 1918 (Pavlova, Volinine, Stowitts).

AVANT, EN, Fr. forward.

AVELINE, Albert, b. Paris 1883, d. Asnières 1968. Fr. dancer and chor. Entered Paris Opéra Sch. 1894 and remained at Opéra all his career. Became leading dancer and ballet master 1917 and later Director of Sch. Cr. rôle of Faun in *Cydalise et la Chèvre-Pied* (1923), partnered Spessivtseva in *Giselle* (1924) at the Opéra, but is most remembered for his long association as partner of Zambelli. Chor. *La Grisi* (1935), *Elvire* (1937), *Les Santons* (1938), *Le Festin de l'Araignée* (1939), *Jeux d'Enfants* (1941), *La Grande Jatte* (1950), *Les Indes Galantes* (Prologue) (1952).

AV PAUL, Annette (Wiedersheim-Paul), b. Stockholm 1944, Swed. dancer. Pupil of R. Swed. B. Sch. becoming soloist R. Swed. B. and principal dancer 1966. Guest artist with the R. Winnipeg Ballet 1966 and created title rôle in *Rose Latulippe* by her husband Brian Macdonald. Guest artist with the Harkness Ballet 1967–68, Grands Ballets Canadiens 1970, returned to R. Swed. B. 1968–72. Dances with d'Amboise's Ballet Spectacular and freelances.

AVRAHAMI, Gideon, b. Tel-Aviv 1941. Israeli dancer. First trained on a kibbutz in folk dancing. After military service studied under Sokolow and appeared in musicals in Israel. Joined Batsheva Co. 1966 and toured, visiting Bath. He remained in England and joined B. Rambert 1968. Chor. *Full Circle* (m. Bartok) 1972.

AZUMA, Tokuho (Azuma IV), b. Tokyo 1909, Japanese dancer. Studied under her father Uzaemon XV (Azuma III, b. 1875, d. 1945), one of the greatest of the Kabuki actors and teachers. In 1954 she founded in Tokyo the Azuma Kabuki Dancers and Musicians, a group which included stars of various Kabuki dynasties and also female players. It toured America 1954 and Europe 1955. The chief actor and dancer is her son Tsurunosuke Bando, b. Tokyo 1928 (dancing name, Azuma Tokutaka).

B

BABILÉE, Jean (Gutmann), b. Paris 1923. Fr. dancer and chor. Studied Paris Opéra and under Kniaseff. Début in Cannes 1941 (*Blue Bird*).

Joined B. des Ch. Élysées on its inception, 1945, as chief dancer. Later danced with Ballet Theatre in U.S. Rejoined Paris Opéra 1952 as étoile, for one season. Danced with Petit's Co. 1953, Charrat's 1954. Chor. *L'Amour et son Amour* (1948), *Til Eulenspiegel* (1949). His outstanding rôles were in *Le Jeune Homme et la Mort* (which he created), *Spectre de la Rose*, and *Blue Bird*. Mar. Nathalie Philippart. Formed his own company, Les Ballets Babilée, which toured Europe, Israel, Brazil and appeared at the Edinburgh Festival 1959. Among the dancers were Clair Sombert, Iovanka Biegovitch, Josette Clavier, Adolfo Andrade, Gerard Ohn. The repertoire: *Sable* (ch. Babilée, m. le Roux), *Divertimento* (ch. Babilée, m. Damase), *La Boucle* (ch. Babilée, m. Damase), *Adagio* (ch. Ohn., m. Albinoni), *Fugue* (ch. Charrat, m. Bach), *L'Emprise* (ch. Dick Sanders, m. Delerue), together with *La Création* of Lichine and Petit's *Jeune Homme et la Mort*. Guest artist Ballet Theatre 1950–52. Now acts in plays and films and in 1968 joined ballet group of Maison de la Culture, Amiens (Ballet-Theatre Contemporain). Director of the Ballet du Rhin at Th. Municipal, Strasbourg, 1972–73.

BABY BALLERINAS, name given to Baronova, Toumanova, and Riabouchinska (q.v.), then aged 13, 14, and 15, when the B. Russe de Monte Carlo was formed in 1933.

BACCELLI (Giovanna Zanerini), b. Venice, d. London 1801. It. dancer. First appeared King's Th., Haymarket 1774. Very popular in London, dancing in ballets by Noverre and M. Gardel (and notably in A. Vestris's benefit 1781, when the House of Commons was adjourned so that Members could attend). Début Paris Opéra 1782. Was mistress of third Duke of Dorset, living with him in Paris, where he was ambassador, and at Knole, where she was painted by Reynolds and Gainsborough. After the Duke had been made a Knight of the Garter she danced at the Paris Opéra wearing a blue bandeau on her forehead inscribed '*Honi soit qui mal y pense*'. Her reclining nude statue is one of the sights at Knole.

BACCHANALE, ballet, ch. Massine, m. Wagner (*Tannhäuser*), dec. Dali, f.p. Met. Op. N.Y. 9 Nov 1939 (Theilade, Kokitch). Ballet involving Ludwig II of Bavaria, Lola Montez, Venus, and Sacher-Masoch.

BACCHUS AND ARIADNE, ballet, ch. Lifar, m. Roussel, dec. Chirico, f.p. Paris Opéra 22 May 1931 (Spessivtseva, Lifar, Peretti). A new version ch. Descombey, dec. Daydé was f.p. Paris Opéra 8 Dec 1967 (Motte, Atanassof, Bonnefous)—in erotic, psychedelic style.

BAILADOS DO CIRCOLO DE INICIAÇÃO COREGRAFICA, Portuguese ballet Co. and private school founded in 1944 by Margarita de Abreu, Professor of the Dance at the Lisbon Conservatoire. This company,

33

in contrast with the Verde Gaio (q.v.), works chiefly in the classical style. They perform at the Teatro San Carlos.

BAILEY, Sally, b. Oakland, Calif. 1932. Am. dancer. Studied at San Francisco B. Sch. and with Volkova and Preobrajenska. Entered San Francisco B. 1951 as ballerina (in *Swan Lake*) where she remains.

BAISER DE LA FÉE, LE, ballet based on Hans Andersen's *The Ice Maiden*. Music Stravinsky. (1) Ch. Nijinska, dec. Benois, f.p. Ida Rubinstein Co., Paris Opéra 27 Nov 1928 (Rubinstein, Shollar, Vilzak). (2) Ch. Ashton, dec. Fedorovitch, f.p. S. Wells B., S. Wells Th. 26 Nov 1935 (Argyle, Fonteyn, Turner). (3) Ch. Balanchine, dec. Halicka, f.p. Am. B., Met. Op., N.Y. 27 Apr 1937 (Mullowny, Caccialanza, Dollar). Later in repertoire of Paris Opéra and N.Y. City B. (4) Ch. MacMillan, dec. Rowell, f.p. Royal Ballet, C. Garden 12 Apr 1960 (Beriosova, Seymour, Macleary). It is in the repertoire of many companies and some notable other Balanchine productions have been by Ballet Russe (Met. Op. N.Y. 1940 and at City Center, N.Y. 1946), N.Y. City B. (City Center, N.Y. 1950). A version, chor. R. Hynd, was performed by Dutch Nat. B., Stadsschouwburg, Amsterdam 16 Oct 1968 (Bovet, de Haas, Campbell).

BAKER, Josephine, b. St Louis, Missouri 1906. Am. negro dancer, singer and music hall artist. Début in Philadelphia. To Paris in 1925 dancing with La Revue Nègre at the Th. des Ch. Élysées and made all her career in France. Levinson wrote: 'Certaines poses de Miss Baker, les reins incurvés, la croupe saillante, les bras entrelacés et élevés en un simulacre phallique, la mimique de la face, évoquent tous les prestiges de la haute statuaire nègre.' She danced at the Folies Bergère and the Casino de Paris and in N.Y. in the Ziegfeld Follies (1936). Now runs an orphanage in the south of France, which she endowed.

BAKRUSHIN, Yuri, b. Moscow 1898, d. there 1973. Russ. writer. Son of A. Bakrushin (1865–1929, founder of Bakrushin Theatre Museum, Moscow). Director of Stanislavsky-Nemirovitch-Dantchenko theatre 1924–39. Teacher of ballet history at Bolshoi Sch. from 1942. Author of *Sixty-Five Years in the Theatre* (with K. Waltz 1928), *Tchaikovsky's Ballets and their History* (1940), biography of *Alexander Gorsky* (1946), *History of Russian Ballet* (1965) etc.

BAKST, Leon, b. Grodno, Russia 1866, d. Paris 1924. Russ. painter, friend of Diaghileff and Benois, and one of the founders of the Ballets Russes. First ballet design *Die Puppenfee*, Maryinsky Th. 1902. For Diaghileff he designed *Cléopâtre* (1909), *Carnaval, Schéhérazade* (1910), *Spectre de la Rose, Narcisse* (1911), *Le Dieu Bleu, Thamar, L'Après-midi d'un faune, Daphnis et Chloë* (1912), *Jeux* (1913), *Good Humoured Ladies* (1917), *Sleeping Princess* (1921). His daring use of bright colours

34

greatly influenced the decorators of the time and was largely responsible for the great impact which Diaghileff's Co. made in Paris and London. He left Russia in 1909 and never returned.

BAL, LE, ballet, book B. Kochno. (1) ch. Balanchine, m. Rieti, dec. Chirico, f.p. Diaghileff's Co., Monte Carlo 7 May 1929. Revived ch. Massine, Monte Carlo 1935. (2) ch. Jooss, m. Rieti, dec. Heckroth, f.p. B. Jooss, Essen, Nov 1930.

BALABINA, Feya, b. 1910. Russ. dancer. Studied at Leningrad Sch. under Vaganova. Graduated 1931 becoming one of the ballerinas of the Kirov Th., Leningrad. Small and with a sparkling technique. Artistic Director of the Leningrad (Vaganova) Sch. 1963–72.

BALACHOVA, Alexandra, b. Moscow 1887. Russ. dancer. Pupil of Bolshoi Sch., début in Bolshoi B. 1905, appointed ballerina 1913. Also danced in Petrograd with Gorsky. Danced in London 1909, partnered by A. Gorsky, in *Dance Dream*. Returned to London 1914 (partnered by Mordkin) to dance *Merry-go-Round* at the Empire Th. Left Russia for good in 1920. Settled in Paris. Mounted *Fille Mal Gardée* (in which she had danced Lise in Moscow) for Cuevas B. 1946, also in Ljubljana 1969 etc., taking the rôle of the Mother herself. Her grand house in Moscow (fully furnished) was the one in which Isadora Duncan was installed (with her school) when she went to Moscow in 1921.·

BALADIN, Fr. word which now means buffoon, comic dancer or mountebank, but originally was used in the Court of the sixteenth century in a different sense. The *baladin du roi* was charged with the education of the young princes in the sports of the time which included horse-riding, fencing, and dancing.

BALANCÉ, a swaying, rocking step from one foot to the other, usually in 3/4 time, en place.

BALANCE À TROIS, ballet, ch. Babilée, m. Damase, dec. Keogh, f.p. Babilée Co., Monte Carlo 25 Apr 1955 (Chauviré, Babileé, Kalioujny). Flirtation in a gymnasium.

BALANCHINE, George (Balanchivadze), b. St Petersburg 1904. Russ. dancer and chor. Trained Imperial (later Soviet) Sch. His first choreographic attempts were made in Russia in 1923. Principal chor. of last Diaghileff period (1925–9), of B. Russes de Monte Carlo 1932, then of his own Co. Les Ballets 1933. Went to the U.S. at end of 1933, to found Sch. of American Ballet and American Ballet with which, and with the N.Y. City B. developed therefrom, he has been continuously associated. Has also staged ballets for Original Ballet Russe, Monte Carlo, and Paris Opéra and created ballets in films and musicals. He has considerably influenced the trend of contemporary choreography.

35

Principal ballets incl. for Diaghileff, *Barabau* (1925), *Triumph of Neptune* (1926), *La Chatte* (1927), *Apollon-Musagète*, *Les Dieux Mendiants* (*The Gods Go A-begging*) (1928), *Le Bal* and *Le Fils Prodigue* (1929); for B. Russes de Monte Carlo, *La Concurrence*, *Cotillon*, and *Le Bourgeois Gentilhomme* (1932); for Les Ballets 1933, *Mozartiana*, *Errante*, and *Les Songes* (all 1933); for B. Russe de Monte Carlo, *Danses Concertantes* (1944) and *Night Shadow* (1946); for Ballet Theatre, *Waltz Academy* (1944) and *Theme and Variations* (1947); for Paris Opéra, *Palais de Cristal* (*Symphony in C*) (1947); for American Ballet *Serenade*, *Transcendence*, and *Alma Mater* (all 1934), *Reminiscence* (1935), *Orpheus* (Gluck) (1936), *Baiser de la Fée* and *Card Party* (1937), *Concerto Barocco* and *Ballet Imperial* (1941); for Ballet Society, *Four Temperaments* (1946), *Renard* (1947), *Divertimento*, *Symphonie Concertante*, *Orpheus* (Stravinsky), and *The Triumph of Bacchus and Ariadne* (all 1948); for N.Y. City B., *Bourrée Fantasque* (1949), *Firebird* (1950), *Swan Lake* (1952), *The Nutcracker* (1954), *Western Symphony* (1955), *Allegro Brillante*, *Agon* (1956), *Stars and Stripes* (1958), *Episodes* (1959), *Monumentum Pro Gesualdo*, *Liebeslieder Walzer* (1960), *A Midsummer Night's Dream* (1962), *Bugaku* (1963), *Tarantella* (1964), *Don Quixote* (1965), *Ragtime* (1966), *Glinkiana* (1967) etc. Mounted *Ballet Imperial* for S. Wells B. (1950) and ch. *Trumpet Concerto* (1950) for S. Wells Th. B. Author of *Complete Stories of the Great Ballets* (1954). Many of his ballets are now in the repertoires of European companies. D.Lit. (Brandeis University) 1965. Mar. Tamara Geva (1922), Vera Zorina (1938), Maria Tallchief (1946), Tanaquil LeClerq (1953). In 1969 he assumed the directorships of the ballets in Berlin and Geneva.

BALANÇOIRE, an exercise, a grand battement made while the dancer at the bar inclines his body forwards and backwards in opposition to the leg movements.

BAL DES BLANCHISSEUSES, LE, ballet, book Kochno, ch. Petit, m. Vernon Duke, dec. Lepri, f.p. B. des Ch. Élysées, Th. des Ch. Élysées, Paris 19 Dec 1946 (Petit, Danielle Darmance). Created to display the acrobatic dancing of Darmance.

BALLABILE, from It. *ballare*, to dance. Term introduced to the dance vocabulary by Carlo Blasis to designate a group dance by a large number of executants. The classical ballets of the Romantic period invariably included one or more ballabiles for the corps de ballet, introduced to rest the ballerina or as a finale.

BALLABILE, ballet 6 sc., ch. Petit, m. Chabrier, arr. Lambert, dec. Clavé, f.p. S. Wells B., C. Garden 5 May 1950 (Elvin, Negus, Dale, Heaton, Navarre, Grant, Chatfield). A ballet of grotesque incidents with magnificent dec.

BALLAD OF MEDIAEVAL LOVE, THE, ballet 7 sc., ch. Pia and Pino Mlakar, m. Lhotka, f.p. Stadttheater, Zurich 6 Feb 1937 (the Mlakars). In repertoire of the Yugoslav Cos.

BALLADE DE LA GEÔLE DE READING, LA, ballet 1 act, ch. Etchevery, m. Ibert, dec. May, f.p. Opéra Comique, Paris 12 Dec 1947 (Kergrist, Rayne, Tcherkas). The Oscar Wilde poem.

BALLERINA, from It. *ballare* and O.F. *baller*, to dance. Title bestowed on the female dancer who sustains the chief classical rôles in a ballet company. At the Maryinsky Th., St Petersburg in 1902 the ballet company (of 180) consisted of ballerinas, first and second soloists, coryphées, and corps de ballet. Only thrice in the history of the Imperial Th. has the additional title of 'prima ballerina assoluta' been bestowed—on Pierina Legnani, on Mathilde Kschessinska, and on Maya Plisetskaya. In the Paris Opéra B. the company (of 120) consists of the following cadres (with corresponding males also), premières danseuses étoiles, premières danseuses, grands sujets, petits sujets, coryphées, premiers quadrilles, seconds quadrilles, élèves ('rats'). See MARGOT LANDER.

BALLERINA, ballet, ch. Baranovsky and Litvinova, m. Mushel, dec. Ryftina, f.p. Tashkent B. 30 Apr 1952 (G. Ismailova, Zavyanov). Ballet on an incident in the life of the dancer Galya Ismailova, who herself danced the leading rôle.

BALLET, probably from It. *ballare*, to dance, *ballate*, a thirteenth- and fourteenth-century sung accompaniment to dancing, 'ballet' (pronounced bal-let, an Elizabethan part-song), and *balli* and *balletti* which, from designating a particular type of dancing, came to designate a court spectacle composed mainly of dancing. It can be defined today as a theatrical entertainment of group and solo dancing usually to a musical, vocal, or percussive accompaniment and with appropriate costumes, scenery, and lighting. See also MODERN DANCE.

BALLET, magazine, published monthly in London and edited by Richard Buckle. The first two issues were dated July–August and September–October 1939. Publishing was resumed after the war with the third number, January 1946, and continued until the issue of October 1952 when publication ceased. From October 1948 to December 1949 it was called *Ballet and Opera* (when the Earl of Harewood edited the opera section).

BALLET, journal in Spanish, founded in 1951, covering the dance in Latin-S. America. Edited from Peru and Chile by J. C. Franco and H. Ehrmann Ewart, and published quarterly until 1956.

BALLET AMBULATOIRE, lit. processional ballet. A processional pageant of mime and dancing to celebrate the visit of some great personage or some important event, such as the canonization of a saint, popular from the fourteenth to the early seventeenth century. The present-day processions with their battles of flowers are probably a relic of the *Ballet Ambulatoire*, which must be included amongst the forerunners of the ballet. Said to have originated in Portugal.

BALLET ANNUAL, THE, a record and year book of ballet published by A. and C. Black in London and edited by Arnold Haskell. Issue No. 1 dealt with the year 1946, No. 2, with 1947, and so on. With the second issue C. W. Swinson and G. B. L. Wilson joined the editorial board, and with the seventh, Mary Clarke and Ivor Guest. The final issue (No. 18, dealing with 1962–63) was in a smaller format. There were indexes in Nos. 2, 8, 9, 10, 11, 12, 13, 14. *Ballet Decade* (1956) was a volume of selections from the first ten issues.

BALLET ASSOCIATES OF AMERICA, an organization founded in 1941 by J. A. Talbot to encourage and help ballet in America. It contributed to and sponsored many Ballet Theatre productions up to 1947, and in 1950 it began to help the N.Y. City Ballet.

BALLET BLANC, lit. white ballet. Those ballets in the classical style in which the danseuses wear a white dress derived from the costume created for Marie Taglioni in *La Sylphide*, e.g. *Les Sylphides*, *Swan Lake*, etc.

BALLET BOOKSHOP, THE, in Cecil Court, London. See EDWARD C. MASON and JOHN O'BRIEN.

BALLET CARAVAN—see AMERICAN BALLET.

BALLET CLUB, THE, see BALLET RAMBERT. For Ballet Clubs, see CLUBS.

BALLET COMIQUE DE LA REINE, spectacle of dancing, singing and music staged by Balthasar de Beaujoyeux (lyrics by La Chesnay, m. de Beaulieu and Thibault de Courville, dec. Jacques Patin), f.p. Palais Bourbon, Paris 15 Oct 1581. Henry III of France wished to have a celebration for the marriage of his Queen's sister, Mlle de Vaudemont, to the Duc de Joyeuse and he called on his mother, the Queen Mother Catherine de Medici, to commission it. This work, based on the ideas evolved by de Baïf (see ACADÉMIE ROYALE DE MUSIQUE), an account of which was printed in 1582 and circulated to the principal European courts, contributed greatly to the development of the court ballet in France and the Masque in England. It is often held to have been the first ballet, although there were almost certainly earlier productions of a similar style in Italy.

BALLET D'ACTION, ballet in which movement, music, dec., and cost.

are subordinated to the unfolding of the theme. Weaver is generally held to have created the ballet d'action, although it is probable that both Angiolini and Hilferding worked in a similar style. A study of the scores used by Noverre and of contemporary descriptions of his ballets suggests that, whilst he ceased to use the corps de ballet as a background for the execution of traditional dance suites by the principal dancers, he had not conceived expressive dance-movement, but interspersed dances in mime scenes, much as arias are set in an opera. See DUCHESSE DU MAINE.

BALLET D'ÉCOLE—see CLASSICAL BALLET.

BALLET DE LA JEUNESSE ANGLAISE, company founded by Lydia Kyasht in 1939, opening at the Cambridge Th., London, and touring England, intermittently until 1946. Performed ballets by Sokolova, Kyasht, Helpmann, and Inglesby. Dancers included Pamela Foster, Béé de Roland, David Latoff.

BALLET DE LA NUIT, court ballet of de Benserade, ch. Chancy, Manuel, Vertpré, Lully, Mollier, m. de Cambefort and Boesset, effects G. Torelli, f.p. Salle du Petit Bourbon, The Louvre, Paris 23 Feb 1653. In this long ballet de cour enacting events throughout the night, Louis XIV (aged 14) played the part of The Sun—he was later called The Sun King. It was performed six times and the Dukes of York and of Buckingham danced with their hosts. J-B Lully was also probably dancing in it.

BALLET DER LAGE LANDEN—see HOLLAND, BALLET IN.

BALLET DU XXme SIÈCLE, LE, see MAURICE BÉJART.

BALLET FOR ALL, a part of the Royal Ballet organization which tours throughout the year giving lecture-demonstrations and performances of ballets to educate the public in the art. It was the idea of Peter Brinson (following a series of extra-mural lectures he gave for Oxford University), who founded the group, devised all the programmes and is the director. The first demonstration was given by him at the Cooperative Hall, Peckham 27 Jan 1961 (a class by Barbara Fewster with Rosemary Cockayne and Keith Martin of the Royal B. Sch., Dudley Simpson at the piano). Then, launched with a grant from the Gulbenkian Foundation, it started its career at Manor Court Modern Sch., Portsmouth 15 Sept 1964 (*Fille Mal Gardée*, danced by Brenda Last and Gary Sherwood). Now it tours continuously in a coach, with dancers from the Royal B. Among its programmes are *The World of Giselle* (f.p. Guildhall, King's Lynn 31 July 1963, Belinda Wright, Y. Yuresha—this was later developed to a full-length programme with actors); *Two Coppelias* (f.p. Civic Th., Rotherham 26 Sept 1967, M. Barbieri, Janet

Francis, V. Wakelyn) contrasting the original 1870 production with the current one—given in a different form for the centenary of the ballet, Richmond Th., Richmond, Surrey 25 May 1970 (N. Christian, Yvonne Cartier) etc. In 1970 two dancers from the London Contemporary Dance Theatre were added to the group to demonstrate the Graham style. In 1972 Alexander Grant became Director and a new work added, *Birth of the Royal Ballet*, f.p. Spa Pavilion, Felixstowe 11 Oct 1972.

BALLET-GIRL, THE NATURAL HISTORY OF THE, a charming little book by Albert Smith, with illustrations by Henning, published in London 1847. It describes in detail the daily life of a dancer of the period, with her aspirations and relaxations (exactly the same today). The author was a well-known comic writer whose lantern lectures on the ascent of Mont Blanc did much to popularize the sport of mountaineering. It was reprinted in 1972.

BALLET GUILD, an organization formed in London in 1941 by Christmas Humphreys and Deryck Lynham and dissolved in 1947. It staged performances and lectures at its St John's Wood Studio, with seasons and an ENSA tour with a company collected by Keith Lester and Molly Lake. Its reference library formed the nucleus of the London Archives of the Dance.

BALLET IMPERIAL, ballet, ch. Balanchine, m. 2nd piano concerto of Tchaikovsky, dec. Doboujinsky, f.p. Am. B. Caravan, Hunter College, N.Y. 29 May 1941 (Marie Jeanne, Caccialanza, Dollar). Frequently revived, notably with dec. Berman, S. Wells B., C. Garden 5 Apr 1950 (Fonteyn, Grey, Somes, Chatfield, Field). In 1963 the designs of C. Toms were adopted. Ballet of pure dancing, recalling memories of the Maryinsky Th. Re-named *Piano Concerto No. 2* in 1973.

BALLET INTERNATIONAL, Am. Co., founded by the Marquis de Cuevas in 1944. It had a single season at the Park Th., N.Y., Oct 30–Dec 23, 1944 which was a financial failure. Its repertoire and dec. were taken over by the Grand Ballet du Marquis de Cuevas.

BALLET INTIME, there have been a number of small ballet companies under this name, incl. that of Adolph Bolm formed in the U.S. in 1916 and reorganized for British tour in 1920, and that headed by Nana Gollner and Paul Petroff in 1938 in the U.S.

BALLETMAKERS, LIMITED, an experimental group of dancers and chors. mostly from the Royal Ballet, founded by Teresa and Fergus Early in London. They worked at Morley College and St Andrews Hall, West Kensington and gave their first performance in the latter in December 1963. For a few years they were doing valuable work in encouraging younger dancers and musicians but they came to an end in 1968.

BALLET-MASTER, see MAÎTRE DE BALLET.

BALLETOMANE (Russ. early nineteenth century), a ballet lover. The balletomanes who attended the performances of ballet at the Russ. Imperial Theatre knew every ballet and every dancer, and would religiously count every fouetté and lend their vociferous support to this or that dancer. The word 'Balletomania' was introduced to the English-speaking public by Arnold Haskell with his book of that title published in 1934, though it had occasionally been seen in print before.

BALLET-PANTOMIME, a spectacle of mime in which dances are inserted.

BALLET RAMBERT, the oldest Eng. ballet company still in existence. The first ballet presented by Madame Rambert was Ashton's first choreographic composition *A Tragedy of Fashion* in Nigel Playfair's revue *Riverside Nights* at the Lyric Th., Hammersmith in 1926. Other occasional productions followed, until on 25 Feb 1930 the Marie Rambert Dancers gave a public matinée at the Lyric Th., Hammersmith, which was sufficiently successful to warrant two further seasons honoured by the appearance of Tamara Karsavina and of Leon Woizikovsky. In October of that year, the B. Club was founded and the first experimental season was staged at the Mercury Th., which soon developed into regular Sunday performances. The limitations imposed by the miniature stage meant that productions could only succeed provided they were perfect in every detail, and this was one of the factors that made of the B. Rambert the ideal nursery of chors. The long list of productions during these early years included Ashton's *Capriol Suite* and *Florentine Picture* (1930), *La Péri*, *Façade* and *The Lady of Shalott* (1931), *Foyer de Danse* (1932), *Les Masques* (1933); Salaman's *Sporting Sketches* (1930–31); Tudor's first ballet *Cross-Garter'd* (1931); Andrée Howard's first ballet (with Susan Salaman), *Our Lady's Juggler* (1933), followed by *Mermaid* (with Salaman) (1934). In addition, there were revivals of excerpts and scenes from a number of the classical ballets. In 1931 they gave seasons in London and Manchester, and in 1934 the first real season at the Mercury opened with Ninette de Valois' *Bar aux Folies-Bergère*. Then followed Ashton's *Mephisto Valse*, Tudor's *The Planets* (1934), and *Jardin aux Lilas* (1936). Dancers to appear with the Co. at this period included Pearl Argyle, June Brae, Margot Fonteyn, Maude Lloyd, Alicia Markova, Agnes de Mille, Kyra Nijinsky, Peggy van Praagh, Ashton, Helpmann, Tudor, and Turner. 1937 saw the B. Rambert's first overseas tour (to France) and brought Tudor's *Dark Elegies* and Howard's *Death and the Maiden*, followed by *Lady into Fox* (1939), whilst yet another choreographer emerged in Frank Staff who, after a few early works, gave in 1939 *Czernyana*. Many of the dancers associated with the earlier years

41

were no longer available, but others had come to the fore, incl. Sally Gilmour, Celia Franca, and Walter Gore. Early in 1940 the B. Rambert joined the Arts Th. Club, and in June of that year joined forces with the London B., an association which lasted until September 1941. They continued to play regularly despite the 'blitz', producing many new works incl. Staff's *Enigma Variations* (his *Peter and the Wolf* was produced in May 1940) and Gore's *Confessional*. In September 1941 production of ballet at the Arts Th. Club ceased and the B. Rambert were prevented by legal complications from resuming their activities until, in March 1943, they began a series of tours sponsored by CEMA (which later became the Arts Council) to factories, camps, and provincial towns (notably Bristol and Salisbury), which not only provided entertainment to war workers and service men, but also did much to build up a vast new audience. The end of the war found the B. Rambert back in its stride with many additions to its repertoire, incl. Howard's *Carnival of Animals* (1943), *The Fugitive* and Gore's *Simple Symphony* (1944), *Mr Punch* and *Concerto Burlesco* (1946), and *The Sailor's Return* (1947). New dancers who began to assume leading rôles at this time included Paula Hinton, John Gilpin, and Belinda Wright. In the autumn of 1947 the Co. left for an eighteen months' tour of Australia and New Zealand, which gave a fresh impetus to ballet in those countries. On their return, yet another new choreographer appeared in the person of David Paltenghi (*Prismatic Variations* and *The Eve of St Agnes*, 1950). Few ballet organizations can boast that they have produced as many choreographers and dancers of merit, or have given as many opportunities to little-known musicians and designers, as the B. Rambert and none can have suffered so many desertions through sheer force of economic circumstances. Whatever may be the final judgement of history when their work is done, their contribution to contemporary Eng. ballet cannot be too often stressed. In 1954 Cranko chor. *Variations on a Theme* for them and in 1955, when their principal dancers were Beryl Goldwyn, Noreen Sopwith, Alexander Bennett. Robert Joffrey chor. *Persephone* and *Pas des Déesses*. In 1960 the principal dancers were Aldous, Martlew, Sandbrook; (men) Chesworth, Morrice, Bannerman. In this year the Bournonville *La Sylphide* was taken into the repertoire and several new ballets by Norman Morrice. David Ellis became Associate Director in 1955. The Company danced in America in 1959 and in China 1957, and had a season at S. Wells Th. during the summer each year. The full-length Petipa *Don Quixote* was mounted in 1962, and about that time the fortunes of the company began to decline. Nothing came of a suggestion in 1964 that they should combine with Festival B. In 1966 David Ellis resigned and the old B. Rambert came to an end. Its final performance was in the open-air theatre in Holland Park, London, on 2 July 1966, forty years and seventeen days after its first performance. Immediately it was re-organized, still the B. Rambert, with Arts Council support and Dame Marie Rambert at its head but with Norman Morrice as its Director. A small company of 16–18 dancers, they produced a new repertoire of very *avant-garde* ballets by young choreographers, though retaining some of the old repertoire (*Lilac Garden, Dark Elegies, Judgement of Paris* etc.) and had a small orchestra under their music-director Leonard Salzedo. Their first performance—at their new London base, the Jeannetta Cochrane Th.—was on 28 Nov 1966 (*Numeros* and *Intermède*, ch. Lacotte, *Time Base*, ch. Chesworth and *Laiderette*, ch. MacMillan). Among many ballets added later, the most successful have been a series by Glen Tetley *Ricercare* (1966), *Pierrot Lunaire, Ziggurat* and *Freefall* (1967), *Embrace Tiger and Return to Mountain* (1968). In 1969 the principal dancers were Patricia Rianne, Sandra Craig, Gayrie MacSween, Marilyn Williams, Mary Willis, Nicoline Nystrom, Julia Blaikie, Amanda Knott, Peter Curtis, Christopher Bruce, Bob Smith, Jonathan Taylor. See also MERCURY THEATRE.

BALLET RUSSE DE MONTE CARLO (including Col. de Basil's and René Blum's companies and Original Ballet Russe). Of the many attempts to gather together the scattered remnants of the Ballets Russes de Serge Diaghileff, two alone were to succeed, the Ballets de l'Opéra de Monte Carlo which remained under the direction of the erudite René Blum (q.v.) from shortly after the death of Diaghileff until the Ger. invasion of France and Monaco, and L'Opéra Russe à Paris. The latter organization, under the joint direction of Col. W. de Basil and Prince Zeretelli, which was seen at the Lyceum Th., London in 1931, revived a number of ballets from the Diaghileff repertoire, incl. *Petrouchka* and *The Dances from Prince Igor*, Nijinska's *Capriccio* and *Etude* (m. Bach, third version), and, with chor. by Boris Romanoff (who was ballet master to the Co.), *Chout, Pulcinella* and *L'Amour Sorcier*. From these two organizations there emerged in January 1932 the Ballets Russes de Monte Carlo, under the general direction of Col. de Basil, with René Blum as artistic director and Serge Grigorieff, who had been with Diaghileff from 1909, as stage director. (After the second season of the company it changed its name to Ballet Russe de Monte Carlo.) Many of the dancers who had collaborated with Diaghileff were no longer available but, as a result of the Russian revolution, a number of the former ballerinas of the Imperial B., incl. Mmes Kschessinska, Preobrajenska, Trefilova and Egorova were teaching in Paris, and it was to their studios that the new company turned to make up its numbers, acquiring the 'baby ballerinas' Toumanova, Baronova and Riabouchinska and strengthened

43

in 1933 by the arrival of Danilova. The first performances given in Monte Carlo were followed by the first London season at the Alhambra, which opened on 4 July 1933 for three weeks and lasted four months, for London, starved of ballet since the death of Diaghileff, welcomed them with open arms. The leading dancers in that season were (in addition to those mentioned) Verchinina, Tchernicheva, Zorina, Lichine, Shabelevsky, Woizikovsky. In addition to revivals of ballets by Petipa, Fokine, Massine and Balanchine, many new works were produced. The first ballet master was Balanchine, who created *La Concurrence* and *Cotillon* before he left at the end of 1932 to form Les Ballets 1933. He was succeeded as maître-de-ballet by Massine, who gave to the company *Les Présages, Jeux d'Enfants, Scuola di Ballo, Le Beau Danube* and *Choreartium*. Early in 1936 René Blum resigned his artistic directorship of the company, which then became known as Col. W. de Basil's Ballet Russe. Blum then founded the René Blum Ballets de Monte Carlo and its subsequent history is given later in this article. In 1938 Massine also left de Basil's company and joined Blum (vid. inf.). In 1938 the Ballet Russe du Col. de Basil, renamed Covent Garden Russian Ballet (where they had their greatest successes), was taken over by Educational Ballets Limited, a company of which the directors were V. Dandré (q.v.), Germaine Sevastianov and W. G. Perkins, and for whom Fokine mounted *Cendrillon* and *Paganini*, whilst Lichine rechoreographed *Le Fils Prodigue* and created *Protée*. During that 1938 season, at Covent Garden in June, René Blum's company were also performing at Drury Lane Theatre just round the corner and balletomanes rushed from one performance to the other to see their favourite ballets and dancers. Because of an impending lawsuit between the two companies de Basil nominally retired. However, at the end of the 1939 season, Col. de Basil became chairman and managing director of Educational Ballets Limited and the company now took the name of Original Ballet Russe. They went to Australia in 1940 (taking Baronova, Riabouchinska, Dolin and Lichine) where Lichine created *Graduation Ball* for them and Schwezoff his *Eternal Struggle*. Thence they performed in New York, presenting Baronova, Toumanova and Riabouchinska again. At the end of 1940 they toured in Mexico and then to Cuba where, in Havana, some of the dancers went on strike on account of non-payment of salaries and alleged breach of contract. There they were stranded but eventually returned to New York, but their new impresario (Fortune Gallo) left them and, at the end of 1941, they went again to Mexico and toured in South America for four years (the Second World War). At the end of 1946 they returned to New York and in 1947 came to Europe, having a season at C. Garden (chief dancers, Jeanmaire, Morosova, Moulin, Riabouchinska, Lichine, Dokoudovski,

Skouratoff, Orloff, Jasinsky). It finally broke up in Paris the same year. After de Basil's death in 1951 an attempt to revive it in England was made by George Kirsta and the Grigorieffs in 1951, but after an Eng. tour and a season at the Festival Hall and Adelphi Th., London, in 1951–52, it was dissolved. In their final season (Jan. 1952 at the Adelphi Th., London) their dancers included Toni Lander, Inge Sand, Sonia Arova, Nina Strogonova, Paula Hinton, Joan Tucker, Dokoudovsky, Spurgeon, Jack Carter, Vassilkovsky. In 1949 the company made two films in Paris, *Graduation Ball* (Bal des Cadets) and *Lac des Cygnes* (Moulin, Dokoudovsky). That completes the story of the Original Ballet Russe of Col. de Basil.

When, early in 1936, René Blum resigned his artistic directorship of the Ballet Russe de Monte Carlo (vid. sup.), he founded the René Blum Ballets de Monte Carlo to carry on the annual season at Monte Carlo. Fokine, as maître-de-ballet, created for him *L'Épreuve d'Amour*, *Don Juan* and *Les Éléments*. Fokine did not, however, continue his connexion and at the beginning of 1938 Massine left Col. de Basil (vid. sup.) and assumed the artistic direction of the René Blum Co., which then took the title of Ballet Russe de Monte Carlo and was sponsored by an Am. corporation, World Art Inc. (subsequently known as Universal Art Inc.). At that time Danilova, Toumanova, Eleanora Marra, Roland Guerard, Marc Platoff, George Zoritch and others left Col. de Basil's company and joined Massine—and Sol Hurok, de Basil's impresario, booked the Blum-Massine company and no longer de Basil's. The Blum-Massine Ballet Russe de Monte Carlo gave its first season at Monte Carlo, marked by the creation of Massine's *Gaîté Parisienne* and *Seventh Symphony*. They then came to Drury Lane, London, when they found the original de Basil company dancing at C. Garden (vid. sup.). Meanwhile a sensational lawsuit was pending between Universal Art Inc. and de Basil, who had purchased the greater part of the Diaghileff cost. and dec., as an outcome of which the latter obtained the exclusive right to perform certain of Massine's ballets. Thus the mantle of Diaghileff had been split between the two Cos. At this period (1938) the Massine B. Russe de Monte Carlo had among its dancers Markova, Krassovska (Leslie), Nini Theilade, Danilova, Toumanova, Slavenska, Massine, Lifar, Eglevsky, Franklin, Youskevitch. They toured America for two seasons and were to have opened at C. Garden in September 1939, but the outbreak of war caused the season to be cancelled. They remained in America and de Mille chor. *Rodeo* for them in 1942. Blum had resigned in 1940 and remained in France, finally dying in a German concentration camp in 1944. Massine resigned in 1945 (to form his own Co., B. Highlights), but the artistic policy was essentially a perpetuation of the Ballets Russes (but not with

45

the *avant-garde* creative urge of the Diaghileff Ballet). The only important new works to be created were Massine's *Nobilissima Visione*, *Bacchanale* and *Rouge et Noir*.

With the interruption of communications with France in 1940 and Blum's death the last visible links with Monte Carlo had been broken. American infiltration had, of course, been slowly taking place in the corps-de-ballet, but when the War ended Am. dancers began to take their places among the principals, and works by Am. chors., composers and designers to be featured in the repertoire. Danilova was the prima ballerina from 1938 to 1951. The fortunes of the Co. (then directed by Sergei I. Denham and a non-profit making concern) began to decline in the 1950s (when its dancers included Ruthanna Boris, Mary Ellen Moyland, Nina Novak, Yvonne Chouteau, Gertrude Tyven, Leon Danielian, Oleg Tupine, Roman Jasinsky) and they did not dance in New York from 1950 to 1957 (when Alicia Alonso, Irina Borowska and Franklin rejoined). They gave their last performances in 1962.

To sum up, the Ballet Russe de Monte Carlo was founded by Col. de Basil (with René Blum) in 1932, changed its name to Original Ballet Russe in 1939 and lasted until 1952. René Blum left the above company in 1936 and founded the René Blum Ballets de Monte Carlo. Massine joined him in 1938 and their company then assumed the name Ballet Russe de Monte Carlo. It continued until 1962. These two companies were the direct descendants of Diaghileff's Ballets Russes.

BALLET RUSSE DU COLONEL DE BASIL, LE, see BALLET RUSSE DE MONTE CARLO.

BALLET RUSSE HIGHLIGHTS, small Co. led by Massine, formed 1945, to tour theatres and stadiums. Dissolved 1946. Dancers included Massine, Eglevsky, Baronova, Hightower, Guelis.

BALLETS AFRICAINS, LES, dancers from French Equatorial Africa, founded by Kéïta Fodéba 1950 while a law student in Paris (he became Minister of the Interior of French Guinea while still the principal dancer). Has danced several times in London.

BALLET SCHOOL, ballet, ch. Messerer, m. Liadov, Liapounov, Glazounov, Shostakovitch (but later changed to Shostakovitch entirely), f.p. Bolshoi B., Met. Op. N.Y. 17 Sept 1962 (Plisetskaya, Maximova, Fadeyechev, Vasiliev). This ballet of the progress of students through the classroom is of the type of Lander's *Étude*.

BALLETS DE LA JEUNESSE, LES, founded in 1937 by Egorova, J.-L. Vaudoyer, and F. Barette in Paris. It only lasted during the year, but it launched the careers of Skibine, Geneviève Moulin, Tatiana Leskowa, Algaroff, Audran, and Bartholin.

BALLETS DE PARIS, Fr. Co. formed by Roland Petit on his secession from the Ballets des Ch. Élysées, at Th. Marigny, Paris 22 May 1948 and, notwithstanding ballets by Janine Charrat, Boris Kniaseff, and a revival, in a reduced version, of Massine's *Beau Danube*, essentially the reflection of his own artistic personality. With a small number of talented artists incl. Janine Charrat, Renée Jeanmaire, Colette Marchand, for a time Nina Vyroubova, Gordon Hamilton, Serge Perrault, Vladimir Skouratoff, and, as guest artist for their first season, Margot Fonteyn, they presented in a short period of time a number of daring works in which a strongly acrobatic element has often been evident. *Carmen*, f.p. London 21 Feb 1949, with its brilliant décors by Clavé and, above all, the inspired interpretation of Jeanmaire in the title rôle, ran for months on end in London, Paris, and N.Y., drawing audiences far wider than the usual ballet public and calling forth violent criticism and excessive praise. The Co. broke up in America in 1950 after plans to film *Carmen* in Hollywood miscarried and most of the dancers returned to Europe. It re-formed in Paris in 1953, with Violette Verdy, Claire Sombert, Hélène Constantine, José Ferran, Serge Perrault, George Reich, Babilée, and Petit, with new ballets *Le Loup*, *Deuil en 24 Heures*, *Cine Bijou*, and appeared in London in 1953 and 1954. It broke up again in America in 1954 as before. It reappeared again at the Th. des Ch. Élysées in 1955, with Verdy, Veronika Mlakar and Petit and again in 1958 at the Alhambra and in N.Y.

BALLETS DES CHAMPS ÉLYSÉES, LES, began with the appearance of Roland Petit and Janine Charrat at the dance recitals organized by Irène Lidova at the Th. Sarah Bernhardt, Paris, in 1944. Soon they were surrounded by a group of artists mostly in their 'teens, who, impatient to give expression to their artistic aspirations, had revolted against the rigid limitations imposed by the Opéra and the Opéra Comique. Their impresario, Claude Giraud, was himself only 20 years of age, and the piano accompaniment was provided by J. M. Damase, then only 16, but later a *Prix de Rome* laureate. Boris Kochno, Jean Cocteau, and Christian Bérard gave their wholehearted support, achieving artistic miracles out of remnants of material and themselves cutting and fitting on the stage. The first recital, on 1 Dec 1944, was an immediate success and was followed by a more ambitious evening on 2 Mar 1945, at the Th. des Champs Élysées, with the first performance of *Les Forains*. Renée Jeanmaire, Éthéry Pagava, Nathalie Philippart, Irène Skorik, Youly Algaroff, Christian Foye, Petit himself, and Serge Perrault had now been joined by Nina Vyroubova, as yet little known outside a small informed circle. Roger Eudes, the director of the Th. des Ch. Élysées, was sufficiently impressed to offer the young company a permanent home, and on 12 Oct 1945 the B. des Ch. Élysées was born. Many of the best contemporary Fr. musicians and designers were soon co-operating. The first London season opened at the Adelphi Th. 9 Apr 1946. The effortless dancing of Babilée as The Joker in Charrat's *Jeu de Cartes* (Janine Charrat was not with the company and had joined the Nouveau Ballet de Monte Carlo), the magnificent dec. of Bérard and Beaurepaire, the essentially Fr. flavour of Petit's chor., and the contagious enthusiasm of the young company, combined to create something of the effect of a window opening on a new world after the dismal war years, and took London by storm. New ballets by Petit, *Les Amours de Jupiter*, *Le Bal des Blanchisseuses*, *Le Rendez-Vous*, the unforgettable *Jeune Homme et la Mort* (devised by Cocteau), Gsovsky's *La Sylphide*, succeeded each other with almost terrifying rapidity as they went from one successful season to another, with Violette Verdy (Guillerm), Leslie Caron and Danielle Darmance appearing in the company. That evil genius of ballet companies, and Fr. companies in particular, internal dissension, was, however, soon to make its appearance. Roland Petit left in January 1948 to form his own Ballets de Paris, joined by Serge Perrault and, for a time until her engagement by the Opéra, Nina Vyroubova. Babilée created his first ballets, *L'Amour et son Amour* and *Til Eulenspiegel*, before he too left to work now with this company, now with that. The death, on 12 Feb 1949, of Christian Bérard, was another serious loss. Lichine and Massine created a number of works, outstanding amongst which was the former's *La Création*. Skorik was engaged as prima ballerina to the Munich Opera House in 1950, and that same year Roger Eudes ceased to present the Co.

BALLETS JOOSS, see JOOSS, KURT.

BALLETS MINERVA, small ballet company founded by Edward Gaillard in London 1953. It tours Britain, visiting the smaller towns and is supported by the Arts Council. The first performance was at St John's Hall, Wembley, 27 Aug 1953. Most of the choreography is by the founder and his associate director and principal dancer Kathleen Gray. Alan Carter and Imre Eck have also created ballets for them. There are 14 dancers and they tour with their costumes in a coach.

BALLETS MODERNES DE PARIS, a small group organized by Françoise and Dominique (Françoise Michaud and Dominique Dupuy) in 1955. They perform small chamber works. Deryck Mendel is a member of the company, which tours.

BALLETS 1933, LES, a company created 1933 by Edward James, Balanchine, Kochno, and Dimitriev. Although it only gave a short season in Paris (Th. des Ch. Élysées) and in London (Savoy Th.) during that year, it was noteworthy in presenting Toumanova, Lubov Rostova,

Nathalie Leslie, and also Tilly Losch (wife of Edward James). Derain, Tchelitchev, Sauguet, and Milhaud all worked for this Co., and Balanchine created for it *Errante*, *Songes*, *Mozartiana*, and *Les Sept Pêches Capitaux* (in which Lotte Lenya played the singing Anna).

BALLET SOCIETY, founded in N.Y. by Lincoln Kirstein and Balanchine 1946 to present new works and generally encourage the lyric theatre. Leon Barzin was musical director, Lew Christensen ballet master, Paul Magriel the editor of publications (which included *Dance Index*), and Jean Rosenthal the technical supervisor. Its first production was at the Central High Sch. of Needle Trades, N.Y. 20 Nov 1946, but thereafter at N.Y. City Center Th. Important works presented have been Balanchine's *Four Temperaments*, *Orpheus*, *Symphonie Concertante*, *Divertimento*, and Taras's *The Minotaur*. From this organization grew the N.Y. City B. (q.v.) with which it continues to work for the benefit of teachers and regional ballets.

BALLET SOPIANAE, a ballet company formed in 1960 in Pecs, Hungary, to give new and experimental works by Imre Eck (q.v.) its Director. It was formed from a single very talented class at school of the National B. in Budapest, with Eck as its principal dancer. Its first season was in 1961 with the programme *Ballad of Horror* (m. Szokolay), *Variations on an Encounter* (m. Vujicics), *Concerto to the Rainbow* (m. Hidas). Among the dancers were Eszter Arva, Gabriella Stimacz, Maria Bretus, Cecilia Esztergalyos, Edith Handel, Sandor Toth, Ferenc Csifo, Antal Fodor. Among Eck's ballets are *Cobweb* (m. Laszlo Gulyas) 1961, *Hiroshima* 1963, *Bartok Concerto* 1965, *Miraculous Mandarin* 1965 (he has made over 40 ballets). The Co. visited London in 1963 and has since toured widely (to Boston, U.S.A. 1969). In 1970 Sandor Toth became director and Eck choreographer.

BALLETS RUSSES, the name of Diaghileff's Co., see under DIAGHILEFF.

BALLETS RUSSES DE MONTE CARLO, LES, see BALLET RUSSE DE MONTE CARLO.

BALLETS SUÉDOIS, a company founded by Rolf de Maré (q.v.) in October 1920, and lasting until March 1925. The chief dancer and chor. was Jean Börlin, who produced a remarkable number of *avant-garde* ballets of considerable interest, amongst them *Nuit de Saint-Jean*, *Tombeau de Couperin*, *La Création du Monde*, *La Jarre*, *El Greco*, *Les Mariés de la Tour Eiffel*, *Relâche*. Borlin gave a recital in Paris in March 1920, and the Co. proper gave its first performance at the Th. des Champs Élysées, Paris 25 Oct 1920. They danced all over Europe and in the U.S. and were finally disbanded in 1925 by the founder. Their principal dancers were chiefly Danes and Swedes, and included Börlin, Carina Ari, Jenny Hasselquist, Kaj Smith, Yolande Figoni, Ebon

Strandin. Their ballets were novel and experimental, and, like Diaghileff's productions, artistically in advance of their time.

BALLETS: U.S.A., Am. ballet company formed by Jerome Robbins in 1958 to perform at the Festival of Two Worlds, Spoleto, and at the Brussels Exposition. Its first performance was at Teatro Nuovo, Spoleto, 6 June 1958. Also in 1958 it appeared in Trieste and at the Florentine Maggio Musicale. In 1959 it toured Europe extensively and made a great impact in Paris, at the Edinburgh Festival (having lost all its property in an air crash en route), and in London. It was typically American in its jazz style and its informal costume. The repertoire consisted of ballets by Robbins *Moves* (no music or dec.), *Afternoon of a Faun* (q.v.), *N.Y. Export: Op. Jazz* (q.v.), *The Concert* (q.v.). There were sixteen dancers, including Muriel Bentley, Barbara Milberg, Wilma Curley, Patricia Dunn, Christine Meyer, Jane Mason, Jay Norman, John Jones, Michael Maule. The company did not dance in 1960, but made a long tour in 1961–62 visiting Paris, London, Germany and Denmark and then disbanded.

BALLET THEATRE, see AMERICAN BALLET THEATRE, which this company has been called since 1957.

BALLET-THÉÂTRE CONTEMPORAIN, Fr. national company founded by the Ministry of Culture in 1968 and first based on the Maison de la Culture, Amiens with Françoise Adret as choreographic director and J.-A. Cartier as artistic adviser. It presents new creations only and using only modern composers and designers. Its first performance was at Amiens 4 Dec 1968 presenting *Danses Concertantes* (ch. Blaska, m. Stravinsky, dec. Delauney), *Salome* (ch. Lazzini, m. Miroglio, dec. Viseux), *Aquathême* (ch. Adret, m. Malec, dec. Singier), *Deserts* (ch. Descombey, m. Varèse, dec. by Group for Visual Art Research). There were 25 dancers in the corps and 10 soloists, among them Marie-Claire Carrié, Martine Parmain, Vera Filatoff, Juan Giuliano, James Urbain, Muriel Belmondo, Don Snyder, with Jean Babilée, Colette Marchand and Magdalena Pope as guests. It also has a small educational group touring factories, schools etc. First appeared in Paris in February 1969 at Th. de l'Est Parisien. Danced in London (Sadlers Wells) 1971. In 1972 the company left Amiens and is based on the Théâtre Municipal, Angers.

BALLETT 1965, 1966 etc., German year book of world ballet, edited by Horst Koegler and others and published by Friedrich's of Hanover. An important annual record of ballet, first appeared in 1965, covering the 1964–65 season—and every year since.

BALLETTO, journal of the ballet, published quarterly in Rome. Edited by Adriano H. Luijdjens. The first number appeared in November 1955. It ceased in 1962.

BALLET TODAY, monthly magazine founded and edited by Miss P. W. Manchester in London. The first issue was March–April 1946. After the April 1952 issue the founder severed her connexion with the magazone. The paper passed through several hands; in October 1953 Peter Craig-Raymond became editor. In January 1954 Mrs Estelle Herf became co-publisher and in June managing editor and publisher. From 1965 it was published every two months and ended with the July–August issue of 1970. It specialized in a good coverage of ballet abroad.

BALLET WORKSHOP, an experimental ballet organization founded by David Ellis and his wife Angela (daughter of Marie Rambert), at the Mercury Th., London. Their first performance was on 14 Jan 1951. At Sunday evening performances throughout the year new works were given by new and by established choreographers, musicians, and artists. The talents of many young creative artists and dancers were discovered at these performances. Its last performance was on 26 Mar 1955.

BALLON, lit. bounce, as of a ball. A term signifying springiness or elasticity of the feet. The term has no connexion with the Fr. dancer Balon, as has sometimes been supposed.

BALLONNÉ or PAS BALLONNÉ, lit. a bouncing step. There are two types, ballonné simple and ballonné composé. In the *ballonné simple* the dancer springs upwards, opening one leg at hip-height to the front, side or back and alights on the other foot, closing the first to the cou-de-pied (or to just below the knee in a *grand ballonné*). The *ballonné composé* is a ballonné simple, then stepping on to the working leg and closing the other leg to the fifth position with a dégagé.

BALLOTTÉ or PAS BALLOTTÉ, lit. a tossing movement. A movement in which the dancer raises the left foot behind the knee of the supporting leg, and, with a slight plié, spring upwards, crossing one foot in front of the other at the cou-de-pied, alighting on the left foot, whilst extending the right in a développé to the front (i.e. unfolding it to its fullest extent) and then bringing it in to the knee, preparatory to repeating the step with a développé of the left leg to the back. The step may of course be executed on the opposite foot. The arms are usually extended to the front. This step is danced by Albrecht and Giselle with arms linked in the first act of *Giselle*.

BALON, Jean (or BALLON), b. Paris 1676, d. there 1739, Fr. dancer and chor. who entered Paris Opéra 1691. He was famous for his lightness and he danced with Mlle Prévost and Mlle Subligny. With the former he mimed to music a version of Corneille's *Les Horaces* at the Duchesse

51

du Maine's (q.v.) château at Sceaux in 1714—a production which fore-shadowed the ballet d'action. So privileged was he that he could greet the King by shaking his hand. He danced in London, when Weaver said he was expressionless. His father François Balon (b. 1644), was also a dancer at the Opéra.

BAMBOULA, a dance, probably originating in the West Indies, to the accompaniment of the native tambourine of that name.

BANOVITCH, Milenko, b. Zagreb 1936. Yugoslav dancer. Pupil of Illitch. Joined Charrat's Co. 1958, Petit's 1959, Tcherina's 1961. Took principal rôle in film *Les Amants de Teruel* (Tcherina) 1962. Danced Prince in Larrain's *Cendrillon*, Paris 1963.

BAR or BARRE, a wooden bar fixed to the classroom wall at approximately hip-height, which the dancer holds to facilitate equilibrium in certain exercises. Every dancing class starts with exercises at the bar. Touring companies carry portable bars which they can erect on the stage for practice.

BAR AUX FOLIES-BERGÈRE, ballet (inspired by Manet's painting) 1 act, ch. de Valois, m. Chabrier, dec. Chappell, f.p. B. Rambert, Mercury Th., London 15 May 1934 (Markova, Pearl Argyle, Ashton).

BARBAY, Ferenc, b. Miskolc 1943. Hungarian dancer. Pupil of Hedvig Hidas and Lepeshinskaya. Joined Hungarian Nat. B., Budapest 1967. To Munich B. 1969 becoming a principal.

BARBERINA, LA (Barberina Campanini), b. Parma 1721, d. Barschau 1799. It. dancer who was a favourite in all the capitals of Europe. Mistress of Prince Carignan, Lord Arundel, Marquis de Thébouville, and the Duc de Denfort. Eloped with Lord Stuart Mackenzie, was loved by Frederick the Great (who engaged her to dance in Berlin), and married the son of his chancellor. Created countess by Frederick the Great and became Abbess of a charitable institution endowed by herself. She first performed the *entrechat huit* in Paris 1739.

BARBIERI, Margaret, b. Durban 1947. S. African dancer, niece of Cecchetti. Pupil of Mannin-Sutton Sch. in Durban and R. Ballet Sch. from 1963. Joined Touring R. Ballet 1965, danced *Giselle* for Ballet for All 1967 and for Touring Royal B. 1968. Became a principal 1970. Danced her first Aurora for Royal B., Leeds 25 Nov. 1969.

BARCLAY, Donald, b. New Malden 1934. Eng. dancer. Studied at Cone-Ripman Sch. 1945–48, Royal Ballet Sch. 1948–50. Royal Ballet 1950–55. Studied under Crofton 1956–57. Joined de Cuevas Co. 1956. Principal dancer Staatsoper Stuttgart, 1957–60. To Oslo 1960–62, Kassel 1962–63, Dortmund 1963–65, Cullberg B. 1965. Ballet master S. Wells Th. 1966–69, Festival B. 1970.

BARI, Tania, b. Treure, Rotterdam 1936. Dutch dancer. Pupil of Netty van der Valk, Nora Kiss and Messerer. Début in Ballets de l'Étoile (Béjart), Paris 1955. Since then has been one of Béjart's principal dancers (1957–58 with his Ballet Theatre, and since 1959 with his Ballet du XXme Siècle at Th. de la Monnaie, Brussels). Cr. chief rôles in Béjart's *Sonate à Trois* (1957), *Orphée* (1958), *Sacre du Printemps* (1959).

BARISHNIKOV, Mikhail, b. Riga 1948. Latvian dancer. Pupil of Riga Ballet Sch. from 1960 and of the Kirov Sch. from 1964 under Pushkin. Joined Kirov B., Leningrad 1967 becoming soloist 1968. Varna Gold Medal 1966. First danced in the West, in London, 1970. Gold Medal, Moscow Competition 1969.

BARKOCZY, Sandor, b. Szolnok 1934. Hungarian dancer and chor. Trained in Leningrad 1950–57. Joined Budapest Opera B. 1957 and now chor. and teacher in State B. Institute. Ch. *Classical Symphony* (m. Prokofieff) 1966, *Dance Suite* (m. Bartok) 1967.

BARN DANCE. (1) Am. rural dance said to have been introduced in the nineteenth century, although it has probably evolved from pagan memories; (2) ballet in 1 act, ch. Catherine Littlefield, m. Guion, Powell, and Gottschalk, dec. A. and S. Pinto, f.p. Littlefield B., Philadelphia 23 Apr 1937 (Dorothie Littlefield, T. Cannon). Revived for B. Theatre, Met. Op., N.Y. 9 May 1944.

BARNARD, Scott, b. Indiana 1945. Am. dancer. Pupil of Joffrey, England, Zaraspe, Verdak. Joined Joffrey B. 1968 becoming soloist.

BARNES, Clive, b. London 1927. Eng. writer on ballet and drama. Educ. Oxford, where he ran the University Ballet Club. Assistant Editor of *Dance and Dancers* from 1951, becoming Executive Editor from 1962. Ballet critic of *The Spectator* 1959–65, *Daily Express* 1956–65, and *The Times* 1961–65. To New York in 1963 as dance critic of *The New York Times* and also (from Sept 1965) its drama critic. Author of *Ballet in Britain Since the War* (1953), *Frederick Ashton and his Ballets* (Dance Perspectives, No. 9, 1961), *Ballet Here and Now* (with others) (1961). London correspondent of *Dance Magazine* (N.Y.) 1956–63. Created Knight of the Order of Dannebrog 1972.

BARON, A., Fr. writer whose *Lettres et Entretiens sur la Danse* (1824) is an important book on the dance up to that date, containing many anecdotes and reflections, and an illustration of choreographic notation.

BARON (Baron Nahum), b. Manchester 1906, d. London 1956. Eng. Court and ballet photographer. His book of photographs *Baron at the Ballet* appeared in 1950, *Baron Encore* in 1952 and *Ballet Finale* in 1958.

BARONOVA, Irina, b. Petrograd 1919. Russ. dancer. Studied under Preobrajenska in Paris and danced at the Paris Opéra in 1930. In 1932 Balanchine made her a ballerina (with Toumanova and Riabouchinska, the three 'baby ballerinas') of de Basil's Co. where she cr. rôles in *Les Cent Baisers, Paganini, Les Présages* (Passion), *Beau Danube* (First Hand), *Jeux d'Enfants*, etc. She was ballerina of various companies in America until 1946, when she retired, married, and lived in England until 1969 when she moved to Switzerland. She also made the films *Florian* (1939), *Yolanda* (1942), and danced in musical comedies. Member of the Technical Committee of the Royal Academy of Dancing.

BARRA, Maximo, b. Melilla 1942. Sp. dancer. Pupil of Irvin, Griffith and Royal B. Sch. Danced in musicals in America then joined Geneva B. 1962. Soloist Frankfurt B. from 1970.

BARRA, Ray, b. S. Francisco 1930. Am. dancer and ballet master. Pupil of Merriweather, the Christensons, Caton, Volkova etc. Joined S. Francisco B. 1949 becoming soloist 1953. Soloist Ballet Th. 1955. To Stuttgart 1958 as principal. Owing to injury stopped dancing 1966 and went to the Deutsche Oper, Berlin 1966 as assistant ballet master and teacher for MacMillan. To Frankfurt 1970 as assistant ballet master and to Hamburg 1973.

BARRETT, Carol, b. London 1948. Canadian dancer. To Canada 1954, pupil of Nesta Toumine, Hightower, Addison. Joined Teatro di balletto di Roma 1967 and Northern Dance Theatre 1969 as principal dancer.

BART, Patrice, b. Paris 1945. Fr. dancer. Pupil of Trailine and at Paris Opéra Sch. under Peretti. Joined Paris Opéra B. 1960 and became premier danseur 1968. Won Gold Medal at first Moscow Competition 1969. Guest artist Festival V. 1970 and 1973. Guest artist R. Winnipeg B. 1972.

BARTHOLIN, Birger, b. Odense 1900. Dan. dancer and chor. Studied with Fokine, Legat, and Volinine. Joined Rubinstein Co. in Paris 1928, and various other companies, returning to Denmark 1931. Formed his own Co. there, and in 1935 joined Blum's Monte Carlo B. and was maître de ballet and chor. of B. de la Jeunesse 1937. Chor. *Symphonie Classique, Romeo and Juliet* (1937), *Parisiana* (1954) which were taken into Royal Danish B. repertoire. Appointed maître de ballet of Nat. Opera, Helsinki 1954, Oslo 1955. Now teaches in Copenhagen and since 1963 has organized an annual International Ballet Seminar there.

BARTOK, Bela, b. Nagyszentmiklós, Hungary 1881, d. N.Y. 1945. Hungarian composer of ballets *The Wooden Prince* (1917), *The Miraculous Mandarin* (1926), and whose music has been much used for ballets, e.g. *Caprichos* (H. Ross), *Medea* (Cullberg), *Concerto Burlesco* (Gore), *The Prisoners* (Darrell), *Sonate à Trois* (Béjart), etc.

BARZEL, Ann, b. Chicago 1913. Am. writer on dance. Studied under Bolm, Volinine, Legat etc. Dance critic of *Chicago Times* 1946–49, *Chicago American* from 1951. Author of many articles on the dance in Am. journals. Made a remarkable private collection of dance films.

BAS, fr. low. See PORT DE BRAS.

BASSE DANSE, lit. low dance. The name variously attributed to the fact that the feet were barely raised from the ground (terre à terre) and to the dance having a humble origin. Solemn dance paced in duple time (in the sixteenth century it was sometimes danced in triple time), popular from the mid-fourteenth to the mid-sixteenth centuries. A collection of some sixty basses danses known as the *Livre de Basses Danses de la Bibliothèque de Bourgogne,* written for Marie of Bourgogne, daughter of Charles the Bold, 1400, is preserved in the Royal Library in Brussels, whilst, in 1521, there was published in England Robert Coplande's *The maner of dauncing of Bace daunces after the use of fraunce,* now in the Bodleian Library. The Basse Danse usually consisted of Branle, Reprise, and Second Reprise, to which was later added the Tordion—see also GALLIARD, MINUET. Ashton has introduced a Basse Danse in his *Capriol Suite.*

BAT-DOR DANCE COMPANY, THE, was founded in Tel-Aviv in 1968 by the Baroness Batsheva de Rothschild, with Jeannette Ordman (from Johannesburg) as Artistic Director. It works in both classical and modern styles, has its own theatre and school and a company of about eighteen dancers. It tours Israel and in 1970 appeared in Italy, and at the Holland Festival 1972.

BATHYLLUS, of Alexandria, the freedman and favourite of Maecenas, brought to perfection, together with Pylades of Cilicia, the imitative dance or ballet called Pantomimus during the reign of Augustus (31 B.C. to A.D. 14). Bathyllus excelled in comic, and Pylades in tragic personifications. At the time street brawls between their respective followers were frequent.

BATSHEVA DANCE COMPANY, the group dancing the Martha Graham and other modern ballets founded in Tel-Aviv in 1964 by the Baroness de Rothschild. It made its first European tour in 1968 and appeared with great success at the Bath Festival in England (Theatre Royal, Bath). Besides many Graham ballets, it has works by McKayle, Pearl Lang, Tetley, Morrice etc. Among its principal dancers are Rina Schenfeld, Linda Hodes, Rena Gluck, Galya Gat, Moshe Efrati, Ehud Ben-David, Anthony Binstead. Its artistic director was Jane Dudley and it first appeared in N.Y. in December 1970. In 1971 William Louther became artistic director.

BATTAGGI, Teresa, b. Milan 1890, d. Rome 1957. It. dancer and teacher. Ballerina of Scala, Milan and then to Rome where she taught at the Opera Sch. with her sister, Placida.

BATTEMENT, lit. a beating. Generic term designating a number of exercises and movements of the leg, executed with a beating motion, e.g.:

Grand Battement Jeté, lit. large thrown beating movement, an exercise to loosen the hip joint and turn out the leg, in which the working leg is raised to the side (à la seconde), in front (à la quatrième devant), or to the back (à la quatrième derrière) quickly and as high as possible, without bending the knee.

Battement Tendu, lit. stretched beating, an exercise in which the working leg is opened to the front, side, or back, with the toe resting lightly on the ground (pointe tendue), and then closed again in the fifth position in front or at the back.

Battement Frappé, lit. struck beating, an exercise for quick extension of the leg and elevation, in which the dancer, standing at the bar, extends one foot briskly to the front, side, or back, striking the ball of the foot on the ground and stretching the toe until it is slightly off the ground, and return it to the position sur le cou-de-pied.

Petit Battement sur le Talon, lit. small beating on the heel, a movement in which the danseuse, on the point and supported by her partner, lightly beats the heel of the supporting foot with the sole of the working foot. This is also performed as an exercise in class on the full or half point.

Petit Battement sur le cou-de-pied, an exercise at the bar in which the dancer beats lightly with the working foot, which may be fully extended or partially relaxed, to the front and back of the cou-de-pied of the supporting leg.

Grands Battements en Cloche, usually executed at the end of barwork, an exercise in which the dancer, with erect body, swings his leg backwards and forwards as high as possible, to loosen the hips.

BATTERIE, lit. a succession of beats. Movements in dancing in which the feet beat together. 'Grande Batterie' where the elevation is large, includes the cabriole, sissonne battue, temps de poisson, etc. 'Petite Batterie' where the elevation is small, includes the entrechat, brisé, etc.

BATTU, lit. Fr. beaten. Pas battu—a beaten step, jeté battu—a beaten jeté, etc.

BAUER, Margaret (Bauer-Pokorny), b. Vienna 1927. Austrian dancer. Studied at Staatsoper Sch. and abroad. Joined Staatsoper B., becoming soloist 1951, principal 1960. Danced *Giselle* in the production Gordon Hamilton made for the opening of the Staatsoper in 1955.

BAUMANN, Helmut, b. Berlin 1939. German dancer and chor. Pupil of Gustav Blank and van Dyk. Joined Hamburg B. 1959, Münster B. 1965 as soloist, and soloist and assistant ballet master Cologne 1966. Chor. *Minimax* (m. Ponchielli) 1964, *Simple Symphony* (m. Britten) 1965, *Wilder Thymian* (m. Baird) 1967, *Fresko* (m. Vivaldi) and (with other chors.) *Choreomatics*, 1969 etc. Appointed director of Cologne B. 1971, forming his Tanz Forum (q.v.).

BAYADÈRE, Indian temple dancer and a popular subject for ballet in the Romantic era. (1) Ballet *Le Dieu et la Bayadère*, ch. F. Taglioni, m. Auber, dec. Ciceri, cost. Lecomte, f.p. Paris Opéra 13 Oct 1830 (Taglioni, Noblet, Nourrit). (2) Ballet *La Bayadère* (Russ. *Bayaderka*), ch. Petipa, m. Minkus, f.p. Bolshoi Th., St Petersburg 4 Feb 1877 (Vazem, Ivanov, Johansson). It was revived in 1900 for Kschessin-skaya, and in 1902 for Pavlova. A shortened version is still in the Soviet repertoire. The 'Kingdom of the Shades' act was produced for the Royal Ballet by Nureyev at C. Garden on 27 Nov 1963 (Fonteyn, Nureyev), with cost. P. Prowse. A notable Russian revival was that by Ponomaryov at the Kirov Th., Leningrad 10 Feb 1941 with Dudin-skaya and Chabukiani (who chor. his own variation) in the leads.

BAYANIHAN PHILIPPINE DANCE COMPANY, a dance group of Fili-pinos (with musicians) which was established in Manila in 1956. It gained international prominence when it appeared at the World's Fair in Brussels (Expo '58) and it has toured the world ever since (Europe in 1958, America in 1959). Its director and chief chor. is Lucrecia Urtula and its most famous dance is the Tinikling in which barefooted couples skip between rapidly clapped bamboo poles held at ankle-level. 'Bayanihan' is a Tagalog word meaning the ancient custom of working together.

BAYLIS, Lilian, b. London 1874, d. there 1937. Eng. theatre manager and the founder of the Old Vic and Sadler's Wells theatre companies. The daughter of a singer, Newton Baylis, she emigrated with her parents to S. Africa in 1890. She settled in Johannesburg and taught music, organized a ladies' orchestra and was a pioneer of musical education. Her aunt Emma Cons invited her to return to London to help her manage the Victoria Theatre (see OLD VIC) and she became acting manager in 1898. On Emma Cons' death in 1912 she became the sole manager. In 1926 Ninette de Valois wrote to her and suggested the establishment of a ballet company at the Old Vic. Lilian Baylis engaged her to arrange the dances in some of the plays and in 1928 the first performance was given there by de Valois' dancers—thence sprung the

57

Royal Ballet (q.v.). See also SADLER'S WELLS THEATRE. She was made a Companion of Honour in 1929. She was intensely religious, like her aunt, and combined her devotion with a shrewd judgement.

BAYLIS, Nadine, b. London 1942. Eng. designer. Pupil of Central Sch. of Art, London. Much associated with B. Rambert and Tetley's ballets. Designed for Rambert *Realms of Choice* (ch. Morrice 1965), *Ziggurat* (ch. Tetley 1967), *Embrace Tiger and Return to Mountain* (ch. Tetley 1968), *Hazard* (ch. Morrice 1965), *Blind Sight* (ch. Morrice 1969), *Living Space* (ch. Bruce 1969), *Rag Dances* (ch. Tetley 1971), *That is the Show* (ch. Morrice 1971) etc. For Nederlands Dans Th. *Circles* (1968), *Imaginary Film* (1969), *Mutations* (1970) etc. For Royal Ballet *Field Figures* (ch. Tetley 1970). For Australian B. *Raymonda* (ch. Petipa-Nureyev 1965), *Gemini* (ch. Tetley 1973). Also worked for Cologne, Hamburg etc. ballets.

BAZ, Irma, b. Buenos Aires 1944. Argentinian dancer. Début in Teatro Argentino, La Plata, joined San Martin B. 1968.

BEALE, Alan, b. 1936. Eng. dancer and teacher. Pupil of Janet Cranmore, Crofton, Royal B. Sch. Joined S. Wells B. 1957. Left 1965 owing to injury. Taught at Dance Centre, London 1966. Went to Stuttgart B. as assistant ballet master the same year. In 1971 became director of the Noverre Ballet (q.v.) in Stuttgart.

BEATON, Sir Cecil, b. London 1904. Eng. photographer and stage designer. His designs include: for C. B. Cochran Revue, *The First Shoot* (1938); for de Basil, *Le Pavillon* (1936); for S. Wells, *Apparitions* (1936), *Les Sirènes* (1946); for B. Theatre, *Les Patineurs* (1946); for de Basil, *Camille* (1946); for N.Y. City Ballet, *Illuminations* (1950), *Swan Lake* (1951), *Picnic at Tintagel* (1951); for S. Wells Th. B., *Casse Noisette* (1951), *Marguerite and Armand* (1963). Awarded C.B.E. 1957. His cost. and dec. for the musical *My Fair Lady* (1956) are especially noteworthy. Awarded a knighthood 1972.

BEATRIX, ballet in 3 acts, ch. Jack Carter, m. Adam (arr. Horovitz), dec. Bardon, cos. Walker. f.p. Festival B., Festival Hall, London 31 Aug 1966 (Dianne Richards, Gilpin, Miklosy, Salavisa, Hayworth). Based on Saint-George's *La Jolie Fille de Gand*, using the same music but with additional pieces by J. Horovitz.

BEATS, a beaten step (see also BATTU). A jumping step in which the dancer beats the lower part of his calves together.

BEAUCHAMP, Pierre, b. Versailles 1636, d. Paris 1705. Fr. dancer and chor. Director of the Académie Royale de Danse. His father and grandfather were Court musicians. He taught dancing to Louis XIV, was responsible for the choreography of many of Molière's and Lully's ballets and made all the Court ballets from 1648. His most famous production was *Le Triomphe de l'Amour*, 1681. Is credited (by Rameau) with the invention of the 'Five Positions', but he may only have codified an established practice. He retired as *maître-de-ballet* in 1687. He was a pioneer of dance notation and appears to have invented the system usually attributed to Feuillet (q.v.), whose book was published in 1700. In 1704 Beauchamp took legal action against Feuillet for the infringement of his system of notation. Neither side won for Beauchamp had not attempted to patent it; he was, however, told by the court to put in a 'privilege' for himself—but he died before he could do so. In the course of the hearing 25 dancing masters testified that Beauchamp had shown them his system of notation 25 years previously; it was similar to that which Feuillet subsequently claimed for himself.

BEAU DANUBE, LE, ballet, ch. Massine, m. J. Strauss and Désormière, dec. Polunin (after C. Guys), cost. E. de Beaumont, f.p. B. Russes de Monte Carlo, Monte Carlo 15 Apr 1933 (Danilova, Baronova, Riabouchinska, Lichine, Massine), being a reconstitution of a 2 sc. ballet of the same name, f.p. at E. de Beaumont's *Soirée de Paris*, Th. de la Cigale, Paris, 17 May 1924 (Lopokova, Massine). It is now one of the most popular ballets and in the repertoire of many companies.

BEAUGRAND, Léontine, b. Paris 1842, d. there 1925. Fr. dancer. Entered Opéra Sch. 1850 and studied under Mme Dominique, taking small solo rôles until 1864, when she made a great success in the principal rôle in the revival of Saint-Léon's *Diavolino*. Nuitter intended her for the rôle of Swanilda in his *Coppélia*, but it was felt that her reputation was not yet great enough and the rôle passed to Bozzacchi, who died shortly after the first performance in 1870. When the ballet was revived the next year, Beaugrand obtained the rôle and was hailed by Gautier as the 'successor of Grisi'. She created the principal rôle in Mérante's *Gretna Green* (1873). After differences with the management of the Opéra she retired in 1880. She was something of a wit.

BEAUJOYEUX, Balthasar de, sixteenth-century (d. 1587) It. violinist (Baldassarino de Belgiojoso) and valet de chambre of Catherine de Medici (and also of Mary Stuart). He arranged the Court *Fêtes* and ballets, the most famous being the *Ballet Comique de la Reine* (q.v.) (1581).

BEAUMONT, Cyril W., b. London 1891. Eng. writer, historian of the ballet, and bookseller. Author of over forty books on ballet, of which the following are especially notable: *Theory and Practice of Allegro in Classical Ballet* (with M. Craske 1930), *Michel Fokine and his Ballets* (1935), *The Complete Book of Ballets* (1937), *The Romantic Ballet in Lithographs* (1938), *The Diaghileff Ballet in London* (1940), *The Ballet*

59

Called Giselle (1944), *The Ballet Called Swan Lake* (1952), *Ballets of Today* (1954). He also translated many important French books on the dance, and edited others. With Idzikowsky he analysed and codified the teaching of Cecchetti (contained in their *Manual of the Theory and Practice of Classical Theatrical Dancing*, 1922), and in 1922 founded the Cecchetti Society. In 1934 the Fr. Government awarded him the *Palmes Academiques* and in 1950 the Legion of Honour. He received the Imperial Society's Imperial Award 1961, the Royal Academy of Dancing's Queen Elizabeth II Award 1962, and in 1962 was made a Knight-officer, Order of Merit (Italy). Member of the Imperial Society's Administrative Council from 1924 and retired as Chairman in 1970. He was President of the Critic's Circle in 1957 and was chairman of its Ballet Section 1951–61. Awarded O.B.E. 1962. In 1965 he closed his bookshop at 75 Charing Cross Road, London, after 55 years.

BEAUMONT, Piers, b. Barcelona 1944. Eng. dancer. Pupil of Royal B. Sch. Danced the leading male rôle in *Pineapple Poll* at School Matinée 1961 and joined C. Garden Opera B. 1961 and the Touring Royal B. in 1963, becoming a principal dancer 1968. Joined Festival B. as principal 1969. Left 1970 to freelance. Danced in Gothenburg B. 1971 as principal. From 1972 he has taught and in 1973 joined the staff of the Royal B. Sch.

BEAUMONT, Tessa, b. Paris 1938. Fr. dancer. Pupil of Kschessinska and Nora Kiss. Début in Béjart's Co., Paris 1954. Soloist in Charrat's Co. 1955, of Béjart's Co. 1955, and of Petit's Co. 1955. In Massine's Balletto Europeo, Nervi 1960. Danced Orlikowski's *Cendrillon*, Paris 1963. Now freelances. Mar. Bozzoni.

BEAUPRÉ, b. 1758, d. 1842. Fr. danseur comique at Paris Opéra. In 1793 he saved twenty-four members of the Opéra who were proscribed.

BEAUTÉS DE L'OPÉRA, LES, Fr. book published 1845 in Paris by Soulie, edited by Giraldon, containing descriptions of the popular operas and ballets. Philarète Chasles wrote the history of the Paris Opéra, Janin the description of *La Sylphide*, Gautier of *Le Diable Boiteux* and *Giselle*, and Chasles of *Ondine*. It was beautifully illustrated by English and French artists, and was simultaneously published in London, in translation and with the same illustrations, by Bogue under the superintendence of Charles Heath.

BEAUTY AND THE BEAST, ballet, ch. Cranko, m. Ravel, dec. Margaret Kaye, f.p. S. Wells Th. B. at S. Wells Th. 20. Dec 1949 (Patricia Miller, David Poole). A pas de deux.

BEAUTY AND THE BEAST, ballet 2 acts, ch. Darrell, m. Musgrave, dec. Minshall. f.p. Scottish Th. B., S. Wells Th. 19 Nov 1969 (D. D.

Washington, T. Sakai). Based on the story by Mme de Villeneuve, with commissioned music.

BECK, Hans, b. Haderslev 1861, d. Copenhagen 1952. Dan. dancer and chor. Pupil at Royal Th. Sch., Copenhagen. Début 1879, solodancer 1881, becoming maître de ballet 1894 until 1915. He was considered one of the greatest male dancers of his time and it was he who lovingly preserved and presented some fifteen of the Bournonville ballets, the Galeotti ballet, and *Coppélia*, which are the treasures of the Danish repertoire. He chor. many ballets, the most famous being *The Little Mermaid* (m. Henriques 1909).

BECKETT, Keith, b. Bletchley 1929. Eng. dancer. Studied Cone-Ripman Sch. and first app. as actor in plays from 1942–46. Won Genée Silver Medal at R.A.D. 1946. Joined Festival B. 1950, becoming a soloist, left in 1959 to become a television producer.

BEDELLS, Phyllis, b. Bristol 1893. Eng. dancer and teacher. Pupil of Cavallazzi, Cecchetti, Genée, Bolm, Pavlova. Début Prince of Wales Th., London 1906 in *Alice in Wonderland*. In 1914 succeeded Kyasht as prima ballerina at the Empire Th. for three years. Toured with Novikoff, prima ballerina in Beecham seasons at C. Garden. Retired in 1921 after illness, but returned in 1925, dancing with Dolin, etc. Danced with the Camargo Society 1930 and 1931, finally retiring 1935. Established a school first in Bristol and then in London until 1966 when she retired and closed her school. Vice-President of the R.A.D. Author of *My Dancing Days* (1954). Received Queen Elizabeth II Award of R.A.D. in 1958 and made Fellow of the R.A.D. 1971. Her daughter Jean Bedells (b. Bristol 1924) was in the S. Wells B. (becoming ballet mistress) and teaches in the Royal B. Sch. Her granddaughter Anne Bedells is in Festival B.

BEELITZ, Claus, b. Berlin 1938. German dancer. Pupil of T. Gsovsky, became soloist of Mannheim and, from 1961, of Deutsche Oper, Berlin.

BEGAK, Alexander, b. Moscow 1935. Russian dancer. Studied at Bolshoi Sch. and graduated to Bolshoi Ballet 1954, becoming soloist 1955. Danced in London 1960.

BÉJART, Maurice, b. Marseilles 1927. Fr. dancer and chor., son of the philosopher Gaston Berger. Pupil and dancer at Marseilles Opéra to 1945, then of Staats in Paris. *Bachelier-ès-Lettres*. 1947–49 toured with Schwarz, Darsonval, Charrat, Petit. Principal dancer International B. 1949–50, and of R. Swedish B. 1951–52. In 1954 formed Les Ballets de l'Étoile in Paris. Chor. many ballets for musicals, films, etc. Made film *L'Oiseau de Feu* (1952) with Ellen Rasch. Chor. *Symphonie pour un homme seul* (1955), *Haut Voltage* (1956), *Orphée* (1959) etc. His Company then became Ballet Th. de Maurice Béjart. In 1959 chor. *Le Sacre de Printemps* and in 1960 was appointed Director of Ballet at the Th. Royale de la Monnaie, Brussels and this became the home of his company which was renamed Le Ballet du XXme Siècle. In the Cirque Royale, Brussels, ch. *Les Quatre Fils d'Aymon* (1961), *IXme Symphonie de Beethoven* (1964) and *Romeo and Juliet* (Berlioz) (1966)—huge productions in the round which had enormous success. Produced Berlioz' *Damnation of Faust* at the Paris Opéra (1964) which was also performed in 1965 in the Epidaurus amphitheatre in Greece. He was offered the Directorship of Ballet at the Paris Opéra but refused. Béjart makes use of great (and often unexpected) spectacular scenic effects and throughout his works runs the theme of the problems of modern man struggling with an oppressive society. His company is in demand all over the world and spends most of its time touring. Béjart's political and social views are strong and after he made a curtain speech in Portugal he and his company were immediately expelled from the country. In Belgium he is something of a national hero, and his audiences are young and enthusiastic. His company danced at the Edinburgh Festival in 1962 (in the ice rink, *Les Quatre Fils d'Aymon*) and in 1960, 1971 and 1972 in London. Its first appearance in America was in 1971 at the Brooklyn Academy, N.Y. Among the principal dancers associated with him are Tania Bari, Tessa Beaumont, Duska Sifnios, Laura Proenca, Jaleh Kerendi, Suzanne Farrell, Germinal Casado, Jorge Donn, Paoli Bortoluzzi, Jorge Lefebre. He embraces Indian styles in some ballets and his school in Brussels is called Mudra Academy. Among his ballets are *Le Sacre de Printemps* (1959), *Bolero* (1960), *Messe pour le temps présent* (1967), *Bhakti* (a section of the triptych *À la Recherche de . . .*) (1968), *Baudelaire* (1968), *L'Oiseau de Feu* (1971), *Nijinsky, Clown de Dieu* (1971).

BELGIUM, BALLET IN, see under BÉJART, VLAANDEREN BALLET VAN and WALLONIE BALLET DE. There is a municipal ballet at Liège.

BELLE HÉLÈNE, LA, ballet, ch. Cranko, m. Offenbach-Aubert, dec. Vertès, f.p. Paris Opéra 6 Apr 1955 (Chauviré, Renault). Ballet based on the operetta.

BELLS, THE, ballet 5 episodes, based on E. A. Poe's poem. Ch. Ruth Page, m. Milhaud, dec. Isamu Noguchi, f.p. Chicago University Composers' Series, Chicago 26 Apr 1946 (Page, Josias).

BELSKY, Igor, b. Leningrad 1925. Russ. dancer and chor. Graduated from Leningrad Sch. 1943 but taken into Kirov B., then in Perm, in 1942. Leading dancer of Kirov B., cr. title rôle of *Shurale* (1950), and of Mako in *Path of Thunder* (1957). Joined Maly Th. Leningrad as principal chor. 1962, becoming Artistic Director. Ch. *Coast of Hope* (1959), *Leningrad Symphony* (1961), *Eleventh Symphony* (1966), *Ovod* (m. Chernov) (1968). Hon. Artist R.S.F.S.R. Mounted *Swan Lake* for Dutch Nat. B. 1965.

BENEATH ITALIAN SKIES, ballet, ch. S. Sergueef and Zakharoff, m. Yurovsky, f.p. Opera House, Kieff 1952 (V. Potapova, Gerasimchuk, Lurye, Segal).

BENESH, Rudolf, b. London 1916. Eng. painter who, with his wife Joan Benesh (b. Liverpool, *née* Rothwell, entered S. Wells B. 1951), copyrighted a system of dance notation in 1955. Author of *An Introduction to Benesh Notation.* Founded Institute of Choreology in London 1960, training students from all over the world in Benesh Notation. See DANCE NOTATION.

BENNET, Alexander, b. Edinburgh 1930, Scottish dancer. Studied under Marjory Middleton. Début Edinburgh Ballet Club, joined B. Rambert, becoming principal dancer 1953. Joined S. Wells Th. B. 1956, becoming a principal dancer 1957. Rejoined B. Rambert 1963. Ballet master Transvaal B. 1965, Western Th. B. 1966. Taught and mounted ballets in America 1968. Founded Anglo-Scottish B. for Edinburgh Festival 1969. B. master C. Garden Op. B. 1969, and of Iceland B. 1970. Joined staff of Arts Educational Schools 1971.

BENNINGTON SCHOOL OF THE DANCE, at Bennington College for Women, Vermont, U.S.A. A summer school of modern dance from 1934 to 1942. It was very influential in drawing attention to the works of Graham, Doris Humphrey etc. In 1948 the summer school of the Connecticut College School of Dance (q.v.) took over its function.

BENOIS, Alexandre, b. St Petersburg 1870, d. Paris 1960. Russ. painter who lived in Paris since 1905. He was one of Diaghileff's friends and the one who most influenced him in the B. Russes, which they founded and of which he was Artistic Director until he resigned in 1911. For Diaghileff he designed *Le Pavillon d'Armide* (which he had created in St Petersburg 1907), *Les Sylphides, Giselle, Petrouchka,* and *Le Chant du Rossignol;* for Ida Rubinstein *La Bien Aimée* (1928) and *Les Noces de Psyché et l'Amour* (1928); for de Basil *Graduation Ball* (1940) (see also ZUCCHI). Author of *Reminiscences of the Ballet Russe* (1941) and *Memoirs* (1960). His son, Nicola Benois (b. St Petersburg 1902), is chief designer to La Scala, Milan, and also made the dec. for Festival B.'s *Esmeralda* (1954). His niece, Nadia Benois (mother of Peter Ustinov), lived in England and designed the dec. for *Hebe, Dark Elegies, Lady into Fox,* etc., for B. Rambert, and in 1939 *The Sleeping Princess* for S. Wells B.

BENSERADE, Isaac de, b. Lyon-le-Forêt 1612, d. Paris 1691. Fr. poet and librettist. Provided libretti and verses for a large number of the Court Ballets of Louis XIV, including *Mascarade en forme de Ballet* (1651), *Ballet de la Nuit* (1653), *Le Triomphe de l'Amour* (1681).

BERAIN, Jean, b. Bar-le-Duc 1638, d. 1711. Fr. engraver and designer. Pupil of Lebrun, succeeded Henry de Gissey as designer to Opéra 1673. Provided cost. (but few dec.) for principal Court and Opéra ballets from his appointment to his death. His designs, based on contemporary court dress, were inspired by a distinguished symbolism. Designed cost. and dec. of *Le Triomphe de l'Amour* (1681) and also the cost. for Louis XIV when he appeared in the ballets.

BERAIN II, Jean, son of the former, whom he succeeded as designer to Opéra 1711, where he remained until c. 1721.

BÉRARD, Christian, b. Paris 1902, d. there 1949. Fr. painter, who was responsible for some of the finest recent stage décors and cost. His work for the ballet includes *Cotillon* (1932), *Mozartiana* (1933), *Symphonie Fantastique* (1936), *Seventh Symphony* (1938), *Les Forains* (1945), *The Clock Symphony* (1948), and *La Rencontre* (1948). His first work for the theatre was the ballet *La Nuit* in Cochran's Revue 1930. He was also a director of the B. des Ch. Élysées on their foundation.

BERCHOUX, M., Fr. poet whose *La Danse ou les Dieux de l'Opéra* (1806) is an account of the rivalry between Vestris and Duport.

BERETTA, Caterina, b. Milan 1840, d. there 1911. It. dancer and teacher. Trained in Milan and a member of the Scala B. Ballerina at Paris Opéra 1855 and later in Turin and the Scala, Milan. To St Petersburg 1877 as ballerina and became ballet mistress there. Returned to Milan and was ballet mistress of the Scala 1902–1908. Trefilova and Pavlova went there to study with her and so, in 1904, did Karsavina (who describes her teaching in *Theatre Street*).

BERG, Bernd, b. E. Prussia 1943. German dancer. Trained from age of 11 in Leipzig, then E. Berlin. Escaped to West 1963, joined Stuttgart B. 1964, became soloist 1967.

BERGSMA, Deanne, b. Pretoria 1941. S. African dancer. Studied under Marjorie Sturman and R. Ballet Sch. Joined Royal Ballet 1959. Soloist 1962. Principal 1967. Cr. girl's solo in Ray Powell's *One in Five* (1960), Lady Mary Lygon in *Enigma Variations* (1968).

BERIOSOVA, Svetlana, b. Kaunas 1932, daughter of Nicholas Beriozoff. Eng. dancer. Pupil of Beriozoff and Vilzak. Début 1941 as Clara in *Casse Noisette* (B. Russe de Monte Carlo). Danced *Sylphides* and *Casse Noisette* for Ottawa B. Co. 1947. Joined de Cuevas Co. 1947, ballerina Metropolitan B. 1947 (cr. *Designs with Strings* and *Fanciulla delle Rose*).

Joined S. Wells Th. B. as joint ballerina 1950. To S. Wells B. 1952 as soloist, becoming ballerina 1955. Danced *Sleeping Beauty* (1954), *Swan Lake* (1955), *Giselle* (1956). Guest artist Belgrade 1954, Scala Milan, Vienna, Stuttgart, Australia etc. Created many rôles in the Royal B., incl. *The Prince of the Pagodas* (1957), *Antigone* (1959), *Le Baiser de la Fée* (1960), *Persephone* (1961), *Les Biches* (1964), *Les Noces* (1966), *Enigma Variations* (1968).

BERIOZOFF, Nicholas, b. Kaunas 1906. Russ. dancer and maître de ballet. Father of Svetlana Beriosova. Studied in Czechoslovakia and danced with Prague Opera B. and with National B. in Kaunas. Joined René Blum Co. in Monte Carlo 1935 where he learned the repertory direct from Fokine. To U.S. in 1938 with Ballet Russe de Monte Carlo and later maître de ballet B. International. Joined de Cuevas Co. 1947 and later in the year Metropolitan B., succeeding Gsovsky as maître de ballet. Maître de ballet at La Scala, Milan 1950–51. Maître de ballet Festival B. 1951, mounting *Petrouchka, Casse Noisette, Schéhérazade* and *Prince Igor*. Chor. *Esmeralda* (1954). Maître de ballet de Cuevas Co. 1956, of Staatsoper, Stuttgart 1957. Maître de ballet de Cuevas Co. 1961–62, of National Ballet of Finland 1962–63, of Zurich Ballet 1964–71. Has mounted Fokine ballets and the classics in many countries. Ballet master San Carlo Opera, Naples 1971. In 1972 mounted Fokine's *Petrouchka, Schéhérazade* and *Prince Igor* on Paris Opéra B. as a filmed record.

BERKAN, Binay, b. Istanbul 1942. Turkish dancer. Studied under B. Appleyard, Molly Lake in Turkey and at Royal B. Sch. Entered Turkish State B. becoming a principal dancer.

BERMAN, Eugene, b. St Petersburg 1899, d. Rome 1972. Russ-Am. painter whose designs are in the tradition of Berain and the Bibienas but seen through twentieth-century eyes. His first designs for the ballet were for Lifar's *Icare* (1938). Since then he has created cost. and dec. for *Devil's Holiday* (1939), *Concerto Barocco* (1941), *Romeo and Juliet* (1943), *Danses Concertantes* (1944), *Le Bourgeois Gentilhomme* (1944), *Giselle* (1946), and *Ballet Imperial* (1950), Tudor's *Romeo and Juliet* (1953), Balanchine's and Robbins' *Pulcinella* (1972).

BERNERS, Lord, b. Bridgnorth 1883, d. Faringdon 1950. Eng. composer and designer. Ballet scores include *The Triumph of Neptune* (1926), *Foyer de Danse* (1932) (from his *Luna Park* suite), *A Wedding Bouquet* (1937), *Cupid and Psyche* (1939), and *Les Sirènes* (1946).

BERNSTEIN, Leonard, b. Laurence, Mass. 1918. Am. composer and conductor. Ballets include *Fancy Free* (1944), *On the Town* (1944), *Facsimile* (1946), *Age of Anxiety* (1950), *Candide* (1956), *West Side Story* (1957). His *Mass* (1971) has dances chor. Ailey.

65

BERTRAM BATELL'S SIDESHOW, a children's programme given by the Ballet Rambert (of which it is an anagram) at the Jeannetta Cochrane Th., London, first given 28 Mar 1970 to 8 Apr 1970. The ballets were frolics chor. by members of the company.

BERYOZKA DANCE ENSEMBLE, a women's dance group formed in Moscow in 1948 by Nadezhda Nadezhdina (b. St Petersburg 1908), a former ballerina of the Bolshoi Th., Moscow, and Stalin Prizewinner. It was founded on a group of dancers from Kalinin who had won a national competition in Russia. Their dances are theatre dances based on folk dances; their most famous is a round dance where the girls glide about the stage as if they were on wheels, holding birch branches ('Beryozka' means birch). They have danced all over the world and first appeared in London in 1954.

BESOBRASOVA, Marika, b. Yalta 1918. Russ. (now Monagasque) teacher. Pupil of Sedowa, Egorova, V. Gsovsky. Joined B. de Monte Carlo 1935, B. de Cannes de M. Besobrasova 1940–43 (director), Cuevas 1947–49, B. des Ch. Élysées 1950–51. Opened her school in Monte Carlo 1949 where she still teaches. In 1966 formed Co. for the centenary of Monte Carlo. Taught Rome Opera B. 1965–69.

BESSMERTNOVA, Natalia, b. Moscow 1941. Russ. dancer. Entered Bolshoi Sch. 1952, graduated into Bolshoi B. 1961. Created rôle of the Young Girl in Liepa's revival of *Spectre de la Rose* (1967). Mar. Y. Grigorovitch. Varna Gold Medal 1965. Her sister Tatiana B., b. 1948, is a soloist of the Bolshoi B. and is mar. M. Gabovitch.

BESSONE, Emma. It. dancer trained at Milan with a brilliant technique. To St Petersburg as prima ballerina 1887, début in *Giselle* and created chief rôle in *The Tulip of Harlem* (q.v.). To Moscow the same year where she remained prima ballerina for several years.

BESSY, Claude, b. Paris 1932. Fr. dancer. Pupil Paris Opéra Sch., becoming première danseuse 1952, nominated étoile 1956. In Gene Kelly's film *Invitation to the Dance* (1953). Guest artist Ballet Theatre 1960, Bolshoi 1961. She suffered a severe car accident in 1967. Wrote her biography *Danseuse Étoile* (1961). Appointed Director of Paris Opéra B. 1970 for a short period, the first woman to hold this post. From 1971 director of Opéra Sch.

BESTONSO, Robert, b. Nice 1942. Fr. dancer. Pupil of Brieux, Peretti, Kniaseff. In Paris Opéra to 1966. Danced in Ballets Roland Petit 1965–67. Joined Festival B. 1967 becoming a principal soloist. Won Blum Prize 1961. To S. Africa 1970 to dance with PACT Ballet. Partnered Aldous in *Sleeping Beauty*, Teheran 1970.

BETTIS, Valerie, b. Houston, Texas 1920. Am. dancer and chor. Her *Virginia Sampler* was the first work in modern dance idiom to be created for a Classical ballet company (B. Russe de Monte Carlo, 1947). Chor. *Streetcar Named Desire* for Slavenska-Franklin Co. 1952. Now teaches in N.Y. and works in television.

BHARATA NATYA SASTRAS, a work of c. 1000 B.C. said to have been written by the sage of Bharata under the divine inspiration of Brahma and preserved in the temple libraries of Tanjore and Malabar. The Classical temple dance of India in its pure form is based on the teachings of the B.N.S.

BHARATA NATYA, the ancient temple dance of the Tanjore bayadères. It is the oldest form of Indian dancing and is always performed by a single dancer (usually female). The sung accompanying music comments on the dance. See KATHAK, KATHAKALI, and MANIPURI.

BIAGI, Vittorio, b. Florence 1941. It. dancer and chor. Pupil of Dell'Ara, Messerer, V. Gsovsky, Lander, Grantzeva. Joined Scala, Milan, B. 1958, B. du XXme Siècle 1960, Opéra Comique, Paris, 1966–69. Appointed director of B. de Lyon 1969. Chor. many ballets.

BIAS, Fanny, b. 1789, d. Paris 1825. Fr. dancer, demi-caractère, who danced at the Paris Opéra (1807 onwards) and in London (1821). A lithograph of her dated 1821 by Waldeck is one of the first illustrations of a dancer standing on her points.

BIBIENA, perhaps the greatest family of scenic artists in the history of the theatre. Founded by Giovanni Maria Galli (1619–65), (they took the name from the village of his birth), succeeded by his sons, Ferdinando (1657–1743) and Francesco (1659–1739), and grandsons, Antonio (1700–76) and Giuseppe Galli (1696–1751). The grandeur and classical proportions of their sets has never been surpassed and their art profoundly influenced stage design. They made Bologna their home but worked all over Europe on Court spectacles, weddings and in theatres.

BICHES, LES, ballet, 1 act, ch. Nijinska, m. Poulenc, dec. Laurençin, f.p. Diaghileff, Th. de Monte Carlo 6 Jan 1924 (Nemchinova, Tchernicheva, Woizikovsky, Vilzak). In England this work was known as *The House Party*. It was in the repertoire of the Markova-Dolin Co. in 1937 (Markova in Nemchinova's rôle of La Garçonne, Dolin in Vilzak's rôle), and the de Cuevas B. in 1947 (Marjorie Tallchief and Skibine). Revived by Nijinska for the Royal B. at C. Garden, 2 Dec 1964 (Parkinson as La Garçonne, Beriosova, Blair, Rosson, Meade). A satire on the 1920s with no plot but a succession of meetings, glances and hints of liaison and flirtation.

BIEGOVITCH, Iovanka, b. Prnjavor, Bosnia 1931. Yugoslav dancer.

Studied at the State Ballet Sch. in Belgrade with Ivanovitch and in Paris with Rausanne and Gsovsky. Danced with Belgrade Opera Ballet 1950–55, Ballets Jean Babilée 1955–59 appearing at the Edinburgh Festival 1959. To Australia in 1959 and joined Borovansky Ballet as ballerina. Returned to Belgrade as prima ballerina 1961. Appointed director of the Belgrade B. 1970.

BIEN AIMÉE, LA, ballet 1 act, ch. Nijinska, m. Schubert, Liszt, and Milhaud, dec. Benois, f.p. Ida Rubinstein Co., Paris Opéra 22 Nov 1928 (Rubinstein).

BIG CITY, THE, ballet 3 sc., ch. Jooss, m. Tansman (*Sonatina Transatlantique*), dec. Heckroth, f.p. B. Jooss, Opera House, Cologne 21 Nov 1932 (Leeder, Mascha Lidolt, Uthoff). An evocation of life in the big city and its evils.

BIGOTTINI, Emilie, b. Toulouse 1784, d. Passy 1858. Fr. dancer. Entered Paris Opéra 1801 and became chief dancer, retiring 1823. Cr. chief rôle in *Nina* 1813. More talented as a mime, for which she was remarkable, than as a dancer. Napoleon flirted with her and instructed the Président du Conseil to send her a present of books. She complained to Napoleon '*Il m'a payé en livres: j'aurais mieux aimé en francs*'. Mar. a millionaire in 1816.

BILLY SUNDAY, or GIVING THE DEVIL HIS DUE, ballet 4 episodes, ch. Ruth Page, m. R. Gassmann, f.p. Ruth Page B., Mandell Hall, Chicago 13 Dec 1946 in practice dress. Revived B. Russe de Monte Carlo, dec. P. du Pont, cost. H. Andrews, N.Y. City Center 2 Mar 1948.

BILLY THE KID, ballet 1 act. Book Lincoln Kirstein, based on life of Wm. Bonney, Am. outlaw of last century, ch. Eugene Loring, m. Aaron Copland, dec. Jared French, f.p. B. Caravan, Civic Th., Chicago 16 Oct 1938 (Loring, Marie-Jeanne, Lew Christensen). Considered by some to be the first really Am. ballet.

BIRDS, THE, ballet, ch. Helpmann, m. Respighi, dec. Chiang Lee. f.p. S. Wells B., New Th., London, 24 Nov 1942 (Grey, Rassine, Moyra Fraser). This was Beryl Grey's first created rôle.

BIRKMEYER, Michael, b. Vienna 1943. Austrian dancer. Trained by Hamilton, Toni Birkmeyer and Georgia Hiden at Staatsoper Sch. Joined Staatsoper B. 1960 becoming soloist 1965 after dancing lead in Nureyev's production of *Swan Lake* in Vienna (1964). To the Australian Ballet as guest artist 1965. Now a principal dancer in Vienna. His father, Toni B., b. Vienna 1897, studied at the Hofoper Sch. joined the Staatsoper B. 1912, soloist 1921, ballet master 1931–34. Made a foreign tour with Greta Wiesenthal and Tilly Losch. Teacher at the State Academy of Music and Dance 1948–63. His grandfather, Adolf B., joined the Staatsoper B. 1852 and was soloist 1870–85.

BISCHOFF, Egon, b. Gotha 1934, German dancer and ballet master. Pupil of Palucca in Dresden and in Kirov Sch., Leningrad. Soloist at the Staatsoper, E. Berlin and later ballet master there.

BIRTHDAY OFFERING, ballet, ch. Ashton, m. Glazounov (*Valse de Concert No. 1, Scènes de Ballet, The Seasons, Ruses d'Amour, Prelude and Mazurka*), dec. Levasseur, f.p. S. Wells B., C. Garden, 5 May 1956 (Fonteyn, Grey, Elvin, Nerina, Beriosova, Jackson, Fifield, Somes, Chatfield, Blair, Grant, Ashbridge, Doyle, Shaw). Composed for the 25th Birthday of the Company, using all its stars.

BJÖRN, Dinna, b. Copenhagen 1947. Danish dancer. Daughter of Niels Björn Larsen. Pupil of Frandsen 1958–63. Joined R. Danish B. 1964 (pupil of Volkova, Brenaa, Ter-Stepanova). From 1957 to 1963 danced in the Tivoli Pantomime B. Chor. *8+1* (also composing the music) at New Stage, Royal Th., 4 Jan 1970. Won Bronze Medal, Varna Comp. 1968.

BJÖRNSSON, Fredbjörn, b. Copenhagen 1926. Dan. dancer. Studied at Royal Th. Sch. and in Paris. Joined R. Danish B. 1943, promoted solodancer 1949. Toured Iceland 1953. Danced most of the principal male rôles in the 1950s and appeared in the film *Black Tights* (1961) as the Thief in Petit's *Carmen*. He worked in America in 1961 and in 1962 mounted (with Kirsten Ralov, his wife) the complete *Napoli* for the New Zealand B. (its first complete production outside Denmark). Chor. *Behind the Curtain* (1954), *Skaelmeri* (1957), *Lykke pa Rejsen* (1959) and others. From 1965 a leading mine with the rôle of Dr Coppelius. Created a Knight of the Order of Dannebrog 1961.

BLACHE, Jean Baptiste, b. Berlin 1765, d. Toulouse 1834. Fr. dancer and chor. To Paris 1776 and studied under Deshayes *père* at Opéra. In 1786 became ballet-master at Montpellier and subsequently in Lyon, Bordeaux and Marseilles. Succeeded Dauberval at Bordeaux, where he produced many ballets and stayed most of his life. In his *La Laitière Polonaise* he introduced, for the first time in ballet, a roller-skating ballet (see MABILLE). He married twice and had thirty-two children. One of his sons Alexis (b. Marseille 1792, d. Bordeaux 1852) was a maître de ballet at St Petersburg and chor. a version of *Jocko ou le Singe de Brésil*.

BLACHER, Boris, b. Newchang, China 1903. German composer and director of the Berlin Hochschule für Musik since 1953. Comp. many ballet scores for T. Gsovsky, Hanka and others, notably *Holiday in the South* (1937), *Chiarina* (1950), *Hamlet* (1950), *Lysistrata* (1951), *The Moor of Venice* (1955).

BLACK CROOK, THE. (1) Extravaganza, book C. M. Barras, f.p. Niblo's Garden N.Y. 12 Sept 1866, which ran for some sixteen months and was revived again and again over a period of years. The ballet-interludes, ch. David Costa, with Rita Sangalli and Maria Bonfanti, from the Paris Opéra, amongst the dancers, were particularly popular and did much to arouse interest in dancing and to create a style which is perhaps the forerunner of the modern musical. Last revived 1929 by Agnes de Mille, Hoboken, N.J. Its history inspired the Am. musical *The Girl in Pink Tights* (1953) (Jeanmaire, Kalioujny). (2) Opera by G. Jacobi produced Alhambra Th., London 24 Dec 1872 and ran for 310 performances. Contained a number of ballet-divertissements. Ch. Hus.

BLACK SWAN, ballet 3 sc., ch. Borovansky, m. Sibelius, dec. Constable, f.p. Borovansky B., Empire Th., Sydney, May 1951 (Busse, Stevenson, Gillespie). On an Australian theme.

BLACK SWAN, THE, the grand pas de deux from Act 3 of *Swan Lake*, danced by Odile and Prince Siegfried (only so-called when danced as a divertissement).

BLACK SWAN, THE, first stereoscopic ballet-film to be made, first publicly shown 24 May 1952 at the Riverside Th., Festival Gardens, London. The story is adapted from the third act of *Swan Lake* by Peter Brinson, who directed it. Ch. Petipa, m. Tchaikovsky, dec. Kenneth Rowell. Odile-Odette—Beryl Grey, Prince Siegfried—John Field, Von Rothbart—David Paltenghi, Benno—Peter Brinson.

BLAIKIE, Julia, b. London 1948. Eng. dancer. Pupil of Royal B. Sch. Joined B. Rambert 1967.

BLAIR, David, b. Halifax 1932. Eng. dancer. R.A.D. scholar, entered S. Wells Sch. 1946 and S. Wells Th. B. 1947, and created the chief rôles in *Harlequin in April* and *Pineapple Poll*. In 1953 became soloist of the S. Wells B. at C. Garden and a principal 1955, becoming Fonteyn's chief partner in 1961. Created rôles in *Prince of the Pagodas* (Prince, 1959), *Antigone* (Polinices, 1959), *Fille Mal Gardée* (Colas, 1960), *Elektra* (Orestes, 1963), *Romeo and Juliet* (Mercutio, 1965). Guest artist in Milan 1957, toured with Fonteyn in Australia, Turkey, Spain 1958–59. In 1965 he staged *Swan Lake* in the Municipal Th., Atlanta, Georgia, with American dancers from Regional Ballets, and *Sleeping Beauty* in 1966, *Giselle* in 1967, and mounted *Swan Lake* Act II for Ballet Th. 1966, and the whole ballet in 1967 (Chicago, 6 Feb 1967, Nerina, Fernandez) and *Giselle* 1968. Retired from Royal B. 1968. Created C.B.E. 1964. In 1970 he returned to the Royal B. and became one of its teachers. Mar. Maryon Lane.

BLAKSTAD, Kari, b. Oslo 1938. Norweg. dancer. Trained by Rita Tori. Entered Norweg. B. 1961, soloist 1964.

BLANCHE-NEIGE, ballet 3 acts, 6 sc., based on Grimm's fairy tale. Ch. Lifar, m. Yvain, dec. Bouchène, f.p. Paris Opéra 14 Nov 1951 (Daydé, Vyroubova, Lifar, Bozzoni, J.-P. Andreani).

BLANK, Gustav, b. Altenbögge 1908. German dancer and teacher. Pupil of Edouardowa, Nikolaijewa, T. Gsovsky. Joined Berlin Staatsoper B. 1931–49, Berlin Stadttheater B. (W. Berlin) 1949–57 as ballet master. Ballet master Hamburg B. 1957–62. From 1962 has taught in Munich. Chor. many ballets.

BLANKSHINE, Robert, b. Syracuse, N.Y. 1948. Am. dancer. Pupil of Sch. of Am. B. and Joffrey Sch. Joined Joffrey B. becoming soloist 1968. Danced in Regional Ballets and at Radio City Music Hall. Deutsche Oper B., W. Berlin as soloist 1970–72. Geneva B. 1973.

BLANTON, Jeremy, b. Memphis, Tennessee 1939. American dancer. Studied under Tudor in N.Y., soloist Robert Joffrey B. 1957, Metropolitan Op. B. 1958–60. Joined Canad. Nat. B. 1962 as soloist.

BLASIS, Carlo, b. Naples 1795, d. Cernobbio 1878. It. dancer, chor., and teacher. Studied under Vigano in Milan. Became chief dancer at La Scala and in 1837 the Director of its Imperial Academy of Dancing. He also was the chief dancer and chor. of the King's Th., London 1847. While in Milan he trained most of the famous It. dancers of the era, who later went to St Petersburg, Paris, etc., during the highest period of Classical dancing. He codified his teaching methods in his books *Treatise on the Dance* (1820) and *The Code of Terpsichore* London 1828), which form the basis of our modern Classical training. The 'Pleiades of Blasis' were six of his pupils who achieved fame—Marietta Baderna, Augusta Domenichettis, Flora Fabbri, Amalia Ferraris, Sofia Fuoco and Carolina Granzini.

BLASKA, Felix, b. Gomel (Russia) 1941. Russ.-French dancer and chor. Pupil of Yves Brieux. Joined de Cuevas B. 1960, Petit's B. 1961, dancing the rôle of the Young Man in a revival of Petit's *Le Jeune Homme et la Mort* 1966. Chor. *Octandre* (1966, m. Varèse) and *Les Affinités Electives* (m. Mestral) for Petit B., *Danses Concertantes* (1968, m. Stravinsky) for Ballet-Theatre Contemporain, Amiens. Founded his own Co., Ballets Felix Blaska, in 1969 for the Festival de Chatillon des Arts and in 1970 they performed in Paris at the Th. de la Ville. Among the dancers of his Co. were Muriel Boulay, Catherine Cardineaux, J.-L. Chirpaz, Vera Filatoff, Peter Heubi, Jean Rochereau. In 1970 his *Deuxième Concerto* was performed by the Marseille B. and by the R. Danish B.

BLAŽEK, Jiri, b. 1923. Czech dancer and chor. Studied under Sacha Machov and in Bolshoi Sch. Joined Schwanda Th. in Prague 1943 and the National B. 1946 becoming principal dancer. Chor. *Spartacus* in Prague 1957, *Daphnis and Chloë* 1960 and many others. Mar. M. Drottnerova.

BLIND SIGHT, ballet, ch. Morrice, m. Downes, dec. N. Baylis. f.p. B. Rambert, Jeannetta Cochrane Th., London 28 Nov 1969 (Craig, Pietje Law, Bruce Taylor, Curtis). The reactions of blind people recovering their sight.

BLONDY, Nicolas, b. 1675, d. 1739. Fr. dancer at the Paris Opéra in the seventeenth century. He was the nephew and pupil of Beauchamp and the teacher of Camargo. Famous for his elevation and nobility and at the time was considered to be the greatest dancer in Europe.

BLOOD WEDDING, ballet 1 act, ch. Rodrigues, m. Ap Ivor, dec. Lambert. f.p. S. Wells Th. B., S. Wells Th. 5 June 1953 (Fifield, Poole, Trecu), An adaptation of the play by Lorca. Also danced by the R. Danish B. and other companies.

BLUEBEARD, ballet in 2 prologues, 4 acts, and 3 interludes (two of which were subsequently eliminated). Book and ch. Fokine, after the *opéra bouffe* by Meilhac and Halévy, m. Offenbach, dec. M. Vertès, f.p. Ballet Th., Palacio de Bellas Artes, Mexico City 27 Oct 1941 (Dolin). The last complete ballet to be composed by Fokine, *Bluebeard* falls far below his earlier works. A ballet of this name, ch. Carlo Coppi, m. Jacobi, was given at the Alhambra Th., London 16 Dec 1895, and Petipa also ch. *Barbe Bleue* (book based on the Perrault fairy tale), m. J. Schneck, dec. Lambini, Ivanov, Levogt, and Perminov, Maryinsky Th., St Petersburg 8 Dec 1896 (Legnani, Gerdt). Pavlova danced it in 1900, during her first season in the Maryinsky Co.

BLUEBELL, Miss (Margaret Kelly), b. Ireland 1915. Eng. dancer and chor. Studied in Liverpool. Joined Alfred Jackson's troupe at Scala, Berlin 1929 and then became leader of the dancers at the Folies-Bergère, Paris. In 1933 started her own BLUEBELL GIRLS, of which there are now six troupes (always employing 180–200 girls) dancing in cabarets and night-clubs on the Continent and in N. and S. America. These troupes are of English girls, not less than 5 feet 8 inches (173 cm) tall, and are extremely well drilled and disciplined, and lavishly dressed. Although the dancing is of the cabaret type (often with Miss Bluebell's chor.) many of the girls are trained in the English ballet schools and the troupes form a regular source of employment for dancers too tall for the Classical ballet companies.

The two main troupes are at the Lido in Paris (where they have performed continuously for 23 years) and at the Stardust in Las Vegas (for 15 years).

BLUE BIRD PAS DE DEUX (*The Blue Bird and the Princess Florine* or *The Blue Bird and the Enchanted Princess*), a pas de deux, ch. Petipa and Cecchetti, from the last act of *The Sleeping Beauty* and often danced separately as a divertissement. It follows the pattern of the Grand Pas de Deux (see PAS DE DEUX) and is of extreme virtuosity. The male dancer flutters his hands throughout the dance and his solo abounds in brisés volés and other beaten steps. See also THE SLEEPING BEAUTY for the dancers of it.

BLUM, Anthony, b. Mobile, Alabama. Am. dancer. Pupil of Sch. of Am. B. Appeared in musicals and joined N.Y. City B. becoming soloist 1963 and principal 1966.

BLUM, René, b. Paris 1878, d. German concentration camp, Auschwitz 1942. Fr. ballet impresario. Brother of Léon Blum, ex-Premier of France. Founded Ballets Russes de Monte Carlo (see B. Russe de Monte Carlo). Director of the ballets at Monte Carlo from death of Diaghileff in 1929 until Nazi invasion of France. A man of great culture and impeccable taste, he was too modest to lay claim to the mantle of Diaghileff, although he had perhaps a better title than anyone, and the survival of ballet after Diaghileff owes not a little to his efforts. The René Blum Prize (founded by Cyril Beaumont in 1950 and given by the Fr. critics to the most promising young Fr. dancer of the year) has been awarded to Xenia Palley (1951), Claire Sombert (1952), Claudine Barbini (1953), Françine Collement (1954), Michèle Seigneuret (1955), J.-J. Delrieu (1956), J.-P. Toma (1957), Gilbert Mayer (1958), Marie Yakimova and Régine Boury (1959), Nanon Thibon and Robert Bestonso (1960), Georges Piletta (1961), Monique Chaussat and J. Bart (1961), Philippe Dahlmann (1963), Noella Pontois and Jacques Valdi (1964), Jacques Dombrovski and Melle Taddei (1965), Chantal Quarrez and J.-P. Gravier (1966), Martine Bonhème and R. Duquesnot (1967). It was discontinued in 1968.

BODENWIESER, Gertrud, b. Vienna 1886, d. Sydney 1959. Austrian teacher. Début 1919 and became Professor of the Vienna State Academy of Music and Dancing. Formed a Central European style dance group and emigrated to Australia 1938 where she founded her school and company.

BOGATYREV, Alexander, b. Tallinn 1949. Esthonian dancer. Studied at the Tallinn Sch. and joined Bolshoi B. 1969. First danced in London with the Young Stars of the Bolshoi 1968.

BOGATYRI, ballet 3 sc., theme based on traditional tales of the Bogatyri,

73

the legendary knights of Vladimir, the first Christian prince of Russia. Ch. Massine, m. Borodin (excerpts from 2nd and 3rd symphonies, and nocturne from String Quartet), dec. N. Goncharova, f.p. B. Russe de Monte Carlo, Met. Op., N.Y. 20 Oct 1938 (Danilova, Franklin).

BOGDANOV, Konstantin, b.c. 1809, d. 1877. Russ. dancer and teacher, father of Nadezhda B. Graduated from the Moscow Th. Sch. and then studied under Didelot in St Petersburg. Returned to Moscow to dance, was the first Gurn in the Moscow *La Sylphide* and partnered Hullin, T. Karpakova (whom he married), Sankovskaya etc. In 1839 became *régisseur* of Moscow B. but left in 1842, opened his own school and concentrated on teaching his daughter.

BOGDANOVA, Nadezhda, b. Moscow 1836, d. there 1867. Russ. dancer. Pupil of her father K. Bogdanov in his private sch. in Moscow until she was 14 when Elssler saw her dance and had her sent to be trained at the Paris Opéra where she joined the *corps* and had a great success, especially in *La Vivandière* when she took over Cerrito's rôle. Returned to St Petersburg 1855 and made her début in *Giselle* 2 Feb 1856. Subsequently she danced in Germany, Hungary, Italy and Poland, retiring in 1867. She was the first Russian dancer to become famous abroad.

BOGOMOLOVA, Ludmilla, b. Moscow 1932. Russian dancer. Entered Bolshoi Sch. 1945, graduated in 1951 and became soloist 1955. Hon. Artist R.S.F.S.R.

BOHNER, Gerhard, b. Karlsruhe 1936. German dancer and chor. Pupil of Hardle-Munz Sch. Danced with Mannheim B. 1958–60, Frankfurt 1960–61, Deutsche Oper, Berlin from 1961. Chor. *Funf Stucke und Glokken* (m. Eimert) 1964, *Varietas* (m. Stravinsky) 1966, *Der Wolf* (m. Dutilleux) 1967, *Science Fiction Story* (m. Ligeti) 1968, *Frustration-Aggression* (m. Xenakis) 1969 etc. Ballet master of Darmstadt B. 1972.

BOLENDER, Todd, b. Canton, Ohio 1914. Am. dancer and chor. Pupil of Vilzak, Sch. of Am. B. With Ballet Caravan, Littlefield Co., and musicals, also Ballet Theatre and B. Russe de Monte Carlo. Joined N.Y. City Ballet 1950. Chor. *Mother Goose* (1948), *Zodiac* (1947), *Souvenirs* (1955), *Still Point* (1956). Director of Ballet, Cologne 1963–66, of Frankfurt 1966–69. Mounted *My Fair Lady* in Turkey 1967. Returned to America to produce musicals.

BOLERO. (1) Sp. dance in 3/4 time to a vocal accompaniment and castanets, said to have been invented in 1780 by the dancer Sebastian Cerezo or Zerezo, who possibly found his inspiration in some existing folk dance. Musically it has a close affinity to the cachucha. (2) Ballet

1 act, ch. Nijinska for Ida Rubinstein, m. Ravel, dec. Benois, Paris Opéra 22 Nov 1928. There have since been a number of revivals in different versions, incl. one for B. International in 1944. This same m. has also been used by a number of other chors., incl. Lifar (Paris Opéra 31 Dec 1941, dec. L. Leyritz), Dolin (S. Wells Th. 6 Dec 1932) and Lander (R. Dan. B. 1934).

BOLM, Adolph, b. St Petersburg 1884, d. Hollywood 1951. Russ. dancer and chor. Trained at Imp. Sch. by Karsavina's father and graduated in 1904. In 1908 organized a troupe headed by Pavlova which toured Riga, Stockholm and Copenhagen. In 1909 danced in Berlin with Pavlova and then at the Empire Th., London, with Kyasht. In Diaghileff's Co. 1909–14. To America 1918, where he did pioneer work in staging ballets for the Met. Op., N.Y., and the Chicago Civic Op. With his Ballet Intime he introduced danced divertissements to the Am. cinema. His influence on the film industry has been exerted both through his ballet *Krazy Kat*, said to have forecast *Mickey Mouse*, and by his creation of the first dance film synchronized to orchestral music (the *Danse Macabre* of Saint-Saëns) in 1929. *Iron Foundry* (1932), since renamed *Ballet Mécanique*, to Mossolov's *Spirit of the Factory*, possibly the best of his choreographic compositions, was also first created for a film *The Mad Genius*. See also *Apollon-Musagète*. As a dancer he will be remembered chiefly for his creation of the Polovtsian Chief in Fokine's *Prince Igor* (1909) and for his Pierrot in *Le Carnaval* (1910). For Ballet Th., chor. *Peter and the Wolf* (1940).

BOLSHAKOVA, Natalia, b. 1943. Russ. dancer. Graduated from Kirov Sch. to the company 1963. Danced leading rôle in *Laurencia* 1967. Varna Silver Medal 1968. Now soloist.

BOLSHOI BALLET. The ballet in Moscow existed long before the building in 1856 of the Bolshoi Th. (q.v.). However, it took a second place to that of St Petersburg until after the 1917 Revolution when the capital was moved to Moscow. Nevertheless it always had a distinguished history of dancers and ballets. Valberg (q.v.) went there from St Petersburg in 1807 to improve the school and produced a number of patriotic ballets connected with the Napoleonic War. From 1912 to 1839 the Gluszkovskys (q.v.)—Adam the ballet master and Tatiana his wife, principal dancer—dominated the theatre and his Pushkin ballets, *Romeo and Juliet* (1821) and *The Prisoner in the Caucasus* (1827), were staged. In 1828 the It. ballet master Bernardelli mounted Vigano's *Othello* and in 1836 Félicité Hullin-Sor (q.v.) produced several important ballets among them *Fenella* (m. Auber, 1836). She was the teacher of many famous dancers, among them Ekaterina Sankovskaya (1816–78) (q.v.) who first danced *La Sylphide* in Moscow (1837). A prominent Moscow ballerina of the 1860s was Nadezhda Bogdanova, the first Russian dancer to become famous abroad. Saint-Léon was moved from St Petersburg to the Bolshoi Th. in 1860, and Muravieva (born in Moscow) worked with him there. Carlo Blasis worked in the Bolshoi School 1861–64.

Vassily Geltzer was the celebrated mime-dancer in the 1870s and his daughter Ekaterina Geltzer was one of its most famous dancers in the 1890s. In 1869 Petipa created his *Don Quixote* for the Bolshoi B., and in 1877 Tchaikovsky's *Swan Lake* had its first performance—unsuccessful with Reisinger's choreography. In 1900 began a great era when A. Gorsky (q.v.) arrived from St Petersburg as *régisseur*. He re-staged many of the older ballets, notably *Don Quixote* and *The Humpbacked Horse* and it is these Moscow reproductions that remain in the modern Moscow repertoire. His principal dancers were E. Geltzer and (also as teacher) V. Tikhomirov, Sophia Fedorova, Vera Karalli, Victorina Kriger, Novikov, A. Volinine, T. Kosloff, Mordkin, I. Zhukov, Leonide Massine—most of whom became known outside Russia.

After the 1917 Revolution the Bolshoi School and Ballet re-opened in 1920, when Gorsky remained in charge until his death in 1924. The great figures of that period were Messerer, Moiseyev, Gabovitch, and Goleizovsky developed as a choreographer. An important ballet of the period was the propaganda ballet *The Red Poppy* (1927).

In the late 1920s and early 1930s the Leningrad dancers began to be transferred to Moscow—among them Semeyonova and Yermoleyev, and also the teachers E. Gerdt and V. Semeyonov. The outstanding Moscow ballerina O. Lepeshinskaya made her début at the Bolshoi Th. in 1937 and a 'Moscow style' began to emerge, more vigorous and flamboyant than the old but pure classical style of the Maryinsky Th. in St Petersburg (where Vaganova remained as teacher). In the 1940s the Bolshoi B. had 200 members and included Sophia Golovkina, Sulamith Messerer, Irina Tikhomirnova and on the German invasion of Russia the company moved to Kuibyshev. In 1944 the great Ulanova was transferred to the Bolshoi B. and also Lavrovsky, the chor. of *Romeo and Juliet*, was made its artistic director—moves which finally established the ascendancy of the Bolshoi, in strength if not in style, over the Kirov B. in Leningrad. Other dancers of that period were Raisa Struchkova, and the young Plisteskaya who, on Ulanova's retirement, became Russia's principal ballerina.

In 1956 the Bolshoi B. made its first visit to London (Covent Garden), with Ulanova, Struchkova, Kondratieva, Fadeyechev, Timofeyeva, Karelskaya. Lavrovsky retired in 1964 and was succeeded by Y. Grigorovitch as artistic director. Among his new generation of dancers were E. Maximova, Bessmertnova, Vassiliev, M. Lavrovsky, Liepa. For the most part the Bolshoi B. repertoire has come from Leningrad choreographers.

BOLSHOI THEATRE, Moscow (*bolshoi* is Russ. for 'great'), the present home of the Bolshoi Ballet, was built in 1856 by the architect Alberto Cavos (grandfather of Alexandre Benois). Originally the ballet in Moscow performed at the Znamensky Th.—from 1776. This was destroyed by fire in 1780 and in the same year a new theatre, the Petrovsky Th., was built by an Englishman Michael Maddox (1747–1822). The ballet performed there from 1780 to 1805 when it was burned down. In 1784 the ballet school of the Orphanage, which supplied most of the dancers, was taken over by Maddox and became a permanent ballet school for the theatre. In 1825 a New Bolshoi Petrovsky Th. was opened on the same site. This was the first Bolshoi Th. The first programme (Jan 6) opened with a prologue *The Victory of the Muses*, ch. F. Hullin-Sor (q.v.), m. Verstovsky, then the ballet *Cinderella*, m. Sor. The architect was Bovet and the building was burnt down in 1853—to be followed by the present building, which has 2000 seats and a stage measuring 85 ft wide and 77 ft deep.

BOLSHOI THEATRE, St Petersburg, was built in 1783 with the name Kamenny (or Stone) Th. It acquired the name Bolshoi after it was rebuilt in 1802. It was burned down in 1811 and rebuilt in 1818 and again in 1836 (see Bolshoi Th., Moscow). Ballet and opera performances were all given here from its opening in 1783 until 1889 when the ballet transferred to the Maryinsky Th. (which had been built, with Cavos as architect, in 1860) (q.v.).

BON, René, b. Montpellier 1924. Fr. dancer. Pupil of Staats and Nora Kiss. Soloist Opéra Comique, Paris 1940–43. At Paris Opéra 1943–44. Joined de Cuevas Co. as soloist, Charrat's Co. 1951, and Massine's Co. Nervi, 1960. Ballet master Dutch National B. 1961 danced in Hamburg, Marseille 1962. Teacher at the Vienna Staatsoper 1963–66. Teacher at Royal Ballet Sch. 1967–68 and Norwegian B., Oslo 1969. Since 1969 has taught in Paris and as a guest teacher.

BONFANTI, Maria (Marietta), b. 1847, d. 1921. It. dancer. Studied under Blasis and made most of her career in America. Début in *The Black Crook* (q.v.) N.Y. 1866 and toured America. Ballerina of Met. Op. N.Y. 1888–94. Opened a school in N.Y. and taught Ruth St Denis.

BONNE-BOUCHE, ballet 3 sc., ch. Cranko, m. Oldham, dec. O. Lancaster, f.p. S. Wells B., C. Garden 4 Apr 1952 (May, Clayden, Shaw, Hart, Grant). A farce and burlesque of Edwardian Kensington.

BONNEFOUS, Jean-Pierre, b. Bourg-en-Bresse 1943. Fr. dancer. Studied

77

at Paris Opéra Sch. and joined corps 1960. Made *premier danseur* 1964 and *étoile* 1966. Joined N.Y. City B. 1970. Mar. Patricia McBride.

BONI, Aida b. Milan 1880. It. dancer. Trained at Scala, Milan, danced at the Opéra Comique 1898–99, Th. Royal de la Monnaie Brussels, Covent Garden 1907, Scala, Milan 1907 and in the same year became étoile of the Paris Opéra. Retired 1922.

BOQUET, Louis-René, chief designer to Opéra, Paris, 1760–82. Designed cost. for several of Noverre's ballets. His designs were largely based on cont. court dress.

BORCHSENIUS, Valborg (née Jorgensen), b. Copenhagen, 1872 d. there 1949. Dan. dancer and teacher. Pupil of Royal Th. Sch., Copenhagen. Solodancer 1895, becoming the leading danseuse (and partner of Hans Beck). Retired 1918. Lander called her back to help him stage many of the Bournonville ballets and she was one of the greatest teachers of the Royal Th. Sch.

BORG, Anne, b. Oslo 1936. Norweg. dancer. Trained by Gerd Kjölaas, entered Norweg. B. 1960, soloist 1962, principal 1968, assistant ballet mistress 1970 and director 1971.

BORG, Conny, b. Stockholm 1938. Swed. dancer. To R. Swed. B. Sch. 1947 and joined R. Swed. B. 1955, premier danseur 1963. Studied in London with Anna Northcote. During 1961–62 was principal dancer in Tudor's ballets in Stockholm. To Gothenburg 1966–70 as Director of Ballet and continued as principal dancer there and as guest in Malmö. Chor. *Ritornell* (1966), *Enjoy Yourself* (1966), *Romeo and Juliet* and *Soirées Musicales* (1968). From 1971 director of the Malmö B.

BORGOGNO, Guigermo, b. Buenos Aires 1939. Argentinian dancer. Début in Teatro Argentino, La Plata. Joined San Martin Ballet, Buenos Aires 1968.

BORIS, Ruthanna, b. Brooklyn 1918. Am. dancer and chor. Studied at Met. Op. Sch. of Ballet N.Y., etc., becoming soloist at Met. Op. 1936. Since 1943 soloist B. Russe de Monte Carlo and dancing in musicals. Director of R. Winnipeg B. 1956–57. Teacher at Univ. of Washington, Seattle from 1965. Chor. *Cirque de Deux* (1947), *Quelques Fleurs* (1948), *Cakewalk* (1951), etc. Mar. Frank Hobi.

BÖRLIN, Jean, b. Haernoesand 1893, d. N.Y. 1930. Swed. dancer and chor. Studied at Royal Th., Stockholm, and admitted to the corps de ballet 1905. Promoted second danseur 1913 and in 1918 left Stockholm to study with Fokine in Copenhagen. Met Rolf de Maré who made him chief danseur and chor. of the Co. he was about to form, the Ballets Suédois (q.v.), from 1920 to 1925. He continued giving dance recitals after this but his health gave way and he died suddenly. See also

ARCHIVES INTERNATIONALES DE LA DANSE (founded in memory of him). Among his ballets are *Nuit de Saint-Jean* (m. Alfvèn) 1920, *Les Mariés de la Tour Eiffel* (m. Auric and others) 1921, *La Création du Monde* (m. Milhaud) 1923, *Relâche* (m. Satie) 1924.

BORNHAUSEN, Angelica, b. Sondershausen 1944. Germ. dancer. Pupil of Hamburg Sch. under Blank and Peter Appel. Joined Hamburg B. 1963. To Cologne 1966–70 as soloist, guest ballerina Canad. Nat. B. 1970. Ballerina in Zürich 1972.

BOROVANSKY, Édouard, b. Přerov 1902, d. Sydney 1959. Czech dancer, chor., and teacher. Pupil of Berger in Prague. Soloist of Czech Nat. B. 1926. Joined Pavlova Co. 1926 and B. Russe de Monte Carlo 1932–39 (cr. rôle of Strong Man in *Beau Danube*). Settled in Australia in 1938 with his wife Xenia Nicolaeva and opened sch. in Melbourne. From the Melbourne Ballet Club he founded the Borovansky Ballet in 1942 and by 1944 was able to stage a fully professional season. His Co. became the leading ballet in Australasia, presenting the classics and modern works (some of which he chor.). The leading dancers in it in 1955 were Peggy Sager, Kathleen Gorham, Paul Hammond, Paul Grinwis. Chor. of *Terra Australis*, *Capriccio Italien*, *Black Swan* (1951), *Outlaw* (1951), etc. In 1960 Peggy van Praagh became Artistic Director of the Company. The principal dancers in 1960 were Gorham, Biegovitch, Christiane Hubert, Marilyn Jones, Grinwis, Robert Pomié, Garth Welch, Frank Bourman. This company was the basis of the Australian Ballet (q.v.) His school is now called the Scully-Borovansky Sch.

BOROWSKA, Irina, b. Buenos Aires 1930. Argentinian dancer of Polish parents (Am. since 1964). Principal dancer of the opera-ballet at Colon Th., Buenos Aires. Joined B. Russe de Monte Carlo as ballerina 1954, Festival B. 1961, remaining ballerina until 1966 when she mar. Karl Musil in Vienna.

BORRI, Pasquale, b. Milan 1820, d. Desio 1884. It. dancer and chor. Pupil of Blasis, début at Scala, Milan 1940. Danced in Venice and Vienna. Principal dancer at Kärntnerthor Th., Vienna 1844–48. Chor. *Rübezahl* (m. Reuling) 1848 and was chor. of Vienna Hofoper 1854–56, 1858–59 and 1879–80. He also worked at the Paris Opéra and Her Majesty's Th. London. Among his ballets are *Redowa* (m. Giorza and Strebinger 1857), *The London Chimney Sweep* (m. F. Doppler 1859), *Dyella or the Tourists in India* (m. A. Bauer 1879), *Der Stock im Eisen* (m. Doppler 1880) etc. Mar. Carolina Pochini.

BORTOLUZZI, Paolo, b. Genoa 1938. It. dancer. Studied under Dell'Ara in Milan, and with Nora Kiss, Gsovsky, Béjart and Messerer. Joined Dell'Ara's Italian Ballet Co. 1956–59. Soloist of Massine's Nervi B. 1960, and Miskovitch's Ballets des Étoiles. Joined Béjart's Ballet du

XXme Siècle 1960 as principal dancer and since 1966 has also been principal dancer in Düsseldorf, commuting between there and Brussels. In 1972 joined Am. B. Theatre and became a guest artist.

BOSCH, Aurora, b. Havana. Cuban dancer. Pupil of the Alonsos and until 1969 principal dancer of the Nat. B. of Cuba. Won Varna Gold Medal 1965. Now chief teacher of the Ballet Clasico of Mexico.

BOSCHETTI, Amina, b. Milan 1836, d. Naples 1881. It. dancer. Pupil of Blasis at Milan, becoming prima ballerina. Cr. rôle in *Flik and Flok* (1862), Milan. Danced Paris Opéra 1864, cr. rôle in *La Maschera*. Beaudelaire addressed a poem to her.

BOSL, Heinz, b. Baden Baden 1946. German dancer. Pupil of Preisser, Blank, de Lutry. Joined Munich B. becoming soloist 1966.

BOSMAN, Petrus, b. S. Africa 1933. S. African dancer. Pupil of Dulcie Howes, Northcote, Cecily Robinson. Joined Festival B. 1951. Royal B. 1958 becoming soloist. Organizes small groups to dance in Africa, West Indies etc.

BOSQUET, LE, ballet, ch. Zullig, m. Rameau (arr. Penny), dec. D. Zinkeisen, f.p. B. Jooss, Cambridge 31 Jan 1945 (de Mosa, Zullig). A ballet of dalliance.

BOSTON. Slow waltz, in Continental countries sometimes called English waltz.

BOSTON BALLET (U.S.A.), founded in 1963, with the help of a Ford Foundation grant, by E. Virginia Williams. Its first performance was 29 July 1964 and it has given regular seasons ever since.

BOTTA, Bergonzio di, b. Tortona 1454, d. Milan 1504. It. chor. responsible for the dinner ballet, on the theme of Jason and the Argonauts, to celebrate the marriage of Galeazzo Visconti, Duke of Milan, and Isabella of Aragon, Tortona 1489. This set a fashion which contributed to the development of the art. Historians have sought to see in this the first production which could be called a ballet but there seems little doubt that there were earlier creations which forecast the ballet.

BOUCHER, François, b. Paris 1703, d. 1770. Fr. painter. Pupil of Servandoni whom he succeeded as official designer to Opéra, Paris, c. 1737. Designed a number of costs. and dec. for ballet.

BOURGEOIS GENTILHOMME, LE, ballet 2 sc. based on scene of the knighting of M. Jourdain in Molière's play. Ch. Balanchine, m. R. Strauss, dec. Benois, f.p. B. Russes de Monte Carlo, Monte Carlo 3 May 1932. Revived B. Russe de Monte Carlo, dec. E. Berman, City Center, N.Y. 23 Sept 1944 (Krassovska, Magallanes, Katcharov).

BOURMEISTER, Vladimir, b. Vitebsk 1904, d. Moscow 1971. Russ. chor. and *maître de ballet*. Studied ballet at the Lunacharsky Th. Tecnicum,

80

Moscow 1925–29. Joined the Moscow Arts Th. of Ballet on its foundation in 1930 by Victorina Kriger, becoming soloist. In 1933 this
became the Stanislavsky and Nemirovitch-Dantchenko Th. B. (q.v.)
and he became its chor. in 1941. Chor. *Le Corsair* (1931), *Straussiana*
(1941), *Merry Wives of Windsor* (1942, m. Oransky), *Les Rives de
Bonheur* (1956, m. Spadaveccia), *Joan of Arc* (1957, m. Peiko) etc. In
1953 he mounted a new *Swan Lake* (q.v.) in Moscow. He also mounted
this version at the Paris Opéra in 1960. In 1961 he chor. *Snow Maiden*
for Festival B. (q.v.).

BOURNONVILLE, Antoine, b. Lyons 1760, d. Fredesborg (Denmark)
1843. Fr. dancer and chor. Pupil of Noverre and danced in his ballets
in Vienna, Paris, and London. In 1782 engaged as premier danseur at
Stockholm by Gustavus III, where he chor. his first ballet *Les Meuniers
Provenceaux* in 1785. In 1792 went to Copenhagen and became famous
as a dancer in many of Galeotti's ballets. Was Dance-Director at
Copenhagen 1816–23 and succeeded Galeotti. Father of August
Bournonville.

BOURNONVILLE, August, b. Copenhagen 1805, d. there 1879. Son of
the above. Danish dancer and chor. Pupil of his father and Galeotti
at the Royal Dan. B. Sch. Début in 1813. In 1920 went to study in
Paris under Vestris and became soloist at Paris Opéra 1826. Danced at
King's Th., London 1828. Returned to Copenhagen 1829 when he
chor. his first ballet. He created thirty-six ballets and divertissements,
among them *Valdemar* (1835), *La Sylphide* (1836), *Toreadoren* (1840),
Napoli (1842, on his return from a period of exile in Italy following a
dispute at the theatre), *Conservatoriet* (1849), *Kermesse in Bruges*
(1849), *Et Folkesagn* (1854), *Far from Denmark* (1860). He retired in
1877 and was knighted. He was ballet master in Vienna 1855–56 and
Director of the Royal Th., Stockholm 1861–64. Wrote his autobiography, *My Theatre Life*. His was the greatest influence in Danish
ballet and his teaching—the Bournonville Style—is virtually the French
style of Vestris and remains little changed to this day.

BOURRÉE, a folk dance of the provinces of Auvergne and Berri in 3/4
or in Alla Breve (2/2) time. Its connexion with the Pas de Bourrée (q.v.)
in the classical ballet vocabulary is on account of its three changes of
weight, as in the folk-dance. The bourrée has been introduced into
ballets with a certain stylization by a number of contemporary choreographers.

BOURRÉE FANTASQUE, ballet 1 act, ch. Balanchine, m. Chabrier, cost.
Karinska, f.p. N.Y. City B., City Center 1 Dec 1949 (Le Clerq,
Maria Tallchief, Janet Reed). Ballet of pure dancing but with a fantastic

twist. Taken into Festival B., Festival Hall, London, 18 Aug 1960 (Burr, Wright, Ferri).

BOUTIQUE FANTASQUE, LA, ballet, ch. Massine, m. Rossini-Respighi, dec. Derain, f.p. Diaghileff's Co., Alhambra Th., London 5 June 1919 (Lopokova, Massine). Revival for S. Wells B., C. Garden 27 Feb 1947 (Shearer, Massine) and again for the touring Royal B., Stratford-on-Avon, 31 Jan 1968 (Wells, Emblen). A fantastic toyshop in the 1860s.

BOVT, Violetta, b. Los Angeles 1927. Russ. dancer. Graduated from Bolshoi Sch. 1944, joined Stanislavsky Th. B. same year and became ballerina and the principal soloist in Bourmeister's ballets. Hon. Artist R.S.F.S.R. 1954.

BOWES, Karen, b. St Catharine's, Ontario 1948. Canad. dancer. Studied at Canad. Nat. B. Sch. and entered Canad. Nat. B. 1966. Promoted to soloist 1967.

BOWMAN, Patricia, b. Washington, D.C. Am. dancer. Studied under Fokine, Legat, Egorova. Principal dancer Roxy Cinema, N.Y., with Massine 1928–31, Mordkin B. 1939, Ballet Theatre 1940, Chicago Op. Co. and in musicals. Teaches in N.Y.

BOZZACCHI, Giuseppina, b. Milan 1853, d. Paris 1870. It. dancer. She was noticed by Amina Boschetti, prima ballerina of La Scala in 1862, who encouraged her to go to study at the Paris Opéra and even paid for some of her lessons under Madame Dominique. In 1869 she was chosen to create the rôle of Swanilda in *Coppélia*, which she did with great success in 1870, at the age of 16. She danced it eighteen times only, and, during the Siege of Paris, fell ill and died on her 17th birthday. Delibes played the organ at her funeral, which was attended by Auber, Nuitter, Perrin, and all the Opéra.

BOZZONI, Max, b. Paris 1921. Fr. dancer. Studied at Paris Opéra, joining Co. 1936, becoming étoile in 1944 and retired 1963. Ballet master Geneva 1964, Director of Ballets des Étoiles de Paris 1965.

BRABANTS, Jeanne, b. Antwerp 1920. Belgian dancer, teacher and chor. Pupil of Jooss, Leeder at Dartington Hall (England), van Damme, and at S. Wells Sch. Founded her own school in Antwerp in 1941, with her sisters Jos and Aimée and her own group, Dansemsemble Brabants, in 1942. From 1951 has been director of the ballet school of the R. Flemish Opera in Antwerp and in 1970 was appointed director of the new Ballet Van Vlaanderen (q.v.). Among her ballets are *Goyescas*, *The Wives of Zalongo*, *Pierlala*, *Game of Chess*, *The Travelling Companion* etc. Won award for choreography at Varna Competition 1968.

BRADLEY, Lionel, b. Manchester 1898, d. London 1953. Eng. writer on ballet. Educ. Manchester G.S. and Oxford. Author of *Sixteen Years of Ballet Rambert* 1946, and was notable for the accuracy of his corrections of the ballet writings of his time.

BRAE, June, b. Ringwood 1917. Eng. dancer. Studied under Goncharov in China and with Legat. Danced for Ballet Club and a principal dancer S. Wells B. 1936–42. Cr. 'Rich Girl' in *Nocturne*, 'Black Queen' in *Checkmate*. Returned as leading dancer on formation of S. Wells Th. B. 1946. Now retired.

BRADLEY, Lisa, b. Elizabeth, New Jersey 1941. Am. dancer. Studied at Sch. of Am. B. Principal dancer in Joffrey's B. since 1961, creating many leading rôles in the ballets of Joffrey, Arpino and Ailey.

BRAHMS, Caryl, b. Surrey. Eng. writer and ballet critic. Editor *Footnotes to the Ballet* 1936, *Robert Helpmann* 1943, *A Seat at the Ballet* 1951, and numerous books with S. J. Simon, notably *A Bullet in the Ballet* 1937 and *Six Curtains for Stroganova* 1945.

BRAHMS QUINTET, ballet, ch. Nahat, m. Brahms, cost. Kim, f.p. Am. Ballet Th., Brooklyn Academy, N.Y. 10 Dec 1969 (Gregory, Nagy, Paul, Young, d'Antuono, Orr, Sorkin, Horvath). Without a plot yet not abstract.

BRANDARD, J., b. Birmingham 1812, d. London 1863. Eng. artist and lithographer whose lithographs and music-covers depict many of the dancers of the Romantic Era (see LITHOGRAPHS). He and A. E. Chalon both drew pictures of the famous *Pas de Quatre* 1845.

BRANDENBURG *Nos 2 and 4*, ballet ch. Cranko, m. Bach (these concertos), dec. Dorothy Zippel, f.p. Royal B., C. Garden 10 Feb 1966 (Park) Sibley, Parkinson, Jenner, Macleary, Usher, Gable, Dowell). Abstract ballet.

BRANLE, probably from the old Fr. *branler*, to sway, because the steps are alternately from left to right. Choral dance, current in Poitou in the fifteenth century, but thought to be of greater antiquity and possibly of Eastern origin. Introduced into England as the Brawl or Brantle early in the sixteenth century. It was popular, in a more sophisticated form, at the court of Louis XIV, whilst Pepys, in 1662, records that he had seen it danced by Charles II. Descriptions of many different branles, in 2/2, 3/4, and 6/8 time, have come down to us and their pantomimic character ranks amongst the early ancestors of the ballet.

BRAUN, Eric, b. Vienna 1924, d. Highland Park, Ill. 1970. Austrian dancer. Studied at Vienna Staatsoper Sch. under Nijinska. Joined Ballet Th. 1944, becoming principal 1955. Taught and chor. in Chicago.

BRAUNSWEG, Julian, b. Warsaw 1897. Polish (now British) impresario. Left Warsaw 1914 for Moscow and took group of dancers to Caucasus 1917. Returned Warsaw 1918 and to Berlin 1919 to study. Organized

83

group of dancers, Russian Romantic B. to Coliseum, London 1924, and worked with Max Reinhardt's German ballet in 1923. To Paris 1929 and in 1939 took Woizikovsky's Polish B. to New York. Settled in England 1939 and in 1949 managed the Markova-Dolin ballet, founding the Festival Ballet (as it then became) 1950 and managing it until 1965. Since then he has arranged and managed the tours of many Cos., including Royal B., Vienna Staatsoper B., Niagara Frontier (Buffalo) etc. His twin brother Marian Norski is also an impresario working in Brazil. Author of *Braunsweg's Ballet Scandals* 1973.

BRENAA, Hans, b. Copenhagen 1910. Dan. dancer. Studied at Royal Th. Sch. Début 1928, becoming solodancer 1943, and also a teacher in the school, and mounted *Aurora's Wedding* 1949. Guest artist B. Jooss 1953. Retired 1955 and now teaches and mounts the Bournonville ballets all over the world. In 1967 mounted Flindt's *The Lesson* for Western Th. B., *La Sylphide* for Scottish Th. B. 1973.

BREUER, Peter, b. Tegernsee 1946. German dancer. Pupil of Gustav Blank. Joined Munich B. 1961. Joined Düsseldorf B. 1963 becoming soloist 1965. Guest artist Festival B. 1969–73, Washington Nat. B. 1972 etc.

BREXNER, Edeltraut, b. Vienna 1927. Austrian dancer. Entered Staatsoper Sch. Vienna 1934. Joined Staatsoper Ballet 1944, becoming soloist 1953 and prima ballerina 1957. From 1962 teacher at Staatsoper Sch.

BRIANSKY, Oleg, b. Brussels 1929. Belgian dancer. Studied Katchourowsky, Gsovsky, Kniaseff. Joined B. des Ch. Élysées 1946, B. de Paris 1950, Festival B. 1951 and 1958. Chor. *Tournoi* at Palais de Chaillot 1950. Guest artist São Paulo 1954. Now teaches in Saratoga with his wife Mireille Lefebvre (Briane) and has his own group.

BRIANZA, Carlotta, b. Milan 1867, d. 1930, possibly in Nice. It. dancer, pupil of Blasis at Milan, where she became prima ballerina. In 1887 she made her début in St Petersburg at the Arcadia Th., and at the Maryinsky Th., in 1889 (in Ivanov's *Tulip of Harlem*). In 1890, as guest artist at the Maryinsky, she cr. the chief rôle in *The Sleeping Beauty*; the audiences called her 'the little brown imp'. She left Russia in 1891 and taught in Paris at the Opéra Comique. Her last appearance as a dancer was as Carabosse in Diaghileff's production of this ballet in London 1921. She had a school in Nice.

BRIGGS, Hedley, b. King's Norton 1907, d. Parkstone 1968. Eng. dancer, actor, and designer. Partnered Penelope Spencer 1928–30, danced at Old Vic and in Camargo Soc. 1930. Designed many ballets for S. Wells B., incl. *Douanes* (1932), *Casse Noisette* (1934), *Tritsch-Tratsch* (1947).

84

BRIGHT STREAM, THE, ballet 3 acts, 4 sc., ch. Lopokov, m. Shostakovitch, dec. Bobishov, f.p. Bolshoi Th., Leningrad 30 Nov 1935.
Comedy ballet about a collective farm called 'The Bright Stream'. It
was criticized in Russia of 'anti-people tendencies' and called 'abstract
and formalistic'.

BRILLANT, Maurice, b. Combrée 1881, d. Paris 1953. Fr. poet and
author of many articles on ballet and the book *Problèmes de la Danse*
1953, and contributed to *L'Art du Ballet*.

BRINSON, Peter, b. Llandudno 1923. Eng. lecturer and writer on ballet.
Educated Denstone and Keble Col., Oxford. Director of Research,
Film Centre 1948–53. Special adviser on cinema to U.N.E.S.C.O.
1949–50. Arranged first stereoscopic film *The Black Swan* 1952
(q.v.), edited *Pavlova* film 1954. Author of pamphlets on films, etc.,
contributor to *The Dancing Times* and *Ballet*, Editor *Films and Filming*
1954–55. Contributor on ballet to *The Times* publications since 1952.
Extension lecturer on ballet to Univs. of Oxford, Cambridge and
London 1954–64. Research fellow The Council of Europe 1961. In
1964 founded and directed the group Ballet for All. Appointed director
of Royal Academy of Dancing 1968, resigned 1969. Author of the
Ballet for All programmes, edited *The Ballet in Britain* (1962), Author
The Choreographic Art (with van Praagh) 1963, *The Polite World* (with
Joan Wildeblood) 1965, *Background to European Ballet* 1966, *Ballet for
All* (with Clement Crisp) 1970. In 1971 appointed Director of the
Gulbenkian Foundation, but continuing his connexion with Ballet for
All.

BRISÉ or PAS BRISÉ, lit. a broken step. A movement in which the dancer
leaps off one foot, breaking the movement in the air by lightly beating
the legs and alighting on both feet. In addition the brisé can be executed two feet to two feet, two to one, one to one, dessus, dessous, en
avant, en arrière.

BRISÉS TÉLÉMAQUES, a series of steps of which the derivation is obscure,
but probably connected with one of the several *Telemachus* ballets (or its
dancers) of the eighteenth century. In 3/4 time it consists of: brisé
over, changement-de-pieds (beaten), entrechat-trois derrière, followed
by brisé back, changement-de-pieds (beaten), entrechat-trois derrière—
all repeated again carried out with the other foot. Forward steps are
done obliquely, backward steps done straight back. In 4/4 time: brisé
over, two changements-de-pied (beaten), entrechat-cinq derrière, brisé
back, two changements-de-pied (beaten), entrechat-cinq derrière—all
repeated again commencing with the other foot.

BRISÉ VOLÉ, lit. a flying brisé, a pas brisé alighting on one foot, the other being extended, pointe dégagé and just off the ground (quatrième demi position), alternately to front and back.

BRITAIN, BALLET IN, see under ROYAL BALLET, BALLET RAMBERT, FESTIVAL BALLET, LONDON, SCOTTISH THEATRE BALLET, WESTERN THEATRE BALLET, NORTHERN DANCE THEATRE, BALLETS MINERVA, INTERNATIONAL BALLET CARAVAN, SADLER'S WELLS OPERA B., HARLEQUIN BALLET, INTERNATIONAL BALLET, METROPOLITAN BALLET, LONDON BALLET, LONDON DANCE TH., CONTEMPORARY DANCE TH. etc.

BRITISH BALLET ORGANIZATION (known as the B.B.O.), a teaching and examining body in Gt Britain and the Dominions. Founded by Édouard Espinosa after he left the Royal Academy of Dancing, and his wife, Louise Kay, in 1930 (see ESPINOSA). Nicola Guerra of the Paris Opéra was choreographical co-director. Examinations are held in the United Kingdom, Australia, New Zealand and Ceylon and an annual Concourse in London. An Espinosa Memorial Scholarship is awarded to the Royal B. Sch. every year and other scholarships to students, known as Grade Incentive Scholarships. The B.B.O. (since 1950) is directed by Edward Espinosa, son of the founder. It preserves the French style of the nineteenth century.

BRITTON, Donald, b. London 1929. Eng. dancer. Studied Maddocks Sch., Bristol, and S. Wells Sch. Joined S. Wells Th. B. 1946 and S. Wells B. 1947. After military service rejoined S. Wells Th. B. 1951 as a principal. Left Royal B. 1965 and taught the boys' classes at Royal Ballet Sch. until 1969. To Oslo 1965 to mount *Pineapple Poll*. From 1969 has danced in musicals.

BRONZE HORSEMAN, THE, ballet, ch. Zakharoff, m. Glière, dec. Bobishov, f.p. Kirov Th., Leningrad 14 Mar 1949 (Dudinskaya, Shelest, Sergeyev). Pushkin's poem. In one scene the River Neva is seen, on the stage, to overflow its banks.

BROOKLYN FESTIVAL OF MODERN DANCE, annual festival at the Brooklyn Academy of Music, N.Y. assembling troupes of modern dancers. The first was held 21 Oct 1968 (opening with the Martha Graham Co.).

BROSSET, Yvonne, b. Stockholm 1935. Swedish dancer. Pupil of the R. Swedish B. Sch. from 1944 and of Royal B. Sch. Joined Royal Swedish Ballet 1953 and became ballerina 1963 and a director of the Co. 1971.

BROWN, Carolyn, b. Fitchburg, Mass. 1927. Am. dancer. Studied with her mother (Marion Rice) and Martha Graham, Tudor and others. Principal dancer of Merce Cunningham Dance Co. from 1953, creating many leading roles. In Paul Taylor Co. 1970.

BROWN, Vida, b. Oak Park, Ill. 1922. Am. dancer and maîtresse de ballet. Danced with B. de la Jeunesse, Paris, and B. Russe de Monte Carlo 1939–48, becoming soloist. Ballerina in Malmö 1949–50. Joined N.Y. City B. 1950 and in 1954 became ballet-mistress and Balanchine's assistant until 1958. Mounted *Symphony in C* (Balanchine) in Copenhagen 1953 and other Balanchine ballets in Europe.

BROWNE, Louise, b. Madison, Wis. 1906. Am. (Brit. by marriage) dancer and teacher. Studied under Kosloff, Vladimiroff, Fokine, de Valois and Craske. Danced leading rôles in Ziegfeld shows in N.Y. from 1922. British première as the Girl Friend in *The Girl Friend* (Palace Th. 1927). Danced in Royal Command perf. 1938. Founded and directed the Ny Norsk Ballet, Oslo 1947–50. Examiner and member of Executive Committee R.A.D., with a school in York. See NORWEGIAN BALLET.

BRUCE, Christopher, b. Leicester 1945. Eng. dancer and chor. Pupil of Rambert Sch. Danced in Gore's London B. 1963 and B. Rambert the same year, of which he is now a principal dancer. Chor. *George Frideric* (m. Handel) 1968, *Living Space* (no music, words by R. Cockburn) 1969, *Wings* (m. Downes) 1970.

BRUEL, Michel, b. Sète 1941. Fr. dancer. Pupil of Nina Lopez, and Lazzini at sch. of Marseille B. Joined Marseille Co. 1958 as soloist becoming étoile 1960. Left in 1964 to freelance, partnering Hightower, Arova, Sombert, Vyroubova etc. and dancing all over the world. Joined Lazzini's Th. Française de la Danse in Paris 1969. Danced *Swan Lake* with Alonso in Cuba and took part in the film of her life, 1970.

BRUGNOLI, Amalia. It. dancer who flourished in the 1820s and was one of the first to exploit the use of the points. Was partnered by her husband Paolo Samengo, who was also famous as a chor. in Italy. They visited London in 1832.

BRUHN, Erik, b. Copenhagen 1928. Dan. dancer. Pupil of Royal Dan. Sch. from 1937, joined Royal Dan. B. 1947, becoming a solodancer 1949. He danced with the Metropolitan B., London, in 1947 and since then, although he has been the principal male dancer of the Royal Dan. B. throughout, he has danced as guest artist in most of the ballet companies of the world—with Ballet Th. in 1949 and regularly ever since, N.Y. City B. 1959–60 and 1963–64, Royal B. 1962, Australian B. 1962–63, Royal Swedish B. 1964, Harkness B. on its formation 1965, Nat. B. of Canada 1964 and subsequently, in Rome Opera B. 1966, Milan Opera B. etc. Danced with Ballet Th. in Russia 1960. Staged a full-length *La Sylphide* for the Canadian Nat. B. 1964 and his own version of *Swan Lake* for them in 1966. Chor. *Concertette* (1953) and *Festa* (1957) for Royal Dan. B. In 1967 he was appointed Director of the

Royal Swedish B. Knight of Dannebrog 1963. One of the greatest male dancers of his generation, he has a remarkable purity of style and is a model exponent of the Bournonville style. Author (with Lillian Moore) of *Bournonville and Ballet Technique* (1962). In 1972 he retired as a dancer and also as director of the R. Swed. B.

BRUNELLESCHI, Elsa, b. Buenos Aires 1908. Sp. dancer, teacher in London, and chor. Studied in Barcelona under Pauleta Panices. Ballets include *Flamenco* (B. Rambert 1943) and dances in *Carmen* (C. Garden 1947). Author of *Antonio* (1958).

BRUNNER, Gerhard, b. Villach 1939. Austrian writer on ballet. Educ. University of Vienna. Writer for *Express, Stuttgarter Zeitung, Neue Zeit, Das Tanzarchiv* and research into eighteenth century Viennese ballet. Commentator for Austrian television. Mar. Christl Zimmerl.

BUCKLE, Richard, b. Warcop 1916. Eng. writer on the ballet. Educated Marlborough and Balliol Coll., Oxford. Founder and editor of the magazine *Ballet*. Author of novel *John Innocent at Oxford* 1939, the play *Gossip Column* 1953. Ballet critic of the *Observer* 1948–55 and of *Sunday Times* from 1960. Organizer of the Diaghileff Exhibition for the Edinburgh Festival 1954. Author of *Adventures of a Ballet Critic* 1953, *In Search of Diaghileff* 1955, *Modern Ballet Design* 1955. Sokolova's memoirs *Dancing for Diaghilev*, 1960, *Nijinsky* 1971. Organized the Epstein Exhibition at the Edinburgh Festival 1961, the Shakespeare 4th Centenary Exhibition at Stratford-upon-Avon 1964. Compiled the catalogues and took a prominent part in presenting Sotheby's (London) sales of Diaghileff material in 1966, 1968, and 1969. In an attempt to raise money to buy Titian's *Death of Actaeon* for the National Gallery he organized a gala at the Coliseum, London on 22 June 1971 *Repetition Generale for The Greatest Show on Earth* at which Fonteyn, Nureyev, Idzikowsky, Ursula Moreton, Sokolova, Gilpin, Danilova, Jeanmaire, Pilar Lopez and himself appeared.

BUGAKU, ballet, ch. Balanchine, m. Mayuzumi, dec. Hays, cost. Karinska, f.p. N.Y. City B., City Center, N.Y. 20 Mar 1963 (Allegra Kent, Villella). Inspired by the attitudes and movements of Japan but not strictly in the style of Bugaku, the dancing performances put on by the Gagaku, the dancers and musicians of the Japanese Imperial Court.

BUJONES, Fernando, b. Miami 1955. Am. (Cuban parents) dancer. Pupil of the Alonsos, Eglevsky and Stanley Williams at Sch. of Am. B. Danced with Eglevsky's group and joined Am. Ballet Th. 1972.

BULGARIAN STATE SONG AND DANCE COMPANY, THE, founded 1951 with Margaret Dikova, previously director of dancing at the Sofia Opera, in charge of the dances. Début in Sofia 1952. Appeared in Paris and London 1955, performing folk dances and songs.

BULNES, Esmée, b. Rock Ferry, England, 1900. Eng. dancer and teacher. Studied under Cecchetti in London, B. Nijinska, Smirnova, Romanoff, Vilzak-Schollar and (in Paris) Egorova. Started teaching at Colon Th., Buenos Aires in 1931 and acted as assistant to Fokine. Organized the ballet schools at Colon Th. and at the Municipal Th. of La Plata. To Teatro alla Scala, Milan, in 1951 as ballet mistress and in charge of the School. She was appointed Director of Ballet in 1954 until 1962 when she was succeeded by Luciana Novaro but remained in charge of the School until 1968 when she retired but continues teaching. Taught Royal B. 1967 and 1969.

BUNDGAARD, Kirsten (formerly Petersen), b. Copenhagen 1936. Danish dancer. Joined R. Dan. B. Sch. 1943, R. Dan. B. 1952 becoming solodancer 1957, ballerina 1961. Guest artist Festival B. In 1955 danced lead in Ashton's *Romeo and Juliet* at Edinburgh Festival.

BURKE, Dermot, b. Ireland 1948. Irish dancer. Pupil of Edith Royal, Joffrey, Zaraspe, Brunson. Joined Joffrey B. 1966 becoming soloist.

BURNE, Gary, b. Bulawayo 1934. Rhodesian dancer. Studied with Elaine Archibald and Ruth French. Joined Royal Ballet 1952, becoming soloist 1956. Created rôles of King of the South in *Prince of the Pagodas* and Etiocles in *Antigone*. Returned to S. Africa 1961, in 1965 principal dancer in the ballets of Cape Town and Johannesburg, mostly partnering Phyllis Spira. Director of Transvaal B. 1963. In 1967 danced with Canadian Nat. B. Chor. *The Misfits, Daphnis and Chloë.*

BURR, Marilyn, b. Paramatta 1933. Austral. dancer. Studied under Kelleway and made debut in the National B. Co. 1948. To England 1952 becoming soloist of Festival B. 1953 and then ballerina. In 1963 joined Hamburg B. as ballerina and in 1964 went to America, dancing with the Washington Nat. B. as ballerina. Danced in New Zealand 1965. Mar. I. Nagy.

BURRA, Edward, b. 1905. Eng. painter. Dec. for S. Wells B. include *Rio Grande* (1935), *Barabau* (1936), *Miracle in the Gorbals* (1944), *Don Juan* (1948), *Don Quixote* (1950).

BURROW, THE, ballet, ch. MacMillan, m. F. Martin, dec. Georgiadis. f.p. Royal Ballet, Covent Garden 2 Jan 1958 (Heaton, Britton). Reminiscent of *The Diary of Anne Frank.* Performed by R. Danish B, 1961.

BUSH, Noreen, b. Nottingham 1905. Eng. teacher. Pupil of Edouard Espinosa. 1924–27 danced at Gaiety Th. London (with Jose Collins) and Daly's Th. (with Evelyn Laye). Head teacher at the Espinosa Sch. Joined her mother's sch. at Nottingham, Pauline Bush Sch. of Dancing (founded 1914). In 1930, with her husband Victor Leopold, founded the Noreen Bush Sch. in Oxford St, London, which became Bush Davies Sch. in 1939 (Marjorie Davies died 1968). In 1945 she opened an additional residential branch at Charters Towers, East Grinstead, with the Adeline Genée Th. built in the grounds in 1967. Member of Grand Council and Major Examiner of R.A.D.

BUSSE, Edna, b. Melbourne. Austral. dancer. Studied under Borovansky and became the first ballerina of his Co. 1943, until 1952 when she retired.

BUTLER, John, b. Memphis 1920. Am. dancer and chor. Trained at Martha Graham Sch. and Am. Sch. of Ballet 1940–41. Member of Graham's Co. 1945–55. Danced in musicals and on television. Chor. many ballets for the Met. Opera, N.Y. City Center and N.Y. Opera TV. For Ballet Th. *Seven Faces of Love* (1957), N.Y. City B. *Unicorn, Gorgon and the Manticore* (1957), Director of Spoleto Festival (dance) 1958. Had his own Co. John Butler Dance Th. which performed in Spoleto 1958 and 1959. Chor. *Carmina Burana* (m. Orff) for N.Y. City Opera Co. in 1959 and for Nederlands Dans Th. 1962. Chor. *Sebastian* (m. Menotti with whose music he has been much associated) 1966 and *After Eden* (m. Hoiby) 1966 both for Harkness B. Since then his choreography has been much in demand all over the world.

BUTSOVA (Boot), Hilda, b. Nottingham. Eng. dancer. Studied under Cecchetti and became member of Diaghileff's Co. Joined Pavlova's Co. and shared many of her rôles with her, holding the title of ballerina. Joined Mordkin's Co. 1927 and danced with Dolin 1929. To America 1930. Now retired and teaches occasionally.

BY THE SEA, ballet, ch. Grivickas and A. Messerer, m. Juzeliunas, dec. Janckus and Surckijavivius, f.p. Lithuanian Ballet, Vilnius 1953 (G. Sabaliauskaite, G. Banys).

C

CABRIOLE, from It. *capriuola*, lit. a she goat, a caper. A step in which the dancer extends one leg to the front, back, or side and, springing upwards, brings the second leg up to the first, which is thus further raised before the dancer alights.

CACCIALANZA, Gisella, b. San Diego 1914. Am. dancer. Studied under Cecchetti and Sch. of Am. B. Soloist B. Caravan and created many rôles for B. Society. Mar. Lew Christensen. She created rôles in several of Balanchine's early ballets.

CACHUCHA, Span. solo dance in 3/8 time with castanets, musically not unlike the bolero (which is in 3/4 time). The word (like 'bluette' in French) indicates something light, smart, sparkling, pretty, and a variety of the bolero was called 'boleras de la cachucha'. It became famous in the Romantic Ballet when Fanny Elssler introduced a cachucha into the first performance of *Le Diable Boiteux* (Paris Opéra, 1 June 1836), vividly described by Gautier. It became Elssler's most famous dance, it was encored at every performance at the Opéra and she danced it wherever she went. She had based it on the dances which she had seen performed in Paris in 1834 by four dancers from Madrid, Dolores Serral, Manuela Dubinon, Francisco Font and Mariano Camprubi. Later it became Pauline Duvernay's most famous dance (f.p. by her in London 1837) who performed it until her retirement in 1851. Many lithographs show both Elssler and Duvernay in this dance. Zorn (q.v.) includes it in his *Grammatik der Tanzkunst* (1887), written down in his notation. In 1967 the dance was reconstructed from this by Ivor Guest, Ann Hutchinson and Philippa Heale and it was taken into the repertoire of Peter Brinson's Ballet for All group (q.v.), f.p. by Virginia Wakelyn, Civic Th., Rotherham 27 Sept 1967.

CADZOW, Joan, b. Melbourne 1929. Austral. dancer. Studied under Miss Brennan and came to London with R.A.D. schol. 1948. Studied at S. Wells Sch. and joined S. Wells Th. B. In 1952 left and took up residence in Paris, dancing in recitals with Chauviré, etc., and soloist of Ballets de l'Étoile at Th. Étoile, Paris 1954–55. Ballerina of Berlin and Frankfurt 1960–66. Prima ballerina of Düsseldorf from 1966. Guest ballerina of many European opera houses. Prix Anna Pavlova 1960.

CAGE, John, b. Los Angeles 1912. Am. composer. Pupil of Buhlig, Weiss, Schoenberg. In 1943 started working on his 'prepared piano' and composing for it. In 1951 organized work on composing direct on to magnetic tape. From 1943 Musical Director of the Merce Cunningham Dance Co. and has composed many ballets for them.

CAGE, THE, ch. Robbins, m. Stravinsky, cost. Ruth Sobotka, f.p. N.Y. City B., City Center, N.Y. 14 June 1951 (Kaye, Mounsey, Magallanes). A horrific ballet based on insect life.

CAHUSAC, Louis de, b. Montauban 1706, d. Paris 1759. Fr. writer. Wrote libretti of many opera-ballets at the Académie Royale with Rameau's music, and published *La Danse Ancienne et Moderne*, The Hague 1754, a complete history of dancing, in which many reforms were urged. He contributed articles on the dance to Diderot's *Encyclopédie* (1751–65).

CAIN AND ABEL, ballet. ch. MacMillan, m. Panufnik, dec. Kay. f.p.

Deutsche Oper B., Deutsche Oper, Berlin 1 Nov 1968 (Frey, Job, Binner). The Bible story.

CAKEWALK, a strutting dance of Am. Negro origin, popular at the beginning of this century. A piece of cake was the prize given to the best performer.

CAKEWALK, ballet 1 act, ch. Ruthanna Boris, m. Gottschalk (arr. Kay), dec. Drew, f.p. N.Y. City B., City Center, N.Y. 12 June 1951 (Reed, Wilde, Hobi, Mounsey). A witty ballet of the period of the cakewalk and Negro minstrels. It was revived by the Joffrey B. at N.Y. City Center 8 Sept 1966.

CAMARGO (Marie Anne de Cupis de Camargo), b. Brussels 1710, d. Paris 1770. Pupil of Mlle Prévost. Famous Fr. dancer who was noted for her light, vivacious style of dancing. She made dancing history by shortening her skirt to a few inches above the instep, thus giving her lower limbs the necessary freedom to perform certain steps of allegro and of elevation. She was also one of the first to wear drawers when dancing (see TUTU). She made her début in Brussels and at the Paris Opéra in 1726 where she was the great rival of Sallé. Retired in 1751 and surrounded herself with parrots and other pets. Lancret's painting of her is in the Wallace Collection, London. Many dishes have been named after her, notably *Bombe Camargo*. Petipa made a ballet *Camargo* in 1872 with Grantzow as Camargo. Her younger sister, Anne Cupis de Camargo, was première danseuse at the Comédie Française 1746 and danced at Drury Lane and C. Garden 1750–1754.

CAMARGO SOCIETY, formed in 1930 on the initiative of Arnold Haskell and P. J. S. Richardson and under the chairmanship of the late Edwin Evans to present performances of ballet to subscription audiences with dancers drawn in the main from the Rambert and de Valois groups and the ballerinas Lydia Lopokova, Olga Spessivsteva and Alicia Markova. Its first performance was at the Cambridge Th., London 19 Oct 1930. Between 1930 and 1933, when the Society, its aim accomplished, was wound up and its repertoire incorporated in that of the Vic-Wells (see ROYAL BALLET) and Rambert Cos., sixteen ballets were produced in addition to revivals of shortened versions of *Swan Lake*, *Giselle*, and a two-act version of *Coppélia*. Cost. and dec. were commissioned from well-known or promising British artists such as John Armstrong, Vanessa Bell, Edward Burra, William Chappell, Edmond Dulac, Duncan Grant and George Sheringham, thus establishing a tradition which has been continued by both the Royal and Rambert ballets. British Ballet owes not a little of its rapid growth to the Camargo Society and its initiators, who had the courage to found it at a time when the possibility of building a national company was derided by most people and the foresight to wind it up as soon as the Vic-Wells Ballet and the Ballet Rambert were strong enough to stand alone. Among the musicians associated with it were Edwin Evans and Constant Lambert. It kept ballet alive in England after the death of Diaghileff.

CAMBIAMENTO, It. for Changement de pieds (q.v.).

CAMBRÉ, a bending back or a leaning to the side from the waist.

CAMPANAS, special beats of the foot in zapateado dances.

CAMPBELL, Sylvester, b. Oklahoma 1938. Am. dancer. Studied at Jones-Haywood Sch. Washington and Am. Sch. of B., N.Y. Joined New York Negro B. 1956 and came to Europe with them. Joined B. de la Tour Eiffel 1959, Dutch Nat. B. 1960 becoming a principal dancer. Also danced as guest with Deutsche Oper B. Berlin and Béjart's B. of XXth Century. From 1972 principal of R. Winnipeg B.

CAMPRA, André, b. Aix 1660, d. Versailles 1744. Fr. composer who composed twenty-five opera-ballets for the Paris Opéra, introducing a new style of entertainment which led up to such works as Rameau's *Les Indes Galantes*. Among his ballets are *L'Europe Galante* (1697), *Le Carnaval de Venise* (1699), *Le Ballet des Sens* (1732). He said, 'There is only one way to popularize opera-ballet and that is to lengthen the dances and shorten the skirts of the danseuses.'

CANADA, BALLET IN, see ROYAL WINNIPEG B., NATIONAL BALLET OF CANADA, LES GRANDS BALLETS CANADIENS, LES FEUX FOLLETS.

CANADA, NATIONAL BALLET OF, based on Toronto and supported by the Canada Council, stems from a performance given at the Variety Arena on 28 May 1951 by Celia Franca and a small group of dancers trained by her, together with soloists Lois Smith and David Adams. Three Toronto ladies, Mrs J. D. Woods, Mrs R. B. Whitehead and Mrs F. J. Mulqueen, had asked the advice of de Valois on the formation of a company in 1949 and as a result Celia Franca had been invited over in 1950 to prospect. She remained and formed the small group which after its first performance danced in Montreal in August 1951, gradually grew, and found a home in St Lawrence Hall, Toronto. In September 1951 a Board of Directors appointed Celia Franca as artistic director, George Crum musical adviser, Kay Ambrose public relations director (artistic adviser 1953–62). Betty Oliphant was appointed ballet mistress and the first performance was given in Eaton Auditorium 12 Nov 1951 (*Les Sylphides*, peasant pas de deux *Giselle*, *Prince Igor*, Franca's *Salome* and Kay Armstrong's *Étude*). The principal dancers were Franca, Lois Smith, David Adams, Irene Apine, Jury Gotshalks and in the group were Angela Leigh, Brian Macdonald, Grant Strate (resident

93

choreographer 1958 onwards), Earl Kraul (principal dancer from 1953). In 1953 the Co. appeared at Jacob's Pillow—the first foreign group so to do. The repertoire is eclectic but based on the Royal and Rambert ballets and with ballets by Grant Strate and productions by Erik Bruhn, Cranko etc. Among the dancers have been Samtsova, Kenneth Melville, Hans Meister, Jeremy Blanton, Lawrence Adams, Veronica Tennant and ballet staff David Scott, Shirley Kash, Joanne Nisbet. It first toured the U.S. in 1955. In Toronto the Co. performs at the O'Keefe Centre. It has its own school, opened in 1959 with Betty Oliphant as principal. The Co. first danced in London (Coliseum) 1972, when the principals were Karin Kain, Veronica Tennant, Nadia Potts, Mary Jago, Vanessa Harwood, Cousineau, Stefanschi, Surmeyan. Nureyev mounted *Sleeping Beauty* for them in 1972, dancing himself, and they toured America with it 1972–73.

CANARIES, or CANARIE, or CANARY, sixteenth-century dance in 3/4 time, possibly owing its name to having originated in the Canary Islands.

CANCAN or CHAHUT. Introduced to Fr. public balls about 1830, the cancan, from being a spirited dance to galop tempo, had by the end of the century become a suggestive entertainment for tourists, complete with high kicks and frilly skirts, still to be seen in its most exuberant form at the famous Bal Tabarin. It has been described as 'a kind of epileptic or *delirium tremens* dance' and as the *enfant terrible* of choral dances. The cancan has been introduced by Massine into his ballets *Gaîté Parisienne* and *La Boutique Fantasque* and has been the theme of countless divertissements. It usually ends with a *grand écart*.

CANTICLE FOR INNOCENT COMEDIANS, ballet, ch. Graham, m. Ribbink, dec. Kiesler, f.p. Graham Dance Co., Juilliard Concert Hall, N.Y. 22 Apr 1952 (Pearl Lang, Yuriko, Ross, Hodes, Cohan). A hymn to life.

CAPAB BALLET, the ballet company based on Cape Town, South Africa, and financed by State funds through the Cape Performing Arts Board. It was founded by Dulcie Howes (q.v.) who opened her own ballet school in Cape Town in 1930. In 1931 W. H. Bell, director of the College of Music at the University of Cape Town, needed some dancers for the operas he was producing there and he invited Dulcie Howes to transfer her school of sixty dancers to the University. It thus became the University of Cape Town School of Ballet and officially opened in 1932. In 1963 it moved into its own building and in 1964 gave its first performance, *The Enchanted Well* (which was in a programme which included an opera and a masque). It then became known as the Univ. of Cape Town Ballet Company (still directed by Dulcie Howes), the first ballet company in S. Africa. Originally it had performed in the Little Theatre, but as it grew began performing in the City Hall and the Alhambra Th. (with the municipal orchestra). In 1941 it visited Johannesburg and Port Elizabeth and since then it has become a touring company, performing all over S. Africa, Rhodesia, S. West Africa etc. In 1949 Markova and Dolin visited S. Africa and danced *Swan Lake* and *Giselle* with a corps drawn from the University of Cape Town (U.C.T.) Ballet and another group the South African National Ballet (which afterwards merged with the U.C.T. Ballet).

To ensure the continuity of the company a non-profit-making trust, the Dulcie Howes Ballet Trust, was formed and in 1963 the State began assisting the company, until 1965 when it was re-named the CAPAB Ballet and financed from public funds, and now maintains over thirty full-time dancers.

When dancing in Cape Town the company is still officially called the U.C.T. Ballet Company, but CAPAB in all performances outside. Guest artists have included Beryl Grey, Nadia Nerina, Maryon Lane, Alexis Rassine, Desmond Doyle, Pat Bosman, Brian Ashbridge etc. David Poole was appointed ballet master in 1963 and director of the company in 1969 on the retirement of Dulcie Howes. In 1965 Phyllis Spira and Gary Burne were appointed principal dancers. Frank Staff was Resident Choreographer, and among the choreographers employed have been Dulcie Howes, David Poole, Alfred Rodrigues, Richard Glasstone, John Cranko etc.

Dulcie Howes continues to direct the U.C.T. School of Ballet and among her colleagues are (or have been) Cecily Robinson (ex-Rambert and de Basil), Pamela Chrimes (ex-S. Wells Th. B.), Yvonne Blake (Blum's Monte Carlo B.), Richard Glasstone (Scapino B.), Patricia Miller (S. Wells Th. B.), Yvonne Honoré (B. Rambert) etc.—all former pupils. Cranko was a student and created his first ballets there.

CAPE TOWN BALLET, UNIVERSITY OF (U.C.T. Ballet)—see CAPAB BALLET.

CAPEZIO AWARD (cash) is given annually in America by a firm of ballet-shoe makers to the person who, in the opinion of a committee, has done great service to the dance. Recipients to date have been Zachary Solov (1952), Lincoln Kirstein (1953), Doris Humphrey (1954), Louis Horst (1955), Geneviève Oswald (1956), Shawn (1957), Danilova (1958), Hurok (1959), Martha Graham (1961), Karinska (1962), Donald McKayle (1963), Limon (1964), Maria Tallchief (1965), de Mille (1966), Paul Taylor (1967), Lucia Chase (1968), John Martin (1969), William Kolodny (1970), La Meri and Gladys Laubin (1971), Isadora Bennett (1972).

CAPRICCIO ESPAGNOL, ballet 1 act, ch. Massine in collaboration with

95

Argentinita, to the m. of that name by Rimsky-Korsakov, dec. M. Andreù originally designed for Fokine's *Jota Aragonesa* in 1937, f.p. B. Russe de Monte Carlo, Th. de Monte Carlo 4 May 1939 (Argentinita, Danilova, Massine). Filmed as *Spanish Fiesta* (1941). Massine staged it for International B., London in 1951 and danced in it.

CAPRICES DU CUPIDON ET DU MAÎTRE DE BALLET, LES (Dan. *Amors og Ballet-mesterns Luner*), ballet, ch. Galeotti, m. Lolle, f.p. R. Dan. Opera 31 Oct 1786. This, with *La Fille Mal Gardée*, is the oldest work in the European repertory, for it is still danced by the R. Dan. Ballet. Now performed with dec. by Pedersen. Lander mounted it at Paris Opéra 27 Feb 1952, dec. Chapelain-Midi. Comic ballet introducing many national pas de deux and ending with a romp.

CAPRICHOS, ballet 4 episodes, ch. Herbert Ross, m. Bartók (*Contrasts for piano, clarinet and violin*), dec. Pons, f.p. Ballet Th., City Center, N.Y. 5 Apr 1950. A grim ballet based on Goya's etchings. It was originally given 24 Jan 1950 at the Choreographer's Workshop, Hunter Coll. Playhouse, N.Y. (Murai, Snyder, Ross etc.). Also in repertoire of Touring Royal B., Wimbledon Th., Wimbledon 12 Oct 1971 (Durant, Strike, Ruanne, Tait, Karras, Jefferies, Morse, Davel).

CAPRICHOS, LOS, ballet, ch. Ana Nevada, m. traditional Sp., dec. Clavé, f.p. B. des Ch. Élysées, Th. des Ch. Élysées, Paris 1946 (Nevada, Petit, Garcia). Typical Sp. theme of a young girl, a duenna and a lover.

CAPRIOL SUITE, ballet, ch. Ashton, m. arr. Warlock (see ARBEAU), dec. Chappell, f.p. Rambert Dancers, Lyric Th., Hammersmith 25 Feb 1930 (Howard, Gould, Turner, Ashton). A suite of Elizabethan dances. Capriol is the name of the young man with whom Arbeau discourses in his *Orchésographie*.

CARACOLE, ballet 1 act, ch. Balanchine, m. Mozart, dec. Bérard, f.p. N.Y. City B., City Center, N.Y. 19 Feb. 1952 (Tallchief, LeClerq, Hayden, Adams, Wilde, Eglevsky, Magallanes, Robbins). Pure dancing. It was revised in 1956 and is now called *Divertimento No. 15*. It is in the repertoire of many Cos.

CARD GAME, also called *The Card Party*, see JEU DE CARTES.

CARDINAL, LA FAMILLE, the classic ballet family, the creation of L. Halévy (1834–1908, who was, with Meilhac, the librettist of *Carmen* and of many of Offenbach's operas). They occur in eight short stories, the first (*Madame Cardinal*) appearing in *La Vie Parisienne* 14 May 1870, and the last (*Le Feu d'Artifice*) in 1880. Halévy was a frequenter of the *Foyer de la Danse* and the *coulisses* of the Opéra and these stories are penetrating vignettes of the Opéra at that time. Madame Cardinal is the archetype of the ballet-mother, watching over her daughters

Virginie and Pauline, in the premier quadrille of the corps de ballet. Virginie marries a marquess and Pauline becomes a courtesan.

CARDUS, Ana, b. Mexico City 1941. Mexican dancer. Pupil of André and Unger in Mexico City. Début with Ballet Concierto de Mexico 1956. Joined Cuevas B. 1960 becoming soloist. To Stuttgart B. 1962 as joint ballerina with Haydee. To Cologne as ballerina 1967–71.

CARLI, Didi, b. Buenos Aires 1943. Argentinian dancer. Studied at the Teatro Colon and under Ruanova. Danced in Frankfurt 1962–64 and a principal at Deutsche Oper, W. Berlin from 1964.

CARMEN, ballet 5 sc., ch. Petit, m. Bizet, dec. Clavé, f.p. B. de Paris, Princes Th., London 21 Feb 1949 (Jeanmaire, Petit, Perrault, Hamilton). A translation of the opera into ballet. Taken into R. Dan. B., Copenhagen 15 Jan 1960 (Simone, Kronstam, Flindt), and into several other Cos. (Transvaal B., S. Africa 1965, with Danielle Jossi and R. Bestonso).

CARMEN, ballet ch. Cranko, m. Fortner (based on Bizet), dec. Dupont. f.p. Stuttgart B., Stuttgart 28 Feb 1971 (Haydee, Madsen, Cragun). Based more on Merimée than on the opera.

CARMEN SUITE, ballet, ch. Alberto Alonso, m. Bizet arr. Schedrin, dec. B. Messerer, f.p. Bolshoi B., Moscow 20 Apr 1967 (Plisetskaya, Fadeyechev, Radchenko). An impression of the opera. Danced by Tchaikovsky Memorial B., Tokyo 1972.

CARMINA BURANA, ballet, ch. John Butler, m. Carl Orff, cost. Butler, dec. Sylbert, f.p. N.Y. City Opera Co., City Center, N.Y. 24 Sept 1959 (Carmen de Lavallade, V. Mlakar, Glen Tetley, Scott Douglas). The dances interpret the bawdy, dog-Latin mediaeval poems which Orff had set to music for choir and soloists. This ballet has been danced by many other companies, notably by the Nederlands Dans Th. and Les Grands B. Canadiens. Also chor. by Heinz Rosen for the Munich B., Prinzregenten Th., cos. Schrock, dec. Jurgens, 6 May 1959 (Hallhuber). The first was in Frankfurt 8 June 1937, ch. Hertling.

CARNAVAL, LE, ballet 1 act, ch. Fokine, m. Schumann, dec. Bakst, f.p. Diaghileff's Co. in its final version at Theater des Westens, Berlin 20 May 1910 (Karsavina, Piltz, Nijinsky). An earlier performance had been given that year 20 Feb 1910 at a charity performance in the Pavlov Hall, St Petersburg, at which Leontiev had taken the rôle of Harlequin and including Nijinska, Karsavina, Fokina, Schollar. The Pierrot was the actor Meyerhold. The Soviet ballet-master V. Bourmeister also produced a ballet to this music at the Stanislavsky Th. Moscow 1946. *Carnaval* is in the repertoire of many companies. It was first revived for S. Wells B. by Evina, dec. E. and M. Williams, S. Wells Th. 24 Oct 1933 (Idzikowsky).

CARNIVAL OF ANIMALS, ballet 1 act, ch. and dec. Andrée Howard, m. Saint-Saëns, f.p. B. Rambert, Mercury Th., London 26 Mar 1943 (Schooling, Scott, Gilmour, Harrold). A zoological suite of dances (omitting *The Swan*).

CAROLINE, Mlle, see DOMINIQUE, Mme.

CARON, Leslie, b. Paris 1931. Fr. dancer. Studied at Paris Conservatoire with Jeanne Schwarz. Début B. des Ch. Élysées 1948, cr. rôles in Lichine's *La Rencontre* and *La Création*. Took lead in Gene Kelly's film *An American in Paris* and *Lili*. Returned to Petit's Co. in London 1954, creating *La Belle au Bois Dormant*. Returned to U.S. to make more films (*Gigi* 1957, *An American in Paris*, *Fanny*). Gave up dancing to become actress in 1956. Her mother was Margaret Petit, musical comedy star.

CAROSO, Fabrizio, It. dancer, composer and author whose books *Il Ballarino* (1581) (a code of dance) was one of the earliest books on the dance. In 1600 he rewrote it and revised it under the title *Nobiltà di Dame*. He describes all the current steps (cabrioles, entrechats, révérences etc.) and enumerates 68 rules of dancing.

CARPEAUX, J. B., b. Valenciennes 1827, d. Courbevoie 1875. Fr. sculptor whose greatest work was the group *La Danse* on the façade of the Paris Opéra (1869). His model was the Princess Hélène de Racowitza. He also made a bust of Eugénie Fiocre. The *Cercle Carpeaux* was founded in 1948 by a group of ballet lovers and *habitués* of the Paris Opéra *'contribuer à accroître en France et à l'étranger le rayonnement de l'art lyrique et chorégraphique tel que celui-ci s'exprime à l'Académie Nationale de Musique et de Danse'*. It has about 250 members and organizes receptions in the Foyer de l'Opéra, endeavouring to bring back to the Opéra the elegance of its former days (its members always wear evening dress at performances).

CARRETILLA, Sp., the rolling beat of the castanet held in the right hand. See GOLPÉ.

CARROLL, Elisabeth (Pfister), b. Paris 1937. Am. dancer. Studied under Besobrasova and Sedowa in Monte Carlo. Début Monte Carlo Opera B. 1951. Joined Ballet Th. 1954, becoming soloist 1961. Joined Joffrey B. 1962 and Harkness B. 1964. Now teaches there.

CARTE BLANCHE, ballet 1 act, ch. Gore, m. Addison, dec. Rowell, f.p. S. Wells Th. B., Empire Th., Edinburgh 10 Sept 1953 (Mosaval, Hill, O'Reilly, Poole, Britton). A series of light, inconsequential scenes related to a circus.

CARTER, Alan, b. London 1920. Eng. dancer and chor. Studied under Astafieva, Legat and Conti Sch. Entered S. Wells (Vic-Wells) B. 1937, soloist 1938–41 and (after war service) of S. Wells Th. B. 1946–47, for whom he chor. *The Catch* (1946). Ballet-master for the films *The Red Shoes* (1947), *Tales of Hoffmann, Invitation to the Dance* (1953) and chor. film *The Man who loved Redheads* etc. Formed the St James's Ballet for the Arts Council 1948–50. Ballet-master of the ballet at the Empire Cinema, London 1951–53. Worked in Amsterdam. Appointed Director of Ballet at Munich 1954–59, of Tel Aviv 1960, Wuppertal B. 1964–68, Bordeaux B. 1968–70. Guest teacher of Royal B. 1962 and chor. for the Touring Royal B. *Toccata* (m. Bach) 1962. At Munich chor. *The Miraculous Mandarin, Prince of the Pagodas, Ondine.* At Wuppertal chor. *Swan Lake, Sleeping Beatuy, Shostakovitch X Symphony.* Appointed director of State Ballet Sch., Istanbul, 1970 (left 1971) and of Finnish Nat. B. 1971 (left 1972). In 1973 became director of ballet in Iceland.

CARTER, Jack, b. Shrivenham 1923. Eng. chor. Studied S. Wells Sch. 1938 and with Volkova, Preobrajenska, Northcote. Danced with Molly Lake's Embassy Ballet 1946 and with Orig. Ballet Russe, B. Rambert, Festival B. In Amsterdam 1954–1957. Chor. many ballets for Ballet der Lage Landen and for Festival B., R. Swed. B. etc. Ballets include *Stagioni* (m. Verdi 1950), *Witch Boy* (1956), *London Morning* (1959), *Señor de Mañara* (1959, m. Tchaikovsky). Mounted full-length *Swan Lake* for Colon Th., Buenos Aires 1963 (using the full 1877 Moscow production score), chor. *Agrionia* (m. Salzedo) 1964 for London Dance Th., *Beatrix* (m. Adam) 1966 for Festival B. Resident chor. Festival B. 1966–70 and mounted his 1963 *Swan Lake* for them 1966 and *Coppélia* 1968, and chor. *The Unknown Island* (m. Berlioz) 1969. For Western Th. B. chor. *Cage of God* (m. Rawsthorne) 1967 etc. Mounted *Cage of God* for Cologne B. and B. Van Vlaanderen, and *Witch Boy* for Washington Nat. B. 1971. To Japan in 1971 and produced *Coppélia* for Tokyo Th. B.

CARZOU, Jean, b. 1907. Fr. painter. His first work for the ballet was the Inca scene in the 1952 production at the Paris Opéra of *Les Indes Galantes.* He also designed *Le Loup* for Petit in 1953 and *Giselle* for the Paris Opéra in 1954.

CASADO, Germinal, b. Casablanca 1934. Moroccan dancer and designer. Studied under Leontieff, Zverev and V. Gsovsky. Danced in the Wuppertal B. and Cuevas B. Joined Béjart's Ballet du XXme Siècle in 1957 becoming a principal dancer. Designed *Tales of Hoffmann* and *Faust* (m. Berlioz) 1964 for Paris Opéra and *Romeo and Juliet* (m. Berlioz) for Béjart's Co. 1966, all to Béjart's choreography.

99

CASATI, Giovanni, b. Milan 1811, d. there 1895. It. dancer and chor. Pupil at Scala Sch. and of A. Vestris in Paris. Danced in Milan 1821–1833. Chor. many ballets in Italy and at C. Garden, Hofoper, Vienna, and in Lisbon. Chief teacher at Scala Sch. Milan 1867 to 1881. Mar. It. dancer Margherita Wuthier, the favourite pupil of Blasis.

CASENAVE, Roland, b. Bordeaux 1923. Fr. dancer and teacher. Pupil of Egorova, Preobrajenska, V. Gsovsky and Northcote. Member of B. des Ch. Élysées 1947 and 1951, in Cuevas B. 1947–51. Danced and taught for the Opera B., Amsterdam, 1952–58, Ballet de France 1958–60. Taught for Dutch Nat. B. 1961–64, London's Festival B. 1965–66. Now a guest teacher and producer of ballets, notably of *Suite en Blanc* and *Paquita*.

CASSANDRE, A. M., b. Kharkov 1901, d. Versailles 1967. Russ.-Fr. painter. Designed *Le Chevalier et la Demoiselle* for Paris Opéra (1941), *Dramma per Musica* for Nouveau B. de Monte Carlo (1946), *Les Mirages* for Paris Opéra (1947), *Coup de Feu* (ch. Milloss) for Cuevas B. (1951), *Chemin de Lumière* (Munich and Paris Opéra, 1957).

CASSE NOISETTE (Nutcracker), ballet 2 acts and 3 sc., based on the tale by Hoffmann, ch. Ivanov, m. Tchaikovsky, dec. Botcharov and Ivanov, f.p. Maryinsky Th., St Petersburg 6 Dec 1892 (dell'Era, Gerdt, Legat, Preobrajenska, Kyasht). Petipa was prevented by illness from carrying out this work and it fell to his assistant Ivanov. The first Sugar Plum Fairy was dell'Era and the Prince, Gerdt. The ballet was revived in its entirety in a version by Serguéeff by the S. Wells B., S. Wells Th. 30 Jan 1934, with Markova and Judson, and by the Festival B., Stoll Th., London 24 Oct 1950 (Markova, Dolin) version by Beriozoff, revised again by Lichine 24 Dec 1957 at Festival Hall, London (Krassovska, Gilpin)—both with dec. Benois. The last act is a divertissement 'The Kingdom of Sweets' and is in the repertoire of many companies. In Russia a new version in 3 acts was given at the Kirov Th., Leningrad 18 Apr 1934, ch. Vainonen, dec. Seleznyov (Ulanova, Sergeyev). In the Russian versions Clara is called Masha and she dances the grand adagio and the Sugar Plum Variation. This version was also given in Moscow until 12 Mar 1966 when the Bolshoi Th. presented a new one, ch. Grigorovitch, dec. Virsaladze (Maximova, Vasiliev).

Other notable versions are (a) New York City Ballet, ch. Balanchine, dec. Armistead, cost. Karinska, f.p. 2 Feb 1954 (Maria Tallchief, Magallanes) and a new version ch. Balanchine, dec. Ter-Arutunian, f.p. N.Y. State Th. 11 Dec 1964 (Farrell, d'Amboise). Always called *Nutcracker*, these versions greatly differ from the original versions of the ballet. (b) ch. Cranko, dec. Adron, f.p. Staatsoper, Stuttgart

4 Dec 1966 (Haydee, Madsen). (c) R. Swedish B., ch. Nureyev, dec. Mongiardino, cost. Gastine and Doboujinsky, f.p. 17 Nov 1967 (Orlando, Selling). This version, with some alterations, was f.p. Royal Ballet, C. Garden, 29 Feb 1968, dec. Georgiadis (Park, Nureyev). (d) chor. by Walter Gore, f.p. Ballet Der Lage Landen, Stadsschouwburg, Amsterdam, 1957. This was revived for his London B., Hippodrome Th., Brighton 4 Oct 1962, dec. Cordwell (Hinton, Karras, Rassine). Also for Norwegian B. 1965, Johannesburg B. 1968.

CASTANETS, a percussion instrument of two hollowed-out pieces of wood, held in the palm of each hand, much used by Spanish dancers. The right-hand castanet is of higher pitch than the left hand. The best castanets are of chestnut wood, but La Argentina preferred those of pomegranate wood.

CASTIL-BLAZE (F. H. J. Blaze), b. Cavaillon 1784, d. Paris 1857. Fr. writer whose *La Danse et les Ballets depuis Bacchus jusqu'à Mlle Taglioni* (1832) and *L'Académie Impériale de Musique* (1855) give a full, intimate account of ballet in France from the earliest times. Music critic of the *Journal des Débats* till 1832.

CATA, Alfonso, b. Havana 1937. Cuban dancer and ballet master. Pupil of Kniaseff 1956, Joffrey and, from 1965, Balanchine. Joined Petit's company in Paris 1957, Joffrey B. 1958, de Cuevas B. 1960, Stuttgart 1961–63, Charrat's Geneva Co. 1963, N.Y. City B. 1964–67. In 1969 appointed by Balanchine to the Geneva B. as ballet master. In 1973 director of Frankfurt B.

CATALYST, THE, ballet ch. Cranko, m. Shostakovitch, dec. Schachteli, f.p. Stuttgart B., Opera House, Stuttgart 8 Nov 1961 (Faure, Barra, Morena, Delavalle). A ballet of transformations.

CATARINA, OU LA FILLE DU BANDIT, ballet 3 acts, 5 sc., ch. Perrot, m. Pugni, dec. Marshall, f.p. Her Majesty's Th., London 3 Mar 1846 (Grahn, Perrot). This ballet, about an incident in the life of Salvator Rosa, remained in the St Petersburg repertoire for many years.

CATON, Edward, b. St Petersburg 1900. Am. dancer and chor. Danced in Pavlova's Co. 1924–25 and has been ballet-master to many companies in the U.S. Teaches in N.Y. and Europe. Ballet-master of de Cuevas Co. 1944 and from 1958. Teaching Pittsburgh B. 1973. Chor. *Sebastian*, m. Menotti (31 Oct 1944) for B. International.

CATULLI CARMINA, ballet, ch. John Butler, m. Orff, cost. Venza and Colisanti-Moore, f.p. Butler's Co. Venetian Pavilion, Caramoor, Katonah, N.Y. 7 July 1964 (Carmen de Lavallade, Robert Powell, Buzz Miller, Veronika Mlakar). The chorus comes on to the stage in this story of Catullus and Lesbia. It is also in the repertoire of Les

Grands Ballets Canadiens (dec. Prévost, cost. Barbeau). Possibly its first appearance as a ballet was in Leipzig 6 Nov 1943. Chor. by T. Gsovsky.

CAULEY, Geoffrey, b. Somerset, Bermuda 1942. Eng. dancer and chor Studied at Royal B. Sch. Joined C. Garden Op. B. 1960 and the Royal B. Chor. *Murmurings* (m. Ravel) 1967 and *Lazarus* (m. Bloch) 1968 both for Royal B. Choreographic Group, *In the Beginning* (m. Poulenc) 1969 for Royal B., *The Listeners* (m. Young) 1969 for Royal B. Sch., *La Symphonie Pastorale* (m. Martinu) 1970, *Ante Room* (m. Martinu) 1971 for Royal B., and the musical *Lie Down I think I Love You* 1970. In 1971 he joined John Field at the Scala, Milan. Director of Zürich B. 1973.

CAVALLAZZI, Malvina, b. Italy, d. 1924. It. dancer. After dancing in many Italian opera houses she became the first prima ballerina at the Met. Op., N.Y. when it opened in 1883. She was a strong mime who excelled in character parts. She was in the Empire Ballets in London 1887–99 (in travesty on every occasion save one, her first appearance at the Empire Th. 1887 in *Diane*) and became in 1909 the first director of the ballet school at the Met. Op., N.Y. She was the wife of Col. Charles Mapleson, the opera impresario.

CAZALET, Peter, b. Kitwe, N. Rhodesia 1934. Eng. dancer and designer. Trained under Dulcie Howes and Pamela Chrimes, Cape Town, after taking degree in architecture. Joined Edinburgh International B. 1958, Festival B. 1959, Western Th. B. 1960. First danced with Univ. of Cape Town B. Contributed regular cartoons on ballet to *Dance and Dancers*. In 1970 retired from dancing to devote himself to designing but rejoined Scottish Th. B. 1971.

CEBRON, Jean, b. Paris 1938. Fr. dancer (son of Mauricette Cebron, of the Paris Opéra 1911–36 and teacher there). Studied oriental dancing, and under Leeder in London. Début in Leeder's Group in London 1956. Worked with the Jooss group in Essen and has developed an individual style of modern dancing. From 1964 with Folkwang ballet in Essen.

CECCHETTI, Enrico, b. in a theatre dressing-room Rome 1850, d. Milan 1928. It. dancer and one of the greatest teachers in the history of ballet. Pupil of Lepri in Florence. Débuts at La Scala, Milan 1870, in London 1875, and St Petersburg (Arcadia Th.) 1887. He became a dancer and teacher in St Petersburg in 1890, and among his pupils at that time were Pavlova, Preobrajenska, Egorova, Karsavina, Kschessinska and Nijinsky. He left in 1902 for Warsaw and in 1905 returned to Italy. Returning to Russia he taught Pavlova privately. He was the teacher of the Diaghileff Co. on its formation in 1909 and opened a school in London in 1918. All the dancers of the Diaghileff era passed through his hands and his strict method of teaching ('The Cecchetti Method') was codified and recorded by Idzikowsky, Craske, de Moroda and Beaumont. He returned to La Scala, Milan, in 1923 as Director of the Imperial Academy of Dancing. He created a number of famous rôles, e.g. Blue Bird and Carabosse in *Sleeping Beauty*, the Charlatan in *Petrouchka*, and the Astrologer in *Coq d'Or*.

CECCHETTI SOCIETY, formed in 1922 in London, at the instigation of Cyril Beaumont, to perpetuate the system of teaching evolved by Maestro Enrico Cecchetti, its first President. The Society was incorporated in the Imperial Society of Teachers of Dancing in 1924. Together with the Royal Academy of Dancing it has, by its system of examinations, done much to raise the standard of teaching and dancing throughout the British Empire. In 1952 an annual Cyril Beaumont Scholarship to the Royal Ballet Sch. was instituted. There is also an annual Cyril Beaumont Award provided by himself and judged at the Royal Ballet Sch., and also the Mabel Ryan Awards (Junior under 13, Senior 13 to under 15 years) for Cecchetti students, and choreographic competitions. The Society also grants the use of the titles Associate, and Fellow, of the Imperial Society of Teachers of Dancing (Cecchetti Society Branch).

CECH, Gisela, b. Vienna 1945. Austrian dancer. Pupil of Staatsoper Sch. under Hamilton, Hiden, Plucis, Krausenecker, Ursuliak. Joined Vienna Staatsoper B. 1960 becoming soloist 1969. Mar. Paul Vondrak.

CÉLESTE, Céline (Celeste Keppler), b. Paris 1811, d. there 1882. Fr. dancer and actress. Danced at Paris Opéra. To America 1827, danced in N.Y. and mar. a Mr Elliott. To London 1830, where she made a great reputation as a dancer and (after the 1850s) as an actress. She also toured America (being the first to dance *La Sylphide* there, 1835) and the Continent. On her second visit to U.S.A. in 1834, General Jackson introduced her to the Members of Congress and congratulated her on being elected a free citizen of the U.S. In 1843 she, with Benjamin Webster, leased the Adelphi Th. and presented ballets and ballet-burlesques until 1859. Retired from the stage 1874 and withdrew to Paris.

CELLI, Vincenzo, It. dancer and teacher. Studied under Cecchetti, becoming principal dancer at La Scala, Milan, in the 1920s and now teaches in N.Y.

CENDRILLON, see CINDERELLA.

CENT BAISERS, LES, ballet 1 act, ch. Nijinska, m. d'Erlanger, dec. Hugo, f.p. de Basil's Co., C. Garden, London 18 July 1935 (Baronova, Lichine). A Hans Andersen fairy tale.

CENTRAL EUROPEAN MOVEMENT, see MODERN DANCE.

CENTRE PRACTICE, those exercises executed in the centre of the class-room in the second part of the class in contrast to those done at the bar in the first part of the class.

CERRI, Cecilia, b. Turin 1872, d. Vienna 1931. It. dancer and teacher who was prima ballerina at the Hofoper, Vienna 1907–19 and taught at their school 1907–31.

CERRITO, Fanny, b. Naples 1817, d. Paris 1909. It. dancer. Pupil Perrot, Blasis, and Saint-Léon. Débuts at Naples 1832, Vienna 1836, Milan 1838, London 1840, Paris 1847, St Petersburg 1855, Moscow 1856. Mar. Saint-Léon 1845, separated from him 1851. Cr. rôles in *Alma, Ondine, Lalla Rookh, Pas de Quatre, Jugement de Pâris, La Vivandière* (of which ballet she was joint chor.). She was also chor. of several ballets, notably *Rosida* (1845) and *Gemma* (1854). She was one of the greatest dancers of her time and second only to Taglioni in international reputation. She was *bondante et abondante*, vivacious, voluptuous and with great strength and brio.

CHABOUKIANI, Vachtang, b. Tiflis 1910. Russ. dancer and chor. Studied under Marie Perrini and at Leningrad, graduated 1929. He became the greatest male dancer in the Soviet Union and twice received the Stalin Prize. His virtuosity was exceptional, although for many years he was troubled with his knee. Chor. of many ballets, incl. *Heart of the Hills* (1938), *Laurencia* (1939), *Sinatle* (1948), *Gorda* (1950), *For Peace* (1953), *Othello* (1957), *The Daemon* (1961). Since 1941 he has been in charge of the ballet at Tiflis. In 1934, with Tatiana Vecheslova, he toured America—the first Soviet dancers so to do. In 1971 mounted *Swan Lake* for Nat. B. of Persia, Teheran.

CHACONNE, dance in 3/4 time introduced towards the end of the sixteenth century, probably of Sp. origin. At first sensual and exotic, it was greatly modified as it was assimilated into the French court ballet. The operas of Lully, Rameau and Gluck frequently end with a chaconne or a passacaglia. The word derives from Sp. *chocuna*, pretty, but Compan derives it from *cecone*, blind, and says it was invented by a blind man.

CHAFFEE, George, b. Oakland, U.S. cont. Am. teacher, dancer and author. Studied under Balanchine, Preobrajenska, Wigman. Soloist of Mordkin B. and B. Russe de Monte Carlo. Collector of prints and iconography of the ballet, and author (with Richard Doubs) of many important articles and monographs on such items.

CHAGOLL, Lydia, b. Brussels 1931. Belgian dancer, teacher and founder of the Ballet Lydia Chagoll. Educated at Brussels Univ. and in Paris, Ghent and Brussels in dancing. Founded the Ballet Lydia Chagoll in Brussels, a small group of classical dancers, which gave its first season in 1966. It toured Belgium and appeared in Germany, England etc. Madame Chagoll was the director and chor. and most of the dancers were English. She is the author of *Plaidoyer Pour le Ballet Belge* (1959) and *Précis d'Enseignement de la Danse Classique* (1966). The company finished in 1970.

CHAHUT, see CANCAN.

CHAÎNÉS (abbreviation of tours chaînés déboulés), a series of quick travelling turns from one foot to the other, on point. Also known as déboulés.

CHALON, A. E., b. Geneva 1780, d. Kensington 1860. Swiss painter (to England 1869), whose paintings and lithographs preserve for us the dancers of the Romantic Era. His best pictures are those of Taglioni and the *Pas de Quatre* 1845. He also painted the young Queen Victoria and was elected an R.A.

CHAMBERS, Barbara, b. Melbourne 1944. Pupil of Borovansky Academy. Joined Borovansky B. 1959 becoming soloist. Joined Australian B. 1962 becoming soloist 1962 and principal 1966. Now teaches.

CHAMBRE, LA, ballet 1 act, ch. Petit, m. Auric, dec. Buffet, f.p. Petit's Co., Th. des Ch. Élysées, Paris, 20 Dec 1955 (Mlakar, Buzz Miller). A Simenon detective story.

CHANGEMENT or CHANGEMENT DE PIEDS (It., cambiamento), lit. a changing of the feet. A spring upwards from the fifth position, in which the feet change during the ascent so that the foot which was at the back at the start is in front on alighting. Whilst in the air the legs should be fully stretched and the feet pointed. If the feet barely leave the ground the movement is described as a petit changement or if maximum elevation is attempted as a grand changement. It is customary to end every class with petits and grands changements (usually sixteen small and eight large).

A *changement battu* is a small changement de pieds with the front foot beating in front, changing and finishing behind. This is also called a royale (see ENTRECHAT).

CHANSON DE L'ÉTERNELLE TRISTESSE, LA, ballet, ch. Ricarda, m. Headington, dec. Stubbing, f.p. de Cuevas Co., Alhambra Th., Paris, 22 June 1957 (Vyroubova, Golovine). Inspired by a poem of the T'ang Dynasty.

CHANT DU ROSSIGNOL, LE, ballet 1 act (based on Hans Andersen's tale), ch. Massine, m. Stravinsky, dec. Matisse, f.p. Diaghileff's Co., Paris

Opéra 2 Feb 1920 (Karsavina, Sokolova). This was a ballet made from the opera *Le Rossignol* (dec. Benois), f.p. Paris Opéra 26 May 1914, which had not been a success. Balanchine made new choreography for it for Diaghileff B., f.p. Gaîte Lyrique Th., Paris, 17 June 1925 (Markova).

CHAPPELL, Annette, b. Liverpool 1929. Eng. dancer and teacher. Pupil of Judith Espinosa and R.A.D. scholar. Joined B. Rambert 1944–49, becoming a principal dancer. In musicals etc. 1949–55. Ballerina Munich B. from 1955 and later teacher there. To Stuttgart B. 1970 to join staff of their school.

CHAPPELL, Meryl, b. Portsmouth 1947. Eng. dancer. Pupil of Royal B. Sch. Joined Royal B. 1965 becoming soloist 1970.

CHAPPELL, William, b. 1908. Eng. designer. Danced with B. Rambert, Camargo Soc., Ida Rubinstein B., and Vic-Wells B. (cr. many rôles, incl. Rake's Friend in *Rake's Progress* and Second Red Knight in *Checkmate*). Prolific and talented designer of ballets, incl. *Capriol Suite, Bar aux Folies-Bergère, Les Rendezvous, Les Patineurs, Giselle*, and *Coppélia*. Author of *Studies in Ballet* (1948) and *Margot Fonteyn* (1951). Now writes and directs revues.

CHARACTER DANCE, described in the eighteenth and nineteenth centuries as *danse comique*—any traditional, national, or folk dance, or dance closely allied thereto, or a dance based on movements inspired by a particular trade, profession, or mode of living.

CHARACTER DANCER, a dancer specializing in or particularly suited by build and aptitude to character dancing as against a demi-caractère (q.v.) or a classical dancer.

CHARISSE, Cyd (née Finklea), b. Amarillo, Texas 1926. Am. dancer. Studied under her father, Bolm, Nijinska, and Nico Charisse, whom she married. Début de Basil's Co. 1939, and in films (*Something to Shout About*) 1942. Since then has danced only in films, notably in *Fiesta, The Unfinished Dance* (1946), *Singin' in the Rain* (1951), *It's Always Fair Weather* (1955), *Brigadoon, Black Tights* (1962).

CHARLESTON, a social dance which, like the polka in 1840, the tango in 1912, and the foxtrot in 1914, took society by storm. Originating as a Negro solo dance in Charleston, S. Carolina, it was first used as a ballroom number by Ned Wayburn in *The Follies*, New Amsterdam Th., N.Y. 20 Oct 1923. It came to London 1925. It is in 4/4 time with a rhythmic beat falling on the first and fourth beats of the bar, and also between the second and third.

CHARNLEY, Michael, b. Manchester 1927. Eng. dancer and chor. Studied under Jooss. Joined S. Wells B., B. Jooss 1943–6. Chor. for

B. Workshop 1952, and for Festival B. *Symphony for Fun* (1952), *Alice in Wonderland* (1953). Also chor. for musicals *A Girl Called Jo* (1955), *The Ballad of Dr Crippen* (1961). Worked in Australia in the 1960s.

CHARRAT, Janine, b. Grenoble 1924. Fr. dancer and chor. Studied under Egorova, Volinine. Was the child in the film *La Mort du Cygne* (1938). Worked with B. des Ch. Élysées 1945–46 and with Nouveau B. de Monte Carlo 1946. In 1951 started her own company (called Ballets de France) which gave its first performance in Grenoble 24 Dec 1951. Chor. *Jeu de Cartes, 'Adame Miroir, Les Algues, Abraxas*, etc. In 1961 she was very severely burned in a Paris television studio while rehearsing *Les Algues*. Director of Geneva B. 1961–63 and returned to dancing in 1962. In 1969 opened a sch. in Paris.

CHASE, Alida, b. Brisbane 1951. Austral. dancer. Pupil Bousloff, Austral. B. Sch. Joined Co. 1969, soloist 1972.

CHASE, Lucia (Mrs Thomas Ewing), b. Waterbury, Conn. 1907. Am. dancer. Founder and director of Am. Ballet Theatre. Studied under Fokine, Nijinska and especially Mordkin of whose company (Mordkin B.) she was ballerina on its foundation, 1938 and 1939 and which she subsidized. In 1940 she founded Ballet Theatre and was its Director and one of its ballerinas (she created the rôle of the Oldest Sister in *Pillar of Fire*) and has remained its head ever since (since 1957 it has been known as Am. Ballet Th.). Ballet in the U.S. owes much to her for the great part this company has played in its development. See AMERICAN BALLET THEATRE.

CHASSÉ or PAS CHASSÉ, a step from a plié in the fifth position, in which the foot is slid out to fourth or second position, maintaining the plié and, without raising the heel, the weight transferred to that foot.

CHATFIELD, Philip, b. Eastleigh 1927. Eng. dancer. Studied S. Wells Sch. Joined S. Wells B. 1943 becoming a principal dancer 1955. Retired to New Zealand 1959 with his wife Rowena Jackson. In 1972 became joint director of Nat. Sch. of B. in Wellington, N.Z.

CHATTE, LA, ballet 1 act, ch. Balanchine, m. Sauguet, dec. Gabo and Pevsner, f.p. Diaghileff's Co., Monte Carlo 30 Apr 1927 (Spessivtseva, Lifar). Based on an Aesop fable. The scenery was of talc. Nikitina and Markova also danced the rôle of the Cat.

CHAUSSAT, Geneviève, b. Mexico City 1941. Swiss dancer. Pupil of Besobrasova and Solange Golovine. Joined the Nice B. then Serge Golovine's Co., and from 1968 a soloist in Munich B.

CHAUVIRÉ, Yvette, b. Paris 1917. Fr. dancer. Studied at Paris Opéra school and under Kniaseff, rising to première danseuse étoile. In 1946 danced with the B. des Ch. Élysées and with Nouveau B. de Monte Carlo. In 1947 she returned to the Opéra but left in 1949 to dance as guest artist in other companies, notably at La Scala, Milan, in N.Y. with B. Russe de Monte Carlo, in London with Festival Ballet, etc. Her Giselle was one of the great interpretations. Returned to Opéra in 1953 as guest artist. Her contract with the Opéra was terminated in 1957 but she was asked to return as guest artist. Danced with Royal Ballet at C. Garden 1958 and in Russia with Algaroff. Appointed director of the ballet school at the Paris Opéra 1963 and from 1970 of the Acad. Internationale de Danse. Awarded Legion d'Honneur 1964, National Order of Merit 1972. Known in Paris as 'La Chauviré nationale' she is the greatest French dancer of this century. Her final perf. at the Paris Opéra was 20 Nov 1972 in *Giselle*.

CHECKMATE, ballet 1 sc. and a prologue, ch. de Valois, book and m. Bliss, dec. E. McKnight Kauffer, f.p. S. Wells B., Th. des Ch. Élysées, Paris 15 June 1937 (Brae, May, Turner, Helpmann). One of de Valois' best ballets, it has always been very popular with Continental audiences. The original costumes and décor were lost in Holland during the German invasion. de Valois also mounted it in Vienna and in Turkey.

CHESWORTH, John, b. Manchester 1930. Eng. dancer and chor. Joined B. Rambert 1952 with little prior training and danced as soloist until 1966. Appointed assistant to the director of the new B. Rambert 1966. Chor. *Time Basé* (m. Lutoslawsky) 1966, *Tic-Tack* (m. Kreisler-Rachmaninoff) 1967, *H* (m. Penderecki) 1968 etc. Appointed associate director 1970.

CHEVALIER ET LA DAMOISELLE, LE, ballet 2 acts, ch. Lifar, m. Gaubert, dec. Cassandre, f.p. Paris Opéra 2 July 1941 (Schwarz, Lifar). A mediaeval legend.

CHICAGO OPERA BALLET, founded in 1955 by Ruth Page from the group which had been appearing in the operas of the Chicago Lyric Opera that year. It gave its first performance on 16 Nov 1955 in Chicago with Markova as guest ballerina. Since then it has given regular seasons in Chicago and tours. The first public perf. of Nureyev in America was for this Co. (*Don Quixote* pas de deux, with Arova, Brooklyn Academy of Music 10 Mar 1962). While touring, from 1966, the Co. was also known as Ruth Page's International B. In 1970 it disbanded and the costumes were sold.

CHILEAN NATIONAL BALLET, based on the Teatro Municipal, Santiago. The visits of European dancers and companies during the last century maintained a sporadic interest in ballet, but it was not until the 1940s that any proper company was maintained. The B. Jooss visited Santiago in 1940 and from it Ernst Uthoff and Lola Botka settled there to maintain a company (dancing in the Central European style). In 1950 a Russ. teacher Elena Poliakova (q.v.) gave it a classical impetus, as did Charles Dickson (from Festival B.) and Denis Carey (Eng. ballet master) with Virginia Roncal as principal dancer (from the de Cuevas Co.). Norman Dixon (ex-Ballet Rambert) worked in Santiago 1970–71. There is also a Ballet Clàsico Nacional and a Ballet Municipal.

CHINA, BALLET IN, the two principal Cos. are in Peking and in Shanghai. Classical ballet first appeared in China in 1954 when Viktor Tsaplin from the Bolshoi B. went to Peking as a teacher, and in 1957 Pyotr Gusev from the Kirov B. mounted *Swan Lake, Giselle, The Corsair* and *The Fountain of Bakhchisarai* for them. The Ballet Rambert toured China in 1957 and the Moiseyev and Bolshoi B. (with Ulanova and Plisetsaya) danced in Peking in 1959. Previous to that there had been visits by Russ. soloists (Dudinskaya, Sergeyev etc.). The Peking Ballet, officially called the China Dance Drama Troupe of Peking, was founded in 1962. All the dancers are pupils of the Peking Dance School founded in 1954 and directed by Dai Ai-lian who had studied at the Rambert Sch. in London from 1930 until 1939 when she returned to China. She chor. the first important ballet of the Co. *The Dove of Peace* (which included ballet with Chinese national dances).

In 1961 Gusev was sent home and ballet was 'reformed' according to the current political condition of China. No more classical ballets could be performed; their place was taken wholly by propaganda ballets of which the most important is *The Red Detachment of Women* (1964), chor. by Wang, who also danced in it. Other revolutionary ballets are *The White Haired Girl, Washing the Liberation Army's Uniforms* (for 7 girls and a boy), *In Praise of Yimon Mountain* etc. These are in the classical style with slight alterations such as hands clenched into fists, or turned outwards to the audience in fourth position in attitude to give a defiant, revolutionary effect. Diao Ke-yuan directs the Co., the ballerinas are Chang Chao and Yu Lie-di, and there are 150 dancers.

In Shanghai the Co. is called the Shanghai Dance School (the school was founded in 1960 but the Co. has taken its name), directed by Li You-ying. The principal dancers are Chang I and Chin Ai-ping and the Co. dances at the Shanghai Municipal Revolutionary Auditorium. There are 135 dancers.

CHIRIAEFF, Ludmilla, b. Riga 1924. Latvian (now Canadian) dancer and director. Studied under Nicolaeva in Berlin, joined de Basil Co. 1936–37 and studied under Fokine and Massine. Danced in Berlin Opera B. during the War and in 1948 opened her own school in Geneva, after having been dancer and ballet mistress in Lausanne. Formed her own troupe in Geneva, Les Ballets des Arts. To Canada in 1952 and made ballets for Radio Canada Television, with Jean Boisvert and formed Les Ballets Chiriaeff 1955. This became Les Grands Ballets Canadiens (q.v.) in 1956, with herself as Director.

CHIRICO, Giorgio de, b. Greece 1888. It. painter. Designed many ballets, including *La Jarre* (B. Suedois 1924), *Le Bal* (Diaghileff 1929), *Les Bacchantes* and *Bacchus* (Paris Opéra 1938), *Protée* (de Basil 1938), *Legend of Joseph* (Scala, Milan 1951) etc.

CHLADEK, Rosalia, b. Brno 1905. Czech dancer and teacher. Studied at Dalcroze Sch., Hellerau 1921–24 and worked there from 1924 (Artistic Director 1930–38). Her work as a modern dancer and as a chor. has mostly been in Austria and from 1942 to 1971 she directed the Vienna High School for Music and Dance, now situated in Schönbrunn Palace.

CHOPINIANA, see LES SYLPHIDES.

CHOREARTIUM, ballet 4 parts, ch. Massine, m. Brahms's Fourth Symphony, dec. Terechkovich and Lourié, f.p. de Basil Co., Alhambra, London 24 Oct 1933 (Baronova, Danilova, Riabouchinska, Verchinina, Jasinski, Lichine, Petroff, Shabelevski). This was Massine's second symphonic ballet, a sombre ballet of mood.

CHORÉAUTEUR, Fr., a composer of ballets or dances. A term coined by Lifar in 1935 in his *Manifeste du Chorégraphe* as a substitute for 'chorégraphe', which he felt to have become susceptible of several meanings.

CHOREOGRAPHER or CHOREGRAPHER (Gr. *khoros*, dance, and *graphein*, write), the composer, or author of the dances and steps of a ballet.

CHOREOGRAPHY or CHOREGRAPHY, term used in the eighteenth century to describe the art of dance notation but now designates the art of dance or ballet composition.

CHOREOLOGY, a term copyright in 1955 by the Beneshes for the writing down of movement and ballets in their system of notation. One who practises Benesh choreology is termed a choreologist. In 1973 there were choreologists attached to the following ballets—Royal B. (Faith Worth, Monica Parker, Jacquie Hollander, Elizabeth Cunliffe), Stuttgart B. (Georgette Tsinguirides), Dutch Nat. B. (Wendy Vincent-Smith), N.Y. City B. (Jurg Lanzrein), B. Rambert (Ann Whitley), Scottish Th. B. (Julie Haydn), Canad. Nat. B. (Suzanne Menk), Australian B. (Elphine Allen, Cherry Trevaskis), Northern Dance Th. (Sandra Curtis), CAPAB B. S. Africa (Susan Smith), PACT B. S. Africa (Mary Garman), Harkness B. (Richard Holden), R. Swed. B.

(Jean Geddis), W. Berlin B. (Louise Blackmore), N. Zealand B. (Pamela Meakins), Festival B. (Bronwen Curry) etc.

CHOREOLOGY, INSTITUTE OF, founded in London 1962 by Rudolf and Joan Benesh to teach the Benesh System of dance notation, to train teachers and to record ballets and other aspects of movement (sport, industrial, medical etc.). It awards an Advanced Diploma in Choreology (two-year course) by examination (A.I.Chor.), a third year leads to membership of the Institute, and for outstanding subsequent work a Fellowship may be gained (F.I.Chor.). See DANCE NOTATION.

CHOREUTICS, a term used by von Laban to describe his analysis of movement and form in dancing.

CHOTA ROUSTAVELI, ballet 4 acts, ch. Lifar, m. Honegger, Tcherepnine, Harsanyi, dec. Schervachidze and C. Nepo, f.p. Nouveau B. de Monte Carlo, Monte Carlo 5 May 1946 (Chauviré, Adjemova, Lifar, Kalioujny). After the fairy tale *A Hero in a Leopard's Skin* by Roustaveli.

CHOURET, Nicole, b. Paris 1944. Fr. dancer. Pupil of Leone Mail and Rita Thalia. Joined Paris Opéra B. 1961, becoming première danseuse 1969.

CHOUT, ballet, ch. Larionov and T. Slavinsky, m. Prokofieff, dec. Larionov, f.p. Diaghileff B. 17 May 1921 Th. Gaîté-Lyrique, Paris (C. Devillier, Slavinsky). A Russian legend.

CHOUTEAU, Yvonne, b. Oklahoma City 1929. Am. dancer. Studied Vilzak-Schollar, Sch. of Am. B., etc. Joined B. Russe de Monte Carlo 1943, becoming their ballerina 1950. To Montevideo 1957–59. Now teaches in Oklahoma City.

CHRIMES, Pamela, b. Cape Town 1923. S. African dancer and teacher. Studied at Univ. of Cape Town and was a member of S. Wells Th. B. 1945–48. Returned to S. Africa and teaches for the Cape Town B.

CHRISTENSEN, Harold, b. Utah 1904. Am. dancer and teacher, brother of Lew and Willam. Director of S. Francisco B. Sch.

CHRISTENSEN, Lew, b. Utah 1908. Am. dancer, teacher, and chor. Soloist in many American companies. Director of S. Francisco B. Chor. *Filling Station* (1938), *Jinx* (1942) *Con Amore* (1953). Mar. Gisella Caccialanza.

CHRISTENSEN, Willam, b. Utah 1902, brother of the above. Am. dancer and chor. Founder of San Francisco B. 1938 for whom he chor. many works. In 1951 became professor at Univ. of Utah, established a school there and in 1952 founded the Utah B. which in 1968 became Ballet West.

CHRISTMAS EVE, ballet 3 acts, ch. Varkovitsky, m. Asafiev, dec. Kolomoytsev, f.p. Maly Th., Leningrad 15 June 1938 (L. Goncharova, Serebrennikov). A fairy tale, this ballet was produced to commemorate the bicentenary of the founding of the Imperial Sch.

CHRISTOUT, Marie-Françoise, b. Neuilly-sur-Seine 1928. Fr. writer on the dance and theatre. D. ès L. and Diplômé de l'Institut d'Art et d'Archéologie de Paris (Sorbonne). Since 1960 has been a librarian at the Bibliothèque de l'Arsenal, Paris, specializing in the theatre collections. Author of *Les Merveilleux et le Théâtre du silence* (1965), *Le Ballet de Cour de Louis XIV*, 1643–72, *Mise en scène* (1967), *Histoire du Ballet* (series *Que sais-je?*, 1966), *The Court Ballet in France 1615–1641* (Dance Perspectives 20), *Maurice Béjart* (1972). Contributor to *Ballet Annual, Dance & Dancers, Dictionnaire du Ballet moderne* (Hazan, 1957), French adviser for *Enciclopedia dello spettacolo* (Rome) etc. Secretary General of Lifar's Université de la Danse, Paris.

CHRONICA, ballet, 3 acts, ch. Jooss, m. Berthold Goldschmidt, dec. Bouchène, f.p. B. Jooss, Arts Th., Cambridge 14 Mar 1939. A struggle for power in an Italian town.

CHRYST, Gary, b. La Jolla, Calif. 1949. Am. dancer. Pupil of Joffrey, Zaraspe, Griffith. Joined Joffrey B. 1968. Previously soloist of Norman Walker Co. (modern) 1966.

CHUJOY, Anatole, b. Riga 1894, d. N.Y. 1969. Am. (since 1931) writer and critic. Studied in St Petersburg. Co-founder and editor *Dance Magazine* 1937–41. Founder and editor *Dance News* (1942–69). Translator of several works on ballet from the Russian. His *Dance Encyclopedia* (1949) is a most important contribution to the literature of ballet, being the first of its kind in the English language. Author of *Symphonic Ballet* (1937), *The New York City Ballet* (1952). Translated Vaganova's *Fundamentals of the Classic Dance* (1947) and edited Fokine's *Memoirs of a Ballet Master* (1961). A revised and enlarged edition of *Dance Encyclopedia* (co-author P. W. Manchester) appeared in 1967. He was member of the Dance Advisory Commission of the High School of Performing Arts, N.Y. and he was the originator of the Regional Ballet Festival Plan in America (1956). He played a prominent part in the development of ballet in America.

CHURCHYARD, ballet, ch. Paul Taylor, m. Savage, cost. Sutherland, f.p. Paul Taylor Co., City Center, N.Y. 10 Dec 1969 (Carolyn Adams, Taylor). Corpses rise from their graves.

CICERI, Pierre, b. Paris 1782, d. 1868. Fr. stage designer, who reigned at the Paris Opéra in its greatest period. He designed the scenery (sometimes in collaboration) for, among others, Didelot's *Flore et Zéphire* (1815), Taglioni's *La Sylphide* (1832) and *La Fille du Danube*

(1836), Coralli's *Giselle*, and Mazilier's *Le Diable à Quatre* (1846), also the famous operas of that era, incl. *Masaniello, William Tell*, and *Robert the Devil*. He introduced gas lighting to the Opéra in 1822 (for the opera *Aladin*, designed by Daguerre, the inventor of the Daguerrotype).

CIEPLINSKI, Jan, b. Warsaw 1900. Polish dancer and chor. Studied in Warsaw and in 1921 toured America and Canada in Pavlova's Co. In Diaghileff B. 1927–27 and ballet master of R. Swedish B. 1927–31. Worked in Budapest 1932–34 and 1943–48 and in the Colon Th. Buenos Aires 1935–36. Ballet master of Anglo-Polish B. in London 1948 and taught in London at the Legat Sch. To N.Y. 1959 where he now teaches. Author of *The History of Polish Ballet* (London 1955).

CIMAROSIANA, ballet 1 act, ch. Massine, m. Cimarosa, dec. Sert, f.p. Diaghileff's Co., Monte Carlo 8 Jan 1924. Originally this ballet (a suite of dances) formed the last act of the *opera buffa Le Astuzie Femminili* which Diaghileff f.p. at the Paris Opéra 27 May 1920.

CINDERELLA (Fr. *Cendrillon*, Russ. *Zolushka*), ballet based on Perrault's fairy-story. (1) ch. Albert, m. Sor, f.p. King's Th., London 26 Mar 1822 (Mercandotti). (2) 3 acts, ch. Petipa, Cecchetti, and Ivanov, m. Schell, dec. Levogt, Shiskov, Botcharov, f.p. Maryinsky Th., St Petersburg 5 Dec 1893 (Legnani, Gerdt). In this, Legnani scored her first success in Russia, see FOUETTÉ. (3) 5 sc., ch. Farren, m. S. Jones, cost. Wilhelm, f.p. Empire Th., London 6 Jan 1906 (Genée). (4) 3 sc., ch. Fokine, m. d'Erlanger, dec. Goncharova, f.p. de Basil, C. Garden, London 19 July 1938 (Riabouchinska, Petroff). (5) 3 acts, ch. Zakharoff, m. Prokofieff, dec. Williams, f.p. Bolshoi Th., Moscow 21 Nov 1945 (Ulanova, Gabovitch). (6) At the Kirov Th., Leningrad, ch. Sergeyev, m. Prokofieff, f.p. 8 Apr 1946 (Dudinskaya, Sergeyev). He revised this in a version f.p. Kirov Th. 11 June 1964 (Kolpakova, Semeyonov). In both the Bolshoi and Kirov versions there is a long divertissement in which the Prince travels the world looking for the slipper, with exotic dances. (7) 3 acts, ch. Ashton, m. Prokofieff, dec. Malclès, f.p. S. Wells B., C. Garden, London 23 Dec 1948 (Shearer, Somes). (8) 3 acts, ch. Rodrigues, m. Prokofieff, dec. Beaurepaire, f.p. Scala, Milan 15 Dec 1955 (Verdy, Perugini). (9) *Cendrillon*, a lavish production by Raymundo de Larrain (nephew of the Marquis de Cuevas), ch. Orlikowsky and Larrain, m. Prokofieff, dec. and cost. Larrain, f.p. Th. des Ch. Élysées, Paris 4 Dec 1963 (Samtsova, Rona, Joyce Graeme; C. Uboldi and Harry Haythorne as the Ugly Sisters). The dec. and cos. were fantastic and the ballet was given nightly until the end of April 1964. Others taking the leading rôles were Tessa Beaumont, Yvonne Meyer, Margot Miklosy, Claire Sombert, Milenko

Banovitch, P. Bortoluzzi and M. Miskovitch. (10) The Nat. B. of Canada presented a version, chor. Franca, dec. Rose, at O'Keefe Centre, Toronto 15 Apr 1968 (Tennant, Blanton).

CIRCUS POLKA, m. Stravinsky for a young elephant. Chor. by Balanchine for Barnum and Bailey's Circus (Elephant Ballet), cost. Bel Geddes, N.Y. 1942. Later versions, for humans, have been given.

CIRQUE DE DEUX, ballet, ch. Ruthanna Boris, m. Gounod, dec. Davison, f.p. B. Russe de Monte Carlo, City Center, N.Y. 10 Sept 1947 (Boris, Danielian).

CISEAUX (pas ciseaux), a step in which the dancer jumps and opens his legs wide apart, starting and ending in the fifth position—like the opening of a pair of scissors. Also known as écart en l'air.

CITO, Marion, b. Berlin 1939. German dancer. Studied under T. Gsovsky since 1950. Joined Deutsches Oper B. Berlin 1960, Frankfurt B. 1962. Principal dancer Berlin 1966–72, Darmstadt 1972.

CITY CENTER, NEW YORK, the theatre at which Am. Ballet Theatre performs (though it also appears at the N.Y. State Th.) and was the home 1966–73 of the City Center Joffrey Ballet. The Moiseyev Dancers also appear there, the Gilbert and Sullivan seasons also, and the Alvin Ailey City Center Dance Co.

CIVIC BALLET (in America)—see REGIONAL or CIVIC BALLET.

CLARKE, Mary, b. London 1923. Eng. writer on ballet. Editor of *The Dancing Times* and Executive Editor of *The Ballroom Dancing Times* since 1963. Asst. Editor and contributor *The Ballet Annual* from 1952 to 1963. London corr. *Dance Magazine* (N.Y.) 1943–55, London Editor *Dance News* (N.Y.) 1955–70. Author of *The Sadler's Wells Ballet—a History and an Appreciation* (1955), *Six Great Dancers* (1957,) *Presenting People Who Dance* (1961), *Dancers of Mercury—The Story of Ballet Rambert* (1962), *Ballet, An Illustrated History* (with Clement Crisp 1973). Sections on dance in *Man the Artist* (1964), *Encyclopedia Britannica*, *Encyclopedia of the Performing Arts* (1974). Reviews ballet for *The Observer, The Sunday Times, The Guardian* etc.

CLARKE, Paul, b. Byfleet 1947. Eng. dancer. Pupil of Grist and Royal B. Sch. Joined Royal B. (Touring) 1964, becoming soloist 1966, principal 1968. Joined Festival B. 1973.

CLASS (German, 'training', Fr. 'classe', 'leçon'), the daily lessons taken by the dancer throughout the whole of his active career. The routine is usually the same throughout the world—first the side practice or bar-work (pliés, battements, développés), then centre practice and the adagio, finishing with the allegro section. At the end of a class there is a pause during which the girls put on their blocked point shoes and the boys practice their turns and leaps. The girls then return and they end the class with their point work, pirouettes, changements and port de bras. In 1971 a class cost a dancer in London 50p, in Paris 15 fr., in N.Y. $3 (or 10 classes for $25).

CLASSICAL BALLET (the *ballet d'école*), ballet in which the movement is based on the traditional technique evolved from the French Court ballet of the seventeenth and eighteenth century, the Italian schools of the nineteenth century, and the Imperial Academy of Dancing, St Petersburg and Moscow, and brought to ultimate perfection by such great teachers as Carlo Blasis, C. P. Johansson, N. Legat and Enrico Cecchetti, and in which dramatic or emotional content is subordinate to form or line—as displayed in the choreography of Petipa and Ivanov. With the dawning of the modern dance movement and the appearance of Isadora Duncan there set in a reaction led by Fokine against the stultification of the classical ballet which had come to consist of set formulae with marches and counter-marches for the supers, ballabiles for the corps de ballet, a variation for the ballerina and a variation for the premier danseur, and the corps de ballet in tutus, pink tights and satin shoes, lined up with a fixed smile, on either side of the stage. That it is possible to compose in the purest classical tradition but in modern form has, however, been amply demonstrated by productions such as Ashton's *Symphonic Variations* and the ballets of Balanchine. The purest classical style nowadays is exemplified by the dancing of the Kirov B. in Leningrad and, in a slightly different form, by the Royal Ballet.

CLASSICAL BALLETS are ballets in the classical style, and the term is usually only applied to ballets created before this century, e.g. *Giselle*, *La Sylphide*, *Coppélia*, *Swan Lake*, *Raymonda*, etc. In period and content some of these ballets are also Romantic ballets, e.g. *La Sylphide*, *Giselle*.

CLASSICAL STYLE, in ballet, is the traditional style as taught in the classroom (danse d'école) with its turn-out, five positions, point work and technique of beats, elevation, etc. The term 'Classical' applies to style only and is not the opposite of 'Romantic' which applies to period and content.

CLAUSS, Heinz, b. Esslingen 1935. German dancer. Studied under Robert Mayer (Stutt.) and Nora Kiss (Paris). Joined Stuttgart B. 1950–57, Zurich B. 1957–59, soloist Hamburg B. 1959–67 and principal dancer Stuttgart from 1967. In Hamburg his *Apollo* (Balanchine) was outstanding and he has danced this rôle in many countries. He has staged Balanchine ballets in Oslo, Stockholm, Rome, Stuttgart etc.

CLAVÉ, Antoni, b. Barcelona 1913. Sp. artist who designed the dec. for many ballets, notably *Los Caprichos* (1946), *Carmen* (1949), *Ballabile* (1949), *Deuil en 24 Heures* (1953), *La Peur* (1957).

CLAVIER, Josette, b. Paris 1933. Fr. dancer. Studied at Paris Opéra Sch. Début as soloist in *Les Malheurs de Sophie* (1948). Première danseuse 1952. Left Opéra in 1955. Guest artist Festival B. 1956. Ballerina of Babilée's Co. 1959 and of Lacotte's Ballets de la Tour Eiffel.

CLAYDEN, Pauline, b. London 1922. Eng. dancer. Studied Cone Sch. début C. Garden Op. Co. 1939. Joined London Ballet 1939 and Ballet Rambert until 1941. Joined S. Wells B. 1942, becoming a principal dancer, and dancing many of Fonteyn's rôles, e.g. in *Nocturne, Daphnis and Chloë, Hamlet,* etc. Danced *Giselle* 1954. Retired 1956. Now teaches.

CLEGG, Peter, b. Cleveleys 1930. Eng. dancer and teacher. Pupil of Sandham and Royal B. Sch. from 1945, also of Volkova, Idzikowsky, Goncharov, A. Phillips. Joined S. Wells B. 1946. War Service 1948–60. Became soloist. To Vancouver to teach 1960. Returned to England 1962 as ballet master C. Garden Opera B. and chor. many dances for them. In 1967 to Johannesburg as ballet master of PACT B. Teacher at Royal B. Sch. 1968–71, ballet master Touring Royal B. from 1971.

CLÉOPÂTRE, ballet 1 act, ch. Fokine, m. Arensky and others, dec. Bakst, f.p. Diaghileff's Co., Châtelet Th., Paris 2 June 1909 (Rubinstein, Pavlova). This ballet, under the title *Une Nuit d'Égypte*, had originally been produced at a children's matinée in St Petersburg 21 Mar 1908.

CLIFFORD, John, b. Hollywood 1947. Am. dancer and chor. Pupil of Loring, and Sch. of Am. B. Joined Western B. Association 1966 and N.Y. City B. the same year becoming soloist. Chor. for N.Y. City B. *Stravinsky Symphony* (1968), *Reveries* (m. Tchaikovsky) (1969), *Saraband and Dance* (m. Debussy 1970), *Symphony in E-flat* (m Stravinsky 1972).

CLOG DANCE, a dance in which wooden-soled shoes are worn, see TAP DANCING. There is a clog dance in Ashton's *La Fille Mal Gardée*.

CLOTHILDE VON DERP, see SAKHAROFF, ALEXANDER.

CLOTILDE, Mlle, see MAFLEUROY, Clotilde.

CLOUSER, James, b. Rochester, N.Y. 1935. Am. dancer. Studied under Caton, Schwezoff. Joined Ballet Th. 1957 and Royal Winnipeg B. 1958, becoming soloist 1959 and ballet-master and assistant director. Chor. many ballets, including *Recurrence* (to his own music), *Quartet* and *The Little Emperor and the Mechanical Court* (1961, m. Delibes). Ballet master Houston B. 1972.

CLOWNS, THE, ballet ch. Arpino, m. Hershy Kay, cost. Edith Bel Geddes, f.p. City Center Joffrey B., City Center, N.Y. 28 Feb 1968 (Blankshine, Erika Goodman, M. Zomosa). Civilization reborn after a holocaust, acted out by clowns.

CLUBS, ASSOCIATION OF BALLET, an organization founded by G. B. L. Wilson at a meeting held at the Royal Academy of Dancing 1 Nov 1947 to link the ballet clubs and study and further their interests. It organizes an Annual Production in London for the member-clubs and publishes a Bulletin.

CLUBS, BALLET. Many of the towns, cities, and universities of Great Britain have clubs whose members meet regularly to discuss and practise ballet. Demonstrations, film-shows, and lectures on ballet are held, and one or more semi-public ballet performances may be given every year. The clubs which give performances are usually organized by a local ballet school or group of schools, and many leading English dancers have had their first stage experience at these shows. There are also similar clubs in the Dominions, the performing sides of which are sometimes semi-professional and form the only ballet company to be seen there. They represent the amateur element in ballet. In Russia there are similar clubs attached to the local Palace of Culture, the one in Leningrad being especially notable. In France there is the Association Française des Amis de la Danse, founded 1948. See REGIONAL BALLET.

CLUSTINE, Ivan, b. Moscow 1862, d. Nice 1941. Russ. dancer and chor. Entered Imp. Sch., Moscow 1872, graduated 1878. Became premier danseur at Bolshoi Th. 1886. Became chor. at Bolshoi Th. 1898, and retired 1903. To Paris 1903 and opened school. Maître de ballet at Paris Opéra 1909–14. Was maître de ballet to Pavlova's Co. 1914–22, chor. for her Snowflakes, The Fairy Doll, Chopiniana, Gavotte (m. Paul Linke), Syrian Dance, etc.

CLYTEMNESTRA, ballet 4 acts, ch. Martha Graham, m. El-Dabh, dec. Noguchi, cost. M. Graham, f.p. Graham's Dance Co., Adelphi Th. N.Y., 1 Apr 1958 (Graham, Bertram Ross). The first full-length modern dance work.

COAST OF HOPE, ballet 2 acts, book Slonimsky, ch. Igor Belsky, m. Petrov, dec. Dorrer, f.p. Kirov Th. Leningrad 11 June 1959 (T. Legat, A. Makarov, A. Osipenko). 'A fairy-tale of truth' about fishermen in semi-abstract style.

COBOS, Antonia (Phyllis Nalte), cont. Am. chor. and dancer. Chor. The Mute Wife (m. Paganini) 1944 for B. International, Madroños (m. Moskowski, Yradier etc.) 1947, The Mikado (m. Sullivan) 1954, both for B. Russe de of Monte Carlo.

COCKERILLE, Lili, b. Arlington, Va. 1946. Am. dancer. Pupil of Leon Fokine, Mary Day, Franklin, Am. Sch. of B. Joined Harkness B. 1964, Joffrey B. 1969.

COCKRELL, Gary, b. Missouri 1932. Am. dancer, actor and chor. Pupil of Lalla Bauman and Matt Mattox. Joined dancers of *Damn Yankees* 1955 and danced in other musicals. Was one of the original dancers in *West Side Story* when it opened in London 1958 and he decided to stay in England. He took the lead in Tennessee Williams' *Orpheus Descending* at the R. Court Th., London 1959 and subsequently acted and appeared in films and television. Acted a leading rôle in the film *Lolita* 1961. Chor. for television and organized a group 'Beat Girls' which toured 1964. In 1965 he created the Dance Centre (q.v.) in Floral St., London.

COCTEAU, Jean, b. Maisons-Laffitte, Paris 1889, d. Milly-le-Forêt, Paris 1963. Fr. writer and artist, and one of the most versatile creative forces of the twentieth century. He was early associated with Diaghileff (who would ever urge him '*Jean, étonne-moi*'), designing posters, writing criticism and descriptions, and providing scenarios for ballets: *Le Dieu Bleu* (1912), *Le Train Bleu* (1924), *Parade* (1917). He has also provided the scenario for a number of other ballets, including *Les Mariés de la Tour Eiffel* (ch. Börlin 1921), and *Bœuf sur le Toit* (Balanchine 1923). He gave his blessing to the young Ballets des Ch. Élysées by writing an introduction to their first souvenir programme and by creating a ballet for them, *Le Jeune Homme et la Mort* (Petit 1947). For the Paris Opéra he made *Phèdre*, for Munich *La Dame à la Licorne* (1953), and he designed the décor for *L'Amour et son Amour* (1948). Elected to the Académie Française 1955. Made many sketches of Diaghileff and his dancers.

CODA, the concluding movement of the Grand Pas de Deux in the classical ballet. It is danced by the prima ballerina and the premier danseur, and not infrequently consists of one or more short solo variations for each in turn and a final pas de deux. Also, as in music, the final section of a classical ballet displaying all the dancers.

CODE OF TERPSICHORE, by Carlo Blasis 1828, is a history of dance and a general treatise on ballet and pantomime. It contains the basis of the classical technique.

COE, Kelvin, b. Melbourne 1946. Pupil of Downes and Rex Reid. Joined Australian B. 1962, soloist 1966 and a principal 1968.

COHAN, Robert, b. N.Y. 1925. Am. modern dancer and chor. Pupil of Martha Graham and entered her Co. 1946 and created rôles in many of her famous ballets (*Deaths and Entrances, Diversion of Angels* etc.).

For eleven years was Graham's partner. In 1956 danced in Broadway musicals and then opened a school in Boston. Joined Graham Co. again in 1962. In 1967 he came to London to become Artistic Director of the London Contemporary Dance Theatre, also dancing leading rôles and choreographing. Among his ballets are *Tzaikerk* (m. Hovhaness), *Hunter of Angels* (m. Maderna), *Stages* (m. Nordheim and Downes) etc.

COHEN, Frederic, b. Bonn 1904, d. N.Y. 1967. Ger. composer and first musical director of B. Jooss. Studied in Leipzig, Bonn, Berlin. Pianist for Yvonne Georgi 1924, joined Jooss in 1932 and remained with him until 1942 when he settled in America. Composed scores for *The Green Table, Seven Heroes, Prodigal Son, Spring Song* etc. Held many teaching posts in America.

COHEN, Selma Jeanne, b. Chicago 1920. Am. writer on the dance. Studied modern dance under Graham, Holm, Limon and at the Dance Notation Bureau. Dance editor of *Collier's Encyclopedia*, catalogued the 'Stravinsky and the Dance' Exhibition, N.Y. 1962. On staff of *Saturday Review* 1964–65. From 1965 editor and publisher of *Dance Perspectives*.

COLEMAN, Emily, b. San Antonio, Texas. Am. journalist. Graduated Am. Univ. Washington D.C. 1935. Editor of *Music and Dance* 1942–64.

COLEMAN, Michael, b. Becontree 1940. Eng. dancer. Studied at Royal B. Sch. Joined Touring Royal B. 1959 and to C. Garden section in 1961, becoming a principal 1968.

COLLÉ (Fr. stuck together), when in jumping the legs and feet remain together.

COLLIER, Lesley, b. Orpington 1947. Eng. dancer. Pupil of Royal B. Sch. Danced leading rôle in School Matinée *Two Pigeons* and joined Royal B. in 1965, soloist 1970, principal 1972.

COLLIN, Darja, b. Amsterdam 1902, d. Florence 1967. Dutch dancer, chor. and teacher. Pupil of Trefilova and Egorova, Wigman and Trümpy. She joined the Münster B., becoming soloist and then became a recital dancer. She joined Alexander von Swaine in 1936 and toured the Far East with him and Rosalia Chladek and also danced in America. In 1949 she was invited to direct a company in Amsterdam, the Opera Ballet Co. (see DUTCH NAT. B.), but in 1951 she moved to Florence and opened an important school there, which was taken over by Antonietta Daviso on her death.

COLLINS, Eugene, b. N.Y. 1934. Am. dancer. Pupil of Dokoudovsky and Stroganova. Joined B. Russe de Monte Carlo 1958–62, Am. Festival B. 1962, Washington Nat. B. 1963 of which he was a principal.

Danced with Festival B. 1964. Now teaches. Mar. Andrea Vodehnal.

COLOGNE, INTERNATIONAL SUMMER ACADEMY OF THE DANCE, an important European summer school with international ballet teachers. Founded in Krefeld in 1957, it moved to Cologne in 1961. It takes place annually in July and during it performances are given by the Cologne Ballet. Directed by Heinz Laurenzen and Peter Appel.

COLOMBO, Vera, b. Milan 1931. It. dancer. Entered Scala, Milan, Sch. 1940 and became a soloist of the Scala Ballet 1952. Appointed ballerina 1954.

COLON, TEATRO (Buenos Aires, Argentina), the leading opera house in South America with a long history of ballet performances and with a strong resident ballet company. The first Teatro Colon was built in 1857 and the Romantic Ballets (*Giselle* etc.) were given. A ballet school was opened in 1865. Various companies (mostly Italian) visited the theatre. In 1908 a new Teatro Colon was opened which was visited by Preobrajenska, Mazzuchelli, Cia Fornaroli, Zucchi between 1912 and 1916. Diaghileff's Co. performed there in 1917. In 1925 Ruth Page became principal dancer and the Co. was reorganized with many Argentinians in it. After that it has been visited by nearly all the great European dancers and chors.—Bolm, Fokine, Lifar, M. Wallmann, T. Gsovsky, Balanchine etc. In recent years Jack Carter has often worked there and the Co. has become an international one. Olga Ferri is prima ballerina and co-director from 1973.

COMAZZANO, Antonio, of Piacenza. It. author of treatise on dancing 1465.

COMBAT, LE (later called *The Duel*), ballet ch. Dollar, m. de Banfield, dec. de Noailles, f.p. B. de Paris, Princes Th., London 24 Feb 1949 (Charrat, Skouratoff). This ballet, with décor by Wakhevitch, is in the repertoire of Am. B. Th. (Hayden, Kriza) 1953 and of many other companies.

COMBES, Jean, b. Paris 1904. Fr. dancer and ballet master. Studied at Paris Opéra Sch. under Ricaux. To Bordeaux B. 1930 then to Vichy and Marseilles. In 1936 became ballet master at Rouen. After working in Geneva, Toulouse and the B. Russe de Monte Carlo he became ballet master in Strasbourg in 1945 until his retirement.

COMMEDIA DELL'ARTE, Italian entertainments of the sixteenth to eighteenth centuries in which certain stock characters, Harlequin, Columbine, Pantalon, etc., appeared. In England, as Harlequinades, they became an essential part of pantomimes, and many ballets (notably *Carnaval*) have been made, using these figures and the situations in which they appear. Originally there was no set text and the actors improvised as they went along (hence also called *commedia all'impro-viso*).

COMPAN, Le Sieur, Fr. author of *Dictionnaire de Danse*, published Paris 1787 and dedicated to Mlle Guimard. A scarce and important work of reference.

COMPANY AT THE MANOR, ballet, 5 sc., ch. Jooss, m. Beethoven's F minor Violin Sonata, dec. D. Zinkeisen, f.p. B. Jooss, Arts Th., Cambridge 15 Feb 1943. A light-hearted frolic at a Victorian manor.

COMUS. (1) ballet, 2 sc., ch. Helpmann, m. Purcell, dec. Messel, f.p. S. Wells B., New Th., London 14 Jan 1942 (Fonteyn, Helpmann). Based on Milton's masque (of 1634, m. Lawes), this was Helpmann's first work for the S. Wells B. and included the speaking of two passages from the poem, later omitted; (2) revival of the actual masque, ch. Inglesby, m. Handel and Lawes, dec. D. Zinkeisen, prod. Leslie French, f.p. International B. 1946 (Inglesby, Algeranoff).

CON AMORE, ballet 3 sc., ch. Lew Christensen, m. Rossini, dec. Bodrero, f.p. San Francisco B., San Francisco 10 Mar 1953 (Bailey, Johnson, Danielian). Based on nineteenth-century lithographs and using three Rossini overtures. In repertoire of N.Y. City B., f.p. City Center N.Y. 9 June 1953 (Bailey, Johnson, d'Amboise), and in repertoires of Joffrey B. and Washington Nat. B.

CONCERT, THE, ballet, ch. Robbins, m. Chopin, cost. Sharaff., f.p. N.Y. City B., City Center N.Y. 6 Mar 1956 (LeClerq, Mounsey, Curley, Bolender). Revised and shortened version f.p. Ballets: U.S.A., Festival of Two Worlds, Spoleto, with two backcloths by Steinberg, 8 June 1958. An audience files in for a Chopin piano recital and they react to the pieces played in a series of witty sketches.

CONCERTO, ballet, ch. MacMillan, m. Shostakovitch (second piano concerto) dec. Jürgen Rose, f.p. Berlin B., Deutsche Oper, Berlin 30 Nov 1966 (Seymour, Carli, Kesselheim, Kapuste). He mounted it for Am. Ballet Th., State Theater, N.Y. 18 May 1967 (d'Antonuo, Toni Lander, Cynthia Gregory, Marks, Douglas), for the Touring Royal B., C. Garden 26 May 1967 (Anderton, Wells, Landon, Wall, Farley), and for R. Swed. B., Stockholm 24 Feb 1968 (Andersson, Arvidsson, Maria Lang, Winquist, Häggbom). An abstract ballet.

CONCERTO BAROCCO, ballet, ch. Balanchine, m. Bach's Double Violin Concerto in D minor, dec. Berman, f.p. Am. B. 29 May 1941, Hunter College Playhouse, N.Y. (Marie-Jeanne, Dollar). In the repertoire of many companies, usually in practice dress. Ballet of pure dancing.

CONCERTO FOR FLUTE AND HARP, ballet, ch. Cranko, m. Mozart, f.p.

Stuttgart Ballet, Stuttgart 26 Mar 1966 (Cardus, Wiedmann, Cragun, Berg).

CONCURRENCE, LA, ballet 1 act, ch. Balanchine, m. Auric, dec. Derain, f.p. de Basil, Monte Carlo 12 Apr 1932 (Baronova, Toumanova, Borovansky, Woizikovsky). Two tailors who pretend to quarrel outside their shops to attract customers. Woizikovsky's dance as the Clochard was memorable.

CONE, Grace, b. London 1892, Eng. dancer and teacher, who with her sisters Valerie (b. 1887) and Lillie (b. 1888, d. 1971) founded the Cone Sisters Sch. originally in Brighton then in Marylebone 1919. This became the Arts Educational Schools (q.v.).

CONE-RIPMAN SCHOOL, see ARTS EDUCATIONAL SCHOOLS.

CONFESSIONAL, ballet in miniature, in one scene to the poem by Browning, ch. Walter Gore, m. Sibelius (death of Mélisande from Pelléas Suite), cost. Andrée Howard, f.p. for the Oxford B. Club 9 May 1941. This work, as interpreted by Sally Gilmour, was one of the most moving in the repertoire of the Ballet Rambert (who f.p. it Arts Th., London 21 Aug 1941).

CONFETTI, ballet, ch. Arpino, m. Rossini, f.p. Joffrey B., City Center, N.Y. 3 Mar 1970 (Corkle, Barnard, Loyd). Bravura classical dance. When danced in London in 1971 it was received as a comic ballet.

CONFLICTS, ballet, ch. Morrice, m. Bloch (Quintet for piano and strings), dec. Koltai. f.p. B. Rambert, S. Wells 23 July 1962 (J. Taylor, Martlew). A choreographer rehearsing dancers whose temperaments conflict.

CONGA, an Afro-Cuban dance in 4/4 time. The dancers step to the first three beats and kick to the fourth beat. In a conga-line each dancer puts his hands on the shoulders or hips of the dancer in front of him and they advance in a line as they dance.

CONLEY, Sandra, b. Hatfield 1943. Eng. dancer. Studied at Brighton Stage Sch. and Royal B. Sch. Joined Touring Royal B. 1962, becoming soloist 1968. Mar. Adrian Grater.

CONNECTICUT COLLEGE SCHOOL OF DANCE, at Connecticut College, New London, U.S.A., the leading summer school of modern dance. It started in 1948 and most of the modern dancers have taught there, with Doris Humphrey as the presiding genius, until her death in 1958. At the end of the six-week course performances are given in the Palmer Auditorium. See BENNINGTON SCHOOL OF THE DANCE.

CONNOR, Laura, b. Portsmouth 1946. Eng. dancer. Pupil of Dugan, Butler and Royal B. Sch. Joined Royal B. 1965 becoming soloist 1970.

CONSERVATORIET, ballet 1 act, ch. Bournonville, m. Paulli, f.p. Royal Th., Copenhagen 6 Mar 1849 and still in repertoire. Incidents during a ballet class. Brenaa mounted it for Joffrey B., City Center N.Y. 20 Feb 1969 (Sutherland, Remington, Martin-Viscount, P. Johnson). Also in repertoire of the Australian B., Festival B. (London Coliseum 9 Apr 1973) and other Cos.

CONSTANTIA, ballet, ch. Dollar, m. Chopin (F minor piano concerto), dec. Armistead, cost. Houston, f.p. B. International, International Th., N.Y. 31 Oct 1944 (Marie-Jeanne, Patterson, Dollar). An abstract *ballet-blanc*. It is called *Chopin Concerto* by Ballet Theatre and *Evocation* by Canad. Nat. B. Named after Constantia Gladowska for whom the concerto was composed.

CONSUELO, Beatriz, b. Porto Alegre, Brazil. Brazilian dancer. Pupil of Verchinina, Leskowa. Joined de Cuevas Co. 1953, becoming soloist 1954, étoile 1958. Prima ballerina Rio de Janeiro 1956. Prima ballerina of Geneva 1964–69, now head of the Geneva school.

CONTEMPORARY DANCE THEATRE, THE LONDON, the Martha Graham style company attached to Robin Howard's London School of Contemporary Dance. Director Robert Cohan. It made its first appearance at the Adeline Genée Th., East Grinstead 11 Oct 1967, with guest artists Noemi Lapzeson and Robert Powell from the Graham Company. Toured Yugoslavia 1970, S. America 1973. It gives regular London seasons at The Place. In 1969 William Louther joined as principal dancer with Lapzeson. The school opened (in Berners St, London and at The Place since 1969), in 1966, principal Patricia Hutchinson. See THE PLACE.

CONTES RUSSES, LES, ballet, ch. Massine, dec. Larionov, f.p. Diaghileff's Co., Th. du Châtelet, Paris 11 May 1917 (Tchernicheva, Sokolova, Woizikovsky). This included *Kikimora* (previously given in 1916).

CONTRACTION-RELEASE, a term used in the Modern Dance Movement, developed by Martha Graham, relating to the breathing (release being when the body is in breath, and contraction when the breath is out).

CONTREDANSE, a term first used in the seventeenth century in England to designate a choral dance. If, as is assumed, the term is derived from the word 'country-dance', gallicized, it had lost all traces of its rural origin by the time John Playford published his *The English Dancing Master* in 1651. This work contains rounds or branles, circle dances in which men and women alternated, and long-ways in which the men in one line faced the women in another, and in both cases the dancers formed patterns much as did the participants in the court ballets. Playford's book contains some 900 of these dances. In France there was evolved from contredanses the English 'round for eight' at the beginning of the eighteenth century, and the *cotillon* (lit. a petticoat), which in time began to consist of six set figures and changed its name to quadrille. By extension, a quadrille came to designate a group of dancers in the court ballet and the hierarchy of dancers at the Paris Opéra includes the first quadrille, second quadrille, etc (see BALLERINA). The 'country dance' has contributed form to the classical ballet much as the folk-dance has contributed steps.

CONTRETEMPS, a step in which the dancer executes a coupé dessous with the left foot, followed by a chassé with the right foot, temps levé with the right foot and chassé passé with the left foot. In the Cecchetti method a *Grand Contretemps* is executed thus: facing croisé right foot front, the dancer raises the left foot slightly off ground, slight temps levé on right foot. Jump forward on to left foot allowing the working leg to bend slightly so that it falls into the fourth position devant croisé and taking care that it passes as closely as possible to the supporting foot. As the left foot comes to the ground bring the right foot through sur le cou-de-pied devant and immediately slide the right foot allowing the knee to bend to second position, transferring the weight to the right foot. As the foot passes to the second position, open the arms to the demi-second position and incline the head to the right. Slide the left foot to the fifth position back, keeping the knees bent. Close the arms to fifth position en bas and execute a demi-contretemps (see DEMI-CONTRETEMPS).

COOKE, Kerrison, b. Bournemouth 1943. Eng. dancer. Pupil of Elizabeth Collins and Royal B. Sch. Joined Touring Royal B. 1962, becoming soloist 1965, principal 1968. To Festival B. 1973.

COPLAND, Aaron, b. Brooklyn 1900. Am. composer. Pupil of Nadia Boulanger. The first composer to win a Guggenheim Fellowship. Wrote the music for *Hear Ye! Hear Ye!* (1934), *Billy the Kid* (1938), *Rodeo* (1942), *Appalachian Spring* (1944), and his music was used for *Time Table* (ch. Tudor 1941), *El Salon Mexico* (ch. Humphrey 1943), *Day on Earth* (ch. Humphrey 1947), *Pied Piper* (N.Y.C.B., ch. Robbins 1951), *Dance Symphony* (ch. Koner 1963), *Ballet in Seven Movements* (ch. Rosen, Munich 3 Dec 1963).

COPLANDE, Robert, Eng. dancing master who wrote as an appendix to a French grammar of 1521 an article *The Maner of dauncynge of Bace daunces after the use of Fraunce*, which is an important document in the history of the dance.

COPPÉLIA OU LA FILLE AUX YEUX D'ÉMAIL, ballet 3 acts, book Nuitter and Saint-Léon from a tale by Hoffmann, ch. Saint-Léon, m. Delibes, dec. Cambon, Despléchin, Lavastre, cost. Lormier, f.p. Paris Opéra 25 May 1870 (Bozzacchi as Swanilda, Fiocre as Frantz, Dauty as Coppelius). This is one of the most popular ballets—a classic

—and it was the most successful of the ballets which marked the return of the *ballet d'action* after the decline of the romantic movement. It was first presented in London 8 Nov 1884 at the Empire Th. arranged by M. Bertrand, the maître de ballet, cost. Chasemore (with Alice Holt as Swanilda, W. Warde as Coppelius)—a one-act version. The full ballet was f.p. at the Empire Th. 14 May 1906 (Genée). The ballet, largely in its original form, was still in the repertoire of the Paris Opéra (by the end of 1952 it had been given 622 times) where the tradition of playing Frantz by a girl en travesti was maintained.

In Russia it was f.p. at the Bolshoi Th., Moscow 24 Jan 1882, chor. J. Hansen. At the Bolshoi Th., St Petersburg it was chor. Petipa 25 Nov 1884 and again by him at the Maryinsky Th. 26 Jan 1894, refurbished by Cecchetti. This version, which had been notated in Stepanoff notation by Sergueeff, was reproduced by him for the S. Wells B. (in two acts) at S. Wells Th. 21 Mar 1933 (Lopokova—later de Valois— Stanley Judson, Hedley Briggs), and it remains in the repertoire (since 1940 in 3 acts with dec. Chappell and since 1954 with dec. Lancaster).

The René Blum Co. gave a version by Zvereff (Nemchinova as Swanilda). The Royal Danish B. have danced it since 27 Dec 1896 (version of Glasemann and Beck, danced by Borchsenius and Beck). The present version is by Lander and it was one of Margot Lander's great rôles (later Inge Sand's). This version was mounted for the Festival B., Festival Hall, London 31 Aug 1956 dec. Maillart (Wright, Gilpin). B. Rambert staged the Petipa version at S. Wells Th. 1 Aug 1957 dec. Doboujinsky (Verdy, Dixon). A new 2-act version for Festival B. was chor. by J. Carter, dec. Farmer, based on the Paris production f.p. Pavilion Th., Bournemouth 29 Oct 1968 (Miklosy, Loggenburg).

Ballet for All (q.v.) give an historic survey and shortened version of the ballet under the title *Two Coppelias*. This compares the original 1870 version (with Frantz *en travesti*) with the Petipa version, f.p. Civic Th., Rotherham 26 Sept 1967 (Janet Francis as Bozzacchi, Margaret Barbieri as Fiocre). The 1870 version was recreated for Ballet for All by Paulette Dynalix who was the last (and one of the greatest) travesti-dancers of Frantz. A new version in 3 acts was chor. Descombey, dec. Clayette, for the Paris Opéra 29 June 1966 (Bessy, Atanassoff, Duthoit).

COQ D'OR, LE, ballet 1 act, ch. Fokine, m. Rimsky Korsakov, dec. Goncharova, f.p. Diaghileff's Co., Paris Opéra 24 May 1914 (Karsavina, Bulgakov, Cecchetti). In the original version there was a cast of singers, but these were not employed in the de Basil Co. version of 1937. A Russ. fairy tale.

CORALLI (Jean Coralli Peracini), b. Paris 1779, d. there 1854. It. dancer and chor. Début at Paris Opéra 1802. Chor. ballets in Vienna, Milan, Lisbon, etc. In 1825 became maître de ballet at Porte St Martin Th., Paris and in 1831 was made chor. at the Opéra, producing such famous ballets as *Le Diable Boiteux* (1836), *La Tarentule* (1839), *Giselle* (1841 with Perrot), *La Péri* (1843). See also ASSOCIATION PHILANTHROPIQUE.

CORALLI, Vera, see KARALLI.

CORELLI, Juan, b. Barcelona 1934. Spanish dancer and chor. Studied with Izard, Preobrajenska, Idzikowsky, Legat. Danced in opera at Liceo Th., Barcelona, and in de Basil and Cuevas Cos. In 1959 he became chor. for French television and chor. *The Nightingale* (m. Stravinsky 1961), *Carmina Burana* (m. Orff 1962), *Til Eulenspiegel* (m. Strauss 1963), *Le Diable à la Kermesse* (m. Barraud 1964) etc.—all for the 'Music for You' programme. For London's Associated Rediffusion chor. *Midsummer Night's Dream* (m. Mendelssohn) in 1964, and for the Washington Nat. B. *Othello* (m. Thiriet) in 1964. For Bulgarian Nat. B. Sofia 1971 *Romeo and Juliet* (m. Prokofieff), *Carmina Burana* (m. Orff). Lives in Canada.

CORKLE, Francesca, b. Seattle 1953. Am. dancer. Joined Joffrey B. as apprentice 1968, and the Co. later in the year, dancing solo rôles.

CORNALBA, Elena, It. dancer trained at La Scala, of the same period as Legnani, Brianza and Zucchi. Danced in Paris at Th. Eden and made début in St Petersburg as ballerina 1887. She was cold, extremely light, and technically brilliant.

CORNAZANO, Antonio, b. Piacenza 1430, d. Ferrara. It. poet and man of letters. Author of *Il Libro dell'Arte del Danzare*, an important book on dancing of the period and setting out some interesting new terms, e.g. *campeggiare*, to stand easily and in a good position, even on one foot, and *ondeggiare*, a slow raising of the body followed by a rapid bending movement.

COROS Y DANZAS of the *Sección Feminina* of the Falange, an important organization in Spain, founded in 1939 to preserve and to dance the many regional dances of their country. They organize competitions throughout Spain and the winners take part in the rallies which take place twice a year. Visited London in 1952.

CORPS DE BALLET, the dancers in a ballet company who are not classed as soloists but usually dance together as one body. At the Paris Opéra the corps de ballet designates the entire company (including the soloists and étoiles), whereas the lower ranks only are called les quadrilles (q.v.).

CORROBOREE, ballet, ch. Rex Reid, m. Antill, dec. Lovejoy, f.p. Australian National B., Sydney 3 July 1950. Another version in 1954 was chor. by Beth Dean. Ballet on Austral. aboriginal dances.

CORSAIRE, LE, ballet. (1) On Byron's poem, ch. Albert, m. Bochsa, f.p. King's Th., London 29 June 1837 (Herminie Elssler, Pauline Duvernay, Albert). Revived at Drury Lane Th. 30 Sept 1844 with Clara Webster as Medora. (2) ch. Mazilier, m. Adam, dec. Despléchin, Cambon, Thierry, Martin, f.p. Paris Opéra 23 Jan 1856 (Rosati, Couqui, Segarelli). At the Bolshoi Th., St Petersburg 12 Jan 1858 it was chor. by Perrot, and again on 13 Jan 1868 there, ch. Petipa, using Perrot's scenario and with Medora danced by Grantzow, and with some music by Delibes added. On 13 Jan 1899 Petipa revised it for Legnani, and made the famous pas-de-deux to extra music by Drigo. This ballet, with its famous shipwreck was very popular and remained for long in the St Petersburg repertoire. During the 1960s the *Corsaire* pas-de-deux had two outstanding pairs of exponents in Fonteyn and Nureyev, and Samtsova and Prokovsky.

CORTESI, Antonio, b. Pavia 1796, d. Florence 1879. It. dancer and chor. Made his début in 1811 at Teatro Canobbiana, Milan, and subsequently danced throughout Italy. He chor. his first ballet, *Inez de Castro* at the San Carlo Th., Lisbon. Chor. many ballets between 1826 and 1859, including a 5-act *Giselle* (m. Bajetti) for Cerrito in 1843 at the Scala, Milan, and an *Ondina* (m. Giaquinto and L. Viviani) in 1850 at Verona. With his production of *La Sylphide* at the Scala, Milan in 1841 (danced by Taglioni), he may be said to have introduced the Romantic Ballet into Italy.

CORYPHÉE, from the Greek *koruphaios*, the leader of the Chorus in the Attic drama. Now a leading member of the corps de ballet and one of the grades in the cadre of the Paris Opéra and Royal B. The word is masculine in gender.

COSI, Liliana, b. Milan 1941. Italian dancer. Entered Scala Sch., Milan, 1951. Graduated 1958, Passo d'Addio 1959 and entered the Scala company, becoming prima ballerina. Studied in Russia. In 1970 she toured Russia dancing the classics. Guest ballerina Festival B. 1971.

COSTUME, the ballet costume has to meet a number of conditions that are not applicable to other forms of stage production. It should give as good a line in movement as in repose, it should not be any heavier than is absolutely necessary, it should not interfere with freedom of movement, and it should be executed in colours which will marry with the décor without being invisible against it, and yet will not strike a discordant note when grouped with other costumes to be used. The costume should help to identify the character to be portrayed, which does not mean that it has to be a literal copy of the dress such a character would wear in reality, for a large measure of stylization is often desirable. In the traditional classical ballets the danseuse wears a *tutu* or 'Sylphide dress' with pink tights and satin shoes, whilst the male dancer is clad in short tunic and tights. Period or national flavour is often suggested by suitable ornament. Such accessories as shoes, tights, and headdress should always be considered in relation to the costume, and the use of jewellery is to be avoided except where definitely demanded by the required characterization.

CÔTÉ COUR (lit. courtyard side) in French theatres, the right-hand side of the stage, as seen by the audience (i.e. the prompt side). For explanation, see CÔTÉ JARDIN.

CÔTÉ JARDIN (lit. garden side), in French theatres, the left-hand side of the stage, as seen by the audience (i.e. the opposite prompt side). In the early days of the French theatre, the King's box was on the left side of the audience and the Queen's on the right. Consequently the sides of the stage were called Côté du Roi and Côté de la Reine respectively. With the coming of the Revolution this nomenclature was deemed unsuitable and new terms had to be found. The old theatre in the Tuileries, successively occupied by the Opéra, the Comédie Française, and the Th. de Monsieur, was situated between the Garden and the Courtyard of the Palace so the new phrases Côté Jardin and Côté Cour were used. See also CÔTÉ COUR. All Fr. scenery is marked 'Jardin' and 'Cour' where ours is marked 'opposite prompt' and 'prompt'. In the Royal Th., Copenhagen, the terms are 'King's side' and 'King's ladies' side'—the sides of the royal boxes. In Italian theatres it is 'lato dextro' and 'lato sinistro', except at the Scala, Milan, where it is 'strada' (for right) and 'cortile' (for left). In Germany it is 'recht' and 'links'.

COTILLON, a ballroom dance known in the eighteenth century, but which enjoyed a great vogue in the nineteenth century, when it usually concluded an evening's entertainment. It was danced by any number of participants with frequent changes of partner but all following the figures performed by the leading couple. The Cotillon, which is said to have its origin in the Contredanse (q.v.) in France, came in time to consist of six set figures and became known as a quadrille.

COTILLON, ballet in 1 act, book Kochno, ch. Balanchine, m. Chabrier, dec. Bérard, f.p. de Basil B., Monte Carlo 12 Apr 1932 (Toumanova, Blinova, Lichine, Woizikovsky). An evocative, nostalgic suite of dances set in a ballroom.

COTON, A. V., b. York 1906, d. London 1969. Eng. ballet critic and journalist. Author *A Prejudice for Ballet* (1938), *The New Ballet* (1946), and critic for the *Daily Telegraph* 1954–69.

COU-DE-PIED (lit. the neck of the foot), in ballet that part of the leg between the base of the calf and the beginning of the ankle.

Sur le cou-de-pied

COULON, a family of dancers of the eighteenth and nineteenth centuries. The most famous was Jean François (b. 1764, d. 1836), a teacher in the Romantic era. Of his two sons, Antoine Louis (1796–1849) was a dancer-mime, and Eugène was renowned as a ballroom teacher in England.

COUPÉ or PAS COUPÉ (lit. a cutting step). A step in which, the weight being on the right foot, the left foot is drawn up to it in the fifth position front and, rising on the full or half point, the weight is transferred to the left foot, thus cutting away the right which is raised sur le cou-de-pied derrière (coupé dessus). If the left foot is drawn up to the right in the fifth position back, the movement is termed a coupé dessous. The step is also executed with a jump in lieu of the drawing up movement. In the now extinct style of the Fr. court dancing of the eighteenth century, there was also a coupé which consisted of a demi-coupé followed by a pas glissé (or, less characteristically, by a pas marché). This demi-coupé was the fundamental step of that technique and could be taken in any direction and with any degree of turn. It consisted of a fondu with the feet in first position, but with all the weight on the foot of the bent leg, the free foot only just off (and parallel with) the floor (called plié sans soi). The free foot now moves outward, towards fourth position in front, the weight coming forward at the same time. When the moving foot reaches the fourth position the knee straightens and the foot, on a low demi-pointe, takes the whole

129

weight of the body poised in momentary equilibrium, while the back leg is brought level into fourth position preparatory to making another step (see also FLEURET).

COURNAND, Gilberte, b. Gerardmer. Fr. writer and bookseller. Opened bookshop in Place Dauphine, Paris, 1951 (now moved to the Rue de Beaune), solely devoted to the dance. Organizes exhibitions and other functions for the cause of ballet in France.

COURONNE, EN, a position of the arms, curved and held above the head so as to frame it. Also called fifth position en haut.

COURT BALLET (ballet de cour), French and Italian, a spectacle of song, dance and verse which was performed at the royal courts of the mid-sixteenth to mid-seventeenth centuries. They were performed by the nobles and dealt with pastoral, allegorical and mythical subjects and the art of ballet stems from them. See BALLET COMIQUE DE LA REINE.

COURU see PAS DE BOURRÉE COURU.

COUSINEAU, Yves, b. Montreal 1932. Canadian dancer. Trained as an actor with experience in the Montreal French theatres. Studied ballet at the Canad. Nat. B. Sch. and mime in Paris under Jacques Lecoq. Entered Canad. Nat. B. 1955 becoming principal character dancer and mime 1959.

COVA, Fiorella, b. Milan 1936. Italian dancer. Entered Scala School, Milan, 1946, graduated 1954, Passo d'Addio 1955 and became soloist 1958. Mar. M. Pistoni.

COVENT GARDEN, THE ROYAL OPERA HOUSE in London built in the middle of the flower and vegetable market. The first theatre (Covent Garden Th.) was built in 1732 by John Rich. This was burnt down in 1808 and the second theatre (The Royal Italian Opera) was opened in 1809. This was destroyed by fire in 1856 and the present building was opened in 1858. During the Second World War it was used as a dance hall and it re-opened on 20 Feb 1946 with the S. Wells B. performing *The Sleeping Beauty*. The Opera House is now the home of the Royal Opera and the Royal Ballet. It is owned by the Covent Garden Trust Ltd, a non-profit-making body working in association with the Arts Council of Great Britain, first with Sir David Webster as its General Administrator succeeded by John Tooley 1970. The theatre has 2,115 seats and the stage is 40 ft wide and 40 ft deep (54 ft with cyclorama.) Seats cost from 80p to £4 (Fonteyn nights, £1·10 to £6) in 1973.

CRACOVIENNE, see KRAKOWIAK.

CRAGUN, Richard, b. Sacramento, Calif. 1944. Am. dancer. Studied in Sacramento (Barbara Briggs) and in Univ. of Fine Arts, Banff (Canada) under Betty Farrally, Gweneth Lloyd, Louise Browne. At Royal B.

Sch. 1961–62, won Genée Schol. of R.A.D. 1962 and studied under Volkova in Denmark. Joined Stuttgart B. 1962 becoming principal dancer and partner of Marcia Haydee. Guest artist Berlin B. 1964 and in Boston (U.S.A.) 1968. Partnered Fonteyn in Touring Royal B. 1968. Created rôle of Petruchio in *Taming of the Shrew* 1969.

CRAIG, Sandra, b. Adelaide 1942. Austral. dancer. Trained in Adelaide and at Royal B. Sch. and Rambert Sch. Joined B. Rambert 1962 becoming a soloist 1964 and in 1966 member of new B. Rambert. Retired 1973.

CRAMÈR BALLET, a Swedish Co. founded in 1967 by Ivo Cramèr. The repertory is based on Scandinavian folklore. There are 12 dancers and the chors. are Cramèr, Tyyne Talvo, Henryk Tomaszewski. The Co. is state supported under the Svenska Riksteatern and it tours Scandinavian countries, mainly Sweden.

CRAMÈR, Ivo, b. Gothenburg 1921. Swed. dancer and chor. Pupil of Alexandrova and Cullberg. An outstanding mime. Ballet-master Verde Gaio Co. (Lisbon) 1948 and Ny Norske Ballet (Oslo) 1952. Chor. *The Message*, *The Prodigal Son* (1957), etc. In 1967 he founded his own company, the Cramèr B., and also took over the Stockholm School of Lia Schubert.

CRANKO, John, b. Rustenburg, 1927, d. over Atlantic 1973. S. African dancer-chor. Cape Town Univ. B. Sch. 1942 and cr. his first ballet *Soldier's Tale* (m. Stravinsky) 1942. To England 1946, joined S. Wells Sch. and later S. Wells Th. B. which took his *Tritsch-Tratsch* (created 1946) into its repertoire. For the R.A.D. Production Club he created *Children's Corner* (m. Debussy, dec. Eberstein), presented at New Th., London, 2 Nov 1947 (Stella Claire, David Poole, Patricia Miller), which created a very favourable impression and was taken into the S. Wells Th. B. repertoire (S. Wells Th. 6 Apr 1948). For S. Wells Th. B., chor. *Sea Change* (1949), *Pineapple Poll* (1951), *The Lady and the Fool* (1954); for S. Wells B. *Bonne Bouche* (1952), *The Shadow* (1953), *The Prince of the Pagodas* (1957); for N.Y. City B. *The Witch* (1950); for B. Rambert *Variations on a Theme* (1954), *La Reja* (1959); for Paris Opéra *La Belle Hélène* (1955); for Scala, Milan *Romeo and Juliet* (1959). Author of revue *Cranks*, London 1955, and *New Cranks* (1960). Chor. for Royal B. *Antigone* (1960). Produced B. Britten's opera *Midsummer Night's Dream* at Aldeburgh 1960. To Stuttgart 1961 as Director of Ballet. Under his directorship he has raised the Stuttgart B. to become one of the leading Cos. of Europe and the best in Germany. In 1963 it danced at the Edinburgh Festival, toured in S. America in 1967 and had a great success at the Lincoln Center, N.Y. in 1969 (and toured America later that year). In 1968 Cranko assumed the directorship of the Munich B. (in addition to

Stuttgart) but relinquished it in 1970. He maintained a steady out-put of original choreography, notable works being *Romeo and Juliet* 1962 (also mounted for Canadian Nat. B. 1964), *Onegin* 1965 and *Taming of the Shrew* 1969. His services as chor. were in demand all over the world. See STUTTGART BALLET.

CRASKE, Margaret, b. 1898. Eng. dancer and teacher. Member of Diaghileff's Co. and taught the methods of her master, Cecchetti, in London. In 1946 she went to the U.S. as ballet-mistress of Ballet Theatre and now teaches in N.Y. at the Metropolitan Opera B. Sch. (of which she is assistant director). With Beaumont, wrote *The Theory and Practice of Allegro in Classical Ballet*, 1930 and with Derra de Moroda *The Theory and Practice of Advanced Allegro in Classical Ballet* (1956)—both on the Cecchetti technique.

CRÉATION, LA, ballet 1 act, ch. Lichine. There is no décor in this ballet and no music, f.p. B. des Ch. Élysées, Princes Th., London 26 Sep 1948 (Caron, Philippart, Sadowska, Babilée, Riabouchinska). Dancers in practice dress are rehearsed for a ballet.

CRÉATION DU MONDE, LA, ballet 1 act, ch. Börlin, m. Milhaud, dec. Léger, f.p. B. Suédois, Th. des Ch. Élysées, Paris 25 Oct 1923 (Börlin, Stranden). A ballet to the same score (dec. E. Wolfe) was made by de Valois for the Camargo Soc., Cambridge Th., London 26 Apr 1931 (Leslie French, Moreton) and was later danced at S. Wells Th. 30 Oct 1933 (Tudor, Moreton). Many chors. have used this score, among them Alvin Ailey and Todd Bolender (see EBONY CONCERTO). MacMillan chor. it for Touring Royal B., dec. Goddard, f.p. Memorial Th., Stratford-upon-Avon 12 Feb 1964 (Wells, Anderton, Farley) in pop-art style.

CREATION OF THE WORLD, THE, ballet, ch. Kasatkina and Vasiliov, m. A. Petrov, dec. E. Steinberg. f.p. Kirov B., Leningrad 23 Mar 1971 (Soloviev, Kolpakova, Barishnikov, Panov). Rehearsals were begun on the Bolshoi B., Moscow but it was moved to the Kirov B. It has a comic conception of God creating man.

CRÉATURES DE PROMETHEUS, LES, ballet. (1) Ch. Vigano, m. Beethoven. This ballet was to honour the Empress Maria Theresa and the music was specially commissioned from Beethoven and written to a book supplied by Vigano. The book has been lost but a summary remains in a theatre-bill. F.p. Vienna 28 Mar 1801 (Cassentini, Vigano). The original German title is *Die Geschöpfe des Prometheus*. (2) Ch. Lifar, m. Beethoven, dec. Quelvée, f.p. Paris Opéra 30 Dec 1929 (Lifar, Spessivtseva, Peretti, Lorcia). (3) Ch. Ashton, m. Beethoven, dec. Meyer, f.p. Royal Ballet (Touring Section), Opera House, Bonn, 6 June 1970 (Wells, Cooke, Thorogood, Last, Davel). A lighthearted ballet set in the time of the composer for his bi-centenary. Many other chors. have used this score.

CREMORNE BALLET, a company formed by Cyril Beaumont and Flora Fairbairn which gave only one performance, at the Scala Th., London 11 Mar 1926, but interesting because Ashton danced in *The Christmas Tree* (ch. Beaumont, m. Adlington)—three months before *A Tragedy of Fashion* (q.v.). Also in the Co. were Penelope Spencer, Betty Scorer, Stanley Judson and Beaumont himself.

CRISP, Clement, b. Romford 1931. Eng. schoolmaster and writer on ballet. Educ. at Oxford and Bordeaux Univs. Ballet critic of *The Financial Times* from 1958. Editor of *Covent Garden Books* 14 and 15. Librarian-archivist of Royal Academy of Dancing from 1968. Author (with Peter Brinson) of *Ballet for All* (1970), *Ballet, an Illustrated History* (with Mary Clarke 1973).

CROFTON, Kathleen, b. Fyzabad, India 1902. Eng. dancer-teacher. Pupil of Novikoff, Legat and Preobrajenska. Joined Pavlova's Co. 1923–28 (soloist from 1924). Joined Chicago Opera B. 1929, de Basil 1932–33, Nijinska's B. 1933, Dandré's Co. 1934. Joined Markova-Dolin Co. 1935–37 as soloist. Retired from ballet 1938–50. In 1950 studied under Preobrajenska and in 1951 opened school in London. Guest teacher of Royal B. and Royal B. School from 1960. To teach at Met. Op. Ballet N.Y. 1966, and in 1967 to Buffalo, U.S.A. to teach and direct the local ballet company (Niagara Frontier Ballet).

CROISÉ, lit. crossed. A position in which the body of the dancer is placed

Croisé Position

obliquely to the audience, termed croisé devant when the leg nearest to the audience is 'crossed' in front (i.e. open to the fourth position in front), or croisé derrière when the leg furthest from the audience is 'crossed' at the back (i.e. opened to the fourth position at the back) on the ground, or extended in the air in arabesque, or bent in attitude, the arms in both cases being in an attitude position. Whereas in an open position the full length of both legs can be seen by the audience, in a croisé position one leg only is fully visible.

CROIX, EN, lit. in the form of a cross. Applied when a movement is executed, consecutively, to the front, side, back, and side again.

CROQUEUSE DE DIAMANTS, LA, ballet 4 sc., ch. Petit, m. Damase, dec. Wakhevitch, f.p. Ballets de Paris, Marigny Th., Paris 25 Sept 1950 (Jeanmaire, Petit, Hamilton). Set in a Paris café. Jeanmaire steals diamonds in order to eat them (and sings of her passion).

CSARDAS, possibly from *Tcharda*, tavern. The Hungarian *csárdás* (pronounced 'chardash'), although only known under that name from the time when it was adopted by the sophisticated nobility in 1840, can be traced back to the close of the ninth century when the Magyars first settled in the Danube lowlands, and is the national dance spontaneously performed at harvest time or wedding festivals to the stirring music of the gipsy fiddler. In its folk dance form it is essentially a free dance with no set steps but falling into two parts, the *lassu* either performed as a circle dance by the men or in couples with the woman's hands on the man's shoulders and his hands on her waist, the steps being terre à terre, and the *gyors* to a quick tempo with many turns and jumps. A characteristic of the *csárdás* is the introduction of a number of steps requiring a turned-in position of the feet. The *csárdás* was first introduced in a ballet in the first act of Saint-Léon's *Coppélia* in 1870.

CUADRO FLAMENCO, a gypsy scene of song and dance. In 1921 Diaghileff presented a *Cuadro Flamenco*, dec. Picasso, in his repertoire.

CUBAN BALLET, stems from the Ballet Alicia Alonso which she founded in 1948 and which danced in Cuba and Latin America. In 1955 its name was changed to Ballet de Cuba and besides dancing in Cuba it toured behind the Iron Curtain in 1961, where it was very welcome for political reasons (although at that time most of the dancers were American). Formerly the Socièdad Pro Arte Musical in Havana had provided a company and school (where Alicia Alonso originally studied). Her school, the Academia de Ballet Alicia Alonso in Havana, directed by herself and her husband Fernando Alonso has in the last few years produced some very fine dancers (among them Loipa Araujo, Mirta Pla, Aurora Bosch, Josefina Méndes, Jorge Esquivel, Roberto

Rodriguez, Osca Gonzales). The Ballet de Cuba danced in the Paris International Festival 1970.

CUBAT'S, the restaurant in St Petersburg where, before the Revolution, the dancers were entertained by the balletomanes, and much intrigue was discussed.

CUCCHI, Claudine, b. Monza 1834, d. Milan 1913. It. dancer who danced in Vienna (Kärntnertor Th.) 1857–68 and made her début in St Petersburg in 1866 in *Catarina*, and later danced in *Esmeralda*.

CUISSE, TEMPS DE, see TEMPS DE CUISSE.

CULLBERG BALLET. Swedish company at the Stockholm City Theatre formed in 1966 as vehicle for the choreography of Birgit Cullberg subsidized by the state through the Swedish State Theatre. In the repertoire are works by Cullberg, Merce Cunningham, Lucas Hoving, Donya Feuer, Flemming Flindt, Eske Holm, Kurt Jooss and Tyyne Talvo. In the first season there were eight dancers, second season twelve, among them Niklas Ek, Karin Thulin, Kari Sylwan, Siv Ander, Lena Wennergren, Mona Elhg, Vlado Juras, Eske Holm, Timo Salin. Guest artists Melissa Hayden, Richard Kuch, Richard Gain, Veronika Mlakar. It gave its first performance 6 Mar 1967, and danced in London (Sadler's Wells 1971).

CULLBERG, Birgit, b. Nyköping 1908. Swed. dancer and chor. Studied Jooss-Leeder in England, and in Paris. Founded own Co. 1944, incl. dancers Ivo Cramer and Tutte Lemkow. Won second prize A.I.D. chor. competition Stockholm in 1945 with ballet *Livsrytmen*. Brought troupe to London 1951, incl. her ballet *Miss Julie*, and dancers Elsa Marianne von Rosen, and Julius Mengarelli. Chor. many ballets for Royal Swedish B., incl. *Miss Julie*, *Medea* and (for R. Dan. B.) *Moon Reindeer*. From 1951 chor. at R. Swedish Opera House. To America 1959. Chor. *Lady from the Sea* (1960) for Ballet Th. Re-founded Cullberg B. 1966 and chor. *Dionysos, Fedra, Eurydice is Dead* (1966–68). Her specially-filmed ballets for television have been very successful, *The Cruel Queen* won Prix d'Italia 1961, *Adam and Eve* etc.

CUNNINGHAM, Merce, b. Centralia, Washington 1919. Am. dancer and chor. Studied at Cornish Sch. Seattle. Joined Martha Graham Co. 1940 and remained as soloist until 1945, also teaching at the Sch. of American B., N.Y. Created many leading rôles in her Co., among them Acrobat (*Every Soul is a Circus*), Christ (*El Penitente*), Revivalist (*Appalachian Spring*). Between 1945 and 1952 gave many solo recitals. In 1952 founded his Merce Cunningham Dance Company which is one of the greatest of the modern dance troupes. In 1964 it toured Europe and the Far East (without a subsidy). He has collaborated much with John Cage who became music director of his Co. 1953 and the painter Rauschenberg. Among the many ballets he has chor. are *Root of an Unfocus* (1944), *The Seasons* (m. Cage) (1947), *Two Step* (1949), *Les Noces* (1952), *Nocturnes* (1956), *Labyrinthian Dances* (1957), *Summerspace* (1958), *Rune* (1959), *Winterbranch* (1964), *How to Pass, Kick, Fall and Run* (1965), *Landrover* (1972).

CUOCO, Joyce, b. Boston 1953. Am. dancer. As a child studied tap dancing and jazz, was 'Clara' in Boston B. *Nutcracker* 1963, danced in television shows, the Danny Kaye Show, Ed Sullivan Show and displayed her pirouettes to millions. Was in Radio City Music Hall. Studied with Ruth Page, Riabouchinska and Lichine and in 1970 came to Europe and joined Cranko's Stuttgart B. In 1971 she was Swanilda in the Noverre B. *Coppélia* and became a principal of the Co.

CUPID OUT OF HIS HUMOUR, seventeenth century ballet, revived with ch. Skeaping, m. Purcell, dec. from old Swedish ballet designs, f.p. R. Swed. Ballet, Drottningholm Palace Th., 14 June 1956 (von Rosen, Holmgren).

CURTAIN-CALL or CALL (Fr. *Révérence*), the acknowledgement by the artist of the applause of the audience. Virginia Zucchi when taking her call in *L'Ordre du Roi* at the Maryinsky Th., St Petersburg in 1886 bowed instead of curtseying, thus creating a precedent followed to this day by certain danseuses. Whether a ballerina should bow or curtsey should be largely determined by the costume she is wearing—the bow is particularly unaesthetic in a *tutu*. The male dancer invariably bows.

According to the *Guinness Book of Records*, there were 89 curtain calls at the Staatsoper, Vienna, after Fonteyn and Nureyev had performed *Swan Lake* there in 1964.

CURTIS, Peter, b. Willesden 1942. Eng. dancer. Pupil of K. Mumford, Andrew Hardie and Rambert Sch. Joined B. Rambert 1961 becoming soloist 1962. Retired 1972.

CYDALISE ET LE CHÈVRE-PIED, ballet 2 acts, 2 sc., ch. Staats, m. Pierné, dec. Dethomas, f.p. Paris Opéra 15 Jan 1923 (Zambelli, Aveline).

CYGNE, LE (*The Dying Swan*), solo dance to music by Saint-Saëns (from *Le Carnival des Animaux*) arranged by Fokine for Pavlova, f.p. Maryinsky Th., St Petersburg 22 Dec 1907 (though in his memoirs Fokine says in the Hall of the Assembly of Nobles, St Petersburg in 1905). It was Pavlova's most famous dance and the costume was by Bakst (now in the London Museum). Other ballerinas have danced it since with varying degrees of success. A film of it exists (lacking a small portion).

CYRANO DE BERGERAC, ballet 3 acts, ch. Petit, m. Constant, dec. Basarte, cost. Yves Saint-Laurent, f.p. Ballets de Paris, Alhambra Th. Paris 17 Apr 1959 (Petit, Jeanmaire, Reich).

CZARNY, Charles, b. Chicago 1931. Am. dancer and chor. Pupil of Bennington College and Martha Graham Sch. N.Y. Joined Limon Co. 1953, danced in musicals, toured Europe with Am. Festival B. With Nederlands Dans Th. 1967 as dancer, and ballet master 1967–70. Chor. *Brandenburg Three* (m. Bach) 1970, for them (later in B. Van Vlaanderen, Scapino B. and Oslo B. repertoires), *Concerto Grosso* (m. Joplin) 1971 for Nederlands Dans Th., Scapino B. etc.

CZECHOSLOVAKIA, BALLET IN. The principal Co. is the National B. based on the Prague Opera House. Although ballet had been performed regularly in Prague from the beginning of the eighteenth century by various groups of dancers (*La Sylphide* was given in 1850, and Grahn danced there), it was not until 1862 that there was a ballet attached to the National Th. with V. Reisinger (b. 1828, d. 1892) as ballet master. Achille Viscusi was ballet master 1900–12 and produced *Swan Lake* in full for the first time in Prague 1907. Sacha Maçhov (q.v.) was ballet master 1946–51 and produced *Romeo and Juliet* in 1950. By this time the Russian influence was becoming strong. Jiri Němeček was ballet master 1957–70 and produced *Flames of Paris*, and Grigorovitch mounted his *Legend of Love* in 1963. In 1970 E. Gabzdyl became ballet director. Among recent notable dancers have been Marta Drottnerova, Olga Skálová, Jiri Blažek.

The other important Co. in Czechoslovakia is that at Brno (where V. Psota was ballet master, on and off, from 1936 to 1952 and was the first to mount Prokofieff's *Romeo and Juliet*). Also see *Prague Ballet*. There are also dancers in the Laterna Magica Th. in Prague.

CZERNYANA, ballet, ch. Staff, m. Czerny, dec. Eve Swinstead Smith, f.p. B. Rambert, Duchess Th., London 5 Dec 1939 (Gilmour, Schooling, Gore). Later another ballet *Czerny II* was f.p. 15 May 1941 Arts Th., London (Gilmour, Schooling, Gore, Staff) and pieces from each were finally incorporated into *Czernyana* when the ballet was revived in 1943. A skit on the various types of ballet.

CZOBEL, Lisa, b. Bamberg 1906. Hungarian dancer. Studied under Preobrajenska, Egorova and joined the Essen Folkwang B. Created rôle of Young Girl in *The Green Table* 1932. Soloist of Berne B. 1940–44. Toured with Trudi Schoop 1945–46. Basel B. 1946–47, taught in America. Returned to Germany 1949, Cologne 1951–56. Danced at Jacob's Pillow 1965.

D

DALCROZE, see JAQUES-DALCROZE.

DALE, Margaret, b. Newcastle-upon-Tyne 1922. Eng. dancer and chor. Trained by Nellie Potts, and after appearing in pantomimes, joined S. Wells Sch. 1937, becoming soloist in the Co. dancing Swanilda in *Coppélia*, Tango in *Façade*, Sugar Plum Fairy in *Casse Noisette*, and many character rôles. Chor. several ballets for television and *The Great Detective* for S. Wells Th. B. 1953. Retired 1954 and became television producer. Her productions for the B.B.C. have been notable: the Bolshoi Ballet *Swan Lake* (Ulanova, 1956), *Coppélia* (Nerina, Helpmann, 1957), *Giselle* (Nerina, Fadeyechev, 1958), *Casse* (Fonteyn, Somes, 1958), *Sleeping Beauty* (Fonteyn, Somes, 1959), *La Sylphide* (Aldous, 1961), *Rake's Progress* (1961), *Les Rendezvous*, *Petrouchka*, *Fille Mal Gardée* (1962), *Checkmate* (1963), *Toccata*, *Coppélia* (1964), *Firebird* (1965), *The Dream* (1967), *Monotones* (1968). Also the Bolshoi B. (1961, 1963) and features on Karsavina (1965), *Cranko's Castle* (1967), Varna Competition (1968), Pavlova (1970), Rambert (1970).

DALI, Salvador, b. Figueras 1904. Sp. surrealist painter, designed dec. for *Bacchanale* (1939), *Labyrinth* (1941), *Mad Tristan* (1944), *Colloque Sentimentale* (1944), *Café de Chinitás* (1944), *Gala* (ch. Béjart, at Venice 1961).

DAMASE, Jean-Michel, b. Paris 1928. Fr. composer who at the age of sixteen was Petit's pianist when the B. des Ch. Élysées was formed. Won Premier Prix du Conservatoire and, in 1947, the Prix de Rome, Composed the music for *Croqueuse de Diamants* (1950), *Piège de Lumière* (1952), *Lady in the Ice* (1953), *Balance à Trois* (1955), *La Tendre Eleonore* (1962).

D'AMBOISE, Jacques, b. Dedham, Mass. 1934. Am. dancer and chor. Pupil of Am. Sch. of B. and Swoboda. Joined N.Y. City B. 1950. becoming soloist 1953. Also danced in films (*Seven Brides for Seven Brothers*, *Best Things in Life are Free*, *Carousel*), and in musical *Shinbone Alley*. Chor. *The Chase* (m. Mozart) 1963, *Quatuor* (m. Shostakovitch) 1964, *Irish Fantasy* (m. Saint-Saëns), *Prologue* (m. sixteenth-century English) 1967, *Tchaikovsky Suite* 1969 for N.Y. City B. Has his own group, Ballet Spectacular.

DAME À LA LICORNE, LA, ballet by Cocteau, ch. Heinz Rosen, m. fifteenth- and sixteenth-century songs, dec. Cocteau, f.p. Gärtnerplatztheater, Munich 8 May 1953 (Mlakar, Lespagnol, Trailine).

138

Based on the Fr. tapestries. Mounted at Paris Opéra 28 Jan 1959 (Bessy, Daydé, Renault).

DAME AUX CAMÉLIAS, LA, ballet 2 acts, ch. T. Gsovsky, m. Sauguet, f.p. Berlin Festival 29 Sept 1957 (Sommerkamp). Revived Paris Opéra, dec. Dupont 3 Feb 1960 (Chauviré, Skibine).

DAMM, Palle, b. Copenhagen 1942. Dan. dancer. Trained by Volkova at R. Danish B. Sch. Joined Norwegian B. 1961, soloist 1963, principal 1968.

DAMNATION OF FAUST, THE, opera-ballet 3 acts, ch. Béjart, m. Berlioz, dec. Casado, f.p. Paris Opéra B., Paris Opéra 13 Mar 1964 (Vlassi, Bonnefous, Atanassoff, Mallarte, Parmain). A new production of the dramatic legend with dancers doubling with the singers.

DANCE AND DANCERS, monthly journal devoted solely to theatrical dancing, published in London. The editor, from its first issue of January 1950, has been Peter Williams.

DANCE CENTRE, THE, in Floral St, Covent Garden, London was conceived by Gary Cockrell (q.v.) and opened in an old school in 1965. The building was converted by him into a collection of dance studios, with changing rooms, showers, a shop and canteen. By 1970 it had become the centre for dancers in London and many of the leading teachers left their own studios and rented studios there. Currently (1972) Anna Northcote, Errol Addison, Maria Fay, Matt Mattox and John O'Brien are giving their classes there and the Royal B., Festival B. and all the visiting Cos. hire studios for their rehearsals. If a studio is hired by a private teacher for $1\frac{1}{2}$ hours and a pianist engaged, at current prices the teacher can only begin to make a profit if thirteen or more students attend. In many respects it corresponds with the Studio Wacker (q.v.) in Paris.

DANCE COLLECTION, of the New York Public Library, was formed in 1947 when the dance section of the Music Division was segregated and a Curator (Geneviève Oswald) appointed to reorganize it. It is probably the most important collection of dance material in the world and since 1965 it has been housed in the Library and Museum of the Performing Arts at Lincoln Center, N.Y. Among the many collections it has acquired are the Gabriel Astruc Diaghileff Archives, the collections made by Lincoln Kirstein, Cia Fornaroli, Sol Hurok, Humphrey-Weidman and much material from the great dancers and photographers (including the photographs by Constantine, George Platt Lynes and Kahn's collection of Ulanova pictures).

DANCE HORIZONS, INC., a non-profit-making organization in N.Y. publishing paperback reprints of classic books on the dance, founded in 1965. Among its titles are *Lambranzi, Noverre*, Beaumont's *Ballet Called Giselle*, Lillian Moore's *Artists of the Dance*, Kirstein's *The Dance*.

DANCE INDEX, a series of monographs on ballet subjects published in U.S.A. from 1942 to 1948, originally edited by Lincoln Kirstein, Paul Magriel, Donald Windham, and Baird Hastings. These monographs were at the time the most important contributions made by America to the literature of ballet. The last issue was Vol. 8, No 6. (Autumn 1948) and the final editors Marian Eames and Lincoln Kirstein.

DANCE MAGAZINE, American monthly journal founded in 1936 by Rudolf Orthwine (d. 1970) devoted to all forms of dance and the teaching profession. Edited by Lydia Joel until 1969 when she was succeeded by William Como.

DANCE NEWS, founded by Anatole Chujoy in U.S.A. in 1942, monthly newspaper devoted to ballet news all over the world. The founder was also the publisher and editor, and P. W. Manchester the Managing Editor. On the death of Chujoy in 1969 the paper changed hands. Miss Manchester resigned and from the September issue the Editor and publisher was Mrs Helen V. Atlas.

DANCE NOTATION. There is no commonly accepted method of recording ballets, in the sense that music may be written down, though many dancers and chors. have made their own systems, intelligible only to themselves. In 1463 Guglielmo Ebreo of Pesaro described a simple system of letters and words with which he recorded a number of *basses danses*. In 1588 Arbeau used alphabetical symbols to note the steps in his *Orchésographie*. Pierre Beauchamp (q.v.) evolved a system but the title of the first notator of dancing must go to Feuillet, who (using Beauchamp's system but claiming it as his own) published in 1701 *Chorégraphie ou l'Art de Décrire la Danse*. This method has curling lines showing the dancers' movements over the stage, along which his steps and positions are indicated. Pécour, ballet composer at the Académie Royale, used this system, and a famous picture of him shows him holding the script. Blasis and Bournonville had their systems, and in 1852 Saint-Léon published his *Sténochorégraphie*, which used simple figures of dancers on a musical stave with an extra line. In 1887 Albert Zorn published a system based on Saint-Léon's which found some favour. In 1891 a ballet teacher at the Imperial Schools at St Petersburg, Stepanoff, published a book which described his own method, using musical notes, and this was taught to the young students at the Sch. (and in the sch. attached to the Bolshoi Th., Moscow). Many of Petipa's ballets were recorded and Sergueeff (q.v.) used this notation

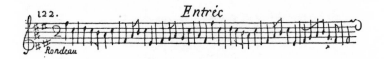

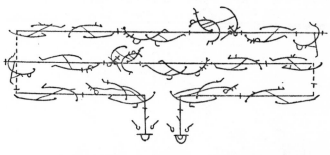

Feuillet's (or Beauchamp's) System of 1700. A 'floor-pattern' system. Using this method he notated a number of the dances at the Paris Opéra in the seventeenth century and Pécour used the system there later.

when mounting *The Sleeping Beauty* and other classics in Western Europe. It was learned by Karsavina, among others. Massine improved it and in this form it is taught in the junior school of the Royal Ballet at White Lodge. Georges Poli's method, using letters only, was published in 1892 and Antonio Cluesa's (music notes) in 1934. Two contemporary systems of notation are those of Pierre Conté, of France (1930) and of Rudolf von Laban (q.v.). Conté uses a nine-line music stave. It has been used by athletes to record their movements and a film of it was made by Painlévé. Von Laban's *Kinetographie*, published 1928, uses three vertical lines, read upwards from the bottom of the page to the right and left of which are placed symbols representing the dancer's movements and positions. This method, also called Labanotation (q.v.), is gaining favour in many countries, especially in America, where classical and modern works are being recorded by it, and a Dance Notation Bureau (q.v.) set up. It is a completely comprehensive system and can be used for any type of human movement. In 1955 a simple method of notation was copyrighted by Joan Benesh,

Saint-Léon's Sténochorégraphie of 1852. A 'pin-figure' system with music staves, used by him at the Paris Opéra during the Second Empire. This example represents: an assemblé with back to audience, temps levé on the cou-de-pied while making a demi-tour en l'air, glissade en tournant, with another demi-tour, temps levé and coupé dessous: the whole is repeated twice with each leg.

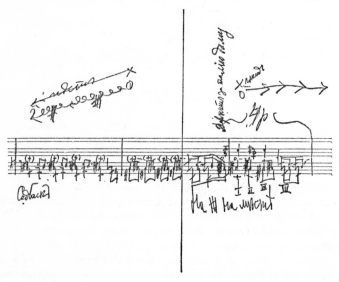

Stepanoff's System, 1891. This uses a specially printed type of music stave, with a 'floor-pattern' above. It was taught in the schools in St Petersburg and Moscow and with this notation the great Russian classics were mounted in Western Europe. This example is the opening of the Black Swan pas de deux from Petipa's 'Swan Lake'.

then a member of the S. Wells B., and her husband, Rudolf Benesh. The Benesh System uses a five-line music stave, one for each dancer or group of dancers, running horizontally across the page. On these staves symbols indicate the movements of the dancers. It was adopted

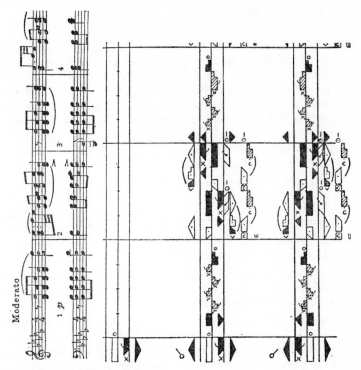

Labanotation, 1953. This uses special symbols moving vertically up the page, and the example is the opening of the Dance of the Little Swans from Balanchine's version of 'Swan Lake'.

Benesh System, 1955. A system using a music-stave now used by the Royal Ballet and other companies. The example is from 'The Lady and the Fool'.

by the Royal Ballet and Sch. in 1955 and is used in mounting the ballets of Ashton, de Valois, Cranko, MacMillan etc. all over the world. It is also the method used by the Stuttgart B., Dutch National B., West Berlin B., Australian B., B. Rambert, Munich B., Scott. Th. B. etc. The mathematically based system invented during 1951–56 by Noa Eshkol (daughter of the then Prime Minister of Israel) and Abraham Wachmann (published 1958) has gained recognition in scientific fields. Eshkol has a small group of dancers who tour the world demonstrating it (visited The Place, London 1970).

DANCE NOTATION BUREAU, founded in N.Y. in 1940 by Eve Gentry, Ann Hutchinson and others to advance the art of dance through the use of notation. All notation methods are studied and that of Laban has been perfected and developed by the Bureau (see Labanotation). Using this method they have notated many ballets (and instructed teachers in it) and have a library of notated works.

DANCE OBSERVER, a monthly magazine published in America since 1933, founded and edited by Louis Horst, largely devoted to the modern dance. Its last issue was January 1964.

DANCE PERSPECTIVES, a series of quarterly monographs on ballet, published in New York and edited by A. J. Pischl and Selma Jeanne Cohen. The first issue appeared in December 1958 and by the end of 1972 had presented 51 numbers of a very high quality in content and presentation.

DANCERS' CIRCLE DINNERS, were instituted in 1920 in London by P. J. S. Richardson. They were indirectly responsible for the Camargo Society, the Association of Operatic Dancing (which became the R.A.D.), the Children's Examinations, the Greek Dance Association etc.

DANCES AT A GATHERING, ballet, ch. Robbins, m. Chopin, lighting Skelton, cost. Eula, f.p. N.Y. City B. 8 May 1969 (Kent, Mazzo, McBride, Verdy, Leland, Blum, Clifford, Maiorana, Prinz, Villella). A ballet of moods and encounters. Taken into Royal B., C. Garden 19 Oct 1970 (Connor, Jenner, Mason, Seymour, Sibley, Coleman, Dowell, Kelly, Nureyev, Wall).

DANCING MASTERS OF AMERICA (D.M.A.), the largest organization of teachers in the United States, was formed in 1926 by the fusion of the American National Association of Masters of Dancing (founded 1884) and the International Association of Masters of Dancing (founded 1894). It holds conventions and schools but does not have an examination system.

DANCING TIMES, THE, first published 1894 as the house magazine of the

Cavendish Rooms, London, it is the oldest monthly devoted to dancing. In 1910 it was bought by P. J. S. Richardson (q.v.) and T. M. Middleton and transformed into a national periodical. It played an instrumental part in the founding of the Royal Academy of Dancing. Richardson remained editor until 1958, succeeded by A. H. Franks (q.v.) until 1963. Mary Clarke then became editor (and part-owner in 1966). In 1956 the ballroom and social dancing sections were split off into a second magazine *The Ballroom Dancing Times*, and in 1962 the format of the *Dancing Times* was doubled. The stated policy is to maintain the highest standards of criticism, give voice to leading authorities and encourage high teaching standards and stress the importance of dance in education.

DANDRÉ, Victor, b. 1870, d. London 1944. Russ. balletomane who associated himself with Pavlova in 1914 and became her manager. In 1931, after her death, he formed his own Co., and in 1938 he assumed control of the de Basil Co. and presented it in London and Australia. Author of *Anna Pavlova in Art and Life*, 1932.

DANHOFF, Christiaan, b. Johannesburg 1947. S. African dancer. Pupil of Conmee, Golman. Joined PACT B., Johannesburg 1964 becoming a principal dancer. Also danced with Capab B. 1965.

DANIAS, Starr, b. N.Y. 1949. Am. dancer. Pupil of Balanchine, Danilova, Williams etc. Joined Festival B. 1968 becoming soloist 1969 and dancing ballerina rôles. Returned to America 1970 to become soloist of Joffrey B.

DANIELIAN, Leon, b. N.Y. 1920. Am. dancer and teacher. Pupil of Mordkin, Dolin, Tudor, Sch. of Am. B. Joined Mordkin B. 1937–39, Ballet Th. 1939–41, B. Russe de Monte Carlo 1942–61. Guest artist San Francisco B. Appointed director of American Ballet Th. School.

DANILOVA, Alexandra, b. Peterhof 1904. Russ. dancer. Studied at Imperial Sch. and entered the Maryinsky Co. In 1924 left Russia to tour in a group with Balanchine. The same year she joined Diaghileff's Co., becoming ballerina in 1927. She joined de Basil Co. in 1933, the Ballet Russe in 1938 and remained their ballerina until 1952. Guest artist of S. Wells B. 1949. Cr. many famous rôles, including Street Dancer in *Beau Danube* and the Sleep Walker in *Night Shadow*. Guest artist Festival B. 1952 and 1955. Formed her own company 1954. Her farewell performance in N.Y. was at the Met. Op. with B. Russe de Monte Carlo 1957. Mounted ballets at Met. Op., N.Y. 1959–61, and *Coppélia* in Milan 1961. Now teaches and lectures.

DANILOVA, Marie, b. 1793, d. St Petersburg 1810. Russ. dancer. Studied Imp. Sch. St Petersburg and graduated 1809. She was altogether exceptional as a pupil and her teacher, Didelot, gave her many rôles while still at school. She made a triumph, partnered by Duport, in *Flore et Zéphire* at the age of 15. She had an unhappy love affair with Duport and died at the age of 17 of consumption hastened, it is said, by a broken heart. She was small and extremely beautiful, and many poets addressed verses to her. The portrait, often reproduced and alleged to be of her, is now known to be of Alexandra Danilova, a coryphée, born 1822 and retired 1858.

DANINA or JOKO THE BRAZILIAN APE, ballet 4 acts, ch. Filippo Taglioni, m. von Lindpaintner, f.p. Stuttgart 12 Mar 1826 (Marie Taglioni, Stuhlmüller, Briol). A very popular work and foreshadowing the Romantic Ballet.

DANISH BALLET, THE ROYAL. Court ballets took place in Denmark in the sixteenth and seventeenth centuries, and a French dancing-master was in charge of the ballets at the Grönnegard Theatre, forerunner of the national theatre, in 1726. In 1748 the Royal Theatre was opened and the first ballet-master was M. des Larches. He was succeeded by a number of foreigners—Neudin, Como, Sacco, J. B. Martin, Gambuzzi, etc.—but it was the Italian, Vincenzo Galeotti, engaged in 1775, who first raised the ballet to its eminent position. He retired in 1816 having built up a fine company with a large repertoire (of which his *Les Caprices du Cupidon* still remains). He was succeeded by Antoine Bournonville, whose son August became ballet-master in 1829 and remained so until his death in 1879. Under August Bournonville the R. Danish B. had its greatest period and obtained the individual character which it still retains. This character lies in the style of its dancing, which was the French style Bournonville learned under Vestris, and in the masculine, pantomimic ballets of which *Napoli* and *Kermesse in Bruges* are typical examples. After his death the ballet declined until the advent of Hans Beck, who was ballet-master 1894–1915, when the Bournonville ballets were revived with himself and his partner Borchsenius dancing the leading rôles. The effects of Fokine's reforms and Diaghileff's productions were not much felt in Denmark, but in 1925 Fokine was engaged as guest-choreographer (producing *Petrouchka* and other works) and in 1930 Balanchine, each leaving his mark. In 1932 Harald Lander a pupil of Beck was appointed ballet-master and under his régime, which closed in 1951, the company had its second great flowering and many Bournonville ballets were revived and new ballets of his own were added, notably *Étude* and *Qarrtsiluni*. During most of this time Margot Lander was the prima ballerina, one of the greatest dancers the country has produced (taking her place with Lucile Grahn, Augusta Nielsen, and Adeline Genée). Although the Bournonville style of dancing was faithfully preserved by Lander, he appreciated that the general trend of ballet throughout the world was turning towards the so-called 'Russian' style as taught by Vaganova at Leningrad. Accordingly he appointed Vera Volkova in 1951 to take charge of the School and her influence is now being felt. Lander was succeeded by Niels Bjorn Larsen in 1951. The attention of the outside world was drawn to the R. Danish B. by visits of enthusiastic groups of English critics in 1950 and succeeding years, and in 1953 the Company made its first visit to Covent Garden, when they achieved the greatest success ever attained by a visiting troupe up to that time. The Royal Th., Copenhagen, has 1,432 seats and the stage measures 33 ft wide and 50 ft deep. In 1960 the leading dancers were (girls) Schanne, Ralov, Vangsaa, Sand, Simone; (men) Schaufuss, Kronstam, Larsen, Jensen, Björnsson, Williams. In 1970 the ballet-master was Fleming Flindt (appointed 1965) and the principal dancers were (girls) Simone, Laerkesen, Ostergaard, Gelker, Englund; (men) Kronstam, Kehlet, Madsen, Larsen, Halby, Ryberg.

The school of the Royal Th. was founded in 1771 by Pierre Laurent, Fr. Master of the Court Ceremonies, housed in Christiansborg Palace but it did not last long. In 1775 Galeotti's own school was accepted as the official school and it was reorganized by August Bournonville into its present form. Pupils enter at 7 and are trained free until 16. There are about 70 students.

DANISH BALLET THEATRE, company founded in 1970 by Frank Schaufuss and his wife Mona Vangsaa, in association with their Danske Balletakademie in Copenhagen, with their son Peter Schaufuss as a principal.

DANSE, LA, Fr. ballet journal published in Paris, edited by G.-G. Duret. It appeared monthly and the first number appeared in July 1954.

DANSE D'ÉCOLE, the classical style (q.v.).

DANSE MACABRE, a theme worked on by painters and sculptors of the Middle Ages in which Mankind is shown frantically and heedlessly dancing to its death, with Death himself as a cloaked skeleton urging them on. Doubtless the prevalence of the Plague inspired artists to the subject, just as violence does now. In German—*Totentanz*, and, perhaps significantly, there is no equivalent in English. It has inspired a number of ballets, mostly German, and Jooss's *The Green Table* is the classic example. Flindt's *The Triumph of Death* (q.v.) is another. Saint-Saëns' symphonic poem *Danse Macabre* depicts a more restricted scene.

DANSE MANU, a dance in the *grand divertissement* of the second act of *La Bayadère* of 1877 (q.v.) ch. Petipa. A dancer bearing a pitcher on her head teases two girls who ask her for water. Originally danced by Vera Zhukova, it has remained popular ever since and is regularly danced by young pupils of the Kirov Sch.—Ulanova among them.

DANSES CONCERTANTES, ballet, m. Stravinsky. (1) Ch. Balanchine, dec. Berman, f.p. B. Russe de Monte Carlo, N.Y. City Center 10 Sept 1944 (Danilova, Danielian); (2) ch. MacMillan, dec. Georgiadis, f.p. S. Wells Th. B., S. Wells Th. 18 Jan 1955 (Lane, Britton, Poole). Suite of dances. Also in the repertoire of Royal Danish B. and other Cos.

DANSEUR (Fr.) dancer (male), DANSEUSE, dancer (female).

DANSEUR NOBLE, lit. noble dancer. A dancer with a noble classical style.

DANSEUR SÉRIEUX, lit. serious dancer. Term used in the eighteenth and early nineteenth centuries to designate the classical dancer.

DANSEUSE TRAVESTIE, lit. disguised dancer. A female dancer in male costume and taking a male part, often in a pas de deux. Except in Russia it was a common practice at the height of the Romantic period in the 1840s and until the beginning of the twentieth century. The rôle of Frantz in *Coppélia* was created for a danseuse travestie and the custom still persists at the Paris Opéra. Adeline Genée was usually partnered thus at the Empire Th., London, where (and at the Alhambra Th.) it was the common practice from 1860 until the outbreak of the 1914–18 War. A great *travesti* dancer was Mme Cavallazzi, who only once appeared in a female ballet dress (in *Diana*, Empire Th. 1888). The custom in Western Europe was killed by the virile male dancing of the Diaghileff Co. See TRAVESTI, EN.

DANTE SONATA, ballet 1 act, ch. Ashton, m. Liszt, dec. Fedorovitch, f.p. S. Wells B., S. Wells Th. 23 Jan 1940 (Fonteyn, Brae, Somes, Helpmann). This powerful ballet, in the modern idiom and danced barefooted, was inspired by the fall of Poland in 1939.

DANTON, Henry, b. Bedford 1919. Eng. dancer and ballet master. Pupil of Volkova and Preobrajenska. Joined International B. 1943, Sadler's Wells B. 1944 and was one of the original dancers in *Symphonic Variations* 1946. Danced with Metropolitan B. 1947, Ch. Élysées B. 1947–48, Australian Nat. B. 1951–52. Artistic Director of Venezuelan Nat. B. 1953–58 and of Caracas Inst. of Fine Arts.

D'ANTUONO, Eleanor, b. Cambridge, Mass. 1939. Am. dancer. Pupil of Papporello and Williams in Boston. Joined B. Russe de Monte Carlo 1954–60. Joined Am. Ballet Th. 1961 as soloist, ballerina 1963.

DAPHNIS AND CHLOË, ballet 3 sc. (1) Ch. Fokine, m. Ravel, dec. Bakst, f.p. Diaghileff's Co., Châtelet Th., Paris 8 June 1912 (Karsavina, Nijinsky); (2) ch. Ashton, m. Ravel, dec. Craxton, f.p. S. Wells B., C. Garden, London 5 Apr 1951 (Fonteyn, Somes, Field). Of the many other versions those by Skibine (Opéra Comique, Paris 1959), Cranko (Stuttgart B. 1962) and Neumeier (Frankfurt B. 1972) are also notable.

DARK ELEGIES, ballet 2 sc., ch. Tudor, m. Mahler's *Kindertotenlieder* (sung), dec. Nadia Benois, f.p. B. Rambert, Duchess Th., London 19 Feb 1937 (Maud Lloyd, van Praagh, de Mille, Gore, Laing). The mourning of a fishing-village. The singer sits on the stage. Also in the repertoire of Ballet Theatre 24 Jan 1940 (Chase, Gollner, Stroganova, Laing, Tudor), the R. Swed. B. (1963) and Nat B. of Canada (1956).

DARMANCE, Danielle, b. 1930. Fr. acrobatic dancer. Studied with Prof. Guichot and joined B. des Ch. Élysées 1946, creating the chief rôle in Petit's *Le Bal des Blanchisseuses* and others.

DARRELL, Peter, b. Richmond, Surrey 1929. Eng. dancer and chor. Studied at S. Wells Sch., was an original member of S. Wells Th. Ballet 1946–47. Danced in musicals and at Malmö Oper. Chor. many ballets for Ballet Workshop 1951–55. Revised Lichine's *Harlequin* for Festival Ballet 1952. Chor. many ballets for Western Theatre Ballet of which he was co-founder. Also chor. for R. Winnipeg B., B. Laage Landen etc. On Elizabeth West's death in 1962 he became the Artistic Director of the company (from 1969 known as Scottish Th. B.). Among his ballets are *The Prisoners* (1957), *Non-Stop* (1957), *Jeux* (1963), *Mods and Rockers* (1963), *Salade* (1961), *Sun into Darkness* (1966), *Beauty and the Beast* (1969), *Tales of Hoffmann* (1972). For Deutsche Oper., W. Berlin, *Carmina Burana* and *Catulli Carmina* (1968).

DARSONVAL, Lycette, b. Coutances 1912. Fr. dancer. Studied Mlle Georgelli Couat, entered Paris Opéra Sch. 1925 and learned from Zambelli, Aveline and Guerra. Became petit sujet 1930 and left Opéra 1931, but returned in 1936 and nominated étoile 1940. Until 1953 was the senior ballerina of the Opéra and danced much in recitals. Her chief rôles were *Sylvia*, *Giselle*, and in *Joan de Zarissa*. Has toured widely. Appointed head of Paris Opéra Sch. 1957–59. Legion of Honour 1959. Director of ballet in Nice 1962 and has her own group and school in Paris and Nice. Sister of Serge Perrault.

DAUBERVAL (Jean Bercher), b. Montpellier 1742, d. Tours 1806. Fr. dancer and chor. Studied under Noverre, début Paris Opéra 1761, becoming chief dancer in 1770 and maître de ballet 1781. To Bordeaux 1785 to 1790, where he chor. *La Fille Mal Gardée* (1789), *The Deserter* (1784), *Le Page Inconstant* (1786), *Télémaque* (1791) etc. Mar. Mlle Théodore.

DAUM, Gerda, b. Munich 1942. German dancer. Pupil of von Sachnowsky and F. Adret. Joined Nice Ballet 1961, soloist in Larrain's *Cendrillon*

(Th. des Ch. Élysées, Paris) 1963. Toured with Babilée. From 1967 to 1972 soloist at Hamburg, to Darmstadt 1972.

DAVEL, Hendrik, b. S. Africa 1939. S. Africa dancer. Pupil of Gwynne Ashton. Joined Festival B. 1959, Gore's London B. 1962, London Dance Th. 1964, Royal B. 1964 becoming soloist 1966, principal 1968. Returned to S. Africa 1972 with his wife Vicki Karras.

DAVID, ballet 6 episodes, book Poppaea Vanda, ch. Lester, m. Jacobson, dec. Meninsky, curtain Epstein, f.p. Markova-Dolin Co., Newcastle-upon-Tyne 11 Nov 1935 (Dolin).

DAVIDSON, Andrea, b. Montreal 1953. Canad. dancer. Studied at Canad. Nat. B. School and entered Canadian National B. 1971, becoming soloist 1972.

DAVID TRIOMPHANT, ballet 2 acts, ch. Lifar, m. Debussy and Moussorgsky, dec. Léger, f.p. Th. de la Maison Internationale des Étudiants, Paris 15 Dec 1936 (Slavenska, Lifar). In Paris Opéra (m. Rieti, dec. Léger) 26 May 1957 (Chauviré, Darsonval, Lifar).

DAY, Mary, b. Washington D.C. Am. teacher and chor. With Lisa Gardiner founded the Washington (D.C.) Sch. of B. 1944 and presented ballets for children. From this developed the Washington Ballet, a regional ballet. In 1962 founded the Washington National B. (q.v.).

DAYDÉ, Bernard, b. Paris 1921. Fr. ballet designer. Designed *Romeo and Juliet* and *Sylphides* (Metropolitan B. London 1948), *Études* (Festival B. 1956 and R. Danish B. 1962), *Prométhée* (Miskovitch B. 1956), *Qartssiluni* (Paris Opéra 1960), *The Lesson* (Opéra Comique 1964) etc.

DAYDÉ, Liane, b. Paris 1932. Fr. dancer. Studied at Paris Opéra under Cebron and Zambelli. Début 1948. Was promoted première danseuse in 1949, and étoile in 1951. Cr. rôle of *Blanche Neige* (1952), *Roméo et Juliette* (1953). Danced in Russia 1958, left Opéra 1959. Danced in Cuevas B. 1961 (*Sleeping Beauty*) and many international tours with Renault (Grand B. Classique de France). Guest artist Festival B., Scala Milan, Colon Buenos Aires. Mar. impresario Claude Giraud.

DEATH AND THE MAIDEN, ballet ch. and dec. Andrée Howard, m. Andante con moto from Schubert's D minor quartet, f.p. B. Rambert, Duchess Th., London 23 Feb 1937 (Howard, Byron). A young girl dies and is borne away by Death and his minions. It was also in the original repertoire of Am. Ballet Theatre N.Y. 1940 (Howard and Annabelle Lyon dancing the rôles).

DEATHS AND ENTRANCES, ballet, ch. Graham, m. Johnson, dec. Lauterer, cost. Gilfond, f.p. Bennington Coll., Vermont 18 July 1943 (Graham, Dudley, Maslow, Cunningham). On the Brontë sisters.

DE BASIL, Col. W. (Voskresensky), b. Kaunas 1888, d. Paris 1951. Russ.

ballet entrepreneur. Joined René Blum in 1932 as co-director of Ballet Russe de Monte Carlo (q.v.) of which he in time obtained complete control. An able administrator rather than an artistic director, he did much to lay the foundations of the present popularity of the ballet. Mar. Olga Morosova.

DE BEAUMONT, Comte Étienne, b. 1885, d. Paris 1956. Fr. painter and patron of the ballet, for whose *Soirées de Paris*, at the Th. de la Cigale, 17 May 1924 to 30 June 1924, a number of ballets afterwards included in the repertoire of the major companies, incl. *Mercure* (1924) and *Le Beau Danube* (1924), were originally created. He designed dec. for *Le Beau Danube* (with V. and E. Polunin after Constantin Guys 1933), *Scuola di Ballo* (1933), *Nocturne* (1933), *Les Imaginaires* (1934), *Gaîté Parisienne* (1938), and *Nobilissima Visione* (with Tchelitchev 1938).

DÉBOÎTÉ, see EMBOÎTÉ.

DÉBOULÉS, a series of quick turns, from one foot to the other, held close together. Also known as chaînés or petits tours.

DEBURAU, Jean-Gaspard (Jan Kaspar), b. Bohemia 1796, d. 1846. Fr. mime and comic dancer. Appeared at the Th. des Funambules, Paris 1830–9, usually as Gilles or Pierrot. Janin called him *le plus grand comédien de notre époque*. He was succeeded by his son Charles (b. Paris 1829, d. there 1873).

DÉCOR, the scenery, backcloth (and sometimes drop-curtain) and costumes of a ballet. The purpose of dec. is to situate the time, place, and mood of the action. It exerts a definite, if passive, influence on the production and contributes to the theatrical illusion and can, in the lines of its design, echo the choreographic pattern, just as it may magnify or dwarf the stature of the dancers, throw them into relief or absorb them according to the degree of colour contrast. The practice of entrusting the décor and costumes to distinguished painters is largely due to Diaghileff, who raised the importance of the décor in a ballet to stand almost on a par with the music and the choreography.

DE CUEVAS, Marquis George, b. Santiago 1885, d. Cannes 1961 (Chilean, but Am. citizen from 1940). Mar. Margaret Strong, granddaughter of the late John D. Rockefeller, the millionaire. Founded the Grand Ballet du Marquis de Cuevas (q.v.) in 1947.

DEDANS, EN, lit. inwards—the opposite of en dehors. The rotated leg, or the body in a pirouette, turns in towards the supporting leg.

DEEGE, Gisela, b. Berlin 1928. German dancer. Studied under T. Gsovsky. Soloist in Opera House, Leipzig 1943–44 and, from 1947 to 1950, soloist at Staatsoper, E. Berlin. Prima ballerina of Städtische

Oper, W. Berlin 1952–66 and also of Gsovsky's Berliner Ballet, 1955–1962.

DEFILÉ, at the Paris Opéra, an occasion when the whole stage is opened up, revealing the Foyer de Danse at the back, and the entire Company from the *petits rats* to the *étoiles* takes the stage to the march from Berlioz' *Les Troyens*. It was an idea of Maurice Lehmann, director of the Paris Opéra, after the Liberation of Paris in 1945 and the now traditional form of the ceremony was chor. by Albert Aveline, the maître de ballet in that year. On 7 May 1964 a *defilé* was arranged in C. Garden in honour of Dame Ninette de Valois. The music was Arnold's *Homage to the Queen* and nearly 500 took part.

DÉGAGÉ, or PAS DÉGAGÉ, lit. a disengaging step. The freeing of the working foot in preparation for a step.

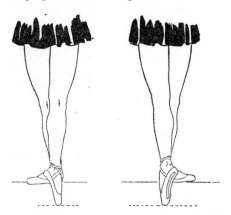

Dégagé à la quatrième devant   *Dégagé à la quatrième derrière*

DEGAS, Edgar, b. Paris 1834, d. there 1917. Fr. painter who made many famous sketches, paintings, and bronzes of dancers in class and at the Paris Opéra. His work has inspired many ballets, notably Lifar's *Entre Deux Rondes* and Ashton's *Foyer de Danse*. The model for his statuette in the Louvre and Tate Gallery was Louise van Goethen (b. 1870, d. 1945) of the Opéra.

D'EGVILLE, J. H., b. c. 1770. Eng. chor. and teacher. Son of ballet-master Peter d'Egville. He was chor. at the King's Th. 1799–1809 and Drury Lane Th., London, also writing the music to the ballets. At the King's Th. he founded an Academy of Dancing to train English soloists owing to the difficulty of importing them during the Napoleonic Wars. This met with opposition and in 1809 he was replaced. Among his ballets are *Le Bon Prince* (1794), *Pigmalion* (1808), *Mora's Harp* (1809), *La Naissance de Vénus* (1826).

DE HAAS, Olga, b. Amsterdam 1944. Dutch dancer. Studied under Sonia Gaskell and entered the Hague Conservatorium 1956, pupil of Valerie Adams. Joined Dutch Nat. B. 1960 becoming soloist 1961 and principal dancer 1964.

DE HESSE, Jean-François, b. The Hague 1705, d. 1779. Fr. chor. who created many ballets at the Comédie Italienne, Paris, 1738–61. He married the daughter of the famous Paris Harlequin, Thomassin (b. 1683, d. 1739).

DEHORS, EN, lit. outwards. This is said of a rotary movement of the leg or in the air executed from the front through the side to the back or of a pirouette in which the body turns away or outwards from the supporting leg towards the working leg (opp. en dedans). See TURN-OUT.

DE LA BYE, Willy, b. Leyden 1934. Dutch dancer. Soloist of Nederlands Dans Th. 1959. She was the first Dutch dancer to dance *Giselle* (1956). Mar. J. Flier.

DEL AMOR Y DE LA MUERTE, ballet, ch. Ricarda, m. Granados and Schelling, dec. Celia Hubbard, f.p. de Cuevas Co., Monte Carlo 28 Apr 1949 (Toumanova, Ricarda, Skibine). A Sp. tragedy of love and death.

DE LAUZE, F. Fr. author of *Apologie de la Danse* in 1623. Little is known of him but his book is valuable inasmuch as it falls between Arbeau (*Orchésographie* 1588) and Pierre Rameau (*Le Maître à Danser* 1725).

DE LAVALLADE, Carmen, b. Los Angeles 1931. Am. modern dancer. Pupil of Lester Horton and joined his group 1953 becoming soloist. Danced solo in *Aida* at Met. Op. N.Y. 1955–56. Joined Alvin Ailey Co. 1962, guest artist B. Theatre 1964 and appears in concerts etc.

DELAVALLE, Hugo, b. Córdoba, Buenos Aires 1933. Argentinian dancer. Studied under Bulnes, Lambrinos, Nora, Peretti. Entered de Cuevas Co. 1956, soloist Staatsoper, Stuttgart 1957–60, Cologne 1960, Düsseldorf 1964.

DELIBES, Léo, b. St-Germain-du-Val 1836, d. Paris 1891. Fr. composer. Accompanist and choir master at the Paris Opéra. In collaboration with Minkus, commissioned to write music for *La Source* (1866) and became the greatest composer of ballet music of his time. Composed *Coppélia* (1870), *Sylvia* (1876).

DE LIGNIÈRE, Aimé, b. Liverpool 1944. Belgian dancer. Pupil of Jeanne Brabants. Entered Royal Flemish B. 1962 becoming soloist 1965 and a principal of B. Van Vlaanderen 1971.

153

DELL'ARA, Ugo, b. Rome 1920. It. dancer. Studied Teatro dell'Opera, Rome. Début 1939, becoming principal dancer 1945. To Scala Milan 1946 onwards as principal dancer. In 1953 edited ballet magazine *Il Cigno*. Left Scala 1959. Ballet master in Naples, Scala, Milan, and from 1965 in Palermo. Chor. many ballets in Rome, Verona, Palermo, Naples. Artistic consultant for World Dance Festival. Nervi 1955–56. Chor. new version of *Excelsior* (q.v.) 1967.

DELL'ERA, Antonietta, b. Milan 1861. It. dancer who came to St Petersburg via Berlin (where she was ballerina 1879–1909) in 1885, making her début in a café-concert but later becoming a guest ballerina at the Maryinsky Th. and creating the chief rôle in *Casse Noisette* in 1892. Her style was reminiscent of Taglioni's and it was she, with Zucchi and Maria Giuri (who all arrived in the same year) who launched the Italian invasion of St Petersburg ballet resulting in great improvements in technique.

DELSARTE, François, b. Solesme 1811, d. Paris 1871. Fr. teacher who was the first to make a complete analysis of gesture and expression. He divided all movements into eccentric, concentric, and normal, and formulated laws controlling the movements of the body. He influenced the work of Laban and Jooss.

DE LUTRY, Michel, b. France 1924. Eng. dancer. Studied under Egorova. Principal dancer at Châtelet Th., Paris. To England 1946 and joined International B. With his wife, Domini Callaghan, danced in television, for B. Workshop, Gore's Co., etc. To Germany 1955 to film. Ballet master at Th. am Gärtnerplatz, Munich 1958–1960, Zürich 1960–63, Dortmund 1963–66, to Munich Staatsoper 1966 in charge of the school.

DE MARÉ, Rolf, b. Stockholm 1888, d. Barcelona 1964. Swed. art patron. Founder of Les Ballets Suedois (q.v.) in 1920, and the Archives Internationales de la Danse, Paris (q.v.) in 1931. Among his many achievements, he first commissioned ballet scores from Poulenc, Auric, Milhaud and Honnegger, he first used Chirico to design a ballet, he got Bonnard to design Debussy's *Jeux*, he put on a negro ballet (*Création de Monde*) designed by Léger, and his *Relâche* was a Dada ballet devised and designed by Picabia and in cluded a René Clair film and music by Satie—a 'mixed media' entertainment of 1924.

DE MARIA, Warren, b. Sydney 1945. Pupil of Leonard, Pomié and Kellaway. Joined Borovansky B. 1959, and Australian B. 1962. To Royal B. Sch. 1963 and partnered Jane Landon in Royal B. Sch. perf. of *Sleeping Beauty* 1964. Member of Royal B. 1964–66 and returned to Australian B. 1966 as a principal.

DE MÉRODE, Cléo, b. Paris 1875, d. there 1966. Fr. dancer. Dancer at the Paris Opéra 1888–1900. A woman of great beauty and the toast of Paris in the 1900s. Her friendship with Leopold II of Belgium earned her the nickname 'Cléopolde'. Published *Le Ballet de ma Vie*, 1955. Danced at the Empire Th. Paris in 1924, partnered by Rupert Doone. The statue of Drama by Falguière in front of the Paris Opéra was a portrait but for reasons of prudery she claimed that it was her head added to the nude body of a professional model. She won the first beauty contest ever organized in Paris, in 1896. Because the hair-style of her period covered the ears, it was rumoured that she had no ears and an enterprising impresario once announced that on such-and-such a day 'Mlle de Mérode will show her ears'.

DEMI-CARACTÈRE DANCE, i.e. semi-character dancing. Carlo Blasis stated that the demi-caractère was 'a mixture of every style' whilst remaining 'noble and elegant but without grand temps of the serious kind': in other words, a dance retaining the form of the character dance but executed with steps based on the classical technique. An example is the rôle of the Street Dancer in *Le Beau Danube*.

DEMI-CARACTÈRE DANCER, a dancer specializing in or particularly suited by physical conformation to the demi-caractère style of dancing.

DEMI-CONTRETEMPS, a spring from one or both feet, extending one leg to the back in a low arabesque before passing it to the front in a chassé and so transferring the weight, or more simply a temps levé in arabesque and a chassé passé en avant, or alternatively, the dancer, with the left foot behind and pointed, jumps off the right foot bringing the left foot round in a small sweep to the front.

DEMI-COUPÉ, see COUPÉ.

DE MILLE, Agnes, b. N.Y. 1909. Am. dancer and chor. Daughter of Cecil B. de Mille. Studied under Kosloff, Winifred Edwards, and Rambert. In London B. cr. rôle in *Dark Elegies* (1937) and of *Venus* in *Judgement of Paris* (1938). Guest artist and chor. B. Russe de Monte Carlo, chor. *Rodeo* (1942); for Ballet Th. *Fall River Legend* (1948). Also chor. the dances in *Oklahoma!*, *Brigadoon*, *Carousel*, etc. Her autobiography, *Dance to the Piper*, published in England 1951, is a remarkable account of a dancer's life. Wrote its sequel *And Promenade Home* (1956), *To a Young Dancer* (1962), *The Book of the Dance* (1963). In 1965 was an original member of the American National Council on the Arts and chairman of its Dance Panel. In 1970 chor. *A Rose for Miss Emily* (m. Hovhaness) for Am. B. Th.

DEMI-POSITION, lit. a half position. Usually qualifies a position of the foot midway between 'on the ground' (à terre) and 'in the air' (en l'air).

DEMOISELLES DE LA NUIT, LES, ballet 3 sc., ch. Petit, m. Françaix, dec. Fini, f.p. B. de Paris, Th. Marigny 21 May 1948 (Fonteyn, Petit). A ballet about cats. Taken into Ballet Theatre repertoire 13 Apr 1951 (Marchand, Kriza).

DE MORODA, Friderica Derra, b. Pozsony 1897. Greek (now British) dancer, writer and teacher. Studied at the school of the Munich Opera, under Jakobleff in Riga and under Cecchetti and Nijinska. Danced in recitals in Riga 1911–13. To London 1913 and danced at the Alhambra and in many revues, musicals and the Palladium pantomime. Returned to Germany to teach. Produced the dances in *The Bartered Bride* for S. Wells B. One of the founders of the Cecchetti Society, translated Lambranzi in 1928. Co-author, with Margaret Craske, of *The Theory and Practice of Advanced Allegro* (1956) and many monographs on dance history. Chor. *Hungaria* for Markova-Dolin B. Since 1952 has had a school in Salzburg and has collected a famous library of books on ballet. Awarded O.B.E. 1974.

DENARD, Michaël, b. Dresden 1944. Fr. dancer. Pupil of Solange Golovine, Y. Brieux, Kalioujny and Franchetti. Joined Nancy B. 1962, soloist at Toulouse and joined Paris Opéra B. 1965, becoming premier danseur. Guest artist of Lacotte's B. National J.M.F. and of Béjart's Ballet du XXme Siecle. In 1970 created eponymous rôle in Béjart's *L'Oiseau de Feu* for the Paris Opéra (then at the Palais des Sports). Guest artist Am. Ballet Th. 1971. Promoted danseur étoile at Paris Opéra 1971. With Ghislaine Thesmar created the principal rôles in Lacotte's reconstruction of *La Sylphide* (m. Schneitzhoeffer) for French television in 1972 and at the Paris Opéra. Won Nijinsky Prize 1971.

DENBY, Edwin, b. China 1903. Am. ballet critic and poet. Studied ballet at Dalcroze Sch., Hellerau. Formerly critic of *N.Y. Herald Tribune*. Author of *Looking at the Dance* (1949), *Dancers, Buildings and People in the Streets* (1965).

DENHAM, Sergei, b. Moscow 1897, d. N.Y. 1970. Russ.-Am. banker who took over the B. Russe de Monte Carlo as Director when Massine left Col. de Basil in 1938 (see B. RUSSE DE MONTE CARLO). In 1954 he organized the Ballet Russe Sch. in N.Y., taking over the Swoboda-Yurieva Sch.

DENISHAWN, see ST DENIS, Ruth, and SHAWN, Ted.

DENMARK, BALLET IN, see under DANISH BALLET, ROYAL. Also see DANISH BALLET THEATRE.

DENYS, Maxine (Goldstein), b. Cape Town 1947. S. African dancer. Pupil of Berman and Royal B. Sch. Joined Royal B. 1964–67, Capab

Cape Town 1967 as ballerina B., PACT B. Jo'burg 1969. Returned to Royal B. 1972. Festival B. 1973.

DEPPISCH, Renate, b. Würzburg 1945. German dancer. Pupil of Munich Sch. and Blank, V. Gsovsky. Joined Munich B. To Düsseldorff B. 1964 becoming soloist. To Dortmund 1973.

DERAIN, André, b. Chatou 1880, d. Chambourcy 1954. Fr. painter and one of the originators of the 'Fauve' movement. His ballet designs include *La Boutique Fantasque* (1919), *Jack in the Box* (1926), *Concurrence* (1932), *Salade* (1935), *L'Épreuve d'Amour* (1936), *Harlequin in the Street* (1938), and *Mam'zelle Angot* (for S. Wells B. 1947).

DERMAN, Vergie, b. Johannesburg 1942. S. African dancer. Pupil of A. Dover and the Royal B. Sch. Joined Royal B. 1962. In 1966 joined the Berlin B. as soloist (when MacMillan was Director) and rejoined Royal B. as soloist 1967, principal 1972.

DERRIÈRE (Fr.) behind, or at the back.

DESCOMBEY, Michel, b. Bois-Colombes (Seine) 1930. Fr. dancer and chor. Pupil of Egorova and Ricaux at Paris Opéra. Joined Opéra corps de ballet 1947 and became premier danseur 1959. In 1963 he succeeded Skibine as maître de ballet. Chor. *Symphonie Concertante* (1962) and *Bacchus and Ariadne* (1964) etc. and many ballets for television. Director of Zürich B. 1970–72. Chor. *Violostries* (m. Erlih and Parmegiani) for Ballet Theatre Contemporain. Mar. Martine Parmain.

DESERTS, ballet, ch. Anna Sokolow, m. Varèse, f.p. Anna Sokolow Dance Co., N.Y. 10 Mar 1967. Taken into repertoire of B. Rambert, Jeannette Cochrane Th., London 25 July 1967. A ballet suggesting despair and loneliness.

DESHAYES, André Jean-Jacques, b. Paris 1777, d. Paris 1846. Fr. dancer and chor. whose father (Jacques-François Deshayes 1741–98) was Director of Paris Opéra Sch. 1780. First appeared in London 1800 in Dauberval's *Les Jeux d'Églé*. He danced in nearly every season at the King's Th. (later Her Majesty's), London, until 1842 and chor. many ballets there, notably *Masaniello* (1829), *Kenilworth* (1831), *Faust* (1833), *Le Brigand de Terracina* (1837). The first performance of *Giselle* in London (Her Majesty's Th. 12 Mar 1842) was produced by him in collaboration with Perrot. His wife, Mme Deshayes, was a famous dancer of the period. See also SYMPHONIC BALLET.

DESIGNS WITH STRINGS, ballet, ch. Taras, m. Tchaikovsky (Trio in A minor), dec. G. Kirsta (later, P. Williams) f.p. Metropolitan B., Edinburgh 6 Feb 1948 (Arova, Beriosova, Franca, Bruhn, David Adams). This ballet of pure dancing is now in many repertoires, including that of the R. Danish B. In France, called *Dessin pour les Six*.

DESPREAUX, Jean, b. Paris 1748, d. there 1820. Fr. dancer and poet. Danced at Paris Opéra, becoming maître de ballet after injuring his foot. Mar. Guimard, the ballerina, in 1789. He was an accomplished writer and poet of the ballet. In 1806 published *Mes Passe-Temps*, which includes a long poem on the dance, the notes of which are particularly valuable.

DESRAT, G. Fr., author of *Dictionnaire de la Danse*, Paris 1895. This is a useful but not very accurate work, with a preface by Ch. Nuitter, famous Librarian of the Paris Opéra, and has a useful bibliography on the Dance.

DESSOUS, lit. 'under', but in dancing indicates that a movement is to be executed so that the working foot passes behind the supporting foot, by contrast with 'dessus'.

DESSUS, lit. 'over', but in dancing indicates that a movement is to be executed so that the working foot passes in front of the supporting foot, in contrast with 'dessous'.

DÉTIRÉ, or LE PIED DANS LA MAIN (Fr. stretched out, or the foot in the hand), an exercise in which the dancer stands in fifth position and raises the right foot, sliding it up the front of the left leg, and seizes the sole of the foot with his right hand (which lies on the inside of the raised leg). Still holding the foot, the dancer raises it to the front, straightens the right leg and then opens it to the right side, flexing his left leg at the same time. The left leg is then straightened while the right foot is still held in the hand outstretched to the right. Also called Shouldering the Leg.

DETOURNÉ and DEMI-DETOURNÉ, swivelling step. In the *demi-detourné* the dancer makes a relevé in fifth position, turns towards the back foot and lowers into a demi-plié in fifth position with the other foot now in front and finishes facing back. In the *detourné*, as above but make a complete turn and finish facing front.

DEUIL EN VINGT-QUATRE HEURES, ballet 5 sc., ch. Petit, m. Thiriet, dec. Clavé, f.p. Petit's Co., Th. de l'Empire, Paris 17 Mar 1953 (Marchand, Lemoine, Perrault). A burlesque in music-hall style. It is also included in the film *Black Tights*.

DEUX PIGEONS, LES, ballet 3 acts, ch. Mérante, m. Messager, dec. Rubé, Chaperon, Lavastre, Bianchini, f.p. Paris Opéra 18 Oct 1886 (Mauri, Sanlaville, Mérante). Revived 1952 by Aveline. Based on La Fontaine's fable. Ch. Ashton, dec. Dupont, f.p. R. Ballet, C. Garden 14 Feb. 1961 (Seymour, Anderton, Gable).

DE VALOIS, Dame Ninette (Edris Stannus), b. Blessington, County Wicklow, Ireland 1898. Irish dancer and chor. Pupil of Espinosa and Cecchetti. Début in pantomime, Lyceum Th., London 1914, and appeared there as principal dancer until 1918. Principal dancer Beecham's Opera Co. 1918 and at C. Garden 1919. Danced with the Lopokova and Massine Cos. at C. Garden and Coliseum 1922. Joined Diaghileff's Co. 1923, becoming soloist until 1925, when she joined Dolin as his partner at Coliseum 1926. In C. Garden Opera again 1928, and became dance director Festival Th., Cambridge 1926, later of the Old Vic and the Abbey Th., Dublin. In 1926 founded her own school in London, the Academy of Choreographic Art, and she and her pupils put on ballets at the Old Vic. For her subsequent history see under ROYAL BALLET. Her ballets include: for the Camargo Society (1931) *La Création du Monde* and *Job*; for Sadler's Wells, *The Haunted Ballroom*, *The Rake's Progress*, *The Gods Go A-begging*, *Checkmate*, *Orpheus and Eurydice*, *The Prospect Before Us*, *Don Quixote*; for Ballet Rambert, *Bar aux Folies-Bergère*. She received the C.B.E. in 1947 and was created Dame of the British Empire 1951. Author of *Invitation to the Ballet* (1937), *Come Dance with Me* (1957). See also under TURKISH BALLET. She was the founder of the Royal Ballet, and with Marie Rambert, of the ballet in England. Mar. Dr A. Connell. She is also *Chevalier de la Legion d'Honneur* (1950) Hon.Mus.D. (London 1947), Hon.D.Litt.Mus. (Reading 1951), Hon.D.Litt. (Oxford 1955), Hon.D.Litt. (Sheffield 1955), Hon.D.Litt. (T.C. Dublin 1957), Hon.LL.D. (Aberdeen 1958). She retired as Director of the Royal Ballet in 1963 but continued to work at the Royal Ballet School until 1971 of which she is a life governor. She carries the title Founder of The Royal Ballet.

DEVANT, in front.

DÉVELOPPÉ or TEMPS DÉVELOPPÉ, lit. a developing movement. A movement which can be executed in various positions of the body, in which the turned-out thigh of the working leg is raised generally until it is at right angles to the body, with the toe in line with the knee-cap of the supporting leg (retiré), and then fully extended to the side (à la seconde), in front (à la quatrième devant), or to the back (à la quatrième derrière), whilst the arms open first to the front (fifth position) and then to the side (second position).

DEVIL IN THE VILLAGE, THE, ballet 3 acts, ch. Pia and Pino Mlakar, m. Lhotka, dec. Clemens and the Mlakars, f.p. Stadt-theater, Zürich 18 Feb 1935 (Panaieff and the Mlakars). A Yugoslav folk story.

DEVILLIER, Catherine, b. Moscow 1891, d. London 1959. Russ. dancer. Graduated in 1908 from Imp. Sch., Moscow, and was ballerina at the Bolshoi Th., Moscow 1909–19. Joined Diaghileff's Co. 1919 to 1922. To London 1936 and taught there until her death.

DE WARREN, Robert, b. Montevideo 1933. Eng. dancer. Pupil of Goncharov, Grigorieva and Royal B. Sch. 1957–58. Joined Nat. B. of Uruguay 1954, C. Garden Op. B. 1957, Royal B. 1958–60, Stuttgart B., 1960, Frankfurt B. 1962–64, Director of Nat. B. of Iran from 1968 to 1970. He then toured Persia studying their folk dancing and collecting dancers. In 1971 formed the Mahalli (q.v.) troupe of folk dancers (and is the director).

DIABLE AMOUREUX, LE, ballet 3 acts 8 sc., ch. Mazilier, m. Benoist and Réber, dec. Philastre, Cambon, cost. Lormier f.p. Paris Opéra 23 Sept 1840 (Noblet, Mazilier, Leroux). Based on a story by Cazotte.

DIABLE À QUATRE, LE, ballet 2 acts, ch. Mazilier, m. Adam, dec. Ciceri, Despléchin, Séchan, cost. Lormier, f.p. Paris Opéra 11 Aug 1845 (Grisi, Maria, Mazilier, Petipa). Romantic Ballet set in Poland.

DIABLE BOITEUX, LE, ballet 3 acts, ch. Coralli, m. Gide, dec. Feuchères, Séchan, Dieterlé, Philastre, Cambon, f.p. Paris Opéra 1 June 1836 (Elssler, Mazilier). This ballet contained the *cachucha*, a dance in which Elssler made a great reputation and introduced into other ballets.

DIAGHILEFF, Serge, b. Novgorod 1872, d. Venice 1929. Russ. connoisseur and impresario. Studied law in St Petersburg in 1890 and formed round him a circle of young artists (among them Benois, Bakst, Nouvel) with whom, in 1899, he founded *Mir Isskoustva* (*The World of Art*) a journal devoted to the arts, which lasted until 1904. In 1899 he was appointed by the director of the Imp. Th. (Prince Volkonsky) to edit their 1899–1900 Annals. Later he was entrusted with the production of *Sylvia*, but differences arose which caused him to resign in 1901. In 1906 he turned his attention to the west and in 1906 staged his first Paris exhibition of Russ. painting. This Diaghileff followed in 1907 with a season of Russ. concerts with the co-operation of such artists as Rimsky-Korsakov (whose pupil Diaghileff had been), Scriabin, Rachmaninov and Chaliapin. In 1908 he presented the last in *Boris Godunov*, which, although it only ran to eight performances, was sufficiently successful to warrant the presentation the following year of a season of opera and ballet directed by a committee which, under the general direction of Diaghileff, included Alexandre Benois as artistic director, Leon Bakst, N. Tcherepnin, conductor at the Maryinsky Th., and the critic Valerian Svetlov, with Michel Fokine as maître de ballet. The opening night at the Théâtre du Châtelet, Paris, on 18 May 1909, with Anna Pavlova, Tamara Karsavina, Bronislava Nijinska, Fokine, Bolm, Nijinsky, Mordkin and Novikov in a programme which included *Le Pavillon d'Armide* and *the Dances from Prince Igor*, marked the beginning of a revolution in Western theatrical art and particularly in the ballet. In that evening, the stultified tradition of dreary productions in several acts with ballerinas in classical tutus laden with jewellery, surrounded by danseuses travesties and a corps de ballet in pink point shoes and conventional dresses, were swept away by one-act ballets in which costumes, décor, music, lighting, dancing and mime formed a closely knit dramatic whole. Gone, too, were the realistic décors and hackneyed music subject to every whim of the chor., to be replaced by a riot of colour, now subtle, now daring, and music which could stand on its own merits, often that Russ. music with which Paris was only just beginning to be familiar. Production followed production and season followed season with *Les Sylphides, Cléopâtre, Schéhérazade, Carnaval, Firebird* (the as yet unknown Igor Stravinsky's first major work), *Petrouchka,* and *Le Spectre de la Rose.* Anna Pavlova and Ida Rubinstein broke away to follow their own paths, but other dancers, incl. Lydia Lopokova, took their places and the great Enrico Cecchetti took the teaching in hand. The year 1911 saw the consummation of the break with Russia, and the first London season at C. Garden and also marked the end of the first period with the resignation of Benois, who continued, however, an occasional collaboration in later years. Fokine, owing to differences over artistic policy, left the Diaghileff Co. in 1912, the year which saw the production of Nijinsky's *L'Après-midi d'un Faune,* followed in 1913 by *Jeux* and *Le Sacre du Printemps.* Consequent on Nijinsky's marriage and his estrangement from Diaghileff, Fokine returned for a time to produce a number of ballets, incl. *La Légende de Joseph,* in which a young dancer from the Bolshoi Th., Moscow, Leonide Massine, made his first appearance with the Co. Faced with the problem of carrying on during the war without Karsavina (who rejoined the Ballets Russes in 1919), Fokine, Benois, and many other of his artists who were caught in Russia, Diaghileff began to assemble a fresh company with Vera Nemchinova, Lydia Sokolova (née Hilda Munnings, the first Eng. ballerina to appear with the Russians), Leon Woizikovsky, Stanislas Idzikowsky, and, later, Olga Spessivtseva. A new era was dawning in which the Russ. ballet was no longer a novelty, and there began the long period of experiment and search for new forms. The blaze of colour of Bakst and the historical feeling of Benois gave way to the cool clear tones and the constructivism and cubism of Picasso, Matisse, Derain, and Marie Laurençin. The lyrical scores of Tcherepnin, Rimsky-Korsakov, and Glazunov were replaced by the subtle music of Poulenc, Auric, and Satie, whilst to Fokine succeeded Massine, Nijinska, and Balanchine. Serge Diaghileff's Ballets Russes had become cosmopolitan and eclectic. To this latter period belong *Parade, La Boutique Fantasque* and *Three Cornered Hat.* In 1921 the failure of the magnificent production of *The Sleeping Princess,* for which the Eng. audience was not yet ready, nearly spelt ruin, but Diaghileff marshalled his forces afresh to present Nijinska's ballets of manners, incl. *Les Biches* and *Le Train Bleu*. Balanchine, Danilova, de Valois, Dolin, Markova, and Lifar joined the company in this last stage. Diaghileff's death at Venice on 19 Aug 1929, left a stunned ballet world wondering how it could survive. In his lifetime Diaghileff had already become a legendary figure with an omniscient instinct for recognizing genius in embryo and bringing it to full flower by his readiness to consider new trends and new ideas, whilst still retaining all that was best in the traditions of the past. To commemorate the twenty-fifth year of his death, a remarkable Exhibition of the work of his collaborators was held at the Edinburgh Festival of 1954, organized by Richard Buckle. This was moved to Forbes House, Halkin Street, London, later in the year. In 1964 the Rue Bayard in Paris was renamed Rue Serge de Diaghilev and the entry to the rear of the Paris Opéra the Place Diaghilev. During 1968 and 1969 a number of auction sales were held at Sotheby's in London of designs and costumes of his ballets, when the high prices showed that interest in his work was still rising (the costumes were worn by students of the Royal Ballet School during the 1968 costume sale at the Scala Th. and also by dancers of Festival B. in 1969 at Drury Lane).

DIDELOT, Charles Louis, b. Stockholm 1767, d. Kieff 1837. Fr. dancer and chor. Pupil of Dauberval, Lany, Noverre, and Auguste Vestris at the Paris Opéra. Début there 1790, with Mlle Guimard. In 1796 produced his most famous ballet, *Flore et Zéphire*, at the King's Th., London, in which he introduced dancers made to fly with the aid of wires. He applied the principles of Noverre both as to costumes and composition. He is said to have introduced flesh-coloured tights for women dancers. From 1801 to 1811 he worked in St Petersburg as maître de ballet and chor. He mounted ballets in London and Paris during the next five years, and returned to St Petersburg in 1816, where he stayed for the rest of his life, producing a great number of ballets and reforming the teaching in the Imp. Schools. His work foreshadowed the Romantic Ballet. He married first Rose Paul or Pohl (d. 1803) and then Rose Colinette, a dancer from Paris popular in London who went to St Petersburg in 1799 and married him in 1807.

DIENES, Gedeon, b. 1914. Hungarian writer on ballet. Educated as a lawyer. Awarded Hungarian Order of Victory 1946. Author of *Reforms in the History of Ballet* 1958, *Reflections on Dance and Mime* 1960.

DIEU ET LA BAYADÈRE, LE, see BAYADÈRE.

DIEUX MENDIANTS, LES, see THE GODS GO A-BEGGING.

DIM LUSTRE, ballet 1 act, ch. Tudor, m. R. Strauss, dec. Motley, f.p.

B. Theatre. Met. Op., N.Y. 20 Oct 1943 (Nora Kaye, Hugh Laing). Nostalgic flirtations in a ballroom.

DINNER BALLET or INTERLUDE. In 1489, for the marriage at Tortona of Isabella of Aragon to Galeazzo Visconti, Duke of Milan, a dinner was arranged at which each dish was served with allegorical songs and dances in which the virtues of the young couple were unfolded. This set a fashion which was imitated in all the courts of Europe. The Dinner Ballet along with the mascarade and the disguising paved the way for the later court ballets.

DIONYSOS, ballet, ch. Cullberg, m. Karl-Birger Blomdahl, cost. Lennart Mörk. f.p. Oscarsteatern, Stockholm 1966 (Niklas Ek, Kari Sylwan, Karin Thulin, Björg Pahle, Juliet Fisher). About the god and the four elements.

DIRECTIONS. To ensure a proper sense of direction and to permit of some codification of movement in space, the acting area is broken up by numbering the corners of an imaginary square round the dancer and the centre of each side. There are several systems of numbering and that adopted in the Cecchetti method of teaching is shown in the illustration.

In practice these numerical systems are little used and the directions usually designated as in the plan.

For directions of the dancer's body, see under CROISÉ, DE FACE, ÉCARTÉ, and EFFACÉ. Directions of movement of the dancer on the stage are en descendant (from the back to the front of the stage), en reculant (from front to back of stage), en diagonale (diagonally across stage), and de côté (from one side to the other).

DIRTL, Willy, b. Vienna 1931. Austrian dancer. Studied in Vienna under Krausenecker, Fränzl, Hanka and Gordon Hamilton. Soloist Vienna Staatsoper 1950 and principal male dancer 1954–70.

DISGENOTEN, DE (The Family Circle), ballet, ch. van Dantzig, m. Bartok (*Concerto for Orchestra*), dec. van Schayk, f.p. Netherlands B. 19 June 1958. A boy becomes homosexual and is alienated from his family. Now in the repertoire of the Dutch Nat. B.

DISPLAY, THE, ballet, ch. Helpmann, m. Williamson, dec. Nolan, f.p. Australian B., Her Majesty's Th., Adelaide 14 Mar 1964 (Gorham, Welch, Lawrence, Kitcher). A lyre bird and an Australian picnic. This was Helpmann's first work for the Australian B.

DIVERSION OF ANGELS, ballet, ch. Martha Graham, m. Dello Joio, dec. Noguchi, f.p. Graham Co., Connecticut Coll., New London, 13 Aug 1948 (O'Donnell, Pearl Lang, Hawkins, Cohan, Hodes).

163

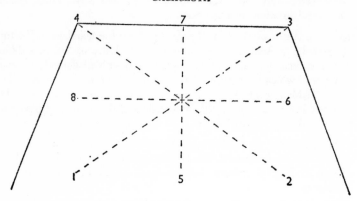

BACKCLOTH

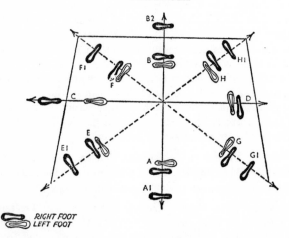

AUDIENCE

A.	De face	E1. Effacé or ouvert en avant
A1.	En avant	F. Facing effacé or ouvert
B.	De face	F1. Effacé or ouvert en arrière
B2.	En arrière	G. Facing croisé
C.	A la seconde or de côté	G1. Croisé en avant
D.	Facing de côté	H. Facing croisé
E.	Facing effacé or ouvert	H1. Croisé en arrière

Directions of the body and feet when using the right foot

About the beauty and pathos of youth. At its first perf. it was called *Wilderness Stair*.

DIVERSIONS, ballet, ch. MacMillan, m. Bliss, dec. Prowse, f.p. Royal B., C. Garden 15 Sept 1961 (Beriosova, Lane, Macleary, Usher). Abstract ballet.

DIVERSITIES, ballet, ch. Jonathan Taylor, m. Badings, dec. Koltai. f.p. B. Rambert, Richmond, Surrey 27 Jan 1965 (Lorraine, Willis, Bruce, Taylor). Electronic music and plastic cost. Taylor's first ballet.

DIVERTIMENTO, ballet 5 parts, ch. Balanchine, m. Haieff, no dec., f.p. Ballet Soc., Hunter Playhouse, N.Y. 13 Jan 1947 (Moylan, Moncion). Pure dancing.

DIVERTIMENTO NO. 15, see CARACOLE.

DIVERTISSEMENT, lit. a diversion. Originally the danced interlude in an opera but now designates a dance complete in itself executed by one or more persons. A series of divertissements inserted in a programme are sometimes described as the Grand Divertissement. The last act of *Coppélia* and the last scene of *The Sleeping Beauty* can be described as divertissements.

DIVINE HORSEMEN, THE, ballet, ch. Tudor, m. Egk, dec. Hugh Laing, f.p. Australian B., Her Majesty's Th. Sydney, 8 Aug 1969. Specially commissioned work.

DIXON, Norman, b. Northampton 1926. Eng. dancer and chor. Studied at Rambert sch. Joined B. Rambert 1949 and became a principal dancer 1953. Chor. many ballets for Sunday Ballet Club, London and Theatre in the Round, Croydon. Left B. Rambert 1958 to work in Portugal 1960, and later to South America, B. Minerva 1967–68, Chile 1968, Yugoslavia 1969 and from 1970 director of SODRE, the Nat. B. of Uruguay in Montevideo.

DOBOUJINSKY, Mstislav, b. Novgorod 1875, d. N.Y. 1957. Russ. painter. Designed dec. for *The Fairy Doll* (m. Bayer, ch. Clustine) for Pavlova 1915, *Casse Noisette* for Vic-Wells B. (1937), *Ballet Imperial* (1941), *Mlle Angot* (Massine 1943), *Graduation Ball* (1944), *Coppélia* (Rambert 1956), *Prisonnier du Caucase* (Cuevas 1951).

DOKOUDOVSKY, Vladimir, b. Monte Carlo 1922. Russ. dancer. Studied under Preobrajenska. Joined de Basil Co. 1935, Mordkin B. and B. Russe 1938–40, Orig. B. Russe 1942, in England 1947 and 1952. Now teaches in America. Mar. Nina Stroganova.

DOLGUSHIN, Nikita, b. Leningrad 1938. Russ. dancer. Trained under Pushkin at Kirov Sch. Leningrad and graduated to Kirov B. 1959. In 1961 he was appointed principal dancer of Novosibirsk B., one of the leading Russian companies (with 120 dancers and in the biggest opera house in Russia), with N. Alexandrova (q.v.). Joined Australian B. 1963 and Moiseyev's new chamber classical ballet 1967 for one season. Varna Gold Medal 1964. In 1969 he became a soloist of the Maly Th. Leningrad.

DOLIN, Anton (Patrick Healey-Kay), b. Slinfold 1904. Eng. dancer. Studied under Grace Cone and Astafieva. Joined Diaghileff's Co. 1921 (under the name Patrikéeff. He became Dolin in 1923). Rejoined as soloist 1924–25 and 1928–29. Cr. rôles in *Le Train Bleu*, *Le Bal*, etc. Danced in revues and films. Cr. rôle of Satan in *Job*, Camargo Soc. 1931. Danced with Vic-Wells B. during 1931–35. Formed Markova-Dolin Co. 1935–38. Cheif dancer in Am. Ballet Th. 1939–46. For this Co. he staged many of the classics and his influence on ballet in America has consequently been very great. In 1948 he returned to S. Wells B., with Markova, as guest artist. In 1949, with Markova, he re-formed a group in England which, in 1950, became the Festival Ballet. His partnership with Markova has been one of the outstanding features of contemporary classical ballet, while as a youth he was capable of remarkable acrobatic feats. In *Bluebeard* and *Vilia* he has shown himself a great comic dancer. Author of *Divertissement* (1931), *Ballet Go Round* (1938), *Pas de Deux* (1949), *Markova* (1953), *Anton Dolin* (1960), *The Sleeping Ballerina* (1966) about Spessivtseva whom he helped rehabilitate. Director of the Rome Opera B. 1962–64. Since then has mounted ballets all over the world. Chor. *Pas de Quatre* (m. Pugni) 1941, *Variations for Four* (m. Keogh) 1957 etc.

DOLLAR, William, b. St Louis 1907. Am. dancer and chor. Studied under Fokine, Mordkin. Member of Am. Ballet 1936–37, Ballet Caravan 1936–38, Ballet Th. 1940, etc. Chor. *Five Gifts* (1943), *Constantia* (1944), *The Duel* (1949), etc. Worked in Teheran 1956, for Th. d'Art du Ballet (Paris) 1964, and in Rio de Janeiro 1965.

DOMENICO DA FERRARA (also known as Domenico da Piacenza), d. 1462. It. dancing master and writer. He came from Piacenza and was dancing master at the court of the Marquis Leonello d'Este of Ferrara early fifteenth cent. He is the author of *Cavalier Piacentino*, the oldest treatise on the dance (fourteenth cent.) describing dances of the period and theorizing on the art. His work is mostly known from the writings of his pupils, Guglielmo Ebreo and Antonio Cornazano.

DOMINIQUE, Madame (Mlle Caroline Lassiat), b. c. 1820, d. 1885. Fr. dancer and famous teacher at the Paris Opéra 1853–79. Among her pupils were Livry, Bozzacchi, and Beaugrand.

DOÑA INES DE CASTRO, ballet, ch. Ricarda, m. Serra, dec. Celia Hubbard, f.p. de Cuevas Co., Th. Municipal, Cannes 1 Mar 1952 (Skibine,

Ricarda, Hightower). The grim story of Pedro of Portugal, in the Middle Ages, who crowns his dead lover as queen.

DONALD OF THE BURTHENS, ballet, ch. Massine, m. Whyte, dec. Mac-Bryde and Colquhoun, f.p. S. Wells B., C. Garden 12 Dec 1951 (Grey, Grant, Edwards). A Scots theme.

DONIZETTI VARIATIONS, ballet, ch. Balanchine, m. from Donizetti's *Don Sebastian*, dec. Hays, cost. Karinska, f.p. N.Y. City B., City Center, N.Y. 16 Nov 1960 (Hayden, Watts). Classical variations.

DON JUAN, ballet 3 sc., ch. Angiolini, m. Gluck (specially composed for this ballet), f.p. Burgtheater, Vienna 17 Oct 1761. In 1936 Fokine, using the same score, made a new *Don Juan* (dec. Andreu), f.p. Blum's Co., Alhambra Th., London 25 June 1936 (Vilzak, Jeannette Lauret, Eglevsky). Another version was chor. for the Vienna Staatsoper B. by R. Adama, dec. Colasanti and Moore, f.p. 26 May 1969 (Musil, Cech, Kirnbauer).

DON JUAN, ballet, ch. Ashton, m. R. Strauss, dec. Burra, f.p. S. Wells B., C. Garden 25 Nov 1948 (Fonteyn, Shearer, Helpmann).

DONN, Jorge, b. Buenos Aires 1947. Argentinian dancer. Pupil of Colon Th. Sch. Buenos Aires. Joined Colon B. and, in 1963, Béjart's Ballet du XXme Siècle, becoming soloist and cr. many rôles incl. Nijinsky in *Nijinsky, Clown de Dieu*.

DON QUICHOTTE (*Don Quixote*), ballet in 4 acts and 8 sc., ch. Petipa, m. Minkus, f.p. at the Bolshoi Th., Moscow 26 Dec 1869 (Sobesh-chanskaya, Sokolov). A revised version by the same chor. was presented at St Petersburg two years later and a new version chor. by A. Gorsky was presented in Moscow 6 Dec 1900, a version still in the Soviet repertoire. A shortened version, with ch. by L. Novikoff, was given by the Pavlova Company. The theme, taken from the novel by Cervantes, had tempted many earlier chors. incl. Noverre, Didelot, Milon, and Paul Taglioni. The Petipa version contains a number of fine classical soli and pas de deux. The National Ballet of Finland has a version, ch. Gé, dec. Nurmimaa, cost. Platonoff, f.p. Helsinki 6 Mar 1958 (Laine, Salin). The Grand Pas de Deux from *Don Quichotte*, often given as a divertissement, is usually the version by Oboukhoff. The current version of the Bolshoi Th. Moscow is that of Gorsky but revised by Zakharoff, f.p. 10 Feb 1940. The Gorsky and Zakharoff version was reproduced by Witold Borkowski for the Ballet Rambert, f.p. Empire Th., Liverpool, dec. Voytek, 28 June 1962 (Aldous, Chesworth, O'Brien). Nureyev mounted his own version, after Petipa, for the Vienna Staatsoper, f.p. 1 Dec 1966, dec. Kay (Wührer, Birkmeyer, Zajetz), and also for the Australian B., dec. Kay, Her Majesty's Th.,

Adelaide 28 Mar 1970 (Aldous, Nureyev, Helpmann). Borkowski also mounted it for Festival B., dec. Luzzatti, f.p. Coliseum, London 1 July 1970 (Samtsova, Prokovsky, Beaumont).

DON QUIXOTE, ballet 3 acts, ch. Balanchine, m. N. Nabokov, dec. E. Frances, f.p. N.Y. City B., N.Y. State Th., N.Y. 28 May 1965 (Farrell, Rapp, Lamont). The music is the first full-length ballet score to be written in America.

DON QUIXOTE, ballet 5 sc., ch. de Valois, m. Gerhard, dec. Burra, f.p. S. Wells B., C. Garden 20 Feb 1950 (Helpmann, Fonteyn, Grant).

DOR, Henriette, b. Vienna c. 1844, d. Neuilly-sur-Seine 1886. Fr. dancer. Ballerina at St Petersburg 1867–69, cr. chief rôle in Petipa's *Le Roi Candaule* (m. Pugni) at St Petersburg 29 Oct 1868.

DORATI, Antal, b. Budapest 1906. Hungarian conductor of B. Russe de Monte Carlo 1935–37. Original B. Russe 1938–41, Am. B. Th. 1941–45. He arranged the scores of *Graduation Ball, Bluebeard, Helen of Troy* and *Fair of Sorochinsk*.

DORIVAL, Anne-Marguerite, d. Marseilles 1788, Fr. dancer. Début at Paris Opéra 1773 with Paul Gardel. She was imprisoned on a *lettre de cachet* obtained by her maître de ballet, Gaetano Vestris. Her admirers then systematically booed Vestris until he obtained her release. She retired 1786.

DOUBLE WORK, movements when one dancer dances with or is supported by another. See also ADAGIO.

DOUGLAS, Scott, b. Texas 1927. Am. dancer. Pupil of Karma Deane and Christensen. Joined San Francisco B. 1946 and Ballet Th. in 1950, becoming soloist 1953, left in 1962. Toured with Robbins' Ballets, U.S.A. 1961, Dutch Nat. B. 1963, returned to Ballet Th. 1964. Artistic Director Nederlands Dans Th. 1969–70. Chor. *Twelve Dances* (m. Handel) 1970. For Hamburg B., *Die heile Welt* (m. Foss) 1972.

DOUTREVAL, André, b. Vienna 1942. Austrian dancer and chor. Entered Vienna Staatsoper B. Sch. 1950. Studied under Adèle Krausenecker and Gordon Hamilton. Joined the company 1956, then danced in Volksoper and Raimund Th., Vienna. To Klagenfurt 1959, Cologne 1961, soloist Bern 1962, Wuppertal 1963, Düsseldorf 1964–67. To Berlin Deutsche Oper B. 1967 as soloist. Frankfurt 1968 as assistant ballet master. Appointed ballet master Kassel 1970.

DOWELL, Anthony, b. London 1943. Eng. dancer. Pupil of the Hampshire Sch. and R. Ballet Sch. Joined C. Garden Opera B. 1960 and the Royal B. 1961 becoming soloist, and now one of the principal dancers. First solo rôle was for Sunday Ballet Club 1959 (in *English Measure* by

168

F. Worth). Cr. the Boy in *Shadowplay*, Oberon in *The Dream*, Troyte in *Enigma Variations*. Usually partners Antoinette Sibley. C.B.E. 1973.

DOYLE, Desmond, b. Cape Town 1932. S. African dancer. Pupil of Dulcie Howes 1946, becoming a member of Cape Town University B. Co. Joined Royal B. 1951, becoming soloist 1953 and ballet master 1970. Cr. rôle of the husband in *The Invitation* (1960).

DOZSA, Imre, b. Budapest 1941. Hungarian dancer. Studied at the Nat. B. Sch. Budapest and joined the Co. becoming soloist. Danced rôle of Colas in Ashton's *La Fille Mal Gardée* in 1971 in Budapest and also in 1972 for the R. Swed. B. in Stockholm.

DRAGADZE, Ivan, b. London 1932. Eng. dancer. Pupil of Goncharov, Newman, Volkova, Preobrajenska and S. Wells Sch. Joined S. Wells B. 1950, Scala B., Milan 1951, Festival B. 1952, Petit B. 1954, Cuevas B. 1955, Étoiles de Paris 1958, Edinburgh International Festival B. 1960, Massine B. 1961, Geneva B. 1962 and then freelancing with his wife Yvonne Meyer.

DRAMMA PER MUSICA, ballet, ch. Lifar, m. Bach, dec. Cassandre, f.p. Nouveau B. de Monte Carlo, Monte Carlo 2 May 1946 (Chauviré, Kalioujny, Trailine, Audran). Without Cassandre's décor it was revived at the Paris Opéra 28 June 1950 (Vyroubova).

DRAPER, Paul, b. Florence 1909. Am. tap dancer (nephew of Ruth Draper), who has danced all over the world and raised the status of his art by his skill and taste. Trained in classical ballet under Vilzak and Oboukhoff. His first performance as a tap dancer was in London 1932. One of his famous pieces is *Sonata for Tap Dancer*, without music.

DREAM, THE, ballet 1 act, ch. Ashton, m. Mendelssohn, dec. Bardon, cost. Walker, f.p. Royal B., C. Garden 2 Apr 1964 (Sibley, Dowell, Grant, Derman, Needham, Drew, Rencher). Ballet of *A Midsummer Night's Dream* cr. for the celebrations of Shakespeare's 400th anniversary. Also in repertoire of Touring Royal B. Oberon was Dowell's first created rôle for Royal B.

DREAM PICTURES, ballet 1 act, ch. Walbom, m. Lumbye, f.p. Royal Th., Copenhagen 15 Apr 1915. This ballet is inspired by Fokine's *Carnaval*.

DREW, David, b. London 1938. Eng. dancer and chor. Studied under Betty Vowles in Bristol and Royal B. Sch. Joined S. Wells B. 1955. Military service 1958 and rejoined Royal B. 1960 becoming soloist. Chor. *Intrusion* (m. Schubert) for Royal B. Sch. matinée 1968 (later taken into Touring Royal B.), *From Waking Sleep* (m. Hovhaness), Touring Royal B. 1970. Also chor. musical *Canterbury Tales* 1968.

DRIGO, Riccardo, b. Padua 1846, d. there 1930. It. composer, for many

169

years music director of the Imp. Theatres, St Petersburg, composing many ballets, notably *The Talisman* (Petipa 1889), *Harlequinade* (Petipa), *The Magic Flute* (Ivanov 1893). The Serenade from *Les Millions d'Arlequin* (Petipa 1900) is well known. See CORSAIR.

DROZDOVA, Margarita, b. Moscow 1948. Russ. dancer. Graduated from the Bolshoi Sch. 1967 and joined Stanislavsky-Nemirovitch-Danchenko Th. B. becoming soloist. Won Varna Silver Medal 1972. Danced in London in 1967 with the Young Stars of the Bolshoi B.

DROTTNEROVA, Marta, b. Gottwaldov 1941. Czech dancer. Pupil of E. Gerdt in Moscow 1962. Soloist Ostrava B. 1954–60. Principal dancer in Prague B. from 1961. Performed in Fonteyn's Gala, London 1963. Mar. J. Blažek. Gold Medal Varna 1966.

DRYAD, THE, ballet in 2 acts, ch. Alexandre Genée, m. Dora Bright, f.p. Empire Th. 7 Sept 1908 (Genée, Cleather). This was one of the best of the Empire ballets and one of Genée's most successful rôles. It was f.p. as an amateur production, Playhouse Th. London, 26 Mar 1907.

DUBREUIL, Alain, b. Monaco 1944. Monagasque dancer. Pupil of his mother, Susan Dubreuil 1956–59, Arts Educ. Sch. 1959–62 and of Addison, Hightower, Lander and Dolin. Danced with Irish Ballet in Dublin in 1962 and then joined Festival B. 1962, becoming soloist 1964 and principal 1968. Mar. Gillian Shane. To Royal B. 1973.

DUBROVSKA, Felia, b. 1894. Russ. dancer. Graduated from Maryinsky Sch. St Petersburg 1913 and joined Co. Left Russia 1920 and joined Diaghileff B. 1921. Danced in the 1921 *Sleeping Princess* in London and created principal rôles in *Les Noces*, *Les Biches*, *Gods Go a-Begging* and *Prodigal Son*. Became ballerina of Met. Op. B. and a teacher in America (Sch. of Am. B.). Mar. P. Vladimiroff.

DUDINSKAYA, Natalia, b. Kharkoff 1912. Russ. dancer. Entered Petrograd Sch. 1923, graduated 1931 after studying under Vaganova, of whose style she was the personification. Promoted to ballerina in 1932. Cr. chief rôles in *Flames of Paris* (1932), *Lost Illusions* (1938), *Gayané*, *Bronze Horseman*, *Laurencia* (1939) etc. She was one of the greatest of the Kirov ballerinas of recent times and since 1951 she has taken the Class of Perfection of the Kirov B. and is principal ballet mistress. She was the first to dance *Cinderella* in Leningrad and was Carabosse in the film of *Sleeping Beauty* (1964). Stalin Prizewinner 1941, 1947, 1949, 1954. People's Artist of U.S.S.R. 1957. Mar. Sergeyev. After Makarova's defection in 1970 she taught the children's class. Order of the Red Banner 1973.

DUDLEY, Jane, b. N.Y. 1912. Am. dancer and teacher. Pupil of Hanya

Holm, Graham. In Martha Graham Co. 1942–54 and has taught ever since. Chor. *Family Portrait* 1954. Artistic director of Batsheva Co. 1964–70. In 1971 came to teach at the London Cont. Dance Sch.

DU MAINE, DUCHESSE, THE, the illegitimate daughter of Louis XIV, who gave at her château at Sceaux in 1708–15 sixteen fêtes. In the 14th (in Jan. 1715), a mimed scene from Corneille's *Les Horaces* was given by the professional dancers M. Balon and Mlle Prevost. This has been called the first *ballet d'action*.

DUMILÂTRE, Adèle, b. Paris 1821, d. there 1909. Fr. dancer, début Paris Opéra 1840 and danced there until 1848. She created the rôle of Queen of the Wilis in *Giselle* and of the statue in *The Marble Maiden* by Saint-Léon (London 1845). Her elder sister, Sophie, was also a dancer.

DUNCAN, Irma (Irma Ehrich-Grimme), b. near Hamburg 1897. German dancer. Pupil of Isadora Duncan's school in Berlin and first appeared on stage with her at the Kroll Op. House, Berlin 1905. One of the founders of the Duncan School in Moscow 1921 and became its principal after Isadora died in 1927. Became Am. citizen 1935 and since then has taught and painted. With Allan Ross MacDougall wrote *Isadora Duncan's Russian Days* 1929. Also *The Technique of Isadora Duncan* 1937 and *Duncan Dancer* 1966.

DUNCAN, Isadora, b. San Francisco of Irish parents 1878, d. Nice 1927. Am. dancer. She was never formally trained, but she evolved her own dances and her own philosophy. Her dancing was essentially of the modern school, of which she was a pioneer in that she saw in danced movement the expression of the mind, and she was strongly opposed to the classical ballets. Her influence on ballet costume was as great as on movement for she discarded the traditional tutu and point shoes for flowing draperies and danced in bare feet, and she was the first dancer to appear without tights on the stage. After an unsuccessful début in Chicago in 1899 she came to Paris in 1900, where she was successful and she opened a school in Berlin in 1904 after dancing all over Europe. In 1905 (and again in 1908 and 1912) she visited Russia and her influence on Fokine is often debated, but it seems certain that whilst he undoubtedly saw much to admire in her work there was also much with which he disagreed, and his ideas had been promulgated in a memorandum to the Imp. Th. before he could have seen her. Duncan established a school in Russia in 1921 and schools in France and America, but none of them survived her death. Her autobiography (up to 1921), *My Life*, was published in 1928. There was a sudden resurgence of interest in her in 1968, and in 1969 a film of her life, *Isadora*, was made with Vanessa Redgrave in the title-rôle.

DUNHAM, Katherine, b. Chicago 1912. Am. dancer and chor. Ph.D. and M.A. Chicago Univ. Danced in Ruth Page's Martinique B. Did research in Caribbean Islands 1937–38. Chor. of several revues. Formed her own Co. with which she has toured Am. and Europe. Author of *The Dances of Haiti, A Touch of Innocence* (1959). Chor. most of the ballets in her repertoire: *Shango, L'Ag'ya, Choros*, etc. Mar. John Pratt who designs her scenery and cost.

DUPONT, Jacques, b. Chatou 1909. Fr. designer. Made cost. and dec. for *Les Indes Galantes* (prologue, finale) 1952 and *La Dame aux Camélias* (m. Sauguet) 1960 for Paris Opéra, *Faust* and *Carmen* for Met. Op. N.Y., *Daphnis and Chloé* (ch. Skibine) for Frankfurt, *The Two Pigeons* (ch. Ashton) 1961 for Royal B., *Carmen* (ch. Cranko) for Stuttgart B. 1971, *Romeo and Juliet* (ch. Skibine) for Colon Th., Buenos Aires 1970 and B. de Wallonie 1972 etc.

DUPORT, Louis (the 'American' Duport), b. c. 1781. The putative son of Pierre Landrin Duport (b. Paris 1762–63, d. Washington 1841, French dancing master) went to America in 1790 with his father. He became a well-known dancer there. Nothing more is heard of him after a performance in Savannah in 1796. It has been suggested that he and Louis Antoine Duport (vid. inf.) were the same person. Lillian Moore discusses the slender evidence for this in her monograph *The Duport Mystery* (*Dance Perspectives* No. 7, 1960).

DUPORT, Louis Antoine, b. Paris 1786, d. Paris 1853. Fr. dancer. After making a great success at the Paris Opéra, being Auguste Vestris's chief rival (*'Vestris a fait naufrage en approchant du port'*), he arrived in Russia in 1808, where he caused a sensation dancing in Didelot's ballets. He seduced Danilova in 1808, left Russia 1812, and made his London début 1819. Having amassed a great fortune, he retired.

DUPRÉ, Louis, b. Rouen 1697, d. Paris 1774. Fr. dancer who taught Noverre. Called 'Le Grand Dupré', he danced in Weaver's *Loves of Mars and Venus*, London 1717. He was a very fine looking man and was principal dancer at the Paris Opéra from 1715 to 1751. He was head of the ballet school until 1743 and J. G. Noverre and G. Vestris were among his pupils. He published a textbook on dancing in 1743.

DUSE, Riccardo, b. Rome 1937. Swiss dancer and ballet master. Pupil of his mother, Dousse, Kniaseff and Zvereff. Joined the Scala, Milan B. then dell'Ara's Balletto Italiano and was soloist of the Nederlands B. Soloist at Cologne 1961–66, N.Y. City B. and from 1968 to 1972 soloist in Frankfurt. In 1972 became ballet master at Lucerne. Mar. Reka Tobias.

DUTCH NATIONAL BALLET (Het Nationale Ballet), based on the Stadsschouwburg Amsterdam, was formed in the autumn of 1961, with Sonia Gaskell as director. Previously there had been a series of companies in Holland, starting with Yvonne Georgi's group in 1936 (from 1938 called Georgi Ballet). This group became the ballet of the Amsterdam Municipal Opera in 1941 and among its dancers were Mascha Ter Weeme, Marie-Jeanne van der Veen, Nel Roos and Lucas Hoving. The Co. was much reduced when the Amsterdam Opera was reorganized in 1946. It included Nel Roos, Max Dooyes—and Darja Collin (who later had a school in Florence) directed it from 1949. She was succeeded by Françoise Adret 1951–58. In 1947 a new Co., Ballet Der Lage Landen was formed with Mascha Ter Weeme as director. In 1958 Sonia Gaskell (who had a group Ballet Recital) was made director of a new Co., Het Nederlands Ballet, in The Hague, with Benjamin Harkarvy and Karel Shook as ballet masters. In 1959 Harkarvy resigned and took some of the dancers to form Het Nederlands Dans Theater (q.v.). This Co. went to The Hague in 1961.

The Amsterdam Opera Ballet and the Ballet Der Lage Landen combined in 1959 to form the Amsterdams Ballet, with Mascha Ter Weeme as director—and in turn the Amsterdams Ballet combined with Het Nederlands Ballet to form the Dutch National Ballet in 1961.

The Co. has over 80 dancers and a very large, eclectic repertoire ranging from the classics to the most modern styles with electronic music. In 1968 Sonia Gaskell retired and was succeeded by Rudi Van Dantzig and Robert Kaesen as joint directors. In 1970 Kaesen resigned and Harkarvy took his place but he also left in 1971. The Co. tours Holland (by coach, always returning to Amsterdam) and abroad. Its first visit to England was in 1969, to Sunderland and later to Sadler's Wells. In 1970 the leading dancers were Maria Bovet, Jessica Folkerts, Olga de Haas, Maria Koppers, Sonja Marchiolli, Helène Pex, Yvonne Vendrig, Simon André, Sylvester Campbell, Toer van Schayk, Istvan Matula, René Vincent, Robert Fisher.

DUVERNAY, Pauline, b. Paris 1813, d. Lynford, Norfolk 1894. Fr. dancer. Studied at Paris Opéra Sch. under Barrez, Auguste Vestris, Coulon, and F. Taglioni. Début at Opéra 1831 in *Mars et Vénus*. In 1831 made unsuccessful début in London, Drury Lane, in Aumer's *Belle au Bois Dormant*, but later became very popular in Paris and London (she was Thackeray's favourite dancer), especially for her *Cachucha* from *Le Diable Boiteux* (Elssler's great dance). Retired 1837 at the height of her fame. She was an extremely beautiful girl, delicate, and something of a wit. In 1835, after an unhappy love affair, she attempted suicide, but in 1845 she married a wealthy Englishman who

173

died in 1860 leaving her over a million pounds. She built a large house, Lynford Hall in Mundford, Norfolk, and devoted the rest of her life to the Roman Catholic Church, building the pro-cathedral at Cambridge and endowing a priest to live at Lynford and say masses for her (which is still being done). She left over £600,000 to charities and some pictures to the National Gallery. She is buried at Roehampton.

DVOŘÁK VARIATIONS, ballet, ch. Hynd, m. Dvorak, dec. Docherty, f.p. Festival B., Theatre Royal, Nottingham 30 Mar 1970 (Samstsova, Prokovsky). Without a story but traces of folk dance in the choreography. Also in repertoire of Munich B. and Festival B.

DYING SWAN, THE, see LE CYGNE.

DYNALIX, Paulette, b. Grenoble 1917. Fr. dancer. Studied at Paris Opéra under Zambelli, entering the company 1931. Promoted première danseuse 1943. She was the youngest of all the Opéra Giselles, which she first danced at the age of 19. At the Opéra she was the last to play the *travesti* rôle of Frantz in *Coppélia*. Awarded the Palmes Academiques 1955. Retired as a dancer 1957. Teaches privately in Paris. In 1967 she came to London to teach the old Opéra version of *Coppélia* to Ballet for All.

DYNASTIES of dancers. In the history of ballet there have been many famous families of dancers, the most notable being the Vestris family, the Taglioni, the Bournonville, the Coulon, the Price, the Petipa, the Espinosa, and the Schwarz, all to be found under the appropriate entries.

E

EAGLING, Wayne, b. Montreal 1950. Canad. dancer. Pupil of Patricia Webster and Royal B. Sch. Joined Royal B. 1969 and became soloist 1972.

EARLY, Fergus, b. Worthing 1946. Eng. dancer and chor. Pupil of Royal B. Sch. and joined Touring Royal B. 1964. From 1963 he was prominent in Balletmakers Ltd (q.v.) and chor. several ballets for them. Joined Ballet for All group, becoming a ballet master and chor. for them *A Yorkshire Marriage* (m. Hewson, poetry Derek Parker) 1966 and *The Twelfth Rose* (m. Hewson) 1969.

EARLY SONGS, ballet, ch. Feld, m. R. Strauss, cost. Simmons, f.p. Am. Ballet Co., Brooklyn Acad. of Music, Brooklyn 2 Apr 1970 (Sarry, Feld, Stirling, Munro, Sowinski). Interpretations of the *Four Early Songs*, sung by three singers.

EATERS OF DARKNESS (*Die im Schatten Leben*), ballet, ch. Gore, m. Britten (*Variations of a theme of Frank Bridge*), dec. Heckroth, f.p. Frankfurt Ballet, Opera House, Frankfurt 29 Jan 1958 (Hinton, Herbinger, Wolfgang Winter). A sane woman imprisoned in a lunatic asylum becomes insane. Also given at Edinburgh Festival, Empire Th. 14 Aug 1961 (Hinton) by Gore's London B. Was also danced by Am. Festival B. (Christine Hennessy) in Europe.

EBBELAAR, Han, b. Hoorn 1943. Dutch dancer. Pupil of Dooyes and Harkarvy. Joined Nederlands Dans Th. on its formation in 1959 becoming principal dancer 1961. Joined Am. Ballet Th. 1968 becoming a principal 1969. To Dutch Nat. B. as principal 1970. Mar. Alexandra Radius.

EBONY CONCERTO, ballet, ch. Taras, m. Stravinsky, dec. Hays, f.p. N.Y. City B., City Center, N.Y. 7 Dec 1960 (McBride, Mitchell). This was Part 3 of an entertainment *Jazz Concert*. The other items were *Creation of the World* (Milhaud, ch. Bolender), *Les Biches* (Poulenc, ch. Moncion) and *Ragtime* (Stravinsky, ch. Balanchine). The music was first used by A. Carter for *Feuilleton*, Munich 28 Aug 1957.

EBREO, Guglielmo, see GUGLIELMO EBREO.

ÉCART, LE GRAND, the splits (q.v.). For écart en l'air, see CISEAUX, PAS. The Italian is 'spaccata'. German 'spagat'.

ÉCARTÉ, lit. separated or spread. A position of the body, oblique to the audience, in which the arm and the leg, on the ground or raised nearest to the audience, are extended on the same vertical and diagonal

Écarté Position

plane as the rest of the body. The other directions of the dancer are 'de face', 'croisé', and 'effacé'.

ÉCHAPPÉ or PAS ÉCHAPPÉ, lit. an escaping or releasing step. A spring into the air from the fifth position, alighting toes first with feet in the second position (échappé à la seconde) or in the fourth position (échappé à la quatrième); also a springing movement from the fifth position on to the points or half points in the second position (échappé sur les pointes). The step can also be done en croix. An *échappé battu* has the beat of an entrechat quatre, landing in second position, and can be closed with the same foot in front with the beat of an entrechat quatre, or the other foot in front with the beat of changement battu.

ÉCHELLE, L', ballet, ch. Dick Sanders, m. Turjak, dec. Ganeau, f.p. Miskovitch Co., 17 Apr 1957 (Beaumont, Sparemblek, Sulich). A murder re-enacted in three ways, as in the film *Rashomon*.

ÉCHO (Fr.), the solo of a dancer in the course of a choreographic ensemble at the Paris Opéra. Another term for Variation.

ECHOING OF TRUMPETS (sometimes erroneously called *Echoes of Trumpets*), ballet, ch. Tudor, m. Martinu (*Fantaisies Symphoniques*), dec. Bergling, f.p. R. Swedish B., Stockholm 20 Sept 1963 (Gerd Andersson, Lindberg, Annette av Paul, Kari Sylwan, M. Mengarelli). The horrors of war and the crimes committed by occupying forces, inspired by events in Lodz in the Second World War. Also performed by Met. Op. B. 1966, Am. Ballet Th. 1968 and by Festival B., Coliseum, London 27 Apr 1973 (Gaye Fulton, Freya Dominic, Diane Hunwin, Alexandra Pickford, Margareet Sietsma, Vivien Loeber, Valerie Aitken, D. von Loggenburg, Alain Dubreuil).

ECK, Imre, b. Budapest 1930. Hungarian dancer and chor. Pupil of Nadasi, joined Hungarian Nat. B. 1946 becoming soloist. In 1960 he was appointed to form a company in Pècs, the Ballet Sopianae (q.v.) of, which he was principal dancer, director and chor. Eck's first ballet was *Csongor and Tunde* (m. Weiner, for Nat. B. at the Budapest Opera 1959). He also chor. *Sacre du Printemps* (m. Stravinsky) for the Opera 1962. See BALLET SOPIANAE for his ballets for that company. He retired as director 1969, becoming chief choreographer.

ÉCOSSAISE. A dance in 2/4 time which enjoyed considerable popularity in the nineteenth century, although it would seem to have been known before that. Historians are now generally agreed that it is not of Scottish origin and perhaps the French name can be taken to indicate that it was evolved in the French ballroom. Although similar to the English country dances it is executed to a faster tempo.

ÉCUYÈRE, L', ballet, ch. Lifar, m. Kosma, dec. Nepo, f.p. at Chauviré

Recital, Salle Pleyel, Paris 21 Feb 1948 (Chauviré, Renault, Bozzoni). Circus life.

EDINBURGH INTERNATIONAL COMPANY, formed by Peggy van Praagh for the Edinburgh Festival of 1958. It presented twelve new ballets during the three weeks at the Empire Th., chor. by Cranko, Skibine, Alan Carter, Parlic, Cullberg and others and danced by Carla Fracci, Kirsten Simone, Marjorie Tallchief, David Poole, Gerard Ohn, Heino Hallhuber, George Skibine and others. Its most notable production was *The Night and Silence* by Walter Gore, danced by Paula Hinton and David Poole. An attempt to keep the company together after the Festival failed.

EDOUARDOVA, Eugenia, b. St Petersburg 1882, d. N.Y. 1960. Russ. dancer and teacher. Graduated from Maryinsky Sch. 1901 and danced with the company until 1917, when she left Russia. Danced with Pavlova in London and on tour with her. Settled in Berlin in 1920 and married Joseph Lewitan ballet critic and editor of *Der Tanz*. From 1920 to 1935 she had her own school in Berlin and was the principal teacher there. Went to live in Paris with her husband in 1935 and then to N.Y. in 1947.

EDWARDS, Leslie, b. Teddington 1916. Eng. dancer. Studied with Rambert and later with Craske, Idzikowsky and Volkova. Début with S. Wells B. 1933. Danced with B. Rambert 1935–37. Returned to S. Wells B. and became a principal mime and character dancer, creating many rôles (the king in *Donald of the Burthens* and in *Prince of the Pagodas*, Thomas in *Fille Mal Gardée*) and was a famous Catalabutte in *Sleeping Beauty*. Guest teacher and director Washington B. 1962. Now a *regisseur* of the Royal B. and from 1967 in charge of the Royal B. Choreographic Group.

EDWARDS, Winifred (Vera Fredowa), b. London 1895. Eng. dancer and teacher. Pupil of Miss Hutton Moss, Freda Grant, Cormani, Mossolova, Cecchetti, Clustine. Member of Pavlova's company 1912–16, Theodore Kosloff's Co. 1916–19 and partner in his schools in S. Francisco and Dallas 1919–34. Teacher at Royal B. Sch. 1947–55 and teacher for R.A.D. 1947–63. Now teaches privately.

EFFACÉ. A position of the body, legs, and head oblique to the audience, from whom the body is partly turned away, with the leg furthest from the audience extended to the fourth position front on the ground or in the air. (See also DE FACE, CROISÉ, ÉCARTÉ.) The word *ouvert* is sometimes used in the same sense.

EFIMOFF, Nicholas, Russ. dancer who came to Western Europe with Balanchine, Danilova, and Gevergeva in 1924 and was engaged at once

177

Effacé Position

by Diaghileff. Later he joined the Paris Opéra, becoming premier danseur and eventually their principal mime.

EGK, Werner, b. Auchesheim 1901. German composer. Wrote music for many German ballets incl. *Joan von Zarissa* (1940), *Abraxas* (1948), *Chinese Nightingale* (1950), *Französischer Suite* and *Casanova in London* (1969).

EGLEVSKY, André, b. Moscow 1917. Russ. dancer brought up in France, and Am. citizen since 1939. Studied in Nice with Nevelskaya, in Paris with Egorova, Volinine, Kschessinska, in London with Nicholas Legat. Joined de Basil's B. Russes in 1931. Principal dancer in B. Woizikovsky 1935, René Blum's B. 1936, B. Theatre 1942 and 1945, B. International 1944, Orig. B. Russe 1946, de Cuevas 1947, N.Y. City B. 1951–58. Cr. rôles in *L'Épreuve d'Amour, Helen of Troy*, etc. Chor. *Colloque Sentimentale*. Partnered Melissa Hayden in Chaplin's film *Limelight* 1952. Has his own group of dancers and school and teaches at Sch. of Am. B. His daughter Marina E. (b. 1951) is a dancer (Harkness B. Am. Ballet Theatre and Hamburg B. 1973).

EGOROVA, Lubov (Princess Trubetskoy), b. St Petersburg 1880, d. Paris 1972. Russ. dancer, graduated from Imp. Sch. 1898, created ballerina 1914. To Paris 1917, ballerina in Diaghileff's Co. Danced Fairy of Song Birds in 1921 London production of *Sleeping Princess* and later Princess Aurora. Had a famous sch. in Paris 1923–68. Organized Ballets de la Jeunesse 1937. Also taught in Copenhagen and mounted

Aurora's Wedding for Royal Danish B. and took classes for the International B. in London. Retired 1968.

EGRI, Susanna, b. Budapest 1926. Hungarian dancer and teacher. Pupil of Nadasi in Budapest. To Italy 1947. Gave recitals, opened Dance Study Centre in Turin 1953 and chor. for Italian theatres, television etc. With her own group toured Germany and Denmark 1957. One of the principal teachers in Italy.

EK, Niklas, b. Stockholm 1943. Swed. dancer, son of Birgit Cullberg. Pupil of Donya Feuer, Juliet Fisher and Lilian Karina and studied with Cunningham in N.Y. 1963. Leading soloist in the Cullberg B. creating many of the rôles. Joined Ballet du XXme Siècle 1972.

ÉLANCÉ, lit. darting. A darting movement.

ELEKTRA, ballet, ch. Helpmann, m. Arnold, dec. Boyd, f.p. Royal B., C. Garden 26 Mar 1963 (Nerina, Mason, Blair).

ÉLÉMENTS, LES, ballet, ch. Perrot, m. Bajetti, f.p. Her Majesty's Th., London 26 June 1847 (Grisi, Rosati, Cerrito). Fokine also produced a ballet of this name for Blum's Co., m. Bach, dec. Bouchène, f.p. Alhambra Th., London 1 Apr 1937 (Theilade, Youskevitch).

ELEVATION, term applied to all aerial movements as opposed to terre à terre movements in which the feet barely leave the ground. Nijinsky, who was possessed of phenomenal elevation, was (erroneously) said to have had the power to remain at the highest point of ascent for a fraction of a second before he descended (a physical impossibility). Whilst there are countless testimonies of Nijinsky's prowess, there are none to Gaetano Vestris's claim that 'If my son (Auguste Vestris) ever comes to earth it is only out of courtesy to his colleagues!'
  Elevation is also applied to the point attained in a dancer's leap or jump. In the Modern Dance the term is also applied to the 'pull up' of the muscles of the abdomen and the general stance when a dancer is erect.

ELFES, LES, ballet 3 acts, 4 sc., ch. Mazilier, m. Gabrielli, dec. Despléchin, Nolau, Rube, Thierry, and Martin, f.p. Paris Opéra 11 Aug 1856 (Ferraris, Marquet, Petipa). In this ballet Amalia Ferraris made a sensational début in Paris. Fokine made a ballet of this name for his own Co. (m. Mendelssohn) Met. Op. N.Y. 26 Feb 1924. Revived with dec. Bérard for Blum's B. Russe 1937 and also in repertoire of Théâtre d'Art du Ballet, Paris.

ELIASEN, Johnny, b. Copenhagen 1949. Dan. dancer. Pupil of R. Dan. B. Sch. but joined Scandinavian B. 1964 as soloist. Joined R. Dan. B. 1967 becoming solodancer 1972.

ELLIS, Angela, b. London 1920, daughter of Marie Rambert. Eng. dancer

179

and teacher. Pupil of Rambert, Volkova, Craske. Joined Pomeroy's
Opera B. 1942, B. Rambert 1943. Taught in Bogota 1949–50. Director
of Ballet Workshop 1951–55. From 1950 associate director (director
from 1966) and teacher of Rambert Sch.

ELSSLER, Fanny, b. Vienna 1810, d. there 1884. Austrian dancer. She
was one of the very great dancers in the history of ballet and the rival
of Taglioni. Her father was Haydn's copyist and the composer be-
queathed money to him which enabled her and her elder sister Thérèse
to learn dancing in Vienna and from Aumer. In 1818 she entered the
corps de ballet of the Hoftheater, Vienna, where she gained her first
stage experience. The impresario Barbaja engaged her to dance in
Naples 1824–27. She had a son by the Prince of Salerno. Returning to
Vienna she became the mistress of Friedrich von Gentz and her name
was romantically linked with the Duke of Reichstadt, although in fact
they never met. In 1833 she and her sister danced at the King's Th.,
London, and in 1834 Dr Véron engaged her for the Paris Opéra. After
her début in Coralli's *La Tempête*, Gautier wrote his famous article
comparing her with Taglioni, 'Taglioni is a Christian dancer—Elssler
a pagan', etc., and Paris was divided into Taglionists and Elsslerites.
When Taglioni left for St Petersburg in 1837, Elssler remained the chief
dancer at the Opéra and rashly and unsuccessfully essayed some of her
rival's rôles, notably *La Sylphide*. From 1840 to 1842 she toured
America with astounding success, being received by the President
van Buren and having triumphs everywhere. There is a legend that on
the voyage she was attacked in her cabin by a sailor who had come to
rob her. She dealt him such a kick that he died a few days later. From
1843 she danced all over the world (except in Paris, to which she never
returned) and after some triumphant seasons in Russia she retired at
the age of 41, her last performance being in Vienna in 1851. She was
essentially a terre à terre dancer (unlike Taglioni who excelled in aerial
movements) and her greatest success lay in her introduction of national
character dances into ballet. Her two most famous dances were the Sp.
Cachucha in Coralli's *Diable Boiteux* (taught her by Dolores Serral)
and the Polish *Cracovienne* in Mazilier's *La Gipsy*. As a dramatic
ballerina she had no equal. Her interpretation of *Giselle* was one of the
very greatest.

Her sister Thérèse (b. Vienna 1808, d. Merano 1878) was tall for a
dancer in those days (5 ft 6 in, 168 cms) and her career was less successful than Fanny's, but she was a very well-known dancer in Europe and
often partnered, *en travesti*, her sister. In 1850 she became the mor-
ganatic wife of Prince Adalbert of Prussia with the title of Freifau von
Barnim, and retired from dancing.

ELVIN, Violetta (née Prokhorova), b. Moscow 1924. Russ. dancer. Studied under Vaganova at Bolshoi Sch. Graduated 1942. Ballerina State Th., Tashkent 1943. Rejoined Bolshoi Co. at Kuibyshev 1944, becoming soloist on return to Moscow. To England 1945. Joined S. Wells B. 1946 becoming one of the ballerinas. Guest artist Scala, Milan 1952, 1953, Copenhagen 1954, S. America 1955, Stockholm 1956, and appeared in several films. Retired 1956 to live in Italy.

ELVIRE, ballet, ch. Aveline, m. Scarlatti-Manuel, dec. Sigrist, f.p. Paris Opéra 8 Feb 1937 (Darsonval, Peretti).

EMBATTLED GARDEN, ballet, ch. Graham, m. Surinach, dec. Noguchi. f.p. Graham Co., Adelphi Th., N.Y. 3 Apr 1958 (Turney, Yuriko, Ross, Tetley). A satire on the Garden of Eden.

EMBLEN, Ronald, b. Port Said 1933. Eng. dancer. Pupil of Northcote, Volkova and Royal B. Sch. 1948–51. Joined International B. 1951, Gore's B. 1954, Festival B. 1954, Western Th. B. 1959, rejoined Festival B. 1960 and Royal B. (Touring) 1962 as soloist, becoming principal.

EMBOÎTÉ or PAS EMBOÎTÉ, lit. an interlocked step. As a very general definition, may be described as a series of steps in which the legs are moved as in plaiting, with the feet interlocking. There are, however, a large number of different steps known incorporating this term, e.g. grand emboîté, emboîté en tournant, emboîté sur les pointes etc. If an emboîté sur les pointes is executed en arrière it is called a *déboîté*.

EMBRACE TIGER AND RETURN TO MOUNTAIN, ballet, ch. Tetley, m. Subotnik, dec. N. Baylis, f.p. B. Rambert, Jeannetta Cochrane Th., London 21 Nov 1968 (Mary Willis, C. Bruce, Gayrie MacSween, P. Curtis). Based on T'ai-chi, callisthenic exercises of the Chinese. Mounted for Nederlands Dans Th. 1969.

E = MC², ballet, ch. Lazzini, m. Mossolov, dec. Hodges, f.p. Marseille B., Th. Municipal, Marseilles 21 Nov 1964. Inspired by Einstein's formula relating mass to energy.

EMPIRE BALLETS, ballets given at the old Empire Th., London, from 1884 to 1914. In the opening year were presented *Coppélia*, and *Giselle*. In 1887, George Edwardes and Sir Augustus Harris became the directors. Katti Lanner was engaged as maîtresse-de-ballet, and among the dancers were Palladino, Cavallazzi, Cecchetti and Will Bishop. In 1897 Adeline Genée made her début in *Monte Cristo*—she was engaged for six weeks and she remained for ten years (and for subsequent performances). She ceased to be permanently employed by the Empire Th. in 1967 and was succeeded first by Topsy Sinden and then by Kyasht and Phyllis Bedells. Also associated with these productions was C. Wilhelm, who from 1887 to 1914 designed most of the costumes and settings, and suggested the themes of many of the ballets. He died in 1925.

ENCHAÎNEMENT, lit. a joining or linking together. A sequence of two or more steps, making up a continuous phrase or movement.

ENGLUND, Sorella, b. Helsinki 1945. Finnish dancer. Trained at the National Sch. Helsinki and joined Finnish Nat. B. 1962. Joined R. Danish B. 1966 becoming soloist 1970.

ENIGMA VARIATIONS, ballet, ch. Ashton, m. Elgar, dec. Julia Trevelyan Oman, f.p. Royal B., C. Garden 25 Oct 1968 (Rencher, Beriosova, Holden, Shaw, Mead, Grant, Lorrayne, Dowell, Parkinson, Doyle, Sibley, Sleep, Edwards, Bergsma). Edward Elgar with his wife and friends at a country house in autumn. He receives a telegram that tells him that Richter will conduct the first performance of his Enigma Variations. One of Ashton's best and most mature ballets, with all the friends depicted in their variations.

Frank Staff also chor. a ballet to this name and music, dec. Sheppard, f.p. B. Rambert Arts Th., Cambridge 26 Nov 1940 (Schooling, van Praagh, Staff, Paltenghi).

ENTERS, Angna, b. N.Y. 1907. Am. painter, author and mime. Has performed ethnic dances in many American museums and is the author of several books.

ENTRECHAT, probably from the It. *capriuola intrecciata* (i.e. cabriole *croisée*). Menestrier says it should be *entrechas*. A spring into the air from the fifth position in which the extended legs, with feet well pointed, criss-cross at the lower calf. In the entrechat quatre, six, huit, the dancer alights with the feet together in the fifth position. In the entrechat trois, cinq, sept, the dancer alights on one foot. The entrechat deux (a term which is never used) is known as a changement battu or a royale (but in Edouard Espinosa's British Ballet Organization Syllabus it is defined as an 'entrechat quatre commenced or ended in a second position'. He explains its feminine gender by deriving it from batterie royale first found in the *Gavotte de Roi*—i.e. of Louis XIV— and later in the *Gavotte de Vestris*). The numbering quatre, cinq, etc., is not that of the number of beats, but is the number of positions taken by the legs in the course of the movement—the 'fifth position' at the commencement and at the finish each counting as one. Camargo is often credited with being the first to cut an entrechat quatre, wearing a heel-less shoe and shortening her skirt above the instep to do so. There are, however, good reasons to believe that, whilst she may have been the first danseuse to do so, the entrechat quatre was executed long before that and was in fact used in such dances as the Gavotte. Nijinsky is said to have been able to execute the entrechat dix. Legat records that Damashoff of the Bolshoi Th. could execute an entrechat huit on rising and descend with straight legs—then reverse the procedure, doing the entrechat huit on the descent.

In January 1973 Wayne Sleep of the Royal B. cut an entrechat douze on B.B.C. television in London. It was filmed in slow motion and counted, to establish what appears to be a world record.

An entrechat ramassé is a sissonne fermée (q.v.) with the beat of an entrechat quatre.

ENTRE DEUX RONDES, ballet, ch. Lifar, m. M. S. Rousseau, dec. Landowski, f.p. Paris Opéra 24 Apr 1940 (Solange Schwarz, Lifar, Efimoff). Later revived for Josette Clavier. The Degas dancer in the Louvre comes to life between two rounds of the night watchman. See VAN GOETHEN.

ENTRÉE, lit. an entrance. The entry on the stage of a dancer or group of dancers and, by extension, a dance or divertissement executed by a dancer (entrée seule) or group of dancers with attributes in common (Red Riding Hood and the Wolf, Furies, Winds). The seventeenth and eighteenth-century Court Ballets were made up of a series of separate entrées of four or more dancers and a final Grand Ballet in which all the dancers participated. With the ballets of the Romantic period and the later four- and five-act ballets of the Petipa period, each act was divided into three, six, nine, or more entrées, each expressing a portion of the theme and frequently made up of a soloist (coryphée) and supporting members of the corps de ballet.

ÉOLINE OU LA DRYADE, ballet 6 sc., ch. Perrot, m. Pugni, f.p. Her Majesty's Th., London 8 Mar 1845 (Grahn, Perrot). A true Romantic ballet in which a mortal falls in love with a wood-nymph, who dies on her wedding day.

ÉPAULÉ, lit. shouldered, so called because in this position the placing of the shoulders is most noticeable. A position in which both shoulders and hips facing either of the downstage corners with the head looking over the shoulder to the audience, the leg nearest the audience is extended to the back in arabesque with the corresponding arm raised in arabesque to the front and the other arm in arabesque to the back.

ÉPAULEMENT, lit. shouldering. The positioning of the shoulders, one forward and the other drawn back, with the head turned to look over the forward shoulder. Good épaulement is one of the most important elements of artistry in dancing and is a characteristic feature of the modern classical style, compared with the Bournonville or old Fr. style, which has little épaulement.

EPISODES, ballet in two parts, f.p. N.Y. City B., City Center, N.Y. 14 May 1959. Part I, ch. Martha Graham, m. Webern, cost. Karinska (M. Graham, Sallie Wilson, Bertram Ross), Part II ch. Balanchine, m. Webern, cost. Karinska (Verdy, Diana Adams, Allegra Kent, Melissa Hayden, Watts, Magallanes, Taylor, Moncion). Homage to Webern. Part I deals with Mary, Queen of Scots, Part II has no story.

EPITAPH, ballet, ch. Van Dantzig, m. Ligeti, dec. Van Schayk, f.p. Dutch Nat. B., Stadsschouwburg, Amsterdam 26 June 1969 (G. Wijnoogst, Van Schayk, Geldorp).

ÉPREUVE D'AMOUR, L', ballet 1 act, ch. Fokine, m. attributed to Mozart but its authorship is in doubt, dec. Derain, f.p. Blum's B. Russe, Th. de Monte Carlo 4 Apr 1936 (Nemchinova, Kirsova, Eglevsky, Obou-khoff). This was one of Fokine's most charming ballets. It is a piece of chinoiserie, with a delightful troupe of monkeys. The score had been composed for a carnival in 1791 and was discovered in Graz in 1928. It is now in the repertoire of the National Ballet of Finland, ch. George Gé, closely following Fokine's choreography, dec. Horvath, cost. Platonoff, f.p. Helsinki 22 Mar 1956 (Rajala, Salin, Lätti).

ÉQUILIBRE. (1) Balance and the ability to hold a pose. (2) Balance on half or full point in any required position.

ERRAND INTO THE MAZE, ballet, ch. Graham, m. Menotti, cost. Gilfond, dec. Noguchi, f.p. Graham Co., Ziegfeld Th. N.Y. 28 Feb 1947 (Graham, Ryder). Journey into a psychological labyrinth.

ERRANTE, ballet 1 act, ch. Balanchine, m. Schubert-Liszt, dec. Tchelit-chev, f.p. Les Ballets 1933, Paris 1933 (Tilly Losch). An obscure allegory.

ESCALES, ballet 1 act, ch. Lifar, m. Ibert, dec. de Bravura, f.p. Paris Opéra 28 July 1948 (Lafon, Kalioujny).

ESCOBIYA, in Sp. dancing, a sweeping or brushing of the sole of the foot in *zapateado* dances.

ESCUDERO, Vincente, b. Valladolid, Spain c. 1889. Sp. gypsy dancer. Danced as a child in cafés, cabarets. Established himself in Paris in 1920 with Carmita Garcia and in 1925 began to work with Argentina as her partner. Danced all over Europe and America and one of the greatest Sp. dancers. In 1931 he danced with Pavlova.

ESMERALDA, LA, ballet 2 acts, 5 sc., ch. Perrot, m. Pugni, dec. Grieve, cost. Copère, f.p. Her Majesty's Th., London 9 Mar 1844 (Grisi, Perrot, Saint-Léon, Frassi, Gosselin, Coulon). Based on Hugo's *Notre Dame de Paris*, it is still in the repertoire in Russia. First danced in Russia by Elssler in 1848, where she had an enormous success with it and chose it for her farewell performance in Moscow in 1851. Also in the repertoire of Festival Ballet, with original ch. by Beriozoff, dec. Nicola Benois, f.p. Festival Hall, London 15 July 1954 (Krassovska, Gilpin, Briansky, Wright, Dolin, Beckett). The first ballet on this theme was Antonio Monticini's *Esmeralda*, f.p. Scala, Milan 1839.

ESPINOSA, famous family of dancers and teachers, of Sp. extraction now settled in England. LEON ESPINOSA (b. The Hague 1825, d. London 1903) studied under Coulon, Taglioni, etc., at Paris Opéra. Début Paris 1845. Danced at Porte St Martin Th., and toured widely (in 1850 in America he was captured by Red Indians). In 1865 danced in Moscow, in Isler's Gardens, but was taken into the Bolshoi Th., making his début as a slave in *Le Roi Candaule*, and stayed seven years. He was so small that a special position was made for him, 'premier danseur de contraste'. Returned to London 1872, opened a school, and presented *Babil et Bijoux* at Covent Garden, with Henriette Dor. His son, ÉDOUARD (b. Moscow 1871, d. Worthing 1950) was the co-founder of the Royal Academy of Dancing in 1920 and founder of the British Ballet Organization 1930. Pupil of Leon, he had a long career as a dancer and producer all over the world and finally as teacher. He was the author of several technical books and an autobiography *And Then He Danced* (1948). Édouard's sisters also became famous teachers—JUDITH (b. London 1876, d. there 1949), LEA (b. Paris 1883, d. 1966) in London, RAY (b. Paris 1885, d. Johannesburg 1934) (as Madame Ravodna) where she trained a generation of S. African teachers. Of the third generation, Édouard's son, EDWARD KELLAND-ESPINOSA (b. London 1906), dancer, producer and teacher studied under his father and danced in music halls, pantomimes, musicals and films. He has been a prolific producer of pantomimes, and on the death of his father in 1950 he became chairman of the British Ballet Organization. Ray's daughter MARCELLE ESPINOSA teaches in Johannesburg. Lea's son, GEOFFREY ESPINOSA (Hughes, b. London 1907), dancer, was for six years ballet master of International Ballet and teacher at their sch. in London, and her daughter RAY ESPINOSA (b. London 1910) taught near London until 1957. Geoffrey's wife, BRIDGET ESPINOSA (Kelly, b. Hampton 1928), Eng. dancer and teacher, studied at Elmhurst Sch. and under Sergueeff, Egorova and Geoffrey Espinosa, joined Embassy B. 1947 and International B. 1948 becoming soloist. Chor. for the B.B.C., teacher and producer she became artistic director of Elmhurst Sch. 1966.

ESQUIVEL, Jorge, b. Havana 1950. Cuban dancer. Studied under Gurov, Leontieva and from 1966 with the Alonsos and Aurora Bosch (Nat. B. Sch.). Joined the Nat. B. of Cuba and immediately became their principal male dancer. Varna Bronze Medal 1970.

ESTAMPIO (Juan Sanchez), b. Spain c. 1883, d. Madrid 1957. Famous Sp. teacher and dancer of flamenco. Teacher of most of the younger generation of Sp. dancers, especially the men.

ESTRO ARMONICO, L', ballet, ch. Cranko, m. Vivaldi, f.p. Stuttgart B., Stuttgart 27 Apr 1963 (Cardus, Delavalle, Barra).

ESTRO BARBARICO, ballet, ch. Milloss, m. Bartok, dec. Clerici, f.p. Cologne 28 Apr 1963 (Söffing, Krisch).

ETCHEVERY, Jean Jacques, b. Paris 1916. Fr. dancer and chor. Studied under Ricaux and Zvereff. Soloist Nouveau B. de Monte Carlo 1942–44. Maître de ballet of the Opéra Comique, Paris 1946–54. Chor. many ballets for them, notably La Ballade de la Geôle de Reading (1947). Ballet-master Th. de la Monnaie, Brussels 1954–55.

ETERNAL STRUGGLE, ballet, ch. Schwezoff, m. Schumann, dec. K. and F. Martin, f.p. B. Russe de Monte Carlo, Sydney 29 July 1940.

ETHERIDGE, Terence, b. Cape Town 1942. S. African dancer. Pupil of Dulcie Howes, Poole, Staff. Joined London Dance Th. 1964, Festival B. 1965 becoming soloist 1967. Joined Northern Dance Th. 1969 becoming assistant director 1970 but resigned same year.

ÉTOILE (Fr. 'star') or Premier Danseur Étoile (Première Danseuse Étoile), a title given to certain of the premiers danseurs of the Paris Opéra by nomination, indicating that they are the leading dancers in the company.

ETORKI (Les Ballets et Choeurs Basques Etorki), French company of singers and dancers founded in 1954 by Philippe Oyhamburu to perform the dances and music of the Basque country. They are based on St Jean de Luz and tour. They performed at Sadler's Wells in 1969.

ETUDE (also ÉTUDES), ballet 1 act, ch. Lander, m. Czerny, arr. Riisager, dec. Nordgren, f.p. R. Danish B., Copenhagen 15 Jan 1948 (Margot Lander, Brenaa, Jensen). Under the title Études Lander mounted it for the Paris Opéra 19 Nov 1952 (Bardin, Renault, Kalioujny), and for the Festival B., R. Festival Hall, London 8 Aug 1955 (Toni Lander, Gilpin, Polajenko, Dolin). A ballet of crescendo and accelerando showing the progress and technique of the dancer. It is now in the repertoire of many Cos.

EURHYTHMICS see JAQUES-DALCROZE.

EURYDICE IS DEAD, ballet, ch. Birgit Cullberg (inspired by the Palle Nielse set of prints, Orpheus and Eurydice, also in décor and costumes), m. Morricone and Pontecorvo, f.p. in Örebro, Sweden 1967 (Niklas Ek, Lena Wennergren, Eske Holm, Karin Thulin). Orpheus seeks his beloved in a war damaged and occupied city.

EVANS, Anya, b. N.Y. 1946. Am. dancer. Pupil of Vilzak-Shollar.

Joined Am. Ballet Th. 1964, Festival B. 1967 as soloist and Royal B. 1969 as soloist.

EVANS, Edwin, b. London 1874, d. there 1945. Eng. music critic who was ballet critic of *Daily Mail* 1933–45. He was particularly interested in modern music and the ballet, and was a friend and adviser of Diaghileff and also the Chairman of the Camargo Society. His articles for *The Dancing Times* were published as *Music and the Dance*. Arr. music *Promenade* (q.v.).

EVDOKIMOVA, Eva, b. Geneva 1948. Am. dancer. Pupil of Munich Opera Sch. 1956–59, Royal B. Sch. 1959–65, Maria Fay 1965–66. Joined Royal Danish B. 1966–69. In 1969 joined Deutsche Oper, Berlin as principal dancer and performed her first *Giselle* there (coached by Chauviré) in 1970. Also guest ballerina in Gothenburg, Festival Ballet in London, Helsinki, Zürich 1971. Won prize at Varna 1968, Moscow 1969 and the only gold medal at Varna 1970. Ballerina R. Danish B. 1972. Guests with Festival B., Geneva B. etc.

EVE OF ST AGNES, ballet, ch. Paltenghi, m. Franck, dec. Furse, f.p. B. Rambert, Bath 31 Aug 1950 (Hill, Pollen, Paltenghi). A medieval story.

EVERY SOUL IS A CIRCUS, ballet, ch. Graham, m. Nordoff, cost. Gilfond, f.p. Graham Co., St James Th., N.Y. 27 Dec 1939 (Graham, Hawkins, Cunningham). Important early work by Martha Graham and the first appearance of Merce Cunningham in her group.

EVTEYEVA, Elena, b. Leningrad 1947. Russ. dancer. Graduated from Kirov Sch. to Kirov B. 1966. First danced in London 1970. Danced Odette-Odile, partnered by John Markovsky, in film of *Swan Lake* 1967. Won Varna Silver Medal 1970.

EXCELSIOR, ballet in 12 sc., ch. Manzotti, m. Marenco, dec. Edel, f.p. Scala, Milan 11 Jan 1881 (Vergani, Montenara). This was Manzotti's most popular ballet (among the characters in it are the scientists Papin and Volta). It was presented at Her Majesty's Th., London 1885 (Limido, Cecchetti). It was revived with chor. dell'Ara, dec. Coltellacci, Maggio Musicale, Florence (Teatro Communale) 27 June 1967 (Tcherina, Fracci, dell'Ara, Labis).

EXTENSION, the extending out of the leg from the body, or the result of so doing (a dancer can be said to have 'a good extension'). Recently it has been applied to the height above her waist that a dancer can raise her extended leg.

F

FABBRI, Flora, b. Florence. It. dancer of the Romantic era. One of the six pupils of Blasis whom he called his Pleiades. Début in Venice, danced in Rome 1838, Bologna 1841 and was an étoile of the Paris Opéra 1845–51. Mar. Louis Bretin, chor. of Opéra in 1842. Danced *La Sylphide, Paquita* etc.

FABLES OF OUR TIME, ballet, ch. Weidman, m. Miller, f.p. Weidman Dance Th. Co., Jacob's Pillow, U.S.A., July 1947. N.Y. première Mansfield Th., N.Y. 18 Apr 1948. Four Thurber fables, and Weidman's most famous ballet.

FAÇADE, ballet 1 act, ch. Ashton, m. Walton (originally written as an accompaniment to poems of Edith Sitwell), dec. J. Armstrong. One of the wittiest of Ashton's ballets, this work was originally created for the Camargo Soc. at the Cambridge Th., London 26 Apr 1931 and included immediately afterwards in the repertoire of the B. Rambert. When the ballet was added to those regularly performed by the Vic-Wells B. in 1935 a new number was included, and when revived by the S. Wells B. in July 1940 further numbers were added and fresh dec. and cost. (also by Armstrong) were introduced. This latter version was subsequently one given by S. Wells Th. B. In the original production by the Camargo Soc. Lydia Lopokova danced the Milkmaid and also the Tango, Markova the Polka, and Ashton the Dago.

FACE, DE, facing the audience.

FÂCHEUX, LES, comedy-ballet by Molière, ch. Beauchamps. First performed at a fête given by Fouquet at Vaux le Vicomte for Louis XIV, 17 Aug 1661. It was repeated at Fontainebleau a few days later with an additional scene suggested by the King. This may have been Molière's first comedy-ballet. It had a great influence on the ballet and set a new fashion at Court.

FÂCHEUX, LES, ballet, ch. Nijinska, m. Auric, dec. Braque, f.p. Diaghileff's Co., Monte Carlo 19 Jan 1924 (Dolin, who danced on his points). A lover delayed on his way to a rendezvous. It was revived in 1927 (ch. Massine).

FACSIMILE, ballet, ch. Robbins, m. Bernstein, dec. Smith, cost. Sharaff, f.p. Ballet Theatre, Broadway Th., N.Y. 24 Oct 1946 (Kaye, Robbins, Kriza). A flirtation on a beach, but deals also with the modern problem of what man shall do with his time.

FADETTA, ballet, ch. Lavrovsky, m. Delibes (for *Sylvia*), dec. Erbstein, f.p. Kirov Th., Leningrad 21 Mar 1934 (F. Balabina, Lapchev). This ballet, with libretto by Slonimsky, to the story of Georges Sand's *La Petite Fadette*, was Lavrovsky's first and was given at the school's graduation performance.

FADEYECHEV, Nikolai, b. Moscow 1933. Russ. dancer. Entered Bolshoi Sch. 1943 and graduated to the Bolshoi Ballet in 1952. Became a soloist in 1953. Danced in London in 1956 and New York 1959. Partnered Ulanova in the film of *Giselle* (London 1956) and Nerina in television *Giselle* (London 1958). People's Artist of the R.S.F.S.R. 1964.

FAILLI or PAS FAILLI, lit. a failed step. A step in which the dancer springs into the air from the fourth or fifth position and, turning the body through 45°, alights on the front foot with the other extended to the back (fourth demi-position in the air) and then swept through to the fourth front with appropriate positions of the arms.

FALCO, Louis, b. N.Y. 1942. Am. dancer and chor. Pupil of Limon, Weidman, Graham. Limon Co. 1960. Chor. *Argot* (m. Bartok 1967). Founded own group 1968, chor. *Huescape* (m. Heary, Schaeffer, Lasry, Baschet) 1968. Chor, *Tutti-frutti*, B. Rambert 1973.

FALLIS, Barbara, b. Denver 1924. Am. dancer. Studied at S. Wells Sch. and under Vilzak. Dèbut in London 1938. Joined Ballet Th. 1940 becoming soloist 1946. N.Y. City B. as soloist 1955. Joined Kovach and Rabovsky 1958. Teaches in N.Y.

FALL-RECOVERY, a term used in the Modern Dance Movement, developed by Doris Humphrey. It is 'a synthesis of two opposites: a period of unbalance and a period of relative balance'. In German, Anspannung-Abspannung.

FALL RIVER LEGEND, ballet, ch. de Mille, m. Morton Gould, dec. Smith, cost. White, f.p. Ballet Th., Met. Op., N.Y. 22 Apr 1948 (Alonso, Bentley). This ballet, of the story of Lizzie Borden the murderer, is de Mille's masterpiece and provides one of the great dramatic rôles in ballet—a rôle shared by Nora Kaye and Sallie Wilson.

FANCIULLA DELLE ROSE, ballet, ch. Staff, m. Arensky, dec. Sheppard, f.p. Metropolitan B., Scala Th., London 10 June 1948 (Beriosova). This was the first rôle to be created for Beriosova.

FANCY FREE, ballet 1 act, ch. Jerome Robbins, m. Bernstein, dec. Oliver Smith, cost. Love, f.p. Ballet Th., Met. Op., N.Y. 18 Apr 1944 (Lang, Kriza, Robbins, Janet Reed, Muriel Bentley, Shirley Eckl). This Am. B. of Manners in a humorous vein, with its slick timing and its clever use of jitterbug and other contemporary dance-hall styles wedded to classical technique, is one of the most delightful productions which has crossed the Atlantic. It was Robbins's first ballet and tells of three sailors and two girls. It inspired a musical and a film *On the Town*. It is always in the repertoire of Am. Ballet Th.

FANDANGO, a Sp. dance in 3/4 or 6/8 time, possibly of S. American origin, for a single couple. Characteristics include the sudden break during which the dancers remain motionless, the castanets, and interpolated songs.

FANFARE, ballet, ch. Robbins, m. Britten (*Young Person's Guide to the Orchestra*), dec. I. Sharaff, f.p. N.Y. City B., City Center, N.Y. 2 June 1953 (Mounsey, Jillana, Larsson, Bolender, d'Amboise, Bigelow, Bliss). This was Robbins's tribute to Elizabeth II, performed on Coronation Night. The dancers represent the various orchestral instruments.

FARANDOLE, an ancient and popular dance in 6/8 time principally found in S. France and Catalonia, in which the participants, to any number, hold hands in a chain as they dance through the streets to the accompaniment of the galoubet and tambourin (a type of pipe and tabor).

FAR FROM DENMARK (Fjernt fra Danmark), ballet 2 acts, chor. August Bournonville, m. Glaeser and Lumbye, dec. Lund and Christensen, cost. Lehmann, f.p. Royal Danish B., Copenhagen 20 Apr 1860. Still in the Danish repertoire. A fancy dress ball on a Danish ship in Buenos Aires harbour.

FARJEON, Annabel, b. Bucklebury 1919. Eng. dancer and critic. Pupil of Phyllis Bedells and S. Wells Sch. Member of S. Wells B. 1935–50. Ballet critic of *Evening Standard* 1959–73.

FARMANYANTZ, Georgi, b. Bezhetsk 1921. Russ. dancer. Entered Bolshoi Sch. 1930, graduated 1940, rising to chief male dancer at the theatre and one of the finest character dancers in Russia. Danced in Prague 1947, Budapest 1949, London 1953 and 1960, Berlin 1954, N.Y. 1959. Honoured Artist of the U.S.S.R. 1951. Now teaches.

FARMER, Peter, b. Luton 1941. Eng. painter and designer. Studied at Central Sch. of Art, London. Designed dec. and cost. for *Agrionia* (London Dance Th. 1964), *Giselle* (Rambert 1965, Stuttgart 1966), *Sleeping Beauty* (Cologne 1967), *Namouna* (Stuttgart, Peter Wright, 1967), *Beauty and the Beast* (Western Th. B. 1967), *The Dream* (Royal B. 1967), *Giselle* (Royal B. 1968), *Night Shadow* (Festival B. 1967), *Bourrée Fantasque* (Festival B.), *Coppélia* (Festival B. 1968), *Sleeping Beauty* (Royal B. 1973). Also designed many plays and book illustrations. Appointed Art Director of London Contemporary Dance Th. 1971.

FARRALLY, Betty, b. Bradford 1915. Eng. dancer and teacher. Studied in Leeds. To Canada 1938 with Gweneth Lloyd and with her founded the Royal Winnipeg B. (and School) in that year. Until 1957 ballet mistress of the Co. Now teaches.

FARRELL, Suzanne, b. Cincinnati 1945. Am. dancer. Pupil of Marian LaCour and of the Sch. of Am. Ballet. Joined N.Y. City B. 1961. Danced her first solo (in *Serenade*) 1962, promoted soloist 1963, principal 1965, and Balanchine created many ballets for her—*Meditation*, *Clarinade*, etc. and gave her most of the principal rôles in the repertoire. She created rôle of Dulicinea in Balanchine's *Don Quixote* 1965 and became a principal dancer of the Co. Left the Co. in 1968 on her marriage to Paul Mejia and has since danced as guest artist in other Am. ballets. Joined Béjart's B. du XXme Siècle 1970.

FARREN, Fred, b. London 1874, d. there 1956. Eng. dancer, chor., and maître de ballet. Début in pantomime 1885. He was one of the principal figures at the old Empire Th., London, and partnered Lydia Kyasht in many ballets, some of which were to his choreography. He was Dr Coppelius in the 1906 (Genée) production of *Coppélia* at the Empire (Frantz was Dorothy Craske).

FARRON, Julia, b. London 1922. Eng. dancer. Studied Cone Sch. and S. Wells Sch. Début pantomime Drury Lane 1934. Joined S. Wells B. 1936, cr. Dog in *Wedding Bouquet*. Became a principal dancer in Co. excelling in character rôles. Retired 1961. From 1964 a teacher at the Royal B. Sch. and guest artist of Royal B. Mar. A. Rodrigues.

FARRUCA, a traditional Andalusian dance introduced by Massine into his ballet *The Three Cornered Hat*.

FASCILLA, Roberto, b. Milan 1937. It. dancer. Entered Scala Sch. Milan 1948, graduated 1956, Passo d'Addio 1957, soloist 1958.

FAUST, ballet 3 acts 7 sc., ch. Perrot, m. Panizza, Costa, Bajetti, dec. Fontana, f.p. Scala, Milan 12 Feb 1848 (Elssler, Catte). One of Perrot's most successful ballets. Elssler chose it for her farewell performance in Vienna in 1851.

FAUST, ballet 3 acts, ch. Béjart, m. Berlioz, dec. Casado, f.p. Paris Opéra B., 13 Mar 1964 (Vlassi, Bonnefous).

FAY, Maria, b. Budapest 1928. Hungarian dancer (British from 1963) and teacher. Studied under Nadasi, Vainonen, Messerer and Moiseyev in Hungary. Member of State Hungarian Th. B. 1948–56. To London 1956 and opened studio 1958. On staff of R.A.D. from 1959, guest teacher at Royal B. Sch. 1961–66. Created system of character dancing for R.A.D. 1960 and at Royal B. Sch. 1961. Guest teacher of B. der Lage Landen 1958, Cuevas B. 1962, Larrain's *Cendrillon* (Paris) 1963,

R. Swed. B. 1967, R. Winnipeg B. 1967–68, 1970. Chor. many character dances for C. Garden Op., Royal B. etc.

FEAST OF ASHES, ballet, ch. Ailey, m. Surinach, f.p. Joffrey B., Fashion Inst. of Technology, N.Y. 30 Sept 1962 (Martinet, Nebrada). Based on Lorca's *The House of Alba*. In the first programme presented by the Harkness B. 1965. Performed by Geneva B. 1973.

FEDIANIN, Vladimir, b. Shakhti 1946. Russ. dancer. Studied at Rostov Sch. 1960 and joined the Ukraine Dance Ensemble. Also trained in the Leningrad Sch., graduating 1968 to the Kirov B. In 1970 soloist Stanislavsky-Nemirovitch-Danchenko Th. B. Won Varna Gold Medal 1972.

FEDICHEVA, Kaleria, b. Ust-Ijory 1936. Russ. dancer. Pupil of Kirov Sch. graduated to Kirov B., Leningrad 1955, becoming principal dancer. Hon Artist R.S.F.S.R. 1963, People's Artist 1967.

FEDOROVA, Alexandra, b. 1884, d. N.Y. 1972. Russ. dancer and teacher. Graduated from Imp. Sch., St Petersburg 1902 and became first soloist at Maryinsky Th. 1904. Left Russia 1922, to Riga 1924 and America 1937 where she taught until 1965. Mar. Alexander Fokine (brother of Michel F.). Her son, Leon Fokine, is a dancer and teacher.

FEDOROVA, Sophia (Fedorova II), b. 1879, d. 1963. Russ. dancer. Trained at Bolshoi Sch. and entered Co. 1899, dancing many principal rôles. Joined Diaghileff 1909 in Paris and created the rôle of the Polovtsian Girl in *Prince Igor*, which was danced on the opening night of the season. Danced leading rôle in *Cléopâtre* and *Schéhérazade*. Returned to Moscow 1913. Rejoined Diaghileff 1928 to dance in *Prince Igor*. Had nervous breakdown in 1930 and retired.

FEDOROVITCH, Sophie, b. Minsk 1893, d. London 1953. Russ. artist. Came to London 1920 and designed the dec. and cost. of many of the finest Eng. ballets and was closely associated with the rise and development of the art in this country. As 'F.E.D.' she made the dec. of *A Tragedy of Fashion*, the first ballet of Ashton (with whom she most often worked). Among her most notable ballets are *Les Masques*, *Horoscope*, *Nocturne*, *La Fête Étrange*, *Symphonic Variations*, *Veneziana*. She was one of the Artistic Advisers to the S. Wells B.

FEDRA, ballet, ch. Cullberg, m. Rosenberg, dec. Mork, f.p. Cullberg B., City Th., Stockholm 6 Mar 1967 (Melissa Hayden, V. Mlakar, Kuch, Ek). The story of Phaedra.

FEET, see POINTE and FIVE POSITIONS.

FELD, Eliot, b. Brooklyn 1942. Am. dancer and chor. Pupil of Sch. of Performing Arts, N.Y. Danced in *West Side Story* on Broadway and was 'Little John' in the film of it (1960). Joined Donald McKayle Co.

and then Am. B. Th. as soloist for whom he chor. his first ballet *Harbinger* (1967), and *At Midnight* (1967). In 1969 he left Am. B. Th. to start his own Co. the Am. Ballet Company. Chor. *Meadow Lark* for R. Winnipeg B. 1968 and for Festival B. 1968. His company disbanded in 1971 and he returned to Am. B. Th.

FELIX (Felix Fernandez Garcia), b. Spain c. 1896, d. Epsom 1941. Sp. dancer. In 1917 Diaghileff met him in Madrid and engaged him to teach Sp. dancing to the Co. and to Massine for the forthcoming production of *Le Tricorne*. He travelled with the Co. to London in 1918, where he lost his reason and died in an asylum.

FEMMES DE BONNE HUMEUR, LES, see GOOD HUMOURED LADIES, THE.

FENSTER, Boris, b. 1916, d. 1960. Russ. dancer and chor. Graduated from Kirov Sch. 1936, joined Maly Th., Leningrad. Chor. *Ashik-Kerib* (m. Asafiev) 1940, and was chief chor. there 1945–53 and of Kirov B. 1956–60. Ch. *False Bridegroom* (m. Chulaki) 1946, *Youth* (m. Chulaki) 1949, *Taras Bulba* (m. Solovyov-Sedoy) 1955, *Masquerade* (m. Laputin) 1960.

FERMÉ, a closed position of the feet (opp. Ouvert).

FERNANDEZ, Royes, b. New Orleans 1929. Am. dancer. Studied under Celli. Joined Original Ballet Russe 1946. Joined Ballet Th. 1951. From 1955 to 1957 was leading dancer in Borovansky Ballet. Rejoined Am. B. Theatre 1957 of which he is one of the principals and also danced with San Francisco Ballet in 1959. Danced with Festival B. 1962. Partnered Fonteyn on a world tour.

FERRAN, José, b. Barcelona 1924. Spanish dancer and teacher. Pupil of Juan Magrina, Preobrajenska, Nora Kiss and Caton. Joined Original Ballet Russe 1947, Cuevas B. 1949–52. Teatro Municipal, Rio de Janeiro 1952, Petit's B. 1952–60. Cuevas 1960. In 1962 he joined Rosella Hightower's school at Cannes as her chief assistant.

FERRARIS, Amalia, b. Voghera 1830, d. Florence 1904. It. dancer, pupil of Blasis. Début Scala, Milan 1844. Danced London 1849 and début Paris Opéra in *Les Elfes*. Cr. rôles in *Marco Spada*, *Sakuntala*, *L'Étoile de Messine*. Retired 1868. One of the 'Pleiades' of Blasis.

FERRI, Olga, b. Buenos Aires 1928. Argentinian dancer. Studied in the Argentine under Bulnes and Borowski and in Paris. Became prima ballerina at Teatro Colon, Buenos Aires and guest artist of Festival Ballet 1960 and 1963. Took rôle of Elssler in Jack Carter's T.V. film *The Life and Loves of Fanny Elssler* 1961.

FESTIN DE L'ARAIGNÉE, LE, ballet, ch. Aveline, m. Roussel, dec. Leyritz, f.p. Paris Opéra 1 May 1939 (Lorcia, Schwarz). Another version, ch. Howard, dec. Ayrton, was f.p. S. Wells B., New Th., London 6 June 1944 (Franca). The book of the earliest version (ch. Staats, f.p. Th. des Arts, Paris 3 Apr 1913) was by Gilbert des Voisins, descendant of Taglioni.

FESTIVAL BALLET. When Markova and Dolin returned to England from America in 1949 and resumed their tours, they chose a corps de ballet largely from the senior members of the Cone-Ripman Sch. at Tring and London. In 1950 this ensemble was called the Festival Ballet, under the management of Dr Julian Braunsweg. They toured England and gave their first London season at the Stoll Th. from 24 Oct 1950 to 20 Jan 1951. Their soloists (with Markova and Dolin) were Gilpin, Krassovska, Anna Cheselka, Paula Hinton, Louis Godfrey, Nicholas Beriozoff, Beckett, Audrey Harman, and (promoted from a talented corps de ballet) Anita Landa, Noël Rossana, Daphne Dale. In 1951 they had a season at Monte Carlo, the first English Co. to be invited, where they made a great impression (Riabouchinska and Lichine were guest artists). Since then they have toured Britain and Europe continuously, having their London seasons at the Festival Hall. In 1954-55 they toured America. Their principal dancers have been Markova (left 1952), Sonia Arova (left 1953), Krassovska, Belinda Wright, Violette Verdy, Dolin, Gilpin, Briansky, Landa, Lander, and as guest artists Toumanova, Chauviré, Danilova, Kovach, Slavenska, Charrat, Svetlova, Miskovitch, Rabovsky. The Co. presented the classical ballets, many of the Fokine ballets (*Petrouchka, Schéhérazade,* etc.) mounted by Beriozoff, their *régisseur,* and new works such as Charnley's *Symphony for Fun* and *Alice in Wonderland.* In 1954 Beriozoff's recreation of *Esmeralda* was presented. Harald Lander mounted *Études* in 1955 and *Coppélia* in 1956. Dr Braunsweg's Company had twelve weeks a year in London's Festival Hall (8 in the summer and 4 at Christmas) and toured the provinces, Europe and the Near East. S. America was visited in 1960 and guest artists included Fonteyn, Beryl Grey, Olga Ferri and V. Skouratoff. In 1960 the principals were Marilyn Burr, Jeannette Minty, Deanne Richards, Anita Landa, Belinda Wright, Gilpin, Godfrey, Prokovsky. The musical director was Geoffrey Corbett, until 1961 when he was succeeded by Aubrey Bowman until 1968. In 1961 Bourmeister chor. *Snow Maiden* for them and in 1963 Orlikowski chor. *Peer Gynt* and later *Swan Lake* which was given in the Verona Arena 1964. Also in 1963, at Christmas they gave an Albert Hall season in combination with a group of Russian stars. In 1965 they visited Sicily and toured S. America, and 1967 Istanbul and Ankara. Samtsova became ballerina in 1965, Prokovsky joined in 1966 and these were the principals with Aldous (1963-67, when she joined the Royal B.) and Gilpin (1950 until he retired in 1970). In August 1965 the Co. suddenly went bankrupt (as it had done several times before) and Dr Braunsweg left. Donald Albery London, theatre-owner and impresario, stepped in with £20,000 and saved the Co. A Trust was formed, with Albery as director and Sir Max Rayne chairman. *Sleeping Beauty* was mounted in 1967. In 1968 Albery resigned and Beryl Grey became artistic director. Japan was visited in 1970. The Co. is now supported by substantial grants from the Greater London Council and the Arts Council and since 1969 has had long summer seasons at the Coliseum and continuing to perform *Nutcracker* at Christmas at the Festival Hall when available. *Don Quixote* was mounted in 1970 and the principal dancers in 1971 were Samtsova, Miklosy, Kessler, Grahame, Prokovsky, Dubreuil, von Loggenburg, Alban, with Breuer and P. Schaufuss as guests. Music director, Terence Kern. The name of the company changed in slight details after the various bankruptcies but since 1968 it has been called London Festival Ballet. In 1973 Massine chor. *Le Tricorne* and *Gaîte Parisienne* for them and Tudor *Echoing of Trumpets*, and Gaye Fulton, Maina Gielgud and Carole Hill were among the principals.

FÊTE ÉTRANGE, LA, ballet, book R. Crichton after Fournier's *Le Grand Meaulnes*, ch. Howard, m. Fauré, dec. Fedorovitch, f.p. London B., Arts Th., London 23 May 1940 (Lloyd, Staff, Paltenghi). Now in repertoire of Royal B. A sensitive ballet of mood, in which a country boy falls in love with the young *châtelaine* on the eve of her marriage. Two songs are sung in it. In repertoire of Scottish Theatre B., f.p. Th. Royal, Norwich 30 Sept 1971 (McDonald, Wells, Aitken).

FEUILLET, Raoul-Auger, b. c. 1660, d. 1710. Fr. dancer and chor. who claimed to have invented a system of dance notation described in his *Chorégraphie ou l'Art de Décrire la Danse* (1700). His *Recueil de Danses* (1704) contains a number of dances at the Opéra notated in this system. It was translated into English in 1706 by P. Siris as *The Art of Dancing*. In fact it would seem that this method of notation was invented by Pierre Beauchamp (q.v.) See DANCE NOTATION.

FEUX FOLLETS, LES, a Canadian dance company based on Quebec and founded in 1952, with Michel Cartier as director. Their name is that of the fireflies which entertained the French Canadian colonists. Their dances are of folk lore, Red Indians, Eskimos and of the early settlers. It danced in London in 1965.

FEWSTER, Barbara. Eng. dancer and teacher. Pupil of Wessex Sch., Bournemouth and entered S. Wells Sch. 1942 and was a member of the S. Wells Opera B. and a founder member of S. Wells Theatre B. 1946 becoming assistant ballet mistress 1947 and ballet mistress 1951–54.,

Ballet mistress of Old Vic *Midsummer Night's Dream* Co. which toured America 1954–55. To Royal B. Sch. as teacher 1955, becoming Deputy Principal in 1967, and Principal (succeeding Ursula Moreton) in 1968.

FIANCÉE DU DIABLE, LA, ballet, ch. Petit, m. Hubeau, dec. Malclès, f.p. B. des Ch. Élysées, Th. des Ch. Élysées, Paris 8 Dec 1945 (Skorik, Petit). A Mephistophelian plot set in a romantic castle.

FIELD, John (Greenfield), b. Doncaster 1921. Eng. dancer and director. Studied under Shelagh Elliott-Clarke and Edna Slocombe. Début with Liverpool B. Club 1938, joined S. Wells B. 1939, becoming a principal dancer of the Co. Partnered Beryl Grey in many rôles and in stereoscopic film *The Black Swan*, also Beriosova in Yugoslavia, Elvin in S. America, etc. Appointed Director of S. Wells Th. B. in 1956 and was in charge of this, the Touring Royal B. (and one of the Assistant Directors of the Royal B.) until 1970 when he was appointed joint Director (with Kenneth MacMillan) of the Royal B. at C. Garden on retirement of Ashton. Resigned 1971. Member of the Committee of the R.A.D. from 1970. Appointed C.B.E. 1967. In 1971 appointed ballet director La Scala, Milan. Mar. Anne Heaton.

FIELD FIGURES, ballet, ch. Tetley, m. Stockhausen, dec. N. Baylis, f.p. Royal B., Theatre Royal, Nottingham 9 Nov 1970 (Bergsma, Derman, O'Conaire, Johnson, Kelly, Clarke, O'Brien).

FIFIELD, Elaine, b. Sydney 1930. Austral. dancer. Studied at Scully Sch. and came to England with R.A.D. Scholarship 1945. Joined S. Wells Th. B. 1947, becoming principal dancer. In 1954, moved to S. Wells B. at C. Garden as soloist. Cr. rôles in *Pineapple Poll, Madame Chrysanthème*. Promoted ballerina 1956. Retired 1958 but returned to Australian B. 1964 and danced with them in London in 1965. Left again 1966 and returned 1969. Her autobiography *In My Shoes* published 1967.

FIGURANT (figurante) (Fr.), a walker-on or supernumerary. (Germ. statist.)

FIGURE IN THE CARPET, THE, ballet, ch. Balanchine, m. Handel (Water and Fireworks Music), dec. E. Frances, f.p. N.Y. City B., City Center, N.Y., 13 Apr 1960 (Verdy, Hayden, Adams, d'Amboise, Moncion, Villella). The weaving of a carpet conceived as a court entertainment.

FILLE DE MARBRE, LA, ballet 2 acts 3 sc., ch. Saint-Léon, m. Pugni, dec. Cambon and Thierry, f.p. Paris Opéra 20 Oct 1847 (Cerrito, Saint-Léon). The sculptor falls in love with his statue. The theme is similar to that of *Alma*.

FILLE DU DANUBE, LA, ballet 2 acts 4 sc., ch. F. Taglioni, m. Adam, dec. Despléchin, Dieterle, Feuchère, Sechan, cost. d'Orchvillers, f.p. Paris Opéra 21 Sept 1836 (Taglioni, Mazilier). Romantic ballet in which a mortal falls in love with the spirit of a girl who has drowned herself.

FILLE DU PHARAÖN, LA, ballet, 3 acts 7 sc., ch. Petipa, m. Pugni, f.p. Maryinsky Th., St Petersburg 30 Jan 1862 (Rosati, M. Petipa). Petipa was made assistant maître de ballet following the success of this ballet, which was for Rosati's last appearance in Russia.

FILLE MAL GARDÉE, LA, or VAIN PRECAUTIONS, ballet 2 acts, ch. Dauberval, m. by an unknown composer f.p. Bordeaux 1 July 1789 (Mlle Théodore as Lise)—original title Le Ballet de la Paille. One of the oldest ballets in the modern repertoire, it was danced by the Pavlova Co., the Mordkin Co., B. Th., de Cuevas Co., etc., and is also in the repertoire of the Soviet ballets. Nowadays different music is used. It was one of the first ballets to be based on the life of the people, thus breaking away from the pre-French Revolution tradition of the mythological ballet. In 1828 the music was rewritten by Herold when Aumer produced it at the Paris Opéra. In 1864 new music by Hertel was used and in 1885 it was restaged by Petipa and Ivanov, using Hertel's score with additions by Delibes, Minkus, Pugni, Drigo and Rubinstein. The ballet was rechoreographed by Ashton, m. Herold arr. Lanchberry, dec. Osbert Lancaster, f.p. Royal Ballet, C. Garden, 28 Jan 1960 (Nerina, Blair, Grant). Ashton was assisted by Karsavina in some of the mime scenes, for she had danced in it in St Petersburg. In repertoire of R. Danish B. 1964 (Ostergaard, Kehlet, Larsen) and Australian B. 1967 (Jones, Alder). The ballet was first performed in Australia at R. Victoria Th., Sydney 21 Aug 1855 (Aurelia Dimier). Ashton mounted his version for Hungarian Nat. B., f.p. Opera House, Budapest 28 Mar 1971 (Kun, Rona) and for Munich B. 17 Mar 1971 (Skroblin, Bosl), R. Swed. B., Stockholm 1 Apr 1972 (Lidstrom, Dozsa).

FILLEULE DES FÉES, LA, ballet 2 acts 7 sc., ch. Perrot, m. Adam and de Saint-Julien, dec. Cambon, Despléchin and Thierry, f.p. Paris Opéra 8 Oct 1849 (Grisi, Perrot, L. Petipa). Typical romantic fairy tale, dramatic but with a happy ending.

FILLING STATION, ballet 1 act, ch. Lew Christensen, m. Virgil Thomson, dec. Cadmus, f.p. B. Caravan, Avery Memorial Th., Hartford, Conn. 6 Jan 1938 (Marie-Jeanne, Bolender, Loring).

FILMS. The cinema is an art form with its own conventions and technique and it does not follow that a good ballet will make a good film, whilst the 'ballet film', as apart from the film used as a record of performance, is as yet in its infancy. The best dance films made to date have on the whole been musicals specially written for the screen such as the Fred Astaire, Ginger Rogers, and Gene Kelly films, and perhaps the most successful ballet film to date has been *La Mort du Cygne*, with choreography by Lifar, featuring Mia Slavenska, Yvette Chauviré, and the young Janine Charrat, in 1938. The many commercial ballet short films made to date, with the possible exceptions of *Capriccio Espagnol* and *Gaîté Parisienne* (ch. Massine, featuring the Ballet Russe de Monte Carlo), have on the whole been neither a true record of the ballets portrayed nor good entertainment as films. *The Red Shoes* (1948) featuring Moira Shearer, was popular with the general public but it conveyed to them a false impression of the art of ballet (though it greatly helped to popularize it).

It has often been suggested that the film offers the ideal solution to the problem of recording choreography, but this has hardly been borne out in practice. This is not to say that the film cannot be a valuable adjunct to notation, and some choreographers, notably Massine, have had small films made of their ballets to aid their memory and for the purposes of copyright. From 1970 Videotape recordings have been much used for this purpose.

It is above all as a method of recording the transient performance of the individual dancer that the camera is invaluable. The art of Nijinsky and of Isadora Duncan, for instance, is already a legend and cannot be brought to life, but audiences in many countries have been able to see Pavlova, Ulanova, and Semeyonova on the screen and to form some idea of the perfection of their art. Many of these films of individual performances have been the work of enterprising amateurs and, imperfect though they often are, they provide an invaluable record to posterity, of which excellent examples are the films in Madame Rambert's private collection featuring Spessivtseva and the late Pearl Argyle. It is to be hoped that in the future it will be possible to have films made by professional cameramen, complete with sound track, of all the principal ballets and of individual dancers of outstanding merit.

In Chicago, Ann Barzel has made a very complete record on film of dancers appearing there. The Royal Ballet has also recorded many of the ballets produced at Covent Garden.

There have been a few experiments in the use of films in the production of ballet. In *Relâche*, produced for the Ballets Suédois in 1924 to music by Erik Satie, with production by Picabia and Jean Börlin, a sequence of surrealist shots devised by René Clair was projected by way of a prologue to each of the two acts, on to a screen used as an act-drop, the intention being to create an appropriate atmosphere for the ballet to follow. In 1928 a similar attempt on a smaller scale was made in

Massine's *Ode*. In 1938 for a special open-air production of Lavrov-sky's *Prisoner of the Caucasus* in the Gorki Park of Culture, Moscow, scenes from the film of Pushkin's poem were thrown on to a gauze screen dropped at intervals during the performance. In 1953 Gene Kelly made an interesting film of dancing (it was not released until several years later), *Invitation to the Dance*. It was a full length film of several balletic episodes and many famous dancers appeared in it—Gene Kelly, Sombert, Toumanova, Diana Adams, Claude Bessy, Youskevitch, Belita, Rall, etc. Two important serious attempts have been made to record ballet in the opera house by Dr Czinner. In 1956 at Covent Garden he filmed the Bolshoi Ballet's *Giselle* (Ulanova, Fadeyechev) throughout one night, in colour (the ballet was danced straight through again after the public had left the theatre). This film was a great success and worthily preserved Ulanova's art. In 1959 he made a film of the Royal Ballet, also in Covent Garden but over several days and with immense preparation. Fonteyn was filmed in *Ondine*, in *Firebird* and in *Swan Lake* (Act II only), and the result was less successful. The film *A Dancer's World*, made in America in 1958, showing Martha Graham and her dancers, demonstrated in a very simple, direct way the rigours of a dancer's life.

With the coming of television there was a great increase in the filming of ballets, for subsequent showing on television. These were usually made direct from stage performances, but for the B.B.C. Margaret Dale (who became their first ballet producer) made a notable series of films in the studios—see the entry Margaret Dale for a list. A list of dance films generally available was published by *The Dancing Times* in 1971 (Apr and Nov) and 1972 (May), another by *Dance News* in their issue of February 1965. In 1954 *The Dancing Times* also published a booklet of *120 Dance Films* by Peter Brinson. In 1968 UNESCO published a catalogue *Ten Years of Films on Ballet and Classical Dance 1956–65*.

In the late 1960s the phrase 'mixed media entertainment' usually meant that films and projections were employed during a dramatic or ballet production. Notable (but by no means the first) were the two ballets presented by the Nederlands Dans Th. in 1970, *Twice* (ch. Van Manen) when a film projected above the dancers repeated their move-ments, and *Mutations* (ch. Tetley and Van Manen) where above the dancers a nude couple were screened. But the effect was negligible.

Some other noteworthy films have been *Cinderella* (Bolshoi B. 1959, Struchkova, Lediak), *Swan Lake* (Bolshoi B., Plisetskaya, Fadeyechev), *Black Tights* (1961, incl. *Carmen* with Jeanmaire-Petit, *Croqueuse de Diamants* with Jeanmaire, *Cyrano de Bergerac* with Moira Shearer-Petit, *Deuil en 24 heures* with Cyd Charisse), *Romeo and Juliet* (Royal B.

1961, Fonteyn, Nureyev), *Sleeping Beauty* (Kirov B. 1965, Sizova, Soloviev), *An Evening with the Royal Ballet* (1965 *La Valse*, and Fonteyn in *Sylphides*, *Corsaire* with Nureyev, *Sleeping Beauty* Act III with Blair), Disney's *Ballerina* (R. Danish B. 1966 with Mette Hönningen, Simone, Kronstam), *Isadora* (1966 with Vanessa Redgrave), *Swan Lake* (Kirov B. 1967, Evteyeva, Markovsky), *Secret of Success* (Bolshoi B., classroom scenes), Keith Money's *Fonteyn* (1969), *Enigma Variations* (Royal B. 1970, Beriosova, Rencher). In 1972 a film was made *I am a Dancer*, showing Nureyev at work and dancing rôles with Fonteyn, Fracci, Seymour and Bergsma. Ashton chor. a charming animal-film *The Tales of Beatrix Potter* in 1971.

FINGER VARIATION, a quick solo dance of one of the fairies in the Prologue of *The Sleeping Beauty* in which the dancer makes pointing gestures. In Petipa's original version this was the variation of the Fairy Violante. The Diaghileff version of 1921 gave the variation to the Fairy of the Humming Birds, and the S. Wells version of 1939 to the Breadcrumb Fairy—mistakes arising from careless scrutiny of the original score. The 1946 Royal Ballet version calls this the Variation of the Fairy of the Golden Vine. In MacMillan's 1973 version, it is the Fairy of the Passion Flower. It was originally danced by Kulichevskaya. The pointing movements are probably the *jettatura* or gesture to ward off the evil eye.

FINLAND, NATIONAL BALLET OF, was founded in 1921 by Edvard Fazer, the director of the Helsinki Opera. Formerly he had been an impresario and in 1908 he had brought a troupe of dancers from the Maryinsky Th., St Petersburg out to dance in Helsinki, Scandinavia, Berlin, Prague and Vienna. They were headed by Pavlova and included Edouardova, Egorova, Bolm and N. Legat—the first time the Russians had danced in the West, a year before Diaghileff's venture. In 1921 he invited George Gé (q.v.) to become the first ballet master in Helsinki and the Co. had its first performance in October 1922 (*Swan Lake*). The repertoire was based on the Maryinsky Th's. In 1934 Gé left to become ballet master of Blum's Ballet (taking with him the leading Finnish dancers Lucia Nifontova and Arvo Martikainen), and was succeeded by Alexander Saxelin. In 1955 Gé returned and remained until his death in 1962. He was succeeded by N. Beriozoff who mounted *Esmeralda, Sleeping Beauty, Les Sylphides* and *Sacre du Printemps*. The ballet master in 1970 was Elsa Silvesterson. The prima ballerina since 1956 has been Doris Laine and among notable recent Finnish dancers have been Klaus Salin, Margaretha von Bahr, Maj-Lis Rajala, Leo Ahonen, Irina Hudova, Sorella Englund. The Co. has toured much abroad, appearing in America, Russia, France etc. and in 1959 danced at the Edinburgh Festival. A regular visiting teacher in the 1960s has been Anna Northcote. In 1971 Alan Carter became ballet master. He resigned and was succeeded in 1972 by Irina Hudova, who left 1973.

FINNEY, Truman b. Quincy, Ill. 1944. Am. dancer. Studied at Stone-Camryn Sch. and Sch. of Am. B. Joined N.Y. City B. 1962, Stuttgart B. 1965 (soloist 1967), Cologne 1968, Frankfurt 1970, Hamburg 1973.

FIOCRE, Eugénie, b. Paris 1845, d. 1908. Fr. dancer, leading dancer Paris Opéra 1864–75. She was one of the great beauties of her age and she excelled in travesty rôles. She cr. rôle of Frantz in *Coppélia*. Carpeaux's bust of her makes her more refined-looking than cont. photographs suggest. Her elder sister, Louise, was also a dancer.

FIREBIRD (*L'Oiseau de Feu*), ballet 3 sc., ch. Fokine, m. Stravinsky, dec. and cost. (except those for the Firebird and the Tsarevna designed by Bakst) Golovine, f.p. Diaghileff's Co., Paris Opéra 25 June 1910 (Karsavina, Fokine). The first ballet-composition by Stravinsky for Diaghileff, the theme is a medley of Russ. fairy tales. The original scenery was damaged and fresh dec. and cost. were designed by Goncharova in 1926. A new version with ch. Balanchine and dec. Chagall, was made for the N.Y. City B. 27 Nov 1949 (Maria Tallchief, Moncion). In 1945 Bolm presented a version (dec. Chagall) for Ballet Theatre (Markova). The ballet was revived by the S. Wells B. for the twenty-fifth anniversary of Diaghileff's death by Grigorieff and Tchernicheva, Empire Th., Edinburgh 23 Aug 1954 (Fonteyn, Somes), dec. by Goncharova (her 1926 version). A new version, ch. Lifar, dec. Wakhevitch, was mounted at the Paris Opéra 7 Apr 1954 (Vyroubova, Algaroff). Many other chors. have used this score. A new version by Balanchine, dec. Chagall (the 1945 designs) was f.p. N.Y. City B., State Th., N.Y. 28 May 1970 (Gelsey Kirkland, d'Amboise). Béjart chor. *Firebird* for the Paris Opéra B. dec. Roustan and Bernard, f.p. Palais des Sports, Paris 31 Oct 1970 (Michaël Denard). He also mounted it for his B. du XXme Siècle, same cost., f.p. Cirque Royal, Brussels 17 Nov 1970 (Bortoluzzi). In this version a new scenario is used; the Firebird rôle (danced by a man) represents the spirit of a group of partisans.

FISH DIVE, the position of the danseuse when, supported almost horizontally by her partner, she holds the position of a temps de poisson. It ends the pas de deux in *Sleeping Beauty* Act III.

FITZJAMES, Louise, b. 1809. Fr. dancer, sister of Nathalie Fitzjames. Début at Paris Opéra 1832, soloist 1835, leaving in 1842. Made a great success in *Le Dieu et la Bayadère* in 1842 in which rôle she succeeded Taglioni. Gautier says she was 'thin as a lizard, transparent as the horn pane of a lantern'.

FITZJAMES, Nathalie, b. 1819. Fr. dancer, sister of the above. Début at Paris Opéra 1837, left 1842. She and Mabille were the original dancers of the peasant pas de deux in *Giselle* 1841. Danced in Italy 1848 and across America 1851. She was also a singer and at Versailles 1842 sang a part of *Lucia di Lammermoor*, mimed *La Muette de Portici* and danced the *Giselle* pas de deux.

FIVE POSITIONS, the basic positions of the feet with one of which most steps in classical ballet are begun and ended, devised to ensure balance in any position of the body. There are also the false or revised positions with the feet and knees turned in, which are now only seen in certain character dances such as the *csárdás*, but were formerly used for the entrances of comic characters. For positions of the arms see PORT DE BRAS.

In the FIRST POSITION the legs are together and the heels touching but not overlapping, with the feet fully turned out in a straight line.

In the SECOND POSITION the fully turned out feet are placed on the same line approximately the length of about one and a half lengths of the dancer's feet apart with the weight evenly distributed.

In the THIRD POSITION (now little used) the fully turned out feet are so placed that the heel of the front foot locks into the hollow of the instep of the back foot.

In the FOURTH POSITION which, like the second, is described as an open position, one foot is placed before the other about one a half lengths of the dancer's foot apart in an extension of the first position with the weight evenly distributed, both feet being fully turned out and separated by a distance of about one foot. There is also a closed or crossed fourth position which is an extension of the fifth.

In the FIFTH POSITION, which, like the first and third, is described as a closed position, the feet are placed together so that the joint of the big toe of the back foot protrudes beyond the heel of the front foot and vice versa.

The positions of the feet are said to be à terre when the feet are flat on the ground, pointe tendue when, in the second or fourth position, the foot is fully stretched with the tip of the toe on the ground and the heel lifted, en l'air demi-position (lit. half position in the air) when the fully stretched leg is raised so as to form an angle of 45° with the supporting leg, or en l'air when the leg is raised at right angles to the supporting leg.

The five positions of the feet are said, on the authority of P. Rameau in his book, *The Dancing Master* (1725), to have been first laid down by the French maître de ballet P. Beauchamp, but it seems probable that he did but codify what was already an accepted practice. Serge

FIVE POSITIONS

A. Feet: First Position
Arms: First Position

B. Feet: Second Position
Arms: Second Position

C. Feet: Third Position
Arms: Third Position

D. Feet: Fourth Position
(open)
Arms: Fourth Position
(en avant)

E. Feet: Fourth Position
(crossed),
Arms: Fourth Position
(en haut)

F. Feet: Fifth Position
Arms: Fifth Position (en
bas–and, dotted, en
avant and en haut)

Positions of the Arms and the Feet

Lifar has introduced a sixth and seventh position but they have not found favour outside the Paris Opéra. See also TURNOUT.

FLAMENCO, a Sp. gypsy. In flamenco dancing a guitarist, surrounded by a group of singers and clapping dancers, accompanies a solo dancer in such dances as the *alegrias, bulerias, farruca, zapateado* etc.

FLAMES OF PARIS, THE, ballet 4 acts, ch. Vainonen, m. Asafiev (pastiche of Gluck, Grétry, Mehul etc.), dec. Dmitriev, f.p. Kirov Th. Leningrad 7 Nov 1932 (the 'Ça Ira' scene only was f.p. the day before) (Balabina, Anisimova, Chabukiani). The triumph of the people in the Fr. Revolution.

FLETCHER, Graham, b. Kersley 1952. Eng. dancer. Pupil of Royal B. Sch. Joined Royal B. 1969.

FLETCHER, John, b. Masjed-de-Sulimian, Persia 1950. Eng. dancer. Studied at Arts Educational Sch. and joined Festival B. 1967. Won R.A.D. Genée Gold Medal 1968. Joined Northern Dance Th. 1969 as principal and Scottish Th. B. 1973.

FLEURET, a step in the eighteenth-century technique (which did not persist after the Fr. Revolution), consisting of a demi-coupé (see under COUPÉ) and two pas marchés sur la demi-pointe.

FLEXMORE, Richard (Dicky), b. Kensington 1824 (son of a dancer at Sadler's Wells), d. Lambeth 1860. Eng. dancer and mime who danced serious ballets and also comic versions of the ballets and in pantomimes. His partner in these productions was his wife Francisca Auriol.

FLIC-FLAC, lit. a crack as of a whip. An exercise in which the working leg is opened to the side (second demi-position en l'air) and sharply closed, brushing the ground, to a little beyond the back and front of the calf alternately. The step may be combined with a turn (flic-flac en tournant).

FLICK UND FLOCKS ABENTEUER (Flik and Flok), comedy ballet in 3 acts, ch. P. Taglioni, m. Hertel, f.p. Berlin 20 Sept 1858. By 1885 this ballet had been performed 419 times in Berlin. The magic adventures of two young men.

FLIER, Jaap, b. Scheveningen 1934. Dutch dancer. Pupil of Gaskell and Harkarvy. Principal dancer of the Nederlands B. 1952 and later of the Nederlands Dans Th. of which he became director 1970. Chor. *The Trial* 1955, *Nouvelles Aventures* 1970. Awarded Knight of Order of Orange 1968. Mar. Willy de la Bye.

FLINDT, Flemming, b. Copenhagen 1936. Dan. dancer. Entered Royal Th. Sch., Copenhagen 1946 and in 1955 the Co. becoming solodancer 1957. Joined Festival B. as soloist 1956. To Paris Opéra as étoile, 1960.

Appointed Director of R. Danish B. 1965, ch. *The Lesson* (m. Delerue) 1963, *The Three Musketeers* (m. Delerue) 1966, *Miraculous Mandarin* (m. Bartok) 1967, *Young Man to Marry* (m. Nörgaard) 1967, *Triumph of Death* (m. Koppel) 1972. Mar. Vivi Gelker.

FLOOR-WORK, the exercises done on the floor at modern dance classes.

FLORE ET ZÉPHIRE, ballet 1 act, ch. Didelot, m. Bossi, dec. Liparotti, f.p. King's Th., London 7 July 1796 (Hilligsberg, Rose, Parisot, Didelot). This, the greatest of Didelot's works, made use of a flying ballet. He danced in it in St Petersburg 1804, re-made the ballet there (m. Cavos) 1806 and danced it with Maria Danilova 1808. A revised version ch. Didelot, m. Venua, f.p. King's Th., London 7 Apr 1812 (Fortunata Angiolini, Armand Vestris). This was given in Paris in 1815 and St Petersburg 1818 and was the ballet in which Taglioni made her début in London in 1830.

FLORESTAN AND HIS SISTERS, a pas de trois introduced into the divertissement *Aurora's Wedding* by Diaghileff in 1923. In the original Petipa version of *The Sleeping Beauty*, and the S. Wells version of 1939, it was a pas de quatre for the Diamond, Gold, Silver, and Sapphire Fairies. In the Diaghileff 1921 version of the ballet it was a pas de quatre danced by Pierrette, Pierrot, Harlequin, and Columbine (ch. Nijinska). In the Royal Ballet version the choreography (for two girls and a boy) was by Ashton.

FOKINE, Michel, b. St Petersburg 1880, d. N.Y. 1942. Russ. dancer and chor. Trained at Imperial Sch., graduated 1898 and entered the Maryinsky as soloist. He became a first soloist in 1904 and began teaching in 1902. In 1905 he staged his first ballet, *Acis and Galatea* for a pupil's performance and *Le Cygne* for Pavlova 1907. First ballet for the Imperial Th. was *Le Pavillon d'Armide* (1907), and in 1909 he joined forces with Diaghileff. Although as a dancer he ranked with the greatest of his time, it is as a chor. that he will be remembered, for his influence on the art of ballet is comparable with that of Noverre, whose ideas he may be said to have embraced and carried a stage further. To appreciate the extent of the revolution operated by Fokine, it must be remembered that at the close of the last century ballets were composed to a formula with set dances in a predetermined order and all designed to show off the virtuosity of the prima ballerina. The dances, whatever the subject, were on the point and the costumes variations of the conventional ballet-dress; the music composed to the dictation of the chor. was more often than not a *pasticcio* and if the ballerina did not like a number another was interpolated, whilst the scene painter would probably work by himself without reference to costume designer or chor.

Fokine summarized his ideas (in a letter to *The Times* 6 June 1914) in five principles which may be paraphrased as follows:

(1) Not to form combinations of ready-made and established dance-steps, but to create in each case a new form corresponding to the subject, the most expressive form possible for the representation of the period, and the character of the nation represented.

(2) Dancing and mimetic gestures have no meaning in a ballet unless they serve as an expression of its dramatic action, and they must not be used as a mere divertissement or entertainment having no connexion with the scheme of the whole ballet.

(3) The new ballet admits the use of conventional gestures only where it is required by the style of the ballet and in all other cases endeavours to replace gestures of the hands by mimetic of the whole body. Man can and should be expressive from head to foot.

(4) The new ballet advances from the expressiveness of the face to the expressiveness of the whole body and from the expressiveness of the individual body to the expressiveness of a group of bodies and the expressiveness of the combined dancing of a crowd.

(5) The new ballet, refusing to be the slave either of music or of scenic decoration and recognizing the alliances of the arts only on conditions of complete equality, allows perfect freedom both to the scenic artist and to the musician. In contradistinction to the older ballet, it does not demand 'ballet' music of the composer as an accompaniment to dancing, it accepts music of every kind, provided only that it is good and expressive. It does not demand of the scenic artist that he should array the ballerinas in short skirts and pink slippers. It does not impose specific 'ballet' conditions on the composer or the decorative artist, but gives complete liberty to their creative powers.

The effect of his reforms was to lift the ballet out of the groove into which it had fallen, introducing a greater plasticity into the technique of dancing, bringing back the male dancer who had degenerated into a mere porteur and replacing the long four- and five-act productions by one act of greater concentration.

His greatest contribution to choreographic art was perhaps his choice and treatment of a subject matter. In ballets such as *Petrouchka* he showed that ballet, far from being confined to the narration of the frivolous and the fantastic, could become the medium for the expression of the most complex human emotions and in this he is the link between Noverre and Vigano, Jooss and Tudor. In *Les Sylphides*, a pure interpretation of the music of Chopin in terms of abstract movement, he paved the way for the later symphonic ballets of Massine and his successors.

He composed over sixty ballets, among them *Prince Igor, Les*

Sylphides, Carnaval, Schéhérazade, Firebird, Spectre de la Rose, Petrouchka, Coq d'Or, L'Épreuve d'Amour.
He lived in France 1911–14. Returned to Russia 1914 but left in 1918. Settled in America, working with many companies. Mar. Vera Fokina (Antonova, b. 1886, d. N.Y. 1958), a soloist at the Maryinsky Th. and of Diaghileff's Co. Their son, Vitale F. (b. St Petersburg 1905), teaches in N.Y.
His *Memoirs of a Ballet Master* (translated by Vitale Fokine and edited A. Chujoy) published 1961.

FOLK DANCE AND SONG SOCIETY, ENGLISH, a society founded by Cecil Sharp in 1911, with headquarters in Regent's Park, London, to study, record, and encourage folk dancing and folk music.

FOLKERTS, Jessica, b. Munich 1941. German dancer. Pupil of Erna Gerbl, V. Gsovsky, M. Rubinstein, Cleo Nordi. Danced in Munich B. 1950–56, Borovansky B. (Australia) 1956–59 as soloist, American Festival B. (in Europe) 1961, ballerina of Dutch Nat. B. 1962–72.

FOLKESAGN, ET (A Folk Tale), ballet 3 acts, ch. Bournonville, m. Gade and Hartmann, dec. Christensen, Lund, and Lehmann, f.p. R. Danish B., Copenhagen 20 Mar 1854 (Juliette Price, Funck). It is still in the repertoire—a fairy tale.

FOLKWANG SCHULE, the theatre academy founded by the city of Essen in 1927, teaching drama, music, dance etc. Jooss was made dance director of it and Leeder, Aiimola, and F. Cohen (composer) joined him there. They started a Folkwang Ballet (or Folkwang Tanzbühne) there in 1929 which produced a number of ballets all chor. by Jooss in the 'Central European' style, culminating in the famous *The Green Table* (q.v.). Because of Hitler's persecution of the Jews, the Co. left Germany in 1933 and settled at Dartington Hall in Devon, at the invitation of Mr and Mrs L. K. Elmhirst. Their dancers were mostly those who had been in Jooss's Neu Tanzbühne when he had been director of dance in the Münster Th. (before going to Essen). This became the B. Jooss. The Folkwang Schule has had some distinguished teachers of classical ballet on its staff, among them Cleo Nordi, Audrey Harman and Anne Woolliams. From 1968 Hans Zullig has been director.

FONDU or PAS FONDU, lit. a sinking or melting step. The lowering of the body by flexing the supporting knee. It is to one leg what the plié is to two.

FONTEYN, Dame Margot (Hookham), b. Reigate 1919. Eng. dancer. Studied under Bosustov and Goncharov as a child, and in 1933 under Astafieva. Joined S. Wells Sch. 1934, début same year in corps de ballet in *Casse Noisette*. First solo rôle was in *The Haunted Ballroom* (the young Tregennis) 1934, and her first important rôle the Creole in the revival of *Rio Grande* (1935). She took over most of Markova's rôles when Markova left the company in 1935, and thenceforth became the prima ballerina of the Royal B., a position which she still holds unchallenged. She danced *Giselle* in 1937 and all the classics, and cr. the leading rôles in most of Ashton's ballets. She has appeared as guest artist in Paris, Milan, Copenhagen, Oslo, etc., and is by common consent the greatest dancer of her era outside Russia. Her dancing with Helpmann during the war was greatly responsible for the rise in popularity of ballet in England and for the rapid development of the S. Wells Co. Among her greatest rôles must be mentioned *Giselle, Swan Lake, The Sleeping Beauty*, the poor girl in *Nocturne, Symphonic Variations, Daphnis and Chloë, Ondine, Apparitions*. She also danced in Petit's *Ballets de Paris* (1948), creating the rôle in *Les Demoiselles de la Nuit*. Created C.B.E. 1950, D.B.E. 1956. Made Hon. D. Litt., Leeds, 1953, and Mus. Doc., London, 1954. Mus. Doc., Oxford, 1959. In 1954 succeeded Genée as President of the Royal Academy of Dancing. Mar. Dr Roberto Arias, Panamanian Ambassador in London 1955. In 1959 she became a guest artist of the Royal Ballet. From 1963 she and Nureyev have danced together as guest artists all over the world.

FOOTBALLER, THE, ballet 3 acts, ch. Laschilin and Moiseyev, m. Oransky, dec. Fedorov, f.p. Bolshoi Th. Moscow 30 Mar 1930 (Messerer). Propaganda ballet. Moiseyev's comic sketch *Football* (m. A. Tsfasman) f.p. his Ensemble 1948 (Bocharnikov, Aristov, Volkov).

FORAINS, LES, ballet 1 sc., by Kochno, ch. Petit, m. H. Sauguet, dec. Bérard, f.p. B. des Ch. Élysées, Th. des Ch. Élysées, Paris 2 Mar 1945 (Éthéry Pagava, Petit). This was one of Petit's most pleasing works, showing the arrival of a circus and its pathetic departure.

FORLANA (or furlana), a favourite dance of the Venetian gondoliers, in 6/8 or 6/4 time.

FORNAROLI, Cia, b. Milan 1888, d. N.Y. 1954. It. dancer. Studied at Ballet Academy of Scala, Milan, and was a favourite pupil of Cecchetti. To America 1910 and became chief dancer at Met. Op., N.Y. 1910–14. Danced with Pavlova on tour and in S. America. Returned to Milan to become prima ballerina at the Scala, until 1934. In 1929 appointed director of the Ballet Academy. Mar. Walter Toscanini who was attacked by the Fascists, and in 1933 Mussolini had her removed from her offices. Retired to N.Y. where she taught. She was the greatest It. dancer of her generation.

FOR PEACE, ballet, ch. Chabukiani, m. Toradze, dec. Askurava and

Lapiashvili, f.p. Opera House, Tiflis 1953 (I. Alexidze, E. Gelovani, Chabukiani).

FOR THESE WHO DIE AS CATTLE, ballet, ch. Christopher Bruce, no music, dec. N. Baylis, f.p. B. Rambert, Young Vic Th., London 9 Mar 1972 (Bruce, Craig, Burge, Scoglio, Avrahami). War and Death.

FOSSÉ, Bob, b. Chicago 1927. Am. dancer and chor. of musicals. Ch. *Pajama Game, Bells are Ringing, Damn Yankees, Little Me, My Sister Eileen, Pal Joey, Sweet Charity* (1966), *Cabaret* (1972).

FOUETTÉ or TEMPS FOUETTÉ, lit. a whipped movement. A step executed by the danseuse on the point, in which the working leg is 'whipped' out to the side (second position en l'air) and in to the knee with a slight circular movement. It is frequently combined with turns on the point (fouettés en tournant). This spectacular step was a speciality of the Italian dancers from Milan who invaded St Petersburg in the 1880s. Bessone (q.v.) turned fourteen in *The Tulip of Harlem* (q.v.) in 1887 and Legnani, in *Cinderella* (1893), did successively three, two and four pirouettes on one preparation. In the same year she turned thirty-two in *The Tulip of Harlem*. This was the first time this feat had been accomplished in Russia, but in London, in 1892, she regularly turned 32 fouettés in *Aladdin* at the Alhambra and this is likely to have been the first achievement of the famous series. Legat records that by watching her carefully he was able to teach the trick to Kschessinska, who became the first Russ. dancer to execute the step. It is now a commonplace.

Although familiarly known as a fouetté, the strict nomenclature of this step is fouetté rond de jambe en tournant en dehors. See also SPOTTING.

According to the *Guinness Book of Records*, Rowena Jackson executed 121 fouettés en tournant in class in Melbourne, Australia, in 1940.

FOUETTÉ SAUTÉ, lit. a jumped fouetté. A step in which the dancer jumps upwards, and whilst in the air turns so as to alight facing in the opposite direction, e.g. the dancer, standing in fourth position facing the stage right, raises the back leg, which is furthest from the audience, in a grand battement to the fourth position front at the same time jumping upwards and, whilst in the air, makes a half turn of the body, alighting facing the stage left so that the raised leg is now in arabesque and nearest to the audience. This is the first step in the Coda of the *Swan Lake* Pas de Trois and is performed six times by the first female soloist in the centre of the stage, but in this case it is beaten (fouetté sauté battu), i.e. the legs are beaten together as in a cabriole. There are many other varieties of fouettés.

FOUNTAIN, GIRLS BY THE (*Les ballerines près de l'eau*), the back row of the corps de ballet. A nineteenth-century term derived from the conventional backcloth of the epoch which always had a fountain in the middle of it.

FOUNTAIN OF BAKHCHISARAI, THE, ballet 4 acts, ch. Zakharoff, m. Asafiev, dec. Khodasevitch, f.p. Kirov Th., Leningrad 28 Sept 1934 (Ulanova, Jordan, Dudko). Pushkin's poem. One of the most important Soviet ballets and performed all over Russia in various versions. The contrasting rôles of Maria (innocent and romantic) and Zarema (passionate) are great test-pieces for Russian dancers. To convey the romantic feeling in the music, Asafiev chose a *Nocturne* of John Field for Maria's *leitmotiv*.

FOUR TEMPERAMENTS, THE, ballet ch. Balanchine, m. Hindemith, dec. Seligman, f.p. Ballet Society, Central High Sch. of Needle Trades, N.Y. 20 Nov 1946 (Caccialanza, Georgia Hiden, LeClerq, Bolender, Lew Christensen, Dollar, Moncion). The 'temperaments' are depicted in the movements. It is in the repertoire of many Cos. Mounted for Royal B., f.p. C. Garden 25 Jan 1973 (Jenner, Bergsma, Dowell, Eagling).

FOYER DE DANSE, ballet ch. Ashton, m. Berners, dec. and cost. after Degas, f.p. B. Rambert, Mercury Th., London 9 Oct 1932 (Markova, Ashton).

FOYER DE LA DANSE, at the Paris Opéra, originally a retiring room at back of the stage, with mirror and bars. Under Dr Véron it became a salon where *abonnés* used to gather to see the dancers exercising before the ballets. Since 1929 it has lost this social aspect and it is now used only for rehearsals and occasional functions. The floor follows the rake of the stage and the walls are decorated with medallions of famous dancers.

FRACCI, Carla, b. Milan 1936. It. dancer. Entered Scala Sch., Milan, 1946, graduated 1954, presented in Passo d'Addio 1955. Promoted to soloist 1956 and prima ballerina 1958. Danced in Edinburgh International Ballet (1958), for Festival Ballet (*Giselle*) 1959 and ballerina of Massine's Balletto Europeo, Nervi and Edinburgh, 1960. Royal B. 1963 (guest), Am. B. Theatre 1967. Since 1963 she has been guest artist of the Scala B. Awarded the prize 'Leopardo d'Oro' in Italy in 1959.

FRAGMENS (Fr.), three or four acts of ballets taken from various operas, unrelated, to make up an evening's programme. An eighteenth-century term.

FRANCA, Celia, b. London 1921. Eng. dancer and chor. Studied R.A.D., Tudor, Idzikowsky. Début B. Rambert 1937. Joined International B. 1941 and S. Wells B. 1941–46, cr. Queen in *Hamlet*, Prostitute in

Miracle in the Gorbals, and appeared with S. Wells Th. B. Ballets include *Khadra* and *Bailemos* for S. Wells Th. B. Joined Metropolitan B. 1948. To Canada 1951 and founded National Ballet Co. of Canada, of which she has always been the Director. In 1968 chor. *Cinderella* (m. Prokofieff, dec. Rose) for her Co.

FRANCE, BALLET IN, see under PARIS OPÉRA BALLET, GRAND BALLET CLASSIQUE DE FRANCE, THÉÂTRE D'ART DU BALLET, BALLET THEATRE CONTEMPORAIN (at Angers), THÉÂTRE FRAN-ÇAIS DE LA DANSE, B. DES CHAMPS ÉLYSÉES, B. DE PARIS. There are also municipal ballets at Rouen (directed by J. P. Ruffier), Nancy (directed by Fred Chrystian), Nantes (directed by Jean Zierrat), Bordeaux (directed by V. Skouratoff and Maria Santesevan), Tours, Rheims, Toulouse, Toulon, Marseilles, Lille (directed by W. Cerullo), Nice, Rennes (directed by P. Juwrevsky), Dijon, Metz, Mulhouse, Limoges, Lyon (directed by V. Biagi). There is a ballet attached to the Opéra Comique in Paris. At Strasbourg is situated the Opéra et Ballet du Rhin (directed by Denis Carey). See also BLASKA (Felix), LAZZINI (Joseph), PETIT (Roland), LACOTTE (Pierre).

FRANCESCA DA RIMINI, ballet 2 sc., ch. Lichine, m. Tchaikovsky, dec. Messel, f.p. de Basil Co., C. Garden, London 15 July 1937 (Tcherni-cheva, Platoff, Petroff). Fokine also created a ballet to this music at the Maryinsky Th. 28 Nov 1915 (Egorova, Vladimiroff).

FRANCHETTI, Jean-Pierre, b. Paris 1944. Fr. dancer, son of Raymond F. Pupil of Paris Opéra Sch. Joined Paris Opéra B. becoming étoile.

FRANCHETTI, Raymond, b. Aubervilliers 1921. Fr. dancer and teacher. Pupil of Ricaux, Egorova, Preobrajenska. Joined Ballet Jeunesse 1937, B. Russes de Monte Carlo 1938 and 1943–45, de Cuevas 1946–47, from 1947 Paris Opéra. From 1963 teacher at Paris Opéra and in 1969 guest teacher of Royal B. and Royal B. Sch. Has own sch. in Paris. In 1971 appointed director of Paris Opéra Ballet.

FRANDSEN, Edite, b. Riga 1914. Latvian dancer and teacher. Pupil of Fedorovna at the Riga Sch. Joined Riga B. 1933 and became ballerina later. To Copenhagen 1951 where she was befriended by Vera Volkova. She opened her own sch. In 1952 was ballet mistress of Malmö B. In 1961 she became a teacher at the sch. of the R. Danish B. until 1972 when she left Denmark and became principal classical teacher at the State Academy for Music and Dance in Vienna. Among her pupils were Lone Isaksen and Dinna Bjorn.

FRANKIE AND JOHNNY, ballet 1 act, ch. Ruth Page and Bentley Stone, m. Moross, dec. Dupont, f.p. Page-Stone Ballet, Chicago 19 June 1938 (Page, Stone). The story of the Am. ballad of that name.

FRANKLIN, Frederic, b. Liverpool 1914. Eng. dancer. Studied under Elliott-Clarke in Liverpool, and Legat. Danced in musicals, etc., and joined Markova-Dolin Co. 1935. Joined B. Russe de Monte Carlo 1938 as premier danseur and since 1944 as maître de ballet. Danced, with Danilova, as guest artist with S. Wells B. at C. Garden 1949 and was Markova's partner in 1952. Cr. the Baron in *Gaîté Parisienne*, the Champion Roper in *Rodeo*, etc. Co-director of Washington Civic B. 1959. Artistic Adviser at Am. B. Th. 1961 and worked at the Scala, Milan. From 1962 Director of Washington Nat. B. and School.

FRANKS, Arthur H., b. Blackheath 1907, d. London 1963. Eng. writer on ballet. Joined staff of *Dancing Times* 1946, Director and Managing Editor 1958–63. Authoı of *Approach to the Ballet* (1948), *Ballet for Film and Television* (1950), *Girl's Book of Ballet* (1953), *Ballet—a Decade of Endeavour* (1955), *Pavlova* (1956), *Svetlana Beriosova* (1958), *History of Social Dancing* (1963).

FRÄNZL, Willy, b. Vienna 1898. Austrian dancer. Pupil of the Opera Sch., joined the Vienna Staatsoper B. 1914 becoming soloist 1921 and principal 1938. He was director of the school 1931 to 1962, while from 1935 to 1962 he was also ballet master. He revived several of the older Viennese ballets. Mar. Lucia Brauer.

FRASER, Moyra, b. Sydney 1923. Austral. dancer. Studied S. Wells Sch. and joined Co. 1938, becoming a principal dancer. Left in 1946 to become principal dancer in *Song of Norway*. Danced in intimate revues in London.

FRASQUILLO (Francisco Leon), b. Seville, c. 1900, d. 1940. Sp. dancer who danced with Argentina in Paris. Famous teacher, and husband of La Quica.

FRENCH, Ruth, b. London 1906. Eng. dancer and teacher. Pupil of Clustine and Morosoff. Principal dancer of Pavlova's Co. and danced with the Vic-Wells B. Principal dancer of London Hippodrome and danced in many revues and musicals. Teaches in London and an Examiner of the R.A.D. Received R.A.D. Queen Elizabeth II Award 1972.

FREY, Frank, b. Munich 1947. German dancer. Studied in Munich B. Sch. and under Blank. Joined Wuppertal B. 1964, then to Basel and Zürich. To Deutsche Oper, W. Berlin 1967 as soloist, danced first in London 1972.

FRIDERICIA, Allan, b. Copenhagen 1921. Dan. writer and manager. Educ. Copenhagen and Stockholm Univs. Wrote scenario of *Miss Julie* (ch. Cullberg 1950) etc. Manager Cullberg B. 1950, Scandinavian B. 1960–65, of Aarhus Th. 1963–66. Author of *Harald Lander* 1951, *Elsa*

Marianne von Rosen 1953 (his wife) etc. Critic of *Information* from 1951.

FRIENDS OF COVENT GARDEN, THE, an organization (functioning like a club, with members paying subscriptions) to help the promotion of opera and ballet at the Royal Opera House, Covent Garden. It was founded in 1962 with the Countess of Harewood as its president and the Hon. Kensington Davison as secretary. Its members have some special facilities for booking seats at the Opera House, they have access to certain rehearsals, and are entertained to lectures, concerts and social events. The subscriptions are devoted to subsidizing cheap tickets for students, giving scholarships to singers and dancers, to making possible the production of new operas and ballets, to providing equipment and facilities for the Opera House etc.—and also to publishing a house-magazine *About The House* (edited by Kensington Davison, first issue was November 1962). It also has a junior section for students and an American Friends organization.

FRIS, Maria, b. Berlin 1932, d. Hamburg 1961. Ger. dancer. Pupil of T. Gsovsky. Début at Opera House, Berlin. Joined Charrat's Co. as soloist 1952. Ballerina at Frankfurt 1956–58, at Hamburg 1960.

FROMAN, Margarita, b. Moscow 1890, d. Boston 1970. Russ. dancer, chor., and maîtresse de ballet. Pupil Bolshoi Th. Sch., Moscow. Entered Co. 1915. Joined Diaghileff's Co. 1916 and toured Europe and America. Returned to Moscow 1917 as ballerina at Bolshoi Th. Toured with her own Co. and settled in Yugoslavia (1921), where she became the head of the Zagreb National Ballet and chief teacher, chor. and producer. Chor. *Romeo and Juliet* (m. Prokofieff, 1949), *The Legend of Ochrid* (1947). To America in 1950s and taught in Connecticut.

FUENTE, Luis, b. Madrid 1946. Spanish dancer. From 1957 studied with Hector Zaraspe (classical and Sp.) in Madrid. Joined Antonio's Co. 1961 to 1964, becoming soloist. Called to N.Y. in 1964 by Zaraspe (who was teaching at the Am. Ballet Center) he joined the Joffrey B., becoming a principal. Left Joffrey B. 1970 following his substituting a traditional *farruca* in *Le Tricorne*, in place of Massine's, and joined Washington Nat. B. In 1972 joined Dutch Nat. B. and 1973 Festival B.

FUGITIVE, THE, ballet in 1 act, ch. Andrée Howard, m. L. Salzedo, book and dec. H. Stevenson, f.p. B. Rambert, Royal County Th., Bedford 16 Nov 1944 (Gilmour, McClelland, Gore). The flight of a political prisoner.

FUKAGAWA, Hideo, b. Nagoya 1949. Japanese dancer. Pupil of Minoru Ochi in Tokyo and Schneider in E. Berlin. Joined Komische Oper, E. Berlin 1969, after winning Bronze Medal at Varna 1965, Silver Medal at Moscow International Competition 1969. Came over to West with his teacher Schneider 1971 and joined Stuttgart B. First danced in London in Buckle's Gala 1971 (Blue Bird, with Lesley Collier). Won Nijinsky Prize, Paris 1969.

FULLER, Loïe, b. Illinois 1862, d. Paris 1928. Am. dancer who gave solo recitals all over Europe and America. She made great use of scarves and other drapery, with concealed lighting under the stage, with which she gained her remarkable effects. Her two most famous dances were the *Serpentine Dance* and *La Danse de Feu*. Painters and poets of the Art Nouveau period fell under her spell after her début at the Folies-Bergère in 1893 and she embodied the dreams of the Symbolist poets. At the Paris Exposition of 1900 she had a theatre designed in Art Nouveau style by Sauvage. She encouraged Isadora Duncan and was distressed by her subsequent ingratitude. She published her autobiography in Paris in 1908 *Quinze Ans de ma Vie*.

FULOP, Viktor, b. Budapest 1929. Hungarian dancer. Trained under Nadasi, and in Moscow under Rudenko and Messerer 1955–56 and also as chor. under Yermolayev and Varlamov 1965–67. Liszt Prize 1960, Kossuth Prize 1962. Merited Artist 1968. Guest artist Festival B. (with Kun) 1961 and 1963.

FULTON, Gaye, b. Manchester 1939. Eng. dancer. Trained at Cone-Ripman Sch. Joined Festival Ballet 1958 and became soloist 1960. Principal ballerina in Zürich from 1964. Guest ballerina Washington Nat. B. 1970, Festival B. 1970–71, and rejoined Festival B. 1972.

FUOCO, Sofia (Maria Brambilla), b. Milan 1830, d. Carate Lario 1916. It. dancer. Danced at the Paris Opéra 1846–50. Retired 1858. She was nicknamed 'La Pointue' for she was the strongest dancer of her time on points. A pupil of Blasis, she was one of his 'Pleiades' (see BLASIS).

FUZELIER, b. 1677, d. 1752. Fr. librettist at the Paris Opéra, producing many ballets between 1713 and 1749. His best-known ballet was *Les Indes Galantes*.

G

GABLE, Christopher, b. London 1940. Eng. dancer and actor. Studied at Royal B. Sch. and entered C. Garden Op. B. 1956. Joined Royal B. 1957, becoming soloist of Touring Section. Transferred to C. Garden section 1963. After an injury he gave up dancing and studied acting, giving his first performance (Dorian in *The Picture of Dorian Grey*) at Watford in 1967. Subsequently he has had a number of acting rôles in television. Cr. The Cousin in *The Invitation*, the Young Man in *The Two Pigeons*, and MacMillan created his *Romeo and Juliet* for him and Seymour (though the rôles were first danced by Nureyev and Fonteyn). In Ken Russell's films for B.B.C.-T.V. he acted Eric Fenby in *Delius* and Richard Strauss in *Strauss* (1970).

GABOVICH, Mikhail, b. Gouv, Kieff 1905, d. Moscow 1965. Russ. dancer. Studied Bolshoi Sch. Moscow and entered Co. 1924, becoming a principal dancer. He was one of the first of the great dancers of the Soviet generation and created rôles in *The Hump-backed Horse* (Gorsky), *Fountain of Bakhchisarai, Prisoner of the Caucasus* (Zakharoff), *Taras Bulba* (Zakharoff) etc. Taught at Moscow Sch. 1951–65 and was its Artistic Director 1954–58. Author of many articles on ballet and a paper on Gorsky, his teacher. Hon. Artist U.S.S.R. 1937, People's Artist 1951, Stalin Prize 1946 and 1950.

GABT, the Russian abbreviation for the institution which comprises the Bolshoi Th., Moscow.

GADD, Ulf, b. Gothenburg 1943. Swed. dancer and chor. Pupil of Garde-meister and R. Swed. B. Sch. Joined R. Swedish B. 1961, Harkness B. 1966–67, Gothenburg B. 1967–70. With Connie Borg founded New Swed. B. 1970. Chor. *Miraculous Mandarin* 1969, *Ebb and Flow* (m. Vivaldi) 1970.

GADES, Antonio, b. Alicante 1936. Sp. dancer. Danced in Pilar Lopez Co., becoming her partner. Left in 1962 to teach at Scala Milan. Formed his own group which danced at N.Y. World Fair 1964 and appeared at Sadler's Wells, London 1970, with Christina Hoyos as his partner.

GAÎTÉ PARISIENNE, ballet 1 act, book and dec. E. de Beaumont, ch. Massine, m. Offenbach and Rosenthal, f.p. B. Russe de Monte Carlo, Monte Carlo 5 Apr 1938 (Tarakanova, Massine, Youskevitch). A rich Peruvian in a Paris night club. This ballet was also filmed in America 1941. It is in the repertoire of several companies. Mounted by Festival B., London Coliseum 9 Apr. 1973 (Gielgud, Dubreuil).

GALA PERFORMANCE, ballet 1 act, ch. Tudor, m. Prokofieff (1st movement, 3rd piano concerto and Classical Symphony), dec. Stevenson, f.p. London B., Toynbee Hall, London 5 Dec 1938 (van Praagh, Lloyd, Larsen). In repertoire of B. Rambert 1940, B. Theatre 1941, and R. Swed. B. A comic ballet and a skit on the pre-Fokine style.

GALEOTTI, Vincenzo, b. Florence 1733, d. Copenhagen 1816. It. dancer and chor. Pupil of Angiolini and Noverre. Danced in London, King's Th. 1769–70. Ballet-master San Moise Th., Venice 1770–75. To Copenhagen 1775, where he became ballet-master and remained there the rest of his life. His first ballets were in the style of Angiolini, but he grew very personal in style and he was responsible for introducing the Romantic Ballet into Scandinavia. Among his ballets are *Dido* (1777), *Les Caprices du Cupidon et du Maître de Ballet* (1786) (still in the repertoire), *Lagertha* (1801) (his most famous, and the first ballet with a Nordic theme), *Nina* (1802), *Romeo and Juliet* (1811). He was made a knight in 1812, which made it impossible for him to appear on the stage in consequence. He was the teacher of Anna Margrethe Schall.

GALINA, Anna (Evelyn Cournand), b. N.Y. 1936. Am. dancer. Pupil of Tatiana Piankova. In 1956 she and her teacher founded a Co. Le Théâtre d'Art du Ballet, based in Paris, with herself as ballerina. It tours the world, with ballets by Fokine, Dollar etc.

GALLEA, Christina, b. Sydney 1940. Australian dancer. Pupil of Danetree, Idzikowsky, Northcote. Joined Australian Th. B. (director, W. Gore) 1955, Frankfurt B. 1958, B. der Lage Landen 1959, Am. Fest. B. 1960, Amsterdam B. 1961, Teatro del Balletto 1962. With her husband Alexander Roy founded International Ballet Caravan 1965.

GALLI, Rosina, b. 1896, d. Milan 1940. It. dancer and ballet mistress. Studied at the Scala, Milan Sch. and in 1912 became soloist at the Chicago Opera. She became the solodancer at the Met. Op., New York from 1914. She took part in the ballets which Bolm chor. there and from 1919 to 1935 was ballet mistress. Mar. Giulio Gatti-Casazza the General Manager of the Met Op., N.Y.

GALLIARD, a gay dance in 3/4 time with leaping steps, said to have originated in Lombardy towards the end of the sixteenth century and usually danced after a pavane. The galliard is referred to by Shakespeare as the sink-a-pace (from the French cinq pas, cinque pas, or five steps which were executed to six beats, the fifth being without a step). The *Tordion* was a form of galliard danced with less elevation. By the mid-seventeenth century the pavane and the galliard were no longer fashionable and had been supplanted by the saraband.

GALOP, a gay round dance in 2/4 time which would seem to have originated in Germany early in the nineteenth century, where it spread to France and England and was subsequently incorporated in the quadrille. Its characteristic is the change of step at the conclusion of every half phrase. A galop has often been used as a finale to a series of ballet-divertissements.

GALSTYAN, Vilen, b. Erevan 1941. Armenian dancer. Pupil of Martykossian and Chabukiani. Joined Tiflis B. 1961 becoming a principal dancer. Danced in London 1963. Varna Gold Medal 1968. Joined Bolshoi B.

GANIBALOVA, Vazira, b. Tashkent 1948. Russ. dancer. Graduated from

Kirov Sch. Leningrad to Kirov B. 1967 (class of Dudinskaya). First danced in London 1970.

GARCIA, Jean, b. Grenoble 1936. Fr. dancer. Pupil of Combes, V. Gsovsky. Joined Strasbourg B. 1951, becoming principal dancer in 1960 and director 1968–72.

GARDEL, Maximilien, b. Mannheim 1741, d. Paris 1787. Fr. dancer, and chor. at the Paris Opéra 1781–87. He was the first to dispense with the customary mask (1773) which he refused to wear in order to show that he, not Vestris, was dancing a rôle. He and Vestris are said to have invented the rond de jambe. Chor. many ballets, notably *La Rosière*, *Mirza*, *Le Premier Navigateur*, and *Le Déserteur*.

GARDEL, Pierre, b. Nancy 1758, d. Paris 1840. Fr. dancer and chor. Brother and pupil of the above. Became premier danseur at Paris Opéra 1780 and in 1787 appointed, succeeding his brother, chief maître de ballet and chor., a post which he retained for forty years throughout the many changes of government. After an accident in 1796 he ceased to dance, but he was also appointed Director of the Ballet School in 1799 until 1815. He was thus the virtual Dictator of the Opéra, and a man of great distinction and personality. He was an accomplished violinist. He chor. many ballets, notably *Télémaque dans l'Ile de Calypso* (1791), *Psyche* (1790), *La Dansomanie*, *Le Jugement de Pâris*. Mar. Marie Miller (q.v.).

GARDINER, Lisa, b. Washington D.C. 1894, d. there 1956. Am. dancer and teacher. Pupil of Protopopovitch, Bolm, Trefilova. Joined B. Intime 1917, Pavlova's Co. 1918–22, Fokine's Co. 1922 and then taught in Washington from 1922. Opened her own school and in 1945 joined Mary Day as Director of Washington Sch. of B. and they founded the Washington B. in 1956.

GARGOUILLADE, probably from Fr. *gargouiller*, to gurgle. A brilliant series of steps in which the left leg describes two small circular movements in the air (rond de jambe en dehors) before the point of the left foot is drawn up to the knee of the supporting leg (retiré). The dancer then springs upwards to alight on the left foot with a small plié bringing the right foot in line with the knee, and executing a rond de jambe en dedans before closing it in the fifth position in front. The arms throughout are usually held down (fifth Cecchetti en bas). The gargouillade is said to have been first introduced by the French danseuse Marie Lyonnois in the middle of the eighteenth century, but, whilst she may have been the first danseuse to perform it, this step would seem to have been known well before this and to have been particularly affected to the entrances of 'Winds' and 'Demons' and to 'Comic dancers' generally. The celebrated Grand Dupré, who was later to train Noverre, excelled at it, we are told. In the cont. Russ. school, called rond de jambe doublé.

GASKELL, Sonia, b. Kieff 1904. Russ. teacher and ballet mistress. Worked with Diaghileff Company and began teaching in Paris in 1936. To Holland 1939 and gave children's classes and formed her own group, Ballet Recital, after the war. From 1955 was Director of The Netherlands Ballet at The Hague and in charge of the school. When Het Nationale Ballet was formed in Amsterdam in 1961 she was appointed the Artistic Director. Retired 1968.

GATOB, the Russ. initials of the organization which includes the Kirov B. in Leningrad.

GAUTIER, Théophile, b. Tarbes 1811, d. Neuilly 1872. Fr. poet and critic. He was one of the great figures in the Romantic movement in literature and in ballet, and his criticisms and descriptions of the dancers of that period (the period of Taglioni, Elssler, and Grisi) are unsurpassed. 'Art for Art's sake' was his phrase and it was the guiding principle in his literary work. He was responsible for the libretto of *Giselle* and was in love with Carlotta Grisi (whose sister he married) though his passion does not appear to have been returned. He sent for her when dying and she came to Paris from Geneva, only to be prevented by his sisters from seeing him, though he died breathing her name.

GAVOTTE, from the old Provençal *gavoto*. A gay dance in two, or frequently four, time evolved from the Branle, known in the sixteenth century and which attained its greatest vogue at the Courts of Louis XIV and XV, after which it declined in popularity. The gavotte usually followed a minuet and sometimes preceded a musette.

GAYANÉ, ballet 4 acts, ch. Anisimova, m. Khatchaturian, dec. Altman, f.p. Kirov B. at Perm 9 Dec 1942, where they were evacuated (Anisimova, Dudinskaya, Shelest, Sergeyev, Andreev). Set in Armenia, a ballet of love, jealousy and war, with the Sabre Dance occurring during the final divertissement.

GÉ, George (Grönfeldt), b. St Petersburg 1893, d. Helsinki 1962. Finnish dancer and chor. Trained in St Petersburg under Legat and studied music under Glazounov. Was the first ballet master of the National B. of Finland 1921 and mounted the first ballet ever staged there, *Swan Lake* (1922). Remained in Helsinki until 1935 and then went to France. Worked with Fokine and joined Blum's Co. in Monte Carlo. Chor. of ballets at Châtelet Th., Paris, the Mogador and the Folies-Bergère. Ballet master of R. Swedish B. 1939–48, the Gothenburg B. and of National B. of Finland again from 1955 to his death.

GEITEL, Klaus, b. Berlin 1924. German writer on ballet. Studied at the universities of Halle, Berlin and Paris. Ballet critic of *Die Welt*.

GELDARD, Kathleen, b. Sydney 1940. Australian dancer. Pupil of J. and M. Halliday. Joined Royal B. 1958. Returned to Australia 1962 as soloist of Australian B. and principal in 1966.

GELKER, Vivi, b. Copenhagen 1942. Dan. dancer. Entered R. Dan. Sch. 1952 and the Co. in 1961. Became solodancer 1967. Created rôle of the girl in Flindt's *Miraculous Mandarin* 1967. Mar. Flemming Flindt.

GELTZER, Vassily, b. 1840, d. 1908. Russ. dancer and mime. Father of Yekaterina Geltzer. He was *regisseur* of the Moscow B. in the 1890s. His talent as a mime was so extraordinary that in the opera *The Song of Triumphant Love* (m. Simon) people used to come for the second act only, just to see him play a part of a deaf-mute.

GELTZER, Yekaterina, b. Moscow 1876, d. there 1962. Russ. dancer. Daughter of Vassily Geltzer. Pupil of Bolshoi Sch. and joined Bolshoi B. 1894. After making her début there she went to St Petersburg to study under Johansson, in 1896. She took a solo rôle in the first performance of *Raymonda* there in 1898. Returned to Moscow, but when Legnani left St Petersburg in 1901, Geltzer went back there to take over the principal rôle in *Raymonda* from her. In 1910 she danced with Volinine in Diaghileff's Co. in Paris and at the Alhambra, London 1911. She was the most popular of the Moscow ballerinas and worked there under Gorsky, excelling in *demi-caractère* rôles (creating the chief rôle in *The Red Poppy* 1927). Mar. her partner Tikhomiroff. She was one of the first artists to receive the title People's Artist of the U.S.S.R. (1925) and she toured Russia in 1935.

GENÉE, Dame Adeline, b. Hinnerup, Aarhus 1878, d. Esher 1970. Danish dancer. Studied with her aunt and her uncle, Alexandre Genée. Début at 10 in Christiania. Première danseuse Centralhallen Th., Stettin at 15, of Imperial Opera, Berlin at 17, of Munich Opera at 18. Guest artist, Copenhagen 1902. To Empire Th., London 1897, and remained leading dancer for ten years. Danced in America 1908 and (with own Co.) 1912. To Australia and New Zealand 1913. Retired 1914, but gave charity performances afterwards. Danced Swanilda in *Coppélia*, one of her greatest rôles, at Empire Th. 1906. One of the founders of the Camargo Society and was President of the Royal Academy of Dancing from its foundation until 1954. One of the great figures in the history of ballet in England and a dancer of exceptional lightness, delicacy, and charm. Created D.B.E. in 1950 and held many Danish decorations. Hon. D. Mus., London. In 1967 the Genée Th. at East Grinstead was named after her, and a rose bears her name. The Genée Gold Medal which she founded in 1931 is the highest award given to a dancer by the R.A.D.

GENZANO, FLOWER FESTIVAL IN, ballet 1 act, ch. August Bournonville, m. Paulli and Helsted, f.p. R. Dan. B., Copenhagen 19 Dec 1858. A pas de deux from it is still performed.

GEOLOGISTS, THE, see HEROIC POEM.

GEORGI, Yvonne, b. Leipzig 1903. German dancer and chor. Studied under Jaques-Dalcroze and Mary Wigman, and under Rausanne in Paris. Toured the world as partner of Harald Kreutzberg. Ballet mistress at Gera 1925, at Hanover 1926, at Amsterdam (and head of the school) 1932, at Düsseldorf 1951 and returned to Hanover 1954 in charge of the ballet until her retirement in 1969. Chor. for film *Ballerina* 1950 (Violette Verdy). Chor. many ballets in Hanover, Salzburg, Vienna etc.

GEORGIADIS, Nicholas, b. Athens 1925. Greek painter. Studied in Athens, N.Y. and London. Closely associated with Kenneth MacMillan as designer of his ballets, notably *Danses Concertantes, House of Birds* (both 1955), *Noctambules* (1956), *The Burrow, Agon* (both 1958), *The Invitation* (1960), *Diversions* (1961), *Romeo and Juliet* (1965), and for Nureyev *Swan Lake* (Vienna 1964, Berlin 1969), *Sleeping Beauty* (Milan 1966), *Casse Noisette* (C. Garden 1968), *Raymonda* (Zürich 1972).

GERBER, Judith, b. Vienna 1946. Austrian dancer. Pupil of Plucis at the Staatsoper Sch. Joined Vienna Staatsoper B. 1961 and coryphée 1967.

GERDT, Pavel, b. St Petersburg 1844, d. there 1917. Russ. dancer and teacher of German extraction. Début St Petersburg 1860, premier danseur 1866. One of the greatest danseurs nobles in the history of ballet in Russia. Cr. chief rôles in Petipa's *Kalkabrino, Cinderella, Halte de Cavalerie, Sleeping Princess*, and Ivanov's *Casse Noisette*. Later he became the teacher of the senior class at the Imp. Sch. (the generation of Karsavina, Nijinsky, Fokine). Celebrated his jubilee as dancer and was still on the stage 1916. Father of Elizaveta Gerdt.

GERDT, Elizaveta Pavlovna, b. St Petersburg 1891 daughter of Pavel Gerdt. Russ. dancer and teacher. Pupil of Anna Johansson at Maryinsky Sch. and graduated 1908 from the class of Fokine. Became soloist 1913 and ballerina 1917. In 1918 she gave company classes and in 1934 she went to the Bolshoi Sch. Moscow to teach, where she has produced such dancers as Plisetskaya, Struchkova, Maximova, Ryabinkina etc.

GERMANY, BALLET IN. There is no private or national ballet in Germany, but the many city opera houses maintain their own ballets, primarily to dance in the operas, and there is considerable activity among them. In a few opera houses the dancers give a regular (two or three times in a month) *ballettabend* or evening solely devoted to ballet. The Ballet Master is responsible for the choreography of the ballets as well as maintaining and training the troupe. As he is usually engaged by the Intendant on a year-to-year contract there is a continuous moving round of ballet masters and dancers, as in the ballet of the nineteenth century. No permanent repertory is built up; the ballet master produces three or four new ballets at the beginning of the season (usually in October or November) and these will be performed throughout the year and then abandoned.

For the most part the ballets were arranged in the 'Central European' style, but in the early 1950s, as a result of the successes of tours by the Sadler's Wells and Cuevas ballets, the classical style attracted the attention of some of the German houses. De Valois' *Rake's Progress* was mounted in Munich, and Alan Carter was appointed ballet master there. At the same time Beriozoff was installed in Stuttgart and mounted, among other ballets, *Sleeping Beauty* with great success. He also assiduously built up his public for ballet and formed a ballet club to maintain interest. From these two cities the revival of the classical ballet spread and many of the 'Central European' ballet masters and mistresses turned to it as best they could.

Only two houses, Stuttgart and Düsseldorf, have had the courage to appoint good ballet masters on a long-term basis and give them full support and in consequence these two cities lead German ballet. Cranko, a choreographer of genius, built up his Stuttgart Ballet (q.v.) to a pre-eminent position and was unique in founding a ballet school in the Russian and English style (though this had been instigated by Beriozoff). Erich Walter established a reputation for his ballet spectacles while working at Wuppertal 1953–64 (notable for his collaboration with Wendel as a scenic designer). The Walter-Wendel combination moved to Düsseldorf and with greater resources made the Düsseldorf Ballet renowned for its productions. Better dancers were engaged (a policy which can only be pursued by giving the ballet master a long period of years in which to operate) and the great classical ballets were mounted there. Also these two cities (alone in Germany) have detached their ballet company from the operatic work, for which they each have a separate group, thus enabling the creative work to be carried on without hindrance. Carter continued Walter's good work in Wuppertal for a time and it remains a leading ballet. No other opera houses have provided the atmosphere for ballet to flourish fully and in spite of the engagement of good ballet masters they have not been able to work on a long-term basis, though Berlin, Munich, Cologne, Hamburg, Frankfurt and Hanover maintain strong companies of dancers. However, none but Stuttgart have been able to build up a repertoire or a stylish corps de ballet. The potentials are great in Germany but the resources are too spread out and inter-city rivalry is too great to form a national ballet. In East Germany there are many companies but little is heard of them. The most important Cos. are the Staatsoper B. and the Komische Oper B.—both in East Berlin. In both, the Russian Olga Lepeshinskaya works. Also see SCHILLING (Tom). Other important Cos. are those in the cities of Leipzig and Dresden. Many dancers from the E. Berlin Cos. have defected to the West in 1970–72.

GIELGUD, Maina, b. London 1945. Eng. dancer. Pupil of Hampshire Sch., London, Karsavina, Idzikowsky, Cameron, Gsovsky, Hightower. Joined Petit's Co. 1961, Cuevas 1962, and Miskovitch B. 1962, Grand Ballet Classique de France 1964–67, Béjart's B. du XXme Siècle 1967–71, Berlin B. 1971, as principal. Guest ballerina Marseilles B. 1970. Danced in London 1971 in Buckle's *Save the Titian* Gala. Ballerina of Festival B. 1972.

GIGUE (It. *Giga*), dance in triple time popular in France in early eighteenth century. See JIG.

GILMOUR, Glenn, b. Hamilton, Ontario 1938. Canadian dancer. Trained at Canad. Nat. B. School, entered the company 1958 and became soloist 1964.

GILMOUR, Sally, b. Malaya 1921. First studied in Singapore. To England 1930, studied with Karsavina and in 1933 entered Rambert Sch., eventually becoming the leading dancer of the B. Rambert and one of the greatest dramatic dancers of her generation. The rôle with which she is always associated, and which she created, is Silvia in *Lady into Fox* (ch. Howard 1939). She also created the rôle in *Confessional* (Gore 1941), Duck in *Peter and the Wolf* (Staff 1940), Younger Sister in *The Fugitive* (Howard 1944), *Simple Symphony* (Gore 1944), *Winter Night* (Gore 1948), Tulip in *The Sailor's Return* (Howard 1947), etc. She first danced *Swan Lake*, Act II, in 1944 and *Giselle*, Act II, in 1945, Act I and the entire ballet in 1946. Married and went to live in Australia 1953. Returned to London 1972.

GILPIN, John, b. Southsea 1930. Studied Cone-Ripman Sch. and Rambert. Was a child actor. Joined B. Rambert 1945, becoming a principal dancer. Joined Festival B. 1950, becoming its premier danseur. Guest artist of Royal B. in 1961 and 1963 and has danced with many companies in Europe and America. From 1969, guest artist of Festival B. He resigned 1970.

GINGERBREAD HEART, THE, ballet 3 acts, ch. Parlic, m. Baranovic, dec. Denic, f.p. Belgrade Opera 15 July 1950 (Peric, Markovic). A folk ballet, also in the repertoire of the Zagreb Opera (ch. Froman).

GINNER, Ruby, b. Cannes 1886. Eng. teacher of dancing. Studied ballet in her youth and did research into the dancing of the ancient Greeks. Formed her own troupe The Grecian Dancers (1913) which gave its first performance at the Tivoli Music Hall, London. Started the Ruby Ginner Sch. of Dancing during the Great War and taught at the Central Sch. of Speech and Drama 1914–18. In 1916 Irene Mawer joined her and her school of 'the Revived Greek Dance' was renamed the Ginner-Mawer Sch. of Dance and Drama. In 1923 the Association of Teachers of the Revived Greek Dance was formed (from 1936 called The Greek Dance Association (q.v.)). From 1924 to 1951 its examinations were held in conjunction with the R.A.D. and in 1951 the Association was taken into the Imperial Society of Teachers of Dancing. In 1930 she took a company to Athens to perform in the Delphic Festival. Awarded M.B.E. 1968. Author of *The Revived Greek Dance* (1933), *Gateway to the Dance* (1960) etc.

GIOJA, Gaetano, b. Naples 1768, d. there 1826. It. dancer and chor., the chief of the Neapolitan school. Studied under Traffieri. Début Rome 1787. Chor. his first ballet, *Sofonisba*, at Vicenza 1789. Famous for his mime, he became known as the 'Sophocles of the Dance'. As a chor. he was the disciple of Vigano and chor. 221 ballets, but the ballet in Italy went into a decline after his master's death. He was a kindly and well-liked man, and several of his ballets inspired other chors., e.g. *Nina* and *Les Mineurs Wallaques* (used by Taglioni as *Nathalie*). His most famous ballet was *Cesare in Egitto*, Scala, Milan 1815.

GIPSY, LA, ballet 3 acts 5 sc., ch. Mazilier, m. Benoist, Thomas, Marliani, dec. Philastre and Cambon, cost. Lormier, f.p. Paris Opéra 28 Jan 1839 (Elssler, Mazilier). This was Elssler's great ballet and the one in which she danced her sensational *Cracovienne*. It is set in and around Edinburgh.

GIRAUDET, Eugène, Fr. author of *Traité de la Danse*, Paris 1890, a useful account of all types of dancing, with 500 illustrations.

GISELLE, or LES WILIS, ballet 2 acts, book by Gautier and Saint-Georges, ch. Coralli and Perrot, m. Adam and some numbers by Burgmüller, dec. Ciceri, f.p. Paris Opéra 28 June 1841 (Carlotta Grisi, Lucien Petipa, with Adèle Dumilâtre as Myrthe). This, the greatest of the Romantic ballets, was inspired by a passage in Heine's *De l'Allemagne* describing the tradition that betrothed girls who have died before their wedding day return, as Wilis, to dance in the misty moonlight. In the first act, Giselle, a country girl, kills herself with a sword on discovering that her lover, Albrecht, has deceived her. In the second act, she rises from her grave and dances with the Wilis and with her lover, who lays her to earth as dawn breaks. The ballet makes the greatest demands on the dramatic powers of the dancer (in Act I) and on her technique and sensitivity (in Act II): consequently it has always been the touchstone by which ballerinas have been judged for over 100 years, and the ballet which all wish to interpret. It was first produced in London in 1842 (Grisi), St Petersburg in 1842 (Andreyanova), in Italy at the Scala, Milan 1843, in America at Boston 1846 (Mary Ann Lee) and N.Y. later the same year (Mme Augusta). Among the famous interpreters of the rôle, besides those mentioned above, must be mentioned Grahn (1843), Cerrito (1843), Elssler (1843), Bogdanova (1856), Ferraris (1859), Rosati (1862), Muravieva (1862), Zina Mérante (1863), Grantzow (1866), Vazem (1878), Gorschenkova (1884), Bessone (1887), Grimaldi (1899), Preobrajenska (1899), Zambelli (1901), Pavlova (1903), Karsavina (1910), Spessivtseva (1924), Ulanova (1932), Markova (1934), Nemchinova (1935), Fonteyn (1937), Toumanova (1939), Chauviré (1944), Grey (1944), Alonso, Gilmour (1945), Struchkova, Goldwyn (1953), Beriosova (1956), Daydé (1953), Maximova (1960), Makarova (1961), Bessmertnova (1965), Haydee (1966), Evdokimova (1971).

Some notable productions were (1) the first in London, Her Majesty's Th. 12 Mar 1842 (Grisi, Perrot), (2) at the Empire Th., London 26 Dec 1884 (Alice Holt, Mlle Sismondi as Loys), (3) by Diaghileff B., dec. Benois, at Paris Opéra 18 June 1910 (Karsavina, Nijinsky). This production was f.p. C. Garden 16 Oct 1911 (Karsavina, Nijinsky), Pavlova also danced the rôle in this London production, (4) by the Paris Opéra for Spessivtseva's début 26 Nov 1924 (Spessivtseva, Aveline), and again 11 Mar 1932 when she danced it with Lifar—his first Albrecht, (5) by the Vic-Wells B., at the Old Vic, London 1 Jan 1934 (Markova, Dolin, Darnborough), (6) by the Camargo Society, Savoy Th., London 24 June 1932 (Spessivtseva, Dolin), (7) by the B. Rambert, Repertory Th., Birmingham, dec. H. Stevenson 31 July 1945 (Gilmour, Gore)—Act II only. The entire ballet was f.p. S. Wells Th., London 11 July 1946 (Gilmour, Mulys), (8) the first in America, at the Howard Athenaeum, Boston 1 Jan 1846 (Mary Ann Lee, George Washington Smith).

GITANA, LA, ballet, prologue, 3 acts, 5 sc., ch. Filippo Taglioni, m. Schmidt and Auber, f.p. Bolshoi Th., St Petersburg 23 Nov 1838 (Taglioni, Goltz). In this ballet Taglioni made her first great success in Russia. The story is of a child stolen by gypsies in Spain and recovered ten years later in Russia. In London, f.p. Her Majesty's Th., 6 June 1839 (Taglioni).

GITIS, the Russian abbreviation for the Lunacharski State Institute of Theatrical Art, founded in Moscow 1958 for the training of all theatrical artists, critics, ballet masters, choreographers in their crafts and in Marxism.

GIULIANO, Juan, b. Cordoba, Argentina 1930. Argentinian dancer. Studied at Colon Th. Sch., Buenos Aires. Début in SODRE ballet Montevideo 1950, then danced with the ballet in São Paolo 1953. Joined Cuevas B. 1956, soloist with Charrat's B. 1957–59, Ballet Russe 1961–62, Opéra Comique 1963 where he choreographs. Joined Ballet Theatre Contemporain at Amiens 1968. Mar. Helene Trailine.

GLADSTEIN, Robert, b. Berkeley, Calif. 1943. Am. dancer. Pupil of the Christensens. Joined San Francisco B. 1959 becoming soloist. Joined Am. Ballet Th. 1967, soloist 1969. Chor. several ballets for San Francisco B.

GLASSTONE, Richard, b. Elisabethville (Belgian Congo) 1935. Brit. dancer and chor. Studied at Cape Town B. Sch. 1952–56 and in London at Rambert Sch. and de Vos 1957. Principal character dancer of Univ. of Cape Town Ballet 1953–56 and 1960–63. Soloist and chor. of Scapino Ballet, Amsterdam 1957–59 and 1963–65. Chor. for them *The Little Mermaid* (m. Van Zanten) 1957, *Alice in Wonderland* (m. Bartok) 1958, *The Golden Key* (m. Ketting) 1964. Resident chor. and director and principal teacher of Turkish Nat. B., Ankara 1965–69. Chor. for them *Lady with the Dagger* (m. Tarcan) 1966, *Sylvia* (m. Delibes) 1967, *Prince of the Pagodas* (m. Britten) 1967, *Iliskiler* (m. Britten) 1968. In 1969 joined staff of Royal B. Sch. and chor. *Primavera* (m. Vivaldi) for Royal B. Sch. Matinée 1970. Mounted *Rake's Progress* (de Valois) for B. van Vlaanderen 1972.

GLAZOUNOV, Alexander, b. St Petersburg 1865, d. Paris 1936. Russ. composer of ballet at Maryinsky Th. (following Tchaikovsky) of Petipa's *Raymonda* (1898), *Ruses d'Amour* (1900), and *Les Saisons* (1900). Ashton's *Birthday Offering* (1956) also has Glazounov's music.

GLIÈRE, Reinhold, b. Kiev 1875, d. Moscow 1946. Russ. composer of the ballets *Chrysis* (1912), *Egyptian Night* (1926), *The Red Poppy* (1927) and *The Bronze Horseman* (1949).

GLINKIANA, ballet, ch. Balanchine, m. Glinka, dec. E. Frances, f.p. N.Y. City B., State Th., Lincoln Center, N.Y. 23 Nov. 1967 (Verdy, Paul, Hayden, McBride, Mejia, Villella). Pure classical dancing.

GLISSADE, lit. a glide. A sliding step executed in any direction (usually a joining step). Starting in the fifth position right foot front with a demi-plié, the right foot is slid out to a dégagé position in second along the ground, the weight is then transferred to the right foot and the left leg, now extended (dégagé) to the second position on the ground, is then closed behind the right foot in a fifth position with a sliding movement. This is a glissade devant. When the step is begun with the back foot and executed without changing the feet it is known as a glissade derrière; when begun with the front foot and the feet are changed in the execution of the step it is a glissade dessous, and when begun with the back foot and the feet are changed it is a glissade dessus. (Both these last two variants are generally known as a glissade changé.) Also en avant and en arrière. In recent years the R.A.D. Grade Work (juniors only) and General Certificate Examinations (G.C.E.) the use of the words dessous and dessus have been interchanged in defining the glissade. But in the Senior Work (and elsewhere in ballet) they remain as given above.

GLISSÉ, a glided step (as in pas glissé).

GLOIRE, lit. glory. A stage-machine in the latter part of the seventeenth century and early eighteenth for lowering from the flies celestial beings on clouds or in chariots.

GLUSZKOVSKY, Adam, b. St Petersburg 1793, d. *c.* 1870. Russ. dancer, teacher, and chor. Favourite pupil of Didelot. Studied abroad under Duport. In 1811 he was sent to Moscow as ballet-master to stage Didelot's ballets (and his own, notably *Russlan and Ludmilla*). From 1812 to 1839 he was principal dancer and ballet master of the Bolshoi B., Moscow and teacher at the new Moscow Sch. (founded 1809) which he built up to such a degree that while he was there the Moscow dancers rivalled those of St Petersburg. Author of *Memoirs of a Ballet Master 1812–68*. His wife, Tatiana, was a ballerina in Moscow of that period.

GNATT, Poul, b. Baden (Austria) 1923. Danish dancer. Pupil at Royal Th. Sch., Copenhagen. Soloist in Metropolitan B. 1947. Danced for Ballet Th. and Orig. B. Russe and, until 1953, Borovansky B. in Australia as a soloist. Brother of Kirsten Ralov. To New Zealand and formed New Zealand Ballet 1953. In 1967 director of Victorian Ballet Co. in Australia. In 1968 produced the first programme of the new Filippino Nat. B. in Manila. Assistant Ballet master Norwegian Nat. B. 1971.

GODFREY, Louis, b. Johannesburg 1930. S. African dancer. Pupil of Sturman, Conmee, Volkova, Addison. Danced in musicals in S. Africa, joined Markova-Dolin B. 1949 and Festival B. on its inception in 1950, becoming soloist and principal until 1964. Danced in musicals in London and returned to S. Africa 1970 to become ballet master of PACT Ballet, Johannesburg. Joint artistic director 1973. Mar. Denise Schultze.

GODOUNOV, Alexander, b. Riga 1949. Latvian dancer. Graduated from

Bolshoi Sch. 1967 and danced the Prince in *Swan Lake* for the Co. in 1971.

GODREAU, Miguel, b. Ponce, Puerto Rico 1946. Am. dancer. Pupil of Pereyaslavec, Wilde and Joffrey Sch. After touring in musicals, joined Ailey Co. 1965, Harkness B. 1966 and returned to Ailey 1967. To Sweden 1967 and chor. *Opera '67* for Swed. television. Danced in *Dear World* 1968 and rejoined Ailey 1970. In *Show Boat*, London 1971, joined Cullburg B. 1972. Mar. Judith Jameson. First appeared in London 1970.

GODS GO A-BEGGING, THE, or LES DIEUX MENDIANTS. There have been a number of ballets of this name using Handel's music (arranged as a suite by Beecham) notably: (1) book Boris Kochno, ch. Balanchine, dec. Bakst, f.p. Diaghileff's Co., His Majesty's Th., London 16 July 1928 (Danilova, Woizikovsky); (2) same book, ch. de Valois, dec. H. Stevenson, f.p. S. Wells B., S. Wells Th. 21 Feb 1936 (Elizabeth Miller, William Chappell); (3) ch. Lichine, dec. Gris after Bakst, de Basil Co. 1937.

GOLDBERG VARIATIONS, THE, ballet, ch. J. Robbins, m. Bach, cost. J. Eula, pianist Gordon Boelzner, f.p. N. Y. City B., N.Y. State Th., N.Y. 27 May 1971 (G. Kirkland, Leland, McBride, Mendl, von Aroldingen, Maiorano, Clifford, Wells, Weiss, Tomasson, Blum, Martins and the company). A ballet of callisthenics and moods with slight eighteenth-century evocations.

GOLDEN AGE, THE, ballet 3 acts 5 sc., ch. Vainonen, m. Shostakovitch (his first ballet), f.p. Kirov Th., Leningrad 26 Oct 1930. A propaganda ballet in which the characters include a Fascist Chief of Police and the Captain of a Soviet Football Team.

GOLDWYN, Beryl, b. Pinner 1930. Eng. dancer. Studied S. Wells Sch. Joined B. Rambert 1949, becoming principal dancer in 1953, dancing *Giselle*. Retired 1955.

GOLEIZOVSKY, Kasyan, b. Moscow 1892, d. there 1970. Russ. dancer and chor. Graduated at Maryinsky Sch. 1909. To Moscow 1909 and joined Bolshoi B., coming under the influence of Gorsky. Danced in London 1910. Began as chor. in 1917 in short works and for variety theatres. From 1918 began teaching and opened his own studio in Moscow which in 1922 became a company, The Chamber Ballet, producing chamber ballets and concert numbers. As his work was very modern for the Russians he fell into disfavour under Stalin, but he was later rehabilitated and he became Russia's most ardent modernist in ballet. On Balanchine's recommendation Diaghileff invited him to Paris 1924 but he remained in Moscow and in 1922–25 he chor. *Faun* (m. Debussy)

227

Teolinda (m. Schubert), *Joseph the Beautiful* (m. Vasilenko) and other works for the Experimental Th. Between 1930–40 he staged parades and sports displays. He had a revival of creativity in the late 1950s producing *Choreographic Compositions* (m. various) 1960, and *Scriabiniana* 1962, *Leili and Mejnun* (m. Balasanian) 1964 for Bolshoi B. At the very end of his life he was actively creating ballets for Moiseyev's Young Ballet. Author of *Forms of Russian National Choreography* 1964.

GOLEM, THE, ballet, ch. Georgi, m. Burt, dec. Schachteli, f.p. Hanover B., Landestheater 31 Jan 1965 (H. Krause, D. Czinady, M. Vitzthum, W. Winter). Also chor. by F. Marteny (Graz 1966) and by A. Mitterhuber (Th. an der Wien, Vienna 1967).

GOLIKOVA, Tatiana, b. 1945. Russ. dancer. Pupil of Bolshoi Sch., Moscow. Joined Bolshoi B. 1965 and dancing leading rôles. First danced in London 1970.

GOLLNER, Nana, b. El Paso 1920. Am. dancer. Studied under Kosloff and in Paris. Prima ballerina. Orig. B. Russe 1941–43, International B. 1947 and Ballet Th. Mar. Paul Petroff.

GOLOVIN, Alexander, b. Moscow 1863, d. Tsarskoe-Selo 1930. Russian painter who was long attached to the Russian Imperial Theatres. He was responsible for the original designs for Fokine's *Firebird* (1910) and, with Korovin, for the sets and costumes for the Diaghileff production of *Swan Lake* (1911). He has also left some remarkable portraits.

GOLOVKINA, Sophia, b. 1915. Russ. dancer and teacher. Pupil of Bolshoi Sch., soloist Bolshoi B. 1933–59. From 1960 director of Bolshoi Sch., Moscow. Hon. Artist R.S.F.S.R. and Order of Red Banner of Labour.

GOLOVINE, Serge, b. Monaco 1924, Fr. dancer. Pupil of Sedowa and Ricaux. Joined Lifar's Monte Carlo B. 1946 and accepted into Paris Opéra. Joined de Cuevas B. 1950 becoming the chief dancer. Chor. *Feu Rouge, Feu Vert* (1953) etc. Started his own group in 1962. Ballet master Geneva B. 1964–69. Now has his own school in Geneva.

GOLPÉ, Sp., the bass beat of the castanet, usually held in the left hand. See CARRETILLA.

GONCHAROV, George, b. St Petersburg 1904, d. London 1954. Russ. dancer, chor., and teacher. Trained in St Petersburg. Toured Russia, dancing and making ballets. Opened school in Shanghai in the 1920s with Vera Volkova, and there gave Fonteyn lessons in 1933. To London in 1945 and taught at S. Wells Sch. Taught in Italy and later became ballet-master of Alonso's Cuban National B. Returned to London and took over Volkova's Sch., where most of the dancers in or visiting

London took lessons. Among his pupils were Fonteyn, Elvin, and Beriosova.

GONCHAROVA, Nathalie, b. Moscow 1881, d. Paris 1962. Russ. painter who lived in Paris, and contributed to the ballet some of its finest décors and costumes, including: *Le Coq d'Or* (1914), *Les Noces* (1921), *Ygrouchka, Poupées Russes* (1921), *Une Nuit sur le Mont Chauve* (1924), *Cendrillon* (1938), *Bogatyri* (1938), and *Ancient Russia* (1943). Mar. the artist Larionov with whom she often collaborated. In 1954 she made the dec. for the S. Wells revival of *Firebird*, based on her 1926 version.

GOOD-HUMOURED LADIES, THE (*Les Femmes de Bonne Humeur*), ballet 1 act, ch. Massine, m. D. Scarlatti, dec. Bakst, f.p. Diaghileff's Co., Teatro Costanza, Rome 12 Apr 1917 (Lopokova, Idzikowsky, Massine, Woizikovsky, Tchernicheva, Cecchetti). Based on Goldoni's comedy. Massine mounted it for Royal B., C. Garden 11 July 1962 (Linden, Sibley, Seymour, Holden, Shaw, Hynd, with Lydia Sokolova as guest).

GOODMAN, Erika, b. Philadelphia 1947. Am. dancer. Studied at Philadelphia Dance Academy, Royal B. Sch. and Joffrey Sch. Joined N.Y. City B. 1965 and Joffrey B. 1967.

GOODWIN, Noel, b. Fowey 1927. Eng. writer on music and ballet. Educ. in France and London Univ. Ballet critic of *Daily Express* from 1956, and music editor from 1965. Executive editor *Music and Musicians* from 1965. London correspondent for Canadian Broadcasting Corp.

GOPAK or HOPAK, a Russ. folk dance in 2/4 time.

GOPAL, Ram, b. Bangalore 1920. Indian dancer and teacher. Studied under Kunju Kurup (Kathakali), Sundaram (Bharata Natya), Misra (Kathak), and Nabakumar (Manipuri). Opened first school of Indian classical dancing in Bangalore 1935. Taught Mrinalini Sarabhai. Début with La Meri in India 1937. To Europe 1938. Début in London at Aldwych Th. 1939 with own Co. and has now danced all over the world. At the 1944 All-India Dance Festival, Bombay, was voted the winner. By his dancing and his lectures he has brought an understanding and an appreciation of the Indian dancer's art to the Western world.

GORDA, ballet, ch. Chaboukiani, m. Toradze, dec. Lapiashvili, f.p. Opera House, Tiflis 30 Dec 1949 (V. Tsignadze, Z. Kikaleishvili, I. Alexidze, M. Bauer).

GORE, Walter, b. Waterside, Scotland 1910. Scottish dancer and chor. Trained at Italia Conti Sch. and by Massine. Danced in Rambert first season at Lyric Th., Hammersmith 1930. In 1935 joined Vic-Wells B. and cr. rôle of Rake in *The Rake's Progress*, but left same year to create dances for musicals. Returned to B. Rambert as soloist and chor. after war service. Chor. *Paris Soir* (1939), *Confessional* (1941),

Simple Symphony (1944), *Mr Punch* (1946), *Plaisance* (1947), *Winter Night* (1947), *Antonia* (1948). Guest chor. B. des Ch. Élysées in Paris 1952 and chor. *La Damnée*. To Australia with his wife, Paula Hinton (1952). Returned same year, formed his New-Ballet Co. and put on more ballets for B. Workshop and productions for other companies; *Carte Blanche* for S. Wells Th. B. (1953). Chor. *Hoops, Peepshow, Street Games* (1952), *Light Fantastic* (1953), *Eaters of Darkness* (1958, Frankfurt). In 1954 he had his own Co. for which he chor. many new ballets. Returned to Australia 1955. Guest chor. Amsterdam 1956, of Miskovitch's Co., Paris, 1956. From 1956 to 1958 director of ballet at Frankfurt. Chor. *Night and the Silence* (m. Bach) for Edinburgh International B. 1958. Founded his own Co. London B. 1961–63. Ballet master Norwegian National B. 1963–65. Ch. *Sweet Dancer* (1964) for B. Rambert. In 1957 ch. *The Nutcracker* for B. Der Lage Landen, Holland and later mounted it for London B. 1962, Norwegian Nat. B. 1965, Johannesburg B. 1968. From 1965–69 ballet master of Gulbenkian B., Lisbon, of Augsburg 1971–72.

GORIANKA, ballet, ch. O. Vinogradov, m. Kajlaev, dec. Marina Sokolova, f.p. Kirov Th., Leningrad 20 Mar 1968 (Komleva, Panov, Barishnikov). Contemporary subject—a country girl leaves her village and her fiancé to lead her life in a city as a student. She falls in love but her old fiancé kills her. This was Barishnikov's first created rôle.

GORHAM, Kathleen, b. Sydney 1932. Austral. dancer. Studied under Norton and Kellaway. Joined Borovansky Co. and then B. Rambert in 1948 in Australia. To England 1949 to S. Wells Sch. Danced with S. Wells Th. B. 1951–52 and was soloist in de Cuevas Co. 1953. Returned to Australia 1954–59 to join Borovansky Co. as chief dancer. Danced again in Europe and in 1962 became principal dancer of Australian B. Retired 1967. Awarded O.B.E. 1968. Now has her own school in Melbourne.

GORSKY, Alexander A., b. St Petersburg 1871, d. Moscow 1924. Russ. dancer and chor. Graduated from Imp. Sch. 1889 and made soloist in 1895 and premier danseur 1900. For the previous four years he had been teaching under Gerdt and in 1900 he was moved to the Bolshoi Th., Moscow, as *régisseur*. Although a pupil of Petipa, he was a rebel against his choreographic methods. In Moscow he restaged a number of older ballets and sought to strengthen and dramatize them by the introduction of additional episodes and by making the dancing of principals and corps de ballet alike an integral part of the action. Among the ballets so treated by him were *Don Quixote* (1900), *Swan Lake* (1901), *The Humpbacked Horse* (1901). In 1911 he staged a ballet *The Dance Dream* at the Alhambra Th., London for the Coronation. Much of his work is still in the Soviet repertoire and he introduced the Stepanoff method of dance-notation to the Imp. Sch. in Moscow, and in 1898, using this method, he staged *The Sleeping Beauty* for the first time in Moscow.

GOSLAR, Lotte, b. Dresden. German dancer-mime. Pupil of Wigman and Palucca. First danced in cabaret, Berlin 1933 and toured with a group. To America 1937 with E. Mann's troupe in nightclubs. To Hollywood 1943. A satirical entertainer. Founded her Pantomime Circus 1954.

GOSSCHALK, Käthy, b. Amsterdam 1941. Dutch dancer. Pupil of Scapino B. Sch., Amsterdam 1953 and joined Co. 1957–60. Studied in N.Y. at Juilliard Sch. and joined Nederlands Dans Th. 1962 becoming principal from 1967.

GOSSELIN, Geneviève, b. 1791, d. 1818. Fr. dancer, sister of Louis Gosselin. Début at Paris Opéra 1809 and had a triumph in *L'Enfant Prodigue*. She died young. She became fat, but was so supple that she was called 'The Boneless'. Her younger sister was also a dancer, Madame Anatole (Petit). See also POINTE.

GOSSELIN, Louis F., b. Paris 1800, d. there 1860. Fr. dancer and teacher. Danced at the Paris Opéra and at King's Th., London (1827–52). Became chief professor at the Opéra 1853, teaching Cerrito, Rosati, Bogdanova, etc. Brother of Geneviève Gosselin.

GOTOB, the Russian abbreviation for State Theatre of Opera and Ballet (applied to all the Russ. opera houses).

GOUBÉ, Paul, b. Paris 1912. Fr. dancer and chor. Pupil at Paris Opéra under Ricaux becoming premier danseur 1933. Chor. and chief dancer of a new company, Ballets de Monte Carlo 1941. Formed his own Co. the Ballets de la Méditerranée at Nice 1955, which danced there and in Addis Ababa. Chor. *Le Lien* (m. Franck, 1952), *Ad Alta* (m. Britten, 1953), *Duo* (m. Scriabine, 1954), etc. In 1969 opened Centre de Danse de Paris in the Salle Pleyel, Paris, where all forms of dance are taught.

GOULD, Diana, b. London 1913. Eng. dancer. Studied under Rambert and Egorova. Was a principal dancer of the early Rambert seasons. Also with de Basil and Markova-Dolin 1935–37. Mar. Yehudi Menuhin.

GOULD, Morton, b. N.Y. 1913. Am. composer of *Fall River Legend* (1948). His *American Concertette* is the music for Robbins's *Interplay* (1945) and his *Derivations for Clarinet and Jazz Band* for Balanchine's *Clarinade* (1964).

GOUNOD SYMPHONY, ballet, ch. Balanchine, m. Gounod Symphony in D, dec. Armistead, cost. Karinska, f.p. N.Y. City B., City Center, N.Y. 7 Jan 1958 (Maria Tallchief, d'Amboise). Taken into repertoire of Paris Opéra Ballet, dec. Bouchène 4 Mar 1959 (Amiel, J. P. Andreani).

GOVILOFF, George, b. Monaco 1932. Fr. dancer, brother of Serge Golovine. Studied Besobrasova, Preobrajenska, Peretti. Joined de Cuevas Co. 1951, soloist 1952, principal dancer 1956. Joined Festival B. 1963–64.

GOVRIN, Gloria, b. Newark, N.J. 1942. Am. dancer. Pupil of Tarassoff Sch. and Sch. of Am. B. Joined N.Y. City B. 1959, becoming soloist 1961. Created rôle of Hippolyta in Balanchine's *Midsummer Night's Dream* 1962.

GRADES, name given to certain elementary examinations in the technique of classical dancing.

GRADUATION BALL, ballet 1 act, ch. Lichine, m. J. Strauss, arr. Dorati, dec. Benois, f.p. B. R. de Monte Carlo, Th. Royal, Sydney 28 Feb 1940 (Riabouchinska, Lichine, Orloff, Runanine). In the repertoire of many companies, it tells of a ball given by a girl's school to which cadets are invited. Danced by Ballet Th. 1944. R. Danish B. took it into their repertoire, Copenhagen 22 Mar 1952 (Sand, Bjornsson) and Festival B., Paris 6 May 1957 (Landa, Muller, Beckett, Flindt).

GRAEME, Joyce, b. Leeds 1918. Eng. dancer and teacher. Studied under Idzikowsky, M. Craske, Volkova, Rambert and S. Wells Sch. Joined S. Wells Ballet 1937. International Ballet 1941–43. Entered B. Rambert 1945 and became a principal dancer. Directed Australian National Ballet 1948–51, assistant-director B. Rambert 1953. Danced at Scala, Milan 1955 and joined the staff of the Scala School. Also danced with Festival B. 1952–54. Now teaches. Mounted *Giselle* for Scottish Th. B. 1971.

GRAF, Uta, b. Berlin 1942. German dancer. Pupil of Blank and joined Hamburg B. becoming soloist and then principal.

GRAFF, Jens, b. Wangerooge, Germany 1942. German dancer. Pupil of Rita Tori. Soloist with Oslo B. 1961. Principal dancer Bordeaux B. 1963–65. Soloist Hamburg B. 1965–68. Cullberg B. 1968–70 and soloist R. Swed. B. 1970.

GRAHAM, Martha, b. Pittsburgh 1893. Am. dancer and chor. Entered school of Ruth St Denis and Ted Shawn 1916 and danced with them until 1923. Since 1930 she has become one of the leaders of the Modern Dance movement (q.v.) as teacher and dancer and is one of the greatest contemporary figures in the Am. dance. She has chor. over 100 dances and ballets, incl. *Punch and the Judy* (1941), *Deaths and Entrances* (1943), *Salem Shore* (1943), *Appalachian Spring* (1944), *Dark Meadow* (1946), *Errand into the Maze* (1947), *Clytemnestra* (1958), *Episodes* (1959), *Acrobats of God* (1960), *Secular Games* (1962), *Circe* (1963). Made Doctor of Arts, Harvard Univ. 1966. Retired as dancer 1970.

Her ballets, mostly intense and tragic, are danced barefooted and with impassive mien. They use a formidable technique (the Martha Graham Style) which has evolved from the Central European Style of the 1920s. Her company of very highly trained dancers has toured Europe and the Middle East (London 1954, 1963, 1967) and two 'Martha Graham' companies have been formed outside America, one in Tel Aviv (the Batsheva Ballet, founded by the Baroness de Rothschild in 1964) and in London (the London Contemporary Dance Company, founded by Robin Howard 1967). Among the great dancers of her company are or were Ethel Winter, Yuriko, Linda Hodes, Helen McGehee, Pearl Lang, Bertram Ross, Erick Hawkins, Merce Cunningham, Robert Cohan. A film of her style of training, *A Dancer's World*, was made in 1958.

GRAHAME, Shirley, b. Teddington 1936. Eng. dancer. Studied at R. Ballet Sch. from 1948. Joined Royal Ballet 1954, becoming soloist 1958. Danced Odette in R. Ballet Sch. *Swan Lake* at Covent Garden in 1960. To Canada 1960. Ballerina of Touring Royal B. 1961–70. Joined Festival B. as ballerina 1970. Retired 1971.

GRAHN, Lucile, b. Copenhagen 1819, d. Munich 1907. Dan. dancer, pupil of Bournonville. Début at Royal Th., Copenhagen 1834, but left Denmark 1839 and became an international ballerina, dancing at the Paris Opéra, in St Petersburg in 1843, and in London in 1845 (in the famous *Pas de Quatre*). In Copenhagen she cr. the title rôle in Bournonville's *La Sylphide* in 1836. She was the chor. of some of Wagner's operas in Bayreuth. She was tall, slim, with blue eyes and blonde hair. In 1856 she ceased to appear as a dancer and became ballet mistress of Leipzig 1858–61, Munich 1869–75. Mar. Austrian tenor Friederich Young, 1856. She left a large amount of money for the poor in Munich and a street in Munich is named after her.

GRAND BALLET CLASSIQUE DE FRANCE, founded in Paris 1963 by the impresario Claude Giraud, a group of French dancers from the Paris Opéra and the former de Cuevas B. which tours intermittently, giving gala performances. The principal dancer is Liane Daydé (Giraud's wife) and among others who have regularly danced in it are Vyroubova, Renault, Giuliano, Hightower, Polajenko, Urbain etc. They visited America in 1965, Australia, the Far East etc. and re-form when the occasion arises. In 1967 they took part in the Paris International Festival. To South America 1972.

GRAND BALLET DU MARQUIS DE CUEVAS, an international ballet Co. deriving from B. International in the U.S. In 1947 the Marquis de Cuevas bought the Nouveau B. de Monte Carlo and combined the two repertoires, naming the new troupe Grand B. de Monte Carlo.

The first performance was at the Vichy Opéra 12 July 1947 and the chief dancers Hightower, Marjorie Tallchief, Pagava, Skibine, Eglevsky, and Dollar. Based on Paris, the Co. toured Europe and had a C. Garden season in 1948. William Dollar was ballet-master in 1948 and was succeeded that year by John Taras, who held that office until 1952. After the 1951 season in Monte Carlo the Co. changed its name from G. B. de Monte Carlo to the above and gave seasons all over Europe, S. America, and the near-East. It drew its dancers from Europe and from the U.S., and its choreographers, designers, and composers also. The Marquis de Cuevas (q.v.) was the artistic Director and owner of the Co. which fulfilled a very important rôle in European ballet. In 1955 its chief dancers were (girls) Hightower, Marjorie Tallchief, Ricarda, Moreau, Bourgeois; (men) Skibine, Golovine, Skouratoff. Taras rejoined as ballet-master. In 1956 Hightower left and Schanne joined. Hightower rejoined and in 1960 the principal dancers were (girls) Hightower, Vyroubova, Melikova, Consuelo, Dale, Mathé, Miklosy, (boys) Golovine, Polajenko, Goviloff, Prokovsky, Nunes, Ferran. In 1960 *The Sleeping Beauty* was mounted in Paris by Nijinska and Helpmann. In 1961 it became International Ballet of the Marquis de Cuevas. After the death of the Marquis in 1961, the company was carried on by his widow and his nephew Raimundo de Larrain but it was disbanded after its final performance in Athens 30 June 1962.

GRAND PAS CLASSIQUE, pas de deux, ch. V. Gsovsky, m. Auber, f.p. Th. des Ch. Élysées, Paris 12 Nov 1949 (Chauviré, Skouratoff). Very popular in the cont. repertoire of Fr. dancers, and of great virtuosity.

GRANTSEVA, Tatiana, Russ.-Fr. dancer and teacher. Pupil of Egorova, Preobrajenska. Danced in B. Russe de Monte Carlo 1938–44. From 1962 has taught in Paris and worked with Béjart's Co. In 1972 joined R. Petit's Co. in Marseilles as teacher.

GRANDS BALLETS CANADIENS, LES, Canadian Co. based on Montreal and founded in 1956 by Ludmilla Chiriaeff (q.v. for early history of the Co). As Les Ballets Chiriaeff the dancers first appeared on stage at the Chalet de la Montagne, Montreal in 1955 and the Co. proper was formed the following year, with 20 dancers. Its repertoire was mostly of works by the founder and by Eric Hyrst, leading dancer and chor. Subsequent ballet masters were Zvereff, Caton, Seillier (1965) and currently Nault who is also co-director. Dolin was appointed Artistic Adviser in 1964 and mounted *Pas de Quatre*, *Swan of Tuonela* and *Giselle*. At Montreal's Expo '67 Nault mounted *Carmina Burana* (m. Orff) and followed it by *Catulli Carmina* and *Trionfo di Afroditi*, which brought great fame to the Co. The Co. toured Europe in 1969, appearing at S. Wells Th., London. Grants are received from the Greater Montreal Council of

Arts, the Canada Council and the Province of Quebec. In 1970 the ballet mistress was Linda Stearns and among the dancers were Richard Beaty, Vincent Warren, Armando Jorge, Lawrence Gradus, Sonia Taverner, Veronique Landory, Erica Jayne, Shelley Osher, Margery Lambert, Ghislaine Thesmar. When *Giselle* was given at Expo '67, Alicia Alonso danced in Canada though as a Cuban she had been refused an American visa since 1960. In 1971 the company had a great success with *Tommy*, rock opera by the pop-group The Who, chor. by F. Nault and showed it at City Center, N.Y.

GRAND TOUR, THE, ballet, ch. Joe Layton, m. Noel Coward (arr. Hershy Kay), dec. Conklin, f.p. Touring Royal B., Theatre Royal, Norwich 10 Feb 1971 (Lorrayne, Wells, O'Conaire, Sherwood, Sleep, Drew, Davel). Scene on a cruise ship in the 1930s with Noel Coward, Mary Pickford, Gertrude Lawrence, Shaw, Douglas Fairbanks etc. on board.

GRANT, Alexander, b. Wellington, N.Z. 1925. New Zealand dancer. In 1944 won R.A.D. scholarship, joined S. Wells Sch. 1946, becoming a soloist of S. Wells B. 1949, creating rôle of the Barber in Massine's revival of *Mam'zelle Angot* (1947), Tirrenio in *Ondine* (1958), Alain in *Fille Mal Gardée* (1960) and many others. The Royal Ballet's most distinguished character dancer, he was appointed C.B.E. 1965. In 1971 he became director of the Ballet for All group of the Royal B.

GRANT, Carol, b. Stockport 1942. Eng. dancer. Trained with Doreen Bird and at Royal B. Sch. Joined Gore's London Ballet in 1961. Soloist of London Dance Th. 1963 and joined Festival B. 1967 as a principal, until 1970. Now dances as guest artist.

GRANT, Garry, b. Wellington, N.Z. 1940, brother of Alexander G. N.Z. dancer. Pupil of Jean Horne, Trevor and Neil, and Royal B. Sch. Joined Royal B. 1962 becoming soloist.

GRANT, Pauline, b. Birmingham 1915. Eng. dancer and chor. Studied Ginner-Mawer Sch. and Tudor. Has chor. the dances in many Eng. musicals, ice-shows and pantomimes. Also for Glyndebourne Opera, S. Wells Opera and C. Garden Opera. In 1969 appointed ballet mistress of Movement Group of S. Wells Opera. Member of Council of Béjart's Mudra School in Brussels 1972.

GRANTZOW, Adèle, b. Brunswick 1845, d. 1877. German dancer, pupil of her father Gustav Grantzow in Brunswick and of Mme Dominique in Paris. She was one of the outstanding prima ballerinas of the period, dancing in Russia, Paris, etc. Cr. title rôle in Petipa's *Camargo*. The ballet *La Source* was created for her but she had to return to Russia before it could be put on. She died after an operation on her leg.

GRAY, Felicity (Andreae), b. Southampton 1914. Eng. dancer and chor.

Studied under Bedells and R.A.D. Scholar. Début in Camargo Society. Danced with Vic-Wells and with Woizikovsky's Co. and in America. Chor. ballets for Carl Rosa Opera, R.A.D. Production Club, musicals, and revues. Her series of explanatory talks and demonstrations for the B.B.C. television service 'Ballet for Beginners' (prod. by Philip Bate), in 1952–53 did much for the general understanding of ballet. Author of *Ballet for Beginners* (1952).

GRECO, José, b. Montorio-Nei-Frentani 1919. It. dancer. Studied in America with Argentinita. Toured in her Co. as her partner till her death in 1945. Continued for two years in her sister's, Pilar Lopez's Co., touring Europe and America. First appeared in London at R.A.D. Production Club Matinée at C. Garden 1950. Founded his own Co., with his wife Nila Amparo, and danced at S. Wells Th. in 1951 and Festival Hall 1956 and subsequently. Danced in films *Around the World in Eighty Days* and *Ship of Fools*. Awarded Spanish Cross of the Knight of Civil Merit 1962.

GREEK DANCE ASSOCIATION, founded 1923 by Ruby Ginner (q.v.) at Stratford-on-Avon for teachers of her Greek Dancing (rhythmic movements in which the dancers are barefoot and wear the traditional Greek tunic). With the R.A.D. they held Children's Examinations. In 1951 it was absorbed into the Imperial Society of Teachers of Dancing.

GREGORY, Cynthia, b. Los Angeles 1946. Am. dancer. Pupil of Maracci and Rosselatt. Joined San Francisco B. 1961 becoming soloist 1964. Joined Am. Ballet Th. 1965 becoming principal dancer. Mar. Terry Orr.

GREGORY, Jill, b. Bristol 1918. Eng. dancer and ballet mistress. Pupil of de Valois, Craske, Egorova, Sergueeff. Joined Vic-Wells B. 1933 and remained with the organization throughout. Appointed ballet mistress of Royal B. 1952, a post which she still holds.

GREEN TABLE, THE, ballet in 8 sc., ch. Jooss, m. Cohen, dec. Heckroth, f.p. Th. des Ch. Élysées, Paris 3 July 1932 (Jooss, Uthoff, Pescht, Liza Czobel). This ballet won the first prize in the first competition organized by the Archives Internationales de la Danse and brought fame to Kurt Jooss, whose finest work it remains. It is a satire inspired by the First World War (the Green Table is that at which the politicians meet and decide the fate of mankind). It is in the repertoire of many Cos., including Joffrey B. 1966, Cullberg B. and Northern Dance Th. 1973.

GREY, Beryl, b. London 1927. Eng. dancer. To S. Wells Sch. 1937, (youngest member) in corps de ballet 1941, becoming soloist in 1942. Danced full-length *Swan Lake* on 15th birthday, *Giselle* in 1944, and Aurora in *Sleeping Beauty* 1946. One of the ballerinas of the Royal B.

Made the first stereoscopic ballet film *Black Swan* (1952). Guest artist Royal Opera House, Stockholm 1953 and 1955, Opera House, Helsinki 1954 etc. In 1943 John Masefield, Poet Laureate, having seen her dance *Les Sylphides* wrote a poem on the occasion. Resigned from Royal B., 1957. Guest artist in Leningrad, Bolshoi Th. Moscow, Tiflis 1957–58 (the first English dancer to be so honoured). Guest artist of Royal Ballet, Festival Ballet etc. Danced in S. Africa and New Zealand 1959–60, Peking 1964. Author of *Red Curtain Up* (1958), *Through the Bamboo Curtain* (1965). In 1966 appointed Director-General of Arts Educational Trust ballet school. In 1968 became Artistic Director of London Festival B. Made Doctor of Music by Leicester University 1970. Appointed C.B.E. 1973.

GRIDIN, Anatoli, b. Novosibirsk 1929. Russ. dancer. Studied in Novosibirsk and Leningrad and joined Kirov B. 1952 becoming principal character dancer. Cr. rôle of Severyan in *The Stone Flower* (Grigorovitch 1957).

GRIEG CONCERTO, ballet (pas de deux), ch. Charrat, m. Grieg pianoforte concerto, f.p. Gala de l'Association des Écrivains de la Danse, Palais de Chaillot, Paris 19 Mar 1951 (Charrat, Perrault). Many other ballets have used this music.

GRIEVE, William, b. 1800, d. 1844. Eng. scenic designer, one of a long line of scenic painters. He designed many of the settings for the ballets of the Romantic period seen in London, incl. *L'Ombre, Alma ou La Fille de Feu, Ondine*, and *La Esmeralda*.

GRIGORIEFF, Serge, b. Tichvin 1883, d. London 1968. Russ. dancer and *régisseur*. Studied at Imp. Sch., graduated 1900 and danced at Maryinsky Th. Joined Diaghileff in 1909 and cr. many rôles, incl. Russian Merchant in *Boutique*. His phenomenal memory of the Diaghileff repertoire made him invaluable to the Co. and to the de Basil Co., for both of which he was *régisseur*. Mar. Tchernicheva 1909. Author of *The Diaghilev Ballet* (1953). Mounted *Firebird* for Royal B. 1954 and at Milan 1955 and *Petrouchka* 1957. Régisseur Festival B. 1956. Lived in London for the latter part of his life.

GRIGORIEVA, Tamara, b. Petrograd 1918. Russ. dancer and ballet mistress. Pupil of Preobrajenska, Balanchine, Vilzak. Joined Balanchine's Ballets 1933 and the same year the de Basil Co. becoming ballerina 1938, until 1944. Settled in Rio de Janeiro 1944 and worked in the Teatro Municipal. Guest ballerina at Colon Th., Buenos Aires 1947–48. Ballet mistress and director of Montevideo B. 1951–54. Ballet mistress Colon Th. 1956–57 and returned in 1961 as director of ballet there.

GRIGOROVA, Romayne (Austin), b. Kenilworth 1926. Eng. dancer and ballet mistress. Pupil of Volkova, de Valois, Goncharov, A. Philips. Joined B. Rambert 1946, Metropolitan B. 1947, S. Wells Th. B. 1951–55. Ballet mistress for *Can-Can* 1955, St Gallen B. 1956. From 1957 ballet mistress of the opera ballet at Covent Garden (now Royal Opera Co.). Chor. many opera ballets.

GRIGOROVITCH, Yuri, b. Leningrad 1927. Russ. dancer and chor. Studied at Kirov Sch. (then evacuated to Perm) and graduated to Kirov B. 1946. Became a leading *demi-caractère* soloist. Showed a talent for choreography and in 1956 chor. Glinka's *Valse Fantaisie* for the school graduation performance. He also chor. a version of *The Baby Stork* (m. Klebanov) and *Tom Thumb* (m. Varlamov) for the Leningrad Palace of Culture. In 1957, while still dancing for the Kirov B., he and some young colleagues began working on a new version of Prokofieff's *Stone Flower*. This was first performed in Leningrad in 1957 and by its novel choreography and production won great credit for the young choreographer. It was also given in Moscow in 1959. Chor. *Legend of Love* (m. Melikov) 1962 at Kirov (Moscow in 1965). In 1964 he was appointed chief chor. and Artistic Director of the Bolshoi in Moscow and produced a new staging of *Sleeping Beauty* (1963) and of *Nutcracker* (1966), *Spartacus* (1968) and *Swan Lake* (1969). In 1966 appointed Artistic Director of the Bolshoi B. Mar. Bessmertnova. People's Artist of R.S.F.S.R. 1966.

GRIMALDI, Joseph, b. London 1779, d. there 1837. Eng. actor and comic dancer. As an infant he appeared at S. Wells Th. His greatest success was in the pantomime *Mother Goose* at C. Garden 1806. Dickens edited his *Memoirs* (1838).

GRINWIS, Paul, b. Ghent. Belgian dancer and chor. Studied at Brussels Opera. Joined de Basil's Co. 1946. To Borovansky B. 1951. Returned to Europe 1952 and rejoined Borovansky B. 1954–61 as principal dancer and chor. of *Les Amants Éternels* (1951), *Los Tres Diabolos* (1954). Returned to Europe 1964. Ballet master Bordeaux 1966. Director of PACT Johannesburg B. 1969–70. Returned 1971 to work in Belgium.

GRISI, Carlotta, b. Visinada, Italy 1819, d. St-Jean, Geneva 1899. It. dancer. Studied Milan under Guillet and entered corps de ballet at the Scala 1829. Dancing in Naples 1833 she met Jules Perrot and became his pupil and mistress. With him she danced in London (1836), Vienna, Milan, Munich, and Naples. Début Paris at Th. de la Renaissance (1840) and at the Opéra (1841) in a dance in the opera *La Favorita* partnered by Lucien Petipa. In the same year she met Théophile Gautier whose great love and inspiration she became. Her greatest triumph was *Giselle* which he wrote for her. She also cr. the rôles in *La Jolie Fille de Gand* (1842), *La Péri* (1843), *Esmeralda* (1844),

Paquita (1845), *Pas de Quatre* (London 1845), and *Le Diable à Quatre* (1845). She danced in London regularly from 1842 to 1851. In 1850 she made her début in the Maryinsky Th., St Petersburg in *Giselle*. She retired in 1853 and settled in Saint-Jean with her daughter, Ernestine Grisi (by Prince Radziwill). She was one of the greatest dancers in the history of ballet, combining something of the spirituality of Taglioni with the brio of Elssler. She was of medium height, with pale auburn hair and blue-grey eyes.

GRISI, LA, ballet, ch. Aveline, m. Tomasi and Metra, dec. Dignimont, f.p. Paris Opéra 21 June 1935 (Bos, Peretti). An imaginary incident in Grisi's life.

GROSSE FUGE, ballet, ch. Van Manen, m. Beethoven (the Grosse Fuge, followed by the Cavatina from string quartet 13, Op. 130), dec. Vroom, f.p. Nederlands Dans Th., Circus Th., Scheveningen 8 Apr 1971 (Sarstadt, Venema, Westerdijk, Waterbolk, Benoit, Vervenne, Christe, Koning). Also danced by Royal B. (touring group), Odeon Cinema, Golders Green 29 Apr 1972 (Ruanne, Barbieri, Strike, Hill, Johnson, Cooke, Clarke, Jefferies).

GROSSVATERTANZ (grandfather dance), a German family dance of the seventeenth century usually played at weddings. It appears (with the same traditional music) in Act I of *Casse Noisette* and in the finale of *Carnaval*.

GRUBER, Lilo, b. Berlin 1915. German dancer and chor. Pupil of Wigman. Appointed ballet mistress Leipzig B. 1943, director of ballet at the Staatsoper, East Berlin, from 1955. Chor. *Flames of Paris* 1953, *Swan Lake* 1959 etc.

GSOVSKY, Tatiana, b. Moscow 1902, Russ. dancer, chor. and teacher (daughter of actress Claudia Issatchenko). Trained at St Petersburg. Ballet-mistress at Moscow Experimental Th. To Germany 1925 and opened school in 1929. From 1945 to 1952 ballet-mistress at Staatsoper, East Berlin. Ballet-mistress at Teatro Colon, Buenos Aires 1952–53. In 1953 she returned to Berlin (Western Zone) to continue her teaching and founded the Berliner Ballet Co. which toured America in 1955. Ballet Mistress of Städtische (now Deutsches) Oper, W. Berlin and also (1959–66) in Frankfurt. Head of the ballet school of the Deutches Oper, W. Berlin. Mar. Victor Gsovsky. Chor. many ballets and is one of the greatest figures in German ballet.

GSOVSKY, Victor, b. St Petersburg 1902. Russ. chor. and teacher. Studied in St Petersburg. Became maître de ballet Berlin Staatsoper 1925, and of Markova-Dolin Co. 1937. Taught in Paris and made maître de ballet at Paris Opéra 1945 and of B. des Ch. Élysées 1946–47 for whom he chor. *La Sylphide* (1945) and of Metropolitan B. for whom he chor. *Dances of Galanta* and *Pygmalion*. In 1949 maître de ballet Munich Staatsoper. Was famous teacher in Paris until 1964 when he became teacher of Düsseldorf B. To Hamburg B. 1968 as teacher. See GRAND PAS CLASSIQUE.

GUELIS, Jean, b. Paris 1924. Fr. dancer. Studied Paris Opéra 1935–37, and became premier danseur Marseilles Opéra 1940. To America 1941, dancing in ballet and musicals. Returned to Paris 1946 and danced with B. des Ch. Élysées 1948. Now organizes the ballets in Paris night clubs, musicals.

GUERRA, Antonio, b. Naples 1810, d. Vienna 1846. It. dancer and chor. Studied under Pietro Hus in Naples. Début San Carlo Th. 1826 and earned the nickname 'Le Petit Duport'. Chor. his first ballet, *Il Primo Navigatore*, in Vienna. Danced also in Milan, Turin, Florence. To Paris Opéra and partnered Taglioni. To Her Majesty's Th., London, as principal dancer 1838 and maître de ballet, where he partnered Elssler in his version of *La Gitana* (1839) and chor. many ballets, incl. *Le Lac des Fées* (1840) for Cerrito. Chor. *Les Mohicans* at Paris Opéra 1837, a failure. To Th. Imperiale, Vienna 1842 as chor. (*Nankin, Angelica, Manfred, Fortuna*).

GUERRA, Nicola, b. Naples c. 1862, d. Cernobbio 1942. It. dancer, chor. and teacher. At age of 17 premier danseur of Scala, Milan. Danced in London, St Petersburg, Paris, and New York. Principal dancer and maître de ballet at Vienna for ten years. Engaged by M. Rouché to mount a revival at the Paris Opéra of *Castor et Pollux* 21 Mar 1918 (ch. Guerra, m. Rameau, dec. Drésa). For Rubinstein's Co. at the Paris Opéra he chor. *La Tragédie de Salomé* Apr 1 1919 (m. Schmitt, dec. Piot), *Artémis Troublée* 28 Apr 1922 (m. Paray, dec. Bakst). Director of the Paris Opéra Sch. of Dance 1927–29 and chor. many ballets, notably *Cyrca* (1927), *Turandot* (1928), *Salamine* (1929). Ballet master in Rome 1929. See BRITISH BALLET ORGANIZATION.

GUERRERO, Maria, b. Madrid 1951. Sp. dancer. Pupil of Maria de Avila 1957–65, Bedells 1965, Royal B. Sch. 1966. Joined Festival B. 1968 becoming soloist 1970. Mar. Peter Schaufuss. To Berlin 1973.

GUEST ARTIST (Fr. *En représentation*, Ger. *am gast*), a solo dancer who dances with a company of which he is not a member, and is usually paid a fee for each performance.

GUEST, Ivor, b. Chislehurst 1920. Eng. writer on the history of ballet. Educated Lancing and Trinity College, Cambs. Mar. Ann Hutchinson. Organized National Book League's Exhibition of Ballet Books, London 1957–58. Adviser on ballet to *Enciclopedia dello Spettacolo*. Editorial

Adviser, *Dancing Times* from 1963. Vice-chairman of British Theatre Museum from 1966. Member of the Executive Committee of Royal Academy of Dancing since 1965 and Chairman from 1969. Associate Editor *Ballet Annual* 1952–63. Author of *Napoleon III in England* (1952), *The Ballet of the Second Empire 1858–1870* (1953), *The Romantic Ballet in England* (1954), *The Ballet of the Second Empire 1847–1858* (1955), *Fanny Cerrito* (1956), *Victorian Ballet Girl* (1957), *Adeline Genée* (1958), *The Alhambra Ballet* (1959), *The Dancer's Heritage* (1960), *La Fille Mal Gardée* (editor, 1960), *The Empire Ballet* (1962), *A Gallery of Romantic Ballet* (1965), *The Romantic Ballet in Paris* (1966), *Dandies and Dancers* (1969), *Carlotta Zambelli* (1969), *Two Coppélias* (1970), *Fanny Elssler* (1970), *Pas de Quatre* (1970).

GUGLIELMO EBREO (William the Jew), of Pesaro. It. dancing master and writer of the fifteenth century. His treatise on the dance *De Practica seu Arte Tripudii*, 1463, is more varied than that of his colleague Domenico da Ferrara, with whom he worked (notably at the wedding of Costanzo Sforza and Camille d'Aragon in Pesaro 1475). He spent his life arranging the dances and festivities at the courts of Milan, Mantua, Urbino, Naples, Venice etc.

GUIGNOL ET PANDORE, ballet 1 act, ch. Lifar, m. Jolivet, dec. Dignimont, f.p. Paris Opéra 29 Apr 1944 (Lorcia, Lifar, Peretti). A light frolic.

GUIMARD, Madeline, b. Paris 1743, d. there 1816. Fr. dancer. Début Paris Opéra 1762 and made première danseuse in 1763. She danced in the ballets of Noverre and M. Gardel and was one of the greatest of her time. She was a terre à terre dancer, very thin (she was called 'Le Squelette des Grâces') with a pockmarked face and had many famous lovers. She married the ex-dancer and poet Despréaux in 1789. Walpole wrote of her that although ugly her features were so fine that at 45 she appeared on the stage to be but 15.

GUIZERIX, Jean, b. Paris 1945. Fr. dancer. Pupil of Bazet and Guillaumin. Joined Paris Opéra B. 1964, becoming premier danseur 1971, étoile 1972.

GULBENKIAN BALLET (Grupo Gulbenkian de Bailado), founded in Lisbon in October 1965 by the Gulbenkian Foundation in Portugal. The artistic director was Walter Gore and the ballets were mainly classical and those of Gore himself. John Auld was ballet master and the principal dancers were Paula Hinton, Isabel Santa Rosa, Patrick Hurde, Joanne O'Hara, Carlos Trincheiras. In 1970 the Co. occupied their new theatre in the Gulbenkian Foundation, and Gore and Hinton left. Geoffrey Davidson was ballet master and later in the year Milko Sparemblek became artistic director, principal dancers O'Hara,

Penelope Wright, Santa Rosa, Hurde, Margery Lambert, Armando Jorge, Candelaria. Repertoire is largely modern with ballets by Sparemblek, Trincheiras, Lubovitch. Danced in London 1973.

GUSEV, Pyotr, b. St Petersburg 1904. Russ. dancer, teacher and chor. Entered Maryinsky Sch. 1918 and graduated to company 1922. In 1934–35 he was a principal dancer at the Maly Th., Leningrad, partnering Olga Mungalova in 'acrobatic' classical pas de deux which Russ. dancers present at concerts. From 1935 became famous teacher at Bolshoi Sch. (especially for *pas de deux*) and became its head in 1937–40 and in 1950. Principal dancer of Kirov B. 1945–51 and of Bolshoi B. 1951. Also ballet master of Stanislavsky and Nemirovitch-Danchenko Th. 1935–41, 1943–46, 1951–57. Directed the Maly B. 1960–61. Retired in 1961. From 1957 to 1960 he worked with the Pekin Ballet as teacher-choreographer and ch. *Le Corsaire* (1955) and *Seven Beauties* (1953) at Maly Th.

GUY-STÉPHAN, Marie, b. 1818, d. Paris 1873. Fr. dancer. At Paris Opéra 1840–41, 1853–55; London 1841–43, 1852. She danced in Madrid and specialized in Sp. dances.

H

H, ballet, ch. Chesworth, m. Penderecki (*Polymorphia*), lighting J.B. Read, f.p. B. Rambert, Richmond Th., Surrey 25 Jan 1968. The hydrogen bomb explodes.

HABANERA, from Havana, a slow Cuban dance in 2/4 time which for a time enjoyed great popularity in Spain and, to a less extent, France.

HÄGER, Bengt, b. Malmö 1916. Swed. administrator and writer on the dance. General Secretary of Archives Internationales de la Danse, Paris 1946. President Swedish Dance Association since 1944. Director of Dance Museum, Stockholm, from 1963. Dean of the Swedish State High School for Choreographic Art, which in 1970 became the Swedish State Dance School. Member of Swed. Government Council for Culture 1969. Author of *Ballet, Classic and Free* (1945), etc. Edited de Maré's (whose assistant he was) *Les Ballets Suedois* (1947). Early in his career he was assistant to Fokine and de Basil, was publicity manager for B. Jooss 1947–49, and touring manager of several Cos. Administrator of the Carina Ari Foundation (q.v.).

HÅGGBOM, Nils Åke, b. Stockholm 1943. Swed. dancer. Pupil of R. Swed. B. Sch. and joined Co. 1959, becoming soloist 1966.

HAIG, Robin, b. Perth, Australia 1937. Australian dancer. Pupil of Linley Wilson. Joined Gore's Australian Theatre B. 1955. To Royal B. Sch. 1956. Joined Royal B. 1957. Joined Gore's London B. 1961. Toured with Fonteyn in Australia 1962. Returned to Royal B. Joined Western Th. B. as principal 1963–69. Joined Australian B. 1973.

HALL, Fernau, b. Victoria B.C., 1915. Canadian dancer and author. Published *Ballet* (1948), *Modern English Ballet* (1950), *An Anatomy of Ballet* (1953). Contributor to *Ballet Today* 1958–70. Ballet critic of *Daily Telegraph* from 1969.

HALLHUBER, Heino, b. Munich 1927. German dancer. Studied at Munich Staatsoper Sch. under Gerbl, Mlakar, V. Gsovsky. Entered Staatsoper 1945 and became soloist 1949. Now a principal dancer in Munich. Danced at Edinburgh Festival 1958.

HALTE DE CAVALERIE, ballet 1 act, ch. Petipa, m. Armsheimer, dec. Levogt, cost. Ponomarev, f.p. Maryinsky Th., St Petersburg 2 Feb 1896 (Legnani, Gerdt). A girl is courted by the officers of a regiment which halts in a village.

HAMILTON, Gordon, b. Sydney 1918, d. Paris 1959. Austral. dancer. Début with Austral. B. Co. Studied under Egorova. Joined B. de la Jeunesse 1939. From 1939 to 1941 danced with B. Rambert and Anglo-Polish B., joining S. Wells B. 1941 and remaining till 1946. With B. des Ch. Élysées 1946–47. Returned to S. Wells B. 1947 and rejoined Petit in his Ballets de Paris 1949. Also danced in musicals in America. To Vienna State Opera as ballet-master 1954 to 1959, contributing greatly to the revival of the company. Mounted *Giselle* there 1955.

HAMLET, ballet 1 sc., ch. Helpmann, m. Tchaikovsky, dec. Hurry, f.p. S. Wells B., New Th., London 19 May 1942 (Fonteyn, Franca, Helpmann, Paltenghi). This mime drama deals with the thoughts which flit across the brain of the dying Hamlet. Revived C. Garden 2 Apr 1964 (Seymour, Nureyev). Nijinska also chor. a *Hamlet* at the Paris Opéra 1934 (her own Co.), m. Liszt, dec. Annenkoff (Nijinska as Hamlet, Chanova as Ophelia). T. Gsovsky made another version at Städtische Oper, Berlin 19 Sept 1953 (m. Blacher). Also with music by Blacher, V. Gsovsky made a *Hamlet* (dec. Jürgens) for Munich B. 19 Nov 1950.

HAMLET, ballet, ch. Sergeyev, m. Chervinsky, dec. S. M. Yunovich, f.p. Kirov B., Leningrad 12 Dec 1970 (Sizova, Panov).

HAMLYN, Brenda, b. London 1925. Eng. dancer and teacher. Pupil of Cone-Ripman Sch. 1934–41, S. Wells Sch. 1941–42. Danced in London Lunch Time B. 1941, B. Guild 1942, soloist B. Rambert 1943–48, Nat. B. of Australia 1948, Empire B., London 1949–51. From 1951–64

243

danced in Italian opera houses (guest at Scala, Milan, 1956, 1957, 1966). Guest in Cologne 1961, Rome 1965. Has had her own school in Florence from 1964.

HANDS (in classical ballet). On the stage the fingers are held together, relaxed and very slightly rounded with the thumb lying close to them. In class, at the bar, pupils are often made to hold their hands with the thumb touching the tip of the second finger (French) or two of the centre flexed fingers (Cecchetti). This accustoms them to the feel of the slightly curved fingers in dancing.

*Position while
dancing* *Position at the bar
(Cecchetti method)* *Position at the bar
(French method)*

HANKA, Erika, b. Vinkovci 1905, d. Vienna 1958. German dancer and chor. Pupil of Bodenwieser and Jooss. Joined Düsseldorf B. 1936–39 as soloist and promoted ballet mistress. Danced for B. Jooss and became ballet mistress successively in Cologne, Essen and Hamburg. In 1941 was invited to chor. *Joan von Zarissa* (m. Egk) for the Vienna Staatsoper B. and was appointed ballet mistress same year and remained until her death. Chor. about 50 ballets there, notably *The Moor of Venice* (m. Blacher), for the re-opening of the Staatsoper 29 Nov 1955. Other ballets were *Hotel Sacher* (1957) and *Medusa* (1957).

HANKE, Suzanne, b. Altdöbern (E. Berlin) 1948. German dancer. Trained under Anne Woolliams and Alan Beale at Stuttgart and at the Royal B. Sch. Joined Stuttgart Ballet 1966 becoming soloist 1968. To CAPAB B. 1973.

HANSEN, Emile, b. 1843, d. 1927. Danish dancer and chor. Pupil of August Bournonville. For R. Danish B., chor. *Aditi* (m. Rung) and *The Gypsy Camp* (both 1880), *Carnival Jest in Venice* (m. Rung) 1890. He is often confused with Joseph Hansen.

HANSEN, Joseph, b. 1842, d. Asnières 1907. Belgian dancer, ballet master and chor. Director of ballet at the Bolshoi Th., Moscow 1879 to 1884. He revived *Swan Lake* 13 Jan 1880 (Odette, Y. Kalmykova) following Reisinger's original production of 1877, with little success. From Moscow he became ballet master of the Alhambra, London 1884–87. Thence he became ballet master of the Paris Opéra, succeeding Mérante from 1889 to 1907. His *La Maladetta* (m. Vidal) of 1893 had 176 performances there. He mounted the first performance of *Coppélia* in Brussels (1871) and the first in Russia (Moscow 1882).

HARANGOZO, Gyula, b. Budapest 1908. Hungarian dancer and chor. Trained under Ede Brada. Entered Hungarian Nat. B. and became principal dancer (an outstanding character dancer) 1928. Appointed choreographer 1936. Kossuth Prize 1956, Eminent Artist 1957, Gold Medal of Socialist Labour 1966. Chor. *Scene in the Czarda* (m. Hubay) 1936, *Janko in Boots* (m. Kenessey) 1937, *Romeo and Juliet* (m. Tchaikovsky) 1939, *The Wooden Prince* (m. Bartok 1935 and 1956), *Coppélia* (m. Delibes) 1953 etc.

HARBINGER, ballet, ch. Eliot Feld (his first), m. Prokofieff (*Piano Concerto in G*), cost. Simmons, f.p. Am. Ballet Th., State Th., N.Y. 11 May 1967. Young people dancing (Feld, Tracey, Verso, Sarry). Plotless but conveying a feeling of the 1960s.

HARDIE, Andrew, b. Edinburgh 1909. Scottish dancer and teacher. Pupil of M. Middleton, Idzikowsky, Sokolova, Craske, N. Legat. Danced in Beecham's opera seasons at C. Garden 1936–37. Danced in Mona Inglesby's group before 1939 and in 1946 joined her International B. Taught in Judith Espinosa's sch. and opened his own in London 1958. Author of *Ballet Exercises for Athletes* (illus. by Fougasse). Guest teacher of B. Rambert 1969–71.

HARKARVY, Benjamin, b. N.Y. 1930. Am. teacher and chor. Pupil of Chaffee, Caton, Sch. of Am. B. and Preobrajenska. Joined Brooklyn Lyric Opera 1948 and did his first choreography (dances in *La Traviata*). Opened school in N.Y. 1955 and in 1957 became director and ballet master of R. Winnipeg B. In 1958 ballet master of the Nederlands Ballet and then formed his own Co. in Amsterdam 1959, the Nederlands Dans Th. (q.v.). Left in 1969 to become joint director of Harkness B. Chor. many ballets, notably *Madrilesco, Le Diable à Quatre, Grand Pas Español, La Favorita* etc. In 1970 he became joint director (with van Dantzig) of the Dutch National B. but resigned 1971. Director of Pennsylvania B. 1972.

HARKNESS BALLET, founded in N.Y. 1964 by Mrs Rebekah Harkness (q.v.). The dancers were rehearsed at Watch Hill, Rhode Island by Volkova, Bruhn and Leon Fokine. George Skibine was appointed Director and its first performance was 19 Feb 1965 at the Casino, Cannes (*Pas de Six* from *Napoli, Feast of Ashes* ch. Ailey, *Scottish Fantasy* ch. Bruhn, *Time Out of Mind* ch. Macdonald). The principal dancers were Marjorie Tallchief, Elisabeth Carroll, Lone Isaksen, Margaret Mercier, Marlene Rizzo, Brunilda Ruiz, Panchita de Peri, Daphne Dale, Bruhn, Polajenko, Jhung, Lawrence Rhodes, Helgi Tomasson, Richard Wagner. The second programme included *Daphnis and Chloë* ch. Skibine and *The Abyss* ch. Hodes. They then moved to the Opéra Comique, Paris, and toured Europe. In 1965 toured America and gave their first N.Y. season 1967. Since then they have established themselves as one of the important Am. Cos. Brian Macdonald was director 1967. In 1968 Lawrence Rhodes was appointed director and in 1969 Harkarvy joined him. In 1965 the Harkness House for the Ballet Arts was opened in N.Y. In 1970 the interest of Mrs Harkness inclined to her newly-formed Harkness Youth Ballet, which she had formed the previous year, and the two Cos. combined, and Rhodes, Harkarvy, Isaksen and others left. Renzo Raiss became ballet master 1971. In 1972 they bought their own theatre in N.Y.

HARKNESS, Mrs Rebekah, b. St Louis 1915. Am. composer and founder of the Harkness B. Studied music under N. Boulanger and ballet with Leon Fokine. As president of the Harkness Foundation (established 1961) she promoted tours of Joffrey, Robbins' Ballets: U.S.A. etc.

HARLEM, DANCE THEATRE OF, all-Negro ballet company founded in New York by Arthur Mitchell in 1968. The associate director is Karel Shook and among the principal dancers are Lydia Abarca, Llanche Stevenson, Walter Raines, Clover Mathis and Mitchell. Danced in the Spoleto Festival 1971.

HARLEQUINADE, the English *Commedia dell'Arte*—a pantomime. See also LES MILLIONS D'ARLEQUIN.

HARLEQUIN IN APRIL, ballet, prologue, 2 acts, and epilogue, ch. Cranko, m. Arnell, dec. Piper, f.p. S. Wells Th. B., S. Wells Th. 8 May 1951 (Miller, Holden, Blair). A symbolical ballet of man's life.

HARMAN, Audrey, b. Penn, Bucks. Eng. dancer and teacher. Pupil of S. Wells Sch. 1942–46 and of Volkova. Joined S. Wells Theatre B. 1946, soloist International B. 1948, soloist Festival B. 1949–52. Teacher at Royal B. Sch. 1956–63, at the Folkwangschule, Essen 1963–64. Teacher in London from 1964 and worked with Massine from 1968 in his courses at the Royal B. Sch.

HAROLD IN ITALY, ballet, ch. Massine, m. Berlioz, dec. Lamotte, f.p. B. Russe de Monte Carlo, Boston 14 Oct 1954 (Danielian, Borowska, Chouteau).

HARRIS, Joan, b. London 1920. Eng. dancer and ballet mistress. Studied under Grandison Clark, Sadler's Wells Sch. and Idzikowsky. In International Ballet 1940–45. Joined S. Wells B. 1945 and a soloist in S. Wells Theatre B. in 1946. To Munich Staatsoper 1954 as soloist and ballet mistress. Director of Norwegian Nat. B. 1961, and from 1965 head of their school. Was ballet mistress of films *The Red Shoes*, *Tales of Hoffman* and *Invitation to the Dance*.

HARROLD, Robert, b. Wolverhampton 1923. Eng. dancer and teacher. Pupil of Preobrajenska, Volinine, Pericet. Joined Anglo-Polish B.

1940. Soloist in B. Rambert 1941–44. After war service danced in films and television. Chor. for Turkish Nat. B., Ankara 1959–60, Glyndebourne Opera from 1959. Now teaches in London and contributes to the *Dancing Times*.

HART, John, b. London 1921. Eng. dancer. Studied under Judith Espinosa, won Genée Gold Medal of R.A.D. Joined Vic-Wells B. 1938, becoming one of the principal dancers. Ballet-master S. Wells B. 1955. Published his photographs *Ballet and Camera* (1956). In 1963 appointed assistant director of Royal B. Resigned 1970. Director PACT B., Jo'burg 1971. Appointed C.B.E. 1971. From 1970 has been ballet-director at Int. Univ. of Performing Arts, San Diego.

HARVARD THEATRE COLLECTION, one of the principal dance collections of America, it is in the Houghton Library of Harvard Univ., Cambridge, Mass. From 1940 to 1960 Dr W. B. Van Lennep was curator and from 1960 to 1970 Helen Willard.

HARWOOD, Vanessa, b. Cheltenham 1947. Canad. dancer. Pupil of Oliphant, Schwenker at Canad. Nat. B. Sch. Joined Canad. Nat. B. 1965, soloist 1967, principal 1970.

HASKELL, Arnold L., b. London 1903. Eng. writer on the ballet. Educated Westminster and Trinity Hall, Cambridge. Was one of the founders of the Camargo Soc. (1930) and a director of the Ballet Club. His books did much to popularize ballet in England and especially in the Dominions. His book *Balletomania* (1934) introduced the word into English usage. He was the founder of the S. Wells Benevolent Fund, is a vice-president of the R.A.D., and has made several lecture tours for the British Council. Among his many books are *Studies in Ballet* (1928), *Diaghileff* (1935), *Dancing Round the World* (1937), *The National Ballet* (1943), the Pelican *Ballet* (1938), *In His True Centre* (autobiography, 1951) and was the Editor of *The Ballet Annual*. He was awarded the Legion of Honour 1951 and C.B.E. in 1954. His strong advocacy of making the Royal B. Sch. a school giving a full academic education was largely responsible for its expansion in 1947, with himself as Director. In 1956 he was appointed a governor of the Royal Ballet. Retired 1964. All his life he has been a connoisseur and he wrote the first book on Epstein, *The Sculptor Speaks*, in 1931. In 1972 published the second volume of autobiography *Balletomane at Large*. Vice-chairman Varna competition 1964–73.

HASSALL, Betty (Taudevin), b. Cheltenham 1909. Eng. teacher. Pupil of Judith Espinosa, Irene Hammond, becoming Head Teacher of the Hammond School, Chester, now her own (boarding) school of ballet. Examiner for Royal Academy of Dancing.

247

HASSELQUIST, Jenny, b. Stockholm 1894. Swedish dancer. Pupil Opera Sch., Stockholm and solodancer 1915. Also studied under Fokine and took the leading rôles in his ballets. Left the Royal Th. to become ballerina of de Maré's Ballets Suédois 1920–25. Now teaching in Stockholm.

HASSREITER, Joseph, b. Vienna 1845, d. there 1940. Austrian dancer, chor. and teacher. Entered the Vienna Hofoper B. Sch. 1851, and studied in Germany. Joined the Vienna Co. (1870) and was a soloist 1870–90 and ballet master 1891–1920, and head of the school. He chor. *Puppenfee* (m. Bayer) in 1888 and it remains in the repertoire of the Staatsoper B. Also chor. many ballets afterwards but his first appears to have been his most successful.

HASTINGS, Baird, b. N.Y. 1919. Am. writer. Educ. France and Harvard. Member of editorial staff *American Dancer* 1941–42. Founder and editor *Dance Index* 1941–46. Editorial staff *Dance News* from 1947. Director of Salle Vital, Archives Internationales de la Danse, Paris 1947. Founder and editor (with Lily, his wife) of art-journal *Chrysalis* from 1948 (published Boston, Mass.). Radio commentator on the arts. Author *Christian Bérard*, Boston (1950). Became teacher at Hartford Coll., Conn. and conductor of the Mozart Festival Orchestra. Now lives in N.Y.

HAUNTED BALLROOM, THE, ballet 1 act 3 sc., ch. de Valois, m. Geoffrey Toye, dec. Motley, f.p. Vic-Wells Ballet, S. Wells Th. 3 Apr 1934 (Markova, Moreton, Appleyard, Helpmann). The names of the characters are from the Christian names of the original dancers, Alicia, Ursula, Beatrice. Revived by Festival B., Cardiff 1 Apr 1965.

HAUT, EN, a position of the arms above the head.

HAUT VOLTAGE, ballet, ch. Béjart, m. Constant and P. Henry, dec. Rilliard, f.p. Charrat's Les Ballets de l'Étoile, Metz 27 Mar 1956 (H. Trailine, Miskovitch). A woman with supernatural power causes the electrocution of a pair of lovers, but the man recovers and kills the woman. Also performed by Massine's Nervi Ballet, Nervi 1956.

HAVAS, Ferenc, b. Budapest 1935. Hungarian dancer. Trained under Nadasi at State B. Institute and joined Budapest Opera B. 1952, becoming principal dancer 1953. Awarded Liszt Prize 1963, Kossuth Prize 1965. Danced *Romeo and Juliet* with Bolshoi B., Moscow (with Struchkova) 1966. Guest artist Festival B. 1960–64.

HAWKINS, Erick, b. Trinidad, Colorado. Am. dancer. Studied at Sch. of Am. B. Joined American B. 1935–37, Ballet Caravan 1936–39. Member of Martha Graham Co. 1938–51 as a principal dancer. Then formed his own company. Chor. many ballets incl. *Early Floating, Here and Now with Watchers* etc.

HAY or HEY, first mentioned in 1529, a country dance having a serpentine movement in which when the two lines of dancers meet they thread through each other, passing right and left alternately. This movement also forms a part of many dances, notably of the Farandole.

HAYDEE, Marcia (da Silva), b. Rio de Janeiro 1939. Brazilian dancer. Pupil of Vaslav Veltchek and Royal B. Sch., Anne Woolliams and Cranko. Joined Teatro Municipal, Rio de Janeiro 1953. Member of de Cuevas B. 1957, becoming soloist 1959. In 1961 joined Cranko's Stuttgart B. as ballerina. Cr. many rôles—Juliet in Cranko's *Romeo and Juliet* (1962), *Las Hermanas* (1963), *Onegin* (1965), *Song of the Earth* (1965), *Taming of the Shrew* (1969). Danced as guest artist Royal B. 1966. Danced *Giselle* 1966. Guest artist Berlin 1964 and 1968, Nat. B. of Canada 1964 etc. A poem in Latin addressed to her, by J. Eberle, appeared in the *Stuttgarter Zeitung* in 1969.

HAYDEN, Melissa (Herman), b. Toronto 1922. Canadian dancer. Studied with Volkoff and Balanchine. Début in Boris Volkoff's Canadian Ballet. Joined Ballet Theatre 1945. Joined Ballet Alonso in S. America. Joined N.Y. City Ballet as leading dancer 1950, cr. rôles *Illuminations, The Duel,* and *Caracole,* etc.; with Eglevsky, danced the leading rôle in the Chaplin film *Limelight* (1953). Rejoined B. Theatre 1953 and N.Y. City B. 1955. Guest artist Canadian Nat. B. 1963, Royal B. 1963 and Les Grands B. Canadiens 1969. Author of *Melissa Hayden—Off Stage and On* (1963). Retired 1973.

HAYTHORNE, Harry, b. Adelaide 1926. Australian dancer and ballet master. Studied under Idzikowsky, Northcote, Leeder and de Vos. Joined Metropolitan B. 1949, International B. 1950–51, ballet master at London Coliseum 1955 and Drury Lane 1956. Ballet master of Massine's Balletto Europeo (Nervi and Edinburgh) 1960. Danced Ugly Sister in *Cendrillon* (Paris 1963) (q.v.) and has worked in Italy and Holland. Notator in Labanotation of Balanchine's ballets in Europe. Ballet master Sadler's Wells Opera B. 1965. From 1967–71 ballet master of Western (later Scottish) Th. B. In 1968 guest teacher of Bat Dor Co., Tel-Aviv. Author of *How to be a Ballet Dancer* (1971). In 1972 appointed Production Co-ordinator of Scottish Th. B.

HAYWORTH, Terry, b. Burnley 1926. Eng. actor and dancer. Pupil of Nicolaeva Legat, Preobrajenska. Child actor 1940–42. Joined Anglo-Polish B. 1943, B. des Trois Arts 1944, Metropolitan B. 1947–49, Massine's B. 1950, B. de R. Petit 1951, in opera ballet at Bordeaux, Brussels, Antwerp 1951–63, Gore's London B. 1963, Festival B. from 1965.

HAZAÑA, ballet, ch. N. Morrice, m. Surinach, dec. Koltai, f.p. B. Rambert, S. Wells Th., London 25 May 1959 (Chesworth, Sandbrook, Martlew, Morrice). In a S. American village a cross is mounted on the church.

HAZARD, ballet, ch. Morrice, m. Salzedo, dec. Baylis, f.p. B. Rambert Th. Royal, Bath 12 June 1967 (Craig, Bruce, Taylor). Morrice's first ballet for the re-formed B. Rambert.

HEART OF THE HILLS, ballet 5 sc., ch. Chaboukiani, m. Balanchivadze, dec. Virsaladze, f.p. Kirov Th., Leningrad 28 June 1938 (Chikvaidze, Chaboukiani). Many Georgian and Caucasian dances are introduced into this ballet.

HEAR YE! HEAR YE!, ballet 1 act, ch. Ruth Page, m. Copland, dec. Remisov, f.p. Chicago Op. House 30 Nov 1934 (Page, Stone). A murder trial, set in a court room.

HEATON, Anne, b. Rawalpindi 1930. Eng. dancer. Studied Cranmore Sch. and S. Wells Sch. Début in S. Wells Op. (*Bartered Bride*, 1945). First soloist of S. Wells Th. B. at its inception in 1945. Cr. rôles in *Assembly Ball, Khadra, Valses Nobles et Sentimentales*, etc. Transferred to S. Wells B. in 1948, becoming soloist and cr. rôles in *Clock Symphony, Mirror for Witches*, etc. Danced *Giselle* (1954). To S. Wells Th. B. 1956 as guest artist. Chief dancer in Coliseum pantomime, London 1959. Mar. John Field. Teacher at Arts Educational Sch. Mounted *Giselle* in Teheran 1971.

HEBERLE, Thérèse, b. Vienna 1806, d. Naples 1840. Austrian dancer. Trained with Horschelt's Children's Dancers at the Th. an der Wien, Vienna, where she was one of his three most gifted pupils. Danced in Vienna 1813–26, finally at the Kärntnertor Th. Then to London where she danced in the Italian Opera. Mar. a banker, Falconet, who lost all her money. She also danced in Italy, at the Scala, Milan, where her reputation was considerable and the Milanese public called the young Carlotta Grisi 'la petite Heberle'. Grillparzer wrote some verses about her and dedicated his poem *Vorzeichen* to her.

HECKROTH, Hein, b. Giessen 1901, d. Frankfurt-a-M. 1970. Ger. designer who worked in close co-operation with the Ballet Jooss for many years. His masks and costumes for *The Green Table* (1932) are an outstanding piece of characterization. His other designs for the Jooss Company include, *The Prodigal Son, The Seven Heroes, The Big City*, and *Pandora*. He also designed the décor for the films *The Red Shoes* (1948), *Tales of Hoffmann* (1951). Designer at Frankfurt Opera in his last years.

HEIDEN, Heino, b. Wuppertal-Barmen 1923. Ger. (now Canadian) dancer and chor. Studied under T. Gsovsky, Preobrajenska, Tudor. Joined Berlin Staatsoper B. 1945, Dresden B. 1947 (as soloist), soloist Komische Oper, Berlin 1948, ballet master Hamburg, Am. B. Th. (touring) 1950, asst. ballet master Gärtnerplatz Th., Munich 1951. To Canada 1952 to teach at Vancouver and chor. many ballets there (some for the young Lynn Seymour). Left Montreal 1960 to become director of Mannheim B. where he chor. *La Fille Mal Gardée*. To Washington D.C. 1964, Royal Flemish B., Antwerp, 1965, Canadian Nat. B. 1966 where chor. *La Prima Ballerina* (m. Ridout). Director of Lübeck-Kiel B. 1967–68. Has private school in Lübeck.

HEINEL, Anne, b. Bayreuth 1753, d. Paris 1808. German dancer. Studied under l'Epy. Début Stuttgart 1767 under Noverre. Début Paris Opéra 1768. She is said to have invented the pirouette à la seconde. Retired in 1782. Mar. Gaetano Vestris 1792.

HEINRICH, Helga, b. Munich 1933. Ger. dancer. Studied in Munich Sch. and with Luipart, V. Gsovsky, Orlikowski. Joined Orlikowski's ballets in Oberhausen and Basel. To Stuttgart 1959, Munich 1964, Düsseldorf 1965. Guest ballerina Festival B. Now teaches in Munich.

HELEN OF TROY, ballet, prologue and 3 sc., ch. Lichine, m. Offenbach, dec. Vertès, f.p. Ballet Th., Palacio de Bellas Artes, Mexico City 10 Sept 1942 (Baronova, Eglevsky, Robbins). Fokine was working on this ballet when he died and its choreography was taken over by Lichine with suggestions from all the members of the Company. It is a burlesque, full of comic touches, notably a skit on *L'Après-midi d'un faune*.

HELPMANN, Sir Robert, b. Mount Gambier, Australia 1909. Austral. dancer, chor., and actor. Studied in Australia, in Pavlova Co., with Novikoff. To London 1933, joined S. Wells B. and danced first solo, Satan in *Job*, that year. Became the chief male dancer and partner of Margot Fonteyn, this partnership, which developed during the War, being a major factor in the development and success of the S. Wells B. His first ch. was for the R.A.D. Production Club *La Valse* (1939). For the S. Wells B. he chor. *Comus* (1942), *The Birds, Hamlet* (1942), *Miracle in the Gorbals* (1944), *Adam Zero* (1946). He left the Co. 1950 to become a successful actor and producer. His chief cr. rôles, besides those in his own ballets, are Red King in *Checkmate*, Mr O'Reilly in *The Prospect Before Us*, the Poet in *Apparitions*, and the Young Man in *Nocturne*. In 1960, with Nijinska, chor. the de Cuevas *Sleeping Beauty* and in 1963, with Ashton, chor. Royal B.'s new *Swan Lake* and chor. *Elektra* for Royal B. the same year. Returned to Australia and chor. for the Australian B. *The Display* (1964), *Yugen* (1965), *Sun Music* (1968) and became joint Director, with Peggy van Praagh, of that Co. 1965.

Awarded C.B.E. 1964 and knighted in 1968. He has also chor. and directed musicals (incl. *Camelot* 1969).

HENNESSY, Christine, b. Providence, R.I. 1936. Am. dancer. Pupil of Swoboda at B. Russe Sch., N.Y., and joined B. Russe de Monte Carlo 1954. In 1956 went to Germany and became principal dancer at Bremen. In 1957 joined a touring group American Concert B. and in 1958 was ballerina of a similar group based in Europe, American Festival Ballet. She returned to America and in 1969 was ballerina of R. Winnipeg B.; best dancer's prize at Paris International Festival that year.

HENRIOT, Henri, b. Nancy 1944. Fr. dancer. Pupil of Julie Sedowa at Cannes and Besobrasova at Monte Carlo. Joined Dutch Nat. B. 1964, Royal Flemish B., Antwerp 1967, becoming soloist.

HENRY, Louis X. S., b. Versailles 1784, d. Naples 1836. Fr. dancer and chor. of over 125 ballets. Studied at Paris Opéra under Deshayes and Coulon. Début there, with Clotilde Mafleuroy, 1803. In 1805 chor. *L'Amour à Cythère* which, on account of his youth, displeased Gardel and Milon who complained to Napoleon about it and succeeded in preventing him from staging any more ballets. Fled to Italy after producing a ballet in 1807 at Porte St Martin Th. and had great success in Milan and Naples and came under the influence of Vigano and Gioja. Also worked in Vienna. Returned to Paris and chor. *Hamlet* (1816) and other ballets at Porte St Martin Th. To Th. Nautique 1834 and chor. *William Tell, Les Ondines, Chao-Kang.* Engaged at Paris Opéra 1834 and chor. *L'Ile des Pirates* (for Elssler) which was not a success and he returned to Naples. See LA SYLPHIDE.

HENRY, Pierre, b. Paris 1927. Fr. comp. Pupil of Messiaen. From 1949, with Pierre Schaeffer (b. Nancy 1910), experimented with *musique concrète*. In 1952 part of his *Symphonie pour un homme seul* was used by Merce Cunningham in N.Y. for his *Collage.* In 1955 Bejart used this score for his *Symphonie pour un homme seul* and subsequently made great use of Henry's music—notably *Haut Voltage* (1956, also with m. by Constant), *Variations for a Door and a Sigh* (1965), *Messe pour le temps present* (1967), *Nijinsky, Clown de Dieu* (1971) etc.

HENZE, Hans Werner, b. Gütersloh 1926. Ger. composer. Pupil of Musikhochschule, Brunswick and of Fortner. Among his ballets are *Jack Pudding* (1950), *Labyrinth* (1950), *The Idiot* (1952), *Dance Marathon* (1957), *Ondine* (Royal B., 1959), *Gemini* (Austral. B. 1973).

HERMANAS, LAS, ballet, ch. MacMillan, m. Frank Martin *Concerto for harpischord*, dec. Georgiadis, f.p. Stuttgart B., Stuttgart 13 July 1963 (Haydee, Keil, Barra, Papendick). Lorca's *Casa de Bernarda Alba.*

Also given by Western Th. B., New Th., Cardiff 22 June 1966 (Haig, McDonald, Cazalet, O'Donohoe). Also in Berlin B. 1967 and Ballet Theatre 1967. By Touring Royal B., S. Wells Th. 2 June 1971 (Seymour, Barbieri, Larsen, Sherwood).

HEROIC POEM (or THE GEOLOGISTS), ballet, ch. N. Kasatkina and V. Vassiliov, m. Karetnikov, dec. Stenberg, f.p. Bolshoi Th., Moscow 21 Jan 1964 (Sorokina, Vladimirov).

HEROLD, Louis-Joseph-Ferdinand, b. Paris 1791, d. there 1833. Fr. composer and on musical staff of Paris Opéra. Composed many ballets, incl. *La Somnambule* (1827), the new version of *La Fille Mal Gardée* (1827 and that used by Ashton 1960), *Sleeping Beauty* (1829).

HERTEL, Peter Ludwig, b. Berlin 1817, d. there 1899. Ger. composer. Conductor at Berlin Royal Opera and composed several of Paul Taglioni's ballets *Flick and Flock* (1858), *Satanella* (1852), *Sardanapal* (1865), and the new 1864 version of *La Fille Mal Gardée* (used in Russia and by Cuevas B. etc.).

HERZBERG, Tana, b. Berlin 1932. Ger. dancer. Pupil of Blank, T. Gsovsky. Joined Berlin B. 1952, becoming soloist 1956. Principal dancer Braunsweg 1964-66.

HEUBI, Peter, b. Bern. Swiss dancer. Studied in Bern and under Lia Schubert in Stockholm. Rambert Sch. 1960. Joined de Cuevas B. 1961. Soloist in Geneva 1962, principal dancer B. de la Jeunesse Musicale 1963-35. Soloist Festival B. 1965-68, B. Felix Blaska 1970. Teaches in Bern.

HIGHTOWER, Rosella, b. Ardmore, Oklahoma 1920. Am. dancer and chor. of Am. Indian extraction. Studied with Dorothy Perkins in Kansas City. With B. Russe de Monte Carlo 1938-41. Ballet Theatre 1941-45, ballerina Original Ballet Russe 1946-47, prima ballerina Grand Ballet du Marquis de Cuevas 1947-61. Chor. for Markova-Dolin in N.Y. *Henry VIII* (1949), for Metropolitan Ballet *Pleasure-drome* (1949), for de Cuevas *Salomé* (1950), *Scaramouche* (1951). In 1961 opened her residential ballet school in the Residence Gallia, Cannes. Gives occasional guest performances and presents her own group in the Casino, Cannes. From 1969-71 Director of Ballet in Marseilles (while continuing to teach in her school). During the 1950s she was the most popular ballerina in Europe on account of her remarkable technical ability. Her daughter, Dominique Robier is also a dancer, in Béjart's Co. Director of Nancy B. 1973.

HILARIDES, Marianna, b. Java 1933. Dutch dancer. Pupil of Gaskell, Egorova, Hightower. Joined Gaskell's group, Ballet Recital, 1951.

Then danced with the Vienna B., and all the Dutch Cos., Cuevas, and Gr. B. Classique de France.

HILFERDING VAN WEWEN, Franz, b. Vienna 1710, d. there 1768. Austrian maître de ballet and dancer. He was trained in Paris 1734–36 under Blondi, and became ballet-master in Vienna, and later at Stuttgart where he greatly influenced Noverre, who succeeded him, in his development of the *ballet d'action*. In 1758 he went to St Petersburg as maître de ballet, where he did much to raise the standard of dancing. He remained there until 1765, when he returned to Vienna, where he had been succeeded by his pupil Angiolini, who took his place in Russia. Another of his pupils was Eva Maria Veigl (q.v.).

HILL, Carole, b. Cambridge 1945. Eng. dancer. Pupil of R. Ballet Sch. Joined Royal B. 1962, coryphée 1966, soloist 1966. Danced *Giselle* in Rhodesia 1970. Joined Festival B. 1972 becoming a principal.

HILL, Margaret, b. Birmingham 1929. Eng. dancer. Soloist of B. Rambert, joined S. Wells B. 1952 as soloist. Cr. chief rôle in *Solitaire* (1956).

HINKSON, Mary, b. Philadelphia 1930. Am. dancer. Pupil of Martha Graham and member of her Co. since 1951. Created title rôle in Graham's *Circe* (1963). Teaches for Graham in N.Y., London etc.

HINTON, Paula, b. Ilford 1924. Eng. dancer. Pupil of Delamere-Wright. Joined B. Rambert 1944, becoming principal dancer and succeeding to many of Sally Gilmour's rôles. Also danced with B. des Ch. Élysées, Orig. B. Russe, and Festival B., Pilar Lopez 1958, Frankfurt Opera 1956–58 etc. Mar. Walter Gore and created leading rôle in many of his ballets (*Antonia*, *Night and Silence*, *Eaters of Darkness*, *Sweet Dancer* etc.). Ballerina of London B. 1961 and of Gulbenkian B., Lisbon 1965–69. Guest artist Western Th. B. 1965, Northern Dance Th. 1971–72.

HITCHINS, Aubrey, b. Cheltenham 1880, d. N.Y. 1969. Eng. dancer. Educ. Cheltenham College. Studied under Cecchetti, Legat. Became Pavlova's partner 1925–30. Danced with Les Chauves Souris in Paris. Founded his own Co. 1943 and since 1947 taught in N.Y.

HODES, Stuart, b. 1924. Am. dancer and chor. Pupil of Martha Graham, Sch. of Am. B. From 1947 to 1958 a principal dancer of Graham Co. Also danced in musicals on Broadway. Chor. many ballets incl. *Suite for Young Dancers* (1959), *Balaam* (1960) and *The Abyss* (1965). Mar. Linda Hodes (Margolies) a principal dancer of the Graham Co. who worked for the Batsheva Dance Co. in Tel Aviv 1965, staging Graham ballets and chor. *The Act* for them.

HOFGEN, Lothar, b. Wiesbaden 1936. Ger. dancer, Pupil of Roleff, van Dijk. Principal dancer Cologne 1959–64, of Béjart's B. du XXme Siècle 1964–67. Ballet master Karlsruhe 1967–69, Bonn 1970–73, Mannheim 1973.

HOLDEN, Stanley, b. London 1928. Studied at Bush-Davies Sch. To S. Wells B. 1944 and S. Wells Th. B. 1948. To S. Africa to teach in 1954, but returned to Touring Royal Ballet 1957 (transferred to C. Garden 1958) as soloist until 1969. To America 1970 to teach in California. Created rôle of Mother Simone in Ashton's *La Fille Mal Gardée* (1960) etc.

HOLDER, Christian, b. Trinidad 1949. British dancer. Pupil of Corona Sch., Isabelle Florence, Laura Wilson Joffrey, Zaraspe. Joined Joffrey B. 1966 becoming soloist. Performed in cabaret in Belgium, London, Jamaica etc. with his father's (Boscoe H.) company.

HOLLAND, BALLET IN, see under the three main Cos. (1) DUTCH NATIONAL B., (2) NEDERLANDS DANS THEATER and (3) SCAPINO B.

HOLM, Eske, b. Copenhagen 1940. Dan. dancer. Pupil of R. Dan. Sch. Entered R. Danish B. 1958 becoming solodancer. Chor. *Tropisms* (1964), *Cicatrice* (1969) etc.

HOLM, Hanya, b. Worms 1898. Ger. (now U.S.) dancer. Studied at Dalcroze Inst. at Hellerau, and under Wigman. Danced in Wigman's Group and founded Wigman Sch., N.Y. (1931) which is now the Hanya Holm Studio. Chor. many modern ballets, incl. the musicals *Kiss Me Kate* and *My Fair Lady*. One of the leading figures in modern Am. dance. From 1961 head of dance department of N.Y. Musical Academy.

HOLMES, Anna-Marie (Ellerbeck), b. Mission City, B.C. 1943. Canadian dancer. Studied under Heino Heiden, Lydia Karpova and Wynne Shaw in Canada 1953–59 and in London 1959–60. Also studied in Leningrad under Dudinskaya since 1962. Danced with her husband, David Holmes, in R. Winnipeg B. 1960–62, Kirov B. 1962–63, Festival B. 1963–64, Grands B. Canadiens 1964–65, Dutch Nat. B. 1965–67, Ruth Page's Chicago B. 1968 and 1969.

HOLMES, David, b. Vancouver 1938. Canadian dancer. Studied under Lydia Karpova in Vancouver 1957–58, R. Winnipeg B. 1958–59, in London (de Vos and Addison) 1959–60 and under Alexander Pushkin in Leningrad every year since 1962. Danced with his wife, Anna-Maria Holmes, in R. Winnipeg B. 1960–62, Kirov B. 1962–63, Festival B. 1963–64, Grands B. Canadiens 1964–65, Dutch Nat. B. 1965–67, Ruth Page's Chicago B. 1968 and 1969.

HOLMGREN, Bjorn, b. Stockholm 1920. Swed. dancer and chor. Pupil of R. Opera Sch., Stockholm, Egorova, Volkova, Kniaseff, Skeaping. Début R. Swed. B. 1939, becoming principal dancer 1946. Guest artist International B. 1949. Chor. *Suite Classique* (m. Lalo), *Variation de Ballet* (m. Brahms). *Swedish Rhapsody* (m. Alfven) 1958 and many musical comedies in Stockholm. Retired from R. Swed. B. 1966 and became ballet master of Cullberg B. 1968. Now on staff of Swedish State Dance School, Stockholm.

HOLZ, Rudolf, b. Berlin 1938. Ger. dancer. Pupil of Blank, T. Gsovsky. Joined Berlin B. 1955 becoming a principal dancer.

HOMAGE TO THE QUEEN, ballet 1 act, ch. Ashton, m. Arnold, dec. Messel, f.p. S. Wells B., C. Garden 2 June 1953 (Fonteyn, Grey, Elvin, Nerina, Somes, Field, Hart, Rassine). F.p. on Coronation Night as part of the Coronation celebrations.

HONER, Mary, b. London 1914, d. London 1965. Eng. dancer. Studied under Judith Espinosa, Craske, Legat. Appeared in musical comedy and début in S. Wells B. 1936, becoming a ballerina and retiring in 1942. Cr. Bride in *Wedding Bouquet* and a Blue Girl in *Patineurs*. Later appeared as an actress. Opened a ballet school in London. In 1946 founded Embassy B. with Molly Lake.

HOPAK, see GOPAK.

HØNNINGEN, Mette, b. Copenhagen 1945. Danish dancer. Graduated to R. Danish B. 1963, becoming solodancer 1967. In 1964 she was chosen by Walt Disney to act and dance the leading rôle in his film *Ballerina*.

HOOPER, Alan, b. Teignmouth 1948. Eng. dancer. Pupil of Spencer-Edwards and Royal B. Sch. Joined Touring Royal B. 1966 becoming a soloist 1969. Retired 1971 to teach.

HORNPIPE, a dance apparently peculiar to Great Britain, where it once enjoyed a greater popularity than at present. It would not seem at first to have been associated with things nautical and derives its name from a musical instrument now obsolete. Originally in three time, it has, since the conclusion of the eighteenth century, been danced in duple time.

HOROSCOPE, ballet 1 act, ch. Ashton, m. Constant Lambert, dec. Fedorovitch, f.p. S. Wells B., S. Wells Th. 27 Jan 1938 (Fonteyn, Somes). Young lovers ruled by the signs of the zodiac. Somes made his first success in this ballet.

HORST, Louis, b. Kansas City 1884, d. N.Y. 1964. Am. musician and composer. Musical Director for Ruth St Denis (1915–25), Martha Graham (1926–48), etc., and one of the leading figures associated with the musical side of the dance in America. Founder and editor of *Dance Observer* (1934). Author of *Pre-Classic Dance Forms* (1937), *Modern Dance Forms* (1960).

HORTENSIA, a step in which the dancer, standing with feet apart and one

256

in front of the other, suddenly jumps and reverses their position, several times.

HORTON, Lester, b. Indianapolis 1906, d. Los Angeles 1953. Am. dancer and teacher. Pupil of Bolm etc. Studied Red Indian dancing and Japanese theatre. Founded his own troupe, the Lester Horton Dancers 1934 in Hollywood and chor. and designed their dances. He was a leader of modern Am. dance and influential in its teaching, having as his pupils Ailey, Trisler, de Lavallade etc.

HOTEL SACHER, ballet, ch. Hanka, m. Hellmesberger and Schönherr, dec. Wakhevitch, f.p. Vienna Staatsoper B. 10 May 1957. Written round Vienna's most famous hotel (Brexner, Brauer, Zlocha, Dirtl, Adama).

HOUSE OF BIRDS, ballet, ch. MacMillan, m. Mompou, dec. Georgiadis, f.p. S. Wells Th. B., S. Wells Th. 26 May 1955 (Tempest, Lane, Poole). From Grimm's *Jorinda and Joringel*.

HOVING, Lucas, b. Groningen. Dutch (now Am.) dancer and chor. Pupil of Georgi, Jooss. Danced with B. Jooss, Graham Co., Limon Co. etc. Taught at Juilliard Sch. and at Swedish State Sch., Stockholm in 1970. In 1971 became director of the Rotterdam Dance Academy.

HOWARD, Andrée, b. 1908, d. London 1968. Eng. dancer, designer and chor. Studied with Rambert from 1924. Member of the B. Club for whom she made her first ballets, for many of which she was her own designer. From 1933–52 devised some twenty-three ballets, the most noteworthy being: for B. Club (and later B. Rambert) *Our Lady's Juggler* (her first ballet 1933), *Mermaid* (1934), *Death and the Maiden* (1937), *Lady into Fox* (1939), *Sailor's Return* (1947). For London B. and later S. Wells Th. B. *La Fête Étrange* (1940). For S. Wells Th. B. *Assembly Ball* (1946), *Mardi Gras* (1946), *Selina* (1948). For Royal B. *Mirror for Witches* (1952), *Veneziana* (1953), *Conte Fantastique* (1957). She designed *Sleeping Beauty* for the Turkish Nat. B. and also danced one of the Ugly Sisters in *Cinderella* at C. Garden and appeared in Festival B.'s *Nutcracker*.

HOWARD, Robin, b. London 1924. Eng. founder of London Contemporary Dance Theatre and benefactor of the dance. Educ. Eton, Trinity Col., Cambridge and served Scots Guards during Second World War. Balletomane from 1945, met Martha Graham 1962 and arranged for her to visit Britain in 1963. Cultivated her art by sending Eng. dancers to study with her in N.Y. (among them Eileen Cropley, Anna Price) and in 1965 started Graham classes in London. Acquired premises in 1966 and opened school. Founded London Contemporary Dance Theatre (Graham style Co.) in 1967. Bought The Place (q.v.) 1969 as a centre for the company and school.

HOWES, Dulcie, b. Cape Province 1910. S. African dancer and teacher. Pupil of Webb, Craske, Karsavina, Brunelleschi. Danced in Pavlova's Co. and returned to S. Africa 1930. Founded University of Cape Town School of Ballet 1932 and in 1934 it gave a public performance and became the Univ. of Cape Town Ballet—the first in S. Africa and having a distinguished record of productions and dancers, many of whom have found their way into the Royal B. In 1963 the State gave financial support to the Co. and in 1965 it was financed with public funds through the Cape Performing Arts Board—and is now known as the Capab Ballet. She retired from the Directorship in 1969 (succeeded by David Poole) but continued as head of the School to 1973. See CAPAB BALLET.

HOYER, Dore, b. 1911, d. Berlin 1967. Ger. dancer. Pupil of Jaques-Dalcroze Sch. at Hellerau-Laxenburg and of Palucca. Gave her first recital 1934 in Dresden. Danced in Wigman's Co. Ballet mistress in Hamburg 1949–51, during which she chor. her most well-known dance *Bolero* (1950). Since then she toured giving solo recitals. Her influence in German dance was very great.

HUDOVA, Irina, b. Finland 1930. Finnish dancer and teacher. Pupil of Nifontova and entered Helsinki Nat. B. Sch. 1945 studying under Saxelin. Came annually to London to Northcote's classes. Joined Finnish Nat. B. 1950, becoming ballerina, and dancing and studying in Leningrad and Moscow. In 1964 gave lessons at the R.A.D., London, and toured with Fonteyn as ballet mistress of a small Royal B. group. Guest teacher of Royal Ballet 1967–68 and also taught in Puerto Rico 1967. From 1969 was teacher of Turkish Nat. B. in Ankara and Scala, Milan. In 1972 became Director of the Nat. B. of Finland in Helsinki. Returned to Scala 1973.

HUISSEN Ineke b. Harlem 1943. Dutch dancer. Joined Dutch Nat. B. 1961, becoming soloist 1966.

HULBERT, Tony, b. London 1944. Eng. dancer, ballet master and chor. Pupil of Andrew Hardie. Joined Béjart's B. du XXme Siècle 1961. Became a principal dancer Festival B. 1965, of Royal B. 1965, of Western Th. B. 1967, of Netherlands Dance Th. 1968. Principal dancer and teacher of R. Winnipeg B. 1970. In 1971 appointed ballet master of B. de Wallonie, Charleroi. Chor. *Jadis* for Netherlands Dance Th. 1969, *Simple Symphony* and *Sextet* for B. de Wallonie 1971.

HULLIN-SOR, Félicité, b. 1805, d. after c. 1850. Fr. dancer. Pupil of Albert in Paris but worked as a dancer, teacher and chor. in Bolshoi Th., Moscow 1823–35. Between 1831 and 1833 she was ballet mistress and produced many ballets and divertissements. Was the teacher of Sankovskaya and was mar. to Fernando Sor, the Spanish guitarist and composer. She and her sister, Josephine Hullin played 'rôles d'amour' at the Paris Opéra in 1818. Her other sister, Virginie, began her career by playing Cupid rôles at the Opéra and later became famous for her wonderful memory, for she could replace a dancer at a moment's notice without having danced the rôle before. Their father, Jean Baptiste Hullin, used to produce ballets with casts of children (including a *Fille Mal Gardée* with a 6-year-old Lise and a 5-year-old Colin).

HUMP-BACKED HORSE, THE (Russ. *Koniok Gorbunok*), ballet 4 acts 9 sc., ch. Saint-Léon, m. Pugni, f.p. Bolshoi Th., St Petersburg 3 Dec 1864 (Muravieva). This ballet was the first to be based on stylized national dance. It was revised by Gorsky in Moscow 25 Nov 1901 and this version is still in the Kirov repertoire. Using a new score by R. Schedrin (b. 1927) A. Radunsky re-chor. the ballet at the Bolshoi, Moscow 4 Mar 1960 (Karelskaya, Vasiliev, Radunsky). A film of this (with Plisetskaya) was made in 1962. In 1963 (also using Schedrin's music), I. Belsky re-chor. it for the Maly Th., Leningrad.

HUMPHREY, Doris, b. Illinois 1895, d. N.Y. 1958. Am. dancer and chor. Studied under Ruth St Denis and Shawn, a member of whose company she became. Founded, with Weidman, her own Co. and school 1928. Has chor. many ballets in the modern style, and a major figure in this movement in America. Chor. *The Life of the Bee* (1929), *The Shakers* (1931), *Theatre Piece, With my Red Fires, New Dance* (all 1936). Artistic Director of Limon Co. 1945 (when she retired from dancing). Founded Juilliard Dance Th. 1955. Author of *The Art of Making Dances* (1959).

HUMPHREYS, Sheila, b. London 1939. Eng. dancer. Pupil of Crofton, Nordi, Royal B. Sch. Joined Touring Royal B. 1958, soloist 1964 becoming ballet mistress.

HUNGARIAN NATIONAL BALLET, THE, dates from 1884 when the Budapest Opera House opened (then the Imperial B.). Before then there were groups of dancers mostly from Vienna (Elssler danced there in 1846, Augusta Maywood chor. *Rendezvous at the Masked Ball* in 1847). The ballet master was Frederico Campilli, *Coppélia* was performed there in 1877 and the most popular ballet was Hassreiter's *Puppenfee* (1884). The younger Marie Taglioni was guest artist. Nicola Guerra was ballet master intermittently 1899-1915. In 1917 Bartok's *The Wooden Prince* was chor. by Ede Brada. The chief chors. 1918–39 were J. Cieplinski and Rezsö Brada (son of Ede B.)—and Gyula Harangozó. The last was one of the greatest figures in Hungarian ballet. A great character dancer, he is also a most successful chor. Their other great master was Ferenc Nádasi, who taught their dancers from 1937 to his death in 1962. In 1950 Vainonen came over from Russia and started a new era, with strong Russian influence. He mounted *Casse Noisette*, *Flames of Paris* etc., Zakharoff mounted *Swan Lake* (1951), and Lavrovsky *Giselle* and later his *Romeo and Juliet*, while the leading dancers went to Russia for training. In recent years the principal dancers have been Zsuzsa Kun, Gabriella Lakatos, Adél Orosz, Ferenc Havas, Viktor Fulop, Viktor Rona. A new chor. Laszlo Zeregi has emerged, with a very successful *Spartacus* (1968) etc. In 1971 Ashton mounted his *Fille Mal Gardée* for the Co. with great success. The Co. danced at Edinburgh Festival 1963, 1973. Director 1973, G. Lörinc.

HUNGARICA, ballet, ch. Milloss, m. Bartók, dec. Sciajola, f.p. Rome Opera House, 10 Jan 1956 (Radice, Lauri, Koellner). An abstract ballet but evoking nostalgia for Hungary.

HUNGARY, BALLET IN, see under HUNGARIAN NATIONAL BALLET, and BALLET SOPIANAE.

HUROK, Solomon, b. Pogar, Russia 1888. Am. impresario who has presented most of the ballet companies and dancers in America from 1920 (incl. Pavlova, Duncan, Royal B., Kirov B., Bolshoi B.). Author of *Impresario* (1947), *S. Hurok Presents* (1955). Awarded Legion of Honour 1960, O.B.E. 1961.

HURRY, Leslie, b. London 1909. Eng. painter and designer. Designed for S. Wells B. *Hamlet* (1942), *Swan Lake* (1943) and new version in 1952.

HUTCHINSON, Ann, b. N.Y. 1918. Am. dancer and teacher of notation. Educ. in England. Studied under Jooss and Leeder (Dartington Hall), Graham, Celli, Craske, Sch. of Am. B. etc. Joined musical *One Touch of Venus* (ch. de Mille) 1943 and danced in many musicals subsequently. Made a special study of dance notation systems (and can interpret 23 of them) and took diploma in kinetography, Laban. Co-founder in 1940 of the Dance Notation Bureau (q.v.) and was president until 1961. Formerly teacher of ballet and Labanotation at Sch. of Performing Arts, N.Y. and head of notation faculty at Juilliard Sch. Author of *Labanotation* (1954) and of an enlarged, revised edition 1970. Since 1962 has lived in London and teaches notation. See CACHUCHA. Mar. Ivor Guest.

HYND, Ronald (Hens), b. Hampstead 1931. Eng. dancer. Studied under Rambert. Joined Ballet Rambert 1949, becoming soloist. Joined Royal Ballet 1951, becoming soloist 1954. Mar. Annette Page. In 1970 appointed Director of Ballet, Munich. Resigned 1973. Ch. *Baiser de la Fée* 1968 for Dutch Nat. B., *Pasiphäe* (1969) for Royal B. Chor. Group, *Dvorak Variations* for Festival B. (1970), *In a Summer Garden* (1972 for Touring Royal B.) etc.

HYWELL, Suzanne, b. Tunbridge Wells 1944. Eng. dancer. Pupil of Bush-Davies Sch. and Royal B. Sch. Joined Western Th. B. 1962 and Northern Dance Th. 1968 as principal.

I

ICARE, ballet 1 act, ch. Lifar, rhythms by Lifar orchestrated by Szyfer, dec. Larthe, f.p. Paris Opéra 9 July 1935 (Lifar). This ballet has no music, only sounds emitted by percussion and other instruments. Revived at Paris Opéra with dec. by Picasso 5 Dec 1962 (Labis).

ICE MAIDEN, THE or SOLVEIG, ballet 3 acts, ch. Lopokov, m. Grieg, dec. Golovin, f.p. Kirov Th., Leningrad 27 Apr 1927 (Mungalova, Gusev, Yermoleyeff).

IDIOT, THE, ballet-pantomime, ch. T. Gsovsky m. Henze dec. Ponelle, f.p. Hebbel Th., Berlin 1 Sept 1952 (Palar, Trofimova, Horn, Leistner). Follows the Dostoievsky novel.

IDYLLE, ballet 1 act, ch. Skibine, m. Serrette, dec. Camble, f.p. de Cuevas Co., Empire Th., Paris 2 Jan 1954 (Marjorie Tallchief, Skibine, Skouratoff). A charming ballet about horses in a field.

IDZIKOWSKY, Stanislas, b. Warsaw 1894. Polish dancer and teacher. Studied under Cecchetti. Début in Empire Th. Ballets. Member of Pavlova's Co. Joined Diaghileff 1914 and cr. rôle of Snob in *Boutique Fantasque*, Dandy in *Tricorne*, etc. Left Co. in 1926 but rejoined in 1928. Danced with Vic-Wells B. 1933 and cr. rôle in *Les Rendezvous*. His elevation and technique were prodigious and comparable with Nijinsky's. He worked with Beaumont in codifying the teaching of Cecchetti. For years he was a famous teacher in London. Now retired.

ILLUMINATIONS, ballet 1 act, ch. Ashton, m. Britten, dec. Beaton, f.p. N.Y. City B., City Center, N.Y. 2 Mar 1950 (LeClerq, Hayden, Magallanes). For tenor and strings, the music is Britten's settings of some Rimbaud songs.

IMAGES OF LOVE, ballet, ch. MacMillan, m. Tranchell, dec. Kay, f.p. Royal B., C. Garden 2 Apr 1964 (Beriosova, Nerina, Parkinson, Seymour, Macleary, Doyle, Rosson, Rencher, Gable, Grant, Nureyev). Episodes from the Shakespeare plays. With *The Dream*, and *Hamlet* formed the Shakespeare Quatercentenary Programme of the Royal B.

IMAGO, ballet, ch. Nikolais, m. Nikolais, cost. Nikolais, f.p. Nikolais Dance Co., Hartford, Conn. 24 Feb 1963 (Louis, Bailin, Lamhut, Frank). A full length experiment in colours and shapes.

IMPERIAL DANCING ACADEMY, the school of dancing at the Teatro alla Scala, Milan, was founded in 1812 under Benedetto Ricci. In 1837, Carlo Blasis was appointed Director and under his rule the school at La Scala had its greatest period, training Italian dancers who became the prima ballerinas of all the capitals of Europe—among them Grisi, Fuoco, Legnani, Zucchi, Cerrito, etc. Cecchetti, also a pupil of the Academy, became Director in 1925. Cia Fornaroli was Director 1928–1933, Ettorine Mazzucchelli 1933–1950, Vera Volkova 1950–51 and Esmée Bulnes from 1951 to 1968. The original title of the Academy was Imperiale Regia Accademia di Ballo. It is now called the Scala Ballet School.

IMPERIAL SCHOOL, ST PETERSBURG, see under LANDÉ.

IMPERIAL SOCIETY OF TEACHERS OF DANCING, a society of dance teachers (founded 25 July 1904) in the British Empire, with headquarters in London. It conducts its own examinations and issues diplomas in ballroom and other types of dancing. The Cecchetti Society (q.v.) was incorporated into it in 1924 and forms one of the ballet sections of the society. Examinations entitle members to use the letters M.I.S.T.D. and F.I.S.T.D. after their name. The Greek Dance Association was also incorporated in 1951.

IMPERIO, Pastora (Rojas), b. Granada c. 1885, d. 1961. Famous Sp. gypsy dancer. Her mother was also a famous gypsy dancer and singer, La Mejorana, who inspired much of de Falla's music. She was the first to chor. his *El Amor Brujo* (1915). Mar. bullfighter El Gallo (of the Ortega family).

IMPRESSIONS DE MUSIC-HALL, ballet, ch. Nijinska, m. Pierné, dec. Dethomas, f.p. Paris Opéra 6 Apr 1927 (Zambelli, Aveline). Revived 1943, dec. Wild.

IMPROMPTU AU BOIS, ballet, ch. Ruth Page, m. Ibert, dec. Wakhevitch, f.p. B. des Ch. Élysées, Th. des Ch. Élysées 1951 (Arova, Fosca, Ohn).

INBAL, the National Ballet and Dance Theatre of Israel. A folk-dance troupe founded in 1950 by Sara Levi-Tanai. The style is that of the dancers of the Yemen and their chief ballet is *The Yemenite Wedding*. First danced in London 1957, N.Y. 1958.

INDES GALANTES, LES, opera ballet in prologue and four entrées. Book Fuzelier, m. Rameau, dec. Servandoni. Of the chor. all that is known is that Sallé arranged her dances in the third entrée, f.p. l'Académie Royale, Paris 23 Aug 1735 but dropped from repertoire 1773. New production at Paris Opéra 18 June 1952. Prologue ch. Aveline, dec. Dupont and Arbus. First entrée, ch. Aveline, dec. Wakhevitch. Second entrée, ch. Lifar, dec. Carzou. Third entrée, ch. Lander, dec. Fost-

Moulène. Fourth entrée, ch. Lifar, dec. Chapelain-Midy (Vaussard, Bozzoni, Dynalix, Vyroubova, Lifar, Bardin, Daydé, Renault, Darsonval, Kalioujny). This is one of the most spectacular and most popular productions of the Opéra. In the third entrée scent is sprayed over the audience.

INGLESBY, Mona, b. London 1918. Eng. dancer and chor. Studied under Craske, Rambert, Egorova, etc. Danced with Ballet Club and B. Rambert, and with Dandré's Russian B. at C. Garden 1939. In 1940 founded her own Co., the International Ballet, which gave its first performance in 1941. She was the prima ballerina of the Co. and chor. for it *Endymion, Amoras, Everyman, Comus*, etc. Retired 1953.

INTERNATIONAL BALLET, Eng. ballet company founded by Mona Inglesby, who was its prima ballerina. The first performance was at the Alhambra Th., Glasgow 19 May 1941. In the early days the repertoire included many one-act ballets, but later the Co. gave only a few of these (*Gaîté Parisienne, Sylphides*, etc.) and concentrated almost entirely on the full-length classics, mounted by their *régisseur* Sergueeff, *Swan Lake, Sleeping Beauty, Coppélia*, and *Giselle*. The company has included among its dancers Harold Turner, Moira Shearer, Sonia Arova, Nina Tarakanova, Dorothy Stevenson, Joan Tucker, Nana Gollner, Paul Petroff, Domini Callaghan, Michel de Lutry, Helen Armfelt, Algeranova, Algeranoff, Errol Addison, Ernest Hewitt, Maurice Béjart, Miskovitch, Holmgren. The Co. also made tours in Italy, Spain, Sicily, and Switzerland. The International Ballet did much to satisfy the demands of the English provincial towns for ballet. It broke up in 1953.

INTERNATIONAL BALLET CARAVAN, a small touring Co. based on London. Founded by Alexander Roy (b. Magdeburg 1937) and his wife Christina Gallea (b. Sydney 1940), it gave its first performance in England at the Questors Th., Ealing, London 10 Jan 1967. Previously it had been performing on the continent from September 1965. It tours Europe continuously in two mini-buses and in 1970 formed the ballet for a musical at the Th. de la Monnaie, Brussels.

INTERPLAY, ballet 1 sc., ch. Robbins, m. Morton Gould, dec. Carl Kent, f.p. Concert Varieties, Ziegfield Th., N.Y. 1 June 1945 (Janet Reed, John Kriza, Robbins). In repertoire B. Th. (dec. O. Smith, cost. I. Sharaff) since 17 Oct 1945, and N.Y. City B. since 23 Dec 1952. This ballet in the modern Am. idiom has greatly influenced cont. choreographers.

IN THE NIGHT, ballet ch. Robbins, m. Chopin (*Nocturnes*), cost. Eula, lighting Skelton, f.p. N.Y. City B., State Th., N.Y. 29 Jan 1970 (Mazzo, Verdy, McBride, Blum, Martins, Moncion). Romantic couples

—Robbins's third ballet to Chopin piano music (after *The Concert* and *Dances at a Gathering*). By Royal B., C. Garden, 10 Oct 1973.

INVISIBLE FRONTIERS, ballet-evening chor. by Neumeier (and dec. also), m. Bliss, Poulenc, Mahler, Simon and Garfunkel etc., in three parts, f.p. Chamber Th., Frankfurt 7 Oct 1970 by the members of the Frankfurt B. (Cordua, Kruuse, von Klenau, Barra, Finney, Tobias etc.). A series of short ballets. The first, *Frontier* (m. Bliss) perf. by Scottish Th. B., Jeannetta Cochrane Th., London 24 Nov 1970, and *Rondo* (m. folk songs etc.) was taken into repertoire of R. Winnipeg B. 1971.

INVITATION, THE, ballet, ch. MacMillan, m. Matyas Seiber, dec. Giorgiadis, f.p. Royal B., New Th., Oxford 10 Nov 1960 (Seymour, Heaton, Gable). At a house-party in the country a young girl loses her innocence.

IPHIGÉNIE EN AULIDE, tragedy-opera 3 acts, m. Gluck, ch. Noverre, f.p. Paris Opéra 12 Apr 1774 (Gardel, Guimard, Vestris, Heinel). This was Gluck's first ballet for Noverre.

IRAN, BALLET IN, see Persia.

IRVING, Robert, b. Winchester 1913. Eng. conductor. Educ. Winchester, New Col., Oxford, and Royal Col. of Music. Associate conductor B.B.C. Scottish Orchestra 1946–48. Musical Director of Royal B. 1949–58. Musical Director of N.Y. City B. since 1958. Also conducts for Martha Graham Co.

ISAAC, Mr, an English dancing master who flourished at the end of the seventeenth and the beginning of the eighteenth centuries and of whom very little is known except that he was highly esteemed by his contemporaries. He was dancing teacher of Queen Anne (b. 1665) and he suggested to Weaver that he should translate Feuillet into English (which he did in 1706). Essex wrote in his translation of Rameau (1728) 'the late Mr Isaac was the prime dancing master in England for forty years . . . and was justly titled the Court Dancing Master . . .' He composed many dances for the stage, notably those in Shadwell's *Psyche* in 1675.

ISAKSEN, Lone, b. Copenhagen 1941. Danish dancer. Pupil of Edite Frandsen. Joined Scandinavian B. 1959 dancing solo rôles. To N.Y. 1961 and studied at Am. B. Center and joined Joffrey B. as soloist, until 1964. Joined Harkness B. 1964 as principal dancer, making great impression in Hodes' *The Abyss*. In 1970 joined Dutch Nat. B. as principal, with her husband Lawrence Rhodes. Returned to America 1971.

ISMAILOVA, Galya, b. Tomsk 1925. Russ. dancer. Pupil of Tashkent ballet sch. becoming prima ballerina of Tashkent Opera House. She dances classical rôles and also the Uzbek dances. Her success in the 1949 Youth Festival led to the creation of the ballet *Ballerina* (q.v.). Stalin Prize 1950. Danced in London 1953.

ISRAEL, BALLET IN, see under INBAL, BATSHEVA DANCE CO. and BAT-DOR DANCE CO. There are also an ISRAEL CLASSICAL B. and several folk troupes.

ISTAR, ballet, ch. Lifar, m. d'Indy, dec. Bakst, f.p. Paris Opéra 31 Dec 1941 (Chauviré). This was a re-creation of the ballet made for Natasha Truhanova in 1912, with ch. Clustine, dec. Desvallières.

ISTOMINA, Avdotia, b. 1799, d. 1848. Russ. dancer. Graduated from Imp. Sch., St Petersburg 1815 and made her début 1816 in *Acis and Galatea*. She reached her peak in 1820 and became première danseuse mime, retiring in 1836. She has been immortalized by Pushkin in his dedication to *Eugène Onegin*, a poem describing her dazzling beauty and technique. Two duels were fought over her.

ITALY, BALLET IN, see under SCALA, TEATRO ALLA, MILAN. There are also companies attached to the opera houses in Rome, Naples, Turin, Genoa, Palermo, etc.

IVANOV, Lev, b. Moscow 1834, d. St Petersburg 1901. Russ. dancer and chor. Graduated from Imp. Sch., St Petersburg 1852, appointed *régisseur* 1882 and second ballet-master 1885. He worked under Perrot and, for most of his career, as deputy to Petipa. He created many ballets at the Maryinsky Th. but rarely received credit for them because Petipa's name, as his senior, had to take precedence. However, it is established that he chor. *Casse Noisette* (1892) and Acts II and IV of *Swan Lake* (1895), two masterpieces which testify to his qualities. In 1890 he chor. the Polovtsian Dances for the first production of *Prince Igor*. Fokine's version for the Diaghileff B., Paris 1909, closely followed the patterns of Ivanov's production.

IVANOVSKY, Nicolai, b. St Petersburg 1893, d. Leningrad 1961. Russ. dancer and teacher. Graduated from Maryinsky Sch. 1911, joined Diaghileff 1912–15. Returned to Maryinsky B. 1915 as soloist. He became artistic director of the Kirov Sch. (called the Vaganova Choreographic Sch.) from 1945 to 1961. Author of *Ballroom Dance of the 16th to the 19th Centuries* (1948).

IVESIANA, ballet, ch. Balanchine, m. Ives, f.p. N.Y. City B., City Center, 14 Sept 1954 (Reed, Wilde, Kent, Adams, LeClerq, Moncion, d'Amboise, Bolender, Bliss). Six episodes of rather surrealist nature.

J

JACK PUDDING, ballet, ch. von Pelchrzim, m. Henze, dec. Ponnelle, f.p. Wiesbaden B. 30 Dec 1950. Based on Molière's *Georges Dandin*. Another version was by Walter in Wuppertal 1954.

JACKSON, Rowena, b. Invercargill, New Zealand 1926. New Zealand dancer. Studied under Powell and Lawson and won first R.A.D. Scholarship in New Zealand. To S. Wells Sch. 1946. Won Genée Gold Medal 1947 and joined S. Wells B., becoming one of its ballerinas 1954. In 1954 gave recitals in New Zealand. Retired 1959. Mar. Philip Chatfield. Awarded M.B.E. 1961. She became famous for her impeccable fouettés (see FOUETTÉ). From 1972 director, with her husband, of Nat. Sch. of Ballet, Wellington.

JACOBI, Georges, b. Berlin 1840, d. London 1906. Ger. composer. Studied in Brussels and Paris. Became 1st violin of Paris Opéra and mar. dancer Marie Pilatte. In 1869 engaged by Offenbach to conduct at the Th. des Bouffes-Parisiens. In 1872 became musical director of the Alhambra, London until 1898. Composed the music of over 100 ballets incl. 45 of the ballets at the Alhambra.

JACOBS, Wini, b. Deurne 1947. Belgian dancer. Pupil of Jeanne Brabants. Entered Royal Flemish B., Antwerp 1965 becoming soloist of B. Van Vlaanderen.

JACOBSEN, Palle, b. Copenhagen 1940. Dan. dancer. Pupil of R. Danish B. Sch., joined Co. Danced in Basel, Düsseldorf and Johannesburg and rejoined R. Dan. B. 1967 becoming solodancer 1969.

JACOBSON, Leonid, b. 1904. Russ. dancer and chor. Pupil of Ponomarev at Leningrad Sch. Character dancer at State Th. (Kirov) 1926–33, soloist and ballet master Bolshoi Th., Moscow 1933–42. From 1942 ballet master at Kirov Th., Leningrad. Ch. *The Age of Gold* (with Vainonen) 1930, *Shurale* (1941), *Solveig* (1952), *Spartacus* (1956). He also chor. *The Hunter and the Bird* (m. Grieg) 1940, *The Blind Girl* (m. Pons) 1941, *Troika* (m. Stravinsky) and *The Snowflake* (m. Prokofiev) and all these, with some others were included in his ballet *Choreographic Miniatures* f.p. Kirov Th., Leningrad 6 Jan 1959. They are very popular items in dance recitals. He made some dances for the children of the Isadora Duncan Studio in Moscow. In 1970 he formed a small company.

JACOB'S PILLOW, an eighteenth-century farm in Massachusetts bought by Ted Shawn in 1930 and where, from 1933 to 1939 he formed and trained his Men's Group and used it as a summer school. In 1940

Mary Washington Ball held a Jacob's Pillow School of Music and Dance festival there and later in the year it was bought from Shawn and an annual Dance Festival held there, with Shawn as director 1941–1972. This summer festival lasts for ten weeks and dancers and groups are brought there from all over the world. In 1959 the Ted Shawn Theatre was built there.

JAGO, Mary, b. Henfield 1946. Eng. dancer. Pupil of Royal B. Sch. Joined C. Garden Op. B. 1965 and Nat. B. of Canada 1966, becoming soloist 1968, principal 1970.

JAHNKE, Karin, b. Jena 1940. Ger. dancer. Studied at Stuttgart B. Sch. under Mörike 1951–57. Joined Dortmund B. 1958–59, to Cologne B. 1959–67. To Berlin Deutsches Oper B. 1967 as soloist.

JAMAICA'S NATIONAL DANCE THEATRE, an amateur group founded in 1962 in Kingston by Eddy Thomas (pupil of Ivy Baxter and Martha Graham, in whose group he danced) and Rex Nettleford, an Oxford Rhodes Scholar, who are the joint artistic directors. There are some 18 dancers and they perform in Jamaica and appeared at the Stratford (Ontario) Festival in 1963. They perform folk dances *Bongo, Bandana Dance, Santa Foulle* etc. and also some ballets *African Scenario, Dialogue for Three, Games at Arms* etc. They appeared at S. Wells Th. 1972.

JAMISON, Judith, b. Philadelphia 1943. Am. dancer. Pupil of Judimar Sch., Philadelphia. Danced in de Mille's *The Four Marys* in 1964. Joined Ailey Co. 1965 becoming a principal. Mar. Miguel Godreau.

JANIN, Jules, b. Saint-Étienne 1804, d. Paris 1874. Fr. writer who became dramatic critic of the *Journal des Débats* in 1836 and held the post until his death, earning the title *le prince des critiques*. His criticisms included all the ballets of the time and he wrote the article on *La Sylphide* in *Beautés de l'Opéra* (q.v.). Two dishes bear his name, *Soles à la Jules Janin* and *Chaud-froid de filets de poulet à la Jules Janin*.

JANOTTA, Monique, b. Paris 1945. Fr. dancer. Pupil of Paris Opéra Sch. Joined Cuevas B., Geneva B. and joined Düsseldorf B. as principal 1970.

JAPAN, BALLET IN. There are no permanent companies in Japan, but there are a number of schools and these often take it upon themselves to mount a season, engaging guest stars. The Tchaikovsky Memorial B. (q.v.) is one of these, and there are also the Tokyo Ballet Theatre, and the Tokyo City Ballet (leading dancer, Noriko from the Royal B. Sch.) and that organized by Ayako Ogawa, who also chor. musicals in Japan.

JAQUES-DALCROZE, Émile (real name Jacob Dalkes), b. Vienna 1865, d. Geneva 1950. Swiss musician and teacher who evolved, while in

Geneva, a system of musical training through movement which he termed Eurhythmics. He founded a college for teaching his system in 1911 at Hellerau, Germany, transferred to Laxenburg near Vienna 1925. There are now schools teaching Dalcroze Eurhythmics all over the world and the system is considered an indispensable part of the early training of a young dancer, teaching him the exact interpretation into movement of the time and intervals of the music. Among Dalcroze's students are Marie Rambert, Mary Wigman, Hanya Holm, and Uday Shankar. Diaghileff was impressed by his method, and he influenced Kurt Jooss.

JARDIN AUX LILAS (Lilac Garden), ballet 1 act, ch. Tudor, m. Chausson, dec. Stevenson, f.p. B. Rambert, Mercury Th., London 26 Jan 1936 (Maude Lloyd, van Praagh, H. Laing, Tudor). Revived by B. Th. N.Y. 1940 and N.Y. City B. 1951. Using a small number of characters, Tudor, in a manner reminiscent of Proust, has succeeded in conjuring up their emotional strain under the restraint of social convention. Also in repertoire of National B. of Canada 1954 and many other Cos. Tudor mounted it for the Royal B., C. Garden 12 Nov 1968 (Beriosova, Parkinson, Dowell, Doyle). The Stevenson costumes were used, but dec. was by T. Lingwood.

JARDIN PUBLIC, ballet 1 act, ch. Massine, m. Dukelsky, dec. Halicka (later by Lurçat), f.p. de Basil's Co., Auditorium Th., Chicago 8 Mar 1935 (Toumanova, Massine). This ballet in modern style of dancing is based on Gide's *Faux Monnayeurs*, and had a famous pas de deux for the Poor Lovers.

JARRE, LA (*La Giara*), ballet, libretto Pirandello, ch. Börlin, m. Casella, dec. Chirico, f.p. Ballets Suédois, Th. des Ch. Élysées, Paris 19 Nov 1924 (Inger Friis, Viber, Börlin). With ch. de Valois, dec. Chappell, f.p. S. Wells B., S. Wells Th. 9 Oct 1934 (Appleyard, Helpmann, Gore).

JARRETÉ, Fr. knock-kneed (opp. *Arqué*). *Cagneux* is also used.

JASINSKI, Roman, b. Warsaw 1912. Polish dancer. Studied in Warsaw. Member of Rubinstein's Co. 1928, de Basil's 1933–47, and B. Russe since. Mar. Moussia Larkina (Moscelyne Larkin). Now teaches in Tulsa, Oklahoma and runs the Tulsa Civic B.

JASON, Josephine, b. Adelaide 1945. Australian dancer. Pupil of Joanne Priest and Austr. B. Sch. Joined Australian B. 1966 becoming soloist 1968. To London 1972 and joined Festival Ballet.

JAVOTTE, ballet 3 sc., ch. Mariquita, m. Saint-Saëns, dec. Amable, f.p. Grand Th., Lyon 3 Dec 1896 (Damiani, de Tondeur), f.p. Paris Opéra 5 Feb 1909. A peasant love-story.

JAZZ, syncopated dance music originating from Am. Negro bands in 1918. Jazz and 'swing' have been suggested rather than introduced as such in some ballets in which it has been desired to emphasize the contemporary setting of the action, e.g. Jooss's *The Big City* and in many Am. ballets.

JAZZ CALENDAR, ballet, ch. Ashton, m. Rodney Bennett, dec. Jarman, f.p. Royal B., C. Garden 9 Jan 1968 (Derman, Park, Lorrayne, Sibley, Trounson, Dowell, Grant, Nureyev). Comic ballet in pop-art style.

JEANMAIRE, Renée (Zizi), b. Paris 1924. Fr. dancer. Studied at Paris Opéra Sch., graduating to the Co. in 1939. Left and gave recitals in Paris. In 1945 danced with Petit at Th. Sarah Bernhardt and in 1946 joined Lifar's Nouveau B. de Monte Carlo as soloist. Joined de Basil's Co. 1947 and Petit's B. de Paris 1948 as ballerina, where she made a sensation in Petit's *Carmen*. To U.S.A. to film in 1951, appearing with Danny Kaye in *Hans Christian Andersen*, and danced in the N.Y. musical *The Girl in Pink Tights* (1953). Mar. Roland Petit. Returned to his Co. 1955. From 1956 she has been a very successful singer in music-halls. In the film *Black Tights* (1962) she was ballerina in *La Croqueuese de Diamants* and *Carmen*. To Casino de Paris 1970, singing and as joint director with Roland Petit.

JEFFERIES, Stephen, b. Birmingham 1951. Eng. dancer. Pupil of Royal B. Sch. Joined Royal B. 1969, danced solo rôles 1970, principal 1973.

JENNER, Ann, b. Ewell 1944. Eng. dancer. Pupil of Marjorie Shrimpton and Royal B. Sch. Joined Royal B. 1961, becoming soloist 1964, principal 1970. Danced *Fille Mal Gardée* 1966, *Sleeping Beauty* 1972.

JENSEN, Svend Erik, b. Copenhagen 1913. Dan. dancer. Studied at Royal Th. Sch., becoming solodancer 1942. A great dancer and, from 1958, teacher in the Royal Danish Conservatory.

JESUIT BALLET. The Jesuits have made great use of the stage for didactic purposes, educational and theological, and in the seventeenth century began presenting ballets at openings of sessions or at prize-givings. Especially in France, these ballets formed an important part of Jesuit drama and in the seventeenth century the scenery and stage effects of the College of Louis-le-Grand in Paris were said to be more varied and numerous than those of the Th. Français but not quite as good as those of the Opéra. Students of the College even gave ballet performances before the Fr. Court. Elaborate programmes were prepared and the ballets were on pious or sacred themes. Much criticism was levelled against the Jesuits for their use of the ballet, which they attempted unsuccessfully to answer in a ballet by P. C. Porée *L'Homme instruit par les spectacles* (Paris 1726). The Jesuit priests Ménéstrier (q.v.) in 1682 and P. Le Jay in 1725 both wrote important treatises on ballet.

JETÉ or PAS JETÉ, lit. a thrown step, probably because the leg seems to be thrown forwards, backward or sideways (en avant, en arrière, de côté). A spring from one foot (which may finish extended to the back, front, or side, or closed in front of or behind the cou-de-pied) on to the other. By derivation grand jeté, lit. a big thrown step. A leap from one foot to the other, finishing in any required position, e.g. en attitude, when the l. leg is extended to the back in attitude position and the dancer leaps upwards off the r. foot, alighting with a plié on the l. leg with the r. in attitude position; en tournant, when the r. leg is extended to the front at hip height (grand battement à la quatrième devant) and the dancer leaps upwards and slightly forwards, with a turning movement, raising the l. leg to the back in a grand battement to alight, having completed a half turn of the body, with a plié on the r. leg with the l. leg extended to the back. This step is usually preceded by a preparation such as a pas de bourrée executed with a half turn so that the entire movement gives a complete turn of the body. These steps can, of course, be executed on the other leg.

A split jeté is a grand jeté in which, at full height, the legs are horizontal as in 'the splits'.

JEU DE CARTES (also called *Card Game* and *The Card Party*), ballet in three hands to Stravinsky's music. (1) Ch. Balanchine, dec. I. Sharaff, f.p. Am. B., Met. Op., N.Y. 27 Apr 1937 with Dollar as the Joker. (2) Ch. Janine Charrat, dec. P. Roy, f.p. B. des Ch. Élysées, Th. des Ch. Élysées, Paris 12 Oct 1945, with Babilée as the Joker. (3) Ch. Cranko, dec. Zippel, Stuttgart B., Stuttgart 22 Jan 1965 with Madsen as the Joker. Cranko mounted this version for the Royal B., C. Garden 18 Feb 1966, with Gable as the Joker. Many other Cos. have produced versions of this Stravinsky ballet.

JEUNE HOMME ET LA MORT, LE, ballet 2 sc., by Cocteau, ch. Petit and Cocteau, m. Bach, dec. Wakhevitch, f.p. B. des Ch. Élysées, Th. des Ch. Élysées, Paris 25 June 1946 (Nathalie Philippart, Jean Babilée). The ballet was originally rehearsed to jazz music, but eventually the conductor, Girard, suggested the use of Bach's Grand Passacaglia in C minor without the fugue (orch. Respighi), played three times. It is one of the most notable ballets of our times (a pas de deux) and has been called 'a *Spectre de la Rose* of our epoch'.

JEUX, ballet, ch. Nijinsky, m. Debussy, dec. Bakst, f.p. Diaghileff's Co., Th. des Ch. Élysées, Paris 15 May 1913 (Karsavina, Shollar, Nijinsky). This was the first Diaghileff ballet on a contemporary theme (the dancers carried tennis rackets). Also ch. Börlin for B. Suédois, Paris

24 Oct 1920. In repertoire of Scottish Th. B. (formerly Western Th. B.), ch. Darrell, f.p. Citizens Th., Glasgow 7 Mar 1963 (Mottram, Roope, Wellman).

JEUX D'ENFANTS, ballet 1 act, ch. Massine, m. Bizet, dec. J. Miro, f.p. de Basil Co., Monte Carlo 14 Apr 1932 (Riabouchinska, Toumanova, Lichine). This was remounted at the Paris Opéra 16 July 1941, ch. Aveline, dec. Dresa and Dasté.

JEWELS, ballet in 3 parts, ch. Balanchine, dec. Harvey, cost. Karinska, f.p. N.Y. City B., N.Y. State Th. 13 Apr 1967 (1) *Emeralds*, m. Fauré (Verdy, Paul, Leland, Schorer, Ludlow, Moncion, Prinz), (2) *Rubies*, m. Stravinsky (McBride, Neary, Villella), (3) *Diamonds*, m. Tchaikovsky (Farrell, d'Amboise)—and corps. Abstract, classical dancing.

JHUNG, Finis, b. Honolulu 1937. Korean dancer. Pupil of W. Christensen and Pereyaslavec. Joined San Francisco B. 1960, Joffrey B., and in 1964 Harkness B. as soloist. Now teaches in N.Y.

JIG, dance of great antiquity in the British Isles (although now usually connected with Ireland, Shakespeare refers to a 'Scotch Jig' and it is mentioned in early English literature). By the middle of the seventeenth century it had made its appearance on the Continent and some authorities have held that the Jig was derived from the Fr. Gigue (q.v.), or the Italian Giga. Usually in 6/8, 12/8, or some other triple time, it is in binary form. Towards the end of the sixteenth and seventeenth centuries, the name jig was given to a farcical stage entertainment of singing and dancing.

JILLANA (Zimmermann), b. New Jersey 1934, Am. dancer. Studied Am. Sch. of B. Joined N.Y. City B. (then B. Society) 1948, becoming a soloist 1955. Joined Ballet Th. 1958 as Jillana Williams, but returned to N.Y. City B. 1960. Retired 1966 as dancer. Now teaches.

JINX, ballet 2 sc., ch. Lew Christensen, m. Britten, dec. Morcom, cost. Fiocca, f.p. Dance Players, Nat. Th., N.Y. 24 Apr 1942 (Reed, Christensen). A ballet of circus life.

JOAN DE ZARISSA, ballet, ch. Lizzie Maudrik, m. W. Egk, dec. Fenneher, f.p. Staatsoper, Berlin, 20 Jan 1940 (Ilse Meudtner, Bernhard Wosien, Rolf Jahnke). With ch. Lifar, m. Egk, dec. Brayer, f.p. Paris Opéra 10 July 1942 (Darsonval, Schwarz, Chauviré, Lifar, Peretti). The story of a fourteenth century Don Juan. Many German Cos. have made versions.

JOAN OF ARC, ballet 3 acts, ch. Bourmeister, m. Peiko, dec. Ryndin, f.p. Stanislavsky and Nemirovitch-Dantchenko Theatre, Moscow 29 Dec 1957 (Bovt, Kuzmin).

JOB, a masque for dancing in 8 sc., book Geoffrey Keynes (after Blake), ch. de Valois, m. Vaughan Williams, dec. G. Reverat, f.p. Camargo Society, Cambridge Th., London 5 July 1931 (Dolin as Satan, J. MacNair as Job). The scenario and score had been offered to and declined by Diaghileff. It was taken into the repertoire of the Vic-Wells B. 29 Sept 1931. In 1948 new dec. was designed by John Piper.

JOFFREY, Robert (Abdullah Jaffa Anver Bey Khan), b. Seattle 1930. Am. dancer of Afghan descent, teacher and chor. Studied under Mary Ann Wells and at School of Am. Ballet where he was noticed by Gordon Hamilton who introduced him to Petit's B. de Paris as soloist in 1948. Worked in American Modern Dance and became ballet teacher at High Sch. of Performing Arts, N.Y. 1950. Started his own sch. American Dance Center. Made ballets for musicals and for Choreographers' Workshop 1952.

Created his first ballet *Persephone* (m. Silverman) 1952. In 1952 formed his own group (see JOFFREY BALLET). Mounted two of his ballets for B. Rambert 1955 (*Pas des Déesses*, m. Field and *Persephone* but using m. by Vivaldi). Among his ballets are *Pierrot Lunaire* (m. Schoenberg 1955), *Within Four Walls* (m. Foster 1956), *Gamelan* (m. Harrison 1962), *Astarte* (m. Syrcus 1967). For his career as Director see JOFFREY B.).

JOFFREY BALLET, CITY CENTER, the name since 1966 of various Cos. which Robert Joffrey (q.v.) has formed and animated. In 1952 a group from his own sch., Am. Dance Center, performed his works at Y.M.H.A. in N.Y. and at Jacob's Pillow. In 1954 (29 May, at Y.M.H.A.) he gave a programme of his ballets (incl. the first performance of *Pas des Déesses*) with dancers from his sch. and called them Robert Joffrey Ballet Concert. In 1956 the group, then called Robert Joffrey's Theatre Dancers (there were six) gave a tour with a repertoire of four of his ballets. In 1958 it was enlarged to 8 dancers and called Robert Joffrey Theatre Ballet and in 1960 it had an orchestra, was again enlarged and became the Robert Joffrey Ballet. It was offered an engagement for the 1962 Spoleto Festival and Mrs Harkness offered to pay their travelling expenses. Instead Joffrey asked that the money should be used to pay the dancers for a rehearsal period prior to their annual tour. This she did and they made a successful tour of the Middle East, India and Pakistan in the winter of 1962–63. The Harkness Foundation sponsored the company, which then worked at Watch Hill, Rhode Island, and they toured Russia in the winter of 1963, with ballets by Joffrey, Arpino, Macdonald, Ailey etc. and then toured America. They severed their connexion with Harkness after this and the Co. broke up. The Ford Foundation gave money which allowed them to start again, at Jacob's Pillow 10 Aug 1965, followed by a very successful appearance at N.Y.

City Center in 1966. The Co. was then renamed the City Center Joffrey B. and was established there 1966–73 with Joffrey director, Alexander Ewing as administrator and Arpino as principal chor. Among his dancers in 1970 were Lisa Bradley, Trinette Singleton, Barbara Remington, Erika Goodman, Robert Blankshine, Luis Fuente, John Jones, Paul Sutherland, Michael Uthoff, Edward Verso, Burton Taylor, Francesca Corkle, Rebecca Wright. First danced in London (Coliseum) 1971. Their school is called American Ballet Center, directed by Joffrey and Arpino, with Ann Parson and Jonathan Watts teaching.

JOHANSSON, Anna, b. 1860, d. St Petersburg 1917, daughter of Christian Johansson. Swed. dancer. Studied at Imp. Sch., St Petersburg, making her début in 1878 in *Esmeralda*. Ballerina at the Maryinsky Th. until 1899 when she retired and became teacher of the Class of Perfection. She was a cold dancer, but with something of Taglioni's grace and elevation. Created rôle Fairy of the Song Birds in *Sleeping Beauty*.

JOHANSSON, Christian, b. Stockholm 1817, d. St Petersburg 1903. Swed. dancer and teacher. Studied at R. Swedish B. Sch. and under Bournonville in Copenhagen. Returned to Stockholm 1837 as premier danseur, partnering Taglioni. To St Petersburg 1841, début in *La Gitana* and made premier danseur at once. Became one of the leading male dancers of his time (chiefly as a partner). He was Taglioni's last partner in Russia, 1842. He began to teach in 1860. In 1869 he retired from the stage and became the chief teacher at the Imp. Sch., St Petersburg, considerably influencing the formation of a Russ. school of dancing. Among his pupils were Kschessinska, Preobrajenska, and Gerdt. In his entire career as a teacher he never repeated an *enchaîne-ment*—each lesson was different and made for each individual pupil. Petipa used to visit his classes and borrowed his *enchaînements* for his ballets.

JOHANSSON, Marie, b. Stockholm 1949. Swed. dancer. Studied at R. Swed. B. Sch. and the Royal B. Sch., London. Joined R. Swed. B. 1966. Joined New Swed. B. 1970 to dance in their first season in London. Returned to R. Swed. B. Joined Am. Ballet Th. 1971.

JOHNSON, Nicholas, b. London 1947. Eng. dancer. Studied at Royal B. Sch. and joined Royal B. (Touring Section) 1965. Became soloist 1968, principal 1970.

JOKO, LO SCIMMIOTTO BRASILIANO, see DANINA.

JOLIE FILLE DE GAND, LA, ballet 3 acts, ch. Albert, m. Adam, dec. Ciceri, Philastre, Cambon, f.p. Paris Opéra 22 June 1842 (Grisi, Petipa, Coralli). A popular pantomime ballet of the Romantic era. See *Beatrice*, ballet, ch. Jack Carter with same music and plot, 1966.

273

JONES, Marilyn, b. Newcastle, Australia 1940. Austral. dancer. Pupil of Norton, van Praagh. Joined Royal Ballet 1957, Borovansky B. 1959 as soloist, de Cuevas B. 1961 as prima ballerina until the Co. dissolved. Returned to Australia in 1962 to become prima ballerina of Australian B. Guest artist Festival B. 1963. Awarded O.B.E. 1972. Mar. Garth Welch.

JONES BEACH, ballet, ch. Balanchine and Robbins, m. Andriessen, cost. by Jansens, f.p. N.Y. City B. at N.Y. City Center 9 Mar 1950 (Le Clerq, Tallchief, Hayden, Robbins, Magallanes). Set on a beach with the dancers in bathing costumes.

JOOSS, Kurt, b. Wasseralfingen 1901. Ger. dancer and chor. Studied music and drama and in 1920 met Rudolf von Laban at Mannheim Th. under whom he studied and danced. In 1924 formed the 'Neue Tanz-bühne' at the Münster Th., with Sigurd Leeder, Aino Siimola (whom he married), and Fritz Cohen, and produced several ballets there. The 'Folkwang Schule' at Essen was founded 1927 and he was made dance director, and in 1930 maître de ballet at Essen Opera House. His Essen group in 1932 won the first competition organized by Rolf de Maré's Archives Internationales de la Danse, in Paris, with his *The Green Table*. The same year he founded his Ballets Jooss and began his series of world tours. His school moved to Dartington Hall, Devon, England, and during the war the company was based on Cambridge. In 1951 he returned to Essen and re-formed his group which began a new tour in 1953, but the company broke up the same year after a season at Sadler's Wells. Jooss, a disciple of the space-movement theories of von Laban and a devotee of the Central European school of dancing, adopts a form of movement free from artificial conventions and which is claimed to be better adapted than the pure classical style to the charac-terization of the mentality and emotional feeling of his characters. His ballets are presented against black backcloths and with the minimum of costume or scenery and with the very effective use of lighting. His ballets include *The Green Table, The Big City, The Prodigal Son, Seven Heroes, A Spring Tale, Chronica, Company at the Manor, Pandora, Journey in the Fog, The Night Train*. In 1934, he chor. *Persephone* for Ida Rubinstein's Co.

JORDAN, Olga, b. 1907. Russ. dancer. Studied under Vaganova at Lenin-grad Sch. graduating 1930, becoming one of the ballerinas of Kirov Th., Leningrad. During the 1942–44 blockade of Leningrad she organized recitals of ballet there, for which she was decorated. Now writes on ballet. Teacher in Moscow from 1963.

JOTA, traditional Northern Spanish dance, in 3/4 time and musically after the waltz style, for one or more couples who both play the castanets and sing. The song is a *cuartela* (usually a four-line stanza of eight syllables to a line, with assonance instead of rhyme in the first and third lines, but for the jota extended by repetition to six lines). Massine has introduced a jota into his *Three Cornered Hat*.

JOTA ARAGONESA, ballet 1 act, ch. Fokine, m. Glinka, dec. Golovin, f.p. Maryinsky Th., St Petersburg 29 Jan 1916.

JOVITA, OU LES BOUCANIERS, ballet 3 sc., ch. Mazilier, m. Labarre, dec. Despléchin, Thierry, and Cambon, f.p. Paris Opéra 11 Nov 1853 (Rosati, Mérante, Petipa). Set in seventeenth-century Mexico.

JUDGEMENT OF PARIS, ballet 1 act, ch. Tudor, m. Weill, dec. H. Laing, f.p. London B., Westminster Theatre, London 15 June 1938 (Langfield, de Mille, Bidmead, Tudor, Laing). Set in a *boîte de nuit*. Danced by B. Rambert, Arts Th., London 1 Oct 1940. Also in repertoire of Canadian Nat. B.

JUDSON, Stanley. Eng. dancer. Joined Pavlova's Co. 1927. Principal dancer Vic-Wells B. 1931 to 1934 and later of Markova-Dolin Co. Joined Blum's B. Russe 1936. Later producer of ice-shows in America. He was the first male member of the Vic-Wells Ballet.

JUILLIARD SCHOOL OF MUSIC, DANCE DEPARTMENT, was instituted in the Juilliard School N.Y. in 1952, with Martha Hill as director. On the original staff were de Mille, Graham, Humphrey, Robbins, Tudor, Horst and Ann Hutchinson. It offers a full programme of instruction and confers degrees. From 1964 has been housed in Lincoln Center with the Sch. of American B.

JUNGLE, ballet, ch. Van Dantzig, m. Henk Badings, dec. Toer van Schayk, f.p. Dutch Nat. B., Stadsschouwburg, Amsterdam 20 Dec 1961 (Koppers, Campbell). Also by London Dance Th., Vaudeville Th., London 19 Mar 1965 (Kristina, Sibbritt). A parable, beasts in the jungle act out the problems of mankind. In repertoire of Nat. B. of Washington 1972.

JUNK, Victor, b. Vienna 1875. Austrian composer and author of *Handbuch des Tanzes* (Vienna 1930)—a dictionary of dance.

JUPONNAGE (Fr.), the long ballet skirt. Term used in the Paris Opéra.

JÜRGENS, Helmut, b. Westphalia 1902. Ger. artist. Designer of many German ballets, working at the opera houses of Düsseldorf (1936–38), Frankfurt (1938–45), Munich from 1947.

K

KABUKI, the popular dance-drama of Japan (as distinct from the Nō plays, a ritual, aristocratic form of entertainment). Female rôles are taken by men, the music is played on the stage, and the dancers make their entries on a platform level with the spectators' heads (the 'hana-michi' or flower-path). Masks are not worn (as they are in Nō plays), make-up is heavy, and the scenery is real and very elaborate. The word 'kabuki' means 'song-dance-skill' and the art is said to be derived from the appearance of a temple danseuse, O'Kuni, in Kyoto, capital of the Japanese Empire, in c. 1586. In 1596 she met Sanzo Nagoya, a great warrior, who may have married her. With the help of his managerial as well as dancing skill, she started a new style of dancing, adding popular and erotic elements to Nō and sacred themes. In 1641 actresses were banished from the Kabuki theatre. In 1655 the short sketches and dances were replaced by long dramas in several acts. The greatest era of the Kabuki drama was 1688–1703. The dancing forms only a part of the full Kabuki programme and the repertoire still contains the great pieces composed over 300 years ago. Styles of Kabuki theatre vary from the oldest, most stylized and static pieces to newer classics some-times mixing realism with stylization. This depends on the era and on the personality of the actor-manager heads of Kabuki Dynasties, all hereditary. See also AZUMA, whose troupe visited London in 1955. In 1972 another troupe with members of the Nakamura dynasty per-formed at Sadler's Wells.

KAESEN, Robert, b. Wilrijk, Belgium 1931. Belgian dancer and chor. Pupil of Brabants in Antwerp. Became a principal dancer of Dutch Nat. B. and from 1969–70 he was joint director (with Van Dantzig) of the Co.

KÅGE, Jonas, b. Solna 1950. Swed. dancer. Joined R. Swed. B. Sch. 1959 and entered the Co. 1967. Danced Romeo in MacMillan's *Romeo and Juliet* 1969 and made soloist 1970. Danced with Am. Ballet Th. 1971.

KAI, Una, b. N. Jersey 1928. Am. dancer. Pupil of Swoboda, Nemchinova, Oboukhoff, Balanchine. Joined Balanchine 1948 (Ballet Society) and became assistant ballet mistress of N.Y. City B. 1956. Left the Co. 1960 and since then has toured the world mounting Balanchine's ballets for him—among them *Bourrée Fantasque* (Festival B., Scala Milan, R. Danish B., Paris Opéra), *Serenade* (Hamburg, Nat. B. of Canada, Atlanta Civic B., Washington, Royal B.), *Concerto Barocco* (Hamburg, Milan, Nat. B. Canada, Paris Opéra). To N. Zealand Nat. B. 1973

KAIN, Karin, b. Hamilton, Ont. 1951. Canadian dancer. Pupil of Canad.

276

PIERRE BEAUCHAMP (1636–1705). *Maître de ballet* to the Court of Louis XIV, codifier of the 've positions' and pioneer of dance notation.

2. AUGUSTE VESTRIS (1760–1842). The greatest male dancer of his time, *premier danseur* at the Paris Opéra and ballet master of the King's Theatre, London.

3. LA CAMARGO (1710–1770), from the painting by Lancret. She excelled in steps of elevation, and she and Sallé (her rival) were the leading ballerinas of the first half of the eighteenth century.

GREAT DANCERS

4. MARIE TAGLIONI (1804–1884) in *La Sylphide*, from the painting by A. E. Chalon. The principal dancer of the Romantic Era, with a light, ethereal style.

5. FANNY ELSSLER (1810–1884) dancing the *cachucha* from *Le Diable Boiteux* (lithograph by Alexandre Lacauchie). The rival of Taglioni, whose style was the very opposite, being *terre à terre*.

6. VIRGINIA ZUCCHI (1847–1930), from the painting by Clairin. She brought to Russia the brilliant technique of the Italian School.

7. ISADORA DUNCAN (1878–1927). The American whose free style of dancing introduced the Modern Dance, as distinct from the Classical Ballet.

ANNA PAVLOVA (1881–1931) in *La
Gavotte Pavlova*. The Russian dancer
who made the whole world conscious of
the art of ballet.

9. TAMARA KARSAVINA (b. 1885) and
VASLAV NIJINSKY (1888–1950) in
Giselle. The principal dancers of
Diaghileff's Ballets Russes.

11. ALICIA MARKOVA (b. 1910) and
ERIK BRUHN (b. 1928) in *Giselle*. Two
outstanding dancers of the immediate
past, she as the first ballerina of the
Sadlers Wells Ballet and subsequently of
American ballet, he as the supreme ex-
ponent of the Bournonville style in the
Royal Danish Ballet.

10. IRINA BARONOVA (b. 1919) and DAVID
LICHINE (1910–1972) in *Les Présages*. Two
principal figures of the 1930s.

13. MARGOT FONTEYN (b. 1919) and RUDOLF NUREYEV (b. 1938) in *La Bayadère*. The *prima ballerina assoluta* of the Royal Ballet and the outstanding Russian dancer, whose late partnership gave a great impetus to the art in the last decade.

12. GALINA ULANOVA (b. 1910) in *Giselle*. The greatest Russian dancer of the period of the Second World War and after.

14. ANTOINETTE SIBLEY (b. 1939) and ANTHONY DOWELL (b. 1943) in *Swan Lake*. The two dancers who personify the Royal Ballet in the 1970s.

15 (*left*). KAY MAZZO (b. 1946) with John Jones in *Afternoon of a Faun*. This Jerome Robbins ballet is typical of a new trend in classical ballet.

16. J. G. NOVERRE (1727–1810), who introduced a new style of ballet and whose writings on the art are without peer.

17. JULES PERROT (1810–1892). The 'male Taglioni', and choreographer of many of the ballets of the Romantic Era.

18. AUGUST BOURNONVILLE (1805–1879), who gave Danish ballet its greatest works, with *Napoli*, *La Sylphide* etc.

19. MARIUS PETIPA (1818–1910). Creator of the great St. Petersburg classics: *The Sleeping Beauty*, *Swan Lake* (with Ivanov) etc.

FOUR EARLY CHOREOGRAPHERS

FOUR CHOREOGRAPHERS OF
THE TWENTIETH CENTURY

20. MICHEL FOKINE (1880–1942).
Diaghileff's choreographer and cre-
ator of *Les Sylphides, Petrouchka,
Firebird* etc.

21. LEONIDE MASSINE (b. 1895).
Choreographer of *The Three
Cornered Hat, Symphonie Fantas-
tique, Les Présages* etc.

22. GEORGE BALANCHINE (b. 1904).
Diaghileff's last choreographer and
the leading figure in American ballet. Choreographer of *Apollon
Musagète, Serenade* etc.

23. FREDERICK ASHTON (b. 1904). The
choreographer of British ballet,
with *La Fille Mal Gardée, Les
Patineurs, Symphonic Variations* etc.

20

21

23

22

24. CARLO BLASIS (1795–1878), whose pupils at Milan became the ballerinas at St. Petersburg and whose code of teaching still forms the basis of the classical technique.

25. ENRICO CECCHETTI (1850–1928). Teacher of the great Russian dancers and of Diaghileff's company.

26. OLGA PREOBRAJENSKA (1870–1962). One of the greatest dancers of the Petipa era, who in Paris trained or polished many of the greatest dancers of the mid-twentieth century.

27. AGRIPPINA VAGANOVA (1879–1951). Teacher of the great dancers in Leningrad, whose style is perpetuated in her book *Fundamentals of the Classic Dance*.

FOUR GREAT TEACHERS

28. SERGE DIAGHILEFF (1872–1929), whose Ballets Russes brought the Russian ballet to the West.

29. MARIE RAMBERT (b. 1888), whose Ballet Rambert was the first ballet company in Britain.

30. NINETTE DE VALOIS (b. 1898). The founder of the Royal Ballet.

31. MARTHA GRAHAM (b. 1893). A leader of the Modern Dance Movement in America, and the originator of a distinctive style.

FOUR CREATORS OF COMPANIES

Nat. B. School, joined National B. of Canada 1970 and promoted a principal 1971.

KALEIDOSCOPE, ballet, ch. Nikolais, m. Antheil, Varèse, Cage etc., f.p. Henry Street Playhouse Dance Co., Connecticut Coll., New London 25 May 1956 (Bailin, Lamhut, Louis, Frank). Mixture of dancers, colours, props etc.

KALIOUJNY, Alexandre, b. Prague 1924. Fr. dancer. Studied under Preobrajenska in Paris. Joined Ballets de Cannes, and in 1946 Lifar's Nouveau B. de Monte Carlo where he made a great impression in *Prince Igor*. Made danseur étoile at the Paris Opéra 1947, left in 1953 and went to America to dance in the musical *The Girl in Pink Tights*. Returned to France 1955, and rejoined Opéra 1956. Retired 1961 and teaches in Nice.

KAMIN DANCE BOOKSHOP, bookshop in Sixth Avenue, N.Y., founded by Sally Kamin, devoted to ballet and all dance forms. She was born in the Ukraine 1897, d. N.Y. 1968. Founded the bookshop 1930 and it lasted to 1961.

KAMOUN, Claudine, b. Algiers 1941. Fr. dancer. Pupil of Gaillard, Perrault, Golovina, Fay. Joined de Cuevas B. 1960 becoming soloist. Joined Golovine's Co. 1963, *Cendrillon* (Paris) 1963, London Dance Th. 1964, Geneva 1968 as principal.

KAPUSTE, Falco, b. Oels (Schlesien) 1943. Ger. dancer. Pupil of Jean de Ruiter and Georgi. Joined Wiesbaden B. 1963, Hamburg B. 1964, Berlin B. 1965 becoming soloist. To Düsseldorf 1970.

KARALLI, Vera (called Coralli in France and Austria), b. Moscow 1888, d. Baden (Austria) 1972. Russ. dancer. Graduated to Bolshoi B. 1906, ballerina 1909. Joined Diaghileff's Co. 1909 in Paris, taking the lead in *Pavillon d'Armide*. Returned to Russia and became the first Russ. 'film-star'—her greatest film was *The Dying Swan*. Settled in Paris in the 1920s and then moved to Austria.

KARELSKAYA, Rimma, b. 1927. Russ. dancer. Graduated to Bolshoi B. 1946, becoming soloist and later ballerina. Now retired. Created the chief rôle in Radunsky's revival of *Humpbacked Horse* in 1960.

KARINA, Lilian, b. St Petersburg 1910. Russ. dancer and teacher. Pupil of Edouardova, V. Gsovsky etc. Opened school in Budapest with Milloss 1937. To Stockholm 1939 and opened school there 1943.

KARINSKA, Barbara, b. Russia 1886. Russ. designer and maker of costumes. To Paris after the Revolution and her first work was to make the cost. for Balanchine's *Cotillon* (1933), designed by Bérard. To N.Y. 1938 and made most of the cost. for N.Y. City B. Won Capezio Award 1962.

KARRAS, Vicki, b. 1942. S. African dancer. Pupil of Gwynne Ashton. Joined Festival B. 1960, London B. 1962, London Dance Th. 1964, Royal B. 1964 becoming soloist 1968. Returned to S. Africa 1972. Mar. Hendriks Davel.

KARSAVINA, Tamara, b. St Petersburg 1885, daughter of dancer Karsavin. Russ. dancer. Studied Imp. Sch. under Gerdt, Kosloff, Johansson, and Cecchetti. Début in *Javotte* (1902) as a soloist and by 1909 had reached ballerina status (though not receiving the title). In 1909 joined Diaghileff's Co. on its inception as chief dancer and was creator of most of the principal rôles in the great Fokine ballets, also dancing *Giselle* and *Swan Lake*. She is one of the great dancers in the history of ballet excelling in dramatic as well as in the Classical rôles. Among the ballets in which she cr. the principal rôles are *Sylphides* (Waltz), *Carnaval* (Columbine), *Petrouchka*, *Spectre de la Rose*, *Thamar*, *Firebird*, *Daphnis and Chloë*, *Coq d'Or*, *Tricorne*. Mar. the late H. J. Bruce. Left Russia 1918 and has lived in London since 1919, where she was Vice-President of the Royal Academy of Dancing until 1955. In 1930 she danced for the B. Rambert and has trained several leading Eng. dancers in her old rôles and given memorable lectures on ballet. In 1930 published *Theatre Street*, an account of her life at the Maryinsky Sch. and Th., one of the classics in the bibliography of ballet. In 1956 wrote *Ballet Technique* and 1962 *Classical Ballet: the Flow of Movement*, both reprints of *Dancing Times* articles.

KARSTENS, Gerda, b. Copenhagen 1903. Danish dancer. Pupil at Theatre Sch., Copenhagen, becoming solodancer 1942 and their greatest mime (which she now teaches). Retired 1956.

KASATKINA, Natalia, b. 1934. Russ. dancer and chor. Graduated into Bolshoi B. 1954. With her husband, V. Vassiliov chor. *Vanina Vanini* (1962), *The Geologists* (or *The Heroic Poem*) (1964) and a new version of Stravinsky's *Sacre du Printemps* (1965) in which she danced the solo of the Possessed Girl. For the Kirov B. chor. *Creation of the World* (1971).

KASTL, Sonja, b. Zagreb 1929. Yugoslav dancer. Pupil of Froman and Roje. Entered Zagreb National B. 1945, becoming ballerina in 1950. Danced in London 1955. Director of Zagreb B. from 1965.

KATALYSE, ballet, ch. Cranko, m. Shostakovitch, f.p. Stuttgart B., Stuttgart 8 Nov 1961 (Micheline Faure, M. Morena, Barra, Delavalle, G. Burne).

KATERINA, ballet 3 acts 7 sc., ch. Lavrovsky, m. Rubinstein and A. Adam, dec. Erbstein, f.p. Kirov Th., Leningrad 25 May 1935. A ballet on the Serfs' Theatre of the eighteenth century.

KATHAK, one of the four main forms of Indian dancing (with Bharata Natya, Kathakali, and Manipuri). It is the style of North India and appears to have been influenced by the Moslems. It is performed with the spectators sitting all round the dancers, on floor level (unlike the other forms which are danced on a platform). It is very elegant and stylized. When a movement has been completed, the dancer moves with a stylized walk and assumes a posture before starting the next movement.

KATHAKALI, the sacred dance-dramas of the Hindus. Costumes and make-up are stylized and the dances are usually performed at night, in the open air. It is primarily a dramatic art and makes much use of *mudras* or gestures. See KATHAK, MANIPURI, and BHARATA NATYA.

KAY, Barry, b. Melbourne 1932. Austral. designer and artist. Designed ballets for Gore in Australia. To England 1957 and designed *The Prisoners* and *Chiaroscuro* for Western Th. B. (both Darrell), *Salade* (ch. Darrell) for Edinburgh 1961, *Raymonda*, Act III, Touring Royal B., 1966, *Sleeping Beauty* (ch. MacMillan) for Berlin 1967, *Don Quixote* (ch. Nureyev) for Vienna B. 1966 and Austral. B. 1970, *Anastasia* (ch. MacMillan) Berlin 1967 and Royal B. 1971.

KAYE, Nora (Koreff), b. N.Y. 1920 of Russian parents. Am. dancer. Studied Met. Op. Ballet School, Fokine, Vilzak, Tudor, Craske. As child danced at Met. Op. and later in Radio City Music Hall ballet. Joined Ballet Theatre on its inception (1940) in corps de ballet. Cr. rôle of Hagar in *Pillar of Fire* (1942), making great impression, and raised to ballerina of the Co., dancing *Giselle*, *Lac*, and many dramatic rôles in which she is unrivalled and has been described as the 'Duse of the Dance'. Joined N.Y. City Ballet 1951. Danced in Japan 1953–4. Returned to Ballet Th. 1954. Retired 1961. Mar. Herbert Ross.

KEHLET, Niels, b. Höbro, Denmark 1938. Danish dancer. Pupil of R. Danish B. Sch. 1948–57. Joined R. Danish B. 1957, becoming solo-dancer 1961. In 1960 he studied at the R. Ballet Sch., London. Guest artist de Cuevas B. 1961. Cr. rôle of Colas in Ashton's *Fille Mal Gardée* for R. Danish B. 1964. Also guest artist with Festival B. and Western Th. B. 1967. Am. Ballet Th. 1971. Guest, Scala, Rome 1972–73.

KEIL, Birgit, b. Kowarschen (Sudetenland) 1944. Ger. dancer. Pupil of Cranko, Stuttgart Sch. and Royal B. Sch. Joined Stuttgart B. 1961, soloist since 1965. Guest artist Wiesbaden B. 1968.

KEITH, Jens, b. Stralsund 1898, d. Berlin 1958. Danish dancer and ballet master. Studied under von Laban in Hamburg. After dancing in the Münster B. etc. he became soloist at the Berlin Staatsoper 1930, ballet master at Essen, of Städtische Oper, Berlin 1945–49. Chor. many ballets in Germany.

KELLAWAY, Leon (Jan Kowsky), b. London. Pupil of Astafieva and Legat. Member of Pavlova's Co. He partnered Kyasht in London and Spessivsteva in Australia. From 1940 to 1955 was ballet master and character dancer of Borovansky B. Has a school in Sydney and for a time was associate ballet master of the Australian B.

KELLY, Desmond, b. S. Rhodesia 1942. British dancer. Pupil of Archibald, Ruth French. Joined Festival B. 1959 becoming soloist 1962, principal 1964. With his wife, Denise Le Comte, guest artist in New Zealand Nat. B., Washington B. 1968. Joined Royal B. 1970 as principal. Guest artist Scala, Milan 1972.

KELLY, Gene, b. Pittsburg 1912. Am. dancer whose dancing in films (tap and ballet) has given an impetus to the general appreciation of the art of the dance. His films include *Anchors Aweigh* (1945), *An American in Paris* (with Leslie Caron), *Singing in the Rain* (1952), *On the Town* (1949), *Invitation to the Dance* (1953). Directed *Flower Drum Song* (1958), *Hello, Dolly!* (1968). Chor. *Pas de Dieux* (m. Gershwin) (1960) for the Paris Opéra. Legion of Honour (1960).

KEMP, William, fl. 1600. Eng. comic actor and dancer who danced a Morris dance from London to Norwich 1599. He danced on the Continent and also in Shakespeare's company. In 1594 he acted with Burbage and Shakespeare before Elizabeth I.

KEMPF, Christa, b. Berlin 1937. Ger. dancer. Pupil of G. Blank. Joined Berlin Staatsoper B. 1953, Berlin B. 1955–58 and principal dancer Hamburg B. 1958–66.

KENT, Allegra, b. Los Angeles 1936. Am. dancer. Studied under B. Nijinska and Sch. of Am. Ballet. Entered N.Y. City B. 1953, became soloist 1957 and now a principal dancer.

KERENSKY, Oleg, b. London 1930. Eng. writer on ballet and broadcaster. Educ. Westminster Sch. and Christ Church, Oxford. Diplomatic corresp. B.B.C. 1955–63, Deputy Editor *The Listener* 1963–68. Ballet critic of *Daily Mail* 1957–71 and *New Statesman* from 1968. Author of *Ballet Scene* 1970, *Anna Pavlova* 1973. Freelance broadcaster on the arts from 1969. Ballet critic of *Int. Herald Tribune* from 1971.

KERES, Imre, b. Szeged 1930. Hungarian dancer and chor. Pupil of Harangozo, Nadasi, Messerer. Joined Szeged B. 1947, Budapest B. 1951, becoming assistant ballet master 1954. In 1956 worked in Th. Châtelet, Paris and became assistant to Yvonne Georgi in Hanover. Ballet master Lübeck 1959–62. From 1962 ballet master of Wiesbaden B. Chor. many ballets. In 1970 he also chor. at Th. am Gärtnerplatz, Munich, and from 1971–73 was ballet master there, together with Wiesbaden.

KERMESSEN I BRUGGE, ballet 2 acts 3 sc., ch. Bournonville, m. Paulli, f.p. Royal Th., Copenhagen 4 Apr 1851 and still in the repertoire. Three brothers fall in love with three girls at the Holy Fair in Bruges.

KERR, Russell, b. Auckland, N.Z. 1930. New Zealand dancer. Pupil of Whitford, Idzikowsky and Royal B. Sch. Joined José Greco Co. 1951, B. Rambert 1953, soloist Festival B. 1954. Returned to New Zealand to teach and became director of the New Zealand B. until 1968.

KERSLEY, Leo, b. Watford 1920. Eng. dancer and teacher. Studied under Idzikovskiy and Rambert. Soloist B. Rambert (1936–39 and 1940–41), S. Wells B. (1941–42), Anglo-Polish B. (1942–43), S. Wells Th. B. (1946). In 1952 he went to U.S.A. to teach and later to Holland. With his wife, Janet Sinclair, published *Dictionary of Ballet Terms*, London (1952). Worked in Holland and returned to teach in England 1959. Has his own school in Harlow, Essex.

KESSELHEIM, Silvia, b. Hamburg 1942. Ger. dancer. Pupil of Gustav Blank 1958. Joined Hamburg B. 1959. To Royal Ballet Sch. 1959–60. Joined Stuttgart B. 1961. To Berlin Deutsche Oper 1965 as soloist, becoming principal. To Darmstadt 1972.

KESSLER, Dagmar, b. Merchantville, New Jersey 1946. Am. dancer. Studied at Sch. of Pennsylvania B. under Frano Jelincic (whom she married) and became soloist of the company in 1964. Joined Hamburg B. 1966 and Festival B. as soloist 1967, becoming principal 1968–73.

KHADRA, ballet 1 act, ch. Celia Franca, m. Sibelius, dec. Honor Frost, f.p. S. Wells Th. B., S. Wells Th. 27 May 1946 (Sheilah O'Reilly, Anne Heaton, Kersley). Scenes from Persian miniatures.

KHACHATURIAN, Aram, b. Tiflis 1903. Russ. composer, who wrote the music for *Happiness* 1939, *Gayané* 1942 and *Spartacus* 1951.

KHOKHLOV, Boris, b. Moscow 1932. Russ. dancer. Graduated from Bolshoi Sch. to the Company 1951 and became soloist 1952. Danced in London 1956 and 1960 and in N.Y. 1959.

KHUDEKOFF, Sergei, b. 1837, d. 1927. Russ. balletomane, publisher and author of *History of Dancing* (published 1914–17) in four volumes. He was a close friend of Marius Petipa and with him made the libretto of *La Bayadère* (1877).

KIDD, Michael, b. N.Y. 1919. Am. dancer and chor. Studied under Vilzak and Shollar. Member American B. 1937, soloist Ballet Th. 1942–47. Chor. *On Stage!* (1945). Became chor. of musicals and in films, creating the ballets in *Finian's Rainbow*, *Guys and Dolls* (1952), the ballet in Danny Kaye's film *Knock on Wood* (1954), *Seven Brides for Seven Brothers* (1955), *Hullo Dolly!* (1967) etc.

KIKIMORA, ballet, ch. Massine, m. Liadov, dec. Larionov, f.p. Diaghileff's Co. Eugénie-Victoria Th., San Sebastian 25 Aug 1916 (Shabelska, Idzikowsky). In 1917 it was included in *Contes Russes.*

KING, Karl-Heinz, b. Cologne 1931. Ger. dancer and teacher. Pupil of S. Wells Sch., Rousanne etc. Danced in Cologne, Düsseldorf, Bielefeld, Th. am Gärtnerplatz, Munich. In 1956 opened (with Peter Roleff, b. Cologne 1906, dancer) the Roleff-King Sch. in Munich.

KING'S THEATRE, Haymarket, London, built 1704–5 and soon became the principal home of opera in London and later of ballet. It was burnt out in 1789 and the second theatre opened for ballet in 1793. Nearly all the dancers of the Romantic era appeared in it, flourishing under the management of Lumley. In 1837 it was renamed Her Majesty's and it was also known as the Italian Opera House (not to be confused with the Royal Italian Opera by which name C. Garden was known from 1847 on). It had a famous Green Room. The story of the fire is told in the ballet *The Prospect Before Us.*

KINNEY, Troy, b. 1872, d. 1938. Am. author and artist who, with his sister Margaret, wrote and illustrated *The Dance, Its Place in Art and Life* in 1924, an important work in the literature of the dance.

KIRKLAND, Gelsey, b. Bethlehem (U.S.A.) 1953. Am. dancer. Pupil of Sch. of Am. B., joined N.Y. City B. 1968 and dancing solo rôles 1969. Cr. rôle in Balanchine's 1970 *Firebird.* Her sister, Johnna Kirkland (b. 1950) is also in the N.Y. City B.

KIRNBAUER, Susanne, b. Vienna 1942. Austrian dancer. Studied at Vienna Staatsoper Sch. Joined Vienna Staatsoper B. 1956. In 1965 to Paris, danced in Charrat's B. de France, 1966, as soloist and in the Charrat-Miskovitch Co. and Grand B. de Paris. Returned to Vienna and Aurora in *Sleeping Beauty.* Soloist of the Staatsoper B. in 1967.

KIROVA, Vera, b. Sofia 1940. Bulgarian dancer. Pupil of Valya Verbeva at Sofia Sch. of Ballet. Joined the Bulgarian Nat. B. in Sofia 1959, becoming prima ballerina. Won first prize and Gold Medal at Varna 1964. Mar. son of President of Bulgaria (Traikov). Hon. Artist of Bulgarian Republic. Dances also as guest artist abroad, notably for the Bolshoi B., Cuban B., and especially for the B. de Wallonie in Charleroi, where she was the principal ballerina until 1973. Lives in Paris.

KIROV BALLET, the company attached to the Kirov Th. (q.v.) in Leningrad and the cradle of Russian ballet. For its beginnings see LANDÉ. As St Petersburg was the capital of Russia and also on account of the great interest in ballet of the Tzar and the Imperial Court, the Maryinsky (now Kirov) Th. attracted the greatest European ballet masters (see DIDELOT, HILFERDING, ANGIOLINI, LE PICQ, PERROT, ST LEON, PETIPA etc.) and dancers (see TAGLIONI, ELSSLER, LEGNANI etc.).

Thus were born many of the great classical ballets and the greatest Russian dancers were produced. Even the 1917 Revolution and the Second World War interrupted but little the continuity of the ballet. But when Moscow became the capital, the resources of the Kirov B. were drained to enhance the Bolshoi B. in Moscow and many of their most talented members were lost—Ulanova among them. In spite of this the Kirov B. continues as the fountain-head of the purest classical style in the world and the spirit of their greatest teacher Vaganova (who would not move to Moscow) remains undiminished. In 1955 the chief dancers were Dudinskaya, Balabina, Shelest, Vecheslova, Makarov, Andreev and a troupe of 180 dancers. During the Second World War the Co. was evacuated to Molotoff (Perm). In 1970 the artistic director was K. Sergeyev and the chief dancers were Kolkapova, Makarova, Sizova, Evteyeva, Osipenko, Komleva, Soloviev, Barishnikov, Panov, Vikulov, Budarin. See GATOB. In 1972 the directors were Sergeyev, Semeyonov and Vinogradov. Director 1973, P. Ratschinsky.

KIROV THEATRE OF OPERA AND BALLET, Leningrad, is the name since 1935 of the Maryinsky Theatre, St Petersburg, with its ballet sch. in Theatre (now Rossi) Street. Up to 1880 the ballet performances were given at the Bolshoi Th. From 1917 to 1935 it was called the State Academic Theatre of Opera and Ballet (or GATOB from its Russian initials). Kirov was head of the Communist Party in Leningrad and, though close to Stalin, was opposed to his revengeful persecution. He was shot in his office in 1934—many think it was on Stalin's order. The theatre has 1,760 seats and the stage is 97 ft wide and 72 ft deep. There is a second ballet theatre in Leningrad, the Maly Th. (q.v.).

KIRSOVA, Helen (Ellen Wittrup), b. c. 1911, d. London 1962. Dan. dancer, teacher and chor. Danced with the Santiago B., and with the Blum and de Basil Cos. Cr. rôle of the Butterfly in *L'Épreuve d'Amour* (Fokine 1936). Toured Australia with de Basil Co. 1936–37 and settled in Sydney. Opened her own school 1940 and started her own Co., Australian National B., in 1941, opening at Sydney Conservatory. Ch. *A Dream and a Fairy Tale* (1940), *Faust* (at Minerva Th., Sydney, using Heine's ballet scenario), *Waltzing Matilda*, etc. Trained Peggy Sagar, Henry Legerton, etc. Author of *Ballet in Moscow Today* (1956).

KIRSTEIN, Lincoln, b. Rochester, N.Y. 1907. Am. writer. Educ. Harvard. Founded Sch. of Am. Ballet (1934) and Ballet Caravan (1936–41). Cofounder and Editor *Dance Index* (1940–46). Co-founded, with Balanchine, Ballet Society (1946), which became New York City Ballet of which he is now Director. Author of *Book of the Dance, A Short History of Theatrical Dancing* (1935), *Blast at Ballet* (1938), *Ballet*

Alphabet (1940), *Movement and Metaphor* (1971), and numerous monographs and articles. One of the chief creative forces in Am. ballet. See AMERICA, IN BALLET.

KISS, Nora, b. Piatigorsk 1908. Russ. teacher. Pupil of Alexandrova, Brianza, Volinin. From 1929–35 danced in Europe in Cos. directed by Romanov and Balanchine. Has taught in Paris since 1946 (and in Rome during 1939–45).

KIVITT, Ted, b. Miami 1942. Am. dancer. Studied with Gavriloff, Milenoff etc. Danced in musicals and night-clubs. Joined Am. B. Th. 1961 becoming soloist 1964.

KLAVSEN, Verner, b. Copenhagen 1931. Danish dancer. Studied under Harald Lander and Volkova in Copenhagen and was engaged as solo-dancer by the Royal Swedish Ballet in 1952, of which he became one of the principal dancers. Also danced with de Basil's Ballets Russes in 1951. Partnered Doris Laine in Russia 1963.

KLEIN, Ethne, b. Johannesburg 1948. S. African dancer. Pupil of Berman, Sturman and de Villiers. Joined Johannesburg City B. 1963, PACT B. 1966, becoming soloist.

KLEMISCH, Dietlinde, b. Vienna 1938. Austrian dancer. Studied under Vondrak and at Staatsoper Sch. Entered Vienna Staatsoper Ballet 1952, beoming soloist 1957.

KLOS, Dieter, b. Essen 1931. Ger. dancer and ballet master. Pupil of Nordi, etc. at Essen Folkwang Sch. Danced with Folkwang B., ballet master Essen 1963–67, Gelsenkirchen 1967–71, Bonn 1971.

KNAPP, Monika, b. Füssen 1946. Ger. dancer. Studied at Munich B. school. Joined Wuppertal B. 1966 becoming soloist, Wiesbaden 1970–71, principal Stuttgart B. from 1971.

KNIASEFF, Boris, b. St Petersburg 1905. Russ. dancer and teacher. Studied under Mordkin and Nelidova. Left Russia 1917 to become maître de ballet in Sofia. Danced with de Basil Co. and formed his own troupe 1931 in Monte Carlo (with Blinova, Chamie, Hoyer in it). Maître de ballet of Opéra Comique, Paris, and later opened his own school (among his pupils were Chauviré, Algaroff, Jeanmaire, Skouratoff, Lafon), then in Switzerland and Athens, where he advocates a 'barre par terre' system with the pupils lying on the floor. Chor. many ballets, incl. *Berioska* (Silver Birch, 1931), *Piccoli* (1947). Was formerly mar. to Spessivtseva. In 1967 taught in Buenos Aires.

KNIGHT ERRANT, ballet, ch. Tudor, m. R. Strauss, dec. Lazarides, f.p. Touring Royal B., Opera House, Manchester 25 Nov 1968 (Davel, Landon, Thorogood, Barbieri, Anderton). An episode from *Les Liaisons Dangereuses* by de Laclos (1782).

KNILL, Hans, b. Schaffhausen 1941. Swiss dancer. Began ballet training 1959, joined Charrat's Co. 1962, Dutch Nat. B. 1963 and principal of Nederlands Dans Th. 1967.

KNOTT, Amanda, b. Sawbridgeworth 1945. Eng. dancer. Pupil of Royal B. Sch. and Rosella Hightower. Joined Teatro Italiano di Balletto touring Italy, and the B. Rambert 1964. Chor. *Singular Moves* (1966) and others.

KNUST, Albrecht, b. Hamburg 1896. Ger. dancer, chor. and teacher and writer on dance notation (Laban system). Studied under Laban and Jooss and joined Laban's ballet group Tanzbühne Laban in 1922. Director of the Hamburg Laban Sch. 1924–25 and appointed ballet master in Dessau 1926. Began his first writings on Laban notation in the Hamburg Dance Notation Bureau 1930 and greatly developed the system. In 1934 he took over the dance section of the Folkwangschule in Essen when Jooss and Leeder emigrated to England. In 1936 the Nazis banned the organization and the Bureaux were closed. From 1939 to 1945 Knust notated the ballets in the Staatsoper, Munich and started writing his great book *Encyclopaedia of Laban Kinetography*, completed in 1950. From 1951 he has been permanently at the Essen Folkwangschule. Chor. *Der Prinz von China* (Gluck) and *Prometheus* (Beethoven) 1927, and published *Handbook of Laban Kinetography* (1943).

KÖCHERMANN, Rainer, b. Chemnitz 1930. Ger. dancer. Studied under T. Gsovsky and Gore in London. In 1949 became soloist at Staatsoper, E. Berlin, and from 1951 to 1955 of the Städtische Oper, W. Berlin. In 1955 became principal dancer of the Frankfurt Opera House and in 1960 of the Staatsoper, Hamburg and later director. Partner of Maria Fris in television.

KOCHNO, Boris, b. Moscow 1903. Friend and secretary of Diaghileff from 1923. For the Diaghileff Co. he conceived the plots of *Les Fâcheux*, *Zéphire et Flore*, *Les Matelots*, *La Chatte*, *The Gods Go A-begging*, *Le Fils Prodigue*, *Ode*, *Le Bal*, etc. For de Basil's Co., *Cotillon* and *Jeux d'Enfants*. He collaborated with Balanchine in the 'Ballets 1933' Co. He was the founder, with Roland Petit, in 1945 of the Ballets des Ch. Élysées, devising more ballets, among them *Les Forains*. Author *Le Ballet* (1954), *Diaghileff and the Ballets Russes* (1970). See SOBEKA.

KOEGLER, Horst, b. Neuruppin 1927. Ger. critic and lexicographer. Studied at Kiel University and Halle/Saale Academy of Theatre. Contributor on ballet and opera to *Die Welt*, *Stuttgarter Zeitung*, *Tanzarchiv*, *Dance Magazine*, *Opera*, etc. Author of *Ballett in Deutschland (II)*, *Bolschoi Ballett*, *Modernes Ballett in Amerika*, *Ballett International* etc. and editor of the annual *Ballett* from 1965, German correspondent of *Dance and Dancers*. His *Ballett-Lexikon* was published in 1972.

KOELLNER, Alfredo, b. Genoa 1933. Italian dancer. Studied under E. Caorsi, P. and T. Battaggi. Entered Rome Opera Ballet 1950, becoming principal dancer 1955. Soloist of Balletto Europeo, Nervi and Edinburgh, 1960. Mar. Vjera Markovic. To Stuttgart 1960. Now works in Italy.

KOESUN, Ruth Ann, b. Chicago 1928. Am. dancer. Studied at Swoboda Sch., N.Y. Joined Ballet Theatre 1946 and became a principal dancer. Mar. Erik Braun.

KÖHLER-RICHTER, Emmy, b. Gera 1918. Ger. dancer and ballet mistress. Pupil of Wigman and T. Gsovsky. Danced Bonn, Berlin, Leipzig. Ballet mistress of Cologne 1947–51, Basel 1953–55, Weimar 1956–58 and since 1958 director of Leipzig B. Chor. many ballets.

KOLO (a Yugoslav folk dance), the name of the National Folk Ballet Co. of Yugoslavia. Founded in Belgrade, May 1948, the repertoire consists of folk-dances of Serbian and Macedonian origin of remarkable beauty and variety, which were for the most part collected and recorded by the sisters Jankovic and have such names as *Kolo, Oro, Sota, Skoplje, Teskoto, Lindjo, Duj-Duj*. The Co. made a great impression when it danced in London (Cambridge Th.) in May 1952.

KOLOSOVA, Eugenie, b. 1780, d. 1869. Russ. dancer and teacher. Was a favourite pupil of Didelot at St Petersburg and became his leading dancer. When he left Russia for a time he left the school in her charge and found it in a finer state on his return. She also acted, and sang in operas.

KOLPAKOVA, Irina, b. 1933. Russ. dancer. Trained at the Kirov Sch. and was the last to graduate from Vaganova's class 1951, becoming soloist of Kirov B. and now prima ballerina. Created rôle of Katerina in Grigorovich's *The Stone Flower* 1957. Member of the Praesidium. People's Artist R.S.F.S.R. 1965. Mar. Vladilen Semeyonov.

KOMAKI BALLET, THE, a Classical ballet Co. founded in Tokyo in 1947 by Masahide Komaki, who had been a member of the Shanghai B. Russe and returned to Japan in 1946. Originally called the Tokyo Ballet Co. it was formed from Japanese dancers who had learned the style from a White Russian teacher, Eliane Pavlova, in Tokyo. The first production was *Swan Lake* with Momoko Tani as ballerina. In 1950 the ballerina was Sakiko Hirose and the principal male dancer Naoto Seki. In 1952 Komaki invited Sonia Arova to be guest ballerina, followed by Nora Kaye (twice). The Co. toured in Japan.

KOMLEVA, Gabriella, b. Leningrad 1939. Russ. dancer. Trained at Kirov

Sch. and graduated to Kirov B. 1958, becoming soloist. Created rôle of Asiat in Vinogradov's *Gorianka* 1968. Varna Silver Medal 1966. Hon. Artist R.S.F.S.R.

KONDRATIEVA, Marina, b. Leningrad 1934. Russ. dancer. Entered Bolshoi Sch. 1944, graduated 1952, and now a leading soloist at the Bolshoi Th., Moscow. Hon. Artist R.S.F.S.R. 1965.

KONDRATOV, Yuri, b. 1921, d. Moscow 1967. Russ. dancer. Studied at Moscow Sch. Pupil of Gusev, making his début 1939 at Bolshoi Th. in *Svetlana*. Graduated 1940 and became a leading dancer the same year. Partnered Lepeshinskaya (1949–50) and Ulanova (1951–52 and in her Italian tour 1951). Stalin Prize 1950. Danced in Sweden 1955. Retired 1959 and made Artistic Director of Bolshoi B. 1960. People's Artist R.S.F.S.R. 1962. Partnered Beryl Grey in Russia 1957–58.

KONER, Pauline, b. N.Y. 1912. Am. modern dancer and chor. Pupil of Fokine, Cansino. Toured as soloist with Michio Ito 1928–29. Joined Limon Dance Co. 1946 and became his principal dancer. Chor. *The Farewell*, a solo for herself, 1962. Now lectures and teaches.

KONSERVATORIET, see CONSERVATORIET (the original spelling).

KOPPERS, Maria, b. Hague 1939. Dutch dancer, pupil of Amsterdam Conservatorium and joined Dutch Nat. B. 1961, becoming soloist 1962 and a principal dancer.

KOREN, Sergei, b. 1907. Russ. dancer. Graduated into Kirov B. 1927, becoming a principal character dancer. To Bolshoi B. 1942, creating rôle of Mercutio in *Romeo and Juliet*. Retired 1961 and became a ballet master at Bolshoi. Honoured Artist R.S.F.S.R. 1939.

KORRIGANE, LA, ballet 2 acts, ch. Mérante, m. Widor, dec. Lavastre, Rube, Chaperon, Lacoste, f.p. Paris Opéra 1 Dec 1880 (Mauri, Sanlaville, Mérante). This ballet, to a book by Coppée, was one of the most successful to be produced at the Opéra, and the waltz-mazurka *La Sabotière* became Mauri's greatest solo. The scene is seventeenth-century Brittany and the ballet is a Breton *Giselle*.

KÖRTVÉLYES, Geza, b. 1926. Hungarian writer on ballet. General Secretary of the Hungarian Dancers Association. Author of various books on ballet, *The Miraculous Mandarin at the Budapest Opera* (1961), *Towards a Modern Ballet* (1970) etc.

KORTY, Sonia, b. St Petersburg 1892, d. Salzburg 1955. Russ. dancer and teacher. Pupil of Fedorova. Danced in Diaghileff's Co. and in 1916 in Copenhagen. Later danced in N.Y., the Opéra Comique, Paris and became ballet mistress of the R. Flemish B., Antwerp. Taught at the Salzburg Mozarteum 1953–55. Wrote many articles on the dance and published *Dance Notation* in 1940.

KOSLOWSKI, Albert, b. Libau 1902. Latvian dancer and teacher. Studied in Moscow. Danced in Riga and Paris (under Fokine). Returned to Riga 1932, becoming ballet master at Nat. Opera until 1944. To Stockholm to teach, becoming ballet master of R. Swedish B. 1949. His wife, Nina (b. Libau, 1908, studied under Fedorova) also teaches with him. Now teaches at R. Swedish B. Sch.

KOVACH, Nora, b. Satoraljaujhely 1931. Hungarian dancer, wife of Rabovsky (q.v.). Pupil of Nadasi in Budapest. Joined Hungarian B. 1948. See RABOVSKY for her escape to West and career. Now American citizen.

KRAANERG, ballet, ch. R. Petit, m. Tchaikovsky and P. Henry, dec. Vasarely, f.p. Canad. Nat. B., Ottawa 2 June 1969 (Piletta).

KRAGH-JACOBSEN, Svend, b. Copenhagen 1909. Danish writer and critic. Dramatic and ballet critic of *Berlingske Tidende* since 1938. Author of *Ballettens Blomstring* (1945), *Margot Lander* (1947), *Ballet-Bogen* (1954), etc. Editor-in-chief *Den Kongelige Danske Ballet* (1952). Editor of *Danish Th. Annual* (from 1955). Contributor to *Dance Encyclopaedia* (1967).

KRAKOWIAK, lit. Cracow dance, gay Polish dance in 2/4 time, characterized by the clicking of heels, sometimes danced by a couple but usually by a large number. As the *Cracovienne* it enjoyed a considerable vogue in the ballet programmes of the Romantic period, and the Cracovienne in *La Gipsy* (1830) was one of Fanny Elssler's greatest solos.

KRAMER, Ivan, b. Cehovec 1942. Yugoslav dancer. Studied in Zagreb and joined Zagreb B. Joined Dutch Nat. B. 1966 becoming ballet master 1970. Mar. S. Marchiolli.

KRASSOVSKA, Nathalie (also danced under her real name Nathalie Leslie), b. Petrograd 1919. Russ. dancer, daughter of Lydia Krassovska of Diaghileff's Co. She called herself Krassovska from 1936 to 1952 and from 1953 onwards. Studied in Russia as a child and with Preobrajenska in Paris and later at Sch. of Am. B. First appeared in Nijinska's B. 1932, joined Les Ballets 1933, with Lifar to S. America 1934, B. Russe de Monte Carlo 1936 (ballerina) to 1950. To Festival B. 1950 as ballerina. Left 1955 and now teaches in Dallas, Texas.

KRASSOVSKAYA, Vera, b. Petrograd 1915. Russ. writer and historian of ballet. Studied at Kirov Sch. and danced in Kirov B. 1933–41. Author of *V. Chabukiani* (1956), *Russian Ballet Theatre from the Beginning to the Middle of the 19th Century* (1958), *Leningrad Ballet* (1961), *Russian Ballet Theatre of the Second Half of the 19th Century* (1963), *Anna Pavlova* (1964).

KRAUL, Earl, b. London, Ontario 1929. Canad. dancer, chor. and ballet master. Pupil of Bernice Harper, Idzikowsky and Betty Oliphant. Joined Canad. Nat. B. 1951, becoming soloist 1954 and principal dancer 1965. Partnered Martine van Hamel at Varna 1966.

KRAUSE, Horst, b. Poland 1930. Ger. dancer. Danced in Lübeck, Braunschweig, Düsseldorf and in 1954 went to Hanover as principal dancer and until 1971 was Georgi's assistant.

KRAUSENECKER, Adèle, b. Vienna 1899. Austrian dancer and teacher. Trained at the Hofoper Sch., Vienna, became principal dancer 1925–48. She was head of the Vienna Staatsoper Sch. 1931–63.

KRESNIK, Hans, b. Bleiburg 1939. Austrian dancer and chor. Danced in the ballets of Graz, Bremen and 1961–68 Cologne. In 1968 appointed ballet master Bremen. Chor. *O sela pei* (m. Pauels) 1967, *Paradies?* (m. Michaletz) 1968, *Ballett-Uraufführung* (m. Niehaus) 1969, *Susi Creamcheese* (m. Zappa) 1970.

KREUTZBERG, Harald, b. Reichenberg 1902, d. Bern 1968. Ger. dancer who studied under Laban and Wigman, and became one of the best known of the male exponents of the Modern German Dance. His principal partner was Yvonne Georgi. In his later years he choreographed for Dore Hoyer and others, and taught in his school in Bern from 1955.

KRIEGER, Victorina, b. St Petersburg 1893. Russ. dancer and writer. Entered Bolshoi Sch. Moscow 1903. Graduated to Bolshoi B. 1910 (from Tikhomirov's class), dancing the ballerina rôles in *Humpbacked Horse* 1915 and *Don Quixote* 1916. In 1921 she joined Pavlova's Co. as ballerina with Pavlova. Danced in Canada but left owing to rivalry with Pavlova. Danced in Europe and America; returned to Russia in 1923 and rejoined the Bolshoi B. in 1925 and also danced in Leningrad. In 1929 founded the Moscow Art Theatre Ballet and toured Russia with it. This became the Stanislavski and Nemirovitch-Danchenko Ballet (q.v.) In 1958 became Director of the Bolshoi Th. Museum. Author of *My Notes* (1930) and writes on ballet in the newspapers. People's Artist of R.S.F.S.R. 1951. As a dancer she had exceptional virtuosity and could perform the 32 *fouettés* alternately *en dedans* and *en dehors*.

KRISCH, Winfried, b. Hamburg 1936. Ger. dancer. Pupil of Sauer, Peters, Kiss, V. Gsovsky. Danced with the ballets in Malmö, of Béjart, Bonn, Essen, Cologne (1959–63), Munich (1963–70) as principal.

KRISTINA, Anita, b. Vienna 1940. Austrian dancer. Pupil of Pfundmayr, Royal B. Sch., Nordi, Northcote, Hightower. Joined Vienna Volksoper 1955, Charrat 1961, London Dance Th. 1964, Berlin 1964, Hamburg 1967. From 1973 principal dancer Tonin's Festival B.

KRIZA, John, b. Berwyn, Ill. 1919. Am. dancer. Studied under Bentley Stone, Dolin, and Tudor. Joined Ballet Theatre 1940, becoming one of the principal dancers. Cr. rôles in *Fancy Free*, *Interplay*, etc. Retired 1966, becoming assistant to the directors.

KRÖLLER, Heinrich, b. Munich 1880, d. there 1930. Ger. dancer and chor. Studied in Munich B. Sch. and became soloist there 1907. Studied in Paris and worked with Zambelli. Principal dancer Dresden and ballet master, Munich 1917, Berlin Staatsoper 1919–22, Vienna Staatsoper 1922–28. Chor. many ballets incl. *Legend of Joseph* (1922), *Schlagobers* (1924), J. A. Carpenter's *Skyscrapers* (1929) etc.

KRONSTAM, Henning, b. Copenhagen 1934. Dan. dancer. Entered R. Dan. B. Sch. 1941, studied under Lander and Volkova. Entered R. Danish B. 1952 and cr. rôle of Romeo in Ashton's *Romeo and Juliet* (1955). Promoted solodancer 1956. Danced in Aix-en-Provence Festival 1955, America 1960. In 1966 made principal dancer and assistant ballet master. He is also Director of the R. Danish B. Sch. Order of Dannebrog 1964. In 1961 he was guest artist with de Cuevas B.

KRUUSE, Marianne, b. Copenhagen 1942. Dan. dancer. Pupil of Bartholin, joined Scandinavian B. 1959–61, Th. d'Art du Ballet 1961–62, Mulhouse B. 1962–63, Stuttgart B. 1965–70 and went with Neumeier to Frankfurt as principal 1970 and Hamburg 1973.

KSCHESSINSKA (also Kschessinskaya), Mathilde (the Princess Romanovsky-Krassinsky), b. Ligovo 1872, d. Paris 1971. Russ. dancer and teacher. Studied at Imp. Sch., St Petersburg, graduating 1890 and becoming prima ballerina assoluta (only one other dancer, Legnani, had ever held this title). One of the greatest of the Imp. Russ. dancers and the first to rival the Italian ballerinas of the time. Morganatically mar. Grand Duke André of Russia (nephew of the Tzar) 1900 and had immense authority in the Maryinsky Th. Danced in Diaghileff's Co. Budapest, London, and Monte Carlo in 1911. Left Russia 1920 and lived in Paris since 1929 where she had a famous school. Her last appearance on the stage was in London 1936. She was the first Russ. to execute the thirty-two fouettés (q.v.). Wrote her autobiography, *Souvenirs de la Kschessinska* (Paris 1960).

KUJIAVIAK, or KUJIAVAK, Polish dance in 3/4 time closely allied to the mazurka.

KUMUDINI, b. Bombay 1930. Indian dancer. To England to join Ram Gopal's Co. in 1948 and became his chief dancer.

KUN, Zsuzsa, b. Budapest 1934. Hungarian dancer. Studied in Budapest, with Nadasi and Vainonen, and for a year in Moscow with E. Gerdt, Messerer, Nikitina. Début Budapest 1949 and now prima ballerina.

Danced at Bolshoi Th. Moscow and in Youth Festivals Bucharest 1953, Warsaw 1955 (1st prize), and on television E. Berlin 1959. Danced *Giselle* in 1958. Guest artist Festival B., London 1961. Won the Critics' Prize at Paris International Festival 1969.

KUNAKOVA, Lyubov, b. Izhevsk 1951. Russ. dancer. Graduated from the Perm Sch. 1970 and joined the Perm Ballet. Won the Varna Gold Medal 1972.

KURGAPKINA, Ninel, b. Leningrad 1929. Russ. dancer. Graduated into Kirov B. 1947 (class of Vaganova) and became ballerina. In 1972 she became director of the Leningrad (Vaganova) Sch.

KURA, Miroslav, b. Brno 1924. Czech dancer and chor. Danced in Katovice 1940–45, ballet master Brno 1947 and from 1964 at Prague.

KYASHT, Lydia, b. St Petersburg 1885, d. London 1959. Russ. dancer. Studied under Gerdt at Imp. Sch., St Petersburg (with Pavlova and Karsavina). Début 1902, becoming second dancer 1905, first dancer 1908. To England 1908 and succeeded Genée as prima ballerina at Empire Th. Also danced in America. In 1919 was a ballerina in Diaghileff's Co. Settled in England and in the 1940s had her own Co., B. de la Jeunesse Anglaise (q.v.). Taught in London and Cirencester and occasionally at S. Wells Sch. Author of *Romantic Recollections* (1929).

KYLIAN, Jiri, b. Prague 1947. Czech dancer. Pupil of Royal B. Sch. and joined Stuttgart B. 1968, becoming a principal, and chor. *Paradox* in 1970 etc.

L

LABAN, Rudolf von, b. Bratislava 1879, d. Weybridge 1958. Hungarian dancer and teacher, and inventor of the Laban System of Dance Notation. He studied in Paris and danced in many German cities and in 1907–10 worked in Vienna. He was the founder in 1911 at Munich of the Central European School of dancing, training Mary Wigman (from 1913) and Jooss (from 1921).

During the Great War he was in Zürich and in 1919 he was in Nuremberg and Stuttgart. Jooss joined him in 1921 and in 1923 he was director of ballet in Hamburg. He founded an Institute of Choreography in Würzburg in 1925 and was in charge of the ballet at the Berlin Staatsoper 1930–34. In 1938 he came to England and joined Jooss who was there with his company during the Second World War. He opened a studio in Addlestone in Surrey, with Lisa Ullman, and remained there until his death. Author of *The Dancers World* (1920),

Choreography (1926), *Dance Notation* (1928), *A Life for the Dance* (1935), *Modern Educational Dance* (1948), *The Mastery of Movement on the Stage* (1950), *Principles of Dance and Movement Notation* (1956). Through his pupils, his plastic style of dancing found much favour and in a few years it was danced in most of the opera houses in Germany and the adjoining countries, and it was not until the 1950s that it was ousted by the classical style. He elaborated a formidable analysis and philosophy of the dance, which found expression through his pupils Jooss and Leeder in the Ballets Jooss. His influence has been very great on the Continent and in America, where it became the basis of the Modern Dance. Author of *Kinetographie Laban* (1928). See LAB-ANOTATION and DANCE NOTATION.

LABANOTATION, a term introduced in America in 1953 to describe a system of dance notation evolved by the Dance Notation Bureau from the method and originally proposed by von Laban. See DANCE NOTATION.

LABIS, Attilio, b. Vincennes 1936. Fr. dancer. Studied at Paris Opéra Sch., entered Co. 1952, soloist 1960 and étoile 1961. Danced in Russia 1961 and partnered Fonteyn in the Royal B. at C. Garden 1965 and regularly afterwards on tour. Chor. *Arcades* 1964.

LAC DES CYGNES, LE, see SWAN LAKE.

LACOTTE, Pierre, b. Chatou 1932. Fr. dancer and chor. Studied at Paris Opéra Sch. 1942–46. Entered Paris Opéra B. 1946 and became premier danseur 1952. Having been refused permission to choreograph outside the Opéra, he left in 1955 and formed his own group, Ballets de la Tour Eiffel, which had its first season that year at the Th. des Ch. Elysées (fifteen dancers with Josette Clavier as principal dancer, ballets chor. by Lacotte). They appeared in N. Africa 1955, Belgium 1958, Monte Carlo 1959. In 1962 he formed a new group, with the assistance of the organization Les Jeunesses Musicales de France, which he called the Ballet National J.M.F., with Ghislaine Thesmar as principal dancer and himself as Director. This group toured France and had a Paris season each year. Chor. *La Nuit est une Sorcière* (m. Bechet) (1954) (winner of television award), *Combat de Tancredi* (m. Monteverdi) 1966, and for Ballet Rambert *Intermede* (m. Vivaldi) 1966. Mar. Ghislaine Thesmar. In 1972 he recreated *La Sylphide* (q.v.) at the Paris Opéra, closely adhering to the original production of 1832, with Schneitzhoeffer's music.

LADY AND THE FOOL, THE, ballet, ch. Cranko, m. Verdi-Mackerras, dec. Beer, f.p. S. Wells Th. B., New Th., Oxford 25 Feb 1954 (Miller, MacMillan, Mosaval). A rich girl who falls in love with a clown. This ballet was revised in 1955 and taken into the S. Wells repertoire (f.p.

C. Garden 9 June 1955, Grey, Chatfield, Powell). Danced by Deutsche Oper. B., Berlin 1965.

LADY FROM THE SEA, ballet, ch. Cullberg, m. Riisager, dec. Hedeby, f.p. Ballet Th., Met. Op. New York 20 May 1960 (Serrano, Bruhn, Glen Tetley). From the Ibsen play. Danced by the R. Swedish B., Stockholm 1 Mar 1961 (Sylwan, Klavsen).

LADY INTO FOX, ballet 3 sc., ch. Andrée Howard, m. Honegger, dec. Nadia Benois, f.p. Ballet Club, Mercury Th., London 15 May 1939 (Sally Gilmour, Boyd). The story of David Garnett's novel, of a girl who changes into a fox. The rôle is the one by which Sally Gilmour will always be remembered.

LADY OF SHALOTT, ballet 2 sc., ch. Ashton, m. Sibelius, dec. Chappell, f.p. Ballet Rambert, Mercury Th., London 12 Nov 1931 (Pearl Argyle, Ashton).

LADY OF THE CAMELLIAS, THE, ballet, ch. T. Gsovsky, m. Sauguet, dec. Ponnelle, f.p. Berlin B. 29 Sept 1957 (Helga Sommerkamp, A. Marlière, Reinholm). There have been many versions of this Dumas story, notably *Camille* (ch. Taras, m. Schubert 1946), by Tudor (m. Verdi 1951), *Marguerite and Armand* (ch. Ashton m. Liszt 1953) etc.

LAERKESEN, Anna, b. Copenhagen 1942. Dan. dancer. Pupil of Edite Frandsen and entered R. Danish Sch. 1959. Joined R. Danish B. 1960. Made solodancer 1964 and principal 1966. She dances the title rôle in *La Sylphide* in which she made her début while still a student 1959. In 1967 and 1968 guest artist Nat. B. of Canada.

LAFONTAINE, MLLE (also La Fontaine), b. Paris 1655, d. there 1738. Fr. danseuse who appeared in 1681 in the principal female rôle in *Le Triomphe de l'Amour*, the first ballet at the Paris Opéra to feature professional female dancers, thus becoming the first première danseuse. She took the veil and was succeeded by Mlle Subligny.

LAGERBORG, Anne-Marie, b. Stockholm 1919. Swed. dancer and director. Studied at R. Swed. B. Sch. from 1926, joined R. Swed. B. 1937 becoming soloist 1942. She was appointed one of the Associate Directors in 1963 and left in 1968 to become Associate Director of the Cullberg B. During her time with the R. Swed. B. she mounted many of the Cullberg ballets for other companies and was assistant to her and to Cramèr and Tudor.

LAGERTHA, ballet 3 acts, ch. Galeotti, dec. Chipart and Lerneur, f.p. R. Danish B., Royal Th., Copenhagen 30 Jan 1801 (Bjorn, Birouste, Antoine Bournonville). An incident from Danish history—the first ballet to have such a theme. Songs are sung in the course of the action. It went out of the repertoire in 1821.

D.B.—20

LAIDERETTE, ballet, ch. MacMillan, m. F. Martin, dec. Rowell, f.p. Sadler's Wells Choreographers' Group, S. Wells Th., 24 Jan 1954 (Maryon Lane, Poole). In repertoire of Ballet Rambert. A fantasy.

LAINE, Doris, b. Helsinki 1931. Finnish dancer. Studied in Finland, Moscow and with Anna Northcote. Joined National Ballet of Finland 1947, becoming soloist 1952 and prima ballerina 1956. Holds the Pro Finlandia Award. Guest artist Bolshoi B., Moscow 1960, and Festival B. 1964.

LAING, Hugh, b. Barbados 1911. Eng. dancer. Studied Margaret Craske, Rambert, Preobrajenska. First appeared in *Unbowed* (1932) for Ballet Club, Mercury Theatre, London, and cr. rôles for them, including *Descent of Hebe, Jardin aux Lilas* (Lover), *Dark Elegies, Judgement of Paris.* Joined Tudor's London Ballet 1938. With Tudor to America 1939. Joined Ballet Theatre 1939, cr. rôles in *Pillar of Fire, Romeo and Juliet* (Romeo), *Bluebeard, Undertow*, etc. Joined N.Y. City Ballet 1950, cr. rôles in *Dame aux Camélias, La Gloire, Miraculous Mandarin*, etc. Now a N.Y. fashion photographer.

LAKATOS, Gabriella, b. Budapest 1927. Hungarian dancer. Trained under Nadasi at State B. Institute from 1938 and joined Budapest Opera B. 1943 becoming principal dancer 1947. She is the only Hungarian soloist not also trained in Russia. Awarded Kossuth Prize 1958 and Merited Artist 1966. Guest artist Festival B. 1960.

LAKE, Molly, b. Cornwall 1900. Eng. dancer and teacher. Studied under Astafieva. Début in Pavlova's Co. and later danced in Markova-Dolin Co. (1935–36). In 1945 with her husband, Travis Kemp, and Mary Honer formed the Embassy Ballet, later called Continental B. Was also an original member of the Ballet Guild. To teach in Turkey 1954 as Director of the Conservatorium, Ankara.

LAMBERT, Constant, b. London 1905, d. there 1951. Eng. composer, conductor, and author. Educ. Christ's Hospital and Royal College of Music. First Eng. composer to be commissioned by Diaghileff, for whom he wrote *Romeo and Juliet* (ch. Nijinska) in 1926. He was Musical Director of the S. Wells B. from its inception, and much of its pre-eminence is due to his influence. He was the Co.'s conductor and, when they were without an orchestra, one of their two pianists. His ballet compositions for S. Wells are *Pomona* (1930), *Rio Grande* (1931), *Horoscope* (for which he also wrote the book, 1938), and *Tiresias* (1951). He arranged the m. for many ballets, incl. *Les Patineurs* and *The Prospect Before Us*, and was the author of a brilliantly witty account of contemporary music *Music Ho!* (1933). He was one of the architects of British ballet.

LAMBRANZI, Gregorio, Venetian teacher whose book for dancing masters *Nuova e curiosa scuolo de' balli teatrali* was published in Nuremberg 1716 (Eng. trans. by Derra de Moroda 1927). The book is illustrated and gives suggestions for composing dances. It also includes dances based on trades and sports.

LAMENT OF THE WAVES, ballet, ch. Ashton, m. Masson, cost. Rencher. f.p. Royal B., C. Garden 9 Feb 1970 (Marilyn Trounson, Carl Myers). Two young lovers drown together.

LAMENTATION, solo dance, ch. Graham, m. Kodaly, f.p. Maxine Elliot Th., N.Y. 8 Jan 1930 (Martha Graham). One of Graham's greatest dances, which she performs sitting on a bench.

LA MERI (Russell Meriweather Hughes), b. Kentucky 1898. Am. dancer, teacher, and writer. Founded Ethnologic Dance Center (1942) in New York, and dances and teaches national and folk dances. Author of many books on the dance.

LANCHBERY, John, b. London 1923. Eng. conductor. Studied at Royal Academy of Music, London, winning the Henry Smart scholarship for composition. Joined Metropolitan B. 1948 as conductor, Sadler's Wells Th. B. 1951 and made principal conductor of Royal B. 1960. Guest conductor R. Danish B. Composed music for many films and for the ballet *Eve of St Agnes* (B. Rambert) and arranged the music for Ashton's *Fille Mal Gardée* (1960), *The Dream* (1964) and his film *Tales of Beatrix Potter* (1971). Appointed musical director of Australian B. 1972.

LANDA, Anita, b. Las Arenas, Vizcaya, of half-Span. parentage 1929. Eng. dancer. Studied Brunelleschi and Cone-Ripman Sch. Début in Esmeralda's Span. Co. 1948. Joined Markova-Dolin Co. 1949 and the Festival B. on its formation in 1950, becoming a principal dancer. Cr. rôles in *Harlequinade*, *Symphonic Impressions*, *Symphony for Fun*. Now retired.

LANDÉ, Jean Baptiste, d. St Petersburg 1746. Fr. dancer and maître de ballet. Went to Russia in 1734 as a dancer. Was made ballet-master of a school for poor children and in 1735 pleased the Empress Anne with an excellent display of dancing by his pupils. He petitioned her in 1737 to found an Academy of Dancing in St Petersburg. His request was granted in 1738 and the Imperial Theatre School was founded with himself in charge. It was situated in the Winter Palace and appears originally to have had twelve boys and twelve girls chosen by the Empress from the servants' children. Landé's deputy was his French pupil Lebrun. The school's first graduation was in 1742 or 1743. In 1742 Rinaldo Fusano, a comic dancer from Italy (who had been the Empress Elizabeth's dancing master), was appointed Landé's assistant and he succeeded him as head in 1746. Thus Landé was the founder of the great Russian school of ballet.

LANDER, Harald, b. Copenhagen 1905, d. there 1971. Dan. dancer and chor. Pupil of Royal Dan. Sch. Début in *Far from Denmark* (1925). Studied in U.S.A. 1926–27 (also in Russia, America, and Spain). Became solodancer 1929 and ballet master from 1932 to 1951, recreating the modern Danish ballet, at the Opera House, Copenhagen, with its veneration for the Bournonville tradition and at the same time receiving the influence of contemporary trends and styles. In 1951 he was guest chor. at the Paris Opéra and became ballet master there 1953–63 and a Fr. citizen 1956. Director of the School 1959. Chor. many ballets, notably *Gaucho* (1931), *Bolero* (1934), *Anna-Anna* (1936), *La Valse* (1940), *Slaraffenland* (1942), *Qarrtsiluni* (1942), *Etude* (1948), for Paris Opéra an act of *Les Indes Galantes* (1952), *Hop Frog* (1953), *Printemps à Vienne* (1954). Mar. Margot Lander 1931, Toni Lander 1950. He returned to Copenhagen 1962 to remount his *Etude* there and since then has mounted his ballets all over Europe. Opened school in Paris 1964. He returned again to Denmark 1970 and reinstated his old ballets in the repertoire. Appointed Knight of Dannebrog.

LANDER, Margot (Margot Gerhardt), b. Copenhagen 1910, d. there 1961. Dan. dancer. Studied at the Royal Th. Sch., Copenhagen. Début as the Esquimo Dancer in *Far from Denmark*. Became solodancer 1931 and prima ballerina 1942 (the first Dane to receive this honour). Retired 1948. Decorated 'Ingenio et Arti' and, on retirement, the Fortjensmedalle. In 1932 she studied in Russia and in Paris (under Egorova and Volinin). Her most famous rôles were Swanilda, Giselle, and in *Swan Lake* and *Napoli*. Mar. Harald Lander in 1931, and later Erik Nyholm.

LANDER, Toni (Toni Pihl Petersen), b. Gentofte 1931. Dan. dancer. Studied at R. Danish Sch. Début 1947, becoming solodancer 1950. Mar. Harald Lander 1950. Soloist Orig. B. Russe (London) 1951, de Cuevas Co. 1953, Festival B. 1954, Ballet Th. 1959. Returned to Copenhagen 1962 to dance *Etude* under Harald Lander. Guest artist with Festival B. 1962. Rejoined Am. Ballet Th. 1964. Mar. Bruce Marks 1966. In 1961 Niels Poulsen named a rose after her. Rejoined R. Danish B. 1971. Appointed Knight of Dannebrog.

LÄNDLER, a dance in 3/4 or 3/8 time originating in Austria. It is for couples and was popular during the time of Mozart, Beethoven and Schubert, all of whom composed numbers of them. From it evolved the Waltz (q.v.). The Tyrolienne is similar.

LANDON (Leach), Jane, b. Perth, Australia 1947. Studied at Royal B. Sch. and danced Aurora in *Sleeping Beauty* at the school matinée 1964.

Joined Royal B. (Touring Section) 1964 and became a principal dancer 1968. In 1969 joined the Stuttgart B. as soloist. From 1972 teaching in Stuttgart B.

LANDORY, Veronique, b. Budapest 1938. Pupil of Nadasi (1946–48) and Royal B. Sch. (1949–53). Joined Les Ballets Chiriaeff 1953 as soloist (later Les Grands Ballets Canadiens), now a principal dancer.

LANE, Maryon, b. Zululand 1931. S. African dancer. Studied in Johannesburg. With R.A.D. Schol. to S. Wells Sch. 1946 and joined S. Wells Th. B. 1947, becoming a soloist of that Co. To Royal B. 1955 as soloist. Danced as guest of B. Rambert 1966. Teacher at Royal B. Sch. from 1971. Mar. David Blair.

LANG, Maria, b. Stockholm 1948. Swed. dancer. Pupil of R. Swed. B. Sch. from 1959, entered the R. Swed. B. 1965 dancing principal rôles from 1968. Also studied under R. Hightower.

LANG, Pearl, b. Chicago 1922. Am. dancer and chor. Studied under Martha Graham and became principal dancer in her company 1942–52. Also danced in Broadway musicals *One Touch of Venus*, *Carousel*, *Finian's Rainbow* and now teaches.

LANNER, Katti (Katharina), b. Vienna 1829, d. London 1908. Austrian dancer, daughter of Joseph Lanner, the composer of waltzes. Début 1845 in Vienna and danced with Elssler and Cerrito. Danced *Giselle* in N.Y. 1870. To London and opened a ballet sch. the National School of Ballet, at which she taught for some ten years, this being one of the first ballet schools in England. In 1887 engaged by George Edwardes and Augustus Harris, joint managers of the Empire Th., as maîtresse de ballet. Chor. of the Empire Ballets from 1887 to 1897, notably *Spirit of England*, *The Press*, *Cleopatra*, *La Danse*, *Monte Cristo*, *Under One Flag*. She is an important figure in Eng. ballet, forming a direct link between the Romantic era and Adeline Genée (whose Eng. début was in *Monte Cristo* in 1897).

LANY, Jean B., b. Paris 1718, d. there 1786. Fr. dancer and ballet master. Entered Paris Opéra 1750 and retired 1769, having become maître de ballet. Excelled at comic rôles (especially as a 'pâtre'), being barely 5 ft high and having very thick legs. Gaetano Vestris's sister, Thérèse, was his mistress, and he taught M. Gardel and Dauberval.

LANY, Louise Madeleine, b. Paris 1733, d. there 1777. Fr. dancer, sister of the above. Début at Opéra 1744, retired 1767. Noverre described her as 'the greatest dancer in the world, who has eclipsed all others by the beauty, precision, and boldness of her execution'. She appears to have been the first danseuse to achieve the entrechat six and huit.

LAPAURI, Alexander, b. Moscow 1926. Russ. dancer. Entered Moscow

Sch. 1935, graduating 1944. A chief dancer at the Bolshoi Th. Mar. Struchkova. Danced in England 1954, 1956. Chor. for the Bolshoi B. *Song of the Woods* (m. Zhukovsky, 1960), *Lieutenant Kije* (m. Prokofieff, 1963). Now teaches at the Bolshoi Sch.

LAPZESON, Noemi, b. Buenos Aires 1940. Argentinian dancer. Studied at Juilliard Sch., N.Y. and with Martha Graham, whose Co. she joined 1961. She also taught in the Juilliard and Graham Schs. Came to London to become a principal of the London Contemporary Dance Theatre in 1969 and also teaches in their school. Chor. *Cantabile* (m. Finnissy) 1970.

LARIONOV, Michel, b. Tiraspol 1881, d. Paris 1964. Russ. painter, librettist, and producer who collaborated with Diaghileff and influenced Massine. His décors include *Soleil de Nuit* (1915), *Contes Russes* (1916), *Chout* (he chor. this ballet with Slavinsky, 1921), *Le Renard* (1922). Mar. Goncharova.

LARSEN, Gerd, b. Oslo 1921. Norwegian dancer. Studied under Craske. Début in London Ballet. Cr. rôle in *Gala Performance* (1938), etc. Joined International B. 1941 and S. Wells B. 1944 as a soloist. Mar. Harold Turner. Now a principal mime of the Royal B. and teacher.

LARSEN, Niels Bjorn, b. Copenhagen 1913. Dan. dancer and chor. Studied at Royal Th. Sch., Copenhagen. With Trudi Schoop 1935–37. Solodancer of Royal Dan. B. 1942 and ballet master, succeeding Harold Lander, 1951–56. Chor. *Sylvia* (1948), *Drift* (1950), *Lunefulde Lucinda* (1954). Director Tivoli Th. 1955. He is one of the greatest living mimes. He retired as Director of the R. Danish B. and resigned 1965. Father of Dinna Bjorn.

LASCAUX, ballet, ch. Lazzini, m. Antill, dec. Chavignier, f.p. Marseille B., Th. Municipal, Marseille 23 Jan 1964. Inspired by the cave drawings.

LASSEN, Elna, b. 1901, d. 1930. Dan. dancer of great promise, pupil of Borchsenius. To America with Fokine 1921–24, dancing chief rôles in his ballets.

LAST, Brenda, b. London 1938. Eng. dancer. Pupil of Pinchard, Volkova and Royal B. Sch. Won Genée Gold Medal of R.A.D. 1955. Joined Western Th. B. 1957 and Royal B. 1963, becoming a principal dancer.

LAUCHERY, Albert, b. Mannheim 1779, d. Berlin 1853. Fr. dancer. Pupil of his father Etienne L. and studied in Paris. Returned to Berlin Opera as soloist 1803 and became head of the ballet school and was still teaching in 1846 when he celebrated his fiftieth year in the Co.

LAUCHERY, Étienne, b. Lyon 1732, d. Berlin 1820. Fr. dancer and chor.

at the courts of Kassel and Mannheim and from 1786 in Berlin. Father of Albert L.

LAUMER, Denise, b. Berlin 1930. Ger. dancer. Pupil of Blank and T. Gsovsky. Joined Berlin Staatsoper B. 1947. From 1953 to 1964 she was ballerina at Wüppertal under Erich Walter and created the chief rôles in most of his ballets.

LAURENÇIA, ballet, ch. V. Chaboukiani, m. Krein, dec. Virsaladze, f.p. Kirov Th., Leningrad 22 Mar 1939 (Dudinskaya, Chaboukiani). Based on Lope de Vega's tragedy *Fuente Ovejuno*. The *pas de six* from this ballet was staged for Royal B. by Nureyev 24 Mar 1965 (Nerina, Sibley, Park, Nureyev, Gable, Usher).

LAURENÇIN, Marie, b. Paris 1885, d. there 1956. Fr. painter and lithographer who designed dec. and cost. for *Les Biches* (1924), *L'Eventail de Jeanne* (1927) and *Le Déjeuner sur l'Herbe* (Ballets des Ch. Élysées 1945). She also created a number of lithographs on dance subjects.

LAVOLTA, see VOLTA.

LAVROVSKY, Leonid M. (Ivanoff), b. St Petersburg 1905, d. Paris 1967. Russ. chor. Graduated Leningrad B. Sch. 1922 and joined Kirov Co. From 1934–38 Artistic Director of ballet of Maly Th., Leningrad and from 1938–44 of Kirov Th. To Bolshoi Th., Moscow 1944 as chief chor. and Artistic Director. His first ballet was *Fadetta* (m. Delibes for *Sylvia* 1934). Chor. *Katerina* (1935), *Prisoner of the Caucasus* (Leningrad 1938), *Red Poppy* (new, Moscow, 1949), *Life* (1949), *Romeo and Juliet* (Leningrad 1940, Moscow 1946). *The Stone Flower* (1954), *Paganini* (1960); Stalin Prize 1946, 1947, 1950. People's Artist R.S.F.S.R. 1965. In 1964 he was made head of the Bolshoi Sch. and it was while presenting a group of his students in Paris that he died.

LAVROVSKY, Mikhail, b. Tiflis 1941. Russ. dancer, son of Leonid L. Entered Bolshoi Sch. 1952 and graduated to the company 1961. Won Varna Gold Medal 1965. Created rôle of the Prince in Grigorovitch's *Nutcracker* 1966. Lenin Prize 1970. Mar. L. Semenyaka.

LAWRENCE, Ashley, b. Hamilton, N.Z. 1934. N.Z. conductor. To England 1956 and studied at Royal Coll. of Music 1956–59. Joined Royal B. 1962 becoming principal conductor of Touring Royal B. and in 1963 went to Berlin, with MacMillan, as Musical Director of the Deutsche Oper. In 1970 was appointed principal conductor of B.B.C. Concert Orchestra and also guest conductor of the Royal B., Berlin B. and of Stuttgart B. 1971. In 1973 became Musical Director of the Royal B.

LAWRENCE, Bryan, b. Birmingham 1936. Eng. dancer. To S. Wells Sch. 1949, S. Wells Th. B. 1954, becoming soloist 1956. Danced the Prince in *Swan Lake* by the R. Ballet Sch., C. Garden 1960. In 1964 became a principal of the Australian B. Retired 1967 to teach in Canberra with his wife, Janet Karin.

LAWSON, Joan, b. London 1907. Eng. writer and teacher. Studied under Margaret Morris and Astafieva. Later in Moscow and Leningrad. Danced in Carl Rosa Operas, revues, and Nemchinova-Dolin Co. Regular visitor to Russia, lecturer on ballet and author of *European Folk Dance* (1953), *Classical Ballet, its Theory and Technique* (1960), *Dressing for Ballet* (with Peter Revitt) (1958), *A History of Ballet and its Makers* (1964) etc. On staff of Royal B. Sch. 1963–71.

LAYTON, Joe (Lichtman), b. N.Y. 1931. Am. chor. Pupil of Joe Levinoff and of Manhattan High Sch. of Music and Art. Début in *Oklahoma!* 1947 and danced in many musicals in N.Y. Joined George Reich's Ballet Ho in Paris 1954–55. Chor. many musicals, incl. *Once Upon a Mattress* 1959, *Sound of Music* 1959, the London production of *On the Town* 1963, the film of *Thoroughly Modern Millie* 1967, *George M!* 1968, and Noel Coward's *Sail Away* 1961. For the Royal B. he chor. *Overture* (m. Bernstein), *The Grand Tour* (m. Coward) 1971, *O.W.* (Oscar Wilde) (m. Walton) 1972. For Joffrey B. *Double Exposure* (m. Scriabin and Pousseur) 1972.

LAZARUS, ballet, ch. Cauley, m. Bloch, f.p. Royal B. Choreographic Group 1968. To Touring Royal B. Grand Th., Leeds 5 Dec 1969 (Davel, Anderton, Emblen). The raising of Lazarus.

LAZZINI, Joseph, b. Nice 1927. Fr. dancer and chor. Pupil of F. Meylach. Joined Nice B. 1945 as principal dancer. To Naples 1949–54, and appointed Director of ballet at Liège 1954–57. To Toulouse 1958 and director of ballet at Marseille 1959–69, where he made a great reputation for his modern and spectacular ballets. In 1963 awarded gold medal for best choreographer at the International Festival in Paris. In 1969 a new Co. was formed in Paris, Le Théâtre Français de la Danse (q.v.), and he was appointed its director. Among his many ballets are *La Valse* (m. Ravel, Toulouse 1959), *Miraculous Mandarin* (m. Bartok, Marseille 1962), $E = MC^2$ (m. Mossolov, Marseille 1964). He mounted *Miraculous Mandarin* at the Met. Op., N.Y. 1965 and in 1966 chor. there the Venusberg scene in *Tannhäuser*. In 1971–72 directed the Strasbourg Opéra du Rhin.

LECLAIR, André, b. Brussels 1930. Belgian dancer and chor. Pupil of Monique Qerida and V. Gsovsky. Danced with the B. des Ch. Élysées and became étoile of the Monnaie, Brussels (1950). Guest artist Norske B., Oslo, 1955, in Babilée's B. 1957, Charrat's partner 1960 and became soloist of Béjart's B. du XXme Siècle until 1967 when he became Director of the Royal Flemish B. at Antwerp. Chor. many ballets. Ballet master B. van Vlaanderen 1970.

LECLERQ, Tanaquil, b. Paris 1929. Am. dancer. Studied School of Am. Ballet, ballerina of Ballet Society at its inception, cr. rôles in *Four Temperaments*, *Symphony in C*, *Orpheus*, etc. Joined N.Y. City Ballet as ballerina in 1950, cr. rôles *Bourrée Fantasque*, *Illuminations*, *Jones Beach*, *Pied Piper*, etc. Retired 1956 on contracting poliomyelitis in Denmark. Mar. Balanchine 1953, now divorced. Author of *Mourka, the Autobiography of a Cat* (1964) and *Ballet Cookbook* (1967).

LEE, Mary Ann, b. Philadelphia, c. 1823, d. 1899. Am. dancer. Pupil of P. H. Hazard (of Paris Opéra) in Philadelphia where she made début 1837 in *Le Dieu et la Bayadère*. Learned Elssler's *Cachucha*, *Cracovienne*, and *Bolero* from Silvain (q.v.), and toured U.S. To Paris 1844 to study under Coralli and returned the following year, bringing with her *Fille du Danube*, *Jolie Fille de Gand*, and *Giselle*, which she was the first to dance in America (at Howard Athenaeum, Boston 1 Jan 1846, partnered by G. W. Smith). Retired 1847.

LEEDER, Sigurd, b. Hamburg 1902. Ger. dancer and teacher. Studied under Laban. In 1920 début as dancer and actor. Danced under Jooss 1924. Principal dancer at Essen 1927–34. Guest artist with Jooss 1932. Teacher with Ida Rubinstein Sch. 1933. Co-director of Jooss-Leeder Dance Studio at Dartington and Cambridge 1934–41. Dancer and ballet-master B. Jooss 1942–47. Chor. *Sailors' Fancy* (1943). Taught in London from 1947 until 1958, when he went to Chile. Returned to Zürich 1965 and opened school.

LEFÈBRE, Jorge. Cuban dancer. Pupil of Alicia Alonso in Havana. Danced in America and studied with Dollar, Mattox and joined Katharine Dunham's group. Joined Béjart's B. du XXme Siècle 1963 becoming a principal dancer. Chor. for B. de Wallonie *New World Symphony* (m. Dvorak 1972). Mar. Menia Martinez.

LEGAT, Nicholas, b. Moscow 1869, d. London 1937. Russ. dancer and teacher, pupil of Johansson and succeeded him as prof. of the Class of Perfection in the Imp. Sch., having first begun to teach 1889. Premier danseur at St Petersburg and made Artist Emeritus in 1913. Among his pupils were Fokine, Nijinsky, Bolm, Karsavina, Pavlova, Preobrajenska, Kyasht, Vaganova, Kschessinska. Left Russia 1923, joined Diaghileff and trained Lifar and Danilova. In 1929 opened a sch. at Colet Gardens, London, attended by most of the dancers of the period, incl. Eglevsky and later Moira Shearer. His wife, Nadine Nicolaeva-Legat (b. St Petersburg 1889, d. Tunbridge Wells 1971), founded a ballet school in England. He was an excellent caricaturist and wrote and illustrated a book on Russian ballet published in St Petersburg and translated in London 1939. His brother Sergei (1875–1905) was also a fine dancer at the Maryinsky Th.

LEGEND OF JOSEPH, ballet 1 act, ch. Fokine, m. R. Strauss, dec. Sert, cost. Bakst, f.p. Diaghileff's Co., Paris Opéra 14 May 1914 (Massine, Kusnetzova). This was Massine's first important rôle. Other choreographers since have made ballets to this music and theme (notably H. Kröller, Vienna Staatsoper B. 18 Mar 1922).

LEGEND OF LOVE, ballet 3 acts, ch. Grigorovitch, m. Melikov, dec. Virsaladze, f.p. Kirov Th., Leningrad 23 Mar 1962 (Kolpakova, Zubkovskaya, Gribov, Gridin). Based on a Turkish play by Nazym Hikmet, in which a queen sacrifices her beauty to save her sister. Produced in Moscow 15 Apr 1965 (Plisetskaya).

LEGEND OF OCHRID, THE, ballet 4 acts, ch. Froman, m. and book S. Hristich, dec. Belozanski, f.p. Belgrade Opera 28 Nov 1947 (Sanina, Parlic). This ballet makes great use of Yugoslav and Croat national dances.

LEGERTON, Henry, b. Melbourne 1917. Austral. dancer and ballet master. Pupil of Idzikowsky, Kirsova, Volkova. Joined London B. 1940 and then served in Australian Army. Joined S. Wells B. 1946 and was chosen by Massine for the Shop Boy's rôle in *Boutique Fantasque* (1947). Ballet master of the Touring Royal B. 1957 and now of C. Garden.

LEGNANI, Pierina, b. 1863, d. 1923. It. dancer. Pupil of Beretta in Milan. Début Milan and later appeared in Paris, London, and Madrid. In 1893 she went to St Petersburg and made her début that year in *Cinderella*. She remained there until 1901 (her last performance was in *La Camargo*)—longer than any foreign dancer had stayed. In *Aladdin* in London in 1892 she turned thirty-two fouettés, a feat hitherto never performed. She created the rôle Odette-Odile in *Swan Lake* in the 1895 (St Petersburg) version of Petipa and Ivanov, in which the fouettés were also introduced. She also appeared in the Alhambra Ballets in London from 1888 (in *Irene*), dancing *The Sleeping Beauty* there (ch. L. Espinosa) in 1890. She and Kschessinska were the only two dancers in the history of the Maryinsky Th. to receive the title prima ballerina assoluta. See FOUETTÉ.

LEISTNER, Wolfgang, b. Zwickau 1933. Ger. dancer. Studied in Leipzig and at S. Wells Sch. Début in Leipzig 1949. Danced with Komische Oper, E. Berlin, Munich, Wiesbaden and became a principal at Städtische Oper, W. Berlin 1956–63. Ballet master Heidelberg B. 1963–65. To Mannheim B. 1967 as principal dancer.

LELAND, Sara, b. Melrose, Mass. 1941. Am. dancer. Pupil of E. V. Williams and first appeared in her Boston B. Joined Joffrey B. 1959–60. Joined N.Y. City B. 1960 becoming soloist 1963.

LEMAÎTRE, Gérard, b. Paris 1936. Fr. dancer. Pupil at Châtelet Th. Sch., Paris. Joined Petit's Co. 1952–56, and also danced with de Cuevas B. Joined Nederlands Dans Th. 1961, becoming principal. A ballet, *Opus Lemaître*, was chor. by van Manen for him 1 Nov 1972 in Paris.

LEMANIS, Osvald, b. Riga 1903, d. Flint, Mich. 1965. Latvian dancer. Pupil of Sergueeff and Fedorova in Riga. Joined Riga B. 1926, soloist 1928. In 1933 partnered Spessivtseva in Riga. Director of Latvian Nat. B. 1934–44. Principal dancer and chor. Stuttgart 1948–50. In 1951 settled in America (Detroit) with his wife, Mirdza Tillak, to teach.

LEMOINE, Jean-Bernard, b. Rouen 1920. Fr. dancer. Pupil of Kschessinska. Début Nouveau B. de Monte Carlo 1945. Joined Paris Opéra 1947. Left in 1953 to join Petit's Co. Became one of the principal dancers in Charrat's Co. 1953. To Opéra Comique 1957.

LENINGRAD SYMPHONY, ballet, ch. Belsky, m. Shostakovitch (1st movement of Seventh Symph.), f.p. Kirov B., Lewisohn Stadium, N.Y. 14 Apr 1961 (Sizova, Soloviev). Dramatic ballet about the siege of Leningrad. The first Soviet ballet to have its première in the West.

LEONOVA, Marina, b. Moscow 1949. Russ. dancer. Pupil of Bolshoi Sch. and joined the Co. 1969. First danced in London 1967 with young stars of the Bolshoi.

LEOTARD, a skin-tight garment combining long-sleeved (or sleeveless) vest and brief trunks, worn by dancers as a foundation for certain stage costumes, or as a practice costume. From Jules Leotard (1830–70), a famous Fr. acrobat of the nineteenth century, who invented the flying trapeze.

LEPESHINSKAYA, Olga, b. Kieff 1916. Russ. dancer. Studied at Moscow Sch. under Tikhomiroff, joined Bolshoi Th. 1926, first soloist 1933 becoming one of chief ballerinas of Russia. Stalin Prize 1941, 1946, 1947, 1950. Honoured Artist of R.S.F.S.R. 1942, People's Artist 1947, 1951. Member of the Supreme Soviet. Taught in Mongolia and in Budapest (1963–65). Now works with the Staatsoper and Komische Oper Ballets in E. Berlin.

LE PICQ (or LE PICK), Charles, b. Strasburg 1749, d. 1806. Fr. dancer. Was Noverre's favourite pupil and one of the chief dancers at the Opéra. In 1786 he went to St Petersburg as ballet master with his wife Gertrude (who was made prima ballerina) and remained there for twelve years, also dancing in London (ballet master at King's Th. 1783 and 1785) and Paris. While at St Petersburg he arranged for the Russian edition of Noverre's *Letters* to be published. Noverre said of

him, 'This Proteus of the Dance who had united in him every style. . . .'
He chor. many ballets and revived many of Noverre's.

LEPRI, Giovanni. It. dancer, pupil of Blasis at Milan. Became premier
danseur at La Scala 1857. Maître de ballet at Academy of Dancing,
Florence, where he taught Cecchetti.

LEROUX, Pauline, b. Paris 1809, d. 1891. Fr. dancer. Danced Paris
Opéra, cr. rôle *Le Diable Amoureux* (1840) and danced in London
1824–33.

LESKOVA, Tatiana, b. Paris 1922. Fr. dancer and ballet mistress. Studied
under Egorova, Kniaseff, Oboukhov. Début at Opéra Comique, Paris,
1937. Soloist of Ballets de la Jeunesse 1938 and of Original Ballet
Russe 1939, creating a rôle in *Graduation Ball* in Australia. To Brazil
1945 dancing and teaching, becoming ballet mistress and chor. of
Teatro Municipal, Rio de Janeiro in 1950, with her own school,
Academia Ballet Society. Ballet mistress for Massine, Nervi 1960.
From 1961 director of the Rio de Janeiro B. To Chile, but returned to
Rio 1969.

LESLIE, Nathalie (see KRASSOVSKA, Nathalie).

LESSON, THE, ballet, ch. Flindt, m. Delerue, dec. Daydé, f.p. Danish
Television (winning prize) 20 Sept 1963 (Amiel, Flindt, Chelton).
First put on stage, Opéra Comique, Paris 6 Apr 1964 (Flindt, Amiel,
Garden) and for R. Dan. B., Copenhagen 7 Dec 1964 (Hönningen,
Kronstam, Kiil). In repertoire of many Cos. The Ionesco play of the
mad teacher who murders his pupils.

LESTER, Keith, b. Guildford 1904. Eng. dancer and chor. Educ. St Paul's.
Studied under Dolin, Astafieva and Legat. Début in Fokine's dances for
Hassan in London 1923. Partnered Kyasht and trained with Karsavina
and partnered her, and appeared with Spessivtseva in Buenos Aires.
Chor. *David* (for Markova-Dolin Co. 1935), *Pas de Quatre* (1936), and
other ballets. Chor. for Open Air Th., Regent's Park 1937, joined
London B. 1939, and formed Arts Th. B. Co. in 1940. In 1945 joined
the Windmill Th., London (non-stop variety) in charge of the dancing
and chor. over 150 ballets for them. From 1965, principal teacher of
the Royal Academy of Dancing, London and director of their Teacher's
Training Course.

LETTER TO THE WORLD, ballet, ch. Martha Graham, m. H. Johnson,
cost. Gilfond. Text by Emily Dickinson, f.p. Bennington Col., Vermont 11 Aug 1940 (Graham, Dudley, Hawkins, Cunningham). One
of Graham's first group dances, with a speaker.

LEVASHEV, Vladimir, b. Moscow 1923. Russ. dancer. Entered Bolshoi
Sch. 1932 and graduated 1941. Leading character dancer and mime of

the Bolshoi B. Created eponymous rôle in *Shuraleh* in Moscow 1955, and of Severyan in *The Stone Flower* 1959. People's Artist R.S.F.S.R. 1965. Danced in London 1960, N.Y. 1959. In 1961 he created a rôle in Lavrovsky's *Night City*

LÉVINSON, André, b. St Petersburg 1887, d. Paris 1933. Russ. critic and historian of the dance. Left Russia 1918 and settled in Paris. He was a great upholder of the classical tradition and originally an opponent of Fokine's reforms. His chief works, *La Danse d'Aujourd'hui* (1929) and *Les Visages de la Danse* (1933), are a series of articles on the leading dancers (Classical and music-hall) who appeared in Paris. His *Life of Taglioni* (1929) is a standard work. Also wrote *La Danse au Theatre* (1924), *La Vie de Noverre* (1925), *Anna Pavlova* (1928), *La Argentina* (1928).

LEZGINKA, Russian dance in 6/8 time deriving its name from the Lezghis, a number of tribes inhabiting Daghestan on the Caspian Sea.

LHOTKA, Nenad, b. Zagreb 1922. Yugoslav dancer and chor. Studied under Anna Roje and Egorova. Entered Zagreb National B. 1942 and became principal dancer. In 1950 he joined Charrat's Co. in Paris as soloist. Returned to Zagreb 1953. Awarded State Prize in 1949 and 1950 (for his Romeo in Froman's *Romeo and Juliet*, which he created). Chor. *Tragedy of Salome* (m. Schmitt 1953) and *Classical Symphony* (m. Prokofieff 1954) in Zagreb. Danced in London 1955. Ballet master at Royal Winnipeg Ballet 1955–56. Mar. Jill Morse.

LICHINE, David (Lichtenstein), b. Rostov-on-Don 1910, d. Los Angeles 1972. Russ. dancer and chor. Studied in Paris under Egorova and Nijinska. Danced in Ida Rubinstein Co. 1928, and with Pavlova. Soloist in Ballet Russe de Monte Carlo 1932–41. Cr. rôles in *Jeux d'Enfants*, *Beau Danube* (King of the Dandies), *Présages*, *Cotillon*, *Choreartium* etc. Chor. many ballets, incl.: for B. Russe de Monte Carlo, *Nocturne* (1933), *Le Pavillon* (1936), *Francesca da Rimini* (1937), *Protée* (1939), *Graduation Ball* (1940), *Helen of Troy* (1942). For B. des Ch. Élysées chor. *La Rencontre*, *La Création* (1948). For Festival B. chor. *Symphonic Impressions* (1951), *Concerto Grosso en Ballet* (1952). *Nutcracker* (1957). Mar. Tatiana Riabouchinska. Taught in Los Angeles 1954–72.

LIDO, Serge, b. Moscow 1906. The leading Fr. ballet photographer since 1939. Among his books of photographs (text by his wife, Lidova) are *Danse* (1947), *Danse No. 2* (1948), *Sauts* (1949), and in 1951 published the first of an annual series of books, *Ballet* (No. 2 1952, No. 3 1953, No. 4 1954, and so on), *Ballet Panorama* (1961), *Ballet d'aujourdhui* (1966).

LIDOVA, Irène, b. Moscow 1907. Fr. critic and writer on the dance. Studied at the Sorbonne. In 1944 instituted 'Soirées de la Danse' at Th. Sarah Bernhardt, Paris, presenting young Fr. dancers (Petit, Charrat, Vyroubova, Babilée, Marchand, Skorik, Pagava, Navada, etc.) which the following year, became the B. des Champs Élysées with herself as General Secretary. Wrote *Les Visages de la Danse Française* 1953, and the text of all her husband's (Lido's) books. Paris correspondent for *Dance News*. General Secretary of French Association of Ballet Critics and Writers.

LIDSTRÖM, Kerstin, b. Stockholm 1946. Swed. dancer. Studied R. Swed. B. Sch. and Royal B. Sch., London. Entered R. Swed. B. 1963, now dancing solo rôles. Joined Nederlands Dans Th. 1970. Returned to R. Swed. B. 1971 and danced Lise in *Fille Mal Gardée* (1972).

LIEBESLIEDER WALZER, ballet, ch. Balanchine, m. Brahms, dec. Rays, cost. Karinska, f.p. N.Y. City B., City Center, N.Y. 22 Nov 1960 (Adams, Hayden, Verdy, Jillana, Carter, Watts, Magallanes, Ludlow). Waltzes in a drawing room with the two pianos and vocal quartet on stage.

LIED VON DER ERDE, DAS, see SONG OF THE EARTH.

LIEPA, Maris, b. Riga 1936. Latvian dancer. Studied in Riga, and at Bolshoi Sch., Moscow. Joined Riga B. 1952, becoming soloist 1955 and after dancing in a Latvian Festival in Moscow 1955 was invited to partner Plisetskaya in Budapest. From 1955–60 soloist of Stanislavsky-Nemirovitch-Dantchenko B. and joined Bolshoi B. 1960 as a principal dancer. In 1967 he revived *Spectre de la Rose* in Russia and danced it with Bessmertnova. Hon. Artist R.S.F.S.R. 1964. People's Artist 1969 and Lenin Prize 1969.

LIEUTENANT KIJE, ballet, ch. Lapauri and Tarasova, m. Prokofieff, dec. B. Messerer, f.p. Bolshoi Th., Moscow 10 Feb 1963 (Struchkova, Bogomolova, G. Bovt). The signature of the Tzar gives 'life' to a non-existent lieutenant.

LIFAR, Serge, b. Kieff 1905. Russ. dancer, chor., and author. Joined Diaghileff's Co. 1923 and became the premier danseur 1925. In 1930 to Paris Opéra as premier danseur and appointed professor 1932. From 1932 to 1958 he was the controlling and creative power at the Opéra and the leading (and most controversial) figure in ballet in Paris. He was one of Diaghileff's greatest male dancers, and chor. for his Co. *Renard* (1929). At the Opéra he chor. most of the ballets in their current repertoire, taking the leading rôles, notably *Prométhée* (1929), *Icare* (1935), *Le Roi Nu* (1936), *Alexandre le Grand* (1937), *Joan de Zarissa* (1942), *Suite en Blanc* (1943), *Entre deux Rondes* (1940), *Nautéos* (1954),

L'Oiseau de Feu (1954). In 1953 he was appointed Technical Adviser on the Dance at the Opéra. His régime at the Opéra was interrupted for a time after the war (1945–46) by political feeling against him, but he was reinstated. He raised the status of ballet at the Opéra to its present position from the low level to which it had fallen by the 1920s, and revitalized it artistically with something of the spirit of his old master Diaghileff. He also introduced the modern Russ. style of dancing there in place of the outdated It. style which had prevailed. He is an active propagandist and his writings include *Le Manifeste du Chorégraphe* (1935), *La Danse* (1937), *Diaghileff* (1939), *Carlotta Grisi* (1941), *Giselle* (1942), *L'Histoire du Ballet Russe* (1945), *Les Trois Grâces du XXᵉ Siècle* (1959). He last performed at the Opéra, in *Giselle* 5 Dec 1956 and he finally left the Opéra 1 Oct 1958 to direct the École Supérieure d'Études Chorégraphiques at the Sorbonne. In military slang 'sergelifars' are the long tight underpants worn by French paratroops. In 1962 he returned to the Opéra as choreographer and again in 1969. Published *Ma Vie* (1965).

LIFE GUARDS ON AMAGER, THE, ballet, ch. A. Bournonville, m. W. Holm, dec. Güllich, cost. Lehmann, f.p. R. Danish B., Royal Th., Copenhagen 19 Feb 1871. An episode of 1808 based on Edouard du Puy, a baritone who was Denmark's first Don Giovanni and who was for a time in the Life Guards. A Shrovetide Party. Its 100th perf. was in 1890. It was revived in 1947 and again in 1971, and given at the Edinburgh Festival the same year.

LIFT, the lifting of the danseuse by her partner. The apparently effortless lift of the ballerina or the run across the stage of the dancer with the danseuse in a supported leap demands considerable skill, allied to sheer muscular strength, as well as good timing. The upward, or forward, lift of the man must synchronize perfectly with the volitation of his partner's spring upwards and forwards. The lift is the more effective if the muscular mechanism and holds employed are concealed from the audience. Choreographers have vied with each other in the invention of new lifts, and modern Russ. choreography makes great use of them. See F. LOPOKOV and E. LUKOM.

LIGHT FANTASTIC, ballet, ch. Gore, m. Chabrier, dec. Rowell, f.p. Walter Gore Ballet Co., Festival Th., Malvern 25 May 1953 (Gore, Hinton). Boys sit on chairs and gaze wistfully at dolls. Revived often, and in Scottish Th. B. repertoire 1970.

LILAC GARDEN (see JARDIN AUX LILAS)

LILAVATI, Devi, b. Calcutta. Indian dancer. Studied under Krishna Rao and joined Ram Gopal company 1947. Married Bengt Häger and lives in Stockholm giving recitals in Scandinavia, China, Italy, France etc. Studied at Stockholm Choreographic Institute 1966–68. Chor. a new *Schéhérazade* (Rimsky-Korsakov) for Malmö B. 1969 and for television.

LIMON, José, b. Culiacán, Mexico 1908, d. New Jersey 1972. Mexican dancer. Studied under Weidman and Doris Humphrey in whose Co. he danced from 1930 to 1940. Had his own group dancing ballets with choreography by Doris Humphrey and himself. His best-known ballet is *Moor's Pavane* (1949). Won Capezio Award 1965. In 1964 the N.Y. State Council on the Arts appointed him director of a new group The American Dance Theatre (first performed 18 Nov 1964 in Lincoln Center). Mounted his ballets for R. Swed. B. 1970. His Co. danced at S. Wells 1957.

LINCOLN CENTER FOR PERFORMING ARTS, New York, a complex of buildings which comprises (1) the N.Y. State Theater, home of the N.Y. City B. and the N.Y. City Opera, (2) the New Metropolitan Opera House, with its seasons of grand opera, the seasons of the Royal B., the Kirov B. and the Bolshoi B. etc., (3) the Philharmonic Hall, with its smaller Alice Tulley Hall for concerts, (4) the Juilliard Sch. of Music which includes the Sch. of American Ballet, (5) the Vivian Beaumont Theatre for repertory and (6) the N.Y. Public Library's section on Performing Arts, which includes the famous Dance Collection (q.v.). The Lincoln Center was opened in 1964.

LINDEN, Anya, b. Manchester 1933. Eng. dancer. Studied in America under Kosloff and Pring. Joined S. Wells Sch. 1947 and entered the Co. 1951, becoming a soloist in 1954 and ballerina 1958. Retired 1965.

LINE, the harmonious disposal of arms, legs, and head in relation to the body. The outline presented by the dancer in action or repose. Line is partly acquired and is partly a natural gift of physique. In the Classical ballet, the development and the display of line is one of the main objects.

LITHOGRAPHS, or prints made from a stone 'plate', were invented by Senefelder (b. Prague 1771, d. Munich 1834) in 1796. By 1830 lithography was the most highly developed and successful method of illustration, and it is from the lithographs of 1830 to 1850 (mostly English) that we have our knowledge of the appearance and costumes of the dancers of the Romantic era. Taglioni, Grisi, Elssler, Grahn, Cerrito, and the rest are all depicted by its means. It was also the method of printing music-covers, many of which show dancers. With the 1850s the lithograph was ousted by the daguerreotype and the photograph. The chief artists whose work was printed in this way were

A. E. Chalon, J. Brandard, and J. Bouvier. The best-known lithographer of their work was R. J. Lane.

LITTLEFIELD, Catherine, b. Philadelphia 1905, d. Chicago 1951. Am. dancer and chor. Studied in Paris and founded the Littlefield Ballet in Philadelphia in 1935, which toured America (and broke up in 1942), and appeared in London in 1937. Chor. *Barn Dance, Terminal*, etc. Also chor. ice-skating revues for Sonja Henie. She was a pioneer of Am. ballet, her Co. was the first to visit Europe (London, Paris 1937) and the first to produce a full-length *Sleeping Beauty* (1937).

LITTLE MERMAID, THE (Den lille Havfrue), ballet, ch. Hans Beck, m. Fini Henriques, dec. T. Petersen, f.p. R. Danish B., Copenhagen 26 Dec 1909 (Ellen Price). Based on the Hans Andersen story. A new version was mounted by Harald Lander in Copenhagen 14 Mar 1936 (Ulla Poulsen).

LITTLE STORK, THE, ballet, ch. Popko, Posspekhine, Radunsky, m. Klebanoff, dec. Zimin, f.p. for the Graduation Performance 2nd stage (Filial) Bolshoi Th., Moscow 6 June 1937. This popular children's ballet is usually performed by pupils of the school. Plisetskaya cr. the rôle of the Cat.

LIVRY, Emma-Marie, b. Paris 1842 (the illegitimate daughter of a member of the Jockey Club and a 16-year-old member of the corps de ballet), d. Neuilly 1863. Fr. dancer. Pupil of Madame Dominique and Marie Taglioni, who saw in her a worthy successor. Début Paris Opéra 1858 in *La Sylphide*, and cr. title rôle in *Le Papillon* (1860). During a rehearsal of *La Muette de Portici* in 1862 her dress caught fire and she was severely burned, dying in great agony eight months later. Her elevation and *ballon* were said to have rivalled Taglioni's.

LJUNG, Viveka, b. Stockholm 1935. Swed. dancer. Entered R. Swed. B. Sch. 1942 and the R. Swed. B. 1952, becoming soloist. Joined Ballet Theatre 1961 and Dutch Nat. B. 1962.

LLOYD, Gweneth, b. Eccles 1901. Eng. teacher and chor. Pupil of Ginner-Mawer Sch. of Dance in London. To Canada and with Betty Farrally (q.v.) founded the Winnipeg (later the Royal Winnipeg) Ballet and the School, in 1938—the first Canadian ballet. Chor. over thirty ballets for them between 1939 and 1958. In 1950 she opened a school in Toronto but remained a Director of the R. Winnipeg B. until 1958.

LLOYD, Maude, b. Cape Town. South African dancer who was one of the principal dancers with Rambert since 1927, creating leading rôles in *Jardin aux Lilas, Dark Elegies, Gala Performance*, etc. Soloist in Markova-Dolin and London Ballets. Now writes on ballet in the

London *Observer* under the name Alexander Bland (with her husband Nigel Gosling).

LLOYD, Margaret, b. S. Braintree, Mass. 1887, d. Brookline 1960. Am. writer on the dance. Was dance critic of the *Christian Science Monitor* 1936–60. Author of the *Borzoi Book of Modern Dance* (1949).

LONDON ARCHIVES OF THE DANCE, or L.A.D., a body founded under a trust deed on 9 Jan 1945 with the object of building up a centre where books, programmes, costume designs, scores, photographs, and other dance material can be made available to all who are interested in the history of the ballet. A considerable collection of material had already been made, but it was held in store since no premises had been found to house and display it. The prime movers of its formation were Cyril Beaumont, Lionel Bradley, Deryck Lynham, and Christmas Humphreys. In 1969 it was handed over to the Enthoven Collection of the Victoria and Albert Museum, London.

LONDON BALLET, THE. When Antony Tudor left the B. Rambert in 1937 and founded his own company, he appeared with Agnes de Mille at the Oxford Playhouse, their joint company being known as Dance Th. In December 1938 his company, then known as the London B., began giving regular performances in London at Toynbee Hall, with a repertoire of ballets originally created at the Mercury Th., incl. *Jardin aux Lilas* and *Dark Elegies*, to which were added a number of new creations such as *Judgement of Paris*, *Soirée Musicale*, and *Gala Performance*. The dancers included Pauline Clayden, Gerd Larsen, Maude Lloyd, Peggy van Praagh, Hugh Laing, Guy Massey, and David Paltenghi. Tudor and Laing then left to join B. Th. in the U.S.A., and the company continued for a time under the joint direction of Maude Lloyd and Peggy van Praagh and, in November 1939, participated in the project for making of the Arts Th. a Ballet Centre in London. Here they produced several works, incl. *Pas des Déesses* (Lester) and *La Fête Étrange* (Howard) before they merged in June 1940 with the B. Rambert, an association which continued until September 1941.

LONDON BALLET, WALTER GORE'S, gave its first performance in Hintlesham Hall, near Ipswich 28 July 1961, with a programme of *Peepshow*, *Night and Silence* and *Scottish Suite*, all chor. Gore. The musical director and joint founder was Michael Pilkington and among the dancers were Paula Hinton, Walter Gore, Anna Price, Jane Evans, Roger Tully, and Harry Haythorne. The Co. appeared at the Edinburgh Festival the same year and later toured. Other dancers included Alexis Rassine, Robin Haig, Vicki Karras, Jill Bathurst and among ballets were Gore's *Nutcracker*, his *Eaters of Darkness* and *Light Fantastic* etc. It came to an end during 1963.

LONDON CONTEMPORARY DANCE THEATRE, THE, see CONTEMPORARY DANCE THEATRE, THE LONDON.

LONDON DANCE THEATRE, ballet company founded by Norman McDowell. Its first performance was at the Th. Royal, Newcastle on 22 June 1964 with ballets by Jack Carter (*Agrionia, I Quattro Stagione*), Charrat (*La Répétition de Phèdre*), Andrée Howard (*The Tempest*), Terry Gilbert (*Rave Britannia*) etc. Among the dancers were Joyce Graems, Carol Grant, Yvonne Meyer, Belinda Wright, Ivan Dragadze, Gerard Sibbritt, Terence Etheridge. The Co. came to an end just a year afterwards.

LONDON FESTIVAL BALLET (see FESTIVAL BALLET).

LONDON MORNING, ballet, ch. Jack Carter, m. and libretto Noel Coward, dec. Constable, cost. McDowell, f.p. Festival B., Festival Hall, London 14 July 1959 (Minty, Gilpin, Dolin). Scenes in front of Buckingham Palace.

LOPEZ, Pilar, sister of La Argentinita, b. San Sebastian 1912. Spanish dancer and chor. Danced in her sister's Co. until 1945. Started her own Co., B. Español, 1946 in Madrid, originally with José Greco, Elvira Real (who danced Argentinita's rôles), Manolo Vargas, and Nila Amparo, which tours widely.

LOPOKOV, Andrei, b. St Petersburg 1898, d. Leningrad 1947. Russ. dancer and teacher. Son of an usher at Alexandrinski Th. and brother of Feodor L. and Lydia Lopokova. Studied under Oboukhoff, Fokine, and Gerdt at Maryinsky Sch. and entered Co. 1916. Became the chief character dancer and began teaching 1925. In 1927 appointed chief teacher of Character Dancing in the Leningrad Sch. and in 1936 of Ethnographic Dance. Hon. Artist R.S.F.S.R. (1939) created rôle of Nur-Ali in *Fountain of Bakchisarai* and Mercutio in *Romeo and Juliet*.

LOPOKOV, Feodor V., b. St Petersburg 1886, d. Leningrad 1972. Russ. dancer and chor. Brother of the above and of Lydia Lopokova. Graduated from Maryinsky Sch. 1905 and entered Co. To Moscow in 1909. With Sedowa and Legat in 1910 on tour to Paris, etc. Promoted to coryphée 1911 and joined Pavlova's Co. visiting America. Returned to Moscow and chor. *Mexican Tavern* (1916), *Sleep, Firebird* (m. Stravinsky, dec. Golovine). Chief chor. Kirov Th., Leningrad, from 1922. To Moscow again in 1926 and returned to Leningrad 1927, where he chor. *Ice Maiden* (m. Grieg), *The Bolt* (1931), *The Bright Stream* (1935), *Christmas Eve* (1938), *Taras Bulba* (1940), etc. Director of Ballet, Maly Th., Leningrad (1930–35). People's Artist R.S.F.S.R. (1956). Retired 1960, but in 1963 chor. Moussorgsky's *Pictures from an Exhibition* one of his most mature works. Wrote *Paths of the Ballet* (1916, published

1925), *Choreographic Confessions* (1971) and his autobiography *Sixty Years in Ballet*, 1966. The choreography of the Lilac Fairy in *Sleeping Beauty* (Royal B. and Kirov B.) is by him. He was an innovator, and chor. a controversial *Dance Symphony* in 1923 to Beethoven's Seventh Symphony. He also introduced the lift where the dancer is carried high above her partner's head. He was given the unique title Honoured Ballet Master.

LOPOKOVA, Lydia (Lady Keynes), b. St Petersburg 1891. Russ. dancer, sister of above. Graduated from Maryinsky Sch. 1909 and joined Diaghileff's Co. 1910. Shared rôle of Aurora in 1921 production of *Sleeping Princess* with Trefilova, Egorova, and Spessivtseva, cr. rôle of Mariuccia in *Good Humoured Ladies*, Can-Can Dancer in *Boutique Fantasque*, Street Dancer in *Beau Danube*, etc. For the Camargo Society, cr. rôle of Tango in *Façade*, and danced Swanilda in S. Wells *Coppélia* 1933. Mar. J. Maynard Keynes 1925 and with him founded Arts Th., Cambridge.

LORCIA, Suzanne, b. Paris 1902. Fr. dancer (pupil of Zambelli) who became étoile of the Paris Opéra 1931, retired 1950 and taught at the School.

LORD OF BURLEIGH, THE, ch. Ashton, m. Mendelssohn (arr. Edwin Evans, orch. G. Jacob), dec. G. Sheringham, f.p. charity perf. Carlton Th., Haymarket, London 15 Dec 1931 (Markova, Gould, Howard, Hyman, Argyle, Chappell, Gore, Ashton, Tudor). Characters from Tennyson's poems meet each other. Produced for Camargo Society at Savoy Th., London 28 Feb 1932. Revived 7 Dec. 1937 for S. Wells B. with dec. Derek Hill.

LORING, Eugene, b. Milwaukee 1914. Am. dancer and chor. Studied at the Sch. of American Ballet and danced in their earliest productions. Chor. *Billy the Kid*, *The Great American Goof*, *Silk Stockings*, *Funny Face*, etc. Now teaching. Chairman of Dance Sch. of Fine Arts, Univ. of California (Irvine). In 1970 founded the Am. Sch. of Dance, Los Angeles, and the Los Angeles Dance Th. of which he is director.

LORRAYNE, Vyvyan, b. Pretoria 1939. S. African dancer. Pupil of Salamon, de Villiers. Entered R. Ballet Sch. 1956 and the Royal B. 1957 (after dancing in the C. Garden Opera Ballet) as soloist becoming a principal 1967. Created the girl's rôle in Ashton's *Monotones* (1965).

LOSCH, Tilly (Countess of Caernarvon), b. Vienna c. 1904. Austrian dancer and actress. Studied at Vienna Opera Ballet Sch. First solo rôle in 1924 in *Schlagobers* (ch. Kröller, m. R. Strauss) in Vienna. Chor. Reinhardt's production of *Midsummer Night's Dream* in 1937. Chief dancer in Balanchine's Ballets 1933 and has acted in many plays (notably *The Miracle*) and films (*The Good Earth*). She was the original Dancing Anna in Balanchine's *Seven Deadly Sins* (1933).

LOST ILLUSIONS, ballet, ch. Zakharoff, m. Asafiev, dec. Dmitrieff, f.p. Kirov Th., Leningrad 1936 (Ulanova, Sergeyev). Balzac's *Splendeurs et Misères des Courtisanes.*

LOUIS XIV, b. St Germain-en-Laye 1638, d. Versailles 1715. The most magnificent of the Bourbon Kings, the Sun King of France. His love of dancing and court entertainments and his foundation of the Académie Royale de Danse make him one of the founders of the art of ballet. He first danced in public in 1645 and appeared as The Sun King in the *Ballet de la Nuit*, 23 Feb 1653 in the Petit Bourbon Palace.

LOUP, LE, ballet 1 act, ch. Petit, m. Dutilleux, dec. Carzou, f.p. B. de Paris, Empire Th., Paris 17 Mar 1953 (Violette Verdy, Petit). A girl falls in love with a wolf and they are hunted to death. Remarkable for its interpretation by Verdy and Carzou's forest scene. In repertoire of R. Danish B., Copenhagen 9 Dec 1967 (Flindt).

LOURÉ, Fr. dance in 6/8 time, probably so called because it was at first danced to the strains of the *louré*, or bagpipe. Of rustic origin, it was subsequently introduced to the court ballet and enjoyed a certain popularity in the mid-eighteenth century.

LOUTHER, William, b. N.Y. 1942. Am. modern dancer. Pupil of Popova, May O'Donnell, Graham, Schurr, Tudor. Joined May O'Donnell Dance Co. 1959, McKayle Co. 1960, Ailey Co. 1964, Graham Co. 1965, London Cont. Dance Th. 1969–71. Chor. *Vesalii Icones* (m. Maxwell Davies 1969), *Divertissement in the Playground of the Zodiac* (m. Quincey 1969). To Batsheva Dance Th. 1971 as artistic director.

LÖVENSKJOLD, Herman, b. Holdernjernvärk 1815, d. Copenhagen 1870. Dan. composer of the Danish version of *La Sylphide* (A. Bournonville 1836), also of his *The New Penelope* (1847) and *Fantasies* (1838).

LOVES OF MARS AND VENUS, THE, *ballet d'action* in 6 scenes. Book and chor. John Weaver, m. Symonds and Firbank, f.p. Drury Lane Th., London 2 Mar 1717. This is the first recorded *ballet d'action* and of great historic importance. Mars was danced by Louis Dupré, Venus by Mrs Santlow and Vulcan by Weaver. Extracts were recreated for Ballet for All (Royal B.), ch. Skeaping, m. Symonds, dec. D. Walker, f.p. Th. Royal, Lincoln 30 Jan 1969 (Jacqueline Lansley, Alison Howard, Sven Bradshaw).

LUBOVITCH, Lar, b. Chicago 1943. Am. dancer and chor. Studied at Juilliard Sch., N.Y. and with Sokolow and Graham. Danced in Graham Co. 1964, and 1967–69 with Harkness B. on production side.

313

Chor. several ballets, for Bat-Dor Dance Th., B. Rambert and Dutch Nat. B.

LUCA, Dia, b. Karansebes, Rumania 1912. Austrian dancer and chor. Pupil of Zina Luca, T. Birkmeyer, H. Kreutzberg. Danced in Volksoper, Vienna 1938–40, ballet mistress Brno 1942–44, at Raimund Th., Vienna 1954–55 and became ballet mistress of the Volksoper B. from 1955–72.

LUCIAN, b. Samosata, c. A.D. 125. Greek author of the time of Marcus Aurelius, whose *Dialogue* on the dance is a classic.

LUDLOW, Conrad, b. Hamilton, Mont. 1935. Am. dancer. Pupil of the Christensens. Joined San Francisco B. 1953, becoming principal 1955. Joined N.Y. City B. 1957, soloist 1960, leading soloist 1961.

LUIPART, Marcel, b. Mühlhausen (Mulhouse) 1912. Ger.-Fr. dancer and chor. Début 1933 in Düsseldorf. Joined Massine's Co. in Monte Carlo 1934. Danced at the Scala, Milan and Opera Reale, Rome, 1940. With Derra de Moroda's Co. during the War. Ballet master Munich 1948 and in 1960 became choreographer at Cologne. Chor. *Abraxas* (1948). From 1971 director of State Academy of Dance, Vienna.

LUISILLO (Luis Perez Davila), b. Mexico City 1928. Mexican dancer. Studied classical and Spanish dancing and was taken to Spain by Carmen Amaya, dancing in her Co. in 1948. He then formed his own Co. with his partner Teresa which toured America and broke up in 1954. He then formed another Co., Luisillo and his Theatre of Spanish Dance, which has toured the world. His dances are often dramatic, e.g. *The Blind Man, The Prisoner and the Rose, Sanlucar de Barrameda* etc. Danced in London 1948 and 1961.

LUKOM, Elena, b. 1891, d. Leningrad 1970. Russ. dancer. Graduated from Maryinsky Sch. 1909 and danced in Diaghileff's Co. in Paris 1910. Soloist of Maryinsky B. 1912 and made ballerina 1918—the last ballerina of the Maryinsky and the first of the Soviet ballet. She cr. the rôle of Tao-Hoa in the Leningrad *The Red Poppy*. Became *repetiteur* of the Kirov Th. and director of the *classe de perfection* 1953–65. Hon. Artist R.S.F.S.R. 1960. Author of *My Work in Ballet* 1940. With her partner Boris Shavrov she was the first to use the high and acrobatic lifts so characteristic of the Soviet ballet.

LULLY, Jean Baptiste, b. Florence 1632, d. Paris 1687. It. composer who became the composer of dance music to Louis XIV in 1653 and director of the court orchestra. He was the King's favourite and was one of the originators of the Académie Royale de Musique of which he became Director in 1672. He collaborated in his operas and ballets with Quinault, Berain, Beauchamp, Molière, and Racine. Among the ballets he composed are *George Dandin* (1668), *Le Triomphe de l'Amour* (1681), *Le Temple de la Paix* (1685). He revolutionized the *ballets de la cour*, replacing the slow stately airs by lively allegros 'as rapid as the pirouettes of the danseuses'. Among Directors of the Paris Opéra, he was remarkable in that he did not take a mistress from the corps de ballet.

LUMBYE, Hans Christian, b. Copenhagen 1810, d. there 1874. Dan. composer of many Bournonville ballets, incl. *La Ventana* (1854), *Napoli* (1842), Called 'the Nordic Strauss'.

LUMLEY, Benjamin, b. 1811, d. Kensington 1875. Eng. lawyer and author. Superintended finances of Her Majesty's Th., London 1836–41 and took over the management 1842 until the theatre closed 1858 (when he returned to the law). He produced the *Pas de Quatre*, among other ballets, in 1845, and engaged Jenny Lind. Published *Reminiscences* 1864.

LUNEFULDE LUCINDA (Capricious Lucinda), ballet 1 act, ch. Niels Bjorn Larsen, m. Jersild, dec. Refn, f.p. R. Dan. B., Copenhagen 9 Oct 1954 (Sand, Björnsson, Williams, Larsen).

ЛХУ, the Russian abbreviation for the Leningrad Sch. (i.e. the Maryinsky, later Kirov and from 1957 the A. Vaganova Sch.).

LYNHAM, Deryck, b. Maisons Laffitte, France, 1913, d. Lausanne 1951. Eng. writer on the ballet. Educated in France. One of the founders of the Ballet Guild and the London Archives of the Dance. Author of *Ballet Then and Now* (1947), and *The Chevalier Noverre* (1950).

LYNNE, Gillian, b. Bromley 1926. Eng. dancer. Studied under Madeleine Sharp, R.A.D., and O. Ripman. Début Arts Th. B. 1940. Joined S. Wells B. 1943, becoming a principal dancer. Left 1951 to become principal dancer at Palladium and has appeared in films and in musicals (notably in *Can-Can*). She is now a producer of musicals, operas etc. in London. Took her own group of dancers (Collages) to Edinburgh Festival 1963. Chor. ballet in Tippett's *The Midsummer Marriage*, C. Garden 1968.

LYONNAIS, Marie, b. Strasbourg, Fr. dancer at the Paris Opéra (1740 to 1767) who, with Mlle Lany and Mlle Carville, shared roles with Camargo. She was the first to make a success of the difficult step the *gargouillade* (in *Zoroastre* 1749).

LYRE, EN, a port de bras in which the arms are held en couronne but with the hands overlapping each other.

M

MAAR, Lisl, b. Vienna 1942. Austrian dancer. Pupil of Hamilton, Plucis, Bon, Hiden, Ursuliak at Staatsoper Sch. Joined Vienna Staatsoper B. 1956, becoming soloist 1966.

MABILLE, BAL, famous open-air dancing place in Paris of the last century. Founded 1840 by Charles Mabille in the (present) Avenue Montaigne, it was first the resort of servant girls but later it became very fashionable. The can-can and polka were the chief dances of the exhibition dancers, among whom were La Reine Pomaré, Céleste Mogador, Rose Pompon, Alice la Provençale, and Rigolboche. Among the men were Brididi, Chicard and Valentin le Désossé, who is the can-can dancer in *Boutique Fantasque*. It declined in the 1870s and finally closed in 1885. Mabille's two sons were dancers. Charles eloped with and married Augusta Maywood, and Auguste was assistant ballet master at the Opéra and chor. *Nisida* (1848) and the roller-skating ballet in *Le Prophète* (1849).

MACARRONA, LA (Juana Vargas), famous Sp. *flamenco* dancer, of the period 1900–20 and a star of the *café-chantant* era.

MCBRIDE, Patricia, b. Teaneck 1942. Am. dancer. Pupil of Sch. of Am. B. Eglevsky B. Co. 1958, N.Y. City B. 1959 becoming soloist 1960, ballerina 1961. Often partnered by Villella. Mar. J. P. Bonnefous.

MACDONALD, Brian, b. Montreal 1928. Canadian dancer and chor. Pupil of Crevier and Leese. Joined Nat. B. of Canada on its inception, 1951 to 1953. Chor. several works for television with the R. Winnipeg B. In 1962 chor. *Time Out of Mind* for Joffrey B. and in 1963 *Prothalamion* for the Norwegian B. Director of R. Swedish B. 1964–65. Chor. *Rose Latulippe* for R. Winnipeg B. 1966 and in 1967 succeeded Skibine as Director of the Harkness B. Resigned in 1968 to mount musicals etc. Mar. Annette Wiedersheim-Paul 1965. Director of Batsheva Dance Th. 1971–72.

MCDONALD, Elaine, b. Tadcaster 1943. Eng. dancer. Pupil of Louise Browne and Royal B. Sch. Joined Gore's London Ballet 1962 and Western Th. B. (now Scot. Th. B.) 1964 becoming a principal dancer.

MCDOWELL, Norman, b. Belfast 1931. Eng. dancer and designer. Pupil of Molly Lake, S. Wells Sch., Volkova etc. Joined S. Wells Op. B. In 1951 joined Orig. Ballets Russes, then B. Rambert, Festival B. and B. der Lagerlande, Amsterdam, where he cr. the eponymous rôle of *The Witch Boy* (J. Carter 1956). Designed *L'Homme et sa Vie* for B. Workshop 1951 and since then has designed some forty ballets (many for

Jack Carter) incl. *Lola Montez* for B. Rambert, *Witch Boy* for Dutch Nat. B., Festival B., Colon Th., Buenos Aires, *London Morning, Beatrix, Sleeping Beauty, Coppélia* etc. for Festival B., *Swan Lake* for Colon Th., Buenos Aires etc. In 1964 formed the London Dance Th. (q.v.) and in 1965 was a director of Festival B.

MCGEHEE, Helen, b. Lynchburg, Va. Am. dancer. Student of modern dance at Randolph-Macon Univ. and joined Graham Co. 1944, becoming a leading dancer and creating rôles in *Acrobats of God, Clytemnestra, Phaedra* etc. Has chor. several ballets and teaches at Graham Sch. and Juilliard Col.

MCGRATH, Barry, b. Dartford 1941. Eng. dancer. Pupil of Legat Sch. Joined Festival B. 1958 becoming soloist 1961. To Zürich B. 1964–68, as principal. Joined Royal B. 1968 as principal.

MCKAYLE, Donald, b. N.Y. 1930. Am. dancer. Pupil of Graham, Cunningham etc. Danced in most of the Am. modern Cos. and has his own group for which he chor. the ballets. Teaches in N.Y. and in 1963 won the Capezio Award. Has also chor. and danced in Broadway musicals.

MACHOV, Sasha, b. Zhor 1903, d. Prague 1951. Czech dancer and ballet master. Was a dancer in Czech theatres 1927–39. Worked in Athens and was regisseur in Brno 1945–46. He worked in London in 1946 and mounted *The Bartered Bride* for the S. Wells Opera at S. Wells Th., using the S. Wells Th. B. in the dancing scenes (which he also chor.). Returned to Czechoslovakia the same year and became director of the Prague Nat. B. until his self-inflicted death.

MACLEARY, Donald, b. Glasgow 1937. Scottish dancer. Pupil of Sheila Ross 1950–51. Entered S. Wells Sch. 1951. Joined S. Wells Th. B. 1954, becoming soloist 1955, principal dancer Royal B. 1959 and partner of Beriosova.

MACMILLAN, Kenneth, b. Dunfermline 1929. Eng. dancer and chor. Studied S. Wells Sch. Joined S. Wells Th. B. on its formation 1946. To S. Wells B. 1948. Returned to S. Wells Th. B. 1952. Chor. *Somnambulism* (1953) and *Laiderette* (1954) for S. Wells chor. group, and *Danses Concertantes* and *House of Birds* for S. Wells Th. B. 1955. For S. Wells B. *Noctambules* (1956), *The Burrow* (1958), *Agon* (1958), *Baiser de la Fée* (1960), *The Invitation* (1961). For Am. Ballet Th., *Winter's Eve* (1957), *Diversions* (1961), *Rite of Spring* (1962), *Symphony* (1963), *Romeo and Juliet* (1965—his first full-length ballet). He was Resident choreographer of the Royal B. 1965–66 and in 1966 he was appointed Director of Ballet at the Deutsches Oper, Berlin, where he chor. *Anastasia* (1967), *Sleeping Beauty* (1967), *Olympiad* (1968). For the Stuttgart B. chor. *Las Hermanas* (1963), *Song of the Earth*

(1965), *Miss Julie* (1970). He has staged his ballets in many countries. In 1970 he was appointed joint director of the Royal Ballet (with John Field who subsequently resigned leaving him as sole director in 1971). He chor. *Checkpoint* (m. Gerhard) for Touring Royal B. 1970, and *Anastasia* (in three acts) 1970 for Royal B. In 1972 chor. *Ballade* (m. Fauré), *The Poltroon* (m. Maros) for Touring R. B. and *Trio* (m. Prokofieff) for Royal B. In 1973 produced their new *Sleeping Beauty*.

MACRAE, Heather, b. Melbourne 1940. Austral. dancer. Pupil of Laurel Martyn. Joined Borovansky B. 1960, London B. 1962, Australian B. 1963 as soloist and ballet mistress from 1969.

MADAME CHRYSANTHÈME, ballet 1 act, ch. Ashton, m. Rawsthorne, dec. I. Lambert, f.p. S. Wells B., C. Garden 1 Apr 1955 (Fifield, Grant). Japanese ballet based on novel by P. Loti.

MADSEN, Egon, b. Ringe, Denmark 1942. Dan. dancer. Pupil of Bartholin, Frandsen, Volkova, Hiden, Cranko. Joined Pantomime Th., Scandinavian B. 1959. Entered Stuttgart B. 1961 becoming soloist 1962, and now principal dancer, creating many rôles in Cranko's ballets. Guest artist in Zürich 1963.

MADSEN, Jørn, b. Copenhagen 1939. Dan. dancer. Entered R. Danish B. Sch. 1949, joined Co. 1958, solodancer 1961. Guest artist Royal B. 1965.

MAD TRISTAN, ballet 2 sc., ch. Massine, m. Wagner, dec. Dali, f.p. Ballet International 15 Dec 1944 (Moncion). A surrealist ballet.

MAFLEUROY, Clotilde-Augustine (Mlle Clotilde), b. Paris 1776, d. there 1826. Fr. dancer who was a premier sujet at the Opéra from 1810 until she retired in 1818. She was much admired by Castil-Blaze, who said that she was the most graceful woman at the Opéra for fifty-four years. Noverre said that her technique was perfect. She was much troubled by emitting an unpleasant smell which she was unable to conceal even with musk. This made it impossible for her to obtain a dancing partner. In 1802 she mar. the composer Boieldieu. It was an unhappy marriage and he soon left her.

MAGALLANES, Nicolas, b. Camargo, Chihuahua, Mexico 1922. Am. dancer. Studied School of Am. Ballet. With Ballet Caravan 1941. Littlefield Ballet 1942, B. Russe de Monte Carlo 1943–47. Joined Ballet Society 1946 and became a principal dancer of the N.Y. City Ballet. Cr. chief rôle in *Orpheus, Illuminations*, etc.

MAGIC FLUTE, THE, ballet 1 act, ch. Ivanov, m. Drigo, f.p. Maryinsky Th., St Petersburg 23 Ap 1893 (Anna Johansson) (after having had a student performance a few weeks before). The ballet was also in the repertoire of Pavlova's Co. It has no connexion with Mozart's opera.

MAGRIEL, Paul, b. Riga 1906. Am. writer on ballet. One of the editors of *Dance Index* (1942). Author of a number of monographs for Ballet Society 1946–48, and of *Bibliography of Dancing* 1936. First curator of Dance Archives in Museum of Modern Art (1939–42).

MAHALLI DANCERS OF IRAN, a national company of Persian folk dancers, founded by Robert de Warren in Teheran 1971. There are about 60 dancers and they perform regional dances collected by de Warren from Kurdistan, Baluchistan, Torbatjam etc. and Whirling Dervishes. They performed at Persepolis during the 2,500th anniversary celebrations of the Persian Monarchy in 1971 and at the opening of the Kennedy Center, Washington in 1971. First performed in London at Sadler's Wells 1972.

MAILLOT, Fr. for tights (and for bathing costume) named after a costumier of the Paris Opéra in the nineteenth century (d. c. 1838).

MAIOCCHI, Gilda, b. Milan 1928. It. dancer. Entered Scala Sch., Milan, graduated 1946, Passo d'Addio 1947, ballerina 1953. Now ballet Mistress.

MAÎTRE (MAÎTRESSE) DE BALLET, Ballet Master (Mistress) (Ger. Ballettmeister, -meisterin). Until recently a person attached to a company of dancers, to a theatre or, in the eighteenth century and before, to a Royal Court, who composed, arranged, and produced dances and ballets, and was responsible for taking or supervising classes to maintain and develop the technique of the dancers entrusted to him (her).

Of recent years it has come to designate the person responsible for the training of the dancers and taking of rehearsals, whilst he or she who composes or arranges ballets has become known as the choreographer, choreographer, or *choréauteur*.

MAKAROV, Askold, b. 1925. Russ. dancer. Joined Kirov B., Leningrad 1942 becoming principal male dancer and receiving Stalin Prize. People's Artist of R.S.F.S.R. 1954. Cr. rôle in *Native Fields* and the title rôle in *Spartacus* (1956). Mar. Petrova.

MAKAROVA, Natalia, b. Leningrad 1940. Russ. dancer. Trained at Kirov Sch. Graduated to Kirov B. 1959, becoming soloist. Created rôle of Beautiful Maiden in Jacobsen's *Country of Wonder* 1967. Danced her first *Giselle* at Covent Garden, London 1961. Varna Gold Medal 1965. First *Cinderella* in Chicago 1964, first Aurora 1968. Hon. Artist R.S.F.S.R. On 4 Sept 1970, the penultimate day of the season of the Kirov B. at R. Festival Hall, London she walked out of the theatre and asked for asylum in England, which was granted. She gave two television performances in London and then joined Am. Ballet Th., Nov 1970. Her *Giselle* is considered by many to be the best interpretation of the time. See also SERGEYEV. In 1972 she made her first appearance as guest ballerina of Royal B. (*Giselle, Swan Lake*).

MALAGUEÑA, a Sp. dance similar to the *fandango*.

MALENA, LA, b. Jaen 1878. Sp. gypsy *flamenco* dancer who came to Paris in the Company of Argentina, and danced with Estampio.

MALHEURS DE SOPHIE, LES, ballet, ch. Quinault, m. Françaix, dec. Hugo, f.p. Paris Opéra 25 Feb 1948 (Clavier, Bari). Clavier was taken from the corps de ballet to cr. the rôle at the age of 14.

MALY THEATRE (Little Theatre) Leningrad, was before 1918 the Imperial Mikhailovsky Theatre. A ballet Co. was installed there in 1932 under Feodor Lopokov. In 1936 Leonid Lavrovsky took over for a year. Boris Fenster went direct from the Leningrad Sch. to the Maly Th. in 1936 and was chief choreographer from 1945 to 1953. It acquired its name in 1926. I. Belsky was chief chor. 1963, Vinogradov 1972.

MAM'ZELLE ANGOT, ballet, 3 sc., based on the opera by Lecocq, ch. Massine, m. Lecocq, dec. Doboujinsky, f.p. B. Th., Met. Op. N.Y. 10 Oct 1943 (Massine, Nora Kaye, Eglevsky, Hightower). Recreated by Massine for S. Wells B., C. Garden (Grant, Fonteyn, Somes, Shearer) 26 Nov 1947, with dec. by Derain. A version of the operetta *La Fille de Madame Angot*. Also in repertoire of Australian B., dec. Derain, f.p. Princes Th., Melbourne 9 Dec 1971 (Aldous).

MANCHEGA, see SEGUIDILLA.

MANCHESTER, P. W. (Miss), b. London. Cont. Eng. writer on the dance. Secretary Ballet Rambert 1944–46. Founded and edited magazine *Ballet Today* 1946–51. Managing Editor and later Editor of the American *Dance News* 1951–69. Author of *Vic-Wells; a Ballet Progress* (1942) and (with Iris Morley) *The Rose and the Star* (1949). Co-editor (with Anatole Chujoy) of the *Dance Encyclopedia* (1967). From 1969 adjunct-professor at Univ. of Cincinnati College of Music, teaching dance-history.

MANÈGE (term borrowed from the circus), an imaginary circle bounding the whole stage, so that tours en manège indicates that the dancer executes the turns while travelling right round the circumference of the stage. It. *in ruota*.

MANIPURI, in Hindu dancing, the style of north-east India. The dances are in the form of dance-drama (supported by dialogues and songs) and many dancers participate. It is mainly lyrical and lighter than the other Indian styles. See also KATHAK, KATHAKALI, and BHARATA NATYA.

MANON LESCAUT, ballet in 3 acts, 5 sc., ch. Aumer, m. Halévy, dec. Ciceri, cost. Lecomte, Lami, Duponchel, f.p. Paris Opéra 3 May 1830

(Mostessu, Ferdinand and, in a minor rôle, Marie Taglioni). The Prévost novel.

MANZOTTI, Luigi, b. Milan 1838, d. there 1905. It. mime dancer and chor. After fourteen years in Rome he went back to La Scala, Milan, and ch. many spectacular ballets there (in some of which horses and elephants appeared on the stage) notably *Sieba* (1876), *Excelsior* (m. Marenco, f.p. 11 Jan 1881, this ballet was given in London 1885 with Cecchetti in the cast), *Amor* (17 Feb 1886, m. Marenco), *Sport* (1897).

MARBLE MAIDEN, THE, ballet by Vernoy de Saint George, ch. Albert, m. Adam, f.p. Drury Lane Th., London 27 Sept 1845 (Adèle Dumilâtre, L. Petipa). This ballet resembles *La Fille de Marbre* and *Alma*.

MARCEAU, Marcel, b. Strasbourg 1923 of Polish parents. Fr. mime. Pupil of Étienne Decroux. Started his own small Co. 1947, won Prix Debureau 1949. He now tours the world with his group (his brother Alain is his assistant), maintaining the traditions of Debureau. A feature of his programmes are the escapades of his character 'Bip'.

MARCEL, M., famous Fr. dancing master of the eighteenth century who took himself and his art very seriously. He was the supreme teacher of the minuet. To an agile English pupil, who had just done a succession of very complicated steps, he said 'Monsieur, l'on saute dans les autres pays; mais on ne danse qu'à Paris'.

MARCHAND, Colette, b. Paris 1925. Fr. dancer. Studied Paris Opéra, which she left and, with Perrault, joined the Metropolitan B. in England as ballerina 1947. Principal dancer in Petit's Ballets de Paris (1948) and made a great success when the Co. visited N.Y., where she remained to dance in a musical and make a film *Moulin Rouge* (1953). Rejoined Petit's Co. 1953. Now appears in musicals and as a guest ballerina.

MARCHIOLLI, Sonja, b. Zagreb 1945. Yugoslav dancer. Pupil of State B. Sch., Zagreb, and entered Zagreb B. 1962. Joined Dutch Nat. N. 1966, with her husband Ivan Kramer, becoming soloist 1968.

MARDI GRAS, ballet, ch. Andrée Howard, m. Salzedo, dec. Hugh Stevenson, f.p. S. Wells Th. B., S. Wells Th. 26 Nov 1946 (Heaton, Nerina, Britton, Kersley). A young girl in a carnival. As the Circus Dancer, Nadia Nerina was first noticed by the public.

MARGUERITE AND ARMAND, ballet, ch. Ashton, m. Liszt (*Sonata in B minor* and *Lugubre Gondole*), dec. Beaton, f.p. Royal B., C. Garden 12 Mar 1963 (Fonteyn, Nureyev, Edwards, Somes). Dumas' *La Dame aux Camélias*. It was the first ballet created for Nureyev after he left Russia.

MARIA, Mlle (Maria Jacob), b. Paris c. 1818. Fr. Jewish dancer at the

Paris Opéra 1837–49. She created leading rôles in *La Jolie Fille de Gand*, *Le Diable à Quatre*, *Paquita* etc., danced *La Fille Mal Gardée* in 1835 and was the first to dance the polka on the Paris Opéra stage (see Polka). In the opera *Jerusalem*, fearing that her dress was about to catch fire from the footlights, she leapt into the orchestra pit. She married the Baron d'Henneville and on her retirement Janin wrote 'Adieu, Maria the dancer . . . you have been all that you should have been, good, simple, not over-vain, nor ambitious, nor clamorous—in short, charming; and your bounding companies will not fill your place for some time to come'.

MARIEMMA, b. Valladolid, c. 1920. Sp. dancer excelling in the pure classical Sp. style. Studied in Paris under Goncharova of the Th. du Châtelet, where she became principal dancer of the children's ballet at the age of 11. Studied Sp. dancing under Estampio. Danced London 1948.

MARIE JEANNE (Pelus), b. N.Y. 1920. Am. dancer. Studied at Am. Sch. of Ballet. Joined B. Caravan 1937–40. Orig. B. Russe 1942, de Cuevas 1944. A leading Balanchine dancer. Retired 1954 to teach. Author of *Yankee Ballerina* and *Opera Ballerina*.

MARIÉS DE LA TOUR EIFFEL, LES, ballet 1 act by Cocteau, ch. Börlin, m. Auric, Poulenc, Milhaud, Honegger, Taillefer, dec. Lagut, cost. J. Hugo, f.p. B. Suédois, Th. des Ch. Élysées, Paris 18 June 1921 (Ari, Figoni, Kaj Smith, Vahlander, Eltorp). A surrealist ballet.

MARIQUITA, b. Algiers in 1830s, d. Paris 1922. Fr. dancer and chor. In 1845 played at the Funambules with Deburau. Became maîtresse de ballet at the Gaîté Th., Paris, and later at the Folies-Bergère. From 1898 to 1920 was maîtresse de ballet at the Opéra Comique, and in 1896 chor. *Javotte* for which Saint-Saëns wrote the music.

MARK, TO (marquer), when a dancer indicates a movement or step by a slight movement of the hands, arms, or legs without executing it in full, as in a rehearsal.

MARKOVA, Dame, Alicia (Marks) b. London 1910. Studied under Astafieva, Legat, Cecchetti and Celli. Joined Diaghileff's Co. 1925, becoming ballerina and remaining until the Co. broke up in 1929. Danced for Camargo Soc. and became ballerina of B. Rambert (B. Club) and Vic-Wells B. until 1935—the first English ballerina. Ballerina of Markova-Dolin Co. 1935–38. In U.S.A. 1938 to 1948 as ballerina of B. Russe de Monte Carlo and (1941–45) Ballet Theatre, etc. Returned to S. Wells B. 1948 as guest artist at C. Garden. Re-formed the Markova-Dolin group in England 1949, which became the Festival B. Left it in 1952 and danced in U.S.A., returning to Royal B. as guest 1953. One of the greatest of dancers, with the light, aerial style of Taglioni. Cr. countless rôles, including the Polka in *Façade*, *Rake's Progress*, *Haunted Ballroom*, etc., and her *Giselle*, *Swan Lake*, and *Sylphides* set standards by which other dancers are judged. Her association with Dolin in pas-de-deux work is part of the history of ballet. Awarded C.B.E. 1958. Wrote *Giselle and I* (1960). Her final appearance was with Festival B. 1962 and she retired at the end of that year. Appointed director of Met. Op. Ballet, N.Y. 1963 until 1969. Created D.B.E. 1963. D. Mus. Leicester Univ. 1966. In 1971 appointed Professor of Ballet and Performing Arts at the Univ. of Cincinatti Conservatory of Music.

MARKOVA-DOLIN BALLET, founded by Markova and Dolin in London in 1935, backed by the late Mrs L. Henderson. Toured Europe and England until 1938. Among its ballets, besides the classics, were *Les Biches*, *David*, *Pas de Quatre*, *La Bien Aimée*. It re-formed in America in 1945. Among its original dancers were Keith Lester, Franklin, Algeranoff, Prudence Hyman, Molly Lake, Kathleen Crofton, Diana Gould. Ended 1948.

MARKOVIC, Vjera, b. Zagreb 1931. Yugoslav dancer. Pupil of Orlova, Froman, Roje and Mme Legat. Entered Zagreb Nat. B. 1945, becoming leading soloist 1949. Danced in Rome, Basel, Stuttgart, Vienna Volksoper and was in Massine's ballet in Nervi 1960. In 1970 ballet mistress of the ballet in Zagreb. Mar. A. Koellner.

MARKOVSKY, John, b. Riga 1944. Latvian dancer. Trained in Riga and graduated from Kirov Sch., Leningrad 1962 and entered Co. Danced Romeo (with Minchenok as Juliet) at Kirov 1967. In Kirov film of *Swan Lake* (1968) danced Prince to E. Evteyeva's Odette-Odile.

MARKS, Bruce, b. N.Y. 1937. Am. dancer. Studied modern dance and then a pupil of Craske and Tudor. Joined Met. Op. B. 1956 becoming soloist 1958. Joined Am. Ballet Th. as a leading dancer 1961. Guest artist R. Swedish B. 1963–64 and Festival B. 1965. Mar. Toni Lander 1966. Danced with R. Danish B. 1966 as guest and joined as a principal dancer 1971.

MARLIÈRE, Andrée, b. Antwerp 1934. Belgian dancer. Studied at S. Wells Sch. 1948, Messerer 1960–62, V. Gsovsky 1962–66. Joined Berlin B. 1957–58, Babilée's Co. 1958, B. du XXme Siècle 1959–64, Düsseldorf B. 1964–66. Ballerina R. Flemish B., Antwerp since 1966 and teacher of B. van Vlaanderen from 1970.

MARTENY, Fred, b. Prague 1931. Czech dancer and chor. Pupil of Prague Conservatorium. In 1949 soloist of Vienna Volksoper B., soloist Strasbourg, and Marseille. Ballet master in Hildesheim 1963–65, in

Koblenz 1965–66, in Graz 1967–70. To Marseille B. 1970–72 as assistant ballet-master. In 1972 teacher of B. Th. Contemporain.

MARTIN, Jean Baptiste, Fr. artist who designed for the Opéra in Paris in the eighteenth century. Among his ballets were *La Provençale*, *Psyche*, and the *Ballet des Éléments*.

MARTIN, John, b. Louisville 1893. Am. critic of the ballet in the *New York Times* 1927–62. Published *The Modern Dance* (1933), *American Dancing* (1936), *Introduction to the Dance* (1939), *The Dance* (1946), *World Book of Modern Ballet* (1952) etc. The most influential ballet critic in America in his time.

MARTIN, Keith, b. Doncaster 1943. Eng. dancer. Pupil of Louise Browne and Royal B. Sch. Entered Royal B. 1961 becoming soloist. From 1971 principal dancer of Pennsylvania B.

MARTINEZ, Menia, b. Havana 1929. Cuban dancer. Pupil of F. Alonso, Pares, and in Russia of Balticheva, Pushkin, Jordan, Semeyonova. Joined B. Alicia Alonso 1952–55, guest ballerina of Bolshoi and Kirov B. while studying there 1955–59, 1965–66. Joined Nat. B. of Cuba as ballerina 1960–69, Béjart's B. du XXme Siècle 1969. Chor. *Imagenes* for Cuba B. 1963. Guest ballerina B. de Wallonie 1972. Mar. Jorge Lefèbre.

MARTINS, Peter, b. Copenhagen 1946. Dan. dancer. Pupil of Stanley Williams at R. Danish B. Sch. Entered R. Danish B. becoming solo-dancer. In 1967 he danced *Apollo*, at short notice, for the N.Y. City B. at the Edinburgh Festival and then joined that company permanently. Guest artist Festival B. 1970 and 1972.

MARTIN-VISCOUNT (formerly Martin), William, b. Winnipeg 1940. Canad. dancer. Pupil of Spohr, Hardie, Turner, Addison. Joined R. Winnipeg B. 1958, Festival B. 1962, rejoined R. Winnipeg B. 1962 becoming soloist. Also studied in Russia. Joffrey B. 1969, B. de Rio de Janeiro 1970. Now teaches in Fort Worth.

MARTYN, Laurel, b. Brisbane 1916. Austral. dancer and chor. Won Genée Gold Medal, R.A.D. Studied S. Wells Sch. and danced (as Laurel Gill) in S. Wells B. 1935–38. Joined Borovansky B. as principal dancer 1947. In 1948 became Director and teacher of Melbourne Ballet Guild. Now Director of Victoria B.

MARTYRE DE SAINT-SEBASTIEN, LE, ballet, ch. I. Rubinstein, m. Debussy, dec. Bakst, f.p. Ida Rubinstein Co., Th. du Châtelet, Paris 22 May 1911 (Ida Rubinstein). It was first given at the Paris Opéra, ch. Fokine dec. Bakst 17 June 1922, (I. Rubinstein). With chor. Lifar, dec. Labisse it was given at the Paris Opéra 8 Feb. 1957 (L. Tcherina). The libretto of this cantata-ballet is by d'Annunzio.

MARUSYA BOGUSLAVKA, ballet, ch. Sergei Sergeeff, m. Svechnikov, dec.

Volchenko, f.p. Opera House, Kieff 23 Nov 1951 (L. Gerasimchuk, E. Potapova, N. Apukhtin, Ivashchenko). Filmed in *Concert of Ukrainian Stars*.

MARYINSKY THEATRE, see KIROV THEATRE, its present name.

MASCARADE, or MASQUERADE, entertainment popular in the fourteenth and fifteenth centuries consisting of a procession of decorated, and usually allegorical, cars from which costumed actors declaimed laudatory poems as they filed past the person to be honoured. In Florence the masquerades were known as *trionfi, carri* and *canti carnascialeschi* in which masked figures went singing and dancing through the streets. In England a similar form of entertainment was the mumming or disguising, in which masked figures would appear, on foot or in allegorical cars, frequently preceded by torchbearers and musicians, and perform with song and dance. In time the miming or disguising became a regular feature of Christmas and Shrovetide festivities until 1513, when it began to be known as a maske or masque.

MASKS. In the seventeenth and eighteenth centuries it was customary for dancers to wear masks; winds would have masks with puffed cheeks, fauns would wear brown masks and tritons masks of green, while grotesque characters would have two faces. Noverre in his letters urged, amongst many reforms of costume, the 'burning of hideous masks' and, in 1773, Gaetano Vestris, being unable to appear in his usual rôle in Rameau's opera *Castor et Pollux*, was replaced by M. Gardel, who refused to dance unless he was allowed to discard his wig and mask; the innovation was so successful that, thereafter, principal dancers abandoned the mask, although until the end of the century masks were frequently worn by the corps de ballet. In the contemporary ballet masks have occasionally been introduced to create a particular effect, as for the nightmarish monsters of Jooss's *Pandora*, the insects in Howard's *Spider's Banquet*, and the Rout in Helpmann's *Comus*. In de Valois's *Gods Go A-begging* the masks for the Negro boys help to create a sense of period, and effective use of masks has been made in Jooss's *Green Table*.

MASQUE, or MASKE. As the mumming or disguising became more elaborate, scenery was introduced and the details of production received more attention until by 1513 it was known as a maske or masque. The masque, influenced by the *Ballet Comique de la Reine* and the Fr. court ballet, attained to its greatest splendour in the reign of James I. The contents of the royal exchequer were lavished on entertainments commissioned from Ben Jonson, Francis Beaumont, Thomas Campion, and others to music by composers such as Purcell and Eccles whilst much of the scenery was due to Inigo Jones. The

English court masque in turn influenced the Fr. Opera-Ballet from which Classical ballet as we know it was evolved.

MASQUES, LES, ballet 1 act, ch. Ashton, m. Poulenc, dec. Fedorovitch, f.p. B. Rambert, Mercury Th., London 5 Mar 1933 (Markova, Argyle, Ashton, Gore). The dec. and cost. were black and white only.

MASON, Edward C., b. Coogee 1929, d. London 1965. Austral. dancer and writer. Pupil of X. Borovansky, Kellaway, Northcote. Assistant Editor *Dance and Dancers* 1957–62, Associate Editor 1963–64. Ballet critic of *Time and Tide* 1959–63, *Glasgow Herald* and *Sunday Telegraph* 1963–65. Founded Ballet Bookshop, in Cecil Court, London 1959.

MASON, Kenneth, b. Darenth 1942. Eng. dancer. Studied at Royal B. Sch. Entered C. Garden Opera B. 1959, Royal B. 1960 becoming soloist 1968. Left Royal B. 1970.

MASON, Monica, b. Johannesburg 1941. S. African dancer. Pupil of Inglestone, Brooking and Royal B. Sch. Joined Royal B. 1958 becoming a principal in 1967. Created the rôle of the Chosen Virgin in Mac-Millan's *Rite of Spring* 1962.

MASSACRE DES AMAZONS, ballet, ch. Charrat, m. Semenoff, dec. Bazaine, f.p. Charrat's Co., Grenoble 24 Dec 1951 (Charrat, Bon, Oukhtomsky).

MASS FOR OUR TIME (Messe Pour le Temps Present), ballet, ch. Béjart, m. Indian, Pierre Henry, chants, speaking etc. dec. Roustan and Bernard, f.p. Béjart's B. du XXme Siècle, Avignon 3 Aug 1967 (Laura Proenca, Paolo Bortolozzi, Jorge Donn). A 'ceremony in 9 episodes' interpreting present day life.

MASSINE, Leonide, b. Moscow 1895. Russ. dancer and chor. Studied at Imp. School, Moscow, graduated 1912. In 1913 Diaghileff visited Moscow and picked him out as a possible successor to Nijinsky, with whom he had then broken. He joined Diaghileff's Co. and worked with Cecchetti, having his first important rôle in Fokine's *Legend of Joseph* in 1914. In 1915 he chor. his first ballet *Soleil de Nuit*. Thenceforth he became Diaghileff's greatest chor. after Fokine. As a dancer has immense personality, riveting the audience's attention even when motionless, and his forte is in character rôles. Has created over fifty ballets, of which the following are notable: for Diaghileff's Co., *Les Femmes de Bonne Humeur* (1917), *Parade* (1917), *Contes Russes* (1917), *La Boutique Fantasque* (1919), *Le Tricorne* (1919), *Le Sacre du Printemps* (2nd version 1920), *Les Matelots* (1925), *Zéphire et Flore* (1925), *Le Pas d'Acier* (1927), *Ode* (1928). In 1926 he went to America for three years and appeared at the Roxy Cinema in ballets which he staged there. When de Basil's Co. started, among the ballets he chor. for them were *Le Beau Danube* (1933), *Scuola di Ballo* (1933), *Jeux d'Enfants* (1933), *Union Pacific* (1934), and the great symphonic ballets (thereby breaking new ground and causing much controversy, finally settled in his favour), *Les Présages* (1933), *Choreartium* (1933), and *Symphonie Fantastique* (1936). He also made ballets for Cochran's productions in London, for the Ida Rubinstein Co. in Paris and at the Scala, Milan. He worked for most of the American Cos. during the war, creating among others, *Rouge et Noir, Capriccio Espagnol* (1939), *The New Yorker* (1940), *Aleko* (1942), *Mam'zelle Angot* (1943). In 1946 he mounted *La Boutique Fantasque* and *Le Tricorne* for the S. Wells B. at C. Garden and danced in them himself. In 1948 he restaged *Mam'zelle Angot* for them. He has also mounted his most famous ballets for companies all over the world. He appeared in the films *The Red Shoes* (1948), *Tales of Hoffmann* (1951), *Carosello Napoletano* (1954), for which he also made the dances, and many others. In 1960 he formed a large ballet company, Balletto Europeo, which danced at the Nervi and Edinburgh Festivals. His daughter, Tatiana, and his son also dance (the latter, Lorca M., is also a chor.). From 1969 Massine became a guest teacher of choreography at the Royal Ballet School. Wrote his autobiography *My Life in Ballet* (1969). Mar. Vera Savina, Eugenia Delorova, Tatiana Orlova.

MASSINE, Lorca, b. N.Y. 1944. Am. dancer and chor. Son of Leonide M. by his third wife, Tatiana Orlova. Pupil of Y. Brieux and V. Gsovsky. Joined his father's Co. in Nervi. Balletto Europeo 1960. Danced with Béjart's Co. 1968–70. Chor. Mahler's *Tenth Symphony* for B. du XXme Siècle (1968), *Ode* (m. Stravinsky) for the N.Y. City B. Stravinsky Fest., N.Y. 1972.

MATELOTS, LES, ballet 5 sc., ch. Massine, m. Auric, dec. Pruna, f.p. Diaghileff's Co., Th. Gaîté-Lyrique, Paris 17 June 1925 (Lifar, Woizikovsky, Slavinsky, Sokolova, Nemchinova). The story was by Kochno and this was the first ballet in which Lifar attracted attention.

MATHÉ, Carmen, b. Dundee 1938. Scottish dancer. Trained at Cone-Ripman (Arts Educational) Sch., Tring. Joined de Cuevas B. 1956 becoming soloist 1958. Joined N.Y. City B. 1961, Am. B. Theatre 1962, Festival B. 1962 becoming ballerina the same year. Left 1970 to become ballerina of Washington Nat. B. 1971.

MATTACHINS, or *bouffons*. Dancereferred to in 1588 by Thoinot Arbeau as derived from those of the Salii and the Pyrrhic, in which the participants clad in armour of gilded cardboard with bells on their legs executed a pantomimic battle dance with sword and buckler.

MATTEINI, Marisa, b. Rome 1932. It. dancer. Studied at Rome Opera B. Sch. and graduated to the Co. 1947 becoming ballerina 1949.

MATTOX, Matt, b. Tulsa 1921. Am. modern dancer and teacher. Pupil of Belcher, Loring, Charisse, Cole. Danced in musicals and now famous teacher of modern Am. dancing. In 1970 came to London to teach at the Dance Centre.

MAULE, Michael, b. Durban 1926. S. African dancer. Studied under Celli in N.Y. Début in *Annie Get Your Gun*, N.Y. 1946. Danced in B. Theatre and Alonso B. Soloist N.Y. City B. 1950. Joined Danilova's Concert Co. 1954, becoming her partner. In Robbins's Ballets: U.S.A. in 1959. Now dancing in touring groups.

MAURI, Rosita, b. Reus 1849, d. Paris 1923. Sp. dancer. Chief dancer Teatro Principal, Tarragona 1868. Danced in Germany, Italy, Vienna. Début Paris Opéra 1878 where she became one of its greatest étoiles and was still dancing there in 1907; cr. the chief rôles in *La Korrigane* (1880), *Les Deux Pigeons* (1886), *La Maladetta* (1893). In the first her solo 'La Sabotière' was her great *tour de force*. Teacher at the Opéra until 1920.

MAXIMOVA, Ekaterina, b. Moscow 1939. Russ. dancer. Entered Bolshoi Sch. 1949. Pupil of E. Gerdt, graduated 1958 and became soloist the same year, the youngest in the Bolshoi B. Danced in America 1959. Trained for *Giselle* by Ulanova, which she first danced in 1960. Now a principal dancer of the Bolshoi B. Created the principal rôle in Grigorovich's *Nutcracker* and *Spartacus* (1968). First danced in London 1963. Mar. V. Vassiliev.

MAY, Pamela, b. Trinidad 1917. Eng. dancer. Studied with Freda Grant and in Paris. To S. Wells Sch. 1933. Début in S. Wells B. 1934 in pas de trois in *Swan Lake*. Became soloist and later ballerina. Cr. Red Queen in *Checkmate*, Moon in *Horoscope*, etc. Danced Scala, Milan, as guest artist and since 1952 appears as guest artist with Royal B. Teacher at Royal Ballet Sch. since 1954.

MAYWOOD, Augusta (called La Petite Augusta), b. N.Y. 1825, d. Leopoldville (Lvov) 1876. Am. dancer. Studied under Hazard in Philadelphia. Début there 1837 in *La Bayadère* (in which her namesake had made her Am. triumph in 1836). Made great success in America and in 1839 made her début at the Paris Opéra in *Le Diable Boiteux* and excited Gautier's admiration. Eloped with a dancer, Charles Mabille of the Opéra, in 1840 and left Paris. Prima ballerina Lisbon 1843 (dancing *Giselle*) and Vienna 1845 (*Giselle* also). To La Scala, Milan, as prima ballerina 1848, one of its greatest seasons, and remained there until her retirement in 1863. She was the first Am. dancer to become a prima ballerina in Europe. She taught in Vienna before her end.

MAZILIER, Joseph, b. Marseilles 1801, d. Paris 1868. Fr. dancer and chor. Début at Th. la Porte Saint-Martin 1822. Character dancer at Paris Opéra 1833 and appointed *maître de ballet* 1839. Chor. of many famous ballets, *La Gipsy* (1839), *Le Diable Amoureux*, *Vert-Vert*, *Jovita*, *La Fonti*, *Paquita*, *Betty*, *Les Elfes*, *Le Corsaire*, and *Marco Spada* (1857).

MAZOWSZE, the Polish State Dance Co. (a folk dance troupe of a hundred dancers) was founded in 1948 by T. Sygietynski and his wife M. Ziminska. Its school is at Karolin, an estate 20 miles from Warsaw at which the dancers are trained in dancing, music, and general education. It has toured widely and first visited London 1957, N.Y. 1961. Mazowsze is a district of Poland in which Karolin and Warsaw lie.

MAZURKA, or *masurek*, Polish choral dance in 3/4 time danced with slight variations through Russia and Central Europe and which for a time, in the second half of the nineteenth century, was introduced into official balls in West Europe. When performed with that combination of *brio* and proud carriage which seems to be innate in the Polish and Russian dancer, it is one of the most stirring national dances and has been introduced into a number of ballets. As many as fifty-six different steps have been described as belonging to the mazurka, but its characteristics are the stamping of feet and the clicking of the heels, and the *holubiec*, a turning step performed in couples.

MAZZO, Kay, b. Chicago 1946. Am. dancer. Pupil of B. Hayes and Sch. of Am. B. Joined Robbins's Ballets U.S.A. 1961, N.Y. City B. 1962 becoming soloist 1965 and principal 1969. Guest ballerina Berlin B. and Geneva B. 1970.

MBT, the Russian abbreviation for the Bolshoi Th., Moscow.

MEAD, Robert, b. Bristol 1940. Eng. dancer. Pupil of Royal B. Sch. Joined Royal B. 1958 Touring Section, to C. Garden section 1962 becoming a principal dancer in 1967. Joined Hamburg B. 1971.

MEADOW LARK, ballet, ch. Feld, m. Haydn (attributed), f.p. R. Winnipeg B., Centennial Hall, Winnipeg 3 Oct 1968. Mounted by Festival B., Hippodrome, Bristol 9 Dec 1968 (Kessler, Grant, Dubrueil, von Loggenburg). A pastoral, with musicians on stage.

MEDEA, ballet, ch. Cullberg, m. Bartok (incl. *Microcosmos*), dec. Grandström, f.p. Riksteater, Gaevle, Sweden, 31 Oct 1950 (Lagerborg, Béjart, Noring). Mounted by Swedish B. Co., Prince's Th., London 12 Feb 1951 (von Rosen, J. Mengarelli). Revised version given by R. Swed. B., Stockholm 11 Apr 1953 (von Rosen, Sandberg, Andersson). By N.Y. City B. 26 Nov 1958 (Hayden, d'Amboise, Verdy) and by

R. Danish B., Copenhagen 25 Apr 1959 (Schanne, Kronstam, Simone). The Euripides tragedy.

MÉDÉE ET JASON, ballet, ch. Noverre, m. Rodolphe, f.p. Stuttgart 11 Feb 1763 (Nency, G. Vestris). One of Noverre's greatest *ballets d'action.*

MEDIAVILLA, André, b. Bordeaux 1938. Pupil of Pierrozi, Celada. Joined Bordeaux B. 1957 becoming soloist 1957 and now principal.

MEDICI, Catherine de, b. Florence 1519, d. Blois 1589. Wife of Henry II of France who introduced into France the court entertainments of her native Italy, the first of which *Ballet Comique de la Reine* (1581) set a fashion from which the art of ballet stems.

MEDITATION FROM THAÏS, pas de deux, ch. Ashton, m. Massenet, f.p. at a charity gala, Adelphi Th., London (Sibley, Dowell) 21 Mar 1971.

MEDUSA, ballet, ch. Hanka, m. von Einem, dec. Wakhevitch, f.p. Vienna Staatsoper B. 16 Nov 1957 (Zimmel, Dirtl, Adam). The Greek legend.

MEISTER, Hans, b. Schaffhaüsen 1937. Swiss dancer. Pupil of Zürich B. Sch. and Royal B. Sch. Joined Canad. Nat. B. 1957, soloist Met. Op. B., N.Y. 1962–66, Zürich 1967–68. To Nat. B. of Finland 1972.

MELBOURNE CUP, ballet, ch. Rex Reid, m. mid-nineteenth cen. (including Suppé's *Light Cavalry* Overture and the gavotte from Thomas' *Mignon*) arr. Mackerras, dec. Church, f.p. Australian B., Her Majesty's Th., Sydney 16 Nov 1962 (Gorham, Welander). The famous Australian horse race—to celebrate its centenary. Fred Archer wins at Flemington.

MELIKOVA, Genia, b. Marseilles. Russ. dancer. Pupil of Sedowa, Vilzak, Schwezoff. Danced at Radio City, N.Y., and musicals. Ballet Th. 1949–50. Joined de Cuevas Co. 1954 as ballerina. Festival B. 1963.

MELVILLE, Kenneth, b. Birkenhead 1929. Eng. dancer. Studied S. Wells Sch., joining the S. Wells B. 1946, becoming soloist. Left 1954. Joined Festival B. 1955. To Canadian National B. 1960–63. Zürich B. 1963 and as teacher there. In 1970 to teach at Bloomington Univ., Indiana.

MENDELSSOHN SYMPHONY, ballet, ch. Nahat, m. Mendelssohn's Italian Symphony, f.p. Am. Ballet Th., City Center, N.Y. 15 July 1971. An abstract ballet. It was mounted for Festival B., Coliseum, London 10 Apr 1972 (Wade, Merrin, Schaufuss, Ito).

MÉNÉSTRIER, C. F., b. Lyon 1631, d. Paris 1705. Fr. Jesuit father whose *Des Ballets Anciens et Modernes selon les Règles du Théâtre,* Paris (1657), is the first printed history of the dance. He took his name from the old Fr. word *ménétrier,* a player of instruments or a dancing master.

MENGARELLI, Julius, b. Stockholm 1920, d. Vastanvik 1960. Swed. dancer (brother of Mario). Studied at R. Swedish B. Sch. and became solodancer of R. Swed. B. 1945. Cr. rôle of Jean in *Miss Julie*.

MENGARELLI, Mario, b. Stockholm 1925. Swed. dancer (brother of Julius). Studied at R. Swed. Ballet Sch. and became soloist of R. Swedish B. 1960.

MEPHISTO VALSE, ballet, ch. Ashton, m. Liszt, dec. Fedorovitch, f.p. Ballet Club 13 June 1934 (Markova, Gore, Ashton).

MER, LA, ballet, ch. T. Schilling, m. Debussy, cost. Reinhardt, f.p. Varna Competition 1968 (Bey, Gawlik). Won chor. prize. Later taken into repertoire of the Komische Oper B., E. Berlin 5 Apr 1969 with dec. Geister.

MÉRANTE, Louis, b. Paris 1828, d. Asnières 1887. Fr. dancer and chor. Début at Liège 1834. In 1846 became premier danseur at Marseilles, and in 1848 he went to the Paris Opéra, where he became the leading male dancer. Cr. leading rôles in *Nemea*, *La Source*, etc. as well as in his own ballets, among which are *Gretna Green* (1873), *Sylvia* (1876), *Yedda* (1879), *La Korrigane* (1880), *Les Deux Pigeons* (1886). Mar. dancer Zina Richard (who later danced under the name Mérante).

MERCANDOTTI, Maria, b. Spain c. 1801. Sp. dancer. To Paris, studied under Coulon and made her début at the Opéra 1821. Début at King's Th., London 1814 and thereafter she was one of the most popular and sought after dancers in London. Her father was erroneously thought to have been the Earl Fife, who served in the Peninsular War. It was he who brought her to London when she was 13 and acted as her manager and patron. He married her to a gambler ('*Le Wellington des joueurs*'), Ball Hughes, in 1823 (caricatures by G. Cruikshank commemorate this incident). She then retired from the stage and later married M. Dufrêne, a composer.

MERCIER, Margaret, b. Montreal 1937. Canadian dancer. Studied at S. Wells Sch. Entered Royal B. 1954. Joined Les Grands B. Canadiens 1958 becoming principal dancer. Joined Joffrey B. 1963 and Harkness B. 1964 as principal. Mar. Richard Wolf and retired.

MERCURY THEATRE, Notting Hill Gate, London, the cradle of English ballet, was originally a church hall built in 1850. It was acquired in 1927 by Ashley Dukes and his wife, Marie Rambert, who reconstructed the interior, making a small theatre and adjoining ballet school. It was opened as a theatre on 16 Feb 1931, with a performance by the Ballet Club (see BALLET RAMBERT). It seated 120 and the stage measures 18 ft wide and 18 ft deep. It was named the Mercury Th. in 1933 and was turned into a ballet studio in 1955.

331

MERRY, Hazel, b. Edgware 1938. Eng. dancer. Pupil of Clarke, Royal B. Sch., Northcote, Sunde. Joined Western Th. B. 1957 remaining until 1963, creating many principal rôles (*Non-Stop*, *Sonate à Trois* etc.). In 1961 also danced for Festival B. Joined Béjart B. 1963, ballerina of Zürich B. 1964 and also danced with R. Danish B. on T.V. To Nederlands Dans Th. 1964, B. Rambert 1966, and Royal B. (Touring) 1967 as a soloist.

MÈRE, PETITE, each petit rat at the Paris Opéra is assigned to one of the soloists or étoiles, who acts as her petite mère and gives her counsel and support.

MESSAGE, THE, ballet, ch. Ivo Cramèr, m. Handel, Gluck, dec. Granstrom, f.p. Concert Hall, Stockholm 16 Nov 1945 (Boman, Qvarsebo, Cramer). The story of Joseph and Mary.

MESSEL, Oliver, b. Cuckfield 1905. Eng. painter and stage designer. Educated Eton. His works for ballet include *Francesca da Rimini* (1937), for de Basil; *Comus* (1942), *Sleeping Beauty* (1946), and *Homage to the Queen* (1953) for S. Wells B. Also decorates C. Garden for Gala Performances. Author of *Stage Designs and Costumes* (1934), etc. C.B.E. 1958.

MESSERER, Asaf, b. Vilna 1903. Russ. dancer and teacher. Pupil of Mordkin. Entered Bolshoi Sch. 1920 and graduated to Bolshoi B. 1921. He became the greatest male dancer in Russia during the 1920s. He chor. several ballets and in 1923 began his teaching career, while still dancing. He began taking the *classe de perfection* in 1942 and became a full-time teacher in 1954 on his retirement from the stage. In the 1920s he toured Europe with his sister Sulamith and his wife I. Tikhomirnova. In 1960 he became ballet master of Béjart's Co. at the Th. de la Monnaie, Brussels. He was ballet master of the Bolshoi B. on several of their tours. Chor. *Ballet School* (1962). He is of a Jewish family and is the uncle of Plisetskaya. People's Artist R.S.F.S.R. 1951. Author of *Lessons in Classical Dance* (1967).

MESSERER, Sulamith, b. Moscow 1908. Russ. dancer, sister of Asaf M. Entered Bolshoi Sch. 1920, graduated to Bolshoi B. 1926, becoming ballerina. Toured Europe with her brother in the 1920s. Began teaching at the Bolshoi Sch. 1938 and the Bolshoi B. 1948. Retired from the stage 1950 and teaches full-time. In 1958 she went to Ceylon to advise on the formation of a national theatre, and in 1960 she taught at the Tokyo ballet school. From 1927 to 1931 she was a national swimming champion. Stalin Prize 1947. People's Artist R.S.F.S.R. 1962.

METAMORPHOSES, ballet, ch. Balanchine, m. Hindemith, cost. Karinska, f.p. N.Y. City B., City Center, N.Y. 25 Nov 1952 (LeClerq, Magallanes, Bolender). Insects are transformed into beautiful winged creatures.

METASTASEIS AND PITHOPRAKTA, ballet, ch. Balanchine, m. Xenakis, lighting Bates, f.p. N.Y. City B., State Th., N.Y. 18 Jan 1968 (Farrell, Mitchell). Two separate ballets, involving mass movements of the dancers.

METROPOLITAN BALLET, a company formed in London by Cecilia Blatch and Leon Hepner in 1947. Among its dancers were Colette Marchand and Serge Perrault, Paul Gnatt, Sonia Arova, Erik Bruhn, and Svetlana Beriosova (who first attracted attention in this company). The ballet-master was V. Gsovsky, and later Beriozoff and Celia Franca. Taras created *Designs with Strings* for this company. The Metropolitan Ballet was unhappily unable to continue and broke up in December 1949.

METROPOLITAN OPERA HOUSE, New York ('The Met'), opened in 1883 and was the leading theatre for opera and ballet in the city until it closed in 1966 (with a performance of the Bolshoi B.). It had 3,612 seats and the stage measured 53 ft wide and 72 ft deep. The new Metropolitan Opera House is at Lincoln Center for the Performing Arts and opened on 16 Sept 1966.

MEUNIERS, LES, ballet, ch. J. B. Blache, m. by an unknown composer, f.p. Montpellier 1787. Very frequently performed in pre-Romantic times. A comic ballet about peasant life (thus preceding *La Fille Mal Gardée*).

MEYER, Laverne, b. Guelph, Ontario 1935. Canadian dancer and chor. Pupil of Volkoff, and from 1956 at Rambert Sch. and Royal B. Sch. Joined Western Th. B. 1957, danced principal rôles, appointed ballet master 1962 and assistant artistic director 1966. Studied modern dancing in New York 1964 and left the Co. in 1968, went to Manchester to study feasibility of starting a ballet there. In 1969 founded Northern Dance Th. (q.v.). Chor. many ballets, among them *The Web* (1962) for Western Th. B. and taken into Nederlands Dans Th. and Les Grands Ballets Canadiens.

MEYER, Yvonne, b. Rio de Janeiro, Brazilian dancer. Studied under Leskowa, Lindenberg and Veltchek. Joined de Cuevas Ballet 1954, becoming soloist. Joined Miskovitch's Company 1957 as ballerina, danced Edinburgh Festival 1958. Soloist of Massine's Balletto Europeo, Nervi and Edinburgh 1960. Ballerina Chicago B. 1961, London B. 1962, to Brazil 1963, Washington B. 1968, Rhodesia 1971 etc. Mar. Ivan Dragadze.

MICHAUT, Pierre, b. Paris 1895, d. there 1956. Fr. writer on ballet and films. Author of *Histoire du Ballet* (1945), *Le Ballet Contemporain* (1950), etc. See ASSOCIATION DES ÉCRIVAINS.

MIDDLETON, Marjory, b. Edinburgh 1908. Scottish teacher. Pupil of Karsavina, Idzikowsky, Craske. Opened school in Edinburgh 1915 and taught until her retirement 1972. Awarded M.B.E. 1964. Chor. many ballets.

MIDSUMMER NIGHT'S DREAM, A, ballet 2 acts, ch. Balanchine, m. Mendelssohn (several pieces in addition to his incidental music to the play), cost. Karinska, dec. Hays, f.p. N.Y. City B., City Center, N.Y. 17 Jan 1962 (Jillana, Hayden, McBride, Mitchell, Villella, Moncion, Vazquez).

MIKLOSY, Margot, b. Budapest 1938. Hungarian dancer. Pupil of Nadasi 1948–56. Joined Hungarian Nat. B. 1954. Escaped from Hungary with her husband Imre Varady 1956. Joined de Cuevas B. 1957 becoming soloist. Joined Festival B. 1961 as soloist, becoming ballerina. Guest artist Gothenburg 1969, etc.

MILLER, Buzz, b. America 1923. Am. dancer. Studied under Slavenska and at Am. Sch. of Ballet, N.Y. Début in musical in Los Angeles 1948. In Roland Petit's Co. 1955–56. Works in Paris, dancing in modern Am. style.

MILLER, Marie Elisabeth Anne, b. 1770, d. 1833. Fr. dancer. Début Paris Opéra 1786, retired 1816. She was the wife of Pierre Gardel and mostly danced under the name of Marie Gardel. See SAULNIER.

MILLER, Patricia, b. Pretoria 1927. S. African dancer. Joined S. African B. 1941 and Cape Town B. Club, dancing leading rôles. Joined S. Wells Sch. 1947 and S. Wells Th. B. same year, of which she became a principal dancer. Cr. rôles *Beauty and the Beast*, *Lady and the Fool*, *Harlequin in April*, etc. Mar. Dudley Davies. Returned to South Africa 1956 to teach. Director of the Natal B. from 1969, with her husband.

MILLIONS D'ARLEQUIN, LES (also known as *Harlequinade*), ballet 2 acts, ch. Petipa, m. Drigo, dec. Allegri, cost. Ponomarov, f.p. Hermitage Th., St Petersburg 10 Feb 1900 (Kschessinska). One of Petipa's last ballets, it was in a remarkably fresh, different style and is said to have inspired some of the dances in Fokine's *Carnaval*. In 1950, Lichine made a short ballet *Harlequinade* to some of the original music for the Festival B.

MILLOSS, Aurel, b. Ujozora, Hungary 1906. Hungarian (It. from 1960) dancer, chor. and producer. Studied Budapest, and in Berlin with Gsovsky and Laban. Succeeded Kreutzberg as first dancer at Berlin Opera and then toured Germany. Succeeded Romanoff as *maître de ballet* at Teatro dell'Opera, Rome 1938–45. Created ballets at the Scala, Milan 1942–52 and also for R. Swed. B., Teatro Colon, de Cuevas B., Béjart's Co. and B. des Ch. Élysées (*Don Quichotte* 1947). Ballet master Cologne B. 1960–63. Chor. over 160 ballets, incl. *Miraculous Mandarin*,

Prodigal Son, Creature di Prometeo, Jeu de Cartes, and always employed very good scenic artists for his works. Director of Vienna Staatsoper B. 1953–66 and of Rome Opera B. 1966–69 when he retired. In 1970 he was re-appointed Director of the Vienna Staatsoper B.

MILON, Louis, b. 1766, d. Neuilly 1849. Fr. dancer and chor. Début Paris Opéra 1787 and was assistant maître de ballet 1799–1826. Chor. many ballets, among them *Nina* (1813), *Clari* (1820).

MIME. The art of using the face, limbs, and body to express emotion and dramatic action. Gesture is a natural means of expression used to underline and complete the spoken word. In dancing, which is as a rule a silent art, mime suitably heightened to make it theatrically expressive, assumes particular importance as the only means of expression.

Weaver and later J. G. Noverre were, in the eighteenth century, the first actually to seek to invest the art of theatrical dancing with a definite dramatic content by the use of mime based on a stylization of natural gesture. Their ideas, however, were largely misunderstood and led to the introduction between the dance pas of scenes interpreted in a conventional mime now largely unintelligible to the uninitiated (e.g. the mime scenes in *Giselle* and *The Swan Lake*).

Some of the conventional mime gestures used in Classical ballet are shown in the illustrations. The construction of a sentence in mime follows the French language, e.g. 'I love you' is conveyed by the gestures for 'I you love' (*je vous aime*).

Fokine was the first fully to realize the value of lyrical gesture, and in his ballets the mime scene gave way to expressive dancing. The first attempt to make a scientific analysis of gesture was made by François Delsarte, whose work has been further elaborated by Rudolf von Laban, from which sprang the modern dance movement and the choreography of Jooss.

MINKUS, Ludwig, b. Vienna 1827, d. there 1890. Hungarian composer who became the official composer to the ballet at the Bolshoi Th., Moscow in 1864. In 1871 he assumed the same position in St Petersburg and became the close associate of Petipa for whom he composed 16 ballets. He retired in 1886 and returned to Austria. Among his most successful ballets were *Fiammetta, Don Quixote, Camargo, La Bayadère, Paquita* (St Petersburg version with Deldevez), and *La Source* (with Delibes).

MINKUS PAS DE TROIS, a short *pas de trois*, ch. Balanchine, m. Minkus, cost. Robier, f.p. N.Y. City B., C. Garden 19 Aug 1948 (Hightower, Marjorie Tallchief, Eglevsky). The music is from *Paquita*. Went into N.Y. City B. 18 Feb 1951, Vienna Staatsoper B. 17 Mar 1958, Festival B. 19 June 1968.

335

MIME

No or Not

Call

Ask

Hear

See

Marry

Love

Dance

Swear

MINOTAUR, THE, ballet, ch. Åkesson, m. Blomdahl, dec. Horlin, f.p.
R. Swedish B., Stockholm 5 Apr 1958 (Holmgren, M. Mengarelli,
Orlando, Brosset, Rhodin). The story of Theseus and the Minotaur.

MINUET, from the Fr. *pas menu* (small step), probably because in contrast to the earlier dances all boisterous movement was excluded and
the stately minuet was executed *terre à terre* with small steps in three
time. Evolved from a folk dance of the Fr. province of Poitou, the
minuet became the most favoured dance at the court of Louis XIV,
when the floor pattern was a figure 8. When, however, the court ballet
declined and the minuet was introduced to the stage the pattern was
modified by the maître de ballet Pécour to that of an 'S' or 'Z'. The
minuet has been introduced by a number of choreographers into ballets
with an eighteenth-century theme.

MIRACLE IN THE GORBALS, ballet I act, book M. Benthall, ch. Helpmann, m. Bliss, dec. Burra, f.p. S. Wells B., Princes Th., London
26 Oct 1944 (Helpmann, Clayden, Paltenghi, Franca). Christ returns to
the slums of Glasgow and is martyred again.

MIRACULOUS MANDARIN, THE, ballet, m. Bartók. (1) f.p. Cologne, ch.
H. Strobach 28 Nov 1926 (Wilma Aug, Ernst Zeiller), but was immediately banned on the grounds of immorality, as it was in Prague in
1927, f.p. in Hungary in 1945. (2) Ch. Bolender, dec. Colt, f.p. N.Y.
City B., City Center, N.Y. 6 Sept 1951. (3) Ch. Rodrigues, dec.
Wakhevitch, f.p. S. Wells B., Empire Th., Edinburgh 27 Aug 1956
(Fifield, Somes). There has been hardly a city or a ballet company
which has not had its own version. Notable productions have been
(a) Hungarian Nat. B., Budapest, ch. Harangozo, dec. Ferencik 9 Dec
1945, (b) ch. Lavrovsky, f.p. Bolshoi B., Moscow 21 May 1961 (Timofeyeva, Liepa, Simochev)—here called *Night City*, (c) ch. Flindt, dec.
Hoanung, f.p. R. Danish B., Copenhagen 28 Jan 1967 (Gelker,
Flindt), (d) Gothenburg B., ch. U. Gadd, dec. Sichter, f.p. 1969
(Jillian Luke). A prostitute who decoys victims but is absolved when she
encounters an immortal mandarin, who dies as she loves him.

MIR ISKUSSTVA (*World of Art*), the magazine founded in St Petersburg
by Diaghileff, Benois, Bakst and Nouvel to express their views. It
started in 1899 and continued until 1904. The original backers were
S. Mamontov a Moscow millionaire and patron of the Moscow Arts
Th. and Princess Tenisheva, a collector of pictures. It contained illustrations and among the articles were one on Beardsley by D. S. McColl,
on Mozart by Grieg and on Wagner at Bayreuth by Nietzsche.

MIRAGES, LES, ballet, ch. Lifar, m. Sauguet, dec. Cassandre, f.p. Paris
Opéra 15 Dec 1947 (Chauviré, Bardin, Dynalix, Lafon, Renault).

337

This ballet was prepared in 1944 but not performed until Lifar's return to the Opéra.

MIRROR FOR WITCHES, A, ballet, prologue and 5 sc., based on a novel by Esther Forbes, ch Howard, m Ap. Ivor, dec. Adams, cost. Howard and Adams, f.p. S. Wells B., C. Garden 4 Mar 1952 (Heaton, Farron, Edwards, Hart, Chatfield).

MIRROR WALKERS, THE, ballet, ch. Peter Wright, m. Tchaikovsky, f.p. Stuttgart B., Stuttgart 27 Apr 1963 (Cardus, Barra, Lechner, Cragun, Haydee, Delavalle). Two dancers who pass through their mirror into a new world. It was taken into the repertoire of the Touring Royal B. and the *Pas de Deux* from it is still performed.

MISKOVITCH, Milorad, b. Yugoslavia 1928. Yugoslav dancer. Studied in Belgrade under Kirsanova and later in Paris under Kniaseff and Preobrajenska. In 1947 danced with International B. and de Basil in 1948 with de Cuevas Co., Festival B. 1952. In 1954 he partnered Markova in her recitals. In 1960 he was the star of Massine's Balletto Europeo in Nervi and Edinburgh and in 1961 danced for the Ruth Page Ballet. Usually he has his own company and he has launched many notable dancers and chors.—V. Mlakar, D. Sifnios, Y. Meyer, M. Sparemblek, Sanders, Sulich etc.

MISS JULIE, ballet, book A. Fridericia based on Strindberg's play, ch. Cullberg, m. Rangström, dec. Fridericia, f.p. Riksteatern, Stockholm 1 Mar 1950 (von Rosen, Mengarelli). When performed at Royal Op., Stockholm 7 Sept 1950 and in London 1951 the dec. was by Erixson. Taken into repertoire of Ballet Theatre 1958. MacMillan also chor. a *Miss Julie*, m. Panufnik, dec. Kay, for Stuttgart B., f.p. Stuttgart 8 Mar 1970 (Haydee, Frey).

MITCHELL, Arthur, b. N.Y. 1934. Am. dancer. Studied at Sch. of Performing Arts and Sch. of Am. B. Danced in musicals and in modern dance Cos. before joining the N.Y. City B. 1956, becoming soloist 1959 and then a principal. Cr. rôles in *Agon* and in *Midsummer Night's Dream* (Puck). Guest artist Stuttgart B. 1963 and in 1970. Founded the Dance Theatre of Harlem in N.Y. in 1968 and became Director (see under HARLEM).

MITTERHUBER, Alois, b. Göstling-Ybbs 1932. Austrian dancer and chor. Pupil of Dia Luca, Willy Fränzl, Lucia Brauer, Nora Kiss, de Lutry. Joined Vienna Volksoper 1958–64. To Munich Staatsoper 1964 as soloist and chor. some ballets in Vienna. In 1967 appointed director of ballet at Th. an der Wien, Vienna. Chor. *The Golem* (m. Burt) 1967, *Peter Schlemihl* (m. Ronnefeld) 1968, *Peter Pan* (m. Bjelinsky 1969), *Alice in Wonderland* (m. Horovitz 1970). Also *Die Fledermaus* in Rio de Janeiro 1967.

MLAKAR, Pia, b. Hamburg 1908. Yugoslav dancer and chor., wife of Pino and mother of Veronika Mlakar. Studied under Laban in Berlin and Poljakova in Belgrade. Début Darmstadt Opera 1929. Principal dancer Dessau 1930–33, Zürich 1935–38, Munich 1939–43, retired 1947. Ch. many ballets with her husband (q.v.).

MLAKAR, Pino, b. Novo Mesto 1907. Yugoslav dancer and chor. Studied under Laban in Berlin and Poljakova in Belgrade. Début at Darmstadt Opera 1929 and became soloist at Dessau 1930. Won Bronze Medal for his *Un Amour du Moyen Âge* (Handel-Vivaldi) at the A.I.D. Competition, Paris 1932. Principal dancer and chor. Zürich 1935–38, Munich 1939–43 and 1952–54. Chor. *Josephslegende* (R. Strauss) Belgrade 1934, *The Devil in the Village* (with his wife, Pia, m. Lhotka) Zürich 1935, *Prometheus* (m. Beethoven) Zürich 1935, *The Ballet of a Medieval Love* (with his wife, m. Lhotka), Zürich 1937, *The Little Ballerina* (with his wife, and his daughter in chief rôle, m. Prek) Ljubljana 1947, etc.

MLAKAR, Veronika, b. Zürich 1935. Yugoslav dancer. Pupil of her parents, Pino and Pia Mlakar. Début at Ljubljana Opera 1947. Became soloist at Munich State Opera 1954. Cr. chief rôle in Cocteau's *La Dame à la Licorne* Munich 8 May 1953, Berlin 10 Apr 1954. Studied at S. Wells Sch. 1952–54. Principal dancer Ljubljana Opera 1954, of Petit's Ballets de Paris, Paris 1955, Ballets: U.S.A. 1961. Joined Ballet Theatre 1964 as a principal. Danced in John Butler's Co. 1967.

MODERN DANCE, the term used to designate a variety of styles which are not founded on the *danse d'école* (i.e. the Classical ballet) as formulated by Blasis. It does not stress the basic technique of turn-out, five positions, etc., but has its own vocabulary. It stems from the work of the American Isadora Duncan, and its chief exponents are to be found in America and in Germany (which gives rise to the term Central European Dancing). Its chief exponent in Europe was von Laban, who trained Mary Wigman (from 1913) and Jooss (from 1921), and these two and their disciples, by their public performances, drew the attention of the world to this new form of dance. Laban also wrote widely on the subject and invented a system of writing it down (also applicable to Classical ballet). The great stronghold of Modern Dance, however, is America where it was developed in its early stages by Ruth St Denis and Ted Shawn, Doris Humphrey and Charles Weidman, and Martha Graham. It is now a very important force in the artistic life of America and their leaders have gone further than the Germans and have exerted more influence. Almost every mixed university and women's college in the U.S. has a Physical Education Department of which Modern Dance is the chief feature, and a Modern Dance Festival, following a teachers' course, is held each year at Connecticut College,

New London. Modern Dance has greatly influenced modern Classical choreographers from the time when Fokine first saw Duncan dance. Most ballet companies include works in the Modern Dance idiom in their repertoires, the first to do so being the B. Russe de Monte Carlo, which in 1947 commissioned Valeria Bettis to arrange a ballet *Virginia Sampler*. The works of Jerome Robbins and Michael Kidd derive from the Modern Dance, and Agnes de Mille (much influenced by Graham) and Hanya Holm have given it a place in musical comedy. Modern Dance claims to make use of 'natural movements' and it is also a reflexion of a state of mind. Levinson says it *'déplace l'équilibre du côté de l'expression. C'est l'émotion qui, à son tour, y détermine la forme, spontanée chez les uns, élaborée chez les autres. La vie intérieure s'y manifeste avec excès sous les aspects complémentaires du paroxysme passioné ou de la charge "grotesque".'*

Recently in England the term Contemporary Dance has rather loosely (and inaccurately) become to be used to describe the current style of the Martha Graham dancers, with Modern Dance referring to the older Central European style. However, nowadays anything which happens on a stage without recourse to dialogue can pass as 'dancing' and audiences and critics are invited to see people climbing up ladders, dropping and breaking eggs and rolling in plastic bags across the stage as current examples of 'modern dance'.

In London, Modern and Contemporary Dance has since 1968 tended to concentrate at The Place (q.v.). In America an Annual Festival of Modern Dance is given (from 1968) at the Brooklyn Academy of Music, N.Y.

MODS AND ROCKERS, ballet, ch. Darrell, m. the Beatles, dec. Downing, f.p. Western Th. B., Prince Charles Th., London 18 Dec 1963 (Wellman, Symons, Curry, Law, Haig, Donaldson, Mottram). Jazz-ballet on the rivalry between the two cults, set in a café in the 1960s.

MOHR VON VENEDIG, DER (*Moor of Venice*), ballet, ch. Hanka, m. Blacher, dec. Wakhevitch, f.p. Vienna B., Vienna 29 Nov 1955 (Dirtl, Zimmerl, Adama). Shakespeare's *Othello*. It has been in the repertoire of many European Cos.

MOISEYEV, Igor, b. Kieff 1906. Russ. dancer and chor. Entered Bolshoi Th. Sch., Moscow 1921, studying under Gorskova and Tikhomiroff. While at the Bolshoi Sch. he was briefly expelled for being a rebel against the old classical tradition. Début Bolshoi B. 1924 becoming soloist 1925. Chor. *Football* (m. Oransky 1930), *Salammbô* (m. Arends 1932), *Three Fat Men* (1935). Founder and Director of the Moiseyev Folk Dance Ensemble (q.v.). People's Artist of the R.S.F.S.R. In 1967 he began to form a new company to give concert performances of classical dancing. It commenced in 1968 (with Tikhomirnova as his assistant) and now tours the world. Its first performance was at the Glinka Festival in Smolensk 30 May 1968 with works by Messerer, Goleizovsky and Vinogradov and it was called the Young Ballet (now the Classical B. Co.). It danced in Australia in 1969. In 1969 he chor. *The Last Vision* for the Australian B. Lenin Prize 1967. His wife Tamara Zeifert and his daughter Olga M. are soloists in his Ensemble.

MOISEYEV FOLK DANCE ENSEMBLE, the leading folk-dance troupe in Russia. Founded by Igor Moiseyev, it gave its first performance in the Hall of Columns, Moscow 17 Oct 1937. It consists of over 100 dancers (many of them Stalin Prizewinners), drawn from all over the Soviet Union and trained in its own school in Moscow. The dancers are trained in the Classical style but the dances (a repertoire of 190) are in the folk idioms of the country (and of countries visited by the troupe), and also based on contemporary themes. Many are chor. by Moiseyev, notably *The Partisans, Football, Poem from the Surroundings of Moscow, Ukrainian Suite*. It has visited China, and Paris and London in 1955 and N.Y. 1958. In 1965 the title 'Academic Ensemble' was bestowed on it.

MOISEYEVA, Olga, b. 1928. Russ. dancer. Studied under Vaganova at Kirov Sch., Leningrad. Début 1947. Cr. ballerina at the Kirov Th. 1953. First danced in London 1961. America 1964. Honoured Artist R.S.F.S.R. 1955.

MOLLERUP, Mette, b. Copenhagen 1931. Dan. dancer. Entered R. Danish B. Sch. 1947, joined Co. 1960, becoming solodancer 1956.

MOMENTS (Ogenblikken), ballet, ch. van Dantzig, m. Webern, dec. van Schayk, f.p. Dutch Nat. B., Stadsschouwburg, Amsterdam 28 Feb 1968. Patterns and groups. Danced by Harkness B. 1969.

MONAHAN, James, b. Arrah, India 1912. Eng. writer on ballet. Educ. Stonyhurst and Christ Church, Oxford. From 1952–72 Controller of European Services of the B.B.C. Ballet critic of the *Manchester Guardian* (now *Guardian*) since 1935 but under the name of James Kennedy. Author of *Fonteyn: a Study of the Ballerina in her Setting* (1958). Cr. C.B.E. 1962.

MONCION, Francisco, b. La Vegas 1922. Dominican Republic. Am. dancer, studied School of Am. Ballet. With Ballet International from 1944, in musicals, Ballet Society 1946, and a principal dancer of N.Y. City Ballet since 1950. Cr. rôles in *Sebastian* (1944), *Four Temperaments* (1946), *Afternoon of a Faun* (1953) etc. He is also a painter.

MONDINO, Nestor, b. Paris 1930. Uraguayan dancer. Pupil of Dalton 1943–48, Kniaseff. Entered B. Alicia Alonso 1949, then Montevideo B.

1953, Munich B. 1957, Basel B. 1958, Hamburg B. 1963, Zürich B. 1965 as principal dancer and assistant ballet master.

MONIN, Janine, b. Nice 1930. Fr. dancer. Pupil of Rousanne, V. Gsovsky. Joined Nice B. 1948, and then with B. des Ch. Élysées, Charrat, Miskovitch etc. and in Marseilles B. from 1964, as principal.

MONOTONES, ballet, ch. Ashton, m. Satie (*Trois Gymnopedies*), f.p. Royal B., C. Garden 24 Mar 1965 (Lorrayne, Dowell, Mead). Tranquil *pas de trois*, danced in white leotards. A second part (using Satie's *Trois Gnossiennes*) was added C. Garden 25 Apr 1966 (Sibley, Parkinson, Shaw).

MONPLAISIR, Hippolyte, b. Bordeaux 1821, d. Besana 1877. Fr. dancer Pupil of Guillemin and Blasis. Début Brussels 1839. Principal dancer Scala, Milan 1844–46 partnering Elssler. In 1847 (with his father-in-law Victor Bartholemin) organized the first large ballet troupe to visit America, presenting *Le Diable à Quatre, Esmeralda, Fille Mal Gardée* etc. Succeeded St Leon as ballet master at San Carlo Th., Lisbon 1856. Ballet master at Scala, Milan 1861–77 and chor. there *La Camargo* (1868), *Brahma* (1869) etc. *Brahma* remained in the repertoire until 1912 and it was danced in the summer theatre 'Abandon Sorrow' in St Petersburg by Zucchi in 1884 and by Brianza in 1896.

MONTE CARLO. When Diaghileff's second Paris season in 1911 ended, he was offered a season at Monte Carlo before going on to Rome. He and his Ballets Russes went there in March and thenceforth they made it their base, where each year they could rest (only three performances a week were given), rehearse, recruit new dancers, and prepare new ballets. In this way Monte Carlo became a nursery for the ballet, and it was there that René Blum formed the Ballets de l'Opéra de Monte Carlo in 1931 from scattered remnants of the Diaghileff Co. which had broken up in 1929. This became, in January 1932, the Ballets Russes de Monte Carlo. Again, in 1945, it provided a home and work for many Fr. dancers when Grünberg formed his Nouveau Ballet de Monte Carlo, which later became the de Cuevas Co. Thus, three times has it given asylum to ballet companies and allowed them to marshal their strength before going out to seek their fortunes in the big capitals. The performances take place in the Salle Garnier, opened 1897, a tiny theatre seating 600 designed by the architect of the Paris Opéra, in the Casino. The intervals are usually very long to give the audience time to go into the adjoining gaming halls to play a little roulette before returning to the performance. The teacher Marika Besobrasova has a school in Monte Carlo and occasionally presents ballets there.

MONTESSU, Pauline (*née* Paul), b. Marseilles 1805, d. Amiens 1877.

Fr. dancer. Sister and pupil of dancer Paul. Début Lyon 1813, début at Paris Opéra 1820. Mar. the dancer Montessu 1822. Left Opéra in 1836 and made great success in London. When *La Fille Mal Gardée* was f.p. at the Paris Opéra with Herold's music, 17 Nov 1828, she danced Lise. She was notoriously promiscuous and her remark on discovering that she was pregnant 'If only I knew who was responsible for this!' was long remembered by the corps de ballet.

MONTEUX, Pierre, b. Paris 1874, d. Hancock (Maine) 1964. Fr. conductor for Diaghileff 1911–14 who conducted the first performances of *Petrouchka* (1911), *Sacre du Printemps* (1913), *Le Rossignol* (1914), *Daphnis and Chloë* (1912) and *Jeux* (1913).

MONTEZ, Lola, b. Limerick 1818 (*née* Eliza Gilbert), d. New York 1861. Irish dancer and adventuress. Mar. a Capt. James in 1837, divorced 1842. After five months with Sp. teacher appeared as Sp. dancer at Her Majesty's Th. 1843, pretending to be a native of Spain. Highly successful on the Continent but not in London. Became mistress of Ludwig I of Bavaria 1847 who made her the Gräfin Landesfeld and exercised full control over his Government 1847–48. Sought to excuse herself in two good letters to *The Times* but was banished 1848. In Paris she stabbed a dancer. Her Covent Garden appearance was cancelled as she had to appear at Marlborough Street Police Court on a charge of bigamy. Fled to Spain, thence to America. Later to Australia where she horsewhipped the editor of the *Ballarat Times*. Lectured in N.Y. on the Care of the Bust, and published *The Art of Beauty*. Became a sincere penitent after her dancing days were over and devoted herself to helping fallen women. Gautier saw her dance and commented that Elssler was the better Spanish dancer. She appears as a character in several ballets, notably Massine's *Bacchanale* (1939).

MONUMENT FOR A DEAD BOY, ballet, ch. Rudi Van Dantzig, m. (electronic) J. Boerman, dec. Toer Van Schayk, f.p. Dutch Nat. B., Stadsschouwburg, Amsterdam 19 June 1965 (T. Van Schayk, Y. Vendrig). The agonies and tribulations of a young boy growing up. The chief rôle has also been danced by Nureyev (in 1969). Mounted by Harkness B. 1969, Am. B. Th. 1973.

MONUMENTUM PRO GESUALDO, ballet, ch. Balanchine, m. Gesualdo-Stravinsky, cost. Karinska, f.p. N.Y. City B., City Center N.Y. 16 Nov 1960 (Adams, Mesavage, Neary, Russell, Consoer, Fitzgerald, Ludlow, Vazquez).

MOON REINDEER, ballet, ch. Cullberg, m. Riisager, dec. Falk, f.p. R. Danish B., Copenhagen 22 Nov 1957 (Vangsaa, Kronstam, Björnsson). Taken into the repertoire of the R. Swed. Ballet, Stockholm 31 Jan 1959 (Orlando, Selling). A Lapland legend of a girl who becomes a reindeer. It has been taken into the repertoire of Cos. all over the world.

MOORE, James, b. Nuncie, Indiana 1930. Am. dancer. Pupil of Stone-Camryn Sch., Chicago. Toured with Stone-Page B., soloist B. Americain in Paris, danced and acted in Broadway musicals. Joined Robbins's Ballets U.S.A. 1958, danced in *West Side Story*, assistant to Robbins in mounting *Les Noces* for Am. Ballet Th. 1965 and mounted it for R. Swed. B. 1969. Appointed director of R. Swed. B. 1972.

MOORE, Lillian, b. Chase City 1911, d. N.Y. 1967. Am. dancer and writer. Studied with Sch. of American B., Fedorova, Karsavina etc. Soloist of Met. Op. B., N.Y., danced with the American B. 1935–38, toured with U.S.O. entertaining the American Forces 1945–48. Retired from dancing 1954 and taught. Author of articles in *Encyclopaedia Britannica, Enciclopedia dello Spettacolo, Dance Encyclopedia, Dance News, Dancing Times, Dance Perspectives* etc. and many historical monographs. Wrote (with Erik Bruhn) *Bournonville and Ballet Technique* (1962). In 1966 wrote *Images of the Dance*, listing the treasures of the Dance Collection of the N.Y. Public Library etc. In 1960 she served on the President's Advisory Commission on the Arts. She was also Dance critic of the *N.Y. Herald Tribune.* Just before she died she was appointed director of the apprentice's programme of the Joffrey B.

MOOR'S PAVANE, THE, ballet 1 act, ch. José Limon, m. Purcell arranged Sadoff, cost. Pauline Lawrence, f.p. Am. Dance Festival, Connecticut College, New London 17 Aug 1949 (Limon, Betty Jones, Koner, Hoving). The story of Othello's jealousy. It has been filmed.

MORDKIN, Mikhail, b. Moscow 1881, d. Millbrook, N.J. 1944. Russ. dancer and teacher. Studied at Imp. Sch., Moscow, and became ballet master of the Bolshoi Th. Joined Diaghileff's Co. 1909 but left the next season to become Pavlova's partner at the Paris Opéra. Danced in England and America with her, and later formed his own groups (including Geltzer, Sedowa, Lopokova, Volinin) which toured. He was director of the Bolshoi B. 1917 but left Russia finally in 1923 and went to America where he toured with his own company. Formed the Mordkin Ballet Co. in 1937 for the students of his school in N.Y. In 1939 this company became the nucleus of Am. Ballet Theatre.

MOREAU, Jacqueline, b. Bandol 1926. Fr. dancer. Studied Paris Opéra Sch. and became première danseuse 1948. Joined B. des Ch. Élysées as soloist 1951, with Skouratoff. Joined de Cuevas Co. 1952–59 as ballerina. Now teaches at the Opéra School.

MORELAND, Barry, b. Melbourne 1943. Austral. dancer and chor. Pupil of Austral. B. Sch. Joined Austral. B. 1962. Danced with Ham-

344

burg B. and in musicals. Studied at London Cont. Dance Th. and joined Co. Chor. *Summer Games, Nocturnal Dances, Kontakion* etc. Joined Festival B. 1971 and chor. for them *Summer Solstice* 1972 (m. Field), *In Nomine* (m. Maxwell Davies) 1973.

MORETON, Ursula, b. Southsea 1903, d. London 1973. Eng. dancer and teacher. Pupil Cecchetti and Zanfretta (mime.) Début with Karsavina 1920. In Diaghileff Co. 1920–22 and in Massine's Co. Joined de Valois as teacher 1926 and was a principal dancer in S. Wells B. from the beginning. On the formation of the S. Wells Th. B. 1946 was Asst. Director until 1952. Director of the Royal Ballet Sch. 1952–68. Cr. O.B.E. 1968.

MORINI, Elettra, b. Milan 1937. It. dancer. Entered Scala Sch., Milan 1947, graduated 1956, Passo d'Addio 1957, promoted soloist 1958. Danced in Massine's *Laudes Evangeli*, London T.V. 1961. Now ballerina.

MOROSOVA, Olga. Russ. dancer, sister of Nina Verchinina, and the wife of the late Col. de Basil, in whose Co. she was a soloist and finally ballerina.

MORRICE, Norman, b. Vera Cruz, Mexico 1931. English dancer and chor. Studied at Rambert Sch. from 1952 and entered B. Rambert 1953, becoming a principal dancer. In 1958 chor. his first ballet *Two Brothers*, followed by *Hazana* (1959), *The Wise Monkeys* (1960) etc. In 1966 when the B. Rambert changed its character and became a group presenting modern works he was appointed the associate director and the leader of the company. Visited America 1961–62 to study Graham and other modern styles of choreography. Chor. *A Place in the Desert* 1961, *Conflicts* 1962, *The Travellers* 1963, *Realms of Choice* 1965, *Hazard* 1967, *Them and Us* 1968—all for B. Rambert. For Royal B. chor. *The Tribute* 1965, *Side Show* 1966 (for Batsheva Dance Co.), *Rehearsal* 1968, *1–2–3* 1968, *Blind Sight* 1969, *The Empty Suit* (m. Salzedo) 1970. In 1970 he was appointed joint artistic director of the B. Rambert.

MORRIS DANCE, old English folk dance possibly evolved from the sword dance known in the fifteenth century or earlier. The participants wore bells tied to the legs, and a number of them were usually disguised to represent certain characters such as a Fool, Maid Marian, or the Queen of the May, whilst a cardboard horse was also frequently introduced. One of the characters would often have his face blackened and this has given rise to the supposition that the name 'Morris' may be derived from the word Moorish, and possibly that the dance itself is a modified form of the *Moresca*, a Moorish dance. The majority of Morris dances are in 2/4 time or in common time, but 3/4 time is not unknown.

MORRIS, Margaret, b. London 1891. Eng. dancer. Pupil of d'Auban of Drury Lane and Raymond Duncan. Started her own school 1910 in London and began to evolve her own method of dancing. Founded her Margaret Morris Movement in 1925 and evolved a notation, Danscript, 1928, for her free style of dancing. Founded her Celtic B. in Glasgow 1947, where she had her school. Author of *Margaret Morris Dancing*, (1925), *Notation of Movement* (1928), *Maternity Post-Operative Exercises* (with Sister Randell 1936) and her autobiography *My Life in Movement* (1969). Mar. J. D. Fergusson, painter.

MORRIS, Marnee, b. Schenectady, N.Y. 1946. Am. dancer. Pupil of Thayer, Nelson and Sch. of Am. B. Entered N.Y. City B. 1961 and became soloist 1964. Guest ballerina of several civic ballets.

MORSE, David, b. Hitchin 1943. Eng. dancer. Studied at Royal B. Sch. and joined Royal B. 1961, becoming soloist 1970.

MOSAVAL, Johaar, b. Cape Town 1928. S. African dancer. Pupil of Dulcie Howes. To S. Wells Sch. 1951, Royal B. 1952, becoming soloist 1956 and a principal dancer 1963.

MOSCOW, INTERNATIONAL BALLET COMPETITION, a quadrennial competition for dancers begun in 1969 (during June), in imitation of Bulgaria's Varna Competition, which is held every two years (during July).

MOSKOWSKY WALTZ, spectacular *pas de deux*, chor. by Vainonen, m. Moskowsky. It was created for the Young Ballet group in Leningrad in the 1920s (founded by Balanchine and Dmitriev). It has remarkable lifts and throws and influenced choreographers in the West when they saw this brilliant technique for the first time in the 1950s. The first time in London was by Natalia Filippova and S. Vlasov of the Bolshoi B. 9 Jan 1954. The girl wears a Russian practice costume, the man is dressed as for cricket. Subsequently made famous by Struchkova and Lapauri.

MOSOLOVA, Vera, b. 1877, d. 1949. Russ. dancer and teacher. Pupil of Moscow Sch. and graduated 1893. Transferred to St Petersburg 1896 and studied under Johansson but owing to a difference with the theatre was not made a ballerina until 1917. Danced with Geltzer at the Alhambra, London 1911 and became teacher of Pavlova's Co. 1913 (also teaching Kyasht). Became teacher at Bolshoi Th., Moscow 1918, teaching Moiseyev, the Messerers, etc. Hon. Artist R.S.F.S.R.

MOSSFORD, Lorna, b. London 1924, d. there 1972. Eng. dancer and teacher. Studied at S. Wells Sch., Volkova, van Praagh, Plucis. Joined S. Wells B. 1941 becoming soloist, until 1951. To Nat. B. of Turkey 1953 and taught at the Ankara Conservatoire, and Chicago 1954–57.

From 1957 ballet mistress of touring Royal B. Mounted MacMillan's *Solitaire* for Stuttgart B. 1961. In 1970 became Benesh Notation teacher at Royal B. Sch.

MOTTE, Claire, b. Belfort 1937. Fr. dancer. Entered Paris Opéra Sch. 1948 and joined Paris Opéra B. 1952. Became première danseuse 1956 and étoile 1960.

MOTTRAM, Simon, b. Woodford 1937. Eng. dancer. Pupil of Rambert and Royal B. Sch. Joined Royal B. 1956, Festival B. 1960, London B. 1961, de Cuevas 1962, Western Th. B. 1962–65 as principal dancer. Danced with R. Swed. B. 1965 and returned to Western Th. B. 1966. Principal dancer of Nederlands Dans Th. 1969–70, of Northern Dance Th. 1971. Chor. *Tchaikovsky Suite* (1972). New London B. 1972.

MOUNSEY, Yvonne, b. Pretoria 1921. S. African dancer. Studied with Schwezoff and Massine. Joined B. Russe de Monte Carlo, later de Basil in Australia. Joined N.Y. City Ballet as soloist in 1950, cr. rôles in Balanchine's *Swan Lake, La Valse, Cakewalk*, etc. Returned to S. Africa 1959 and helped to found the Johannesburg B.

MOVES, ballet, ch. Robbins, performed in silence and in casual dress, f.p. Robbins's Ballets U.S.A., Teatro Nuovo, Spoleto, 3 July 1959. In repertoire of Joffrey B. 1968.

MOYLAN, Mary Ellen, b. Cincinnati 1926. Am. dancer. Studied Am. Sch. of Ballet. Appeared in musicals and principal dancer B. Russe de Monte Carlo 1943 onwards. Danced in Ballet Theatre 1951. Retired 1957.

MOZARTIANA, ballet 1 act, ch. Balanchine, m. Mozart-Tchaikovsky, dec. Bérard, f.p. Les Ballets 1933, Th. des Ch. Élysées, Paris 7 June 1933 (Toumanova, Jasinsky).

MR PUNCH, ballet 5 sc., ch. Gore, m. Oldham, dec. R. Wilson, f.p. B. Rambert, S. Wells Th. 2 July 1946 (Gilmour, Gore). Ballet of Punch and Judy.

MUDRA, the name of the dance school in Brussels attached to the Ballet du XXme Siècle and directed by Maurice Béjart. All forms of dance are taught, pupils are selected by audition and tuition is free.

MUDRAS, in Hindu dancing, is the language of the dancer's gestures.

MÜLLER, Horst, b. Lahr 1933. Ger. dancer and ballet master. Studied at Essen Folkwang Sch. and Juilliard Sch. Joined Graz B. 1959–61, ballet master Oldenburg 1961–63, and of Mannheim 1963–73. Chor. many ballets.

MULYS, Gérard, b. Strasbourg 1915. Fr. dancer. Studied under Ricaux and Aveline. Danced with Blum and Monte Carlo Cos. Ballet master at Monte Carlo 1941 and at Nice 1948–56. Danced in *Giselle* for B.

Rambert 1946. Author of *Les Ballets Russes de Monte Carlo*. Ballet master at Opéra Comique, Paris 1957. Taught at Paris Opéra 1958. Assistant to Director, Paris Opéra 1971.

MUSETTE, gavotte danced to the strains of the *musette*, a type of bagpipe which enjoyed a great vogue at the courts of Louis XIV and XV, when a pseudo-rustic style was greatly affected.

MUSICAL COMEDY or MUSICAL. The development of ballet and of the modern dance movement in the United States has had a salutary influence on the ballet in musical comedies, which from being mere leg-shows and pretty but meaningless gyrations of lavishly dressed or undressed girls supported by all the colour that modern lighting can provide, have come to add a heightened dramatic note to the underlying theme of the production. There are signs that the 'dream' approach used so successfully by Jerome Robbins in *Billion Dollar Baby* and by Agnes de Mille in *Oklahoma!* has now given place to a wider range of subjects, and most English and American musical comedies now contain long ballet or dance sequences. This association with modern dance and ballet choreographers has been beneficial to the art of ballet, both by interesting new and wider audiences, as did the early Russian ballet performances inserted in music-hall programmes in England, and by restraining choreographers, faced with the need to cater for mass audiences, from becoming too intellectual in their approach.

MUSIL, Karl, b. Vienna 1939. Austrian dancer. Studied under Fränzl and at Staatsoper Sch. Entered Vienna Staatsoper Ballet 1953 and became soloist 1957 and principal. Guest artist Nice 1961, Stuttgart 1962, Hanover 1962, Festival B. 1963, Ruth Page B. 1965 etc. In 1970 joined Hanover B. as principal dancer and assistant ballet master. Mar. Irina Borowska. Partnered Fonteyn on Staatsoper B.'s American tour 1972.

MUTATIONS, ballet, ch. Tetley, m. Stockhausen, dec. N. Baylis, cost. Van Leersum, f.p. Nederlands Dans Th., Circustheater, Scheveningen 3 July 1970 (Sarstadt, Lemaître, Licher, E. Hampton). A girl and two men dance in the nude and there is a film of Anja Licher and Gerard Lemaître dancing nude shown simultaneously, f.p. in London, S. Wells Th. 2 Nov 1970 (Sarstadt, Licher, Benoit).

MUTE WIFE, THE, ballet, ch. Antonia Cobos, m. Paganini, dec. Lebrun, f.p. B. International, N.Y. 22 Nov 1944 (Cobos, Moncion). For Original B. Russe with music D. Scarlatti, cost. Castillo, Met. Op., N.Y. 16 Sept 1949. Was also in repertoire of de Cuevas B. Castanets are used to indicate the return of speech to the wife.

MYERS, Carl, b. Loughborough 1950. Eng. dancer. Pupil of Cissie Smith and Rosella Hightower. Entered Royal B. Sch. 1967 and joined Royal B. 1968. He and Marilyn Trounson had *Lament of the Waves* created for them by Ashton in 1970. Mar. Marguerite Porter.

MYTHICAL HUNTERS, ballet, ch. Tetley, m. Partos, cost. Binstead, f.p. Batsheva Dance Co., Ohel-Shem, 25 Nov 1965. Nederlands Dans Th., Royal Th., The Hague, 10 Jan 1968 (de la Bye, Flier).

MXY, the Russian abbreviation for the Bolshoi Sch., Moscow.

N

NADASI, Ferenc, b. Budapest 1893, d. there 1966. Hungarian dancer, ballet master and teacher. Pupil of J. Holczer and Henrietta Spinzi, also studied in St Petersburg and with Cecchetti. In Imperial (later National) B. in Budapest, soloist 1913 during the time that Nicola Guerra was in charge. He became ballet master 1936 and eventually the director. In 1949 he headed the new State Ballet School. Trained most of the present generation of Hungarian dancers, won many State prizes and awards. Retired 1962 and headed the committee which produced the book (edited by György Lörinc) *Methodik des klassischen Tanzes* in 1964—a complete textbook of classical training.

NAGY, Ivan, b. Debrecen 1943. Hungarian dancer. Pupil of Hungarian Nat. B. Sch., Budapest under Bartos. Joined Nat. B. 1960. Won Varna Silver Medal 1965. To America in 1965 as guest artist for Washington Nat. B. Joined N.Y. City B. 1968, Am. Ballet Th. 1968 as soloist and became a principal 1969. Mar. Marilyn Burr.

NAHAT, Dennis, b. Detroit 1947. Syrian dancer and chor. Pupil of E. Ricardean, Joffrey. Joined Detroit City B. 1958, Joffrey B. 1960–62, Am. Ballet Th. from 1962 for whom he chor. *Momentum* (1969), *Brahms Quintet* (1969). Also danced lead in *Sweet Charity* on Broadway. Chor. *Ontogeny* (m. Husa) for R. Swed. B. 1970, *Mendelssohn Symphony* 1971 for Am. Ballet Th. and Festival B. 1972.

NAÏADE, LA, see ONDINE.

NAMOUNA, (1) ballet 2 acts, ch. Lucien Petipa, m. Lalo, dec. Rube, Chaperon, Lavastre, f.p. Paris Opéra 6 Mar 1882 (Sangalli, Mérante). This was Lalo's finest score and has been used again in Lifar's *Suite en Blanc* (q.v.), (2) ballet, ch. Peter Wright, m. Lalo, dec. Farmer, f.p. Stuttgart B., Stuttgart 2 June 1967 (Keil, Cragun)—using the same story.

NAPAC BALLET (Natal Performing Arts Council), the company based on Durban in South Africa. It was founded in 1969 with Dudley Davies as director assisted by his wife Patricia Miller.

NAPOLI, ballet 3 acts, ch. Bournonville, m. Paulli, Helsted, Gade, and Lumbye, dec. Christensen, f.p. Royal Th., Copenhagen 29 Mar 1842 (Bournonville, Fjeldsted, Stramboe). This, the most popular of the Danish ballets, was inspired by Bournonville's visit to Italy where he went after his banishment from Denmark and was presented on his return. It contains every kind of theatrical trick, has magnificent mime and crowd scenes, and ends with a delirious Tarantella danced by the principals. When danced at the R. Theatre, Copenhagen, the King of Denmark sent champagne to the dancers in the interval before the last act. Lander mounted a condensed version for the Festival Ballet in London 30 Aug 1954, Festival Hall (Toni Lander, Briansky). Erik Bruhn mounted the last act divertissement for the Royal B. at C. Garden 3 May 1962 (Sibley, Park, Seymour, Parkinson, Lawrence, Usher, Bennett). In 1971 Elsa Marianne von Rosen produced the ballet in full at the Stora Th., Gothenburg (Evdokimova, Beaumont).

NASRETDINOVA, Zaituna, b. 1923. Russ. dancer. Pupil of Leningrad Sch., graduating in 1941 becoming ballerina of Bashkir Ballet, Ufa. Honoured Artist of U.S.S.R. 1955.

NATHALIE, OU LA LAITIÈRE SUISSE, ballet 2 acts, ch. F. Taglioni, m. Gyrowetz, f.p. Vienna 8 Oct 1821. With dec. Ciceri, cost. Lami, it was f.p. Paris Opéra 7 Nov 1832 (Taglioni). Later Elssler danced it in Vienna and it became one of her most famous rôles in the early part of her career. The heroine mistakes a statue for her lover and then her lover for a statue.

NATIONAL FOUNDATION ON THE ARTS AND HUMANITIES, is the American equivalent of Britain's Arts Council. It gave its first grants 15 Nov 1965 of about 3 million dollars (of which Am. Ballet Theatre got 350,000 dollars). Agnes de Mille was chairman of the dance panel. The first chairman was Roger L. Stevens.

NATIVE FIELDS, ballet, ch. A. Andreev, m. Chervinsky, dec. Veselikin, f.p. Kirov Th., Leningrad 4 June 1953 (Kurgapkina, Dudinskaya, Makarov, Sergeyev, A. Andreev).

NAULT, Fernand, b. Montreal 1921. Canadian dancer and chor. Pupil of Morenoff, Leese, Vilzak, Craske. Joined Ballet Th. 1944 becoming soloist, regisseur and ballet master. Staged a version of *La Fille Mal Gardée* for Joffrey B. 1959. Became co-director (with Ludmilla Chiriaeff) of Les Grands Ballets Canadiens, choreographing many works for them, incl. *Danses Concertantes*, *Pas Rompu* (m. Glière), *Carmina Burana* (m. Orff), *Mobiles* (m. Suk).

NAUTÉOS, ballet 3 acts, ch. Lifar, m. Leleu, dec. Brayer, f.p. Paris Opéra 12 July 1954 (Chauviré, Lafon, Renault). Originally made for Nouveau B. de Monte Carlo 1947 and shortened for the Paris Opéra 1954. Story of a water nymph and a shipwrecked sailor.

NAVARRO, Armando, b. Buenos Aires 1930. Argentinian dancer and chor. Studied with Bulnes, M. Borowski, Gema Castillo, at Colon Th. Joined Taetro Colon B., Buenos Aires 1947, B. Alicia Alonso 1950, soloist 1951, returned to Colon. In 1956 joined de Cuevas B., soloist 1958, first character dancer 1961. Joined Scapino B. 1962 as teacher, ballet master 1963, artistic director 1970. Chor. (for Colon B.) *Scaramouche* (m. Milhaud) 1946 (for Scapino B.) *Coppélia, Ongerijmd* (m. Stravinsky), *Surprise* (m. Britten) etc. Mar. Marian Sarstädt.

NEARY, Patricia, b. Miami 1942. Am. dancer. Pupil of Milenoff and the Sch. of National B. of Canada, Toronto. Joined Nat. B. of Canada 1956, N.Y. City B. 1960 becoming soloist 1962. To Geneva B. 1969 as guest ballerina. Ballet mistress Deutsche Oper, Berlin 1971–73. For Balanchine mounted *Symphony in C* for Vienna B. 1972, *Agon* and *Four Temperaments* for Royal B. 1972, *Apollo* for Rome B. 1973, *Episodes* for Dutch Nat. B. etc. Director of Geneva B. 1973. Her sister Colleen N. (b. 1952) is soloist in N.Y. City B.

NEDERLANDS DANS THEATER, HET, was founded in Amsterdam by Benjamin Harkarvy, in April 1959. He had resigned from Sonia Gaskell's Het Nederlands Ballet and he took some of the dancers for his new company. Survival was difficult but in 1961 it moved to The Hague and now receives a city subsidy. Hans van Manen joined Harkarvy as joint-director 1961. They resigned in 1969 and were succeeded in 1969 by Glen Tetley and Scott Douglas. These resigned in 1970 and were succeeded by Carel Birnie (for long their business manager) and Jaap Flier. They danced in N.Y. for the first time in 1968 (City Center). Their first appearance in England was in Sunderland 4 Nov 1963 and in London (Sadler's Wells) 22 May 1967. Danced in Edinburgh Festival 1970. Their leading dancers in 1970 were Marian Sarstädt, Käthy Gosschalk, Anja Licher, Rita Poelvoorde, Mea Venema, Arlette van Boven, Kerstin Lidström, Jaap Flier, Hans Knill, Gerard Lemaître, Jan Nuits, Jon Benoit. Ballet mistress, Hanny Bouman. Toured round the world 1972.

NEGENDANCK, Fred, b. Helsinki 1937. Finnish dancer. Started ballet lessons in 1956 under Karnakoski and joined National B. 1958, becoming soloist 1966. Also studied in Paris and with Northcote in London.

NEGRI, Cesare, b. Milan 1530. It. writer whose book *Le Gratie d'Amore* (di Cesare Negri Milanese, detto il Trombone), Milan 1602 and its revised edition *Nuovi Inventioni di Ballo* of 1604 are early works on the

351

dance similar to those of Carosio. He was at Malta at the time of the Battle of Lepanto and danced on a warship before the admirals after the defeat of the Turks.

NEIL, Sara, b. Wellington, New Zealand 1932. New Zealand dancer. To England with R.A.D. scholarship and joined S. Wells Th. B. 1951, becoming a principal dancer 1955. Returned to New Zealand 1959 to become principal dancer of their United Ballet Co. Came to London 1968 to teach, with her husband, Walter Trevor, at Royal B. Sch.

NELIDOVA, Lydia, b. 1863, d. 1929. Russ. dancer (her father was English). Graduated from the Moscow Sch. 1884 and joined Bolshoi B. In 1890 she danced at the Empire Th., London. When she claimed the title of prima ballerina in the Bolshoi B. (following a successful *Fille Mal Gardée*) she was refused, so she opened a private school in Moscow One of the teachers was Anna Sobeshanskaya (b. 1842, d. 1918) who created the rôle of Kitri in *Don Quichotte* and was the second to dance Odette in *Swan Lake*. From this school Diaghileff obtained several of his dancers, incl. Nemchinova and the Lydia Nelidova who cr. rôle of the Nymph in *L'Apres Midi d'un Faun* (she was the daughter of Nelidova and her real name was Lydia Redega).

NEMCHINOVA, Vera, b. Moscow 1899. Russ. dancer. Studied privately under Nelidova in Moscow. Joined Diaghileff's Co. 1915, becoming a principal dancer in 1924. Ballerina Kaunas Opera 1930–35. Also danced with Blum Co. and Ballet Th. Created the chief rôles in *Les Biches* (1924) and *L'Épreuve d'Amour* (1936). In 1927 and 1928 she organized the Nemchinova-Dolin Ballet in London, with Dolin and Oboukhoff (her husband). Now teaching in N.Y.

NÉMEČEK, Jiri, b. Prague 1924. Czech dancer and chor. Pupil of Nikolskaya and V. Psota in Prague. Joined Brno B. In 1939 joined Czech Nat. B., Prague, ballet master of Pilsen B. 1951–57. From 1957 to 1970 artistic director of Prague (Czech Nat. B.). For 16 years he has been producer of the Laterna Magica (Magic Lantern) shows in Prague (multiple film projections and dancers).

NERINA, Nadia, b. Cape Town 1927. S. African dancer. Won many prizes there and from 1942 toured the Union. To England 1945 to Rambert Sch. and then to S. Wells Sch. Joined S. Wells Th. B. 1946 and cr. Circus Dancer in *Mardi Gras*. To Royal B. 1947 as soloist, promoted ballerina 1952. Toured S. Africa and S. Rhodesia during 1952 with Rassine as partner, and again in 1954. For a short time in S. Wells Th. B. she was known as Nadia Moore. In 1960 she danced at the Bolshoi Th., Moscow, as guest artist. Created principal rôle in *La Fille Mal Gardée* 1960. Guest artist Western Th. B. 1965. Retired 1966.

NERVI INTERNATIONAL BALLET FESTIVAL, held nearly every summer in an open-air theatre at Nervi, near Genoa, since 1955. Companies from all over the world take part. The artistic director is Mario Porcile, with the Genoa Opera House. Among Cos. appearing have been Royal B. (1962, 1968), Massine's Co. (1960), Vienna B. (1967), Jooss B. (1964), Scala B. (1962), Brno B. (1967), Festival B., Bolshoi B. Béjart Cullberg etc.

NEUMEIER, John, b. Milwaukee 1942. Am. dancer and chor. Studied with Bentley Stone, Sybil Shearer and Volkova. R. Ballet Sch. 1962–63. Joined S. Shearer's group 1961, Stuttgart B. 1963 becoming a principal dancer. Chor. ballets for Noverre Soc., Stuttgart and for Stuttgart B. *Separate Journeys* (m. Barber) 1968. For Harkness B. *Stages and Reflections* (m. Britten) 1968. Appointed Director of Frankfurt B. 1969–73, ch. *Firebird* (m. Stravinsky) 1970, *Daphnis and Chloe, Romeo and Juliet* 1971, *Nutcracker, Don Juan* (m. Gluck), *Sacre* 1972. Chor. Scott. Th. B. *Frontier* (m. Bliss) 1969. Director of Hamburg B. 1973.

NEW LONDON BALLET, founded Samsova-Prokovsky 1972 (after dancing in Trieste, Nov 1971) for Brit. Council tour Turkey, Far East (guest Margot Fonteyn). To America, Spain etc 1973. F. p. Britain, Th. Royal, Brighton 9 May 1973. Dancers also incl. Dianne Richards, Mottram, Salavisa. Chor. J. Carter.

NEWMAN, Claude, b. Plymouth 1903. Eng. dancer and teacher. Studied under Bedells, Astafieva. Début under Fokine 1924, one of early members S. Wells B., becoming a principal dancer. Maître de ballet S. Wells Th. B. 1946, taught S. Wells Sch. until 1952. Overseas examiner for R.A.D. Became Director of Rome Opera B. 1963 and of the ballet of Bahia, Brazil in 1965. Retired 1970.

NEWTON, Joy, b. Wimbledon 1913. Eng. dancer and teacher. Studied under de Valois at her Academy of Choreographic Art, and was one of the original members of the Vic-Wells B. Ballet mistress of the Co. 1942–46. First teacher and director at the Turkish Ballet Sch. 1947–51 in Istanbul. Teacher at Royal B. Sch. 1963–69. Now retired.

NEW YORK CITY BALLET, THE. The fifth programme of the Ballet Society, at the N.Y. City Center 28 Apr 1948, included Balanchine's *Symphonie Concertante, Symphony in C* (see PALAIS DE CRISTAL), and, a new production, *Orpheus.* The success of these ballets made a great impression on the Chairman of the Executive Committee of the City Center, Moreton Baum, a lawyer. He proposed to Lincoln Kirstein that the performing company of Ballet Society be incorporated into the activities of the City Center as The New York City Ballet. The first season of this new company opened at the City Center on 11 Oct 1948 (*Concerto Barocco, Orpheus, Symphony in C*) with Balanchine as Artistic Director, Barzin as Musical Director, and Kirstein as General Director.

The chief dancers were Maria Tallchief, Marie Jeanne, Tanaquil LeClerq, Beatrice Tompkins, Jocelyn Vollmar, Magallanes, Moncion, Bliss, and Bolender. It was then a subsidiary of the N.Y. City Opera, but in January 1949 it had its first season as an entirely independent unit of the City Center. Tudor and Robbins joined for this season to chor. new works. For their November 1949 season Balanchine staged his version of *Firebird*, and among the dancers who joined the company were Janet Reed, Melissa Hayden, and Frank Hobi. Some of these performances were watched by de Valois and David Webster (General Administrator of Covent Garden), for the S. Wells B. were touring America at the time. The Company were invited to perform at Covent Garden in the summer of 1950 and again in 1952, when they made a great impression though there was considerable controversy about the choreography of Balanchine, which was alleged by some to make the programmes monotonous, although magnificently danced. At the end of 1950 Diana Adams and Hugh Laing joined, and early in 1951 Nora Kaye and Eglevsky. Ashton chor. for them *Illuminations* in 1950 and *Picnic at Tintagel* in 1952. The 1952 European tour also took them to Barcelona, Paris, Florence, The Hague, Switzerland, the Edinburgh Festival, and Berlin. In 1953 they visited Europe again, dancing at the Scala, Milan. In 1954 they staged the full-length *Nutcracker* at City Center, N.Y. Toured Europe again in 1955, appearing in Monte Carlo (the first Am. company to do so). The leading dancers in 1955 were (girls) LeClerq, Maria Tallchief, Hayden, Adams, Wilde, Jillana, (men) Magallanes, Moncion, Bliss, d'Amboise, Bolender, Eglevsky. In 1960 they were (girls) Maria Tallchief, Verdy, Adams, Hayden, Kent, Wilde, Jillana, (men) Bolender, d'Amboise, Bruhn, Fernandez, Magallanes, Moncion, Watts, Villella, Tobias. They first danced in Russia in 1962 (Moscow, Leningrad, Kiev, Tiflis, Baku). In 1964 they became the first Am. company to give its dancers a full 52-week paid employment. And in the same year they gave their first season at the new N.Y. State Th. in the Lincoln Center. In 1965 they danced at Covent Garden again (after an absence of 13 years) and at the Edinburgh Festival 1967. Among their dancers in 1970 were Patricia MacBride, Violette Verdy, Allegra Kent, Suki Schorer, Kay Mazzo, Marnee Morris, Gelsey Kirkland, Karin von Aroldingen, Jacques d'Amboise, Edward Villella, Arthur Mitchell, Francisco Moncion, Peter Martins, Anthony Blum, Conrad Ludlow, Helgi Tomasson.

A feature of the years from 1969 has been the mounting of new ballets by Robbins (*Dances at a Gathering, Goldberg Variations*, etc.) and the emergence of a new generation from a young corps de ballet—for example Gelsey Kirkland, Colleen Neary etc. A remarkable Stravinsky Festival was held at the State Theater, N.Y. 18–25 June 1972, at which the Co. performed 31 ballets to Stravinsky music, of which 21 were new creations. They were—chor. Balanchine, *Pas de Deux, Symphony in 3 Movements, Violin Concerto, Danses Concertantes, Divertimento from Baiser de la Fée, Scherzo à la Russe, Duo Concertant, Rubies* (from *The Jewels*), *Orpheus, Apollo, Agon, Choral Variations on Bach's Von Himmel Hoch, Monumentum pro Gesualdo, Movements for Piano and Orchestra.* Chor. by Robbins, *Scherzo Fantastique, The Cage, Circus Polka, Dumbarton Oaks, Requiem Canticles.* Chor. by Balanchine and Robbins together, *Firebird, Pulcinella.* Chor. by Taras, *Concerto for Piano and Wind, Ebony Concerto, Scènes de Ballet, Song of the Nightingale.* Chor. by Bolender, *Serenade in A, Piano-Rag-Music.* Chor. by Clifford, *Symphony in E flat.* Chor. by Lorca Massine, *Ode.* Chor. by Tanner, *Concerto for Two Solo Pianos, Octuor.*

From 1958 Robert Irving has been the company's distinguished Director of Music.

NEW YORK EXPORT: OP. JAZZ, ballet, ch. Robbins, m. Prince, dec. Ben Shahn, f.p. Ballets U.S.A., Spoleto Festival 8 June 1958 (Curley, Dunn, Milberg, Jones). A jazz ballet, in jeans. Danced by Harkness B. 1969 (Ruiz, Sutherland).

NEW ZEALAND, BALLET IN, began in 1953 when Poul Gnatt toured with a group, New Zealand Ballet Inc. In 1957 several N.Z. dancers from London returned (Russell Kerr, Rowena Jackson, Philip Chatfield, Sara Neil, Walter Trevor) and gave a season in Auckland. A Board was constituted and in 1961 Russell Kerr was appointed artistic director of a New Zealand Ballet Co., based on Wellington, with N.Z. Arts Council support. During the ensuing years seasons have been given with guest stars, among them Beriosova, Musil, Burr, J.-P. Comelin Alexander Grant etc. In 1967 Shabelevsky became ballet master. The same year a fire destroyed all its property but it struggled on. In 1971 Bryan Ashbridge, directing the Auckland Festival, mounted *Swan Lake* (Elaine Fifield as guest) but at the end of the year the Queen Elizabeth II Arts Council withdrew its support. However, it was later restored and *Coppélia* was produced in 1972. The National Sch. of Ballet in Wellington opened in 1967 with Russell Kerr and Sara Neil in charge. Dorothy Daniels took over in 1969 and in 1973 Rowena Jackson and Philip Chatfield became the directors and Una Kai director of the Co.

NICOL, Noleen, b. Johannesburg 1947. S. African dancer. Pupil of de Villiers and Royal B. School. Joined PACT Ballet 1963–68. Joined Festival B. 1969 becoming principal 1973.

NIEHAUS, Max, b. Wesel 1888. Ger. writer on ballet. Author of *Ballet* (1954), *Junges Ballett* (1957 and 1972), *Himmel, Hölle und Trikot— Heinrich Heine und das Ballett* (1959), *Nijinsky* (1961). From 1958 he

355

has published an annual Ballet Calendar (photographs for each month.)

NIELSEN, Augusta, b. 1822, d. 1902. Danish dancer. Succeeded Grahn as solodancer in R. Danish B. Guest artist in Stockholm, Berlin, Paris, Oslo. Was the mistress of the Prince of Hessen and was forced to retire after a scandal. Her most famous dance was *La Lithuanienne* (ch. Lefebvre, m. Lumbye, 1845).

NIEMINEN, Arja, b. Helsinki 1943. Finnish dancer. Studied at the Finnish B. Sch. and entered the National B. 1961, becoming soloist in 1967.

NIGHT AND SILENCE, THE, ballet, ch. Gore, m. Bach, arr. Mackerras. dec. R. Wilson, f.p. Edinburgh International B., Empire Th., Edinburgh 25 Aug 1958 (Hinton, Poole). An outstanding ballet of jealousy. Later performed by B. Rambert and other Cos. (Northern Dance Th. in 1972).

NIGHT CITY (see THE MIRACULOUS MANDARIN).

NIGHTINGALE, THE, ballet 3 acts, ch. Yermolayeff, m. Kroshner, dec. Matrunine, f.p. Odessa 5 Apr 1939 (later in Minsk and Moscow).

NIGHT ISLAND, ballet, ch. Van Dantzig (his first), m. Debussy, dec. van Schayk, f.p. Nederlands B., Royal Th., The Hague 20 Jan 1955 (van Leeuwen, Colcher, Zwartjes, Van Dantzig). Two contrasting couples. Danced by B. Rambert 1967.

NIGHT JOURNEY, ballet, ch. Graham, m. Wm. Schuman, dec. Noguchi, f.p. Martha Graham Group, Cambridge High and Latin Sch., Cambridge, Mass. 3 May 1947 (Graham, Hawkins, Ryder). Oedipus and Jocasta.

NIGHT SHADOW, ballet, ch. Balanchine, m. Rieti after Bellini, dec, Dorothea Tanning, f.p. B. Russe de Monte Carlo, N.Y. City Center 27 Feb 1946 (Danilova, Magallanes, Maria Tallchief, Katcharoff). Called *La Somnambule* in France. Mounted for de Cuevas B., dec. Robier, f.p. Cambridge Th., London 26 Aug 1948 (Pagava, Skibine, Marjorie Tallchief); R. Danish B., dec. Delfau, f.p.Copenhagen 9 Jan 1955 (Schanne, Kronstam, Vangsaa); N.Y. City B., dec. E. Francès, cost. Levasseur, City Center, N.Y. 6 Jan 1960 (Kent, Bruhn, Jillana); B. Rambert, dec. Stone, S. Wells Th. 18 July 1961 (Sandbrook, Morrice, Aldous); Festival B., dec. Farmer, Fenice Th., Venice 20 Mar 1967 (Richards, Gilpin, Mathé). A poet encounters a sleep-walker at a *fête-champêtre*.

NIJINSKA, Bronislava, b. Minsk 1891, d. Los Angeles 1972. Russ. dancer and chor. Sister of Nijinsky. Studied Imp. Sch., St Petersburg and joined corps de ballet 1908. Joined Diaghileff 1909, and left Maryinsky Th. 1911 with her brother and toured with Diaghileff as a soloist. She chor. the dance of the Three Ivans in the 1921 revival of *The Sleeping Princess* in London and also chor. *Le Renard* (1922), *Les Noces* (1923), *Le Train Bleu* and *Les Biches* (1924). For the Ida Rubinstein Co. chor. *La Bien Aimée* and *Le Baiser de la Fée* (1928) and *La Valse* (1929). In 1930–31 she mounted ballets for the Opéra Russe à Paris (founded by Prince Zeretelli, Kachouk, and Col. de Basil) and in 1932 she founded her own Théâtre de Danse in Paris. For de Basil's Co. she chor. *Les Cent Baisers* (1935), revived *Les Noces* (1936), and arranged the dances in Reinhardt's film *A Midsummer Night's Dream*. In 1938 she went to live and teach in America, producing *Brahms Variations* (1944) for Ballet Theatre, etc. She was ballet mistress at the Colon Th., Buenos Aires several times and also for the de Cuevas Co. In 1960 she helped with the mounting of *Sleeping Beauty* in Paris by de Cuevas B. Ashton invited her to mount *Les Biches* and *Les Noces* for the Royal B. in 1964 and 1966 respectively. Director of Buffalo B. 1967.

NIJINSKY, Vaslav, b. Kiev 1888, d. London 1950. Russ. dancer and chor. Entered Imp. Sch., St Petersburg 1900, studied under Legat, Oboukhoff and Cecchetti. First appeared in public at the age of 18 in Mozart's *Don Giovanni*. Later partnered Kschessinska, Preobrajenska, Pavlova, and Karsavina, and created great impression. Met Diaghileff, who was to become the greatest influence in his life. Shortly after his début he joined Diaghileff's Co. on its formation (with leave of absence from the Imp. Th.) and made a sensational personal success dancing in its first Paris season in 1909. He danced *Le Pavillon d'Armide*, *Les Sylphides*, and *Cléopâtre*, and the following year *Schéhérazade* and *Carnaval*. He resigned from the Imp. Th. in 1911 (to which he had returned between the Diaghileff tours) over a dispute about his dress in *Giselle*. The same year, with Diaghileff again, he danced *Le Spectre de la Rose* and *Petrouchka* and chor. *L'Après-midi d'un Faune*, which was a *succès de scandale*. In 1913 chor. *Le Sacre du Printemps* and *Jeux*. Later that year the Diaghileff Co. went to tour America, but without Diaghileff, and on it Nijinsky married one of the dancers, Romola de Pulsky, a Hungarian. Diaghileff, on hearing this, dismissed him and their association ended. He rejoined Diaghileff's Co. in 1916 and danced in the U.S.A. where he was in charge of the company, and chor. *Tyl Eulenspiegel*. After touring S. America he settled in Switzerland and his mind became deranged. His wife faithfully looked after him until his death in London 1950. He had a daughter, Kyra (b. 1914, British, in B. Rambert and taught in Italy). He was the greatest male dancer of his generation and his astonishing *ballon*, elevation, beats, and quality of movement were unsurpassed. He seemed to merge himself completely in all his rôles, and no other dancer, with the possible exception of Taglioni, has had such a myth attached to himself, during or after his lifetime.

NIJINSKY—CLOWN DE DIEU, ballet, ch. Béjart, m. Pierre Henri (and from Tchaikovsky's Pathetic Symphony), cost. Roustan and Bernard, f.p. Ballet du XXme Siècle, Forest National Auditorium, Brussels 8 Oct 1971 (Jorge Donn, Bortoluzzi, Suzanne Farrell). A full-length ballet evoking Nijinsky and his tragic life. Performed at the Coliseum, London 3 May 1972.

NIKITINA, Alice, b. St Petersburg 1909. Russ. dancer and singer. Studied at Maryinsky Sch. under Poliakova, Preobrajenska and N. Legat. Fled Russia during the Revolution, danced in Ljubljana, Berlin etc. Joined Diaghileff's Co. 1923 and became a leading dancer. Cr. rôle of Flore in *Zéphire et Flore* (1925) etc. Danced in Cochran's revues and studied singing in Rome and Milan (having lessons from Tetrazzini). Became professional singer in Italy. In 1949 opened a ballet school in Paris and offers an annual scholarship, the Prix Nikitina, to young dancers. Wrote her autobiography *Nikitina by Herself* 1959. Was befriended by Lord Rothermere, one of Diaghileff's patrons.

NIKOLAIS, Alwin, b. Southington, Conn. 1912. Am. dancer, chor. and composer. Studied dance with Hanya Holm and Graham. Previously he had worked as a musician and as a puppet master. In 1939 he produced an evening's entertainment (with Ernst Krenek the composer) *Eight Column Line* at Hartford, Conn. where in 1948 he was later appointed director of the Henry Street Playhouse. He devised a number of spectacles (from 1953) of moving lights, sounds, figures, scenery, props etc.—using dancers almost as props themselves or just to support them. Among these are *Masks, Props and Mobiles* (1953), *Kaleidoscope* (1956), *Totem* (1960), *Imago* (1963), *Limbo* (1968), *Tent* (1968), *Tower, Structures, Echo* etc. The music is mostly electronic and composed by himself. Among his dancers are Phillis Lamhut, Carolyn Carlson, Murray Louis. Many of his works have been shown on television throughout the world. His Co., Dance Th. of Alwin Nikolais, first appeared in England at Sadler's Wells Th. 23 June 1969.

NINA, OU LA FOLLE PAR AMOUR, ballet 2 acts, ch. Milon, m. Persuis, f.p. Paris Opéra 23 Nov 1813 (Bigottini, Albert). Galeotti first chor. *Nina* in Copenhagen 26 Nov 1802 (Schall).

NINTH SYMPHONY, ballet, ch. Béjart, m. Beethoven, f.p. B. du XXme Siècle, Cirque Royale, Brussels 27 Oct 1964 (Lise Pinet, Sifnios, T. Bari, Hofgen, Bortoluzzi, Casado). This production included a prelude of drum-rolls, monologue etc.

NOBILISSIMA VISIONE, ballet 5 sc., ch. Massine, m. Hindemith, dec.

Tchelitchev, f.p. de Basil's Co., Drury Lane, London 21 July 1938 (Massine, Theilade). Called *Saint Francis* in America.

NOBLET, Lise, b. Paris 1801, d. there 1852. Fr. dancer of the Romantic era, danced at Paris Opéra 1817–41, London 1821–24. Cr. *La Muette de Portici* (1828) and the rôle of Effie in *La Sylphide* (1832). '*Une danseuse qui ne fait jamais de faux pas, qui préfère le cercle d'amis à la foule des amants, qui vient au théâtre au pied, et qui retourne de même.*' Her sister Félicité, Madame Alexis (Dupont), was also a dancer and later an actress.

NOCES FANTASTIQUES, LES, ballet, ch. Lifar, m. Delannoy, dec. Chastel, cost. Levasseur, f.p. Paris Opéra 9 Feb 1955 (Vyroubova, Bessy, van Dijk). A shipwrecked captain and his ghostly wedding under the sea.

NOCES, LES, ballet 4 sc., ch. Nijinska, m. Stravinsky, dec. Goncharova, f.p. Diaghileff's Co., Th. Gaîté Lyrique, Paris 13 June 1923 (Doubrovska). There was a chorus, with wailing and chanting, and four grand pianos on the stage (with four pianists), with percussion. In London the four pianists were Auric, Poulenc, Rieti, and Dukelsky— each one of whom wrote a ballet for Diaghileff. In the controversy which followed in the English press H. G. Wells wrote a vigorous support of the ballet to *The Times*. It was not published but he gave a copy to Diaghileff who used it in his publicity. Nijinska revived her ballet for Royal B. at C. Garden with the original dec., f.p. 23 Mar 1966 (Beriosova, Parkinson, Mead, Dowell). The pianists were Richard Rodney Bennett, John Gardner, Edmund Rubbra, Malcolm Williamson. Another version was chor. by Robbins, dec. Smith, cost. Zipprodt, f.p. Ballet Theatre, N.Y. State Th., N.Y. 30 Mar 1965 (Erin Martin, William Glassman). Bernstein conducted on stage. This was also danced by the R. Swed. B. Stockholm in 4 June 1969. At Paris Opéra 1965, Béjart chor. another version.

NOCTAMBULES, ballet, ch. MacMillan, m. H. Searle, dec. Georgiadis, f.p. S. Wells B., C. Garden 1 Mar 1956 (Nerina, Lane, Linden, Edwards). A hypnotist hypnotizes his audience.

NOCTURNE, ballet 1 act, book E. Sackville-West, ch. Ashton, m. Delius (*Paris*), dec. Fedorovitch, f.p. S. Wells B., S. Wells Th. 10 Nov 1936 (Fonteyn, Brae, Helpmann, Ashton). An outstanding ballet of atmosphere, one of Ashton's best, it was removed from the repertoire.

NOGARET, Nicole, b. Marseilles 1940. Fr. dancer. Pupil of Gsovsky. Danced in the companies of Petit, Tcherina, Charrat, Miskovitch, and soloist in Massine's Balletto Europeo, 1960.

NOGUCHI, Isamu, b. Los Angeles 1904. Japanese-Am. sculptor and stage designer. Made the dec. for many of Martha Graham's ballets, incl. *Frontier* (1935), *Appalachian Spring* (1944), *Errand into the Maze* (1947), *Diversion of Angels* (1948), *Clytemnestra* (1958), *Acrobats of God* (1960) etc. Also made décor for R. Page's *The Bells* (1946), Cunningham's *The Seasons* (1947) and Balanchine's *Orpheus* (1948).

NOIR ET BLANC, see SUITE EN BLANC.

NON-STOP, ballet, ch. Darrell, m. Williams/Palmer, dec. Kay, f.p. Western Th. B., Dartington Hall, Devon 24 June 1957 (Hazel Merry, Oliver Symons, Jeffery Taylor). A rock 'n roll scene.

NORBERG, Charlotte (Törner), b. 1824, d. 1892. Swedish dancer. Studied R. Swedish B. Sch. and in Copenhagen. Début Stockholm 1842 in *La Fille Mal Gardée*. Became solo dancer and retired 1859.

NORDI, Cleo, b. Kronstadt 1899. Finnish dancer and teacher. Studied in Russia and under Gé in Finland. Then with Preobrajenska and Trefilova. Joined Paris Opéra 1924 and Pavlova's Co. 1926–31. Danced in England and taught in London from the 1940s until she joined the Folkwangschule in Essen. Returned to London and continues teaching there. Guest teacher at Royal Ballet School and for London Contemp. Dance Th.

NORTH, Robert (Dodson), b. Charleston, S. Carolina 1945. Am. dancer. Pupil of Crofton, Royal B. Sch., Graham and Cunningham. Joined London Contemporary Dance Th. 1967 (on its inception). Then in Graham's Co. in N.Y. and returned to Lond. Contemp. Dance Th. as principal 1969.

NORTHCOTE, Anna (Stafford-Northcote), b. Southbourne 1907. Eng. dancer and teacher. Pupil of Euphan Maclaren, Craske, Legat and Preobrajenska. As Anna Severskaya danced in Oumansky B. 1930, Levitoff-Dandré B. Russes 1934, B. Russes de Paris 1936, de Basil B. 1937–39. Began teaching in West St, London 1941–69 and at the Dance Centre from 1969. Her studio became the principal centre for professional dancers in London and for visiting foreign dancers. Guest teacher for many Continental Cos.

NORTHERN DANCE THEATRE, the first regionally based ballet company in Britain, founded by Laverne Meyer in Manchester in 1969 and serving the North West. Its funds are derived from local sources (private, municipal and commercial) and with an Arts Council grant. Its first trial performance was on 24 Mar 1969 in the University Th., Manchester, with students from the Royal Manchester College of Music playing. There were 10 dancers, among them Carol Barrett, Calliope Micklem and Terence Etheridge, and ballets by Andrée Howard, Meyer and Clover Roope were performed. Its first season opened in Manchester on 28 Nov 1969 and the first London appearance was at The Artists' Place on 26 June 1970. In 1973 the Co. had 20 dancers.

NORWAY, BALLET IN, see under NORWEGIAN BALLET.

NORWEGIAN BALLET, began in 1948 when Gerd Kjölaas and Louise Browne founded the Ny Norsk Ballet (New Norwegian Ballet) in Oslo. It toured in England and Scandinavia. Fonteyn and Helpmann appeared as guest artists in 1950. It closed in 1958 when the dancers were absorbed into the first state-subsidized company, Den Norske Opera Ballett (Norweg. Opera B.). The first director was Algeranoff and the first perf. was *Coppélia* 25 Feb 1959. In 1960 Nicolas Orloff became director. In 1961 the Co. was enlarged to 20 dancers with Joan Harris as director (until 1965). First perf. was 14 Sept 1961 (*Lilac Garden*, *Judgement of Paris* and *Soirée Musicale*—all ch. Tudor, with *Pas Gracieux* by Rita Tori). In 1965 Joan Harris became director of the Norweg. Opera B. School and the ballet was directed by Brian Macdonald and Henny Mürer. Sonia Arova became director in 1966 until 1970. She was succeeded by Anne Borg. Their National B. Sch. is attached to the Co., takes R.A.D. examinations and since 1965 has been directed by Joan Harris.

NOTARI, Giovanni, b. Rome 1936. It. dancer. Pupil of Gennaro Corbo in Rome. Soloist Scala, Milan, in 1958. In 1959 became primo ballerino in Rome Opera House.

NOTRE DAME DE PARIS, ballet 2 acts, ch. Petit, m. Jarre, dec. Allio, cost. Yves Saint-Laurent, f.p. Paris Opéra 11 Dec 1965 (Motte, Petit, Atanassoff, Bonnefous). The Hugo novel. This was Petit's first work for the Opéra—20 years after he had left.

NOUVEAU BALLET DE MONTE CARLO, founded during the Second World War in 1942 in Monte Carlo with dancers from the Paris Opéra who had escaped to the south of France, together with students from Sedowa's School. In 1945 the Paris impresario Eugene Grünberg took it over and it formed a home for many Fr. dancers in the disruption which followed the War. Yvette Chauviré was the ballerina and the company included Janine Charrat, Jeanmaire, Tcherina, Kalioujny, Skouratoff, and later Lifar as artistic director. After Monte Carlo there were seasons in France and at the Cambridge Th., London, in 1946. In 1947 the Marquis de Cuevas bought the company and re-formed it as the Grand B. de Monte Carlo—later du Marquis de Cuevas (q.v.).

NOVARO, Luciana, b. Genoa 1923. It. dancer and chor. Entered Scala, Milan, Sch. 1933, studying under Giussani, Mazzucchelli, Volkova, and Bulnes. Became prima ballerina 1946. Has also danced in Brazil.

361

Since she gave up dancing she has chor. many ballets for the Scala, Milan and is one of the leading figures in It. ballet. Director of ballet at Scala, Milan 1962–64.

NOVERRE, Jean-Georges, b. Paris 1727, d. St-Germain-en-Larye 1810. Fr. dancer and chor. Pupil of Dupré in Paris. Dancer at Paris Opéra Comique in 1743 and produced his first ballet there 1749. He foresaw and advocated most of the reforms which were to be carried out a century later by von Laban, Fokine and Jooss. His ideas, however, met with such opposition that he had to seek their realization outside his own country, and it was at the Courts of Württemberg (1760–67) and Vienna (1767–74), and at the King's Th., London in 1782, 1788–89 (he had studied mime from Garrick in 1775 while at Drury Lane), that he staged his greatest ballets. He set out his ideas in his *Letters on Dancing* (Stuttgart 1760) which, although today much of their content is taken for granted, when they were written and indeed until the beginning of the twentieth century, were revolutionary. At a time when the court ballet had degenerated into a meaningless succession of conventional dances, to miscellaneous airs hastily strung together, and selected to display the virtuosity of the leading dancer, Noverre advocated unity of design and a logical progression from introduction to climax in which the whole was not sacrificed to the part and all that was unnecessary to the theme was eliminated. Movement, he felt, should be defined by the tone and time of the music and he compared the relationship of music to dancing to that of words to song, but he criticized much of the ballet music of his time (which was still based on the work of Lully) as old fashioned and of too slow a tempo. He told choreographers to abandon entrechats, cabrioles, and overcomplicated steps, and turn to nature for natural means of expression which could be understood by all and not merely by a small élite, which is no more or less than has been done by the exponents of the Modern Dance Movement. His efforts to bring about a reform of costume were successful and he lived to see masks, full-bottomed wigs, and cumbersome hooped and panniered dresses abandoned in favour of attire better suited to the rôles portrayed. None of Noverre's 150 ballets has been handed down to us, but it has been given to few to have so great and lasting an influence on the art of ballet, and it can be said without exaggeration that he is the grandfather of the ballet as we know it today. In 1776 he became maître de ballet at the Paris Opéra, a post he had failed to obtain earlier in his career. He fled to England during the Revolution, where he was welcomed, and he produced his last ballet in London. His principal ballets were *La Toilette de Vénus, Médée et Jason, Les Horaces*. He was engaged in writing a *Dictionary of Ballet* when he died. His brother Augustin (b. 1729, d. Norwich 1805) came to Norwich 1794 and opened a school, founding a long line of dancing masters in that city.

NOVERRE BALLET, the second company of the Stuttgart B. founded by Cranko in 1971 to perform in Stuttgart while the main Co. was on tour and also independently of it, and supplying dancers for the operas. Directed by Alan Beale, its first performance was *Coppélia* (arr. Beale) on 16 Apr 1971 (Cuoco, Oxenham). It ceased in 1973.

NOVERRE SOCIETY, founded in Stuttgart in 1958 to further the cause of the Stuttgart Ballet. It promotes lectures, film evenings and performances of ballets by young chors. from the Stuttgart B.

NOVIKOFF, Laurent, b. Moscow 1888, d. Buffalo 1956. Russ. dancer. Graduated from Imp. Sch., Moscow 1906. Début 1908 at Bolshoi Th. Joined Diaghileff's Co. for 1909 season in Paris. Became partner to Pavlova 1911 and toured with her until 1914, when he returned to Moscow. Rejoined Diaghileff in London 1919 and partnered Karsavina. Again became Pavlova's partner from 1921 to 1928. Opened school in London 1928. Ballet master at Met. Op., N.Y. 1941–45.

NOVOTNY, Richard, b. 1926. Austrian dancer. Soloist of Vienna Staatsoper B. 1962–67 and from 1965 assistant ballet master. Mar. Edeltraut Brexner.

NUIT, LA, ballet 1 act by Kochno, ch. Lifar, m. Sauguet, dec. Bérard, f.p. C. B. Cochran's 1930 Revue, Palace Th., Manchester 4 Mar 1930 (Nikitina, Lifar, Balanchine). The B. des Ch. Élysées f.p. this ballet with ch. Charrat, at the Th. des Ch. Élysées, Paris 19 Apr 1949 (Skorik, Algaroff).

NUITTER, Charles-Louis-Étienne, b. Paris 1828, d. there 1899. Fr. writer, lawyer and Director of the Archives of the Paris Opéra. He wrote the libretti for many of Offenbach's operettas, and of ballets— with L. Mérante, *Les Jumeaux de Bergame* (1866), *Gretna Green* (1873), with Lucien Petipa, *Namouna* (1882) and with Saint-Léon *La Source* (1866) and *Coppélia* (1870).

NUREYEV, Rudolf, b. in a train near Lake Baikal 1938. Russ. dancer. After dancing in local amateur groups and in Ufa Opera B., studied at Leningrad Sch. under A. Pushkin 1955–58. After success in competition in Moscow was offered contracts by Kirov, Bolshoi and Stanislavsky Ths. Chose Kirov B. which he entered 1958 as soloist. Made a great success when Kirov B. danced at Paris Opéra in May 1961 and was praised by all critics. Was reprimanded by Russ. authorities for being friendly with the French. When the Kirov B. were about to board aeroplane at Le Bourget, to fly to London to dance, Nureyev was separated from them by Soviet officials who tried to put him on an aeroplane for Moscow. He eluded the two Russians who had been following him wherever he went in Paris and threw himself into the arms of two French police inspectors and asked for asylum. This was granted and he joined the de Cuevas B. and danced *Blue Bird* with Rosella Hightower. His début in England was on 2 Nov 1961 at Th. Royal, Drury Lane in Fonteyn's Royal Academy of Dancing Gala (*Don Quixote* pas de deux with Hightower, and *Poème Tragique*, ch. Ashton, m. Scriabin—chor. for the occasion). Left Cuevas in Venice after a dispute. To America 1962 to dance on television and with Sonia Arova in Ruth Page's Chicago B. 10 Mar 1962. Guest artist Royal B. first dancing *Giselle* with Fonteyn (C. Garden 21 Feb 1962) and has remained guest artist ever since. Mounted *Raymonda* for Touring Royal B. 1964, *Swan Lake* for Vienna Staatsoper 15 Oct 1964 (his own chor. and danced in it), Kingdom of the Shades scene from *La Bayadère* for R. Ballet 1964, cr. rôle of Romeo in MacMillan's *Romeo and Juliet* (q.v.) 1964, staged full-length *Don Quixote* (q.v.) for Vienna Staatsoper 1966 and Australian B. 1970, staged full-length *Nutcracker* (q.v.) for R. Swedish B. 1967 (his own chor. and danced in it) and for R. Ballet 1968. Ch. *Tancredi* (m. Henze) for Vienna Staatsoper 18 May 1966. Ch. *Sleeping Beauty*, Scala, Milan 1966, etc. Author of *Nureyev*, an autobiography (with Alexander Bland) 1962. He became the most widely-known and most talked-of male dancer since Nijinsky (Karsavina has said that he is his equal) and his partnership with Fonteyn (whose help and encouragement after his escape launched his career in the West) gave her a stimulus which raised her to even greater heights of dancing than before, while his effect on the general public gave an enormous impetus to ballet in the 1960s. In 1972 he became the subject of a film *I am a Dancer* showing him at work and in rôles with Fonteyn, Seymour and Bergsma.

NUTCRACKER, see CASSE NOISETTE.

NUYTS, Jan, b. Antwerp 1949. Belgian dancer. Pupil of Brabants at R. Flemish B. Sch. 1961–67. Joined R. Flemish B. 1967 becoming soloist. Won Gold Medal at Varna Competition 1968 (and partnered Rita Poelvoorde). Joined Nederlands Dans Th. 1969.

NYMPHE DE DIANE, LA, see SYLVIA.

NYSTROM, Nicoline, b. Alexandria 1943. Trained in Malaya and at Rambert Sch. Joined B. Rambert 1967.

O

OBERTAS, Polish round dance in three time, of a somewhat wild character.

OBOUKHOFF, Anatole, b. St Petersburg 1896, d. N.Y. 1962. Russ. dancer. Graduated from Imp. Sch. 1913, and became premier danseur 1917. Joined Blum's Co. 1935 and de Basil's in 1939. To America 1940 and taught at the School of Am. Ballet until his death. In 1927–28 he organized, with Dolin, the Nemchinova-Dolin Ballet in London. Mar. Nemchinova.

O'BRIEN, John, b. Hopetown, Australia 1937. Austral. dancer, teacher and bookseller. Pupil of X. Borovansky 1952–54, Goncharov, Turner, Royal B. Sch., Crofton, Rambert 1955–63. Joined S. Wells Op. B. 1957, B. Rambert 1957–67. In 1966 he took over the Ballet Bookshop (assisted by David Leonard) in Cecil Court, London, on the death of E. C. Mason and in 1968 began giving classes in the Dance Centre.

O'CONAIRE, Deirdre, b. Colwyn Bay 1938. Eng. dancer. Studied with Madame Legat and Ana Roje in Split. Became soloist of Split Ballet 1954. Joined Festival Ballet 1957 and became soloist 1960. Joined London B. 1962 and Royal B. 1962 becoming soloist. Now retired.

ODE, ballet 2 acts, ch. Massine, m. Nabokov, dec. Tchelitchev, f.p. Diaghileff's Co., Th. Sarah Bernhardt, Paris 6 June 1928 (Beliamina, Lifar). The dancers were intertwined with ropes, and use was made of flashing lights and cinema projections. It was one of the earliest examples of what is now called 'mixed media' and it was not a success.

O'DONNELL, May, b. Sacramento 1909. Am. dancer and teacher. Studied with Martha Graham, joined her group and was a soloist 1932–38, and guest artist 1944–52 creating many leading rôles in her ballets. Chor. many ballets and formed her own dance Co. in 1949. Now teaches in N.Y.

ŒUF À LA COQUE, L', ballet, ch. Petit, m. Thiriet, dec. Lepri, f.p. B. de Paris, Princes Th., London 16 Feb 1949 (Marchand, Jeanmaire, Vyroubova, Petit). A burlesque in cabaret style; the scene is set in a kitchen.

OFFENBACH IN THE UNDERWORLD, ballet 1 act, ch. Tudor, m. Offenbach, f.p. Philadelphia B. Co., Convention Hall, Philadelphia, 8 May 1954 (Essen, Lland). A can-can ballet. Also in repertoire of Canadian Nat. B. using different Offenbach music (*Gaîté Parisienne* re-scored), f.p. R. Alexandra Th., Toronto 1 Feb 1955 (France, Leigh, D. Adams,

Earl Kraul). Mounted by Am. Ballet Th., Met. Op., N.Y. 18 Apr 1956 (Kaye, Serrano, Laing, Scott Douglas).

OGOUN, Lubos, b. Prague 1924. Czech athlete, dancer and chor. Joined Czech Nat. B. in Prague 1945 after being in the national gymnastic team. Succeeded Sacha Machov as dance director of the Army Opera Ballet. Director of ballet in Pilsen 1957–61 and then of the Brno ballet. In 1964 founded the Ballet Prague with Pavel Smok and was artistic director until 1968. Chor. of the Laterna Magica in Prague and chor. many works for B. Prague, incl. *Miraculous Mandarin, Students Life* etc.

OHN, Gerard, b. Liège 1928. Belgian dancer. Pupil of Katchourowsky, V. Gsovsky, Kniaseff. Joined B. des Ch. Élysées 1947–57, de Cuevas B. and toured with the groups of Chauviré, Darsonval and Babilée. Now retired.

OISEAU DE FEU L', see FIREBIRD.

OLD-TIME DANCING the dancing at the present time of ballroom dances of the period 1900–14, such as the waltz, polka, lancers etc.

OLD VIC THEATRE, THE, in Waterloo Road, London, was originally the Coburg Th. and was built by subscription helped by a very large donation from one Glossop, a tallow-chandler. It opened 11 May 1818 with *Trial by Battle, or Heaven Defend the Right* (about a murder trial) followed by a Grand Asiatic Ballet and a Harlequinade. Edmund Kean played there in 1831, and in 1833 it was renamed the Victoria Th. after the Queen (who had once visited it as a Princess). It became a music hall in 1871 and later Emma Cons (b. 1838, d. 1912), the first woman member of the London Council, bought the freehold. She re-opened the theatre in 1880 as the Royal Victoria Coffee Music Hall and it became known as The Old Vic and eventually the home of the National Theatre. For its important connexion with English ballet, see LILIAN BAYLIS.

OLIPHANT, Betty, b. London 1918. Eng. teacher and ballet mistress. Danced in musicals in London and arranged dances for the productions of Emile and Prince Littler. To Canada 1947, opened a school in Toronto 1949 and in 1951 taught at Celia Franca's first Summer School for her new Nat. Ballet of Canada. She was appointed first ballet mistress of the Co. and in 1959 became the first director of the Nat. Ballet Sch. (then 27 pupils). In 1967 went to Stockholm at Bruhn's invitation to advise on the reorganization of the R. Swedish B. Sch.

OLYMPIAD, ballet, ch. MacMillan, m. Stravinsky (*Symphony in Three Movements*), f.p. Berlin B., Deutsche Oper, Berlin 11 Mar 1968 (Seymour, Peters, Holz, Kapuste, Doutreval). Also in repertoire of the

Royal B., f.p. C. Garden 2 Dec 1969 (Bergsma, Parkinson, Derman, Rosson, Mead). Dancers in track suits.

OMBRE, L', ballet 3 sc., ch. Filippo Taglioni, m. Maurer, dec. Fedorov, Serkov, Shenian, Roller, Mathieu, f.p. Bolshoi Th., St Petersburg 10 Dec 1839 (Taglioni). It contained two famous *pas*, one in which Taglioni tries to dance with and seize her shadow, and the other, a *Pas des Fleurs*, exploiting her lightness to the utmost and alighting on to tulips, which supported her. She danced both these *pas* at her farewell performance at the Paris Opéra 29 June 1844.

ONDINE, or LA NAÏADE, ballet in 6 sc., ch. Perrot, m. Pugni, dec. Grieve, f.p. Her Majesty's Th., London 22 June 1843 (Cerrito, Perrot). This ballet contained one of Cerrito's most celebrated solos, the *pas de l'ombre* (no connexion with the ballet *L'Ombre*) in which she dances with her shadow. This ballet, but with the title *The Naiad and the Fisherman* was f.p. St Petersburg 30 Jan 1851 (with Grisi) and Perrot used Petipa as his assistant, influencing him in his own ballets later. There was also a ballet *Undine*, ch. Henry, m. Gyrowetz, put on in Vienna in 1825.

ONDINE, ballet in 3 acts, m. Henze (1) ch. Ashton, dec. de Nobili. f.p. Royal Ballet, C. Garden 27 Oct 1958 (Fonteyn, Somes, Farron, Grant), (2) ch. Alan Carter, dec. von Gugel, f.p. Opera House, Munich 25 Jan 1959 (Anaya, Baur, Bertl, Hallhuber), (3) in 2 acts, as *Undine*, ch. T. Gsovsky, dec. Schachteli, f.p. Städtische Oper, W. Berlin 22 Sept 1959 (J. Dornys, Leistner, S. Preisser, Taubert). These are all modern versions of the Romantic ballet above but with Henze's score. Ashton's was filmed in 1959. Also chor. by N. Beriozoff for Zürich B. (1965) and Nancy B. (1973).

ONEGIN, ballet 3 acts, ch. Cranko, m. Tchaikovsky (not from *Eugène Onegin*), dec. Jürgen Rose, f.p. Stuttgart B., Stuttgart 13 Apr 1965 (Haydee, Cardus, Barra, Madsen). The Pushkin poem.

ONE IN FIVE, ballet, ch. Ray Powell, m. Josef and Johann Strauss, cost. D. Rencher, f.p. Sunday Ballet Club, Lyric Th., London 12 June 1960 (Bergsma, Ruffell, Sale, Newton, Rencher). Five similarly dressed clowns—one a girl. Also in repertoires of Western Th. B. (Hazell Merry), Australian B., Nat. B. of Canada and Met. Op. Ballet Studio.

ONE-NIGHT STAND, a single performance in a town given by a touring company.

ON STAGE!, ballet 1 act, ch. Michael Kidd, m. dello Joio, dec. O. Smith, cost. A. Colt, f.p. B. Theatre, Boston, Mass. 4 Oct 1945 (Janet Reed,

Nora Kaye, Kriza, Kidd). A tender ballet on a young girl's first audition for a ballet company.

OPERA-BALLET. The first opera-ballet would seem to have been *La Liberazione di Ruggiero dall'Isola d'Alcina* given at Florence on 2 Feb 1625 for the visit of Wladislaw Sigismund of Poland to the Grand Duchess of Tuscany, but the opera-ballet evolved largely as a combination of the It. opera and the Fr. court ballet in the opera-ballets of Lully, Campra and Romeau. Noverre, in his arrangements of the ballets in the operas of Jomelli at Stuttgart in the second half of the eighteenth century, raised this type of choreographic composition from a mere divertissement between the acts, to an integral part of the production. In the nineteenth century it was the custom for operas produced at the Paris Opéra to have elaborate ballets, hence those in *Robert the Devil, Tannhäuser,* and *Faust.*

OPERATIC DANCING, a term formerly used for ballet dancing—e.g. the Royal Academy of Dancing was called on its foundation The Association of Operatic Dancing of Great Britain.

OPPOSITION, a natural relationship between arms and legs, as in walking when the right leg is forward and the left arm is swung back. It occurs also in static positions such as the *croisé* position and in *épaulement* where the positions of the shoulders, forward and back, are in opposition.

OPUS 1, ballet, ch. Cranko, m. Webern (Passacaglia), f.p. Stuttgart B., Stuttgart 7 Nov 1965 (Birgit Keil, Cragun). Birth of man groping into life, his love and death. Danced Nederlands Dans Th. 1973.

OPUS '65, ballet, ch. Sokolow, m. Macero, f.p. Joffrey B., Delacorte Th., Central Park, N.Y. 1965. Taken into B. Rambert repertoire, f.p. Jeannetta Cochrane Th., London 14 May 1970 (Bruce, Law, Knott). Leather jackets, motor cycles and youthful violence.

ORBS, ballet in six parts, ch. Paul Taylor, m. Beethoven (the three last quartets), dec. Katz, f.p. Paul Taylor Dance Co., Royal Th., N.Y. 4 July 1966 (de Jong, Carolyn Adams, Eileen Cropley, Waggoner, Taylor).

ORCHÉSOGRAPHIE, the title of a book written in 1588 by Arbeau describing the dances of the sixteenth century, and an account of the history of dancing. It is in the form of a dialogue between Arbeau and 'Capriol'. See CAPRIOL SUITE.

ORDMAN, Jeannette, b. Germiston, S. Africa 1935. S. African dancer and director. Studied under R. Berman, Marjorie Sturman and Anna Northcote. Joined Johannesburg Festival B. becoming soloist in 1954. To London and danced on television, S. Wells Op. B. etc. Introduced

R.A.D. teaching into Israel 1965. With the Baroness Batsheva de Rothschild formed the Bat-Dor Dance Co. (q.v.) in 1968, with herself as artistic director and principal dancer.

O'REILLY, Sheilah, b. Bexley 1931. Eng. dancer. Studied under K. Danetree and S. Wells Sch. Original member of S. Wells Th. B. 1946, of which she became a principal dancer, cr. rôles in *Khadra, Sea Change.*

ORIGINAL BALLET RUSSE (Col. de Basil's)—see BALLET RUSSE DE MONTE CARLO.

ORLANDO, Mariane, b. Stockholm 1934. Swed. dancer. Pupil of R. Swed. and Royal B. Schs. Joined R. Swed. B. 1948, became solodancer 1952 and ballerina 1953, the youngest ever to receive the title. Studied in Leningrad 1960. Guest artist Ballet Th. 1961–62. Awarded Order of Vasa 1967.

ORLIKOWSKY, Vaslav, b. Kharkov 1921. Russ. dancer and chor. Pupil of V. Sulima and V. Preobrajensky. Danced in Russia, Poland and Czechoslovakia after the Second World War and in 1952 became ballet master in Oberhausen. His *Swan Lake* there won great acclaim and in 1955 he was appointed ballet master in Basel, taking most of his dancers with him. There he worked up the ballet company to a pre-eminent position on the Continent, with big productions of the classical ballets. From 1966–71 he was director of ballet at the Staatsoper, Vienna. He mounted his *Peer Gynt* (m. Grieg) for Festival B. in 1963, and in the same year *Cendrillon* (m. Prokofieff) for Raymundo de Larrain at the Th. des Ch. Élysées, Paris. In Vienna, chor. *Sleeping Beauty* (1963), *Prince of the Pagodas* (m. Britten) 1967, *Rite of Spring* (1968) etc. In 1971 he became a producer of ice-shows in Vienna.

ORLOFF, Nicholas, b. Moscow 1914. Studied in Paris with Preobrajenska and Gsovsky. De Basil's Co. 1939. Cr. rôle of Drummer in *Graduation Ball.* Ballet Th. 1941–44, de Basil 1947, de Cuevas 1950. Mar. Nina Popova. Ballet master Denver Civic B. See NORWEGIAN B.

OROSZ, Adèl, b. Budapest 1938. Hungarian dancer. From 1947–54 studied under Nadasi at State B. Institute, Budapest. Entered Budapest Opera B. 1954, becoming soloist 1957. Also studied in Leningrad 1959 under Pushkin, Dudinskaya and Shelest. Awarded Liszt Prize 1961 and Kossuth Prize 1965. Danced in Gala at Nice for Picasso's 80th birthday 1961. Principal (with L. Sipeki) in full-length ballet film *Girl Danced into Life* (ch. Horangozo, Rabai and Sergei) 1964. Usually partnered by V. Rona.

ORPHÉE, ballet 2 acts 8 sc., ch. Béjart, m. concrète by Henry, dec. Küfner, f.p. Béjart's Co., Opera House, Liège 17 Sept 1958 (Béjart,

Seigneuret, Tania Bari). The first full-length ballet with musique concrète.

ORPHEUS, ballet 3 sc., ch. Balanchine, m. Stravinsky, dec. Noguchi, f.p. Ballet Society, N.Y. City Center 28 Apr 1948 (Magallanes, Maria Tallchief). The remarkable décor by the Japanese sculptor is a feature of this work. Another version, ch. Cranko, m. Stravinsky, f.p. Stuttgart B., Stuttgart 6 June 1970 (Keil, Heinz Clauss).

ORPHEUS AND EURYDICE, ballet 2 acts, 4 sc. (based on the original libretto by Calzabigi 1762), ch. de Valois, m. Gluck, dec. Fedorovich, f.p. S. Wells B., New Th., London 28 May 1941 (Fonteyn, May, Honer, Helpmann).

OSATO, Sono, b. Omaha 1919. Jap.-Am. dancer. Studied with Egorova. Principal dancer Orig. Ballet Russe 1936–41 and Ballet Theatre 1944–45. Cr. rôle of Lover in Experience in *Pillar of Fire*. Danced in musicals, notably *On the Town*. Now retired.

OSIPENKO, Alla, b. 1932. Russ. dancer. One of Vaganova's last pupils at Kirov Sch. (now called Vaganova Sch.) Leningrad. Joined Kirov B. 1950 becoming soloist 1954. Created the rôle of Mistress of the Copper Mountain (with its sinuous acrobatic movements) in Grigorovich's *The Stone Flower* 1957. Won Pavlova Prize, Paris, 1956. Hon. Artist R.S.F.S.R. 1957, People's Artist R.S.F.S.R. 1960.

ÖSTERGAARD, Solveig, b. Copenhagen 1939. Danish dancer. Pupil of R. Danish B. Sch. 1947–57. Entered R. Danish B. 1958, becoming solodancer 1962. Dances Lise in *Fille Mal Gardée*.

OSWALD, Geneviève, b. Buffalo 1923. Am. writer and librarian. Became curator of the Dance Collection of the New York Public Library 1947 and by 1964 had raised it to such a position that it was separated from the music collection to become an independent division of the library.

OTERO, Caroline (*La Belle Otero*), b. Cadiz 1869, d. 1965. Sp. dancer and singer. Début in Paris 1889. Danced and sang, chiefly in *cafés-chantants*, all over Europe and America. Sang *Carmen* at the Opéra Comique, Paris 1912. Led an adventurous life, described in her autobiography, *My Story*, which ends: 'Ever since my childhood, I have been accustomed to see the face of every man who passed me light with desire.' A film about her was made in 1954. Spent her last years in the south of France.

OTHELLO, ballet 4 acts, ch. Chaboukiani, m. Machavariani, dec. Virsaladze, f.p. Opera House, Tiflis 27 Nov 1957 (Chaboukiani, V. Tsignadze, Kikaleishvili), f.p. at the Kirov Th., Leningrad 24 Mar 1960 (Chaboukiani).

OUTLAW, ballet 3 sc. and prologue, ch. Borovansky, m. Williams, dec.

Constable, f.p. Borovansky B., Empire Th., Sydney January 1951 (Gorham, Stevenson, Grinwis).

OUVERT, an open position of the feet (opp. fermé). Sometimes used in the sense of *effacé* when referring to the body.

OUVERTURE DE JAMBE, customary preliminary exercise in France for loosening the limbs at the beginning of a class. Starting in fifth position, the dancer extends the right leg forward on a plié. Keeping the plié, she circles the leg to the back, closing in fifth, and straightens the legs. The dancer then extends the leg to the side in second position, executes a full plié in second, extends the same foot, and closes to fifth position.

OVOD, ballet, ch. I. Belsky, m. Chernov, f.p. Maly Th., Leningrad 6 Nov 1967.

OZAI, ballet 2 acts 6 sc., ch. Coralli, m. Gide, dec. Ciceri, f.p. Paris Opéra 26 Apr 1847 (Plunkett). This ballet is about the voyages of the navigator de Bougainville, who appears as one of the characters.

P

PACOFS, the name of the Orange Free State Ballet, S. Africa. The newest of their Cos. Frank Staff was appointed director just before he died.

PACT BALLET, the ballet company based on Johannesburg (S. Africa) and subsidized by the Performing Arts Council Transvaal. It was formed in April 1963 when the Johannesburg City B. merged with PACT. In 1943 Marjorie Sturman (q.v.) formed a Pretoria Ballet Society and (with teachers Ivy Conmee and Poppy Frames) in 1944 founded the Johannesburg Festival Ballet Society. This was an amateur Co. of the pupils of the Sturman, Conmee and Frames schools. It gave regular performances in Johannesburg; Markova and Dolin and Nerina and Rassine came as guest stars, and in 1956 Fonteyn and Somes (dancing *Swan Lake*, Act 2). By this time only Sturman remained of the founders and later in the year the Society closed for lack of funds.

A Cecchetti teacher in Johannesburg, Faith de Villiers, had started a Ballet Theatre in 1947 which gave some performances. She also started a National B. in Cape Town but returned to Johannesburg in 1959 to form the Johannesburg Ballet which became the Johannesburg City B. Its first performance was in November 1959 and included Balanchine's *Serenade* mounted by Yvonne Mounsey a Johannesburg dancer in the N.Y. City B. It then received support from the Municipality and gave most of its performances in the open air. PACT took over in April 1963 when the Co. was first called the Transvaal B. and

371

then became the PACT Ballet. Between 1963 and 1972 among the guest stars have been Beryl Grey (*Swan Lake* 1964), Samtsova and Prokovsky (*Giselle* 1963), Merle Park, A. Dowell (*Fille Mal Gardée* 1969), Fonteyn, Labis (*Sleeping Beauty* 1971), Makarova, Nagy (*Giselle* 1972), Ashton, Helpmann (*Cinderella* 1972). Faith de Villiers resigned as director in 1971 and was succeeded in 1972 by John Hart. In 1972 the ballet mistress was Denise Schultze, ballet master Louis Godfrey, principal dancers Dawn Weller, Ethne Klein, Faye Daniel, Keith Rosson, Edgardo Hartley, Hans Wrona.

PAGANINI, ballet 1 act 3 sc., ch. Fokine, m. Rachmaninoff, dec. Sudeikin, f.p. de Basil Co., C. Garden, London 30 June 1939 (Rostoff, Baronova, Riabouchinska). The legend of the 'diabolical' Paganini. Another version, ch. Lavrovsky, m. Rachmaninoff, dec. Ryndin, f.p. Bolshoi Th., Moscow 7 Apr 1960 (Yaroslav Sekh as Paganini, Kondratieva as his Beloved).

PAGAVA, Éthéry, b. Paris 1932. Russ. dancer. Studied under Egorova. Danced pas de deux with R. Petit 1942. In 1945 soloist in B. des Ch. Élysées to 1947 when she became soloist of Grand B. de Monte Carlo (later de Cuevas Co.). Since 1952 danced as guest star in Holland, France, etc. Ballerina of Massine's Balletto Europeo at Nervi 1960. Chor. *Façettes* (m. P. Schaeffer 1969), *The Cage* (m. Penderecki and Serocki 1971) for Dutch Nat. B.

PAGE, Annette, b. Manchester 1932. Eng. dancer. Studied at S. Wells Sch. from 1945 and entered S. Wells Th. B. 1950, becoming soloist 1954. To Royal B. 1955 as soloist becoming ballerina 1959. Retired 1967. Mar. Ronald Hynd.

PAGE, Ruth, b. Indianapolis, b. 1905. Am. dancer and chor. Studied under Clustine, Bolm, and Cecchetti. Danced in Pavlova's (1918) and Diaghileff's Co. 1925 and with Kreutzberg 1932–34. Formed Page-Stone Co. 1938 and has danced in many groups all over the world. Chor. *The Bells* (1946) for B. Russe de Monte Carlo, *Impromptu au Bois* and *La Revanche* (1952) for B. des Ch. Élysées, *Vilia* (1953) for Festival B. Formed the Chicago Op. B. (q.v.) 1955 which performed there and on tours until disbanded in 1969. For its tours it was re-named Ruth Page's International B. in 1966.

PALAIS DE CRISTAL, ballet 4 movements, ch. Balanchine, m. Bizet (*Symphony*) dec. Fini, f.p. Paris Opéra 28 July 1947 (Darsonval, Toumanova, Kalioujny, Ritz). This ballet was later danced by Ballet Society at N.Y. City Center, without dec. on 22 Mar 1948 under the title *Symphony in C* (Maria Tallchief, LeClerq, Magallanes, Moncion), and was taken into the repertoire of the R. Danish B. in 1953, and of

R. Swedish B. and many other Cos. Balanchine conducted it on 8 Nov 1948, in the season that Ballet Society became N.Y. City B.

PALLADINO, Emma, b. Milan c. 1860, d. London 1922. It. dancer. Studied Academy of Dancing, Milan, and later appeared at La Scala. Toured America and first danced England at Drury Lane 1879 in a pantomime. Début at the Alhambra Th. 1881, and in 1888 took Carlotta Brianza's place at the Empire Th. in Katti Lanner's *Dilara*. She danced at the Empire until 1893 and also toured Europe. She was called 'The Complete Palladino' and had a remarkable technique. She married an Englishman and settled in London.

PALLEY, Xenia, b. Chicago 1933. Fr. dancer. Pupil of Sedowa, Kniaseff, and Rousanne. Début de Cuevas B. 1948. Joined Charrat's Co. as soloist 1951. Awarded the René Blum Prize 1952. From 1957–61 prima ballerina in Stuttgart during Beriozoff's régime and was Juliet in Ulbrich's *Romeo and Juliet* there in 1959.

PALMAS, the hand clapping in Sp. dancing.

PALTENGHI, David, b. Bournemouth 1919, d. Windsor 1961. Eng. dancer and chor. Studied under Tudor and Rambert. Début London B. 1939 and danced for B. Rambert. Joined S. Wells B. 1941, becoming a principal dancer. Left 1948 for films. To B. Rambert as principal dancer and chor. Ballets include *Eve of St Agnes*, *Scherzi della Sorte*, etc.

PALUCCA, Gret, b. Munich 1902. Ger. dancer and teacher. Studied with H. Kröller and joined Wigman's group 1923. In 1924 she began giving solo recitals, which became celebrated. She opened a school in Dresden in 1925. It was made to close down in 1939, but she began again 1945 and it is now one of the most important centres of the dance in E. Germany.

PANADER, Carmen, b. Buenos Aires 1933. Argentinian dancer. Pupil of Esmée Bulnes and M. Borowsky. Danced in the Teatro Colon becoming prima ballerina 1952. Danced with de Cuevas, in Stuttgart B., Cologne 1960–63, in Rome and Toulouse. Now teaches in Bordeaux.

PANAIEFF, Michel, b. Novgorod 1913. Russ. dancer. Studied under Legat, Egorova. Début in Belgrade. Soloist in de Basil's and Blum's Cos. and Ballet Theatre. Now teaches in Los Angeles.

PANDORA, ballet 2 parts, 6 movements, ch. Jooss, m. Gerhard, cost. Heckroth, f.p. Ballet Jooss, Arts Th., Cambridge 26 Jan 1944 (de Mosa, Zullig). The story of Pandora's box.

PANICKER, Chatunni, b. Kerala. Indian dancer. Became Sarabhai's partner 1945 and from 1948 has taught in her school. A leading Kathakali dancer.

PANOV, Valery, b. Vitebsk 1938. Russ. dancer. Grad. from Kumysnikov's class at Leningrad Sch. to Maly Th. 1957 and studied there under Semen Kaplan. Joined Kirov B. 1963 as a soloist. He cr. rôle of *Petrouchka* when Maly Th. revived it in 1961. State Prize 1969 and Lenin Prize. Hon. Artist R.S.F.S.R. 1970. He has not been allowed to dance in the West, except for a single performance in Madison Square Garden, N.Y. 1958 when he was suddenly recalled under the false pretext that his father was dying. Mar. G. Ragozina. In 1972 he applied as a Jew for a visa for himself and his wife to emigrate to Israel. This was refused and he was dismissed from the Kirov B. and imprisoned. Dancers from all over the world appealed for him. See HAMLET.

PANTOMIME, (1) a dumb-show. The miming or gesture scenes which develop the story of a ballet; (2) a traditional English entertainment (now usually performed at Christmas) dating from the early eighteenth century, of music, dance, and mime, usually following set lines and ending with a transformation scene and a harlequinade, though of recent years its character has greatly changed.

PANTZ, Serge. Russ. dancer, pupil of Youpushoff. Cr. rôle of *le chien* in *Le Dernier Lampadaire*. His most famous rôle was that of The Guard in *Southern Railway*. This is all, or rather more than all, that is known of Nicolas Bentley's character in *Ballet-Hoo* (1937).

PAPILLON, LE, ballet, ch. Marie Taglioni, m. Offenbach, f.p. Paris Opéra 26 Nov 1860 (Emma Livry). This was Taglioni's only ballet, made for her favourite pupil Emma Livry, with libretto by V. Saint-Georges. A new version with m. Minkus, dec. Lagorio, Botcharov, Wagner, cost. Ponomarov, was f.p. St Petersburg 6 Jan 1874 (Vazem).

PAPILLON, PAS DE, see PAS DE CHAT.

PAQUITA, ballet 2 acts 3 sc., ch. Mazilier, m. Deldevez, dec. Philastre, Dieterlé, Sechan, Despléchin, f.p. Paris Opéra 1 Apr 1846 (Grisi, L. Petipa). A Spanish gypsy discovers that her father is a nobleman, at a magnificent First Empire ball in the last act. Marius Petipa produced it in St Petersburg 24 Sept 1847, making his début as a dancer and partnering Y. Andreyanova (b. 1819, d. 1857) in it. Years later in St Petersburg he mounted a scene which included the now-famous *Grand Pas* and a mazurka, all with new music by Minkus. The *Grand Pas* was danced by Vazem and the other pieces by soloists and students, on 27 Dec 1881. This scene remains in the Russian repertoires (in 1896 Cecchetti added a *pas de quatre*). In 1964 Nureyev mounted this act for the R.A.D. Gala at Drury Lane, danced by Fonteyn and himself, with some students. For Festival B., Roland Casenave mounted it, f.p. New Th., Oxford 9 Mar 1967, dec. McDowell, danced by Samtsova and Prokovsky.

PARADE, ballet 1 act, book Cocteau, ch. Massine, m. Satie, dec. Picasso, f.p. Diaghileff's Co., Châtelet Th., Paris 18 May 1917 (Lopokova, Massine). A Cubist ballet. Revived by Joffrey B., N.Y. 1973.

PARIS INTERNATIONAL FESTIVAL, an annual festival of ballet held at the Théâtre des Champs Élysées each November (first Festival was in 1963) at which companies from all over the world are invited to take part. Prizes were given for the best dancers, best company, best choreographer etc. but these were discontinued in 1972.

PARIS OPÉRA BALLET, the national ballet of France. Its origin is described under 'Académie Royale de Musique' and it has had a continuous history since 1669. It has had many changes of title, according to the political situation, and its present name (since 1871) is *Théâtre National de l'Opéra*. Its first home of any permanence was the Salle Molière in the old Palais Royal, from 1673 to 1763, when it was burnt. From 1794 to 1820 it was in the Salle Montansier in the present Rue Richelieu. From 1821 until it was burnt down in 1873, it was in the Rue le Peletier. The present building (the fifteenth home of the Opéra), designed by Garnier (hence its familiar name, Palais Garnier) was opened in 1875. The theatre has 2,300 seats and the stage is 52 ft wide and 85 ft deep (120 ft with Foyer de Danse). The first Director of the Opéra (which always includes the ballet company) was the Abbé Perrin, who was succeeded by Lully in 1672. The great Director of the Romantic era was Dr Véron, who had two remarkable successes in the opera *Robert le Diable* and Taglioni in *La Sylphide*. The Opéra ballet went into a decline during the latter half of the nineteenth century, but was revived by Jacques Rouché, Director 1914–44. In 1929 he appointed Serge Lifar as maître de ballet, under whom the status of the ballet was raised to a height it had not reached since the time of Taglioni. The characteristic 'French' style still persisted, but Lifar introduced the elements of the great 'Russian' style and his new neo-classical style of choreography, influenced by his training in Diaghileff's Co. In 1952 Maurice Lehmann was appointed Director, and he reverted to the practice of the eighteenth century and mounted lavish opera-ballets (e.g. *Les Indes Galantes*), employing all the resources of the opera and ballet troupes. The École de Danse de l'Opéra was founded in 1713, of which famous Directors (later Professors) were Lany (1750), M. Gardel (1770), Coulon, Vestris, Mérante, Marie Taglioni, Mme Dominique, Carlotta Zambelli. In 1963 Chauviré was appointed Director. Among the most famous ballet masters have been Beauchamp and Pécour (seventeenth century), J. B. Lany, Noverre, G. and A. Vestris, M. and P. Gardel, F. Taglioni, Mazilier, Saint-Léon, Mérante, Staats, Aveline, Lifar. For a description of the ranks of the dancers, see BALLERINA. The dancers are employed by the State and are pensioned. In recent years the Company has left Paris and danced in Copenhagen, New York (1948), Moscow (1958 and 1970), etc., and in 1954 made its only appearance at C. Garden. Among its greatest dancers have been in order of date: (female) Lafontaine Subligny, Sallé, Camargo, Guimard, Heinel, Mme Gardel, Bigottini, Noblet, Taglioni, Grisi, Elssler, Cerrito, Rosati, Livry, Sangalli, Mauri, Subra, Zambelli, Spessivtseva, Darsonval, Chauviré; (male) Balon, Dupré, G. and A. Vestris, Duport, Paul, Albert, Perrot, L. Petipa, Mérante, Vasquez, Aveline, Peretti, Lifar, Renault. Its most successful ballets have been *La Sylphide*, *Giselle*, *Coppélia*, *La Source*, *Les Deux Pigeons*, *La Korrigane*, *Soir de Fête*, *Suite en Blanc*, and *Les Indes Galantes*. In 1955 the leading dancers were (girls) Chauviré, Vyroubova, Bardin, Lafon, Vaussard, Daydé; (men) Lifar, Renault, Bozzoni, Algaroff, van Dijk, with Lander as maître de ballet. The troupe comprises ninety dancers. In 1960 the principals were (girls) Marjorie Tallchief, Chauviré, Darsonval, Vaussard, Lafon, Bessy, Amiel, Motte (men) van Dijk, Skibine, Bozzoni, J.-P. Andreani, Attilio Labis, Algaroff. Soloists (girls) Collement, Rayet, (men) Bari, Duthoit, Descombey, Franchetti, with Skibine as ballet master. In 1962 Descombey became director and in 1969 John Taras. In 1970 Roland Petit was appointed director; but quickly resigned and Claude Bessy took his place as ballet mistress. Among the dancers in 1970 were Claire Motte, Jacqueline Rayet, Christiane Vlassi, Noella Pontois, Ninon Thibon, Wilfriede Piollet, Martine Parmain, Francesca Zumbo, Attilio Labis, Cyril Atanassoff, J.-P. Bonnefous, Georges Piletta, Patrice Bart, J.-P. Franchetti. In 1971 the Paris Opéra closed down. In 1972 yet another attempt was made to reorganize the ballet, always fraught with intrigue and patronage, and Raymond Franchetti became director, with Gerard Mulys as assistant.

PARISOT, Mlle, Fr. dancer, pupil of Barrey, who made great success in London 1796–1807. Contemporary prints usually show her dancing with her bosom partly uncovered.

PARK, Merle, b. Salisbury, Rhodesia 1937. Rhodesian dancer. Studied under Betty Lamb and at Elmhurst Sch. Entered Royal B. 1954, becoming soloist 1958, principal 1959. Danced her first *Giselle* 1967, *Swan Lake* 1973. Has danced several European engagements partnered by Nureyev.

PARKINSON, Georgina, b. Brighton 1938. Eng. dancer. Trained at S. Wells Sch. Entered Royal Ballet 1957 becoming soloist 1959. Danced Odette in R. Ballet Sch. *Swan Lake* at C. Garden 1960. Created rôle of La Garçonne in Royal B.'s revival of *Les Biches* 1964,

Juliet in MacMillan's *Romeo and Juliet*, R. Swed. B., Stockholm 1969. Danced her first *Swan Lake* for Royal B. 1965.

PARLIC, Dmitri, b. Salonika 1919. Yugoslav dancer and chor. Pupil of Boskovic, Poliakova, T. Gsovsky, Preobrajenska. Entered Belgrade Opera 1938, becoming principal dancer 1941. Danced in Germany, Greece, Austria, Edinburgh. Ballet master in Vienna 1958–62, in Rome 1963–66. Returned to Belgrade. In 1969 became director of Nat. B. of Finland to 1970.

PARMAIN, Martine, b. Parmain, Val. d'Oise 1942. Fr. dancer. Pupil of Perrault, R. Thalia, Franchetti, Opéra Sch. Joined Paris Opéra B. 1960, becoming première danseuse 1964. Guest artist B. Th. Contemporain, Amiens 1968, Opéra Comique as principal 1970, and Ballet Studio Opéra 1966. Guest ballerina Zürich B. 1971. Mar. Michel Descombey.

PARNEL, Ruth, b. Belgrade 1928. Yugoslav dancer. Pupil of Jovanovic and Frankfort Conservatoire. Entered Belgrade Opera 1941, becoming ballerina 1946. Danced in Edinburgh 1951. Now teaches.

PAR TERRE, steps on the ground. Also called à terre.

PAS, lit. a step. (1) A single complete movement of one leg in the act of walking or dancing, and, by extension, the transference of the weight of the body by simple or compound movement. (2) A dance for one or more persons similarly attired or with common attributes, e.g. Pas des Déesses, Pas des Patineurs.

PAS ALLÉ, a simple walking step.

PAS D'ACIER, LE, ballet 1 act, ch. Massine, m. Prokofieff, dec. Iakoulov, f.p. Diaghileff's Co., Th. Sarah Bernhardt, Paris 7 June 1927 (Tchernicheva, Lifar). Glorification of the factory. At the end, the décor began to move, like machines.

PAS D'ACTION, lit. action dance. A dance expressive of a theme or telling a story, in opposition to absolute dance—e.g. the Rose Adagio in *Sleeping Beauty*.

PAS DE BASQUE, lit. Basque step. A step (said to have been invented by Camargo) which gives the impression of swaying from side to side, in which the right leg executes a circular movement from the hip (demi rond de jambe) before the dancer springs (pas de basque sauté) sideways on to it, and with a plié, slides the left foot through the first position to the fourth open, so transferring the weight of the body before straightening the right knee and bringing the right foot up to the left, which can then be raised on to the right cou-de-pied in front (coupé dessous) if the step is to be repeated on the other side. It can also be done glissé. There are many variations of the Pas de Basque

377

such as that executed travelling round the stage by Princess Odile at the end of her solo in the third act of *Swan Lake*: with a demi rond de jambe, jeté on the right point, closing the left smartly in the fifth position front, and, still on the point, executing a quick soutenu.

PAS DE BOURRÉE, lit. a bourrée step; a step probably deriving its name from the Bourrée, a folk dance originating in the Province of Auvergne (France), with which, however, it has now no apparent connexion. 'It is basically no more than three transfers of weight from one foot to one foot. But its complete analysis and, further, its perfection in execution has shown it to have numerous variations (twenty-three is the usual number acknowledged); these are all known to the technician and are easily recognized in execution and it is easy to find these variations in many folk dances' (Ninette de Valois, *Invitation to the Ballet*). The dancer standing in the fifth position right foot front with a demi-plié, opens the left foot to the second position (dégagé just above the ground) and brings it in front of the right foot in fifth position on half point; then, still on the half point and without bending the knees, extends the right foot in the second position à terre and closes the left foot in front, executing a plié with both knees at the same time. The entire movement is executed with the right leg to the left. This is known as a pas de bourrée devant with the back foot, but a pas de bourrée may be done dessous, dessus, en tournant in any direction, on half or full point, and with or without changing the feet, and, of course, be on the opposite foot.

PAS DE BOURRÉE COURU, term designating a succession of small, rapid pas de bourrée and, by extension, to bourrée, to perform a series of small, even, staccato steps on the points (sometimes described as a couru, which can also be done on the flat feet, often as a linking step).

PAS DE CHAT, lit. a cat's step. A springing movement in which one foot jumps over the other, executed on the diagonal. A jumping step in which the feet are one after the other drawn up to the knee of the opposite leg (i.e. starting from fifth position, the back foot is drawn up into a retiré position to the side of the supporting knee and jumped on to at the same time bringing the other foot to the front of the now supporting leg in retiré position and closing fifth front). This step appears very frequently in the dance for Puss-in-Boots and the White Cat in the last act of *The Sleeping Beauty*. Also called pas de papillon.

PAS DE CHEVAL, a pawing movement of one foot while the dancer hops on the other. It is seen in the *Don Quichotte* pas de deux (ballerina's solo).

PAS DE DEUX, a dance for two persons. Grand pas de deux—name given in the Classical ballets to the pas de deux for the prima ballerina

378

and the premier danseur, designed to display their virtuosity, and usually consisting of entrée, adage, variation for the premier danseur, variation for the ballerina, and concluding with a Coda.

PAS DE DIEUX, ballet, ch. Gene Kelly, m. Gershwin, dec. A. François, f.p. Paris Opéra B., Paris 6 July 1960 (Bessy, Labis, Descombey). Gods in a modern setting. The first ballet chor. by an American at the Opéra (he was awarded the Legion of Honour afterwards).

PAS DE QUATRE, LE, divertissement by Jules Perrot, m. Pugni, f.p. Her Majesty's Th., London 12 July 1845, with Marie Taglioni, Carlotta Grisi, Fanny Cerrito, and Lucile Grahn, which caused a sensation for never before had the four greatest dancers of the time appeared together. The event has been recorded in one of the most beautiful lithographs of the period by A. E. Chalon. The idea of this ballet was Lumley's (q.v.) and he had to use all his diplomacy to avoid a quarrel between the dancers. It was performed four times only in 1845 (Queen Victoria and the Prince Consort attended the second performance). In 1847 it was performed twice (with Rosati in Grahn's place)—six performances in all. A revival to the original music (orchestrated Leighton Lucas) with ch. by Keith Lester has been produced by a number of companies, including the Markova-Dolin Ballet (1936 Molly Lake, Diana Gould, Kathleen Crofton, Prudence Hyman), Arts Th. Ballet, Ballet Guild. The version now most often seen in the one chor. by Dolin, for Ballet Th., f.p. Majestic Th., N.Y. 16 Feb 1941 (Nana Gollner, Katia Sergava, Alicia Alonso, Nina Stroganova). He mounted it for Festival Ballet, Monte Carlo 21 May 1951 (Markova, Riabouchinska, Hinton, Rossana), by R. Danish B. 1955 etc. When the Kirov B. were in Canada in 1965 Dolin taught them his version and it was f.p. by them Philharmonic Hall, Leningrad 16 May 1966 (Makarova, Komleva, Bolshakova, Nina Gruzdeva). Lester's version is taught annually to the students of the Teachers' Training Course of the Royal Academy of Dancing. In 1970 Ivor Guest wrote a book *Pas de Quatre* describing its history and including the music in full.

PAS DE REPOS, a piece of 'padding' to rest a dancer in the course of a long pas de deux or solo (Karsavina).

PAS DES DÉESSES, ballet, ch. Joffrey, m. J. Field, cost. in style of the famous lithograph of that name, f.p. YM-YWHA, N.Y. 29 May 1954 (Lillian Wellein, Barbara Gray, Jacquetta Kieth, Michael Lland). Danced by B. Rambert, S. Wells Th. 30 June 1955 (Goldwyn, Sopwith, Dyer, Dixon).

PAS DE TROIS (de quatre, de cinq, de six etc.), a dance for three (four, five, six, etc.) persons.

PAS DE TROIS (GLINKA), ballet, ch. Balanchine, m. Glinka, cost. Karinska, f.p. N.Y. City B., City Center, N.Y. 1 Mar 1955 (Hayden, Wilde, Eglevsky).

PAS DE TROIS (MINKUS), see MINKUS PAS DE TROIS.

PAS DE ZÉPHIRE, *battements en cloche* but with a small jump when the moving leg is at its height (in front or at back). A *pas de zéphire battu* is when a beat (a cabriole) is added to the movement.

PAS MARCHÉ, a walking step with the foot arched and set down toe first, then heel, finishing in a demi-plié.

PASSACAGLIA, probably from the Spanish *pasacalle*, street-song. Dance of It. or Sp. origin in three time, probably derived from the chaconne, to which it is closely related musically, which attained its greatest popularity in the reign of Louis XIV who would often perform its grave and solemn movements in his court ballets. Today it is only preserved as a musical term.

PASSAMEZZO, dance popular in the sixteenth century in England, France and Germany, but probably of It. origin. It was performed in 2/4 time to an air sung by the dancers and frequently followed a *Saltarello*.

PASSÉ, a movement in which the position of the legs changes from front to back (or vice versa).

PASSEPIED, dance in 3/8 time in the style of a quick minuet, so called because the feet crossed and uncrossed with a sliding movement, not unlike the pas de bourrée. Originally a choral dance of Brittany, it is said that Henry IV of France travelled to Blois in order to learn it, but it was not until the reign of Louis XIV that it attained to real popularity at the French court. It was later performed on the stage by Marie Sallé and other dancers in the first half of the eighteenth century.

PASSO D'ADDIO, a term used in the Italian ballet schools attached to opera houses (notably the Scala, Milan) indicating a performance of ballet in which the dancers who have just graduated are presented to the public. Lit. 'farewell dance'.

PASTORALE. (1) Ballet, ch. Balanchine, m. Auric, dec. Pruna, f.p. Diaghileff's Co., Th. Sarah Bernhardt, Paris 29 May 1926 (Doubrovska, Lifar, Woizikovsky). A cont. subject, the film star elopes with a telegraph boy. (2) Ballet, ch. Cranko, m. Mozart, dec. Stevenson, f.p. S. Wells Th. B., S. Wells Th. 19 Dec 1950 (Miller, Beriosova, Trecu, Blair). A re-creation of the mood of an eighteenth-century pastoral.

PATH OF THUNDER, ballet, ch. Sergeyev, m. Karayev, libretto Slonimsky, dec. Dorrer, f.p. Kirov B., Kirov Th., Leningrad 31 Dec 1957 (Dudinskaya, Sergeyev). Based on the S. African book by P. Abrahams, the story of a white girl and a black girl who are killed by white people. Also given at Bolshoi Th., Moscow 27 June 1959.

PATINEURS, LES, ballet, ch. Ashton, m. Meyerbeer (from *Le Prophète* and *L'Étoile du Nord*), dec. Chappell, f.p. S. Wells B., S. Wells Th. 16 Feb 1937 (Fonteyn, Honer, Helpmann, Turner). Taken into repertoire of Ballet Th., Broadway Th., N.Y. 2 Oct 1946, with dec. Beaton. A skating ballet, using the Classical technique in its full virtuosity.

PAUL, Mimi, b. Nashville 1943. Am. dancer. Pupil of Gardiner, Day and Franklin at Washington and Sch. of Am. B. Joined Washington B. 1955–60, N.Y. City B. 1961, becoming soloist 1963, principal 1966. Guest artist Festival B. 1969. Joined Am. Ballet Th. 1969 as principal.

PAULLI, Holger, b. Copenhagen 1810, d. there 1891. Danish composer and conductor. He composed the music for a number of A. Bournonville's ballets, incl. *Napoli* (with Helsted, Lumbye, Gade 1842), *Conservatoriet* (1849), *Kermesse in Bruges* (1851), *Brudefaerden i Hardanger* (1853), *Flower Festival of Genzano* (with Helsted 1858).

PAVANE, prob. from the Latin *pavo*, peacock, or from Padua, an Italian city. A sixteenth- and seventeenth-century dance in 2/4 time believed to be of Spanish origin, although certain historians have claimed for it Fr. parentage, danced in France and Italy early in the sixteenth century. The early pavanes were usually danced to a melody played on the hautboys, lutes, and viols with a sung accompaniment of which the pavane *Belle qui tien ma vie* is a beautiful example. A solemn and dignified dance, the pavane was at first reserved to kings, princes, and their consorts in regal robes and trains, which were thus displayed in all magnificence much as a peacock displays its feathers. Although the pavane as such is rarely introduced into modern ballet other than as a divertissement, Ravel's *Pavane for a Dead Infanta* has tempted a number of choreographers.

PAVILLON D'ARMIDE, LE, ballet 1 act 3 sc., book and dec. Benois, ch. Fokine, m. Tcherepnin, f.p. Maryinsky Th., St Petersburg 25 Nov 1907 (Pavlova, Nijinsky, Gerdt). This was Benois's first ballet and it was also danced on the first night of Diaghileff's first season in Paris (Châtelet Th. 19 May 1909, Karalli, Nijinsky, Mordkin). Gobelin tapestries come to life. Based on Gautier's story *Omphale*.

PAVLOVA, Anna, b. St Petersburg 1881, d. Hotel des Indes, The Hague 1931. Russ. dancer. Studied at Imp Sch., under Oblakhov, Vazem, Gerdt, becoming ballerina 1905 and prima ballerina 1906. In 1908 she began to appear in the European capitals on leave from the Maryinsky Th., going to Stockholm, Copenhagen, Berlin, etc., partnered first by Bolm and later by Legat. She was Diaghileff's first ballerina in Paris in

1909. Début in N.Y. and in London 1910 partnered by Mordkin. In 1912 she bought Ivy House, Hampstead, and made London her home. She danced for the last time in St Petersburg 1913, Moscow 1914. In 1914 she formed her own Co. (largely of English girls) and began the tours of the world which lasted the rest of her life. Everywhere she had triumphant successes, in countries which had never seen ballet before, and more than any single person she made the world conscious of the art of the ballet-dancer and of ballet. Her dancing was light, graceful and simple, and to everything she did she brought her own indefinable genius which made her the greatest ballerina of the age. Although her most famous dances were small solos or pas de deux, such as *Le Cygne* and *Autumn Bacchanale*, she excelled in *Giselle*, *Swan Lake*, *Les Sylphides* (the chief rôle of which she created), etc. The repertoire of her own Co. was undistinguished, except for her own dancing, and her taste in music and décor was mediocre, but she shares with Taglioni the most enduring reputation of all dancers. After leaving Russia, Cecchetti remained her principal teacher until his death in 1928. In 1956 a notable exhibition on her life was arranged at the London Museum by John Hayes, to commemorate the 25th anniversary of her death. The 'old girls' of her company meet each year in London for a mass for her in the Russian Church on the day of her death, 23 Jan. The Pavlova Memorial Fund subsidized a series of lectures for several years and in 1969 the remaining money went to provide support for her old dresser, Madame Manya (CHARCHEVNIKOVA).

PAVLOVA, Nadeshda, b. Perm 1957. Russ. dancer. Trained at the Perm Sch. Won All-Soviet Ballet Competition, Moscow 1972.

PEASANT PAS DE DEUX, the name given to the pas de deux in Act I of *Giselle* danced by two soloists. The chor. is by Coralli, the music is by Burgmüller (*Souvenir de Ratisbon*) interpolated into Adam's score and it was first danced by Nathalie Fitzjames and Mabille.

PEAU DE CHAGRIN, LE, ballet, ch. P. Van Dijk, m. Semenoff, dec. J. P. Ponelle, f.p. Opéra Comique, Paris, 1 Apr 1960 (Rayet, Lebertre, van Dijk). The Balzac story.

PÉCOUR, Louis (also Pécourt), b. Paris 1653, d. there 1729. Fr. dancer and chor. who succeeded Beauchamp in 1687 as maître de ballet at Paris Opéra where he introduced a great variety into the ballets. He was one of the lovers of Ninon de Lenclos. Retired from dancing 1703. See MINUET.

PEER GYNT, ballet 3 acts, ch. Orlikowsky, m. Grieg, dec. Bothas and Schröck, f.p. Basel B., Basel 30 Oct 1956 (D. Christensen, Deege, Helga Heinrich, H. Sommerkamp, M. Panitzki). A version of Ibsen's

382

play. Orlikowsky mounted it for Festival B., dec. E. Delany, cost. Yvonne Lloyd, f.p. Monte Carlo 13 Apr 1963 (Gilpin, Skorik, Burr, Borowska, Ferri).

PENCHÉ, a bending forward.

PENNEY, Jennifer, b. Vancouver 1946. Canadian dancer. Pupil of Gweneth Lloyd and Betty Farrally, and from 1962 at R. Ballet Sch. Joined Royal Ballet 1963, becoming soloist 1966, principal 1970.

PENNSYLVANIA BALLET, a professional company founded in 1963 with the help of a Ford Foundation grant. Its director, Barbara Weisberger, directed a regional ballet and opened a school in Pennsylvania. Its first performance was at the Irvine Auditorium in the Univ. of Pennsylvania 19 Apr 1964. They performed at the N.Y. City Center in 1972 and Benjamin Harkarvy became joint-director.

PERCIVAL, John, b. Walthamstow 1927. Eng. writer on ballet. Edited with Clive Barnes *Arabesque* (Oxford B. Club magazine) 1950. On staff of *Dance and Dancers* from 1951, associate editor from 1965. Archivist for *Ballet Annual* 1960–64. Contributor to *Enciclopedia dello Spettacolo*. Ballet critic of *The Times* from 1965. London correspondent of *Dance Magazine*, *N.Y. Times* and *Ballett*. Author of *Antony Tudor (Dance Perspectives* 1963), *Modern Ballet* (1970), *The World of Diaghilev* (1971).

PERETTI, Serge, b. Venice 1910. Fr. dancer. Studied at the Paris Opéra Sch., joined the Paris Opéra Ballet and became étoile in 1941. This was the first time in the history of the Opéra that a male dancer had received this title. He became ballet master in 1944, chor. *L'Appel de la Montagne* in 1945 and soon afterwards retired. He now teaches in Paris.

PEREYASLAVEC, Valentina, b. Ukraine 1908. Russ. dancer and teacher. Joined Bolshoi Sch., Moscow, graduated 1926 and joined Kharkov B., becoming soloist. Also danced in other Ukraine Cos. In Sverdlovsk B. in 1937 as ballerina. Then studied under Vaganova for three years and in 1940 became ballerina in Lvov. Sent by the Germans to do factory work in Leipzig. Liberated by the Americans, and returned to dancing. Reached America 1949, worked in factory in Philadelphia and taught in Tatiana Semeyonova's studio. In 1951 became teacher in Am. Ballet Th. Sch., N.Y. where she remains. Taught Royal B. in London 1963–64 and 1965, and guest teacher at Cologne Summer Academies.

PERFORMING ARTS, SCHOOL OF, New York, founded in 1939 to give a full education and training in drama, music and ballet. In 1962 it combined with the High School of Music and Art and is an annex of it.

PÉRI, LA, ballet. (1) 2 acts 3 sc., book Gautier, ch. Coralli, m. Burgmüller, dec. Séchan, Dieterlé, Despléchin, Philastre, Cambon, cost.

Marilhat, Lormier, f.p. Paris Opéra 17 July 1843 (Grisi, L. Petipa). It was famous for its leap when the Peri falls from a cloud into her lover's arms. An Englishman never missed Grisi's performances for he was convinced that one evening she would fall to her death. (2) ch. Clustine, m. Dukas, dec. Piot, f.p. Châtelet Th., Paris 22 Apr 1912 (Trouhanova). Diaghileff had hoped that Dukas would let him have his score of the ballet for a ch. Fokine, dec. Bakst production but the composer had promised it for Trouhanova and her company. (3) ch. Clustine, m. Dukas, dec. Piot, cost. Stowitts, f.p. Paris Opéra 20 June 1921 (Pavlova). Later in the year this ballet was remade for the Paris Opéra Co., ch. Staats (Bourgat). (4) ch. Ashton, m. Dukas, dec. Chappell, f.p. Ballet Club, Mercury Th., London 16 Feb 1931 (Markova, Ashton). (5) ch. Lifar, m. Dukas, f.p. Nouveau B. de Monte Carlo, Monte Carlo 1946. (6) ch. Ashton, m. Dukas, dec. Hitchens, cost. Levasseur, f.p. S. Wells B., C. Garden 15 Feb 1956 (Fonteyn, Somes). A pas de deux. (7) ch. Skibine, dec. Cernovich and Mitchell, f.p. Paris Opéra 14 Dec 1966 (Motte, Bonnefous). (8) ch. Darrell, dec. Fraser, Festival B. 9 Jan 1973 (Samsova, Prokovsky).

PERI, Ria (Banocs), b. Hungary 1944. Hungarian dancer (now British). Pupil of Budapest State Sch. To England 1960 and entered Royal B. Sch. Joined Royal B. 1964 becoming soloist 1967.

PERRAULT, Serge, b. 1920. Fr. dancer, brother of Lycette Darsonval. Studied at Paris Opéra Sch. Member of the Paris Opéra but left in 1947, with Colette Marchand, to become principal dancer of Metropolitan B. Has danced in most of the Fr. companies and cr. rôle of Toreador in *Carmen* (1948). Teaches in Paris.

PERROT, Jules, b. Lyon 1810, d. Paramé 1892. Fr. dancer and chor. He was one of the greatest male dancers in all ballet, though he was short and ugly (but exceptionally agile). Studied under Auguste Vestris who told him to keep moving during his dancing in order that the audience might not have time to see what he looked like. Gautier called him the greatest dancer of the time, and said that he had the torso of a tenor but with the perfect legs of a Greek statue, somewhat feminine in their roundness, or like those of the youth who breaks the wand in Raphael's *Lo Sposalizio*. He made his début at the Paris Opéra in 1830. He danced with Taglioni and drew so much of the applause that she would no longer dance with him, and in 1835 he left the Opéra to tour Europe as a dancer in his own ballets. He met the young dancer Carlotta Grisi when working at the Teatro San Carlo, Naples, in 1833 when she was 14. He became her teacher, and she his mistress for seven years. They danced together in London, Vienna, Munich, Milan, and Naples, and first app. in Paris at the Th. de la Renaissance in 1840 in *Le Zingaro*. In 1841 *Giselle* was first produced at the Paris Opéra and although his name does not appear in the original programme, it appears certain that Perrot arranged for Grisi all her scenes and dances, thus making him joint chor. with Coralli of this ballet. From 1842 to 1848 he produced the ballets at Her Majesty's Th., London, remounting *Giselle* there, and creating *Alma, Ondine, Esmeralda, Éoline, Pas de Quatre, Catarina, Lalla Rookh, Le Jugement de Pâris, Les Éléments, Les Quatre Saisons*. In 1848 he went to St Petersburg as premier danseur, becoming maître de ballet in 1851 and remaining until 1858, during which time he produced eight new ballets and revived many of his old ones. There he mar. a pupil at the Imperial Sch. Capitoline Samovskaya. He left Russia in 1859 and retired to a village in France, where he died.

PERSEPHONE, ballet, ch. Ashton, m. Stravinsky, dec. N. Ghika, f.p. Royal B., C. Garden 12 Dec 1961 (Beriosova, Grant, Rosson, Larsen). The words by André Gide were spoken in French by Beriosova and transmitted by radio to amplifiers. The work was created in honour of the composer's 80th birthday.

PERSIA, BALLET IN. An Academy of Dance was founded in 1955 by Nejad Ahmadzadeh, at the suggestion of the Ministry of Culture and Arts. This mostly taught and performed Persian dances. In 1958 Ninette de Valois went out to Teheran to develop a classical ballet, and sent Ann Cock, Miro Zolan and his wife Sandra Vane and Marion English to teach and mount ballets. In 1966 Robert de Warren became director of the Iranian Nat. B. In 1967 a new opera house, the Rudaki Hall, was opened, in which the Co. performs, with Aida Ahmadzadeh as prima ballerina. In 1970 de Warren spent a year studying the folk dancing throughout Persia and gathered together a troupe of national dancers, the Mahalli Dancers of Iran, with himself as director. His place as director of the National Ballet was taken by Ahmadzadeh in 1971. In recent seasons Ann Heaton has mounted *Giselle, Schéhérazade, Pas de Quatre* and Chaboukiani produced *Swan Lake* in the 1971–72 season.

PERUGINI, Giulio, b. Rome 1927. It. dancer. Studied at Teatro dell' Opera Sch., Rome. Became principal dancer, Scala, Milan 1949 and has also danced in Spain, Austria, etc. Ballet master at Scala, Milan 1959.

PERUGINI, Mark E., b. 1876, d. Cheltenham 1948. Eng. writer on the dance. Author of *The Art of Ballet* (1915), *A Pageant of the Dance and Ballet* (1935), *The Omnibus Box* (1933). Mar. Irene Mawer.

PETER AND THE WOLF, ballet to Prokofieff's music. (1) Ch. Bolm, dec. Ballard, f.p. Ballet Th., N.Y. 13 Jan 1940 (Loring, Essen, Dollar);

(2) ch. Staff, dec. Sheppard, f.p. B. Rambert, Arts Th., Cambridge 1 May 1940 (Lulu Dukes, Franca, Gilmour, Kersley). A narrator unfolds the story. Revived for PACT B., Johannesburg and for Northern Dance Th. 1969.

PETERS, Kurt, b. Hamburg 1915. Ger. writer and critic. Studied under Fedorova in Riga and Mariska Rudolph. Editor and publisher of *Das Tanzarchiv*, Germany's ballet magazine, first in Hamburg and from 1966 in Cologne. His large personal collection of dance archive material has been presented by him to Cologne. He is one of the directors of the Cologne Institute of Stage Dancing.

PETERSEN, Kirsten, see BUNDGAARD, KIRSTEN.

PETIPA, Jean Antoine, b. Paris 1796, d. St Petersburg 1855. Fr. dancer, chor. and teacher. Father of Lucien and Marius P. After dancing in Paris he moved his family from Marseilles to Brussels in 1819 where he stayed for 12 years. Was chor. in Bordeaux and in Madrid. To St Petersburg in 1848 as teacher in the Imperial School and remained there until his death.

PETIPA, Lucien, b. Marseilles 1815, d. Versailles 1898. Fr. dancer and chor. Brother of Marius P. Studied under his father Jean P. Début in Brussels where his father was maître de ballet. Later danced in Bordeaux and made his début at the Paris Opéra 1840, partnering Elssler in *La Sylphide*. A good-looking man and a very fine dancer, he created many famous rôles, notably Albrecht in *Giselle*, *La Jolie Fille de Gand*, *La Péri*, etc., all partnering Grisi. Chor. *Sakountala* 1858 and *Namouna* (m. Lalo) 1882, becoming maître de ballet at the Paris Opéra 1860–68. Mérante was one of his pupils. He chor. the ballet in Wagner's *Tannhäuser* at its first performance at the Paris Opéra 13 Mar 1861.

PETIPA, Maria M., b. 1857, d. 1930. Russ. dancer, daughter of Maria S. Petipa and Marius Petipa. Début at Maryinsky Th. 1875. She was a famous dancer in Russia and cr. the rôle of The Lilac Fairy in *The Sleeping Beauty*.

PETIPA, Maria S. (née Surovshchikova), b. 1836, d. Novocherkassk 1882, first wife of Marius Petipa. Russ. dancer. She was his favourite *premier sujet* when he was teacher at the Imp. Sch., St Petersburg, 'the most graceful of all dancers, with the body of a Venus'. She married him in 1854, the year she left the Sch. She danced all over Europe and was chiefly famous for her character dancing. Her husband created for her a dance, *The Little Moujik*, in which she appeared en travesti. This was against tradition in Russia and it caused something of a scandal, though it remained her most famous dance. She separated from Petipa in 1867. Her great rival in Russia was Muravieva. Maria M. Petipa was her daughter.

PETIPA, Marius, b. Marseilles 1818, d. Gurzuf 1910. Fr. dancer and chor. After dancing in Brussels, Nantes, and in the U.S. he came to Paris and danced with Carlotta Grisi at the Comédie Française in 1840. From 1843 to 1846 he worked at the King's Th., Madrid, producing five ballets and he also toured Andalusia with Mlle Guy-Stephan and learned Sp. dancing. In 1847 he went to St Petersburg as premier danseur and was appointed maître de ballet in 1862 in succession to the veteran Jules Perrot. Between then and his death in 1910 he produced fifty-four new ballets, besides reviving seventeen old productions and providing the dances for some thirty-five operas. His ballets, in most cases to a romantic theme, were in the accepted style of the period, lengthy productions in five or six acts destined to provide an evening of spectacular entertainment. They contained the inevitable pas de deux followed by a variation for the ballerina, a variation for her partner, a coda, several pas d'action and pas de caractère, and a ballabile for the corps de ballet, whilst marches and processions of supers formed a background for the evolutions of the ballerina for whom the ballet was a vehicle. Petipa's variations, however, have rarely been equalled, for, although reared in the traditions of the Fr. school, he made full use of his imported It. dancers, evolving a style which was a blend of the Adagio of the Fr. *Ballet de Cour*, and the It. Allegro, and exploring the Classical technique to its utmost limits. He may be said virtually to have created the Russ. dancer, and it was with the magnificent technique with which they had been endowed in the Imp. Sch. at St Petersburg under Petipa's reign that the Russ. dancers who made up the Diaghileff Co. commanded world admiration. Amongst the best known of his productions still in the repertoire of various companies are *Don Quichotte* (1869), *La Bayadère* (1876), *Swan Lake* (with Ivanov 1895), *Raymonda* (1898), *The Sleeping Beauty* (1890), *The Seasons* (1900). The *Coppélia* performed by the Sadler's Wells (Royal B.) is the version chor. by him and Cecchetti in Russia in 1894. His first wife was Maria S. Petipa and his second Lubov Leonidova of the Moscow Ballet.

PETIT, Marie-Antoinette, Fr. dancer of eighteenth century. In 1741, she was banned in perpetuity from the Opéra for having been found under the stage, in the costume of Venus rising from the waves, flirting with the Marquis de Bonnac.

PETIT, Roland, b. Villemomble 1924. Fr. dancer and chor. Studied at the Paris Opéra Sch. but left in 1944 to form (with Kochno, Lidova, and others), the B. des Ch. Élysées for which he chor. *Les Forains, Le*

Rendez-vous, Les Amours de Jupiter, Le Jeune Homme et la Mort (with Cocteau), etc. In 1948 he left and formed another Co., Les Ballets de Paris, for which he chor. *Les Demoiselles de la Nuit, Carmen, La Croqueuse de Diamants*, etc. In 1950 he chor. *Ballabile* for S. Wells B. To Hollywood to film in 1949 and formed the B. de Roland Petit on his return to Paris in 1953, with many new ballets, *Le Loup, Deuil en 24 Heures*, etc. He is one of the most original chors. of the era and was a fine premier danseur. Gave N.Y. seasons 1949 and 1954, and his Co. broke up again in Hollywood. Chor. *Cyrano de Bergerac* 1959, *Notre Dame de Paris* (Paris Opéra 1965, in which he danced himself). In 1966 he formed the B. de Roland Petit and presented *In Praise of Folly* at the Th. des Ch. Élysées (m. Constant) and revived *Le Jeune Homme et la Mort*. In 1967 chor. *Paradise Lost* (m. Constant) for the R.A.D. Gala in London (Fonteyn, Nureyev) which was later danced at the Opéra the same year. In 1969 chor. *Pelléas et Melisande* (m. Schonberg) also for R.A.D. Gala (Fonteyn, Nureyev). In 1970 appointed director of the Paris Opéra Ballet (but resigned after a few months of turmoil), and also became, with his wife Renée Jeanmaire, director of the Casino de Paris. Chor. *Kraanerg* (m. Tchaikovsky and P. Henry) for Canadian Nat. B. (Ottawa 1969). In 1971 took charge of the Marseille B. Michaut wrote of him *'Petit assume la charge et l'honneur . . . du rôle de l'éclaireur d'avant-garde: partout ou il passe on entend battre le cœur du jeune ballet.'* Formed a new B. de Marseille 1973.

PETITS RIENS, LES, ballet. (1) Ch. Noverre, m. Mozart and others, f.p. Acad. Royale (Opéra) Paris 11 June 1778 (Guimard, Dauberval). Noverre commissioned Mozart for the music for this ballet, the score of which was not discovered until 1872 in the library of the Opéra. It was revived at the Opéra Comique in 1912. (2) Ch. Ashton, m. Mozart, dec. Chappell, for B. Rambert, Mercury Th. 10 Mar 1928 (Rambert, Argyle, Turner, Ashton). (3) Ch. de Valois, m. Mozart, dec. Smyth, f.p. Old Vic, London 13 Dec 1928. It was the first ballet produced by de Valois for the Old Vic, and it was also the first ballet in the first programme given by the Vic-Wells B., S. Wells Th. 5 May 1931.

PETROFF, Paul, b. Elsinore 1908. Danish dancer. Studied in Copenhagen and became premier danseur of de Basil's Co. 1932–43, Ballet Th. 1943–45, International B. 1947 etc. Mar. Nana Gollner. Teaches in California.

PETROUCHKA, ballet 4 sc., ch. Fokine, m. Stravinsky, dec. Benois, f.p. Diaghileff's Co., Th. du Châtelet, Paris 13 June 1911 (Karsavina, Orloff, Nijinsky, Cecchetti). One of Fokine's greatest masterpieces and with a brilliant score by Stravinsky, this ballet is in repertoire of many large companies today. Mounted by Grigorieff for Royal

Ballet C. Garden 26 Mar 1957 (Fonteyn, Grant, Clegg). The emotions of a puppet.

PHAEDRA, ballet, ch. Graham, m. Starer, dec. Noguchi, f.p. M. Graham Co., Broadway Th., N.Y. 4 Mar 1962 (Graham, Ross, Winter, Taylor). The chor. calls it 'a phantasmagoria of desire'.

PHÈDRE, ballet by Cocteau, ch. Lifar, m. Auric, dec. Cocteau, f.p. Paris Opéra 14 June 1950 (Toumanova, Lifar). A mimed version of Racine's high classical tragedy.

PHILADELPHIA BALLET, see LITTLEFIELD, CATHERINE who founded the Littlefield B. in 1935. The present Pennsylvania B. (q.v.) gives regular seasons, using guest stars.

PHILIPPART, Nathalie, b. Bordeaux. Cont. Fr. dancer. Pupil of Egorova and V. Gsovsky. Début B. des Ch. Élysées 1945. Cr. many rôles for them (notably in *Le Jeune Homme et la Mort*). Mar. Jean Babilée. Their daughter Isabelle Babillé is also a dancer in Béjart's Co.

PHILLIPS, Ailne, b. Londonderry 1905. Irish dancer and teacher. In musical comedies and ballet mistress of her father's Carl Rosa Opera Co. until 1931, when she became an early member of Vic-Wells B. until 1937. Joined S. Wells Sch. as teacher 1940, and in 1953 became the personal assistant of de Valois. In 1960 to teach in Turkey. From 1946 to 1955 she was ballet principal of the S. Wells Sch. In 1971 she returned from retirement and gives occasional lessons at the Royal Ballet Sch.

PHOTOGRAPHERS. Ballet up to about 1820 was depicted by engravings. From that date the lithograph and the Romantic ballet flowered and declined together. From 1850 onwards we depend on the photographers to recreate the dancers for us. Photographs exist of Rosati, Livry, Bozzacchi, and of the Opéra and St Petersburg dancers, but mostly by anonymous studio photographers. From the time of Diaghileff, however, each period of ballet has been recorded by its own photographers who by their interest in ballet and the rapport which they establish with certain dancers have captured something of the spirit of the epoch, and they play an important part in preserving the art. Diaghileff had the *Baron de Meyer* in Paris and *E. O. Hoppé* (b. Munich 1878, d. London 1972) and *Bert* in London. Isadora Duncan had *Arnold Genthe*. In Monte Carlo, *Raoul Barba* photographed most of the full stage sets; in Barcelona, *Battles*, and in Paris, *Studio Iris* and *Lipnitzki*. From 1933 the de Basil and Blum companies were photographed by *Gordon Anthony*, using shadows from cut-out models as evocative backgrounds. He also photographed most of the S. Wells dancers (especially Fonteyn) and produced books on the Company. The earliest Wells and Rambert dancers were recorded by *J. W. Debenham*. In the New Theatre period of S. Wells B., *Mandinian*, and *Tunbridge-Sidgewick* were active. They were followed by *Baron* (d. 1956), *Paul Wilson, Houston Rogers* (1901–70), *Mike Davis, Zoë Dominic, Roy Round*, and others. In America, *Maurice Seymour, George Platt Lynes, Constantine, Walter E. Owen, Martha Swope*, and *Bascome* are the best known, in Germany *Enkelmann*, in Sweden *Rydberg*, and in Denmark *Mydtskov* (father and son). The action-photograph, taken during a performance by stage lighting, conveys much more of the character of the dancer and the ballet than the posed photograph, and one of the earliest was taken by *The Times*, who photographed Dolin in *Le Train Bleu* at the Coliseum, London, in 1924. The pioneer of action photography with a miniature camera was *Merlyn Severn* who covered the de Basil and Blum seasons in 1936–38. *Peggy Delius* was working at the same time. *G. B. L. Wilson*, from 1941, and *Roger Wood*, from 1944, have photographed in action most of the companies appearing in Europe, as has *Fred Fehl* in New York. In France, *Serge Lido* has an individual style of posing his dancers against unusual (often open-air) backgrounds. Among the current English photographers now are (in addition to those mentioned above) *Anthony Crickmay, Donald Southern, Michael Stannard, Frederika Davis, Reg Wilson, Jennie Walton, Keith Money*. It may be noted that in photographing the Sadler's Wells B. at the New Th., London in 1942 on normal black-and-white film the correct exposure was 1/20 sec. at f. 2, and at C. Garden in 1970 it was about 1/100 sec. at f. 4.

PICASSO, b. Malaga 1881, d. Mougins, Cannes 1973. Sp. painter who designed for Diaghileff B. *Parade* (curtain, dec. and cost. 1917), *Tricorne* (curtain, dec. and cost. 1919), *Pulcinella* (dec. and cost. 1920), *Cuadro Flamenco* (dec. and cost. 1921), *L'Après Midi d'un Faune* (backcloth 1922), *Le Train Bleu* (curtain 1924). For Count E. de Beaumont *Mercure* (curtain, dec. and cost. 1924). For B. des Ch. Élysées *Le Rendez-vous* (curtain 1945). For Paris Opéra *L'Après midi d'un Faune* (curtain 1960, but first used at Toulouse 1965), *Icare* (curtain and dec. 1962). His first wife was Olga Khokhlova (d. 1955, sister of Nemchinova) of the Diaghileff B. The front curtain of *Le Train Bleu* was sold by auction at Sotheby's, London, for £69,000 in 1968.

PICHLER, Gusti, b. Vienna 1893. Austrian dancer. Studied at the Hofoper Sch., Vienna, joined the Staatsoper B. 1908, becoming soloist, and ballerina 1925–35. Created one of the principal rôles in Kröller's *Schlagobers* 1924.

PICNIC AT TINTAGEL, ballet 1 act, ch. Ashton, m. Bax, dec. Beaton, f.p. N.Y. City B., City Center, N.Y. 28 Feb 1952 (Adams, d'Amboise,

Moncion). Picnickers of Edwardian days are transported back to the time of Tristram and Iseult.

PIED DANS LA MAIN, LE, see DÉTIRÉ.

PIED PIPER, THE, ballet 1 act, ch. Robbins, m. Copland's Clarinet Concerto, f.p. N.Y. City B., City Center, N.Y. 4 Dec 1951 (Adams, Reed, Jillana, Hayden,¦ LeClerq, Magallanes, Bolender, Robbins, Bliss, Tobias, Bocher). Dancers on an empty stage improvise dances as a member of the orchestra practices his concerto in a corner.

PIÈGE DE LUMIÈRE, ballet 3 sc., ch. Taras, m. Damase, dec. Labisse, cost. Lavasseur, f.p. de Cuevas B., Empire Th., Paris 23 Dec 1952 (Hightower, Golovine, Skouratoff). Fantasy of escaped convicts who catch butterflies in a forest. Revived for N.Y. City B., State Th., Lincoln Center, N.Y. 1 Oct 1964 (Maria Tallchief, Mitchell, Prokovsky). Revived for Festival B., f.p. Fenice Th., Venice 22 Apr 1969 (Samtsova, Prokovsky, Bestonso).

PIERROT LUNAIRE, ballet, ch. Glen Tetley, m. Schönberg, f.p. Glen Tetley Co., N.Y. Sch. of Fashion Design, N.Y. 5 May 1962. Taken into Ballet Rambert, Richmond Th., Surrey 26 Jan 1967, dec. Ter-Arutunian (Christopher Bruce, Gayrie MacSween, Jonathan Taylor). Sung to poems of Albert Giraud. Flirtation of Pierrot, Columbine and an intriguer Brighella.

PILATO, Boris, b. Görz 1921. Yugoslav dancer and ballet master. Studied in Belgrade and with Kniaseff and Preobrajenska. Joined Belgrade B. 1940, danced in Dantzig, Ljubljana. To Paris and danced at the Th. Mogador. In Vienna Volksoper 1945, in Switzerland, Bonn, Lübeck, ballet master Gelsenkirchen 1967. To Essen as ballet master 1968.

PILETTA, Georges, b. Paris 1944. Fr. dancer. Pupil of Paris Opéra Sch., joined Paris Opéra Ballet, becoming étoile 1970. Won René Blum Prize 1961 (with Bestonso).

PILLAR OF FIRE, ballet 2 sc., ch. Tudor, m. Schönberg (*Verklärte Nacht*), dec. Mielziner, f.p. Ballet Th., Met. Op., N.Y. 8 Apr 1942 (Nora Kaye, Chase, Lyon, Laing, Tudor). Tudor's first major work in the U.S.A. and his masterpiece. Nora Kaye's interpretation of the leading rôle established her as one of the greatest dramatic dancers in ballet. Danced by R. Swed. B., Stockholm 30 Dec 1962 (Orlando, Connie Borg, Klavsen), and Ballet Th., State Th., N.Y. 1966 (Sallie Wilson, V. Mlakar, Marks, Young).

PINEAPPLE POLL, ballet 3 sc., ch. Cranko, m. Sullivan (arr. Mackerras), dec. Osbert Lancaster, f.p. S. Wells Th. B., S. Wells Th. 13 Mar 1951 (Fifield, Claire, O'Reilly, Poole, Blair). Also in repertoire of Borovansky B., Australian B., Nat. B. of Canada, and Joffrey B. 1970. Televised on

B.B.C. by Margaret Dale 1 Nov 1959. W. S. Gilbert's Bab Ballad *The Bumboat Woman's Story*.

PIOLLET, Wilfride, b. Drôme 1943. Fr. dancer. Pupil of Paris Opéra Sch. from 1955 and Egorova, Franchetti, Reznikoff etc. Joined Paris Opéra B. 1960, becoming première danseuse 1966 and étoile 1969. Guest artist Festival B. 1969. Mar. J. Guizerix.

PIPER, John, b. 1903. Eng. artist and designer. Ballets include: For S. Wells Co. *The Quest* (1943), *Job* (1948), *The Shadow* (1953). For S. Wells Th. B. *Sea Change* (1949), *Harlequin in April* (1951). For Royal B. *Prince of the Pagodas* (dec. only, 1957).

PIQUÉ, a direct stepping on to the point, without bending the knee.

PIROUETTE, probably derived from the Burgundian *pirouelle*, a spinning top, or from the French *pied*, foot, and *roue*, wheel. Lit. a whirligig. One or more turns of the body accomplished on one leg on the full, $\frac{3}{4}$, $\frac{1}{2}$, or $\frac{1}{4}$ point, with the point of the other leg touching the supporting leg at the level of the knee. It is described as being *en dedans* when the impetus is inwards (i.e. towards the supporting leg) or *en dehors* when the impetus is outwards (i.e. away from the supporting leg). The danseuse in her adagio frequently executes supported pirouettes in which her partner assists her to maintain her balance, gives impetus to her turns, and checks her momentum after the required number have been executed.

Pirouette à la seconde or *grande pirouette*, a pirouette executed with the working leg extended to the side at right angles to the supporting leg (à la seconde en l'air) and usually ended with two or more straight pirouettes. This step, now essentially a man's step, is said to have been first performed by the German Mlle Heinel at Stuttgart in 1766 or 1767, and introduced by her to the Paris Opéra in 1768.

Pirouette en attitude, a pirouette in attitude position.

Pirouette en arabesque, a pirouette in arabesque position.

Pirouette sur le cou-de-pied, a pirouette with the working foot on the instep of the supporting foot.

PISTOLET, see AILES DE PIGEON.

PISTONI, Mario, b. Rome 1932. It. dancer. Studied at Teatro dell'Opera, Rome, becoming principal dancer 1951. To Scala, Milan, 1951 as principal dancer. Chor. many ballets, among them *La Strada* (m. Rota) from the Fellini film, *Prodigal Son* etc. Mar. Fiorella Cova.

PITOS, the finger-snapping in Sp. dancing.

PITTSBURGH BALLET THEATRE, founded in 1970 by Nicolas Petrov, has made remarkable progress in its first three years with performances of *Nutcracker, Swan Lake, Beethoven's Ninth* etc. Guest stars have been Verdy, Villella, Cuoco, Dagmar Kessler etc.

PLA, Mirta, b. Havana. Cuban dancer. Pupil of the Alonsos, Fedorova, Skeaping. Joined B. Alicia Alonso 1954. Now prima ballerina of National B. of Cuba. Silver Medal at Varna 1964 and 1966.

PLACE IN THE DESERT, A, ballet, ch. Morrice, m. Surinach, dec. Koltai, f.p. B. Rambert, S. Wells Th. 25 July 1961 (Martlew, Chesworth). A village which is to be submerged on the building of a dam.

PLACE, SUR, on one spot (indicating that a step or series of steps is executed without moving from the original position on the stage).

PLACE, THE (abbreviated from The Artists' Place), the London headquarters of the London School of Contemporary Dance and its company, the London Contemporary Dance Theatre. Adjacent to St Pancras Church, W.C.1, it was formerly the headquarters of the Artists' Rifles Regiment and was taken over by Robin Howard (q.v.) in 1969. It includes a theatre, seating 260, classrooms and a restaurant. The theatre is used also by small and experimental groups for their dance productions and film showings.

PLACING, a term borrowed from singing. When well-placed, the dancer has acquired the physical requirements of a well-poised head on a vertical neck and spine, level hips and well turned out legs—and this stance has become natural and unforced. In Italian, *impostazione*.

PLANÉ, lit. soared or hovered, as in temps plané, a term applied to such steps as temps de poisson or temps de l'ange, indicating that the dancer should convey the effect of hovering in the air.

PLANETS, THE, ballet, ch. Tudor, m. Holst, dec. Stevenson, f.p. B. Rambert, Mercury Th., London 28 Oct 1934 (Argyle, Laing, Lloyd). Suite of dances to Holst's *The Planets*. With a fourth section, Mercury, added, f.p. London B., Toynbee Hall, London 23 Jan 1939. In this ballet Kyra Nijinsky (Nijinsky's daughter) first danced in London. The first ballet to this music was chor. H. Kreutzberg at Berlin Staatsoper 9 May 1931 (Spies, Moser, Junk, Albu).

PLATOFF, Marc, b. Seattle 1915. Am. dancer, member of de Basil's Co. and Ballet Russe de Monte Carlo 1938–42, later dancing in films as Marc Platt. In original cast of *Oklahoma!* (1943). In 1962 became director of the ballet at Radio City Music Hall.

PLAYFORD, John, b. 1623, d. 1686. Eng. musician who almost monopolized music publishing under the Commonwealth. In 1651 published *The English Dancing Master*, a collection of dances and their tunes.

PLESCHEEF, Alexander, b. Russia 1858, d. Paris 1944. Russ. critic and historian. Author of *Nash Balet* (Our Ballet) 1899, *From the Wings* (1936). Settled in Paris, 1918.

PLIÉ, lit. a bending. Exercise in which the dancer, standing erect, slowly bends the knees in line with the fully turned out feet, with the heels firmly on the ground and the weight on the outside of the feet. When a point is reached beyond which the heels must be raised to continue the plié, it is termed a demi-plié; when the plié is continued to its fullest extent, i.e. when the heels are still as near the ground as possible and the buttocks as near the heels as possible it is termed a full plié. The back should be held erect throughout the exercise. Pliés can be executed in all five positions of the feet but in the second and open fourth positions the heels are kept on the ground during the entire exercise.

Pliés are the first exercises done in every class to loosen up muscles and tendons and develop balance, and pliés are done by every dancer in dressing room or wings before a performance. A plié or demi-plié is the start of nearly every step and may be likened to the coiling of a spring: likewise the dancer alights with a plié to absorb shock and prevent a heavy thud which, echoing throughout the auditorium, would destroy all illusion.

PLISETSKAYA, Maya, b. Moscow 1925. Russ. dancer, niece of Asaf and Sulamith Messerer. Trained Bolshoi Sch. under E. Gerdt and, for a year, Vaganova. Graduated 1943, and joined the Bolshoi B., Moscow, although owing to the war she had been dancing solos in it for some time (she was never in the corps). In 1945 she was made a ballerina and danced her first *Swan Lake* in 1947 and her first *Juliet* 1961. On the retirement of Ulanova in 1962 she became to be considered as the leading dancer in Russia and is the only one to hold the title 'prima ballerina assoluta'. She was guest artist of the Paris Opéra in 1961 and 1964 and first danced in London in 1963 and in New York 1966. Her style is very strong and brilliant rather than lyrical and in this she is the antithesis of Ulanova. Mar. R. Schedrin, composer. People's Artist of U.S.S.R. 1959. Lenin Prize 1964. In 1972 chor. *Anna Karenina* (m. Schedrin).

PLUCIS, Harijs, b. Riga 1900, d. Vienna 1970. Latvian dancer and teacher. Trained in the Riga ballet school, joined the Riga B. and became principal dancer. Studied under Legat in Paris 1927 and joined Rubinstein B. 1928. Founded Riga State Ballet Sch. 1932 and was its director until 1944. To London and became ballet master of S. Wells B. 1947–56. Taught in Switzerland 1957–61 and from 1961 to 1968 was head of the school of the Vienna Staatsoper B.

PLUNKETT, Adeline, b. Brussels 1824, d. Paris 1910. Belgian dancer.

A principal dancer at the Paris Opéra 1845–52 and 1855–57. Danced London 1843–57. Cr. rôles in *Ozai*, *Nisida*, and *Vert-Vert*.

POCHINI (Carlotta) Carolina, b. Milan 1836, d. Naples 1901. It. dancer. Pupil of her aunt and later of Carlo Blasis. Début at Scala, Milan at the age of 13 (in 1849) of which theatre she became ballerina in the 1850s. She also danced extensively in Europe and in Italy. Retired 1874. Mar. Pasquale Borri.

POELVOORDE, Rita, b. Antwerp 1951. Belgian dancer. Pupil of Brabants at R. Flemish B. Sch. from 1962. Entered R. Flemish B. 1968, becoming soloist. In 1969 joined Nederlands Dans Th. Winner of Silver Medal at Varna Competition 1968.

POÈME DE L'EXTASE, ballet, ch. Cranko, m. Scriabin, dec. Jürgen Rose, f.p. Stuttgart B., Opera House, Stuttgart 24 Mar 1970 (Fonteyn, Cragun, Madsen, Clauss, Stripling). An ageing diva spurns a young lover and recalls her former admirers. The *jugendstil* cost. and dec. are based on the art of Klimt. Cranko mounted it for the Royal B., C. Garden 15 Feb 1972 (Fonteyn, Coleman, Wall, Kelly, Drew, O'Brien).

POINTE or POINT, the extremity of the toe. The foot may be à pointe or on full point, à trois quarts or raised on the flexed toes, à demi (sur la demi-pointe) or on the ball of the foot (à quart) with the heel barely raised off the ground. Dancing on the point or 'point work' is said to have been practised by the cossacks since time immemorial but it is not known exactly when it was first used in stage dancing, where it is the

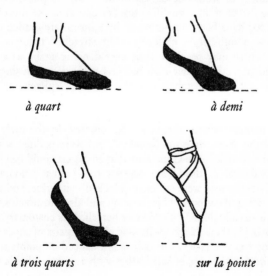

à quart   *à demi*

à trois quarts   *sur la pointe*

privilege of the danseuse (although it was introduced into Nijinska's *Les Fâcheux* 1924 as an acrobatic trick for Anton Dolin). Amongst the earliest reproductions of a dancer standing on her points is a lithograph dated 1821 by F. Waldeck of Fanny Bias in *Flore et Zéphire*. The fact that contemporary critics did not comment on 'point work' would seem to indicate that it was no great novelty, but the gradual development of an already accepted practice. For example, Castil-Blaze said, when he saw Taglioni on her points in 1827, that many would recall Mlle Gosselin who could stand on her point 'for a full minute'. Gosselin died in 1818 and he probably referred to her Paris performance of *Flore et Zéphire* in 1815. It is probable that the use of this mode of progression, providing as it does a compromise between the terre à terre and aerial movement, was extended to lend colour to the wilis, péris, and other supernatural beings which peopled the stage of the Romantic period. The point, by reducing the area of friction, facilitates brilliant pirouettes and lengthens the line of the leg, whilst movement on the point can give an impression of effortless progress. 'Point work' can also, unhappily, be used as an end in itself instead of as a means to an end. The dancers of the so-called Modern or Central European school have ruled out 'point work' from their vocabulary as artificial and unnatural and it cannot be too often repeated that a danced stage performance need not necessarily include 'point work' to be termed ballet, for the history of the art can be traced back to the Middle Ages whilst 'point work' was first seen on the stage well over a century ago. The young dancer or would-be dancer should only be put on her points under the direction of a qualified teacher and after the muscles of the foot and leg have been strengthened by appropriate graded exercises. Every year a number of children suffer stretched tendons and torn muscles, which may preclude their ever dancing again, as a result of misguided parents or their own reckless enthusiasm causing them to attempt to get on their points prematurely. Ger. 'spitzentanz'.

POINT SHOES, the silk or satin shoes, tying up the ankle with ribbon, used by dancers when dancing sur les pointes. In the early days (of Taglioni) the shoes were not 'blocked', but were padded with cotton wool. Gautier told the de Goncourts that an expert could feel inside the shoe of a dancer of the Opéra and say to whom it belonged. Later (about 1862) the toes were stiffened (blocked) with glue, and darned to give strength and support. This darning, and also the attachment of the ribbons, is usually done by the dancer herself. It is customary for ballet Cos. to provide their dancers with one or more pairs of shoes per week in addition to their salary. For ballets not danced on points the dancer wears close-fitting shoes of soft leather with a narrow pliable sole.

POISE, TO, term used by the Royal Academy of Dancing to indicate the slight turning of the head to the right or left while held erect.

POLAJENKO, Nicolai, b. N.Y. 1932. Am. dancer. Pupil of Vilzak. Début in musicals. To Europe 1948, joined Metropolitan B. and B. des Ch. Élysées 1949. To N.Y. with Petit's Co. 1951. Danced at Met. Op., N.Y., and with Grantseva's Ballet Quartet. Joined Festival B. as soloist 1954–55. Principal of de Cuevas B. 1956–62. Guest artist Harkness B. 1964–65. Now has school in Geneva.

POLIAKOVA, Elena, b. St Petersburg 1884, d. Santiago 1972. Pupil of P. Gerdt, Johansson, N. Legat, graduated to the Maryinsky Co. 1902 and danced in it until 1918, also appearing in Diaghileff's first Paris season 1909. Taught Alice Nikitina and left Russia with her and her family 1920. Prima ballerina in Belgrade (and taught Youskevitch, Anna Roje and Parlic). To Chile 1949 and worked with E. Uthoff's National B. of Chile, becoming ballet mistress 1958. In 1965 her library (named after her) was presented to the Santiago Municipal Th.

POLKA, from the Czech *půlka*, half or chain step. A dance in 2/4 time with a step on each of the first three half-beats and a hop on the fourth, which would seem to have been first danced in Bohemia in the 1830s, and took Paris and London by storm in 1840 when fashions and furnishings were named after it, whilst students polkaed to college and sedate citizens polkaed in the street—a craze immortalized in the witty illustrations of Daumier and Gavarni. It was first danced at the Paris Opéra by Maria (Maria Jacob) partnered by Eugene Coralli 25 Mar 1844 to a polka specially composed by Burgmüller. Thereafter the choreographers and serious composers incorporated it into ballets. On the stage it long preserved its central European link through spurs and boots worn by the male dancer and the charming costume reproduced in the lithographs and music covers by Bouvier and Brandard.

POLKA-MAZURKA, dance derived from the polka, from which it differs in that it is in 3/4 time, and from the mazurka, by which it is distinguished by having an accent on the 3rd instead of the 2nd beat.

POLONAISE, probably at its origin a martial or choral peasants dance, it had become by the middle of the seventeenth century a solemn processional dance in 3/4 time to gliding steps, with which court ballets were opened, and as such it is still to be seen on the stage today.

POLOVTSIAN DANCES, see PRINCE IGOR.

POMONA, ballet, ch. Ashton, m. Constant Lambert, dec. J. Banting, f.p. Camargo Society, Cambridge Th., London 19 Oct 1930 (Ludmila,

397

Dolin). It went into the S. Wells repertory in 1933 (dec. V. Bell) (Appleyard, Dolin).

PONNELLE, Jean-Pierre, b. Paris 1932. Fr. designer and producer who works mostly in Germany. Among his ballets are *Jack Pudding* (Wiesbaden 1950), *The Idiot* (T. Gsovsky, Berlin 1952), *Sleeping Beauty* (T. Gsovsky, Berlin 1955), *Josephslegende* (Rosen, Munich 1958), *Swan Lake* (Beriozoff, Stuttgart, 1960), *Peau de Chagrin* (van Dyk, Paris 1960).

PONOMARYOV, Vladimir, b. 1892, d. 1951. Russ. dancer and teacher. Graduated from Maryinsky Sch. 1910 to the company. Danced with Diaghileff B. 1911–12 and became principal dancer of the Maryinsky B. 1912. In 1913 he began to teach in the Maryinsky Sch. and produced a remarkable series of male dancers, among them P. Gusev, A. Yermolayev, V. Chabukiani, K. Sergeyev, N. Zubovsky and the chors. L. Lavrovsky, R. Zakharoff. From 1919 he also took the *classe de perfection* at the Kirov Th. For the graduation class of 1922 he produced *La Sylphide* to present P. Gusev.

PONTOIS, Noella, b. Vendôme 1943. Fr. dancer. Pupil of Janine Schwarz, Devanel, Brieux at Paris Opéra Sch. Entered Paris Opéra B. 1960, becoming étoile 1968. Guest artist Festival B. 1967 as Aurora in *Sleeping Beauty*.

POOLE, David, b. Cape Town 1925. S. African dancer. Studied under D. Howes and C. Robinson, becoming principal dancer Cape Town B. Club. Joined S. Wells Sch. 1947 and S. Wells Th. B. same year, becoming a principal dancer. Joined B. Rambert 1956. Danced in Edinburgh International B. 1958 and returned to S. Africa to teach. Appointed ballet master of Cape Town University B. (CAPAB) in 1963 and in 1969 he became director on the retirement of Dulcie Howes.

POPA, Magdalena, b. 1941. Rumanian dancer. Studied at Kirov Sch., Leningrad. Soloist in Bucharest from 1961. Joined Ballet Théâtre Contemporain, Amiens, 1969.

POPESCU, Gabriel, b. Bucharest 1932. Rumanian dancer. Studied in Moscow. Joined Bucharest B. 1951, becoming soloist. Joined Zürich B. 1965 as a principal.

POPKO, Nikolai, b. 1911. Russ. dancer and chor. Danced in Bolshoi B. 1930–56. With L. Posspekhine and A. Radunsky, chor. *The Little Stork* (1937), *Svetlana* (1939), *Red Sails* (1942).

PORT DE BRAS, carriage of the arms, also a series of exercises designed to develop carriage of the arms. Just as there are five positions of the

feet so there are a number of positions of the arms. In the Cecchetti method the arms in the *first position* are slightly rounded and held at the sides; in the *second position* the lightly rounded arms are extended to either side slightly below shoulder level; in the *third position* one rounded arm rests upon the thigh (en bas) whilst the other is opened slightly to the side; in the *fourth position* one rounded arm is extended in front of the body (quatrième in front) or above the head (quatrième en haut) and the other is extended to the side as in the second position; in the *fifth position* the well rounded arms are extended downwards so that they rest upon the thighs (en bas) or in front of the body (en avant) or above the head (en haut). There are likewise five principal positions of the single arm, the first and second being as described above for both arms, the third being slightly opened to the side, the fourth being rounded and extended to the front (en avant) or above the head (en haut) or fully extended to the front or back (en arabesque) and the fifth being as described above for the fifth en bas. For illustrations, see
FIVE POSITIONS.

There are many alternative names for these positions according to the system of teaching, thus the fifth Cecchetti position en bas is known as 'Bras bas' and the fifth en haut as 'double bras' or 'couronne' (so called because the arms should form a crown about the head). The fifth Cecchetti en avant is (in R.A.D. terminology) very aptly termed the 'gateway' as when a port de bras is executed the arms, generally speaking, will never be extended in any position without passing through the fifth en avant; this lengthens the movement and should prevent the dancer's arms having a cramped or bent look. It can be safely said, in Classical ballet, that a noticeably bent arm is a bad arm.

Generally speaking, it will be found that, in the Classical ballet, when the foot is placed in a given position, the corresponding arm is also placed in that position. A graceful disposition of the arms in relation to the body, head, and legs is just as important to the dancer as good foot work.

PORTER, Andrew, b. Cape Town 1928. English writer on music and the dance. Educ. Diocesan Col. C.T., University Col., Oxford. Principal ballet critic *The Financial Times* from 1953. To N.Y. 1972.

PORTER, Marguerite, b. Doncaster 1948. Eng. dancer. Pupil of Louise Browne and Royal B. Sch. Joined Royal B. 1966, soloist 1973. Mar. Carl Myers.

PORTEUR, Fr. lit. one who carries, a porter. A male dancer whose sole function is to lift the ballerina in supported leaps and similar movements. The male dancer in Western Europe was relegated to the rôle of a porteur during the half century preceding the coming of the

Diaghileff Ballet and male dancing rôles were taken by the danseuse travestie.

POSE, a static position as against the dancer in movement.

PORTUGAL, BALLET IN, see under GULBENKIAN BALLET and VERDE GAIO.

POSE, a static position as against the dancer in movement.

POSÉ (EN AVANT, EN ARRIÈRE), the poising of the body (forwards, sideways, or backwards) by stepping with a straight leg on to the full or half point.

POSÉ EN TOURNANT, a transference of the weight on to one foot and at the same time turning once or more. The working leg is usually held against the supporting leg at cou-de-pied or passé retiré. Familiarly known as 'lame duck' when done en dehors.

POSITIONS, see FIVE POSITIONS.

POSSPEKHINE, Lev, b. 1909. Russ. dancer and chor. Studied in Moscow, joined Bolshoi B. 1928. With Popko and Radunsky (q.v.), chor. *The Little Stork* (1937) and *Svetlana* (1939), *Red Sails* (1942). Now teacher to Bolshoi B.

POTTER, Joan, b. Melbourne 1927. Australian dancer. Studied under Borovansky. Joined Festival B. 1950. Returned to Borovansky B. 1953 and rejoined Festival B. 1959 becoming soloist 1960. Mar. Vassilie Trunoff. Now assistant ballet mistress, Festival B.

POTTS, Nadia, b. London 1948. Canadian dancer. Trained at Canad. Nat. B. Sch. and entered company 1966, becoming soloist 1969.

POTTS, Nellie, b. Newcastle-upon-Tyne 1909. Eng. teacher. Studied with Phyllis Bedells, Craske and Preobrajenska. Opened her school in Newcastle in 1929 and became a Major Examiner for Royal Academy of Dancing 1949. In 1957 emigrated to Australia and joined Kathleen Danetree (formerly head of a school in Birmingham who went to Australia 1947 becoming partner of Frances Scully in Scully-Borovansky Sch., Sydney and an O.B.E. in 1972) as co-director of of the Scully-Borovansky School.

POULSEN, Ulla (*née* Iversen), b. Copenhagen 1905. Dan. dancer. Entered R. Danish Th. Sch. 1913 and became principal dancer of R. Dan. B. 1924. Studied in London under Karsavina 1927–30. Toured Scandinavia, France, Germany 1927–33. Retired 1939. Awarded Danish medal 'Ingenio et Arte' 1934.

POWELL, Graham, b. Cardiff 1948. Eng. dancer. Pupil of Royal B. Sch. and joined Touring Royal B. 1956, becoming soloist. Joined C. Garden section of Royal B. and in 1969 joined Festival B. as soloist. To Australian B. 1970 and Nederlands Dans Th. 1972. Retired 1973.

POWELL, Ray, b. Hitchin 1925. Eng. dancer. Studied at S. Wells Sch., joining the Co. 1947, becoming soloist. Cr. rôle of Gluttony in *The Quest*, Punchinello in *Veneziana* etc. Chor. *One in Five* (1960). From 1962 ballet master of Australian B.

PRAGUE BALLET, THE, a group founded in 1964 with L. Ogoun as artistic director and Pavel Smok ballet master. Their ballets are modern in style and deal with modern themes and of an experimental kind. They appeared at the Paris International Festival in 1967 and in London (Sadler's Wells Th.) 1969. They tour Europe most of the year. Among their ballets were *Rossiniana* (m. Rossini), *Frescoes* (m. Martinu), *Gangrene* (m. Mingus) all chor. Smok, and *Hiroshima* (m. Bukovy), chor. Ogoun. Their dancers include Rozina Kamburova, Petr Kozeluh, Jiri Halamka. In 1970 Smok went to Basel as ballet master and took many of the dancers with him.

PREISSER, Suse, b. Leipzig 1920. German dancer. Studied under Abendroth at Leipzig and E. Mazzucchelli in Milan. Début in Leipzig. Danced in Weimar and became soloist at Städtische Oper, W. Berlin 1947–62. In 1963 became assistant ballet mistress of Munich B.

PREMIER DANSEUR (première danseuse), a leading dancer of a company. *Premier danseur étoile* is the highest rank in the cadre of the Paris Opéra.

PREOBRAJENSKA, Olga, b. St Petersburg 1870, d. Paris 1962. Russ. dancer and teacher. Graduated from the Imp. Sch., St Petersburg 1889, becoming prima ballerina 1898 and one of the greatest dancers in the history of the Imp. B. Taught at the Imp. Sch. 1917 to 1921, left Russia and opened famous sch. in Paris (after three years in Berlin) training, among others, Baronova, Toumanova, and Golovine, and almost every dancer who visited Paris went to her classes. Her gay, witty personality was a feature of her dancing and of her teaching. When over ninety years of age she was giving daily classes in the Studio Wacker. She danced at the Scala, Milan in 1904, Paris Opéra 1909, and in 1910 she was the first to dance *Swan Lake* in England (Hippodrome, London).

PREOBRAJENSKY, Vladimir, b. Russia 1912. Russ. dancer. Studied Leningrad Sch. and was a character dancer at the Kirov Th., Leningrad 1931–35. To Sverdlovsk 1935 to teach. Transferred to Kiev 1939 to dance leading rôles in new Ukrainian ballets and in classical rôles. Joined Bolshoi Th. 1943 as leading dancer in classical ballets. Cr. chief rôles in *Bronze Horseman*, *Prisoner of the Caucasus*, *Fountain of Bakhchisarai*, *The Peasant Maiden*. Usually partnered Lepeshinskaya. Stalin Prize 1946. Now teaches at Moscow Ballet Sch.

PREPARATION, a movement made to prepare for another, e.g. preparation for a pirouette, in which the working leg is opened to the second position and sometimes swept round to the fourth position back.

PRÉSAGES, LES, ballet in 4 parts, ch. Massine, m. Tchaikovsky's 5th Symphony, dec. Masson, f.p. de Basil Co., Monte Carlo 13 Apr 1933 (Baronova, Verchinina, Riabouchinska, Lichine, Woizikovsky). Massine's first symphonic ballet. Tells of Man's conflict with his Destiny.

PRÉVOST, Françoise, b. 1680, d. 1741. Fr. dancer. Début Paris Opéra in *Atys* 1699, she succeeded Subligny and became the greatest dancer in France. She was displaced by her pupils Sallé and Camargo and retired in 1730. She excelled in the passepied. See also BALON.

PRICE, a famous family of dancers (of English extraction) at the Royal Th., Copenhagen, founded by JAMES PRICE, b. London 1761, d. Copenhagen 1805. He was a pierrot in Casorti's troupe and later director of Vesterbros Morkabsteater. JULIETTE PRICE, b. Copenhagen 1831, d. there 1906, was a private pupil of Bournonville. Début at Royal Th., Copenhagen 1849, becoming solodancer. Cr. rôle of Hilda in *Et Folkesagn* 1854. Guest artist in Vienna. Her sister SOPHIE PRICE, b. 1832, was also a solodancer at the Royal Th., and so was her cousin, AMALIE PRICE, b. at sea 1831, d. Copenhagen 1892, Juliette's younger brother VALDEMAR PRICE, b. Copenhagen 1836, d. there 1908, made his début at the Royal Th. 1857 and became a solodancer, one of the great *danseurs nobles* of the Danish Ballet, ELLEN PRICE (de Plane), b. Copenhagen 1879 d. there 1968, the grand niece of Juliette and pupil of Hans Beck, was also a solodancer, creating the chief rôle in Beck's *The Little Mermaid* 1909 and the model for Eriksen's Little Mermaid statue at Langelinie. In 1959 she helped Elsa Marianne von Rosen and Allan Fridericia to mount *La Sylphide*.

PRIEST, Josias, d. London 1734. Eng. dancer and chor. He had a dancing school in London in 1669. Her chor. the dances for the first production of Purcell's *Dido and Aeneas* in 1689, and for the same composer's other operas *The Prophetess* (1690), *King Arthur* (1691), *The Faerie Queene* (1692) and *The Indian Queen* (1695).

PRIMUS, Pearl, b. Trinidad 1919. Am. dancer who studies and performs native dances, mainly Negro. Now teaches at Hunter Col., N.Y.

PRINCE DU DÉSERT, LE, ballet, ch. Skibine, m. Damase, dec. Camble, f.p. Th. des Ch. Élysées, Paris 4 Nov 1955 (Tallchief, Skibine). A parody of Rudolf Valentino and the silent films.

PRINCE IGOR (POLOVTSIAN DANCES FROM), ballet 1 act, ch. Fokine, m. Borodin, dec. Roerich, f.p. Diaghileff's Co., Th. du Châtelet, Paris 19 May 1909 (Fedorova, Smirnova, Bolm). This ballet, one of Fokine's best (and his own favourite) came as a revelation to a public accustomed to the conventional ballets of the period. It also, more than any other, helped to restore the male dancer to the stage in Western Europe where for several decades he had been but a porteur and all male parts had been taken by a danseuse travestie. The ballet is in the repertoire of many contemporary companies. Mounted by Grigorieff for Royal B., C. Garden 24 Mar 1965 (Nureyev).

PRINCE OF THE PAGODAS, THE, ballet, 3 acts, ch. Cranko, m. Britten, dec. Piper, cost. Heeley, f.p. Royal B., C. Garden 1 Jan 1957 (Beriosova, Farron, Blair, Edwards). A fairy story. This was the first full-length British ballet and in May 1957 Cranko mounted it for the Scala B., Milan (Beriosova, Farron, Blair). Also chor. by Alan Carter, dec. Gugel for Munich B., Prinzregenten Th. Munich 17 Mar 1958 (Trofimova, Hallhuber). Original was revived by Cranko at Stuttgart (same dec. and cost.) 6 Nov 1960. By Orlikowski, Vienna Staatsoper, dec. Schneider-Siemssen, cost. Schröck 12 May 1967 (Zimmerl). Score used by several other chors. Chor. by Vinogradov for Kirov B., f.p. Kirov Th., Leningrad 30 Dec 1972 (Sizova, Barishnikov).

PRINZ, John, b. Chicago 1946. Am. dancer. Pupil of Ellisdu Boulay, Lunnon, Joffrey, Am. Sch. of B. Joined N.Y. City B. 1964, becoming soloist, and Am. Ballet Th. 1970.

PRISM, ballet, ch. Nikolais, m. Hovhaness, Antheil, electronic, colour design Constant. F.p. by Co. of Henry St. Playhouse, N. Y. 27 Dec. 1956 (Bailin, Lamhut, Schmidt, Louis).

PRISONER OF THE CAUCASUS, THE, ballet based on Pushkin's poem: (1) 4 acts, ch. Didelot, m. Cavos, f.p. Bolshoi Th., St Petersburg 27 Jan 1823 (Istomina, Goltz); (2) 3 acts 7 sc. ch. Lavrovsky, m. Asafiev, dec. Khodasevitch, f.p. Maly Th., Leningrad 14 Apr 1938; (3) ch. Zakharoff, f.p. open-air th. Moscow 17 Aug 1938; (4) ch. Skibine, m. Khachaturian (ballet *Gayané*), dec. Doboujinsky, f.p. de Cuevas B., Th. de l'Empire, Paris, 4 Dec 1951 (Skibine, Marjorie Tallchief).

PRISONERS, THE, ballet, ch. Darrell, m. Bartok, dec. Kay, Western Th. B., Dartington Hall, Devon 24 Jun 1957 (Musitz, Salt, Sunde). Two political prisoners escape.

PRODIGAL SON, THE. (1) ballet 3 sc., ch. Balanchine, m. Prokofieff, dec. Rouault, f.p. Diaghileff's Co., Th. Sarah Bernhardt, Paris 21 May 1929 (Lifar, Doubrovska). Revived for N.Y. City B. 23 Feb 1950 (Robbins, Mounsey). It was mounted for Royal B. by Patricia Neary, C. Garden 25 Jan 1973 (Nureyev, Bergsma). (2) ch. Lichine, same m. and dec., f.p. de Basil's Co., Sydney 30 Dec. 1938 (Lichine, Osato).

(3) ch. Jooss, same m., dec. Heckroth, f.p. Essen 28 May 1931. (4) ch. Jooss, m. Cohen, f.p. B. Jooss, Stadsschouwburg, Amsterdam 6 Oct 1933. (5) ch. Jooss, m. Cohen, dec. Bouchène, f.p. B. Jooss, Prince's Th., Bristol Oct 1939. (6) ch. Cramer, m. Alfven, dec. Lindstrom, f.p. R. Swedish B., Stockholm 27 Apr 1957 (von Rosen, Holmgren). In the style of the Biblical wall paintings of Dalarna. Famous for its Polka.

PROKOFIEFF, Serge, b. Ekaterinberg 1891, d. Moscow 1953. Russ. composer who wrote *Ala and Lolly* (Berlin 1914). For Diaghileff, *Chout* (1921), *Pas d'Acier* (1927), *Prodigal Son* (1929). He returned to Russia 1934 and composed *Romeo and Juliet* (1938), *Cinderella* (1948), *The Stone Flower* (1954). His m. is also used in *Gala Performance*, *Lieutenant Kije*, *Peter and the Wolf*, etc.

PROKOVSKY, André (Pokrovsky), b. Paris 1939. Fr. dancer. Studied under Zvereff, Egorova, Peretti, Nora. Début dancing with Comédie Française, Paris 1954. Joined Charrat Ballet 1955, Petit's Ballet 1956. Won silver medal at Moscow Youth Festival 1957. Joined Festival B. 1957 as principal dancer, and de Cuevas 1960–62. Soloist N.Y. City B. 1963–66. Principal dancer Festival B. 1966–72, partnering Samtsova, his wife. In 1972 started his own group the New London B.

PROMENADE, (1) a slow turn on one foot while the body is held in a set position, such as an arabesque; (2) a slow turn in a pas de deux when the danseuse, on point, is turned round by her partner.

PROMENADE, ballet 1 act, ch. de Valois, m. Haydn, arr. Edwin Evans, dec. Stevenson, f.p. S. Wells B., King's Th., Edinburgh 25 Oct 1943 (Fonteyn, Hamilton, Paltenghi). The chief rôle was created for Beryl Grey, who was ill for the première. A lepidopterist in a park peopled by girls in the style of the Directoire and Les Merveilleuses.

PROMETHEUS, see CRÉATURES DE PROMETHÉE, LES.

PROMPT SIDE etc., see CÔTÉ JARDIN.

PROPERT, W. A., b. 1867, d. 1946. Eng. doctor and writer on art. He was the first recorder of the Russian Ballet in England and his *The Russian Ballet in Western Europe 1909–1920* (1921) and *The Russian Ballet 1921–1929* (1931) are among the most important accounts of Diaghileff's Co. He was a friend of Bakst and arranged the first exhibition of his work in London 1912.

PROSPECT BEFORE US, THE, ballet, 7 sc., ch. de Valois, m. Boyce, dec. Furse, f.p. S. Wells B., S. Wells Th., London 4 July 1940 (May, Honer, Helpmann, Ashton, Newman). Taken into the repertoire of the S. Wells Th. B. Based on a Rowlandson print of the name, it depicts the rivalry between the King's Th. and the Patheon in 1789.

PROTÉE, ballet 1 act, ch. Lichine, m. Debussy, dec. Chirico, f.p. de Basil's Co., C. Garden, London 5 July 1938 (Lichine). In this ballet the dancer's turnout was not used.

PROTHALAMION, *pas de deux*, ch. Brian Macdonald, m. Delius, dec. Prevost, f.p. Sch. of Fine Arts, Banff, Canada, Aug. 1961 (Annemarie and David Holmes). Taken into R. Winnipeg B. Mar 1962.

PSOTA, Vania, b. Kieff 1908, d. Brno 1952. Czech dancer and chor. Studied in Prague and joined the Prague B. 1924. Soloist in Brno B. 1926–32. With de Basil's B. Russe 1932–36. Returned to Brno as director of the Co. In 1941 regisseur Ballet Theatre. Ballet master de Basil's Original B. Russe 1942–47. Returned to Brno 1947–52 as director again. Chor. many ballets incl. *Romeo and Juliet* in Brno 1938 and was the first to use this Prokofieff score (and danced Romeo), *Slavonic Dances* (m. Dvorak 1941 for B. Th.) etc.

PUGNI, Cesare, b. Genoa 1802, d. St Petersburg 1870. It. composer who, after contributing the scores of many of the ballets created in France and England during the Romantic period, went to St Petersburg, where he was appointed official ballet composer to the Imperial Theatres. Out of his amazing output of some 300 ballets, in addition to ten operas, forty Masses, and some chamber music, the ballets *Le Pas de Quatre, La Esmeralda, Ondine, Catarina* and *The Hump-backed Horse* are alone well known today.

PULCINELLA, ballet 1 act, ch. Massine, m. Pergolesi-Stravinsky, dec. Picasso, f.p. Diaghileff's Co., Paris Opéra 15 May 1920 (Karsavina, Massine). A Commedia dell'Arte ballet.

PUPPENFEE, DIE, ballet with music by Joseph Bayer, f.p. in Vienna, ch. J. Hassreiter, dec. Brioschi 4 Oct 1888 (Camilla Pagliero). With ch. by Sergueeff and Legat another version was given in 1906 at St Petersburg which was revived by Pavlova, under the title *The Fairy Doll* (ch. Clustine, dec. Doboujinski, f.p. N.Y. c. 1914). Another version of the same ballet was danced at the Empire Th., London, by Genée in 1905, and the story was used for Massine's *Boutique Fantasque*. The ballet is still in the repertoire of the Vienna Staatsoper.

PUSHKIN, Alexander, b. Mikulino 1907, d. Leningrad 1970. Russ. dancer and teacher. After his dancing career in the Maryinsky Th. (1931–53) he became a famous teacher of male dancers at the Kirov Sch. Taught Semeyonov, Soloviev, Nureyev, Panov, Makarov and Barishnikov.

ПХУ, the Russian abbreviation for the Petrograd choreographic academy.

PYGMALION, ballet, ch. Sallé, C. Garden 14 Feb 1734. Marie Sallé wore, instead of panier or skirt, a plain muslin dress like a Greek robe with her hair down and unadorned—causing a furore at Covent Garden.

Q

QARRTSILUNI, ballet 1 act, ch. Lander, m. Riisager, dec. Johansen, f.p. Royal Th., Copenhagen 21 Feb 1942 (Niels Bjorn Larsen). An Eskimo priest's ritual dance to welcome the breaking through of the sun after the dark winter.

QUADRILLE. (1) Square dance which attained to its greatest popularity at the court of Napoleon I, whence it was imported into England. It is made up of five figures and the Lancers was a variant of it. (2) Premiers and seconds quadrilles are two of the lowest ranks in the cadre of the Paris Opéra.

QUATRE SAISONS, LES, ballet 1 act, ch. Perrot, m. Pugni, f.p. Her Majesty's Th., London 13 June 1848 (Grisi, Rosati, Cerrito, the younger Taglioni). This ballet appears to have resembled in execution and intention the *Pas de Quatre*. It was the last of Perrot's *divertissements* in London and marked the end of the Romantic Era. Another version, m. Verdi (from *Sicilian Vespers*) and ch. L. Petipa was given at H. Majesty's Th., London 10 May 1856. It marked the début in London of Amina Boschetti (as Winter).

QUATRIÈME, the fourth position (see FIVE POSITIONS).

QUATRIÈME DERRIÈRE (DEVANT), À LA, to the fourth position behind (in front). Two terms indicating that the foot is brought to these positions. See DÉGAGÉ.

QUEST, THE, ballet 5 sc., ch. Ashton, m. Walton, dec. Piper, book D. Langley Moore (from Spenser's *Faerie Queene*), f.p. S. Wells B., New Th., London 6 Apr 1943 (Fonteyn, Helpmann).

QUICA, LA (Francisca Gonzalez), b. Seville c. 1907, d. Madrid 1967. Sp. dancer and teacher. Début at the age of six in *café chantant*. First became a classical Sp. dancer and then learned the flamenco dance from her husband Frasquillo. Became the most famous teacher of flamenco and regional dances in Spain. First danced in London in the lecture demonstration by Doña Dolores de Pedroso organized by the R.A.D. Production Club at Covent Garden in 1951 and in the Company of José Greco.

QUINAULT, Philippe, b. Paris 1635, d. there 1688. Fr. poet who wrote the libretti for the ballets and operas of the court of Louis XIV. His ballets incl. *Le Triomphe de l'Amour* (1681), *Les Fêtes de l'Amour et de Bacchus* (1672) etc.

QUINTET, ballet, ch. Peter Wright, m. Ibert, dec. Gayer, f.p. Stuttgart B., Opera House, Stuttgart 13 July 1963 (Heinrich, Barra, Cragun). Also by Royal B. (Touring) dec. Wood, f.p. New Th., Oxford 29 Oct 1964 (Last, Emblen, Wall). A light-hearted frolic.

R

RABOVSKY, Istvan, b. Szeged 1930. Hungarian dancer. Pupil of Nadasi in Budapest and joined Hungarian B. 1947. Also studied in Leningrad 1949–50. While dancing with the Hungarian B. in East Berlin in May 1953 he and Nora Kovach (q.v.) escaped to the West and immediately appeared as guest artists with Festival B. in London. Then to America the same year where they settled, dancing in cabarets, on television and as guest artists (Festival B. 1955, Petit's B. de Paris etc.). Now American citizens.

RACCOURCI, the turning back of the leg by bringing the toe of the working leg to touch the knee of the supporting leg.

R.A.D., see ROYAL ACADEMY OF DANCING.

RADAMM, Monika, b. Berlin 1950. Ger. dancer. Pupil of T. Gsovsky. Joined Deutsche Oper B., Berlin 1967, soloist 1969.

RADICE, Attilia, b. Taranto 1913. It. dancer. Entered Scala, Milan, Sch. 1923 and studied under Gini and Cecchetti, becoming prima ballerina assoluta of the Scala 1935–57. Prima ballerina of the Teatro dell'Opera, Rome. Since 1957 director of Rome Opera B. Sch.

RADIUS, Alexandra, b. Amsterdam 1942. Dutch dancer. Pupil of Nel Roos. Joined Dutch Nat. B. 1956, Nederlands Dans Th. 1959–68. Joined Am. Ballet Th. 1968 as soloist becoming a principal 1969. Returned to Dutch Nat. B. as principal 1970. Mar. Han Ebelaar.

R.A.D. PRODUCTION CLUB, THE, an activity of the Royal Academy of Dancing, formed in 1932 to give stage experience to young dancers and chors. It gave a series of Sunday performances in London theatres at which many young dancers and chors. were given their first opportunities (Helpmann and Cranko produced their first ballets at these). It also organized lecture courses on choreography and stagecraft. It no longer functions.

RADUNSKY, Alexander, b. Moscow 1912. Russ. dancer and chor. Graduated from Bolshoi Sch. 1930 and in his first season in the Bolshoi B. was given the eponymous rôle in *Don Quixote*. Became one of the company's greatest mimes and created rôle of Lord Capulet in *Romeo and Juliet* (Bolshoi 1946), chor. *The Little Stork* (1937), *Svetlana* (1939) and *Red Sails* (1942)—all in collaboration with Popko and Posspekhine.

407

Chor. new version of *The Hump-backed Horse* with music by Schedrin 1960. Retired from Bolshoi B. 1962 and became chief chor. of the Red Army Song and Dance Ensemble. Hon. Artist R.S.F.S.R.

RAGOZINA, Galina, b. Archangel 1949. Russ. dancer. Pupil of Perm ballet sch. graduating to the Perm B. 1967. Won Gold Medal in senior section of Varna Competition 1968, while still eligible for the junior section. Entered Kirov B. 1970 as soloist. Mar. V. Panov (q.v.) and was dismissed with him in 1972.

RAIMUND, Carl, b. Vienna 1871, d. there 1951. Austrian dancer and teacher. Studied at Hofoper Sch. Joined Staatsoper B. and became principal dancer 1892 and teacher at the school 1899–1930. His son, Carl R. junior b. Vienna 1914, was in the Staatsoper B. from 1933, soloist 1946–63.

RAINÒ, Alfredo, b. Rome 1938. It. dancer. Studied at Rome Opera House Sch. 1947–57, primo ballerino in Rome 1961.

RAISS, Renzo, b. Rome 1927. Am. dancer and ballet master. Pupil of Magda Karsten in Augsburg, joined Augsburg B. 1946. To Kassel 1948, and in 1953 taught in the Boston Conservatory of Music. Ballet master Bremen 1955–57, then started his own Co. American Festival B. (q.v.). In 1965 worked at Met. Op., N.Y. and in 1970 became assistant director of Harkness B.

RAJALA, Maj-Lis, b. Tempere 1930. Finnish dancer. Studied at sch. of National Ballet of Finland and joined the company 1948. Became soloist 1952 and ballerina 1956.

RAKE, the slope of the stage down towards the footlights. The floor of the ballet rehearsal room in some opera houses (notably the Rotonde in the roof of the Paris Opéra) is sometimes constructed to have the same rake as the stage itself so that the dancers are always accustomed to the sloping floor beneath them. In Italian, 'pendenza', Fr. 'pente', Ger. 'Schräg'.

RAKE'S PROGRESS, THE, ballet 6 sc., ch. de Valois, m. Gavin Gordon, dec. Whistler, f.p. S. Wells B., S. Wells Th., London 20 May 1935 (Gore, Markova). The ballet is based on the Hogarth paintings. Mounted by the Munich B., same décor, Prinzregenten Th. 18 May 1956 (Kühl, Hallhuber), by the Turkish B. 1969, by B. van Vlaanderen, Opera House, Ghent 20 Sept 1972 (M. L. Wilderyckz, Aimé de Lignière) and by many other Cos. Massine chor. another ballet on the same theme *The Rake*, for C. B. Cochran in 1935 in which Gore also danced.

RALOV, Borge, b. Copenhagen 1908. Danish dancer and chor. Pupil of Royal Dan. Sch. Début 1927, solodancer 1933, ballet instructor 1934, first solodancer 1942, teacher at the Theatre Sch. 1945. Chor. *The*

Widow in the Mirror (1934), *Twelve for the Mail Coach* (1942), *The Courtesan* (1953). Now retired.

RALOV, Kirsten (*née* Gnatt, sister of Poul Gnatt), b. Vienna 1922. Danish dancer. Pupil of the Royal Sch., Copenhagen. Solodancer 1942. Retired 1962. Knight of the Order of Dannebrog 1953. Mar. first Borg Ralov and then Fredbjorn Björnsson.

RAMBERT, Dame Marie (Ramberg), b. Warsaw 1888. Polish teacher and dancer, founder and director of the B. Rambert. Studied in Warsaw. Influenced by Isadora Duncan. To Paris in 1906 to study medicine and gave private dance recitals. In 1910 went to Jaques-Dalcroze's summer sch. in Geneva, remained with him for three years, going in a group of his pupils who demonstrated his method in St Petersburg. Taught in the Dalcroze Sch. (which had moved to Dresden) arranging ballets. When Diaghileff and Nijinsky came to Dresden while working on *Sacre du Printemps* they chose her to help them with the complicated rhythms. She remained with Diaghileff's Co. (1912–13) and became a pupil of Cecchetti. She left Diaghileff, studied in London with Astafieva, and put on a ballet for the Stage Soc. in 1917, *The Golden Apples* which was afterwards used by C. B. Cochran. Mar. Ashley Dukes 1918. Opened Rambert Sch. 1920 and with her pupils presented *A Tragedy of Fashion* (q.v.) in 1926. The Marie Rambert Dancers gave public performances in 1930 and she founded the B. Club in 1930, in her husband's Mercury Th. This became the B. Rambert (q.v.), the oldest Eng. Co. still in existence. Thus she was one of the founders of modern English ballet, and countless dancers, choreographers, designers, and musicians have received their training and encouragement from her. Awarded C.B.E. 1954. Chevalier of the Legion of Honour 1957. Appointed D.B.E. 1962. D.Litt. Sussex Univ. 1964. Wrote autobiography *Quicksilver* 1972.

RAMEAU, Jean Philippe, b. Dijon 1683, d. Paris 1764. Fr. composer and author of works on harmony. Composed many ballets (incl. *Les Indes Galantes*) often collaborating with Cahusac, the maître de ballet. His partisans were in conflict with those of Lully—the *Guerre des Bouffons*.

RAMEAU, Pierre. Dancing master to Elizabeth Farnese (later 2nd wife of Philip V of Spain) and author of *Le Maître à Danser* (The Dancing Master) Paris 1725, which provides one of the most valuable records of eighteenth-century dancing technique.

RAO, Shanta, b. Mangalore 1930. Indian dancer. Studied Kathakali under Ramuni Menon, Mohini Attam under Krishnan Pannikar, Bharata Natya under Minaksisunderam Pillai. Danced in Peking 1953, America and Europe 1955.

409

RASCH, Albertina, b. Vienna 1896, d. Hollywood 1967. Austrian dancer. Studied Opera Sch., Vienna. To America 1911 and formed the Albertina Rasch Girls troupe in 1924, which danced in many musicals and films. From 1925 she taught in N.Y. and staged dances in musicals.

RASCH, Ellen, b. Geneva 1920. Swedish dancer. Pupil of Franchi, Preobrajenska and R. Swed. B. Sch. Entered R. Swedish B. 1939 becoming solodancer 1946. In 1954 danced in Paris. Danced title rôle in film *Firebird* (ch. Béjart) 1952. Retired 1962.

RASSINE, Alexis, b. Lithuania 1919 of Russ. parents. S. African dancer. Brought up in S. Africa. Studied under Preobrajenska in Paris. Début in Bal Tabarin. Danced in B. Rambert 1938, Trois Arts B. 1939, Anglo-Polish B. 1940. Joined S. Wells 1942 and became a principal dancer. Toured S. Africa and S. Rhodesia with Nadia Nerina 1952 and 1955. Partnered Chauviré C. Garden 1958. Now retired.

RAT, *les petits rats* are the lowest rank of dancers in the cadre of the Paris Opéra (see BALLERINA). Castil-Blaze says that the term is derived from their appearance, with lean faces, and their tendency always to be nibbling at something. At La Scala, Milan, called 'spinazit'.

RAVN, Hanne Marie (formerly Petersen), b. Copenhagen 1937. Danish dancer. Entered R. Danish Ballet Sch. 1946 and danced first solo rôle for R. Danish B. 1958. Guest artist at Jacob's Pillow 1960.

RAYET, Jacqueline, b. Paris 1932. Fr. dancer. Pupil of Paris Opéra Sch., becoming première danseuse 1956, étoile 1961. To Hamburg 1960 as guest ballerina.

RAYMONDA, ballet 3 acts, 4 sc., ch. Petipa, m. Glazounov, dec. Allegri, Ivanov, Lambini, f.p. Maryinsky Th., St Petersburg 7 Jan 1898 (Legnani, Preobrajenska, Gerdt). This ballet is still in the repertoire of the Soviet Ballet and has been revived in Europe and America. Ballet of Crusaders and Saracens, set in Hungary. Revived by Danilova and Balanchine for B. Russe de Monte Carlo, dec. Benois, f.p. N.Y. City Center 12 Mar 1946 (Danilova). Nureyev mounted a version (after Petipa) for Touring Royal B., dec. Montresor, at Spoleto Festival 19 July 1964 (Doreen Wells, Nureyev) but it was not thereafter taken into the repertory. However, the Third Act was redecorated by Barry Kay and became one of the Touring Royal B.'s ballets, f.p. C. Garden 16 July 1966 (Wells, Wall). Nureyev mounted the complete ballet for the Australian Ballet, dec. N. Baylis, f.p. Birmingham Th., Birmingham, Eng. 6 Nov 1965 (Fonteyn, Nureyev)—the rôles were later taken in Australia by Marilyn Jones and Garth Welch. He rechoreographed the complete ballet for the Zürich B., Opernhaus, Zürich 22 Jan 1972 (Haydee, Nureyev), dec. Georgiadis.

RAYMONDA VARIATIONS, ballet (originally called *Valses et Variations*), ch. Balanchine, m. Glazounov (*Raymonda*), dec. Armistead's backcloth for *Lilac Garden*, cost. Karinska, f.p. N.Y. City B., N.Y. City Center 7 Dec 1961 (Wilde, d'Amboise, Simon, Schorer, Govrin, Sumner, Neary). Abstract ballet.

RECITAL FOR CELLO AND EIGHT DANCERS, ballet, ch. Harkarvy, m. Bach, f.p. Nederlands Dans Th., The Hague 14 Oct 1965. The cellist sits on stage.

REDOWA, Bohemian dance in a rapid 3/4 time closely related to the mazurka. Popular in the Romantic era.

RED FLOWER, THE, see THE RED POPPY.

RED POPPY, THE, ballet 3 acts, ch. Lashchilin and Tikhomiroff, m. Glière, dec. Kurilko, f.p. Bolshoi Th. 14 June 1927 (Geltser, Tikhomiroff, Messerer). A Chinese tea-house dancer saves the life of a Soviet ship's captain—it was the first 'revolutionary' ballet and was immensely popular (showed 300 times in 10 years at the Bolshoi). Not produced in Leningrad until 20 Jan 1929, ch. Lopokov, Ponomaryov, Leontiev (Lukom danced Tao Hoa, the heroine). It had famous dances—the *Sailors' Dance* (The Little Apple), *Acrobat with Ribbon* and the *Golden Acrobat* (both danced by Messerer). Ulanova danced Tao Hoa in a new Leningrad version by Lavrovsky in 1949. He also produced a new version with title *The Red Flower* at the Bolshoi Th. Moscow 24 Nov 1957. Other versions are by Zakharoff and by Andreev.

RED SAILS, ballet 3 acts, ch. Popko, Posspekhin, Radunsky, m. Yurovsky, dec. P. Williams, f.p. Bolshoi Th. (Moscow Co.) at Kuibyshev 30 Dec 1942 (Tikhomirnova, Preobrajensky, Messerer). A fairy tale.

REECE, Judith, b. Washington D.C. 1942. Am. dancer. Studied at Miami Conservatory and Sch. of Am. B. Joined Washington Nat. B. Soloist Munich B. 1968–70. Returned to Pennsylvania B. 1970 as principal.

REED, Janet, b. Tolo, Oregon 1916. Am. dancer. Studied with Christensen. With San Francisco Opera Ballet 1937–41, Dance Players 1941–42, Ballet Theatre (guest artist) 1943–46, cr. rôles in *Fancy Free*, *On Stage!* etc. Went into N.Y. musicals. Joined N.Y. City Ballet 1949 and cr. rôle in *Bourrée Fantasque*, *Pied Piper*. Ballet mistress N.Y. City B. 1959–64. Now teaches.

REEL, Scottish and Irish dance for two or more couples in a rapid common time. The Highland Fling is a variant.

REFLECTION, ballet, ch. Cranko, m. Gardner, dec. New, f.p. S. Wells Th. B., Empire Th., Edinburgh 4 Sept 1952 (Fifield, O'Reilly, Miller, Poole, Britton, Trecu).

REGATTA, ballet 1 act, ch. Ashton, m. Gavin Gordon, dec. Chappell, f.p. S. Wells Th. for Vic-Wells B. 26 Sept 1931 (de Valois, Judson). This was Ashton's first ballet for the Wells.

REGIONAL or CIVIC BALLETS (in America) are amateur or semi-professional ballet companies drawing their dancers from the schools of a particular city or region and giving occasional local performances—very similar to the Ballet Clubs of Great Britain. The first was the Atlanta Civic Ballet founded in 1929 by Dorothy Alexander, and it is still flourishing. The movement has grown enormously and there are about seventy in America in four regional associations. Some are of near-professional standard, notably the Washington Civic B. founded by Mary Day and the late Lisa Gardiner which gave its première in Washington 28 Feb 1959 and appeared at Jacob's Pillow in 1960 (the first to do so), with Frederic Franklin as a director and Mimi Paul as principal soloist. Among the others were the New England B. Co. of Boston, the Kansas City Civic B., the Tulsa Civic B., the Ballet Guild of Chicago etc. The first Regional B. Festival was held in Atlanta in 1956 and a North Eastern in Scranton in 1960 (now annual festivals held in different cities), which have given impetus to this important movement.

RÉGISSEUR, the official who is responsible for mounting and rehearsing ballets in the repertoire.

REGNER, Otto F., b. Hersbruck 1913, d. Munich 1963. Ger. writer on the ballet. He was art-editor of the *Frankfurter Allgemeine Zeitung* and the leading ballet critic in Germany. Author of *Ballettbuch* (1954) and *Ballettfüher* (1956).

REICH, George, b. Long Island 1926. Am. dancer and chor. Studied under Balanchine and Gsovsky and modern dance under Hanya Holm and Limon. Début 1944 in N.Y. Broadway shows. In Markova-Dolin Co. 1947, Petit's Ballets de Paris. Dances in musicals, cabarets etc. in Paris, with his own troupe.

REINHOLM, Gert, b. Chemnitz 1923. Ger. dancer. Studied in Berlin under von Sachnowsky, Blank and T. Gsovsky and with Bulnes in Buenos Aires. Début as soloist in 1946 in Staatsoper, E. Berlin. Principal dancer there until 1950, then to Teatro Colon, Buenos Aires, 1952, Städtische Oper, W. Berlin 1953, Berliner Ballett 1955–56, and Munich 1960. Ballet master at Deutsche Oper, W. Berlin from 1960, and administrator from 1969.

REISINGER, the chor. of the first *Swan Lake* to Tchaikovsky's music, Moscow 1877. Little is known of him and it is even doubtful if his christian name was Julius or Wenzel. Krassovskaya gives his dates as b. 1827, d. 1892. He came to Moscow in 1871 at the Bolshoi Th. and chor. *The Magic Slipper*. He appears to have worked in Leipzig 1864–72.

REJDOVÁK, Bohemian dance in 2/4 time of which the Redowa is said to be a variant. The Rejdovák and the Redowa enjoyed considerable popularity in ballet programmes in the 1840s.

RELÂCHE ballet, 2 acts, a cinematographic entracte and a 'queue de chien'. Libretto Picabia, ch. and production, Picabia and Börlin, m. Satie, cinematographic entracte by René Clair, f.p. Ballets Suédois, Th. des Ch. Élysées 4 Dec 1924 (Edith Bonsdorff, Börlin, Kaj Smith). *Relâche* means 'no performance'. A surrealist ballet of which Picabia said '*C'est beaucoup de coups de pied dans beaucoup de derrières ou non.*' Nowadays we would say that it was an example of mixed media and a 'happening'.

RELEVÉ or TEMPS RELEVÉ, lit. a lifted step. The raising of the body on half or full-point or points. In cont. Russ. nomenclature, a relevé on one foot is known as a sissonne simple.

REMINGTON, Barbara, b. Windsor, Ont. 1936. Canadian dancer. Pupil of Severo in Detroit and Royal B. Sch. Joined Ballet Th. 1958, Royal B. 1959 becoming soloist 1961. Returned to America and joined Ballet Th. 1964 and Joffrey B. 1966–69.

RENARD, LE, ballet 1 act, ch. Nijinska, m. Stravinsky, dec. Larionov, f.p. Diaghileff's Co., Paris Opéra 18 May 1922 (Nijinska). New version, ch. Lifar, f.p. Th. Sarah Bernhardt, Paris 21 May 1929. In this ballet the dancing rôles were doubled by a troupe of acrobats and there was a chorus. There have been later versions, by Lifar 1929, Balanchine 1947, G. Blank 1954 (Berlin), Rosen 1962 (Munich), Béjart 1965 (Paris Opéra).

RENAULT, Michel, b. Paris 1927. Fr. dancer. Studied at Paris Opéra Sch. and nominated premier danseur étoile 1946, the youngest in the history of the Opéra. Left Opéra 1959. Danced in Moscow, 1958. Tours with group of Paris Opéra Stars, is teacher at the Opéra School and chor. revues.

RENCHER, Derek, b. Birmingham 1932. Eng. dancer. Pupil of Vernon and Gregory. Joined Royal B. 1952 becoming a principal 1969. Cr. rôle of Lysander in *The Dream* 1964, Paris in *Romeo and Juliet* 1965, Elgar in *Enigma Variations* 1968.

RENCONTRE, LA, OU OEDIPE ET LE SPHINX, ballet 1 act, ch. Lichine, m. Sauguet, dec. Bérard, f.p. B. des Ch. Élysées, Th. des Ch. Élysées, Paris 8 Nov 1948 (Caron, Babilée), The riddle of the Sphinx.

RENDEZ-VOUS, LE, ballet 1 act, ch. Petit, m. Kosma, dec. Brassai, cost. Mayo, f.p. B. des Ch. Élysées, Th. des Ch. Élysées, Paris 15 June 1945

(Petit, M. de Berg, Seillier). Ballet of Paris underworld. The decs. are much-enlarged photographs.

RENDEZVOUS, LES, ballet 1 act, ch. Ashton, m. Auber (ballet music in *L'Enfant Prodigue*), dec. Chappell, f.p. S. Wells B., S. Wells Th. 5 Dec 1933 (Markova, Idzikowsky, de Valois, Helpmann). A lightly-linked suite of dances.

RENDEZ-VOUS MANQUÉ, LE, ballet 3 acts by Françoise Sagan, ch. Taras (Acts 1 and 3), and Don Lurio (Act 2), m. Magne, dec. Buffet (Act 1, cost. Laurenti), f.p. Monte Carlo 3 Jan 1958 (Toni Lander, Noelle Adam, Skouratoff) and subsequently toured Europe and America. A contemporary drama.

RENÉ, Natalia (Roslavleva), b. Kieff 1907. Russ. writer on ballet. Educ. Univ. of Moscow and studied at Lunacharsky Choreographic Technicum, Moscow. Author of *Maya Plisetskaya* (1956), *English Ballet* (1959), *Beryozka* (1960) collaborated on *Vaganova* (1958) and *Fokine* (1962) almanacs, *Era of the Russian Ballet* (1966). Contributor to *Soviet Encyclopaedia*, *Enciclopedia dello Spettacolo*, *Dance Encyclopedia*, and *The Dancing Times* and *Dance and Dancers*.

RENVERSÉ, lit. overturned. A deliberate disturbance of the normal poise without loss of equilibrium, as for instance in a backward bend. The bending of the body during a turn (it can take a variety of forms).

RÉPÉTITION, (Fr.) rehearsal. Ger. 'probe'.

RÉPÉTITION GÉNÉRALE, (Fr.) dress rehearsal (attended by the press and invited audience). Ger. 'hauptprobe'.

REQUIEM CANTICLES, ballet, ch. Robbins, m. Stravinsky (including six pieces from the *Requiem Mass*), in practice costume, f.p. N.Y. City B., N.Y. State Th. 25 June 1972 (Allegra Kent, Anthony Blum, Susan Hendl, Robert Maiorano, Ashley Merrill). Mounted for Royal B., C. Garden 15 Nov 1972 (Bergsma, Derman, Eagling, Ashmole).

RESQUILLEUR, (Fr.) a gate-crasher at a theatrical performance. A Provençal word for a skater. The phrase derives from a production of Meyerbeer's opera *Le Prophète* at the Municipal Opera in Marseille, c. 1880. In it the famous skating ballet was performed by members of the local Roller Skating Club (the normal practice with this opera). As the members passed through the stage door they showed their skates wrapped in paper to the doorkeeper and said 'Resquilleur'. After the third performance the doorkeeper realized that the number of skaters had risen from the prescribed number of seven up to twenty—they were gate-crashers, and the phrase has survived.

RETIRÉ or TEMPS RETIRÉ, lit. a withdrawing movement. The raising, from the fifth position, of the fully turned out thigh until it is at right angles to the body with the toe in line with the knee-cap of the supporting leg and closing front or back, in the fifth position. When the working foot starts from the front and closes at the back, the temps is described as a retiré passé en arrière (a withdrawing movement passing to the back), or if *vice versa*, as a retiré passé en avant (a withdrawing movement passing to the front) and when executed with a relevé, as a relevé retiré passé en avant or en arrière, e.g. in the solo in the coda of *Swan Lake*, Act II, Odette executes an entrechat quatre, relevé passé en arrière twice, followed by four relevés passés en arrière.

RETURN OF SPRING TIME, THE, ballet after F. Taglioni, ch. Skeaping, m. Cesare Bossi, cost. David Walker, f.p. Ballet for All (Royal B.) at Abbeydore Festival, Herefordshire 10 Sept 1965 (Ann Dennis, Gail Thomas, Oliver Symons). Subsequently by the R. Swedish B., Drottningholm Court Th., Sweden 31 Aug 1966 as part of the theatre's bicentenary celebrations. In 1818 F. Taglioni presented this ballet in Stockholm, based on *Flore et Zephire* (q.v.).

REVANCHE, ballet 4 sc., book and ch. Ruth Page, m. Verdi, dec. Remisoff, f.p. Ruth Page Co., University of Chicago 27 Jan 1951 (Page, Stone). For the B. des Ch. Élysées, dec. Clavé, Th. de l'Empire, Paris 17 Oct 1951 (Arova, Moreau, Skouratoff, Ohn). Based on *Il Trovatore*.

REVELATIONS, ballet, ch. Ailey, m. traditional Negro, cost. Harper, f.p. Alvin Ailey Dance Th., YM-YWHA, New York 31 Jan 1960. Negro spirituals are sung by a choir and the dancers dance out their emotions (Pilgrim of Sorrow; Take me to the Water; Move, Members, Move; Rocka' my Soul). One of Ailey's greatest works.

RÉVÉRENCE, (Fr.) a curtsey. Compan describes three types—en avant, en passant, and en arrière (the most respectful). See also CURTAIN CALL.

REVITT, Peter, b. Northampton 1916, d. London 1968. Eng. artist. Studied stage design and sketched at ballet classes. Published *Ballet Guyed* 1948 (caricatures of dancers, some of which had appeared in *Ballet Today*). Illustrated *Dictionary of Ballet Terms* (Kersley 1952), *Mime* (Lawson 1952), *Dressing for the Ballet* (Lawson and himself 1958), *Dictionary of Ballet* (Wilson 1957), *Ballet Physique* (Sparger 1958), *Classical Ballet* (Lawson 1960), *Dictionary of Ballet* (Wilson 1974), *Ballet and the Dance* (Woodward 1967).

REYN, Judith (Fisher), b. Rhodesia 1942. British dancer. Pupil of Dorothy Ainscough (Rhodesia) and Royal B. Sch. Joined Royal B. 1962–66. Soloist of Stuttgart B. from 1966. Guest artist in Munich B. 1967.

REYNA, Ferdinando, b. 1899, d. Paris 1969. French writer on ballet.

Author of *Des Origines du Ballet* (1955,) *Histoire du Ballet* (1964) and the Larousse *Dictionary of Ballet* (1968.) Founded the ballet club in Paris.

RHODES, Lawrence, b. Mt Hope, Virginia 1939. Am. dancer. Pupil of Armand, B. Russe Sch., Joffrey, Williams. Joined B. Russe de Monte Carlo 1958, Joffrey B. 1960–64, Harkness B. 1964 as principal, becoming Director 1968. In 1970 joined Dutch Nat. B. as principal. Returned to America (Pennsylvania B.) 1972. Mar. Lone Isaksen.

RHODIN, Teddy, b. Stockholm 1919. Swed. dancer and chor. Pupil of Franchi 1926–37, Egorova, Gé 1940–48 and Royal Swed. B. Sch. Joined Royal Swed. B. 1937, solodancer 1942 and retired 1964. Appointed ballet master of Malmö B. 1967–70. Chor. for operas, television etc. Has school in Malmö.

RIABOUCHINSKA, Tatiana, b. Moscow 1917. Russ. dancer and one of the 'baby ballerinas'. Studied under Volinine and Kschessinska in Paris. Début *Chauve Souris* in Paris. Ballerina (with Toumanova and Baronova) de Basil's Co. 1932 until 1941. Since then, with her husband Lichine, she has danced with many Cos., Ballet Theatre (1944), Orig. B. Russe (1947), guest artist in Buenos Aires, B. des Ch. Élysées (1948), de Cuevas Co. (1950), etc. Among her cr. rôles are in *Paganini*, *Graduation Ball*, *Cinderella*, *Jeux d'Enfants*, *Beau Danube*, *Présages* (Frivolity), *Choreartium*, etc. Now teaches in California.

RIABYNKINA, Elena, b. Sverdlovsk 1941. Russ. dancer. Trained at Bolshoi Sch., Moscow 1950–59 when she joined Bolshoi B. becoming their youngest soloist. Danced Odette-Odile 1959, at Bolshoi. First danced in London 1965. Cr. title rôle in Vanina Vanini 1962. Her sister, Xenia R., is also in the Bolshoi B.

RIANNE, Patricia, b. Palmerston, N.Z. 1943. N.Z. dancer. Pupil of her mother and joined New Zealand B. 1959. Studied at Royal B. Sch. and joined Marseilles B. 1963. Joined B. Rambert 1966 and Scottish Th. B. 1969 as soloist.

RICARDA, Ana, b. San Francisco. Am. dancer and chor. Pupil of Minnie Hawke in Washington, Celli and Vladimiroff in N.Y., and in Europe of Escudero, Argentina, La Quica. With Markova-Dolin in America. Joined de Cuevas Co. 1949 as ballerina and appeared as guest artist Festival B. 1951. Chor. *Del Amor y de la Muerte* (1949), *Fiesta* (1950), *Doña Inez de Castro*, *La Tertulia* (1952), *Saeta* (1955), *Chanson de l'Éternelle Tristesse* (1957) and for the Royal B. Sch. *Divertimiento Español* (m. Salzedo 1968), *Tertulia* 1971. Teacher at Royal B. Sch. from 1967.

RICAUX, Gustave, b. Paris 1884, d. Aubagne 1961. Fr. dancer and teacher. He was trained at the Paris Opéra Sch. and for many years a

416

principal dancer. He then became a famous teacher in Paris with his own school. Among his pupils were Petit, Babilée, Renault, Peretti.

RICERCARE, ballet (pas de deux), ch. Tetley, m. Seter, dec. Ter-Arutunian, f.p. Am. Ballet Theatre, State Th., N.Y. 25 Jan 1966 (Mary Hinkson, Scott Douglas). B. Rambert, f.p. Playhouse, Nottingham 24 Feb 1967 (Sandra Craig, J. Taylor). Lying on a concave structure a man and a girl embrace after love-making.

RICH, John, b. c. 1682, d. Hillingdon 1761. Eng. dancer and impresario, who built the first Covent Garden Th. in 1732. Thought to have produced the first pantomime in England c. 1720. Brought Sallé and Noverre to London. Under the name of 'Lun' was the best-known Harlequin of his day. He took over from his father (Christopher Rich, d. 1714) the Lincoln's Inn Th. and produced there Gay's *The Beggar's Opera* (1728), thereby 'making Gay rich and Rich gay'.

RICHARDS, Dianne, b. Rhodesia 1934, Rhodesian dancer. Studied under Marjorie Sturman. Joined Festival Ballet 1951, soloist 1955 and ballerina 1959. Guest Am. B. Th. 1963–64. New London B. 1972.

RICHARDSON, P. J. S., b. Newark 1875, d. London 1963. Educated Beaumont Col. and University College School. Senior Director of the *Dancing Times* (q.v.), which he edited 1910–51. Co-founder Royal Academy of Dancing (Hon. Sec. and Vice-President), organized Dancers' Circle Dinners (from 1920), Sunshine Matinées (1919–30). Co-founder Camargo Society. Founder (1929) and Chairman Official Board of Ballroom Dancing 1929–59. Author of many books on ballroom dancing and articles on ballet. His contribution to the organization and the development of the dance in England is immeasurable. In 1932 he took the rôle of Job's spiritual self in performances of Job when the British Ballet danced in Copenhagen. Author of *Who's Who in Dancing* with Haskell (1932), *History of English Ballroom Dancing 1910–1945* (1946), *Social Dances of the Nineteenth Century* (1960). Awarded O.B.E. 1951, Knight of the Order of Danneborg 1952.

RIESTSTAP, Ine, b. The Hague 1929. Dutch dancer. Pupil of ter Weeme, Kyasht, Northcote. Soloist B. der Lage Landen 1948–58, and Scapino B. Writes on ballet and in 1967 retired to teach.

RIGAUDON, or RIGADOON, lively folk dance of Provençal or It. origin, usually in duple time, popular in the seventeenth and eighteenth centuries, which gave its name to the now little used pas de rigaudon.

RIGOLBOCHE (Marguerite Badel), b. Nancy, d. Paris 1920. Fr. dancer, fl. 1860–65, and was the greatest exponent of the can-can of that time. Her invented name gave rise to the word 'rigolbocher' meaning to dance in her eccentric manner. Her *Autobiography* appeared in 1860.

RINALDO AND ARMIDA, ballet 1 act, ch. Ashton, m. Arnold, dec. Rice, f.p. S. Wells B., C. Garden, London 6 Jan 1955 (Beriosova, Somes).

RIO-BALLET, ballet journal founded December 1952 by Elsa Chaise in Rio de Janeiro, covering ballet in Brazil and South America.

RIPMAN, Olive, b. Teddington 1886. Eng. dancer and teacher. Studied under Miss Wordsworth in London. Founded Ripman Sch., London and in 1944 joined with Grace Cone to form the Cone-Ripman Sch.— later becoming the Arts Educational Trust of which she was co-director until 1965.

RITE OF SPRING, THE, see SACRE DU PRINTEMPS, LE.

RIVERA, Chita, b. Washington D.C. 1933. Am. dancer. Studied at Sch. of Am. B. Danced in N.Y. in *Call Me Madam, Guys and Dolls* and then created rôle of Anita, singing and dancing, in *West Side Story* 1957. She also danced the rôle in the London production. Cr. chief rôle in *Bye Bye, Birdie* (ch. Champion, N.Y. 1960), and danced the lead in London production of *Sweet Charity* (1966).

RIVOLTADE, a step in which the dancer turns as he jumps and passes one leg over the other, landing facing the direction from which he jumped.

RIZZO, Marlene, b. Portland, Oregon 1936. Am. dancer. Pupil of S. Williams, Volkova. Joined Am. Ballet Th. 1955, de Cuevas, B. Russe de Monte Carlo, Joffrey B., and Harkness B. on its formation 1964 as soloist. Mar. Helgi Tomasson.

ROAD OF THE PHOEBE SNOW, THE, ballet, ch. Talley Beatty, m. Duke Ellington and Strayhorn, lighting Cernovich, f.p. YM-YWHA, N.Y. 28 Nov 1959 (Caldwell, Collins, Peters, Gore, Gordon, Johnson, Howell, Parham, Jeffery). Jazz ballet of love and violence on the railway tracks near a city (title from an old railway run). This was the first ballet to be financed by the Lena Robbins Foundation (created by Jerome Robbins in memory of his mother). Performed by the London Cont. Dance Th. at The Place, London 10 Feb 1971 (Linda Gibbs, Wm. Louther).

ROBBINS, Jerome, b. N.Y. 1918. Am. dancer and chor. Studied Tudor, Loring. Joined Ballet Theatre 1940–44 (and London 1946). Joined N.Y. City Ballet, becoming Associate Artistic Director 1949. Chor. *Fancy Free* (and cr. rôle) his first ballet 1944, *Interplay, Facsimile, Age of Anxiety, Pied Piper, Fanfare, Afternoon of a Faun*, and numerous musicals incl. *The King and I* and *West Side Story* (1957). In 1958 he formed the Ballets: U.S.A. (q.v.). Won two 'Oscars' in 1962 for film of *West Side Story*, for direction and for chor. (the first time the award had been given for this). Directed and chor. *Fiddler on the Roof* (also called *Anatevka*) 1964. Chor. *Les Noces* (m. Stravinsky) for Am. B. Th. 1965, *Dances at a Gathering* (m. Chopin) for N.Y. City B. 1969 (and for Royal B. 1970), *In the Night* (m. Chopin) 1970, *Goldberg Variations* (m. Bach) 1971, *Watermill* (m. Ito) 1972. Formed the Am. Lyric Th., Workshop, N.Y. 1966 with Government subsidy.

ROCHE, Nora, b. London 1906. Eng. teacher. Pupil of Dore Desnaux, M. Craske and N. Legat. Joined Ross B. 1924, Carl Rosa Opera B. 1925–39 (soloist 1932). Had her own sch. in London 1942–59, taught at Rambert Sch. 1955–63 and Royal B. Sch. from 1960. Major Examiner Cecchetti Soc., going on overseas tours from 1956.

RODE, Lizzie, b. Copenhagen 1933. Dan. dancer. Entered R. Danish B. Sch. 1940, became a member of the Company 1952.

RODEO, OR THE COURTING AT BURNT RANCH, ballet 3 sc., ch. de Mille, m. Copland, dec. Smith, cost. Love, f.p. B. Russe de Monte Carlo, Met. Op. N.Y. 16 Oct 1942 (Mladova, Franklin, de Mille). This ballet introduces an American square dance with a caller.

RODRIGUES, Alfred, b. Cape Town 1921. S. African dancer and chor. Joined Cape Town University B. Club, studied with Cecily Robinson, and appeared in some productions. To London 1946, studied Volkova; joined S. Wells B. 1947. Chor. *Les Ingénues* for R.A.D. Production Club, *Île des Sirènes* (1950) for Fonteyn-Helpmann tour, *Blood Wedding* (1953), *Café des Sports* (1954) for S. Wells Th. B., *The Miraculous Mandarin* (1956) for S. Wells B., *Jabez and the Devil* 1961 (m. A. Cooke) and the dances in many musicals. Also chor. *Romeo and Juliet* (m. Prokofieff) Verona 1955, *Cinderella* for Scala, Milan 1955. Maître de ballet C. Garden 1953–55. Has produced many works in Turkey and Italy, among them *Casse Noisette* at the Scala, Milan 1957. Chor. *Vivaldi Concerto* for R. Dan. B. 1960, worked in Warsaw and chor. musicals. Mar. Julia Farron.

ROI CANDAULE, LE, ballet 4 acts, 6 sc., ch. Petipa, m. Pugni, dec. David, f.p. Maryinsky Th., St Petersburg 29 Oct 1868 (Dor). The story of Gyges, King of Lydia.

ROI NU, LE, ballet, (1) ch. Lifar, m. Françaix, dec. Pruna, f.p. Paris Opéra 15 June 1936 (Chauviré, Lifar); (2) ch. de Valois, m. Françaix, dec. Briggs, f.p. S. Wells B. 7 Apr 1938 (Pearl Argyle, Helpmann, with Margaret Dale as the child who speaks). These ballets are based on the Hans Andersen story.

ROJE, Anna, b. Split 1909. Yugoslav dancer and teacher. Début Split 1926. Studied under Margarita Froman at Zagreb. To Opera House, Belgrade, as soloist 1930 and studied under Poliakova. To London 1933 and studied under N. Legat, becoming his assistant and protégée.

With Blum's Co., Monte Carlo 1938, as soloist and teacher. 1941–51 ballerina at Zagreb. Opened school in Split 1953, with her husband, Oskar Harmos, and in 1954–55 taught in New York at Sch. of B. Russe de Monte Carlo. Now teaches in Bermuda, Boston and in Split.

ROLEFF, Peter (see KING, KARL-HEINZ).

ROMANESCA, or ROMANESQUE, a type of galliard.

ROMANOFF, Boris, b. St Petersburg 1891, d. N.Y. 1957. Russ. dancer and chor. Graduated Imp Sch. 1909. With Diaghileff 1910–14 and chor. *La Tragédie de Salomé* (1912). Chor. ballets in operas at Maryinsky Th. Left Russia 1918. Founded his own Co. 1921 and toured Europe. Chor. at Scala, Milan 1925 and mounted ballets in Rome, Turin, etc. To America 1938 (for many years he was maître de ballet at Met. Op., N.Y.).

ROMANOFF, Dmitri, b. Tzeritzin 1907. Russ. dancer and ballet master. Studied under Koslov, Bolm, Mordkin, Fokine. Début with Nini Theilade in film *Midsummer Night's Dream* 1935. Danced as principal of San Francisco Op. B., Mordkin B. 1937–39, Ballet Th. 1940, becoming *régisseur* 1946. Now teaches in California.

ROMANTIC AGE, ballet 1 act, ch. Dolin, m. Bellini, cost. Merida, f.p. Ballet Theatre, Met. Op., N.Y. 23 Oct 1942 (Markova, Dolin, Kriza). See AGLAË.

ROMANTIC BALLET, used, somewhat narrowly, to describe the ballets produced during the period of the Romantic revival in literature in the early nineteenth century, or roughly from 1830 to 1850, taking as their theme the odyssey of mortal man in love with some female spirit of the air or water or with some maiden risen from her tomb to dance by moonlight in a forest glade. In point of fact *The Swan Lake* produced in 1877 or *Les Sylphides* created in 1909 are as much romantic ballets as are *La Sylphide* or *Giselle*. Many of the romantic ballets are also classical ballets, but examples of classical ballets that are not romantic ballets will spring readily to mind, e.g. *The Sleeping Beauty*, *Symphonic Variations*. The dividing line is a slender one, i.e. in the romantic ballet the accent is on colour or mood rather than on form and design which is predominant in the classical ballet.

ROMEO AND JULIET, ballet. (1) ch. Galeotti, m. Schall, f.p. R. Danish B., Copenhagen 2 Apr 1811 (Schall and Antoine Bournonville). (2) 1 act, ch. Nijinska-Balanchine, m. Constant Lambert, dec. Miro and Ernst, f.p. Diaghileff's Co., Monte Carlo 4 May 1926 (Karsavina, Lifar). The music was the first to be commissioned by Diaghileff from an English composer. The ballet was not a straightforward telling of the story but was styled a rehearsal without scenery in two parts. (3) 3 acts, ch. Vanya Psota, m. Prokofieff, dec. Skrušhny, f.p. Brno Ballet, Czechoslovakia 30 Dec 1938 (V. Psota as Romeo, Zora Šemberova as Juliet). This was the first production using Prokofieff's music. When originally composed (to the libretto of Radlov and Piotrovsky) the story had a happy end—a normal Communist requirement. There were delays in Leningrad, and the Bolshoi Th., Moscow rejected the music as 'unsuitable' (the composer had been disgraced politically). So the State Th. in Brno offered to mount it, with the proper tragic ending, for which Prokofieff wrote a new finale. A year later the Kirov Th., Leningrad took it (with the tragic ending). (4) 3 acts, ch. Lavrovsky, m. Prokofieff, dec. Peter Williams, f.p. Kirov Th., Leningrad 11 Jan 1940 (Ulanova, Sergeyev). (5) 1 act, ch. Tudor, m. Delius, dec. Berman, f.p. Ballet Th., Met. Op., N.Y. 6 Apr 1943 (Markova, Hugh Laing). This version was performed by the R. Swed. B., Stockholm 30 Dec 1962 (Berit Skold, Conny Borg). (6) 3 acts ch. Lavrovsky, m. Prokofieff, dec. Williams, f.p. Bolshoi Th., Moscow 28 Dec 1946 (Ulanova, Gabovitch). (7) 1 act, ch. Lifar, m. Tchaikovsky, f.p. Nouveau B. de Monte Carlo, Monte Carlo 1946 and at Paris Opéra (dec. Moulène) 13 Apr 1949 (Chauviré, Lifar). (8) 1 act, ch. Bartholin, m. Tchaikovsky, dec. Pedersen, f.p. R. Danish B., Copenhagen 8 Dec 1950 (Vangsaa, Bruhn). Bartholin originally produced this ballet for the Ballets de la Jeunesse, Paris 1937 (Moulin, Bartholin). (9) ch. Parlic, m. Prokofieff, dec. Denic, f.p. Belgrade Opera 25 June 1948 (Parnel, Parlic). (10) ch. Froman, m. Prokofieff, dec. Gedrinsky, cost. Kostincer-Bregovac, f.p. Zagreb Opera, June 1949 (Roje, Lhotka). (11) 3 acts, ch. Ashton, m. Prokofieff, dec. Rice, f.p. R. Danish B., Copenhagen 19 May 1955 (Vangsaa, Kronstam). (11) 2 acts, ch. Lifar, m. Prokofieff, dec. Wakhevitch, f.p. Paris Opéra 28 Dec 1955 (Daydé, Renault). (13) ch. Cranko, m. Prokofieff, dec. Jürgen Rose, Stuttgart B., Staatsoper, Stuttgart 2 Dec 1962 (Haydee, Barra). This production was also mounted for the Munich B., f.p. National Th., Munich 12 Nov 1968 (Vernon, Clauss), and for the Canadian Nat. B. 14 Apr 1964. (14) ch. MacMillan, m. Prokofieff, dec. Georgiadis, f.p. Royal B., Covent G. 9 Feb 1965 (Fonteyn, Nureyev—but it was choreographed on Seymour and Gable). He mounted this for the R. Swed. B., Stockholm 5 Dec 1969 (Georgina Parkinson, Jonas Kage). (15) ch. van Dantzig, m. Prokofieff, dec. van Schayk, f.p. Dutch Nat. B., Stadsschouwburg, Amsterdam 22 Feb 1967 (Vendrig, André). (16) ch. Neumeier, dec. Sanjust, m. Prokofieff, Städtische Bühnen, Frankfurt-am-Main 14 Feb 1971 (Kruuse, Finney).

ROMEO AND JULIET, ballet, ch. Béjart, m. Berlioz, dec. Casado, f.p. B. du XXme Siècle. Cirque Royal Brussels 17 Nov 1966 (Bortoluzzi, Laura Proenca). In modern 'beat' style with singing and speaking.

RONA, Viktor, b. Budapest 1936. Hungarian dancer. From 1945–54 studied under Nadasi at State B. Institute, Budapest. Joined Budapest Opera B. 1950 and became principal dancer 1956. Also studied in Leningrad 1959 under Pushkin. Awarded Liszt Prize 1963, Kossuth Prize 1965. Partnered Fonteyn in R.A.D. Gala at Drury Lane 1963 (danced *Gayané* pas de deux), the Prince in Larrain's *Cendrillon* (ch. Orlikowski), Paris 1963 (with Samtsova) etc. Usually partners A. Orosz.

ROND DE JAMBE, lit. circle of the leg. *Rond de jambe à terre*, a rotary movement on the ground of the working leg, executed from the hip, said to be en dehors, or outwards, when the leg is extended first to the front with the foot fully pointed and then swept round to the side and back and through (foot in first) to the front again, or en dedans (inwards) when executed in reverse direction starting from the fourth position back and sweeping round to the side and front. *Rond de jambe en l'air*, a rotary movement in the air with the thigh in second position, executed from the knee downwards en dedans or en dehors. The French dancers Gardel and Vestris have been credited with being the first to execute the rond de jambe en l'air. *Grand rond de jambe en dehors*, a rotary movement of the whole leg, executed from the hip, in which the leg passes through the fourth position en avant, second position and fourth position en arrière. When executed in reverse direction the movement is a *grand rond de jambe en dedans*. *Rond de jambe sauté*, a rond de jambe executed with a leap off the supporting foot. See also FOUETTÉ.

ROOMS, ballet, ch. Anna Sokolow, m. Hopkins, f.p. at YM-YWHA, N.Y., 24 Feb 1955 (Seckler, Beck, McKayle etc.). The terror of loneliness. Also in repertoire of Nederlands Dans Th., Ailey Dance Th. and Joffrey B.

ROOS, Nel, b. Ridderkirk 1914, d. 1970. Dutch dancer and teacher. Pupil of Jooss, Wigman, Georgi, Preobrajenska, Kiss etc. Gave solo recitals from 1920, then assistant to Georgi 1942–47. Ballet mistress Amsterdam Opera B. 1947. Opened school in Amsterdam 1948. Director of Rotterdam Dance Academy 1961. Member of Dutch State Scholarship Board. Correspondent of *Dance News*, contributor to *Dance Encyclopedia*.

ROPES OF TIME, THE, ballet, ch. van Dantzig, m. Boerman (electronic), dec. T. van Schayk, f.p. Royal B., C. Garden 2 Mar 1970 (Nureyev, Vere, Mason). A lonely traveller, always accompanied by Life and Death. The first ballet at the Royal Opera House to have electronic music and van Dantzig's first work for the Royal B.

ROQUEPLAN, Nestor, b. Montreal 1804, d. Paris 1870. Fr. writer and impresario. Editor of *Figaro* (1830). Wrote *Les Coulisses de l'Opéra*

(1855). Director of the Paris Opéra (1847–54) and of the Opéra Comique.

ROSARIO (Rosario Perez), b. Seville 1918. Sp. dancer. Studied under Realito. Cousin and partner of Antonio. In 1954, partnered by Roberto Iglesias, she formed her own Co. Iglesias left in 1956. She rejoined Antonio for his 1964 seasons in London and N.Y.

ROSATI, Carolina, b. Bologna 1826, d. Cannes 1905. It. dancer. Pupil of Blasis. Début at Verona. At Paris Opéra 1853–59. She danced in London 1847–58 and at St Petersburg 1859–61, retiring in 1862. She was a great dramatic dancer and cr. rôles in *Jovita*, *La Fonti*, *Le Corsaire*, and *Marco Spada*. The salary she received was the biggest ever paid by the Opéra up to that time and for a considerable time afterwards.

ROSE ADAGIO, brilliant pas d'action (ch. Petipa) danced by the Princess Aurora with her four suitors, from each of whom she receives two roses, in *The Sleeping Beauty*, Act II, and occasionally presented apart from its context as a divertissement.

ROSE, Jürgen, b. Bernburg (E. Germany) 1937. Ger. artist. Designed ballets for Cranko, Tudor and Franca. For Cranko: *Romeo and Juliet*, Stuttgart 1963, Munich 1969; *Swan Lake*, Stuttgart 1964, Munich 1970; *Fire Bird*, Berlin and Stuttgart 1964–65; *Onegin*, Stuttgart 1965, N.Y. 1969; *Poème de L'Extase*, Stuttgart 1970. For Tudor: *Giselle*, Berlin 1964. For Franca (Nat. B. of Canada): *Nutcracker*, Toronto 1966, *Cinderella*, Toronto 1968. *Daphnis and Chloë*, Frankfurt 1972.

ROSE LATULIPPE, ballet, ch. Macdonald, m. Freedman, dec. Prevost. f.p. R. Winnipeg B., Avon Th., Stratford, Ont. 16 Aug 1966 (Annette Wiedersheim-Paul, Rutherford, Sheila Mackinnon, Goulet). A romantic tale set in Quebec in 1740.

ROSEN, Heinz, b. Hanover 1908, d. Lake Constant 1972. Ger. dancer and chor. Pupil of von Laban, Jooss. Toured with Ballets Jooss. Chor. *Die Dame und das Einhorn* (m. Chailley, dec. Cocteau) Munich 1953 and 1958. Appointed director of Munich B. 1959–67. Chor. *Josephslegende* (1958), *Carmina Burana* and *Catulli Carmina* (1959), *La Buffonata* (m. Killmayer 1961) etc. Also produced opera and operettas.

ROSENTHAL, Jean, b. N.Y. 1912, d. N.Y. 1969. Am. lighting consultant who contributed to the success of so many of the productions of N.Y. City B. from 1946 to 1957. She also worked for N.Y. City Opera 1945–51, Martha Graham from 1958, Robbins' Ballets: U.S.A. 1959–60, and many musicals.

ROSIN, a resin, or solid residue left after the oil has been distilled from crude turpentine. A tray of rosin is to be found in the wings of every

423

stage used for ballet and every rehearsal or classroom so that the dancers may rub their shoes in it to prevent their slipping. Rosin is also often sprinkled on a slippery stage before a performance.

ROSLAVLEVA, see RENÉ, NATALIA.

ROSS, Bertram, b. Brooklyn 1925. Am. dancer. Joined Martha Graham Co. 1953 and became leading dancer and her partner. Created rôles in many of her most famous ballets (*Canticle for Innocent Comedians, Embattled Garden* 1958, *Clytemnestra* 1958, *Acrobats of God* 1960 etc.). Teaches in Graham Sch.

ROSS, Herbert, b. Brooklyn 1926. Am. dancer and chor. Studied under Doris Humphrey 1947 and classical ballet under Platova. Chor. *Caprichos* (1950), *Thief who loved a Ghost, Paean, The Maids* (1957), *Serenade for Seven*. Also for musicals chor. *A Tree Grows in Brooklyn, House of Flowers*. Mar. Nora Kaye. His Co., Ballet of Two Worlds, appeared at Spoleto Festival 1960 and toured Europe. Now directs films and musicals.

ROSSON, Keith, b. Birmingham 1937. Eng. dancer. Studied at Royal B. Sch. 1953–55 when he entered the Royal B., becoming soloist, and 1964 a principal. To PACT B., Johannesburg 1971.

ROSTOFF, Dmitri, b. Kharkoff 1898. Russ. dancer. Cavalry officer in White Russ. army, came to London in 1924 and joined Leonidoff's Russ. B Co. at C. Garden. To Italy and studied under Grassi in Rome, then Volinin and Legat in London. Joined Dandré's Co. 1934 and de Basil 1936. When this Co. broke up in S. America, went to Peru and opened school in Lima 1943, with occasional performances. Created the eponymous rôle in *Paganini* (Fokine 1939).

ROTONDE, LA, at the Paris Opéra, the dome-shaped room with porthole windows where the ballets are rehearsed. It is situated over the library and the floor has the same rake as the Opéra stage.

ROUCHÉ, Jacques, b. 1862, d. Paris 1957. Fr. business man and director of theatres. Founded and directed Théâtre des Arts, Paris, producing ballets (ch. Staats) to music of Ravel, Roussel, etc. (1910–14). Nominated Director of the Paris Opéra for a period of seven years from 1914 and held the post until 1944, when he retired. In 1929 made Lifar ballet-master at the Opéra. During his directorship he raised the ballet of the Opéra to its greatest height since the Romantic era, drawing heavily on his own private fortune as a *parfumier* in the process. Author of *L'Art théâtral moderne* (1910). He introduced the Wednesday ballet-evenings at the Opéra.

ROUGE ET NOIR, ballet, 1 sc., ch. Massine, m. Shostakovitch (1st Symphony), dec. Matisse, f.p. B. Russe de Monte Carlo, Monte Carlo

11 May 1939 (Markova, Youskevitch). The struggle between Man's spiritual and material forces.

ROUND, a dance in which the dancers form a circle.

ROUSANNE, Madame (Rousanne Sarkissian), b. Baku 1894, d. Paris 1958. Armenian teacher. Began studying ballet when she was 30, in the Paris schools (Trefilova, Clustine, Volinine) and started giving classes in 1928. She became a very fine teacher, at the Studio Wacker, and had Violette Verdy, Darsonval, Chauviré, Schwarz among her pupils.

ROWE, Marilyn, b. Sydney 1946. Austral. dancer. Pupil of Frances Letl and Austral. Ballet Sch. Joined Australian B. 1965, principal 1970. Moiseyev chor. *The Last Vision* for her, 1969. Silver Medal, Moscow, 1973.

ROWELL, Kenneth, b. Melbourne 1922. Austral. designer and artist. Designed cost. and dec. for *Winter Night* (B. Rambert, Melbourne 1948). To London 1950 and designed *Alice in Wonderland* (for Festival B.) 1953, *Carte Blanche* (S. Wells Th. B.) 1953, *Laiderette* (Rambert) 1954, *Light Fantastic* (W. Gore's B.) 1953, *Baiser de la Fée* (Royal B.) 1960, *Solitaire* (R. Danish B.), and for Australian B. *Coppélia* (1960), *Giselle* (1965), *Sun Music* (1968), *Sleeping Beauty* (1973) etc. Author of *Stage Design* (1972).

ROY, Alexander, b. Magdeburg 1935. Ger. dancer and chor. Pupil of Steinweg, T. Gsovsky, Blank, Kiss, Northcote. Joined Leipzig B. 1951, Berlin Staatsoper 1953, Komische Oper 1954, Am. Fest. B. 1960, Amsterdam B. 1961, Teatro del Balletto 1962, Nederlands Dans Th. 1963 and founded International Ballet Caravan (q.v.) 1965. Mar. Christine Gallia.

ROYAL ACADEMY OF DANCING, THE, founded on 31 Dec 1920 by P. J. S. Richardson and E. Espinosa as the Association of Operatic Dancing of Great Britain. Granted Royal Charter in 1936 and henceforth became the Royal Academy of Dancing. The first President, Dame Adeline Genée, resigned in 1954 and was succeeded by Margot Fonteyn. It received the patronage of Queen Mary in 1928 and of Queen Elizabeth II in 1953. The aim of the R.A.D. is to improve the standard of operatic (ballet) dancing in Gt Britain and the Commonwealth (it is not concerned with ballroom dancing). It conducts examinations in many countries of the world, awards scholarships to children, and holds lectures, demonstrations, classes, and conferences for its members (who, if qualified, may write after their names A.R.A.D.). To maintain and ensure a high standard among its teachers, a residential Teachers' Training Course was started in London in 1947, awarding diplomas (L.R.A.D.). Among its scholarships are the Leverhulme (£720), the four Overseas—one to S. Africa, one to New Zealand, two to Australia (each paying for a year at the Royal B. Sch.)—and the ordinary scholarships. Among the awards are the Gold, Silver, and Bronze Medals (annual competitions), the Pavlova Casket, and the Plender Cup. A silver plaque given by Genée, the Queen Elizabeth II Coronation Award, is awarded annually to a person who has done outstanding work for British ballet. The recipients have been de Valois (1954), Karsavina, Rambert, Dolin, Bedells, Ashton, Helpmann, Moreton, Beaumont, Markova and (posthumously) Philip Richardson, Kathleen Gordon, Van Praagh, Grigorieff and Tchernicheva, Sokolova, Idzikowsky, John Hart, Gilpin, Louise Browne, Ruth French (1972). In 1972 the R.A.D. moved to Battersea. Kathleen Gordon was Director 1924–68. Ivor Guest has been Chairman since 1969.

ROYAL BALLET, THE, the title of the Sadler's Wells Ballet after it was granted a Royal Charter in October 1956.

SADLER'S WELLS BALLET, THE. From 1926 to 1928 Lilian Baylis, Director of the Old Vic Th., invited Ninette de Valois to arrange the dances in the productions of that Th. At Christmas 1928 (13 Dec 1928) de Valois presented there her first ballet *Les Petits Riens*, which met with sufficient success to justify the occasional production of further ballets. When Lilian Baylis (q.v.) opened her new Sadler's Wells Th. in 1931 she asked de Valois to start a ballet school there, and the first performance of the Vic-Wells B., as it was then called, was given on 5 May 1931 at the Old Vic. The ballets included *Les Petits Riens*, *Danse Sacrée et Danse Profane*, *Hommage aux Belles Viennoises*, *The Jackdaw and the Pigeons*, *Scène de Ballet* from *Faust*—all ch. by de Valois. The dancers included de Valois, Beatrice Appleyard, Freda Bamford, Sheila McCarthy, Ursula Moreton, Joy Newton, with Dolin, Leslie French, and Stanley Judson as guest artists. The first performance at Sadler's Wells Th. was on 15 May 1931, and by September 1931 fortnightly performances were being given. In 1932 Markova joined as ballerina and remained until 1935. Ashton joined as guest chor. in 1933, his first production being *Les Rendezvous*, though he had chor. *Regatta* for them in 1931. In 1935 the Co. made their first West End appearance at the Shaftesbury Th. after which Markova left and the Co. made a provincial tour. The dancers now included Pearl Argyle, June Brae, Alan Carter, William Chappell, Margot Fonteyn, Mary Honer, Robt. Helpmann, Pamela May, Elizabeth Miller, Claude Newman, Michael Somes, Harold Turner. New productions in 1935–37 included *Rake's Progress*, *The Gods Go A-begging*, *Apparitions*, *Nocturne*, and *Les Patineurs*. In 1937 the Vic-Wells B. danced in Paris (Th. des Ch. Élysées) and gave the first performance of *Checkmate*. When war broke out the S. Wells Th. was requisitioned and a provincial tour (with two pianos) was undertaken. In 1940 the Co. was nearly trapped in Holland, but succeeded in returning to England and in 1941 they found a home at the New Th. where their seasons, starring Fonteyn and Helpmann, played a prominent part in the wartime life of London. Beryl Grey, Moira Shearer, Julia Farron, Margaret Dale, David Paltenghi, Leslie Edwards, and others now emerged as soloists. In 1945 they returned to S. Wells Th. and on 20 Feb 1946 they opened C. Garden with *The Sleeping Beauty*. Ashton's *Symphonic Variations* was created the same year and his *Cinderella* in 1948. Under the auspices of the British Council they made several tours of Europe and in 1949 they first danced in America, with great success. In 1955 the leading dancers were (girls) Fonteyn, Grey, Elvin, Nerina, Jackson, Beriosova; (men) Somes, Field, Ashton, Hart, Grant, Rassine, Shaw, Blair.

ROYAL BALLET, THE. A charter of incorporation dated 31 Oct 1956 was granted by H.M. Queen Elizabeth II to Sadler's Wells Ballet, the Sadler's Wells Theatre Ballet and the Sadler's Wells School under the general title of The Royal Ballet, with herself as Patron and administered by governors and a council. The purposes of The Royal Ballet are to promote the art of ballet, to maintain and conduct the activities of the two Sadler's Wells Cos. and the School, to produce ballets, to train dancers, to solicit and receive subscriptions and to borrow or raise money. Princess Margaret was the first President and Lord Waverley the Chairman. Briefly, the Sadler's Wells Ballet, Sadler's Wells Th. B. and School became the Royal Ballet and School in November 1956. In 1960 (when Ashton's *La Fille Mal Gardée* was created) the principal dancers were Fonteyn, Nerina, Beriosova, Linden, Page, Farron, Larsen, Lindsay, Park, Seymour, Wells, Anderton, Lane, Sibley; (men) Somes, Shaw, Grant, Blair, Ashbridge, Macleary, Britton, Doyle, Burne, Edwards, Hynd, Powell, Usher, White. In 1962 John Hart and Michael Somes joined John Field (who was already directing the *Touring Royal Ballet* (q.v.)) as Assistant Directors, and Nureyev became a regular dancer with the Co. and giving a great fillip to ballet in general. de Valois retired in 1963 (with the title of Founder of the Royal Ballet) and was succeeded by Ashton who continued to contribute masterpieces to the repertoire and also invited Nijinska to mount her *Les Biches and Les Noces*. Ashton retired in 1970 (with the title Founder Choreographer of the Royal Ballet) and Kenneth MacMillan (then Resident Choreographer and whose *Romeo and Juliet* had been produced in 1965) and John Field jointly took over the Directorship. The latter resigned the same year and Peter Wright was appointed Administrative Director (and later Associate Director). In 1970 Jerome Robbins mounted his *Dances at a Gathering* for the company. In 1972 the principal dancers included Fonteyn, Sibley, Park, Mason, Seymour, Beriosova, Bergsma, Parkinson, Penney, Barbieri, Collier, Wells, Jenner, and (men) Dowell, Coleman, Cooke, Clarke, Mosaval, Edwards, Johnson, Shaw, McGrath, Kelly, Rencher, Wall. Ballet master, Desmond Doyle, principal conductor Ashley Lawrence. The whole troupe (including the Touring Section and Ballet for All) numbered 45 principals, 23 soloists, 20 coryphées and 49 corps de ballet. Among the guest artists who have appeared with the Co. are Markova, Danilova, Verdy, Chauviré, Makarova, Massine, Franklin, Dolin, Nureyev, Musil.

TOURING ROYAL BALLET. In 1946 de Valois founded a junior Co. to play at Sadler's Wells Th. and to tour the provinces, when the Sadler's Wells B. had its headquarters at Covent Garden. This was the Sadler's Wells Theatre Ballet (originally named Sadler's Wells Opera Ballet) and its first performance was at S. Wells Th. on 8 Apr 1946. This was under the direction of Ursula Moreton, with Peggy van Praagh as ballet mistress and in direct control from its inception until she left in 1955. The original dancers included June Brae, Barbara Fewster, Anne Heaton, Sheilah O'Reilly, Nadia Nerina, Joan Harris, Claude Newman, Leo Kersley, Anthony Burke, with Margaret Dale as guest artist. It toured America 1951–52, and visited Rhodesia 1953 and S. Africa 1954, also performing on the Continent for the British Council. Many of the dancers moved into the senior Co. and in 1955 the leading dancers were Elaine Fifield, Patricia Miller, Maryon Lane, David Blair, David Poole. In 1955 John Field became the Director, while the Co. became wholly a touring organization, with only a short season at S. Wells Th. Consequently their dancers no longer danced with S. Wells Opera as hitherto (and the Opera formed its own small troupe). The principal dancers were then Maureen Bruce, Doreen Tempest, Sara Neil, Margaret Hill, Donald Britton, Michael Boulton. The Co. had a large repertoire of its own and took over some of the early ballets of the S. Wells B. John Cranko was an early member of the Co. and produced some of his first ballets for it, including *Pineapple Poll* (1951) and *Lady and the Fool* (1954) and it became a breeding ground for future ballet masters and directors (van Praagh to Australia, Cranko to Stuttgart, Poole to S. Africa, Fewster to Royal Ballet Sch., MacMillan to Royal B., Dale to the B.B.C., Darrell to Scottish Th. B. etc.). On the granting of the Royal Charter in 1957 it became known as the Touring Section of the Royal Ballet, was billed in the provinces as The Royal Ballet (as indeed it was) but was familiarly always called *The Second Company*. It came to an end on the reorganization of the Royal Ballet in 1970 (last performance was at

Wimbledon Th. 25 July 1970, *Swan Lake* with Doreen Wells, who had been their permanent ballerina from 1960, and Desmond Kelly). At that time the principal dancers were Doreen Wells, Elizabeth Anderton, Shirley Grahame, Lucette Aldous, Brenda Last, Alfreda Thorogood, David Wall, Johaar Mosaval, Ronald Emblen, Kerrison Cooke, Paul Clarke, Desmond Kelly, Barry McGrath, with ballet masters Henry Legerton and Sheila Humphreys. The policy then changed and a small group from the Royal Ballet at Covent Garden (fortified by a ballerina) was sent out to tour the provinces, giving smaller ballets and never *Swan Lake* or *Sleeping Beauty*. This group gradually got larger and more permanent in its members and, though billed as the Royal Ballet, was first known as the Splinter Group (in 1971) and the New Group (in 1972). The nomenclature still seems to be fluid and it seems likely to revert to the Touring Section of the Royal Ballet or Second Company. Among the dancers in 1972 were Vyvyan Lorrayne, Margaret Barbieri, Brenda Last, Lois Strike, Patricia Ruanne, Kerrison Cooke, Paul Clarke, Stephen Jefferies, Johaar Mosaval, with John Auld as company manager and Peter Clegg ballet master.

The Royal Ballet, the creation of Dame Ninette de Valois, now ranks as one of the finest in the world, having the great classical ballets as the backbone of its repertoire, and creating ballets of an essentially British style. Credit for its achievement is also shared by Constant Lambert, its first musical director, and Frederick Ashton.

Also see BALLET FOR ALL which is a part of the Royal Ballet organization.

ROYAL BALLET BENEVOLENT FUND (formerly the SADLER'S WELLS BENEVOLENT FUND) was founded in 1936 by Arnold Haskell to assist members of the dancing profession who are in need or sick. A Gala Performance is given every year at C. Garden to augment its funds. In its early days it contributed to the expenses of the ballet seasons, notably to the first production of *The Sleeping Beauty* and *Dante Sonata*, and to replace cost. and dec. lost in Holland during the war. It guaranteed the 1939–40 season at S. Wells Th. Its benefits are not confined to members of the Royal B. organization but can be applied to all those who are connected with the art of ballet.

ROYAL BALLET CHOREOGRAPHIC GROUP, the organization within the Royal B. which presents ballets choreographed and danced by members of the company. It is directed by Leslie Edwards and gave its first performance at the Yvonne Arnaud Th., Guildford, 2 Apr 1967, with new ballets by Cauley, Drew, Grant, Killar, Newton, Park and Zolan. Its second performance was at the same theatre 12 Nov 1967. Also see SADLER'S WELLS CHOREOGRAPHERS GROUP.

429

ROYAL BALLET SCHOOL, THE (originally The Sadler's Wells School), was opened at the S. Wells Th. on 12 Jan 1931 by de Valois. In September 1947 it was moved to Baron's Court and expanded to give a full academic education under the Directorship of Arnold Haskell. The Junior School (entry 11 or 12 years, Direct Grant from 1973) moved to White Lodge, Richmond Park, 1955. In 1973 it had 84 girls, 39 boys (boarders £1452 a year, day-pupils £900). The Upper School (Baron's Court, entry 15 years) had 145 girls, 31 boys (£600 a year, teachers' Course £642). Director, Michael Wood; Ballet Principal, Barbara Fewster; Head of Education, K. G. Bowles. The School gives a matinée performance at Covent Garden in the summer followed by short season at Richmond Theatre (incl. White Lodge pupils) and in the open air at Holland Park. Senior pupils perform with the Royal B. at C. Garden throughout the year.

ROYALE, see ENTRECHAT for two steps of this name.

ROYALTIES, the payments made to choreographers or composers for the use of their created work—paid at so-much a performance. Usually the composer and the designer are paid a lump sum, but the choreographer is paid a royalty for each performance.

RUANNE, Patricia, b. Leeds 1945. Eng. dancer. Studied at Royal B. Sch. Joined Royal B. 1962 becoming a principal in 1969. To Festival B. 1973.

RUANOVA, Maria, b. Buenos Aires 1912. Argentine dancer. Pupil of Smirnova, Romanoff and Nijinska. Entered Colon Th. B. 1926, becoming ballerina 1932. Ballerina of Blum's B. Russe de Monte Carlo 1936 and toured Europe. Retired from Colon Th. 1956 and teaches in the National B. Sch., Buenos Aires. Director Colon Th. B. until 1972.

RUBINSTEIN, Ida, b. St Petersburg 1885, d. Vence 1960. Russ. dancer. Studied privately under Fokine. Joined Diaghileff's Co. and cr. the chief rôles in *Cléopâtre* (1909) and *Schéhérazade* (1911). In 1928 formed her own Co., the Ida Rubinstein Co. in which she danced the principal rôles, partnered by Vilzak, in ballets at the Paris Opéra, chor. for her by Nijinska, Nicola Guerra, Massine, Jooss, etc., and with décors by Bakst, Benois, etc. Among the ballets she produced were *Le Martyre de Saint Sébastien* (Châtelet Th., Paris 1911), *La Bien Aimée*, *Bolero* (1928), *La Valse* (1929). She gave up her Co. in 1935. It had a C. Garden season in 1931. In it many subsequently famous young dancers appeared, notably Jasinsky, Lichine, Shabelevsky, Verchinina, Ashton, Nathalie Leslie, Zoritch.

RUIZ, Brunilda, b. Puerto Rico 1936. Am. dancer. Studied at Sch. of Performing Arts and joined Joffrey B. 1956, Harkness B. on its formation in 1964 as a principal dancer. Returned to Joffrey B. 1968. Mar. Paul Sutherland.

RUMJANTSEVA, Marianna, b. Helsinki 1940. Finnish dancer. Studied under Karnokoski in Helsinki and at Finnish B. Sch. Joined National B. 1956, becoming soloist 1957. Studied in London with Anna Northcote.

RUSES D'AMOUR, ballet 1 act, ch. Petipa, m. Glazounov, f.p. Hermitage Th., St Petersburg 29 Jan 1900 (Legnani, Gerdt). In the style of a Watteau painting.

RUSSELL, Francia, b. Los Angeles 1938. Am. dancer and ballet mistress. Pupil of de Luce, Sch. of Am. B. and Am. Ballet Th. Sch. Joined Dollar's group 1955. N.Y. City B. 1956 becoming soloist 1960. Joined Ballets: U.S.A. 1961, and rejoined N.Y. City B. 1962. In 1966 became one of Balanchine's assistants, mounting his ballets in Europe (Düsseldorf, Cologne, Vienna).

RUSSIA, BALLET IN, see under KIROV B., BOLSHOI B., MALY TH., STANISLAVSKI AND NEMIROVITCH-DANTCHENKO TH. B. There are also important Cos. in Tiflis (Tblisi), Perm, Novosibirsk, Erevan etc. Also in the Russian sphere of influence are the Cos. in Riga (Latvia), Tallinn (Esthonia), Kaunas (Lithuania) with their best dancers finding their way into the Kirov and Bolshoi Cos.

RUSSIAN TEA ROOM, a restaurant in New York much patronized by dancers and those connected with the ballet—see also CUBAT'S.

RUSSKAIA, Jia (lit. 'I am a Russian') (Eugenia Borisenko), b. Kerch 1900, d. Rome 1970. Russ. dancer and teacher. She went to Rome in 1923, danced and then opened a school in Milan. In 1933 she became director of the Scala Milan Ballet but left in 1934 to open a private school in Rome, which won Olympic Laurels in the 1936 Berlin Olympic Games. With Fascist influence her school received government support and became the National Academy of Dance with herself as head. She taught there until her death. She attained great power under the Fascist régime and retained it after the War. She was an exponent of Modern Dance but had the exclusive privilege of granting to others the right to teach classical ballet in Italy which she rarely exercised. Consequently teachers would resort to the ruse of calling themselves 'teachers of gymnastic dance' though secretly teaching ballet. Wrote *La Danza come modo di essere* 1928.

RUTHERFORD, Richard, b. Augusta, Ga. Am. dancer. Studied at Ballet Th. Sch., Caton and with Harkarvy. Joined R. Winnipeg B. 1958 becoming a principal dancer and in 1970 assistant to the director Arnold Spohr.

RYBERG, Flemming, b. Copenhagen 1940. Danish dancer. Studied at R. Danish B. Sch. from 1953. Joined R. Dan. B. 1959, becoming solo-dancer 1966. Brother of Kirsten Simone.

S

SABLE, ballet, ch. Babilée, m. Damase, dec. de Nobili, f.p. Babilée's Company, Th. des Ch. Élysées, Paris 19 June 1956 (Biegovitch, Sombert, Kalioujny, Dick Saunders, Jane Mason). Set on a beach.

SACHS, Curt, b. Berlin 1881, d. N.Y. 1959. German writer on music and author of a monumental *World History of the Dance* (1933).

SACRE DU PRINTEMPS, LE (The Rite of Spring), ballets 2 acts, ch. Nijinsky, m. Stravinsky, dec. Roerich, f.p. Diaghileff's Co., Th. des Ch. Élysées, Paris 29 May 1913 (Piltz). There was an uproar at the first performance and it was only danced six times. It was given again at the same theatre 15 Dec 1920 and with the same décor, but with ch. by Massine, and Sokolova as the chief dancer. Martha Graham danced this version in Philadelphia 11 Apr 1930. Primitive ritual in which a Chosen Maiden is sacrificed as a fertility offering. Massine revived it for Scala, Milan, same dec. 18 Jan 1962 (Vera Colombo). Also ch. Béjart, dec. Caille, f.p. Béjart's Co., Th. de la Monnaie, Brussels 9 Dec 1959 (Tania Bari, G. Casado). Another version ch. MacMillan, dec. Nolan f.p. Royal B., C. Garden 3 May 1962 (Monica Mason). In Russia, on the gradual lifting of the ban on Stravinsky's music, it was first per-formed at the Bolshoi Th., Moscow 28 June 1965, ch. Vladimir Vasiliov and his wife Natalie Kasatkina, cost. Goncharov (Kasatkina, Yuri Vladimirov). In this a different story was told. Many other choreographers have made this ballet; a notable version is that chor. Erich Walter for the Düsseldorf B., Düsseldorf 19 Apr 1970, dec. Wendel, cost. Kappel (Söffing, Rothe, Breuer, Vondruska).

SADDLER, Donald, b. California 1920. Am. dancer and chor. Pupil of Maracci, Dolin, Tudor. Started dancing 1937, joined Am. B. Th. 1946, chor. *Wonderful Town* (musical, m. Bernstein 1953), danced in musicals and in 1966 was assistant director of Harkness B. Chor. revival of *No, No, Nanette* in 1971.

SADLER'S WELLS BALLET, see ROYAL BALLET, which it became in 1956.

SADLER'S WELLS BENEVOLENT FUND, see ROYAL BALLET BENEVO-LENT FUND.

SADLER'S WELLS CHOREOGRAPHERS GROUP, presented its first programme on Sunday 1 Feb 1953 at S. Wells Th., its second on

14 June 1953. The group gave opportunities to members of the Wells Cos. to present their own ballets in public. Its function was taken over by the Sunday Ballet Club (q.v.) *See* ROYAL BALLET CHOREOGRAPHIC GROUP.

SADLER'S WELLS OPERA BALLET, the original name of the Sadler's Wells Theatre Ballet which in turn became the TOURING ROYAL BALLET (see ROYAL BALLET). Up to 1955 the dancers of the Sadler's Wells Theatre Ballet danced in the operas of the Sadler's Wells Opera Co. but when the company became a wholly touring organization (in 1955), an independent group of dancers, directed by Phillippe Perrottet, was formed at Sadler's Wells solely to dance in the operas. When the Sadler's Wells Opera Co. moved to the Coliseum in 1968, a new group was formed, directed by Pauline Grant, called the Sadler's Wells Movement Group, to appear in the operas.

SADLER'S WELLS SCHOOL, THE, see ROYAL BALLET SCHOOL.

SADLER'S WELLS THEATRE, the oldest in London, was built as a music house for singers and acrobats at Islington by Mr Sadler, after finding in 1683 a mineral spring which he hoped would rival the wells of Tunbridge and Epsom. In 1765 it was rebuilt in brick by Rosoman. Joe Grimaldi, the clown, appeared there 1800–28. During the Napoleonic Wars the theatre was managed by Dibden, the composer, who staged water-spectacles. From 1844 to 1862 it was managed by S. Phelps, the actor—the greatest period of its old history. From 1893 to 1913 it was a music hall, in 1914 a cinema, and it was closed in 1915, becoming derelict. It was rebuilt by Sir Reginald Rowe and others, reopened 6 Jan 1931, coming under the management of Lilian Baylis as a home of opera and drama alternating with her other theatre, the Old Vic. The theatre has 1,738 seats and the stage is 30 ft wide and 26 ft deep. The Royal Ballet (formerly Sadler's Wells B.) originated there (see ROYAL BALLET, TOURING ROYAL BALLET, and SADLER'S WELLS OPERA BALLET) but it is no longer associated with the theatre, though the Touring Royal Ballet has seasons there. The Sadler's Wells Opera Co. left the theatre in 1968 and moved to the Coliseum. Now visiting ballet and opera companies perform at Sadler's Wells.

SADLER'S WELLS THEATRE BALLET, see ROYAL BALLET.

SAGA OF FREEDOM, ballet, ch. Change, m. Janson, dec. Lapinsh, f.p. Opera House, Riga 1950 (Priéde, Pankraete, Ozoly).

SAGER, Peggy, b. Auckland, N.Z. New Zealand dancer. Studied with Nettleton and Edwards, Joined Kirsova Sch. 1942 and danced in her Co. Joined Borovansky 1946. To England 1947, danced in *Red Shoes*, Metropolitan B., Glyndebourne and Brussels Operas. Rejoined Borovansky B. 1950 as prima ballerina. Now teaches.

433

SAILOR'S RETURN, THE, ballet 6 sc., ch. Howard, m. Oldham, dec. Howard, f.p. B. Rambert, S. Wells Th., London 2 June 1947 (Gilmour, Gore, Gilpin). Based on David Garnett's novel of the same name.

ST DENIS, Ruth, b. New Jersey 1877, d. Hollywood 1968. Am. dancer, chor., and teacher. In 1906 had her first success with a Hindu ballet she created, called *Radha*, and thenceforth she toured Europe and America with similar ballets of her own creation and execution, *The Nautch, O-Mika, Egypta*, etc., all derived from folk or national sources. Mar. Ted Shawn in 1914 and founded the Denishawn Sch. which trained many dancers in her style and gave performances in America until 1932. In many respects she resembled Isadora Duncan in the free nature of her dance. Many of her creations were drawn from Oriental sources. She occupied a highly respected and loved place in the Am. dance. Wrote *Ruth St Denis: An Unfinished Life* (1939).

SAINT FRANCIS, see NOBILISSIMA VISIONE.

SAINT-LÉON, Arthur, b. Paris 1821, d. there 1870. Fr. dancer and chor. Studied under his father, ballet-master at Stuttgart. Début Munich, dancing and playing violin. Mar. Cerrito 1845, separated 1851. Danced and mounted his ballets all over Europe and made début at St Petersburg 1859. Chor. *La Vivandière* (1844), *La Fille de Marbre* (1847), *Le Violon du Diable* (1849, in which he played violin), *Fiammetta* (1864), *The Hump-backed Horse* (1864), *La Source* (1866), *Coppélia* (1870). He wrote *La Sténochorégraphie* (1852), a method of recording ballets. He was at the Paris Opéra 1847–52 and maître de ballet there 1863–70.

SAISONS DE LA DANSE, LES, French dance periodical edited by André-Philippe Hersin in Paris and appearing ten times a year. The first issue was February 1968.

SAISONS, LES, see SEASONS, THE.

SAKHAROFF, Alexandre, b. Marioupol 1886, d. Siena 1963. Russ. dancer. He began his dancing career at Munich in 1910, dancing alone on the stage rather in the manner of Isadora Duncan. With his wife, the German dancer Clothilde von Derp (b. Berlin 1895), he developed a highly individual style of modern dancing, 'abstract mime', of great perfection of execution which greatly influenced Massine. They retired from dancin 1953 and taught in Rome.

SALADE, ballet, ch. Lifar, m. Milhaud, dec. Derain, f.p. Paris Opéra 13 Feb 1935 (Lorcia, Simoni, Peretti, Serry, Lifar). This ballet was to the same score as a previous ballet of the same name, ch. Massine, dec. Braque f.p. at one of Comte Étienne de Beaumont's Soirées de Paris at the Th. de la Cigale on 17 May 1924. In the style of an Italian comedy, with sung and spoken words by Flamant. Revived at Paris

Opéra 21 Nov 1962 (Vlassi, Duflot, Bozzoni). Also ch. Darrell dec. Kay, Edinburgh Festival Society, Empire Th. Edinburgh 4 Sept 1961 (Last, Meyer).

SALAMMBÔ, ballet (based on Flaubert), ch. A. Gorsky, m. Arends, dec. Korovine, f.p. Bolshoi B., Bolshoi Th., Moscow 10 Jan 1910 (E. Geltzer, Mordkin). This ballet put into practice all Gorsky's theories about dramatic action, costume etc., which were not unlike Fokine's.

SALARIES. Such are the charms and the opportunities of ballet dancers that it is only of comparatively recent years that they have been expected to live on their earnings from the theatre. Now, however, salaries in all the great opera houses have settled down to a fairly uniform level, taking into account the cost of living in the various countries (and, in the case of America, the fewer weeks of annual employment).

At the time of writing (1972) monetary inflation is proceeding so rapidly and the value of the pound declining, that it is of little use to give foreign salaries, while those in England are not likely to remain constant for long. However in general it may be said that a corps de ballet dancer in any country earns just a little more than the current rate for a shorthand-typist.

In *England*, ballet dancers' salaries and conditions are watched over by the British Actors' Equity Association (founded 1931), which fixed a minimum salary in 1972 for a dancer at £18 a week (£9 in 1960). For English dancers dancing overseas Equity required a minimum of £18 a week clear of board and lodging (£5 in 1960). Dancers in musicals and television, however, would expect to receive about £45 a week.

At *Covent Garden* (1972), the Royal Ballet, the corps de ballet received weekly salaries of £25 (first year), £28 (second year), £33 (third year). Coryphées £40. Soloists from £50. Principals from £70. Senior principals from £90. Touring allowances in the provinces £14 per week or 40% of weekly salary. Overtime rate of 1/66th of artist's salary a half-hour after a 33-hour week has been worked (a performance counts as 3 hours). Contracts are seasonal and there was no pension scheme or rule for retirement. Holidays and rehearsal periods on full pay.

London Festival Ballet (1972), the corps de ballet received between £22–£30·50 a week. Soloists £34–£43 a week and Principals' salaries are by negotiation. A subsistence allowance of £14 a week was paid for touring the provinces in England, and subsistence is negotiated for touring abroad depending on the cost of living in each country. The salaries are paid for 52 weeks each year and include 4 weeks' holiday.

Ballet Rambert (1972) salaries began at £20 a week and rose thereafter by negotiation, for all the dancers are ranked as soloists. The touring

435

allowance in Britain was £12 a week. As with all British companies, there was no retiring age and no pension scheme; all contracts are yearly.

Scottish Theatre Ballet (1972) had a minimum salary (first year) of £18 a week, thereafter contracts are negotiated individually. Touring allowances in Britain were £12 a week. The basic company members are on permanent contract and the salaries paid 52 weeks a year, including 4 weeks' holiday.

Northern Dance Theatre (1972), the salaries ranged from £20 to £45 a week. There was a subsistence payment of £12 a week when dancing away from Manchester. In 1973 a pension scheme was introduced for all the British ballet cos.

In *America*, salaries are governed by the American Guild of Musical Artists contracts (AGMA). There are set rates (1st, 2nd, 3rd year corps, soloists, principal) for companies of under 40 dancers, and another scale (about 10% higher) for companies of over 40 dancers, with a daily 'sustenance' payment when on the road (touring). Most dancers are signed to 2-year agreements but are only paid when working (and have special rehearsal rates). The *New York City Ballet* had (1972) a special agreement with AGMA. Corps de ballet for *all* rehearsal and performance weeks 150 dollars (1st year) to 275 dollars (4th year). Solo dancers, for performance weeks only, 325 dollars but only 50% of this in rehearsal weeks. Principals—as for soloists, but about 50 dollars more. There is a guaranteed 34 weeks of employment (exceeded in practice). This agreement was to 21 Aug 1973.

At the *Bolshoi Th., Moscow*, the Bolshoi B., the dancers (women and men) are retired after 20 years' service, regardless of their age. In practice this usually occurs at 38 because they now graduate from the school at 18 (formerly it was at 19). However they do often go on past this age and pass on to mime rôles.

At the *Royal Th., Stockholm*, the Royal Swedish B. (1972) the corps de ballet receive a basic salary with an increment after each year of service plus 'competence money' according to their excellence, plus 'performance money' (depending on the part they dance on a particular night, e.g. Florestan or Blue Bird etc.). The soloists receive the *same* money (made up as above) but *also* an additional salary as soloist. Principals receive approximately double the basic salary plus a payment for each appearance. Contracts are for one year with six weeks' paid holiday and the dancers are pensioned at 41 (women) and 45 (men) on 60–65% salary.

At the *Paris Opéra* contracts are annual and the dancers are pensioned at 35–40. Promotion up to the rank of grand sujet is made on the results of annual examinations.

In *Germany*, salaries vary according to the class of the opera house to which they belong. There are three classes, in the first are W. Berlin, Hamburg, Munich, Düsseldorf, while Frankfurt, Cologne, Stuttgart are in the second. All have twelve-month contracts with a paid holiday of at least five weeks. The first soloists have another two-month paid holiday for guest engagements.

At the *Royal Danish B.* there are two months' paid annual holidays. Engagements are on a 'lifetime' basis and dancers are retired at 40 on pension (about two-thirds salary).

At *La Scala, Milan*, every year the salaries are increased by a definite percentage and there is a contributory pension scheme.

In the *French* companies only one or two have 12-month contracts and most are for 6 or 8 months only(and paid for that duration). The dancers find work in the many summer music festivals.

In the *Canadian National B.* contracts are for a 'season' (not necessarily twelve months paid), and there are no pension arrangements.

In the *Austrian* ballets (Vienna, Graz, Linz, Salzburg, Klagenfurt etc.), the monthly salary is paid 14 times in the year.

SALAVISA, Jorge, b. Lisbon. Portuguese dancer. Pupil of Mascolo, V. Gsovsky, Egorova. Joined Cuevas B. 1959–62. Joined Petit's Co. 1962, Festival B. 1963 becoming soloist 1965. Joined Scottish Th. B. 1971. New London B. 1972.

SALIN, Klaus, b. Helsinki 1919. Finnish dancer. Studied in Finland and under Nora Kiss in Paris. Joined National Ballet of Finland 1945 becoming principal dancer. Received Pro Finlandia Award.

SALLÉ, Marie, b. 1707, d. Paris 1756. Fr. dancer. First mentioned as dancing in London 1716 and 1717. Studied under Françoise Prévost at the Paris Opéra and made début there 1721. Became principal dancer and the great rival of Camargo. She danced much in London and became the friend of Garrick, Voltaire, and Noverre, who approved of reforms she attempted but which were not widely adopted until afterwards (e.g. dancing in *Pygmalion* in a thin muslin costume instead of in the conventional heavy costume of the day. This was at C. Garden 14 Jan 1734, ch. by herself). Retired in 1740. In her rivalry with Camargo, on which Voltaire, Pope, and Gay wrote verses, she excelled in sensitive interpretation, whereas Camargo had a brilliant technique. She had dealings with Handel and danced in his operas 1734–35, including *Alcina* and *Ariodante* at C. Garden.

SALON MEXICO, EL, ballet, ch. D. Humphrey, m. Copland, dec. Parsons, f.p. Studio Th., N.Y. 11 Mar 1943 (J. Limon, Florence Lessing).

SALTARELLO, Roman dance in 3/4 or 6/8 time performed with lively steps, hence its name (*saltare*, to jump), and increasing its tempo as it progressed. It has been related to both the tarantella and the galliard. In the sixteenth century it was also an after-dance in triple time to the passamezzo.

SALTIMBANQUE, (Fr.) originally a tight-rope dancer, later applied to a clown or dancer at a fair.

SALVIONI, Guglielma, b. Milan 1842. It. dancer who was a principal dancer at the Paris Opéra 1864–67 and created the rôle of Naila in *La Source* 1866. Her début was at the Scala, Milan 1856. She was prima ballerina of the Vienna Hofoper 1870–73 and danced in P. Taglioni's *Sardanapal* at the opening of the new Vienna Opera House in 1869.

SALZEDO, Leonard, b. London 1921. Eng. composer. Trained at R. Col. of Music. Composed music for *The Fugitive* (ch. Howard) 1944, *The Travellers* (ch. Morrice) 1963, *Realms of Choice* (ch. Morrice) 1965, *Hazard* (ch. Morrice) 1967, *The Empty Suit* 1970—all for B. Rambert. Also *Mardi Gras* 1946 for S. Wells Th. B. (ch. Howard), *The Witch Boy* (ch. Jack Carter) 1956 for B. der Lage Landen, *Agrionia* (ch. Carter) 1964 for London Dance Th. Musical director of new B. Rambert 1966–72.

SAMAROPOULO, Persephone, b. Cairo 1941. Greek dancer. Pupil of Ivanova, Y. Metsis and Kniaseff. To London and studied with Rambert, Eileen Ward and Winifred Edwards. Début on television in Cairo 1959, in Athens operas 1966–67, Stuttgart B. 1967–68 and soloist at Zürich 1968–70. Joined Frankfurt B. 1970 as ballerina.

SAMENGO, Paolo, see BRUGNOLI.

SAMTSOVA (properly Samsova and so called from 1972), Galina, b. Stalingrad 1937. Byelorussian dancer. Pupil of N. Verekundova at Kieff B. Sch. Joined Kieff B. 1956 becoming soloist. Mar. Canadian, Alexander Ursuliak, and became British. Danced Jacobs Pillow 1961. Joined Can. Nat. B. 1961 (danced *Giselle* 1962). Cr. chief rôle in Larrain's prod. of *Cendrillon* (ch. Orlikowski), Paris 1963 (q.v.) and awarded Gold Medal for Best Danseuse of Paris Festival. Ballerina Festival B. 1964–73. Has also danced in Hungary, S. Africa, Japan etc. Now mar. André Prokovsky (q.v.) and heads his group.

SANCHEZ, Juan, b. Gerona 1945. Spanish dancer. Pupil of Juan Magrina. Joined Mariemma's Co. 1964, Zizi Jeanmaire's Co. 1964. To S. Africa and joined PACT Ballet 1965–69. Joined Festival B. 1969, soloist 1970.

SAND, Inge, b. Copenhagen 1928. Danish dancer. Pupil of Theatre Sch., Copenhagen, and solodancer since 1950 with the rôle of Swanilda. Guest artist of Orig. Ballet Russe in London 1951. Appointed assistant director R. Danish B. 1967.

SANDERS, Dick (or Dirk), b. Java 1933. Dutch dancer and chor. Pupil of

Jooss 1950 to 1952 and then settled in Paris. Chor. *Récréation* for Béjart's Co. *L'Échelle* for Miskovitch's Co. in 1956, and *L'Emprise* (1957) for Babilée's Co. Also *Maratona di Danza* (m. Henze and production by Visconti) which caused a furore at the Berlin Festival 1957. Chor. *Hopop* (pop-music) for B.Th. Contemporain, Amiens 1971.

SANDERS, Job, b. Amsterdam 1929. Dutch dancer and chor. Pupil of A. Govrilov and Sch. of Am. B. Début with Ballet Society. Subsequently a soloist with B. Russe de Monte Carlo, Chicago Op. B., Am. Fest. B., Nederlands B. Became principal dancer and chor. Nederlands Dans Th. 1962. Chor. *Contretemps* (m. Fauré 1956) for Joffrey B., *The Taming* (m. Creston 1962) for Nederlands Dans Th. etc. Directed the B. Clásico, Mexico 1971–73. Now teaches in The Hague.

SAN FRANCISCO BALLET, THE, was formed in 1933 as part of the San Francisco Opera, with Bolm as its first choreographer. In 1937 Willam Christensen became its director and true founder, and ballet performances were given in addition to the appearances in the Opera. In 1951 he became Professor of Ballet at the University of Utah and his brother Lew Christensen became the director. His other brother, Harold, is director of the San Francisco Ballet School. The Co. gives short seasons of ballet in the San Francisco Opera House and also tours (Far East 1957, S. America 1958, Middle East 1959). Among the dancers it has produced are Janet Reed, Jocelyn Vollmar, Harold Lang, Sally Bailey, Cynthia Gregory and Scott Douglas.

SANGALLI, Rita, b. Milan 1851, d. there 1909. It. dancer. Pupil Augusto Hus. Danced Italy, London, N.Y. (cr. principal rôle in *The Black Crook*, 1866). Début Paris Opéra 1872 in *La Source*. Cr. rôles in *Sylvia*, *Yedda*, *Namouna* at the Opéra. Mar. Baron de Saint-Pierre 1886. In 1881 she wrote a foreword to a charming little book on ballet, *Terpsichore*.

SANINA, Mira, b. Zagreb 1922. Yugoslav dancer. Pupil of Jooss and Jovanovic. Prima ballerina Belgrade Opera 1944. Danced in Zagreb, Ljubljana, Edinburgh, etc.

SANKOVSKAYA, Ekaterina, b. Moscow 1816, d. there 1878. Russ. dancer. Pupil of Hullin-Sor. She was the first to dance *La Sylphide* in Moscow (1837) and was known as 'the Russian Taglioni'. Her supporters resented the presence of her rival Andreyanova (from St Petersburg) in Moscow and threw a dead cat on to the stage when Andreyanova danced there in 1848. In her old age she became a private teacher and the young Stanislavsky was one of her pupils. One of the greatest Russ. romantic dancers. She died in poverty.

SAN MARTIN BALLET (Ballet del Teatro Municipal General San Martin de Buenos Aires), founded in 1968 by Oscar Araiz (q.v.). Supported by the city of Buenos Aires it toured Paris, Madrid and London 1969. The principal dancers are Irma Baz, Guigermo Borgogno, Oscar Tartara and Oscar Araiz. The ballets are in the modern style and chor. by Araiz, Hoyer, Urbani and others. Its first performance was on 8 June 1968 at the Teatro San Martin, Buenos Aires, giving *Presentaçion* (m. Lopez), *El Unicornio, La Gorgona y La Manticora* (m. Menotti) and *Desiertos* (m. Varèse)—all chor. by Araiz. Danced in London at the Place 1969. Now called B. Contemporaneo de la Ciudad de Buenos Aires. Ilse Wiedmann was the ballet mistress.

SANTESTEVAN, Maria, b. Buenos Aires 1933. Argentine dancer. Pupil of Bulnes, Taras, Massine. Joined de Cuevas Co. 1956, becoming soloist 1958 and ballerina 1959. Ballerina Stuttgart B. 1959, of Bordeaux B. 1961 and in 1972 ballet mistress there.

SANTONS, LES, ballet 1 act, ch. Aveline, m. Tomasi, dec. Hellé, f.p. Paris Opéra 18 Nov 1938 (Chauviré, Peretti). This ballet was also filmed. The figures round the Christmas crib come to life.

SAPATE, (It.) the customary surprise (fully expected) which ended the *ballets de la cour* under Louis XIV—sometimes a banquet was served, or a concert given, or a present given to each guest.

SARABANDE, dance in 3 time, accented on the second beat, introduced into Western Europe in the sixteenth century, it is assumed from Spain, although its origin is uncertain (different historians have traced it to Central America, Persia, and the Saracens). At first of licentious pantomimic character it was gradually transformed and introduced into the Fr. Court ballet of the seventeenth century. Suggested derivations of the word are from Sarabanda, a dancer who is said to have first danced it in France, from 'Saracen', or (most likely) *sarao*, Sp. for a ball, or from an Arabic word meaning 'noise'.

SARABHAI, Mrinalini, b. Madras 1923. Ind. dancer. Studied Duhni Devis Kalakshetra Academy of Dramatic Art. Début Madras 1939. To Europe 1949 and first app. in London for R.A.D. Production Club. Since has had seasons with her own Co. in Europe and S. America. Author of novel *This Alone is True*. In 1949 she founded in Ahmedabad the Darpana Academy of Dance, Drama, Music and Puppetry and has been its director ever since.

SARDANA, the national dance of Catalonia revived in the mid-nineteenth century by a village musician, P. Ventura, and set in 6/8 and 2/4 time. It includes a movement performed with linked hands not unlike the farandole.

SARDANAPAL, ballet 4 act, ch. Paul Taglioni, m. Hertel, f.p. Royal Opera, Berlin 24 Apr 1865—where it was very popular. When the new

440

Vienna Opera House, in the Ring, was opened in 1869, it was the first ballet to be given there (on June 16th with Salvioni as principal dancer). The theme is Assyrian.

SARSTÄDT, Marian, b. Amsterdam 1942. Dutch dancer. Pupil of Sybranda, Poons, Rebel. Joined Scapino B. 1957 becoming soloist 1958, and Cuevas B. 1960 as soloist. In 1962 became a principal dancer of Nederlands Dans Th. Retired 1972 to become ballet mistress of Scapino B. Mar. Armando Navarro.

SAUGUET, Henri, b. Bordeaux 1901, Fr. composer of ballets. Wrote *Les Roses* (ch. Massine 1924), *La Chatte* (ch. Balanchine 1927, for Diaghileff B.), *La Nuit* (ch. Massine 1930), *Fastes* (ch. Balanchine 1933), *Les Forains* (ch. Petit 1945), *Les Mirages* (ch. Lifar 1947), *La Rencontre* (ch. Lichine 1948), *La Dame aux Camélias* (ch. T. Gsovsky 1959) and many others.

SAULNIER, Mlle. Fr. dancer. Début at the Opéra 1785, retired 1794. She had a superb figure and was described as *majestueuse*, whereas her rival, Mlle Miller, was *svelte et legère*. She cr. rôle of Calypso in Gardel's *Télémaque* in 1791.

SAUT, (Fr.) a jump off both feet, landing with the feet in the same position.

SAUT DE BASQUE, lit. a Basque jump. Turning step performed in the air with one leg straight and the other in a retiré position, e.g. the dancer standing in the fifth position, right foot front, steps on to the right foot on the right diagonal, raises the left leg in a grand battement to the corner at the same time jumping off the right foot, turns in the air to face the front, bringing the right foot up in a retiré position and lands on the left foot. This is the second step in the coda of the *Swan Lake* Pas de Trois and is performed by the first female soloist eight times, making one complete circle of the stage.

SAUT DE L'ANGE, lit. angel's jump. Similar to a temps de poisson (q.v.) but the body is held obliquely to the ground in the direction of travel. Some teachers call this Temps de l'Ange (q.v.).

SAVINA, Vera (*née* Clark), Eng. dancer. Studied at Sledman's Academy and Loeffler. Danced in Pavlova's Co. 1911. Engaged by Diaghileff 1919 and cr. Poodle's dance in *Boutique Fantasque*. The only English danseuse to take a leading rôle in *Les Sylphides* in Diaghileff's Co. Mar. Massine and went to S. America in his Co. 1921. Rejoined Diaghileff 1924 and danced *Blue Bird*, etc.

SCALA, TEATRO ALLA (Milan), the principal centre of opera and ballet in Italy. Built in 1778 it was destroyed by bombs in 1943. Re-opened 1946, it seats 3,600 and the stage measures 125 ft wide and 130 ft deep.

Outside Italy it is usually called La Scala. Guest artists are usually engaged for the principal ballet productions. The *corps de ballet* had in 1970 26 girls and 18 boys, with 13 dancers from the school. The attached ballet school, formerly called the Imperial Dancing Academy (q.v.), is now called the Scala B. Sch. The adjoining Piccola Scala was opened in 1955. Luciana Novaro was artistic director 1962–64 but now there is not one. The ballet director in 1970 was G. Perugini (having held the post from 1959) and the principal dancers (ballerini) Carla Fracci (guest), Vera Colombo, Liliana Cosi, Fiorella Cova, Elettra Morini, Roberto Fascilla, Mario Pistoni, Bruno Telloli; (soloists) Aida Accolla, Anna Razzi, Luciana Savignano, Alfredo Caporilli, Giancarlo Morganti, Aldo Santambrogio, Dario Brigo, Assistant ballet mistress Gilda Maiocchi. John Field became ballet director 1971.

SCANDINAVIAN BALLET, THE, a ballet company organized jointly by the Riksteatern of Sweden and the Andels-Teatret of Denmark. Its first performance was at Waxjo in Sweden, 2 Feb 1960 and it danced throughout Scandinavia and into Germany. The principal dancer was Elsa Marianne von Rosen and also in the company were Ulla Paulsson, Tyyne Talvo, Lone Isaksen, Margrethe Brock-Nielsen, Svend Buck, Egon Madsen. The company had in its repertoire *La Sylphide* (Bournonville) and V. Skouratoff was the guest artist for the opening season. It disbanded in 1961.

SCAPINO BALLET, the oldest Dutch ballet company founded in 1945 by Hans (Johanna) Snoek, to entertain and instruct children. It is based on Amsterdam and gives occasional performances in the Stadsschouwburg (opera house) when it is not touring Holland. In 1963 it appeared in N.Y. It has a charming repertory of ballets for young people and some of its dancers later graduate into the Dutch National B. It performed in England 1968 in Felixstowe. From 1971 Armando Navarro has been the director. It is state supported.

SCARAMOUCHE, ballet, ch. E. Walbom, m. Sibelius, f.p. R. Danish B. at Copenhagen 12 May 1922. A diabolical fiddler at a ball. The ballet was next given in Riga in 1936 (ch. O. Lemanis). It eventually reached Finland (it was Sibelius's only ballet score) 1955, ch. I. Koskinen, by the Nat. B. of Finland, Helsinki 9 Dec 1955 (Taxell, Salin, Latti).

SCARLET SCISSORS, THE, see A TRAGEDY OF FASHION.

SCÈNE D'ACTION, lit. action scene. A mimed scene introduced in the ballets of the latter part of the eighteenth and nineteenth centuries, to provide the narrative, the dances being meaningless in themselves. In the modern ballet, as a direct result of the influence of Fokine, the separate mime scene has become superfluous as the very dancing itself is fully expressive of the theme, where theme there is. See PAS D'ACTION.

SCÈNES DE BALLET, ballet, ch. Ashton, m. Stravinsky, dec. Beaurepaire, f.p. S. Wells B., C. Garden 11 Feb 1948 (Fonteyn, Somes). The music was originally written for a revue *The Seven Lively Arts*, Ziegfield Th., N.Y. 7 Dec 1944, ch. Dolin (Markova, Dolin). A ballet of pure dancing.

SCHALL, Anna Margrethe, b. Copenhagen 1775, d. Friedricksborg 1852. Dan. dancer. Pupil of Galeotti and was principal dancer of R. Danish B. 1802–24. Cr. chief rôle in Galeotti's *Nina* 1802.

SCHANNE, Margrethe, b. Copenhagen 1921. Dan. dancer. Pupil of R. Th. Sch., Copenhagen, becoming solodancer of R. Danish B. 1942, taking over the rôle of La Sylphide. Danced with B. des Ch. Élysées 1946. Joined de Cuevas Co. 1955 as guest artist. Retired 1966. She was the greatest of the recent interpreters of *La Sylphide* and a postage stamp of her in this rôle was issued in Denmark 1959. Knight of Dannebrog. She now teaches her rôles to the Co.

SCHAUFUSS, Frank, b. Copenhagen 1921. Dan. dancer and chor. Pupil of Theatre Sch., Copenhagen, and solodancer 1949. Also danced with Metropolitan B. and Ballets de Paris. Chor. *Idolon* (1953), *Opus 13* (1959) etc. Mar. Mona Vangsaa. Ballet master of R. Danish B. 1956–59. Guest artist de Cuevas B. Now teacher in his sch., Danish Academy of Ballet, in Copenhagen and in 1970 formed his own Co. in association with it, the Danish Dance Theatre.

SCHAUFUSS, Peter, b. Copenhagen 1949. Danish dancer, son of Frank Schaufuss. Pupil of R. Danish B. Sch. Entered the R. Danish B. and in 1967 spent a year on leave from it to dance with the Canadian Nat. B. In 1970 was guest-principal of Festival B. and joined the Co. 1971. Mar. Maria Guerrero. Won Silver Medal, Moscow 1973.

SCHÉHÉRAZADE, ballet 1 act, ch. Fokine, m. Rimsky-Korsakov, dec. Bakst, f.p. Diaghileff's Co., Paris Opéra 4 June 1910 (Ida Rubinstein, Bulgakov, Nijinsky, Cecchetti). This ballet caused a furore at the time of its production and was the most sensational of all Diaghileff's productions, partly because of its sensuous theme (and the dancing of Nijinsky) and partly because of the entirely new type of dec., with its brilliant masses of colour and costumes which followed Paul Poiret's oriental influence which caused a gasp of admiration and surprise from the audience when the curtain rose. This dec. revolutionized the art of interior decoration and greatly influenced the fashion artists of the period. The critics argued and disagreed among themselves over the

443

use of the music and the cutting of one of the four movements. The ballet has often been revived and is in many cont. repertoires, notably of the Paris Opéra and the Festival B. To whistle a snatch of the music of this ballet is a universal sign of recognition between members of ballet companies descended from Diaghileff's—the shibboleth of the de Basil, Ballet Russe de Monte Carlo and the de Cuevas ballets.

SCHEUERMANN, Lilly, b. Vienna 1945. Austrian dancer. Pupil of Hiden, Plucis, Ursuliak, Denisova. Joined Vienna Staatsoper B. 1961 becoming soloist 1970, principal 1972.

SCHILLING, Tom, b. 1928. East German dancer and chor. Soloist in Dresden and Leipzig ballets 1946–52. Ballet master at Weimar 1953–56, director of Dresden B. 1956–65. With Lepeshinskaya founded the Komische Oper B., East Berlin 1965. Won Varna Prize 1968 for his ballet *La Mer* (m. Debussy) and mounted it for Cullberg B. at R. Dramatic Th., Stockholm 25 Jan 1970 (Ander, Simonsen). Also chor. *Faust Symphony, Abraxas* etc. Pupil of Hoyer and Wigman.

SCHLAGOBERS (whipped cream), ballet 2 acts, ch. Kröller, m. R. Strauss, f.p. Vienna Opera 9 May 1924 (Pichler, Losch). Fairy story in which Sweets and Fairies dance round a boy ill in bed. It was Tilly Losch's début.

SCHLEMMER, Oscar, b. Stuttgart 1888, d. Baden-Baden 1943. Ger. painter and dancer. He developed a form of Abstract Dance (q.v.) while at the Bauhaus at Weimar and at Dessau in which the main interest lay in the figures, the colours, the textures of the costumes, rather than in the actual dancing. It had great influence on the Central European dancers of the 1920s. His ballet *Triadic Ballet* performed at the Landestheater, Stuttgart 30 Sept 1922 with its dancers in various planes and forming geometric figures was the exemplar of his work.

SCHMUCKI, Norbert, b. Switzerland 1940. Swiss dancer. Pupil of Paris Opéra Sch. and danced in the Co. In 1971 to Zürich as assistant ballet master and chor. Has chor. many ballets.

SCHNEIDER, Jürgen, b. Berlin 1936. Ger. dancer and teacher. Pupil of Staatsoper Sch., Berlin 1952–56. Joined Weimar B. 1956 becoming soloist, then soloist of Komische Oper, E. Berlin. From 1959 to 1966 studied under N. Tarassov at the Lunacharski Institute, Moscow, and under A. Pushkin at the Vaganova Institute, Leningrad, and returned to found a new ballet Co. at the Komische Oper, E. Berlin. From 1966 to 1968 studied teaching with the Bolshoi B. and from 1968 was ballet master and principal dancer at the Komische Oper. In 1971 he came over to the West while the Co. was in Helsinki and became a teacher and répétiteur of the Stuttgart B. B. master, Munich B. 1973.

444

SCHNEITZHOEFFER, Jean-Madeleine, b. 1785, d. 1852. Fr. composer who wrote the original score for *La Sylphide* in 1832. He also composed *Proserpine* (1818), *Le Séducteur du Village* (Albert, 1818), *Zémire et Azor* (Deshayes, 1824), *Mars et Venus* (Blache, 1826), *La Tempête* (Coralli, 1834). He was on the musical staff of the Paris Opéra and teacher at the Conservatoire. His name was so difficult to pronounce that his colleagues in the Opéra called him Chênecerf. He himself put on his visiting cards 'Schneitzhoeffer (pronounced Bertrand)'.

SCHOOLING, Elisabeth, b. London 1915. Eng. dancer. Studied with Rambert and from 1930 danced with the Ballet Club, the Camargo Society, and B. Rambert, of which she became a principal dancer and cr. many rôles. Now teaches privately. Chor. ballets for Rambert Sch. and Royal B. Sch. 1970.

SCHOOL OF AMERICAN BALLET, see AMERICAN BALLET, SCHOOL OF.

SCHOOP, Trudi, b. 1903. Swiss dancer. Studied in Vienna and entered the Zürich Sch. and Co. Danced in Paris 1931–32. Toured Europe 1932–39 and America 1940–46. Artistic director of Cornichon Cabaret, Zürich. Created many comic ballets, the most famous, *Fridolin* (m. Kruse and Kasics), won second prize in Paris 1933 when Jooss's *Green Table* won the first prize. Now retired.

SCHORER, Suki, b. Cambridge, Mass. 1939. Am. dancer. Studied at San Francisco B. Sch. and toured with San Francisco B. 1956. Joined N.Y. City B. 1959 becoming soloist 1963. Retired 1971 and teaches.

SCHOTTISCHE, round dance in 2/4 time, sometimes known in the mid-nineteenth century, when it attained its greatest popularity, as the German polka; it is, however, danced to a slower tempo than the polka.

SCHUBERT, Lia, b. Vienna 1926. Austrian dancer and teacher. Pupil of Zagreb Sch., Preobrajenska etc. Danced in Marseille, Lille and Malmö. From 1953 to 1968 was one of the principal teachers in Stockholm. In 1968 she moved to Israel to open a school.

SCHULLER, Stefan, b. Cape Town 1943. S. African dancer. Pupil of Royal B. Sch. Joined Festival B. 1962, Zürich B. 1965–70 and principal dancer B. Van Vlaanderen from 1971.

SCHULTZE, Denise, b. Johannesburg 1933. S. African dancer. Pupil of de Villiers, Poole. Joined Johannesburg City B. 1960, Cape Town B. 1963 and 1965, PACT B. Johannesburg 1967 becoming principal. Ballet mistress 1968, joint artistic director 1973.

SCHULZ, Claus, b. Rostock 1934. Ger. dancer. Pupil of T. Gsovsky and Blank. Joined Schwerin B. 1949. To Komische Oper. B., E. Berlin 1951 and E. Berlin Staatsoper 1956 where he became director of ballet until 1972, when he defected to the West in Paris. He is also a popular singer and People's Artist.

SCHWAARZ, Heidrun, b. Munich 1943. Ger. dancer. Pupil of the Mlakars and A. Carter. Joined Munich B. 1960. To Frankfurt as principal dancer 1965–70. From 1970 soloist at Deutsche Oper, W. Berlin.

SCHWARZ, famous family of Fr. dancers and teachers. JEAN A. SCHWARZ, b. Paris 1884, d. there 1936. Entered Paris Opéra 1896, retired 1909. Famous teacher and father of Nelly, Solange, Jane, Juanina. JEANNE SCHWARZ, b. Paris 1887 (sister of Jean). Entered Opéra 1897, becoming étoile 1919. Retired 1928. Principal teacher at Opéra-Comique 1935–51, and of Conservatoire National de Musique since 1938. NELLY SCHWARZ, b. Berck-plage 1909 (eldest daughter of Jean). Entered Opéra Sch. 1920, retired 1947. Now teaching privately. SOLANGE SCHWARZ, b. Paris 1910 (second daughter of Jean). Entered Opéra Sch. 1920. Became étoile of Opéra-Comique 1933. Re-entered Opéra 1937, becoming étoile 1940–45. Étoile of B. des Ch. Élysées 1945. Étoile of Opéra-Comique 1949–51. Now retired. JANE SCHWARZ, called JHANYNE, b. Asnières 1912 (third daughter of Jean). Entered Opéra 1923, grand sujet 1937, becoming teacher at the Opéra Sch. 1950. Retired 1952. JUANINA SCHWARZ, b. Asnières 1914 (fourth daughter of Jean). Entered Opéra Sch. 1926. Danced Opéra-Comique (as Juanina) 1933–46 when she retired. Also ANNIE BOUFFLET, daughter of Jhanyne, b. 1939, entered Opéra Sch. 1952, and LUCIEN LEGRAND, cousin of the Schwarz sisters, is a teacher.

SCHWEZOFF, Igor, b. Yermolina, Russia, 1904. Russ. dancer and chor. Studied Leningrad and danced there, leaving through China to Europe. Joined B. Russes de Monte Carlo 1932. Dancer and chor. in various Cos. in N. and S. America. Formed his own Co., Rio de Janeiro 1947. Chor. many ballets, incl. *Eternal Struggle* (1933) and *The Red Poppy* (1943). Author of *Borzoi* (1935), his autobiography, which won him a prize of £1,000 from the publishers. President of Federation of Classical Ballet. Now teaches in U.S.A.

SCOGLIO, Joseph, b. New York 1943. Am. dancer. Studied under Danilova and Eglevsky at Sch. of Am. B. and Joffrey Sch. In Hoving's Co. 1968, worked with Lotte Goslar. Came to London with Les Grands B. Canadiens 1968 and joined B. Rambert 1969.

SCOTCH SYMPHONY, ballet, ch. Balanchine, m. Mendelssohn's Scottish Symphony (omitting the first movement), dec. Armistead, cost. Karinska, f.p. N.Y. City B., City Center, N.Y. 11 Nov 1952 (Maria Tallchief, Eglevsky).

SCOTT, David, b. Colombo 1928. Eng. dancer and ballet master. Pupil of Espinosa Sch. and Northcote. Joined Orig. B. Russe 1951, Festival B. 1952 becoming soloist. Joined Nat. B. of Canada 1959 becoming joint ballet master with his wife Joanne Nisbet (b. Karachi 1931, member of S. Wells Th. B., and from 1955 to 1959 of Festival B.).

SCOTT, Margaret, b. Johannesburg 1922. S. African dancer and teacher. Pupil of Conmee, S. Wells Sch. and Rambert Sch. Joined S. Wells B. 1941, B. Rambert 1943 becoming soloist. Stayed in Australia after the B. Rambert tour 1947–48. Joined Rex Reid and Joyce Graeme in founding Australian Nat. Th. B. Company and from 1964 Director of Australian B. Sch.

SCOTTISH THEATRE BALLET, the company which was formerly the Western Theatre Ballet (q.v.) (and still directed by Peter Darrell) when it moved its base to Glasgow in 1969. It shares with the Scottish Opera a building which houses their rehearsal rooms. Its first performance was at Perth Th., Perth 9 April 1969 (*La Ventana*) and on 3 May 1969, when the whole co. appeared in *Les Troyens* at King's Th., Glasgow. The chor. was by Laverne Meyer and the principal dancers Elaine McDonald, Susan Carlton, Peter Cazalet, Kenn Wells. Since then the ballet company has toured Scotland and England and had a season at S. Wells Th. 1970. In 1970 the principal dancers were Elaine McDonald, Marian St Claire, Hilary Debden, Patricia Rianne, Michael Beare, Kit Lethby, Cristian Addams, Jorge Salavisa, with Gordon Aitken as ballet master, Harry Haythorne as production co-ordinator and Muriel Large (until 1973) as administrator. From April 1974 called The Scottish Ballet.

SCRIABINIANA, ballet, ch. Goleizovsky, m. Scriabin, dec. Klementiev, f.p. Bolshoi B., Moscow 17 Oct 1962 (Adirkhaeva). In modern plastic style.

SCUOLA DI BALLO, ballet, ch. Massine, m. Boccherini-Françaix, dec. de Beaumont, f.p. Monte Carlo 25 Apr 1933 (Baronova, Delarova, Psota, Woizikovsky). Based on Goldoni's comedy of the name.

SEA CHANGE, ballet 1 act, ch. Cranko, m. Sibelius (*En Saga*), dec. Piper, f.p. Gaiety Th., Dublin 18 July 1949 (O'Reilly, Hogan, Shore, Zullig). Tragedy of fisher-folk bereaved by a shipwreck.

SEASONS, THE, ballet-divertissement, ch. Petipa, m. Glazounov, dec. Lambin and Ponomariov, f.p. Hermitage Th., St Petersburg, 7 Feb 1900 and then at Maryinsky Th. 13 Feb 1900 (Pavlova, Preobrajenska Kschessinska, N. Legat). There have been many versions since and the music is used in Ashton's *Birthday Offering*. The *Bacchanale* from it was one of Pavlova's most famous solos.

SEBASTIAN, ballet, ch. Caton, m. Menotti, dec. Smith and Milena,

447

f.p. B. International, International Th., N.Y. 31 Oct 1944 (Moncion, Essen). Tragedy of Renaissance Venice. Also chor. by John Butler for Nederlands Dans Th. 22 Oct 1963 and for the Harkness B. 1966.

SECOND COMPANY, THE, the familiar name for the Sadler's Wells Th. B. (q.v.), later applied to the touring section of the Royal Ballet.

À la seconde

SECONDE, À LA, (Fr.) to the second position—see FIVE POSITIONS and PORT DE BRAS—and hence applied to movements and positions of the legs and arms directly to the side of the dancer, e.g. plié à la seconde, pirouette à la seconde, etc.

SEDOWA, Julie, b. St Petersburg 1880, d. Cannes 1970. Russ. dancer. Trained at Imp. Sch., St Petersburg. Made her début 1898, première danseuse 1903, and became one of the ballerinas of the Maryinsky Th. with Pavlova, Trefilova and Preobrajenska. Retired in 1916. From 1918 she taught at Nice.

SEGERSTRÖM, Per-Arthur, b. Stockholm 1952. Swed. dancer. Pupil of Hightower, Franchetti and R. Swed. B. Sch. Joined R. Swed. B. 1970 and danced solos. Varna prize 1972 (with Alhanko), junior class.

SEGUIDILLA, Spanish dance of considerable antiquity to be found to this day in different parts of Spain under different names and with slight variations, e.g. the *Manchega*, a lively variety found in the province of La Mancha and said to be the original form; the *Sevillana* found in Seville; the *Seguidilla Bolera*, in a stately tempo but not related to the Bolero; the *Seguidilla Gitana*, a slower and more sentimental Gipsy type; and the *Seguidilla Taleada*, a more energetic form not unlike the Cachucha. In a rapid 3/4 time, the Seguidilla is danced to the accompaniment of the guitar with sung *coplas* in alternate lines of 7 and 5 syllables with assonance in lieu of rhyme and the playing of the castanets.

SEGOVIA, Rosita, b. Barcelona 1926. Sp. dancer. Pupil of La Tanginesa and Verchinina. Joined Co. at Liceo Th., Barcelona, 1938 Morosova B. 1949 and Antonio's Co. 1953.

SEIGNEURET, Michèle, b. Paris 1934. Fr. dancer. Studied under Jeanne Schwarz. Début 1953 with Béjart's Ballets de l'Étoile and created many leading rôles in his ballets. Won René Blum Prize 1956.

SEILLIER, Daniel, b. Villiers-sur-Marne 1926. Fr. dancer and ballet-master. Studied Ricaux, Egorova, Gsovsky. Danced Paris Opéra 1934–46, de Cuevas 1951–61 (as soloist and ballet master). Ballet master of San Carlos Opera B., Lisbon 1961, Les Grands B. Canadiens 1963 and Nat. B. of Canada from 1965.

SEKH, Yaroslav, b. Ukraine 1930. Russ. dancer. Was not fully trained as a dancer. In 1944 in Lvov he joined an amateur dancing group at a vocational school and in 1946 was noticed by a dancer at the Lvov Opera. He joined the ballet school there. Danced in Lvov B. 1948–49. Entered Bolshoi Sch., Moscow 1949 and graduated into the company 1951 becoming soloist same year. A remarkable character dancer, he created the rôle of *Paganini* in Moscow (1960) and Baitemir in *Asel* (1967), and is a famous Mercutio in *Romeo and Juliet*.

SELINA, ballet 1 act (a satire on the Romantic Ballet by Andrée Howard and Peter Williams), ch. Howard, m. Rossini, dec. Howard, cost. P. Williams, f.p. S. Wells Th. B., S. Wells Th. 16 Nov 1948 (Fifield, Zullig, Holden).

SELINDER, Anders, b. Stockholm 1806, d. there 1874. Swedish dancer and the first native ballet master of the R. Swedish B., solodancer R. Swedish B. 1829, ballet master 1833–45, and 1851–56. Retired from the Opera 1871 and opened a school for children. He introduced the Romantic ballet to Sweden and preserved many Swedish folk dances by putting them into his ballets.

SELLING, Caj, b. Stockholm 1935. Swed. dancer. Took up ballet comparatively late. Engaged by R. Swedish B. 1954 and became solodancer 1959. Guest artist Royal Ballet, C. Garden, for two months (1959) partnering Beryl Grey. Awarded scholarship by King of Sweden 1956. Studied in Moscow and Leningrad 1960. Guest artist of Royal B. 1959, Am. B. Th. 1961–62 and 1964, Australian B. 1962–64. Returned to R. Swed. B. 1964 as principal and now retired.

ŠEMBEROVA, Zora, b. 1913. Czech dancer. Pupil of Preobrajenska and Chladek. Danced in Brno 1922–28, in the Prague Nat. B. 1931–32 and Brno again 1932–42. In Prague 1942–60. She danced Juliet (with

449

Psota as Romeo) in the 1938 *Romeo and Juliet* in Prague (ch. Psota)—the first time the Prokofieff score had been used.

SEMENYAKA, Ludmilla, b. Leningrad 1952. Russ. dancer. Entered Kirov Sch. 1962 and graduated to Kirov B. 1970. Moved to Bolshoi B. 1972. Won Second Prize in Moscow Competition 1972. Mar. M. Lavrovsky.

SEMEYONOV, Vladilen, b. Kuibyshev 1932. Russ. dancer. Pupil of Ponomoryov at Leningrad Sch. Grad. to Kirov B. as soloist 1950, becoming principal dancer. Hon. Artist R.S.F.S.R. Mar. Irina Kolpakova. In 1970 succeeded Sergeyev as Artistic Director of Kirov B. and was joint director with him in 1972.

SEMEYONOVA, Marina, b. St Petersburg 1908. Russ. dancer. Studied under Vaganova at Leningrad Sch., graduating 1925, later becoming prima ballerina at Kirov Th., Leningrad. Transferred to Bolshoi Th., Moscow 1930. In 1935 she danced *Giselle* at the Paris Opéra with Lifar. Stalin Prize 1941. Retired 1952. People's Artist R.S.F.S.R. She has taught for many years.

SEPTUOR, ballet 1 act, ch. Lifar, m. Lutèce, dec. Bonnat, f.p. Paris Opéra 25 Jan 1950 (Bessy, Dynalix, Lacotte, Efimoff). The stories of seven murderers who are hanged.

SEREGI, Laszlo, b. Budapest 1929. Hungarian dancer and chor. Trained under Nadasi, joined Army Ensemble 1949 and the Hungarian Nat. B. 1957. Chor. *Spartacus* (m. Khatchaturian) 1968, *Wooden Prince* (m. Bartok) 1970, *Miraculous Mandarin* (m. Bartok) 1970, *Sylvia* 1972 —all for Hungarian Nat. B., Budapest.

SERENADE, ballet 1 act, ch. Balanchine, m. Tchaikovsky (*Serenade for Strings*), dec. Lurçat, f.p. Sch. of Am. Ballet, Hartford 6 Dec 1934. Its first official performance was by American Ballet 1 Mar 1935 at Adelphi Th., N.Y. (Anchutina, Boris, Caccialanza, Mullowney, Dollar, Laskey). With various changes of cost. this has been danced by many companies and was mounted at the Paris Opéra 30 Apr 1947. Ballet of pure dancing. Given by Royal B., C. Garden 7 May 1964 (Beriosova, Nerina, Page, Blair, Macleary). Since 1948 the cost. have been by Karinska. Also danced by N.Y. City B. 18 Oct 1941, B. Russe de Monte Carlo 1940, R. Danish B. 1957, Scala, Milan 1960, Netherlands B., R. Swedish B. and others.

SERGEYEV, Konstantin, b. St Petersburg 1910. Russ. dancer and chor. In 1924 attended evening ballet classes under Semenoff. In 1928 became principal dancer Kschessinsky Co. (touring). Returned to Leningrad to study at Maryinsky Sch. and entered the Co. 1930 as a soloist, thereafter becoming one of the initiators of the new Soviet Ballet. Cr. a leading male rôle in *Fountain of Bakhchisarai, Bronze*

Horseman, Romeo and Juliet and in the ballets which he chor. at the Kirov Th. *Cinderella* (1964), *Paths of Thunder* (1957), *Distant Planet* (1963). Chor. film of *Sleeping Beauty* (1964). He was one of the greatest *danseurs nobles*, partnering Ulanova and his wife Dudinskaya. He became artistic director of the Kirov B. 1951–56. He resigned, having been attacked in the press in 1955 in a letter signed by Ulanova and other dancers who accused him of restricting their opportunities. However, he returned in 1960 but was dismissed in 1970 following the defection from the Co. of Makarova. He was partly reinstated in 1971 when he became, with Vinogradov, associate to the new artistic director of the Kirov B., V. Semeyonov, and chor. *Hamlet* (m. Chervinsky 1970). When Nerina danced *Giselle* at the Kirov Th. 1960–61 he partnered her. Awarded Stalin Prizes 1946, 1947, 1949. Honoured Artist of R.S.F.S.R. 1939, People's Artist 1957. Lenin Prize 1970.

SERGUEEFF, Nicholas, b. St Petersburg 1876, d. Nice 1951. Russ. dancer and ballet master. Graduated from Maryinsky Sch. 1894, became *régisseur* 1904 and *régisseur-général* 1914. Left Russia 1918, and mounted *The Sleeping Princess* for Diaghileff in 1921. For the S. Wells B. he mounted *Swan Lake* (1934), *Casse Noisette* (1934), *Coppélia* (1933), *Giselle* (1934), *Sleeping Beauty* (1939). For de Basil, *Casse Noisette* (1938). For the International Ballet (whose *régisseur* he became) the same ballets from 1941 onwards. He, more than anyone, was responsible for the preservation of the classical ballets outside Russia. The Russians themselves now show some bitterness to him in their writings. He wrote down the ballets in the Stepanoff notation and brought twenty-one out of Russia in this way. These passed to Mona Inglesby who sold them to the Harvard Library.

SERPETTE, see SICKLING.

SERRANO, Lupe, b. Santiago, Chile 1930. Pupil of Dambre, Schwezoff, Tudor. Joined Mexico City B. at 13. Toured with B. Alicia Alonso 1949, soloist B. Russe de Monte Carlo 1949–51. Ballerina of Am. Ballet Th. from 1953 and made many guest performances. Teaches in Illinois.

SERRER LES REINS (Fr. compress the small of the back), to hold oneself erect and with shoulders well back—term used in the classroom.

SERTIC, Ivan, b. Zagreb 1928. Yugoslav dancer. Pupil of Ana Roje, entered Belgrade National B. 1947, becoming a principal dancer 1953. To Frankfurt 1956 as a principal dancer. Ballet master Lübeck 1963–65, assistant ballet master Wuppertal 1965–67, ballet master Wuppertal 1967–73. Guest chor. Basel B. 1969. In 1973 became ballet master Th. am Gärtnerplatz, Munich.

SEVEN DEADLY SINS, THE, (*Les Sept Péchés Capitaux*), ballet, libretto by Brecht, ch. Balanchine, m. Weill, f.p. Les Ballets 1933, Th. des

Ch. Élysées, Paris 7 June 1933 (Tilly Losch, Lotte Lenya). When at the Savoy Th. in London, it was called *Anna-Anna*. An entirely new version, with dec. Ter-Weill, was given by N.Y. City B., City Center, N.Y. 4 Dec 1958 (Allegra Kent, Lotte Lenya). Other productions: ch. Lander, R. Danish B. 1936; ch. Cullberg, R. Swed. B. 1963; ch. MacMillan, dec. Spurling, Edinburgh Festival 4 Sept 1961 (Anya Linden, Cleo Laine), Royal B., C. Garden 19 July 1973 (Penney, G. Brown).

SEVEN SISTERS, ballet, ch. Gusev and G. Almas-zade, m. Kara-Karayev, dec. Gusak, f.p. Opera House, Baku 1952 (Batashov, Kuznetsov, Almas-zade, and Vekilova).

SEVENTH SYMPHONY, ballet 4 parts, ch. Massine, m. Beethoven, dec. Bérard, f.p. de Basil Co., Monte Carlo 5 May 1938 (Markova, Franklin, Youskevitch). Massine's least successful symphonic ballet. Chaos to Creation, Descent from the Cross, etc.

SEVERSKAYA, Anna, see NORTHCOTE, ANNA.

SEYMOUR, Lynn, b. Wainwright, Canada 1939. Canadian dancer. Studied in Vancouver (Jepson and Svetlanoff) and at S. Wells Sch. 1954–56. Joined C. Garden Op. B. 1956, Touring Royal B. 1957 and became soloist of Royal B. 1958–66. Became ballerina of Deutsche Oper, Berlin 1966–69 (while MacMillan was director). Guest artist Festival B. 1969 and 1970. Created rôles in *The Burrow* 1958, *Baiser de la Fée* 1960, *The Invitation* 1960, *Les Deux Pigeons* 1961, *Anastasia* 1967, etc. She has been MacMillan's main subject for his ballets (and he cr. his *Romeo and Juliet* for her, but Fonteyn danced it first). Guest artist of Canadian Nat. B. 1965. Returned as ballerina to Royal B. 1970. Guest artist of Alvin Ailey ballet 1971.

SHABELEVSKY, Yurek, b. Warsaw 1911. Polish dancer. Studied at Teater Wielki, Warsaw, and with Nijinska. Joined Ida Rubinstein Co. 1928, soloist de Basil Co. 1932–39, and many Am. ballet groups. Guest artist B. Theatre 1940 and in S. America and in Italy. Cr. rôles in *Jeux d'Enfants, Scuola di Ballo, Choreartium, Symphonie Fantastique*. Appointed ballet master New Zealand B. 1967.

SHADOW, THE, ballet 1 sc., ch. Cranko, m. Dohnányi, dec. Piper, f.p. S. Wells B., C. Garden 3 Mar 1953 (Beriosova, Lindsay, Chatfield, Shaw, Ashbridge). Romantic theme of a man who has two loves.

SHADOWPLAY, ballet, ch. Tudor, m. Koechlin, dec. Annals, f.p. Royal B., C. Garden 25 Jan 1967 (Dowell, Rencher, Park). Inspired by Kipling's *Jungle Book* as was Koechlin's music *Les Bandar-Log*. Tudor's first created work for the Royal B.

SHANE, Gillian, b. New Malden 1943. Eng. dancer. Pupil of Lettie

Littlewood. Danced in pantomimes. Joined Festival B. 1960 becoming soloist 1961 and principal. Mar. Alain Dubreuil.

SHANKAR, Uday, b. Udaipur 1900. Indian dancer who was greatly responsible for introducing the art to European audiences. He taught the elements of Indian dancing to Pavlova, and danced himself in her *Radha-Krishna*. He toured the world with his own Company, and founded a dance school in India in 1938.

SHARP, Cecil, b. London 1859, d. 1924. Eng. collector of folk music. Was attracted to folk dancing by seeing the Morris Dancers in Headington, Oxford, in 1899. Founded Eng. Folk Dance Soc. 1911 and devoted his life to the collection and teaching of folk dances. He established centres in the provinces and Cecil Sharp House in Regent's Park is the headquarters of the folk dance movement in England. He also collected folk songs and dances in U.S.A., esp. in the S. Appalachian Mountains.

SHAW, Brian, b. Golcar, Yorks, 1928. Eng. dancer. Studied with Ruth French, S. Wells Sch. First app. in ballet in S. Wells Opera B. Joined Royal B. 1944, becoming a soloist and principal. Cr. rôle in *Symphonic Variations*. Teacher and répétiteur for Royal B. A famous Blue Bird (q.v.).

SHAWN, Ted, b. Kansas City 1891, d. Orlando, Florida 1972. Am. dancer and chor. Mar. Ruth St Denis (1914) and founded Denishawn School (1915) in which all styles of dancing were taught and combined to form a distinctive American style which has had great influence there. He formed a Men's Group of dancers in 1933, which until it was disbanded in 1940 did much to destroy the prejudice against male dancers. His property, Jacob's Pillow (q.v.) in Massachusetts, has become a famous Summer School, of which he was director from 1941. Author of a number of books on the dance and chor. many ballets. Has been called 'Father of American Dance'. Appointed Knight of Dannebrog.

SHEARER, Moira, b. Dunfermline 1926. Scottish dancer. From 1932 studied in Rhodesia and from 1936 in London under Flora Fairbairn and the Legat Sch. Joined S. Wells Sch. 1940. Début International B. 1941. Rejoined S. Wells Sch. 1942 and became a ballerina of the Co. 1944. Made film *The Red Shoes* 1948. From 1952 guest artist of Royal B. From 1953 she has made a successful career as an actress and has appeared in several films. Acted Titania in *Midsummer Night's Dream* with Helpmann at Edinburgh Festival 1954, which then toured America. Now retired.

SHEINA, Svetlana, b. 1918. Russ. dancer and ballerina at Maly Th., Leningrad 1938–59. Stalin Prize 1949. Cr. rôles in *Twelve Months* and *Youth*.

SHELESNOVA, Eleonora (also Olga), b. Moscow c. 1932. Russ. dancer and teacher. Studied in Baku and danced in the ballet there. To Sofia and in 1966 to East Berlin as soloist at the Komische Oper B. Came to the West in 1971 with her husband (a musician) and from then has been teacher to Deutsche Oper B., West Berlin. To Munich B. 1973.

SHELEST, Alla, b. Smolensk 1919. Russ. dancer. Studied at Kirov Sch., Leningrad (cont. of Ulanova and Dudinskaya) becoming prima ballerina and sharing rôles with Ulanova. Appeared in London 1953, Berlin 1954. Stalin Prize 1949. She was the first Russian dancer to appear in London after the Second World War. Now a regisseur of the Kirov B.

SHERWOOD, Gary, b. Swindon 1941. Eng. dancer. Pupil of Royal B. Sch. Joined C. Garden Opera B. 1959, Touring Royal B. 1961, Western Th. B. 1965, Festival B. as soloist 1966 and returned to Royal B. 1967 as soloist, principal 1970–73. Mar. Diana Vere.

SHIRAH, ballet, ch. Pearl Lang, m. Hovhaness, cost. Pearl Lang, f.p. Am. Dance Festival, Connecticut 19 Aug 1960 (Lang, Bruce Marks). In the repertoire of Dutch Nat. B., Stadsschouwburg, Amsterdam 18 June 1962 (Hilarides, Voorembergh, Wilson).

SHOES, see POINT SHOES.

SHOLLAR, Ludmila, b. St Petersburg 1888. Russ. dancer and teacher. Entered Maryinsky Sch. 1900, pupil of Fokine and cr. rôle of Estrella in *Carnaval*. Character dancer at Maryinsky Th. 1906–21. Also in Diaghileff Co. 1909–14 and cr. rôle of Gipsy in *Petrouchka*. Returned to Maryinsky 1917–21 and rejoined Diaghileff 1921 (danced White Cat in London *Sleeping Princess*). Also in Ida Rubinstein Co., Karsavina-Vilzak Co. and Nijinska's Co. To America 1935 and taught in N.Y. with her husband Anatole Vilzak until 1963. Taught at Washington Sch. of B. 1963–65 and then at San Francisco B. Sch. In 1951 she was director of Am. Ballet Th. Sch. and taught at the Washington Sch. 1963–65, then at the San Francisco Sch.

SHORE, Jane, b. London 1929. Studied with Rambert and S. Wells Sch. Joined S. Wells Theatre B. 1946 on its inception until 1950 when she joined the S. Wells B. at C. Garden. Left 1952. Joined Drama Department of British Council 1961 and in 1970 entered the Arts Council as Dance Officer.

SHURALE, ballet 3 acts, ch. Jacobson, m. Yarullin, dec. Ptushko, Milchin, Vano, f.p. Kirov Th., Leningrad 28 May 1950 (Dudinskaya, Belsky). A Tartar fairy story. The ballet was prepared in 1941 but the War stopped it. Its original performance was in Kazan 12 Mar 1945, chor. by L. Zhukov and G. Tagerov.

SIBLEY, Antoinette, b. Bromley 1939. Eng. dancer. Pupil of Cone-Ripman and R. Ballet Sch. Entered Royal Ballet 1956 becoming soloist 1959. Danced Swanilda in *Coppélia*, the first performance by the Royal Ballet Sch. at C. Garden 1959, and danced her first *Swan Lake*, at Golders Green, Hippodrome, London 26 Sept 1959 with Somes. Toured S. Africa with Royal B. as ballerina 1960. Cr. rôle of Titania in *The Dream* 1964 and now one of the leading dancers of the Royal B. dancing all the classical rôles. Awarded C.B.E. 1973.

SIBBRITT, Gerard, b. Perth, Australia 1942. Austral. dancer. Studied with Kyra Bousloff and in London. Toured New South Wales with Kathleen Gorham 1959 and danced in musicals. Joined Larrain's *Cendrillon* Co. in Paris 1963, and then London Dance Th. in 1964. Returned to Australian Ballet 1965. Dir. Maki Asami B. Tokyo 1973.

SICILIANO, or SICILIENNE. Dance in a slow 6/8 or 12/8 time, presumed to be of Sicilian origin, which enjoyed great popularity in the eighteenth century.

SICKLING, of the feet, a fault in which the foot in turned over (inwards or outwards) relative to the leg, like a sickle. In Fr., *serpette*.

SIFNIOS, Duska, b. Skoplje 1934. Yugoslav dancer. Pupil of Kirsanova, Messerer, Gsovsky. Joined Belgrade Ballet 1952, soloist 1953. In 1959 joined Miskovitch B. as principal dancer and in 1960 Massine's Co. at Nervi. In 1961 became principal dancer of Béjart's B. du XXme Siècle. In 1962 danced *Giselle* at Bolshoi Th. as guest.

SIIMOLA, Aino, b. Narva 1901, d. Essen 1971. Esthonian dancer. Studied in Gatschino and Berlin. From 1922 she was with Laban in Stuttgart, Hamburg and soloist of his Co., at Münster 1924-27. To Essen and danced with the Folkwang Dance Th. Married Kurt Jooss 1939 and was his assistant and dancer in his B. Jooss and afterwards in Düsseldorf.

SILVAIN, James (Sullivan), d. Paris 1856. Eng. dancer, brother of Barry Sullivan the actor. Danced at King's Th., London 1824, 1826 (as Sullivan). To Paris Opéra 1831-33. Danced in London throughout the 1830s and 1840s, partnering Grisi and Grahn. Toured America 1840-42 as Elssler's partner.

SIMONE, Kirsten, b. Copenhagen 1934. Dan. dancer. Entered R. Dan. B. Sch. 1947 (pupil of Volkova), joined the Co. 1952 and promoted solodancer (with rôle of *La Sylphide*) 1956 and now the leading ballerina. Knight of Dannebrog 1965—the youngest. Guest ballerina Ruth Page and R. Winnipeg Bs. In 1968 guest ballerina of Bolshoi B. in Russia and 1969 of Am. B. Th.

SIMONEN, Seija, b. Helsinki 1935. Finnish dancer. Pupil of Nat. B. Sch.

of Finland, Kiss and Northcote. Joined Nat. B. of Finland 1952 becoming soloist 1954. To Washington Nat. B. 1968.

SIMPLE SYMPHONY, ballet 1 act, ch. Gore, m. Britten, dec. Ronald Wilson, f.p. B. Rambert, Th. Royal, Bristol 29 Nov 1944 (Gilmour, Gore). A gay and sentimental frolic on the beach.

SINCERETTI, Francis, b. Grasse 1942. Fr. dancer. Studied in Nice and with S. Golovine and V. Gsovsky. Joined Nice B. and was soloist in Hamburg 1966–71. From 1971 soloist of Dutch Nat. B. Mar. Monique Sand.

SINFONIETTA, ballet ch. Ashton, m. Malcolm Williamson, cost. Rice, optical sets by Hornsey Col. of Art, f.p. R. Shakespeare Th., Stratford-upon-Avon, Touring Royal B. 10 Feb 1967 (Wells, Last, Anderton, Wall, Farley). Abstract ballet with changing lighting effects.

SINGLETON, Trinette, b. Beverly, Mass. 1945. Am. dancer. Studied at Am. B. Center, joined Joffrey B. 1965 and soloist 1970.

SIRÈNES, LES, ballet, ch. Ashton, m. Berners, dec. Beaton, f.p. S. Wells B., C. Garden 12 Nov 1946 (Fonteyn, Ashton, Helpmann, who sang). An evocation of the Edwardian era of rich dresses and parasols.

SISSONNE, or PAS DE SISSONNE, probably from *pas de ciseaux*, a scissor-like movement. A movement possibly derived from a step of that name popular in the early eighteenth century court dancing and attributed to Mme de Maintenon. Its invention is also attributed to a Comte de Sissonne. With a slight plié, the dancer springs into the air from the fifth position, alighting on one foot with a demi-plié, with the other leg extended to the back, front, or side; the back foot is then closed to the supporting foot (a sissonne fermée, which is also termed a faux entre-chat cinq). The step, which may be beaten, can be performed in series travelling forward, or from side to side, changing the position of the feet on alighting. If the dancer lands on one foot with the other on the cou-de-pied, as a relevé, it is a sissonne simple (or ordinaire). The word is sometimes debased to *si-sol*. See also RELEVÉ and ENTRECHAT.

SISYPHUS, ballet, ch. Åkesson, m. Blomdahl, dec. Horlin, f.p. R. Swed. Ballet, Stockholm 18 Apr 1957 (Orlando, Holmgren).

SITUATION, ballet, ch. van Manen, m. (sounds of running water etc.), dec. Vroom, f.p. Nederlands Dans Th., Circus Th., Scheveningen 20 Apr 1970 (Licher, Gosschalk, Sarstadt, Vervenne, Hampton, Knill, Lemaître). A series of encounters and reactions in a closed room.

SIZOVA, Alla, b. Moscow 1939. Russ. dancer. Graduated from Kirov Sch. to the company as soloist in 1958. Danced her first Aurora with the Kirov B. at C. Garden, London in 1961, and, partnered by Soloviev, in the film of the ballet 1965. Created rôle of the Girl in Belsky's *Lenin-*

grad Symphony 1961 and Ophelia in *Hamlet* 1970. Her career has been troubled by periods of illness. Hon. Artist R.S.F.S.R. 1966. Varna Gold Medal 1964.

SJÖSTRAND, Hervor, b. Gothenburg 1938. Swed. dancer. Pupil of M. Gardemeister. Entered R. Swed. B. 1958, becoming soloist 1964.

SKÁLOVÁ, Olga, b. Brno 1928. Czech dancer. Pupil of Psota and at the Bolshoi Sch. Joined the Brno Co. and then became principal dancer of the National B. in Prague.

SKEAPING, Mary, b. Woodford 1902. Eng. dancer and teacher. Studied under Zanfretta, Novikoff, Egorova, Craske, Laban. With Pavlova's Co., Nemchinova-Dolin Co. Ballet mistress S. Wells B. 1948–52. Made film *The Little Ballerina* 1947. Has mounted many of the classical ballets all over the world, notably in Helsinki, Havana, Stockholm, Winnipeg. Director of R. Swedish B. 1953–62. Awarded M.B.E. 1958, Order of Vasa 1961. Ch. *Cupid out of his Humour* (m. Purcell), Drottningholm Th., Stockholm 1956 for visit of Queen Elizabeth II to Sweden. Ch. *Atis and Camilla* at Drottningholm Th. 1964. A great expert on the technique of the *ballet de cour* of the seventeenth century she arranged that part of the Ballet for All (q.v.) programmes from 1965.

SKIBINE, George, b. Yasnaya Poliana 1920. Russ. dancer and chor. Studied under Preobrajenska, Lifar, etc., at Paris. Son of dancer in Diaghileff's Co. Joined Blum's Co. 1938 and de Basil's 1940, and several American Cos. Am. citizen since 1945. Joined de Cuevas Co. 1947 becoming the premier danseur. Étoile Paris Opéra 1956–58. Chor. *Tragedy at Verona* (1950), *Annabel Lee* (1951), *Prisoner of the Caucasus* (1951), *Idylle* (1953), *Achille* (1955), etc. Succeeded Lifar as ballet master at Paris Opéra 1958. Resigned 1962. First director of Harkness B. 1964–67. Among his other ballets are *Daphnis and Chloë* (1954), *Fâcheuses Rencontres* (1959), *Pastorale* (1961), *Romeo and Juliet* (1969). Mar. Marjorie Tallchief Dir. Dallas Civic B. Acad.

SKÖLD, Berit, b. Stockholm 1939. Swed. dancer. Entered the Royal Swedish B. Sch. 1948 and joined the Company in 1956, dancing solo rôles in 1960. Danced Juliet in Tudor's *Romeo and Juliet* (m. Delius) 1962.

SKORIK, Irène, b. Paris 1928. Russ. dancer. Studied under Preobrajenska and Gsovsky. Début B. des Ch. Élysées 1945, of which she was chief classical dancer. Became prima ballerina of Munich, Berlin, Basel etc. 1950 onwards, and made guest appearances in Paris and London. Danced in Miskovitch B. 1957–60. Guest artist Festival B. 1963. Now teaches in Paris.

SKOURATOFF, Vladimir, b. Paris 1925 of Ukrainian parents. Fr. dancer. Studied Preobrajenska and Kniaseff. Joined Lifar's Monte Carlo B. 1946, partner of Renée Jeanmaire. Joined de Basil Co. 1947, Petit's Ballet de Paris 1948, B. des Ch. Élysées 1951 with Jacqueline Moreau, de Cuevas Co. 1952, as a principal dancer. Guest artist Scandinavian B. 1960 and Festival B. 1960, R. Swed. B. Ballet master Strasbourg 1967–69, of Bordeaux B. 1970.

SKRAM, Hanne, b. Oslo 1937. Norwegian dancer. Trained by Alfrild Grimsgaard, entered Norwegian B. as soloist 1959, principal 1968.

SLANG, apart from abbreviated or debased forms of technical terms (e.g. *chaîné, couru, si-sol, sus-sous*, etc., q.v.), every country has its own familiar terms in ballet, of which the following are a selection of English phrases: *cow hop*, the dance of the two leading Swans in *Swan Lake*, Act II, from a particular step, posé temps levé en arabesque, pas de bourrée couru en avant into grand jeté en avant. *Catching the feather*, in music hall dancing, when a man does a series of pas de bourrée renversés sautés. *Fish Dive*, see entry. *Lame Duck*, a posé en tournant en dehors. *The Miseries*, the two leading dancers of the corps de ballet in *Les Sylphides*. *The Rounds*, coupé posé turns done en manège. *The Washes*, a port de bras done by the corps de ballet in *Swan Lake*, Act II. They take the left arm down from the hand of the right extended arm, across the body down to the left foot. *The Splits* (q.v.). In America some young children are taught classical steps by such names as *perches* (piqué positions), *hitch-kick* (saut de flèche), *rope-hop* (jeté en tournant—as in skipping), *big and little booties* (grands and petits battements), *toe-sink* (lowering the foot to the ground from half-point), etc. In England *camp* can mean effeminacy in a male dancer and also exaggeration in the interpretation of a rôle. In *Swan Lake* Benno is called *The Catcher*. Dancers wish each other luck when about to go on stage by saying 'Merde' (Fr.) or 'Chuckers' (Austral.) or 'toi-toi-toi' and spitting three times over the shoulder (Ger.), or 'in bocca al lupo' (Ital. 'into the wolf's mouth') or 'ne pooha ne perà' (Russ. 'not a fluff, not a feather') to which the reply is 'k chertyam'—'go to the devils'.

SLASK, the Polish folk dance Co., founded in 1953 by Stanislav Hadyna. It tours the world and first appeared in London (Coliseum) in 1958. The ballet mistress is Elwira Kaminska.

SLAUGHTER ON TENTH AVENUE, ballet, ch. Balanchine, m. Rodgers, cost. Sharaff, dec. Mielziner, f.p. in the revue *On Your Toes*, Imp. Th., N.Y. 11 Apr 1936 (Geva, Vilan, Bolger). The ballet formed part of the story of the revue. Taken into repertoire of N.Y. City B., State Th., N.Y. 30 Apr 1968 (Farrell, Mitchell).

SLAVENSKA, Mia, b. Slavenski-Brod 1914. Yugoslav dancer. Studied in

Zagreb under Margarita Froman and in Paris. In 1936 Olympic Games, Berlin, awarded prize for dancing (with Kreutzberg and Wigman). Ballerina of Ballet Russe de Monte Carlo in America 1938–42. Formed her own companies (incl. Slavenska-Franklin B. 1952–55) which have toured America. Guest artist of Festival B. 1952. Star of film *La Mort du Cygne* (1938). Chor. many ballets for her own companies. In 1933 she danced in Nijinska's Co. under her real name, Mia Corak.

SLAVINSKY, Tadeo, b. Warsaw 1901, d. Australia 1945. Polish dancer. Studied at Warsaw Opera. Joined Diaghileff's Co. 1921. Cr. rôle of a Sailor in *Les Matelots* 1925. Chor. *Chout* (with Larionov) for Diaghileff 1921. To Australia with de Basil's Co. 1938 and remained, joining Borovansky's Co., and teaching.

SLEEP, Wayne, b. Plymouth 1948. Eng. dancer. Pupil of Muriel Carr and Royal B. Sch. Joined Royal B. 1966, becoming soloist 1970. Created solos in *Jazz Calendar* and *Enigma Variations*. Also acts in films and plays. Also see ENTRECHAT.

SLEEPING BEAUTY, THE *(The Sleeping Princess, La Belle au Bois Dormant)*, ballet 4 acts 5 sc., ch. Petipa, m. Tchaikovsky, dec. Levogt, Botcharov, Shishlov, Ivanov, cost. Vsevolojsky, f.p. Maryinsky Th., St Petersburg 15 Jan 1890 (Carlotta Brianza, Paul Gerdt, with Cecchetti as Carabosse, Marie Petipa as Lilac Fairy, Cecchetti and V. Nikitina in Blue Bird). In 1921 Diaghileff revived the ballet, reproduced by Sergueeff using the Stepanoff Notation, Alhambra Th., London 2 Nov 1921 (Spessivtseva, Vladimiroff, with Carlotta Brianza as Carabosse, Lopokova as Lilac Fairy, Idzikowsky and Lopokova in Blue Bird). In this production the Princess Aurora was later danced by Trefilova, Egorova, and Lopokova. The Lilac Fairy was also danced by Nijinska (who also chor. the hunting dances and part of last act). The dec. was by Bakst and a fortune was lavished on the production in anticipation of a long run, but the audience, used to the short one-act ballets and not yet ready for the revival of a classical ballet, gradually fell off and the ballet had to be withdrawn after three months, with great financial loss. Revived by S. Wells B., also by Sergueeff and dec. Nadia Benois, S. Wells Th. 2 Feb 1939 (Fonteyn, Helpmann, with June Brae as Lilac Fairy, Honer and Turner in Blue Bird). With dec. by Oliver Messel it was revived again by the S. Wells Co. to reopen C. Garden after the war, 20 Feb 1946 (Fonteyn, Helpmann, with Beryl Grey as Lilac Fairy, Pamela May and Rassine in Blue Bird, Helpmann as Carabosse). The chor. of the Lilac Fairy variation was (and remains) that of F. Lopokhov. By February 1973 it had been danced over 460 times at C. Garden. Sergueeff also revived it for International B. (May 1948) with Mona Inglesby as Aurora.

The R. Swedish B. revived the ballet (version by Mary Skeaping) 13 Jan 1955, dec. Gamlin (von Rosen, Holmgren, with A.-M. Lagerborg as Lilac Fairy, Gerd Andersson and Bengt Andersson in Blue Bird). Mounted for de Cuevas B. by Nijinska and Helpmann, dec. R. de Larrain, Th. des Ch. Élysées, Paris 27 Oct 1960 (Hightower, Polajenko). Other recent productions (based on the Petipa chor.) have been: Turkish Nat. B., dec. Andrée Howard, mounted by Lorna Mossford, Opera House, Ankara, f.p. 8 Nov 1963 (Meric Sumen); Bolshoi B., Moscow, ch. Grigorovitch, f.p. 7 Dec 1963; Festival B. (version by Ben Stevenson and Beryl Grey), dec. McDowell, f.p. R. Festival Hall, London 24 Aug 1967 (Noella Pontois, Gilpin); Deutsche Oper B., Berlin (version by MacMillan), dec. Kay, f.p. 8 Oct 1967 (Seymour, Holz); Cologne B. (version by Peter Wright), dec. Farmer, f.p. 18 Nov 1967 (Cardus, Watts); Royal B. (version by Peter Wright and Ashton) dec. Bardon, cost. de Nobili, R. Doboujinsky, f.p. C. Garden 17 Dec 1968 (Sibley, Macleary) and a new version (ch. MacMillan, dec. Peter Farmer) f.p. C. Garden 15 Mar 1973 (Sibley, Dowell). The Kirov Th., Leningrad version is Petipa in a version by K. Sergeyev mounted c. 1952. Also see AUMER.

SLINGSBY, Simon. Eng. dancer, pupil of R. Aldridge. He was one of the greatest dancers at the Paris Opéra at the end of the eighteenth century —a remarkable achievement in an era when Auguste Vestris and Le Picq were dancing—and probably the first Eng. dancer to achieve fame in Paris. He danced at the Kings Th., London, during the 1780s with Baccelli and Vestris, but little is known of his career. An anonymous author puts into the mouth of G. Vestris, in a poem addressed to Heinel 1781, 'The connoisseurs with one consent declare Slingsby to Vestris is a dancing bear'—an expression of his jealousy.

SLONIMSKY, Yuri, b. St Petersburg 1902. The *doyen* of the Russ. writers on the dance. Educ. Univ. of Petrograd and Inst. for History of Arts. Critic since 1919. Trans. Noverre's *Letters* (1922) and many books and articles on history of ballet. Outstanding are *Masters of the Ballet in the 19th Century* (1937), *Tchaikovsky and the Ballet Theatre of his Time* (1956), a life of *Didelot* (1958) etc. Editor of *All about Ballet* (lexicon) (1966). Contributor to *Ballet Annual*. Author of librettos to many Russ. ballets, incl. *Youth* (1949), *Path of Thunder* (1957), *Coast of Hope* (1959). Was on staff of Leningrad Institute of Theatre etc. until 1961.

SMIRNOVA, Elena, b. St Petersburg 1888, d. Buenos Airés 1934. Russ. dancer. Pupil of the Maryinsky Sch. and soloist, then ballerina of the Maryinsky Ballet (the last to be nominated in the old régime, 1916). She danced in Diaghileff's first Paris season in 1909, and was the ballerina in her husband's, Boris Romanoff's, Théâtre Romantique Russe in Buenos Aires, whither they emigrated 1920.

SMITH, Bob, b. Liverpool 1946. Eng. dancer. Pupil of Shelagh Elliott Clarke and Rambert Sch. Joined B. Rambert 1966 and danced with Ballet for All 1970–71.

SMITH, George Washington, b. c. 1820, d. Philadelphia 1899. Am. dancer. Début Philadelphia 1838. Originally a stonecutter, he first became a clog dancer, and then joined Elssler and studied under Silvain in America. Partnered Mary Ann Lee (q.v.) and was the first Albrecht in *Giselle* in America. Became ballet-master to Lola Montez. In 1859 principal dancer in the Ronzani Troupe (which included the Cecchetti family) at the Melodeon Beer Hall, N.Y. In 1881 opened a dance school in Philadelphia.

SMITH, Kathleen, b. Austin, Texas 1940. Am. dancer. Pupil of Danilova, Caton etc. Joined Am. Festival B. 1961, and in 1962 the Dutch Nat. B. becoming principal dancer. To Hanover B. 1969 as ballerina, Gelsenkirchen 1970, B. Van Vlaanderen 1971, B. de Wallonie 1973.

SMITH, Lois, b. Vancouver 1929. Canadian dancer. Pupil of Deveson, McBirney and Loring and many teachers in Europe, including Royal B. Sch. In 1946 toured America in *Song of Norway*. Joined Canad. Nat. B. 1951, became the prima ballerina 1958 until she retired in 1969. Awarded Canad. Centennial Medal 1967. Danced the film *Swan Lake* (with Bruhn and Canad. Nat. B.) 1967.

SMITH, Oliver, b. Wisconsin 1918. Am. artist and designer of the décor for many ballets, notably *Rodeo, Fancy Free, On Stage!, Interplay, Fall River Legend, Les Noces* etc. Co-director of Am. Ballet Th. since 1945. Also designer of many musicals.

SMOK, Pavel, b. Prague 1927. Czech dancer and chor. Pupil of Prague Conservatoire. Soloist of the Army Ensemble in Pilsen 1952–58. Ballet master of the new Prague Ballet 1964–70. Chor. *The New Odyssey* 1960, *Victorka* 1960, *Picassiada* 1963. From 1970 ballet master in Basel. Returned to Prague 1973.

SMOLTZOFF, Victor V., b. Moscow 1900. Russ. dancer. Studied at Moscow Sch. Début 1918, and becoming a leading classical dancer. Honoured Artist 1924. Stalin Prize 1950, 1951.

SMUIN, Michael, b. Missoula, Montana 1938. Am. dancer and chor. Pupil of the Christensens. Joined Univ. of Utah Ballet Theatre 1954, San Francisco B. 1957–62. In Broadway musicals until 1966 when he joined Am. Ballet Th., becoming principal 1968–72. Among his ballets are *Vivaldi Concerto* (m. Vivaldi), *Symphony in Jazz* (m. Liebermann), *Three Colors* (m. Offenbach) all 1960 for S. Francisco B., *Highland*

Fair (m. Arnold) 1964 for Harkness B., *The Circle* (m. Thompson) 1966 for Pennsylvania B., *Panambi* (m. Ginistera) 1969 for Ailey Dance Th., *Schubertiade* (m. Schubert) 1970 for S. Francisco B. For Am. Ballet Th. he chor. *The Catherine Wheel* (m. Thompson) 1967, *Pulcinella Variations* (m. Stravinsky) and *Gartenfest* (m. Mozart) in 1969, *The Eternal Idol* (m. Chopin) 1970. Associate Director S. Francisco B. 1973.

SNIJDERS, Ronald, b. Amsterdam 1937. Dutch dancer. Pupil of Kennemen B. Sch., Haarlem 1952–56, of Karel Shook at Dutch Nat. B. Sch. 1956 onwards. Studied with Zaraspe in N.Y. 1968. Joined Dutch Nat. B. 1958 becoming a principal dancer.

SNOEK, Hans (Johanna), b. Geertruidenberg, Holland 1906. Dutch dancer and chor. Pupil of Jooss and Leeder. Founder and director of Scapino B. and Sch. 1945 and chor. for them many ballets incl. *The Magic Flute, The Golden Swan* etc. Author of *Dance and Ballet* (1959). Knight of Order of Orange-Nassau 1960.

SNOW MAIDEN, THE, ballet 3 acts, ch. Bourmeister, m. Tchaikovsky, dec. Pimini and Epishin, f.p. Festival B., Festival Hall, London 17 July 1961 (Belinda Wright, Burr, Briansky, Yuresha). The music is drawn from the score of incidental music written for Ostrovsky's play *Snow Maiden*, the first two movements of the 1st Symphony and other small pieces. It was a great success and the first Soviet-British collaboration in ballet. It was later revised and mounted at the Stanislavsky and Nemirovitch-Dantchenko Th., Moscow 6 Nov 1963 with dec. Volkov (Vlassova, Vera Danilovitch, A. Klein).

SOBEKA, pseudonym of Boris Kochno, as author of the libretti of many ballets for Diaghileff.

SOCIÉTÉ DES ARTISTES ET AMIS DE L'OPÉRA, founded in 1904 by the Count Isaac de Camondo, a benevolent society to help the artists and employees of the Paris Opéra, and their widows and orphans. In 1947 it absorbed the older Association Philanthropique des Artistes de l'Opéra (q.v.).

SODERBAUM, Ulla, Swedish dancer. Joined Jooss Sch. at Dartington and became a principal dancer in his Co. until 1947. Danced in Switzerland 1947–51 when she rejoined Jooss.

SÖFFING, Tilly, b. Apolda 1932. Ger. dancer. Pupil of Bornhacke-Urlichs and Uhlen in Jena. Joined Gera B., then Weimar, Aachen and Augsburg. To Cologne 1960 becoming soloist, Düsseldorf as principal 1965.

SOIR DE FÊTE, ballet, ch. Staats, m. Delibes (from *La Source*), f.p. Paris

Opéra 30 June 1925 (Spessivtseva, Ricaux). Suite of classical entrées, formerly one of the most performed of the Opéra ballets.

SOIRÉE MUSICALE, ballet 1 act, ch. Tudor, m. Rossini-Britten, dec. Stevenson, f.p. for Cecchetti Soc. Matinée, Palladium Th., London 26 Nov 1938 (Larsen, Lloyd, Laing, Tudor, van Praagh). Suite of dances in a ballroom. Danced by B. Rambert from 1940. Mounted for Joffrey B. 1959. Scottish Th. B. 1972.

SOIRÉES DE PARIS, LES, a short season of ballet at the Th. de la Cigàle, Paris, promoted by the Count Etienne de Beaumont, giving ballets by Massine. Although it only lasted from 17 May 1924 to 30 June 1924 it presented the following new ballets: *Romeo and Juliet* (a Cocteau production) dec. J. Hugo, *Mercure* (m. Satie, dec. Picasso), *Salade* (m. Milhaud, dec. Braque), *Beau Danube* (m. J. Strauss, dec. after Guys), *Gigue* (dec. Derain) and *Scuola di Ballo* (m. Boccherini, dec. Count Beaumont).

SÖKMEN, Sait, b. Conakry (Africa) 1942. Turkish dancer and chor. Studied under Molly Lake in Turkey and Royal B. Sch., entered Turkish State Ballet, becoming a principal dancer. Chor. *Wheel* (Ankara 1968) the first ballet to be chor. by a Turk. He left in 1971.

SOKOLOVA, Eugenie, b. 1850, d. Leningrad 1925. Russ. dancer. Graduated from Imp. Sch. 1869, becoming ballerina at the Maryinsky Th. in the 1870s, with Vazem. She was a dancer of charm and warmth and created many rôles in Petipa's ballets. Retired 1886 and became a famous teacher, who taught Pavlova, Karsavina, etc.

SOKOLOVA, Lydia (Hilda Munnings), b. Wanstead 1896. Eng. dancer and chor. Studied under Pavlova and Mordkin. Toured with Mordkin's Co. 1911. Joined Diaghileff's Co. 1913, the first Eng. girl to be taken by him, becoming a principal dancer and remaining until the Co. broke up. Cr. rôles in *Le Train Bleu*, *Boutique Fantasque* (Tarantella), etc., and took the chief rôle in Massine's version of *Le Sacre du Printemps* 1920. Chor. the dances in some London musicals. Author with R. Buckle of *Dancing for Diaghilev* (London 1960). In 1962 she danced Giuseppina Cecchetti's rôle (the Marquise de Silva) in Royal B.'s *Good Humoured Ladies* at C. Garden.

SOKOLOW, Anna, b. Hartford, Conn. 1912. Am. dancer and chor. (of Polish extraction). Pupil of Martha Graham and member of her Co. 1930–39. Formed modern group in Mexico 1939 where she worked for many years. On retiring as a dancer 1954 formed group in America. Works regularly in Israel and teaches their Inbal Ballet. Chor. many solos for herself (*Lament for the Death of a Bullfighter*, *Kadisch* etc.), also many group dances incl. *Rooms* (m. Hopkins 1955), *Opus '58*,

463

Opus '60, Opus '65 (all m. Teo Macero), *Dreams* (m. Webern 1961), *Deserts* (m. Varèse) etc. Many of these have gone into repertoires of other Cos. (e.g. Nederland Dans Th., B. Rambert).

SOLEIL DE NUIT, LE, ballet, ch. Massine, m. Rimsky-Korsakov, dec. Larionov, f.p. Diaghileff's Co., Grand Th., Geneva 20 Dec 1915 (Massine). This was Massine's first ballet and Larionov's first work for Diaghileff. Russian folk dances.

SOLITAIRE, ballet, ch. MacMillan, m. Arnold, dec. Heeley, f.p. S. Wells Th. B., S. Wells Th. 7 June 1956 (Hill, Neil, Britton, Boulton, MacLeary). A solitary girl who plays with groups of boys and girls, but is always left alone in the end. Also danced by R. Danish B. 1961 (dec. Rowell).

SOLODANCER, the highest rank in the cadre of the Royal Danish Ballet, which has only given the rank of prima ballerina once (to Margot Lander).

SOLOV, Zachary, b. Philadelphia 1923. Am. dancer and chor. Appeared in night clubs and joined Littlefield B. 1939, B. Caravan 1941, Loring's Dance Players 1943 (under name of Carlson), B. Theatre 1946–49. Appointed choreographer Met. Op., N.Y. 1951–58, 1963–65. Now works with Kansas City B.

SOLOVIEV, Yuri, b. Leningrad 1940. Russ. dancer. Entered Leningrad Sch. 1949. Grad. to Kirov B. 1958 as soloist from classes of Shavrov and Pushkin. Principal dancer. People's Artist R.S.F.S.R. 1963. Nijinsky Prize, Paris 1963. Mar. Tatiana Legat. An outstanding Blue Bird (q.v.).

SOLVEIG, see THE ICE MAIDEN.

SOMBERT, Claire, b. Courbevoie 1935. Fr. dancer. Pupil of Yves Brieux, Preobrajenska, Rausanne. Danced in Charrat's Co. 1952–53, Petit's Ballets de Paris 1953–54, Scala, Milan 1955 (with Babilée in *Le Jeune Homme et la Mort*). Soloist of de Cuevas Co. 1955, Festival B. 1961. Received René Blum Award 1952. In Babilée B. 1959. Ballerina in Larrain's *Cendrillon* (1963–64). In 1972 became ballerina of B. du Rhin, Strasbourg.

SOMES, Michael, b. Horsley, Glos. 1917. Eng. dancer. Studied under Miss Blott at Weston-super-Mare and Espinosa at Bristol. First boy to win (in 1934) scholarship to S. Wells Sch. Became chief male dancer in S. Wells B. 1938, partnering Margot Fonteyn. First cr. leading rôle The Young Man in Ashton's *Horoscope* (1938). Cr. rôles in most of the S. Wells ballets, including *The Wanderer*, *Symphonic Variations*, *Daphnis and Chloë*, *Tiresias*, *Sylvia*, etc. Chor. *Summer Interlude* for S. Wells Th. B. 1950. Awarded C.B.E. 1959. Appointed assistant director of Royal B. 1963–70 and a principal teacher and *répétiteur* 1970, with special responsibility for Ashton's ballets.

SOMMERKAMP, Helga, b. Berlin 1937. Ger. dancer. Pupil of T. Gsovsky, V. Gsovsky, Egorova. Joined Berlin Staatsoper B. 1948, then danced in Basel, principal Berlin 1957–59, Frankfurt, Am. Festival B., Gelsenkirchen 1962, then toured.

SOMNAMBULISM, ballet, ch. MacMillan, m. Kenton, f.p. S. Wells Choreographic Group, S. Wells Th. 1 Feb 1953 (Lane, MacMillan, Poole). Revised version f.p. S. Wells Th., B., S. Wells Th. 29 May 1956 (Heaton, Hill, Britton). MacMillan's first ballet.

SONATE À TROIS, ballet, ch. Béjart, m. Bartók, dec. Bert, f.p. Béjart's Ballet Th., Th. Marigny, Paris 19 June 1957 (Seigneuret, Tania Bari, Béjart). It had previously been performed in Essen 27 April 1957 (same cast). Danced by Western Th. B., f.p. S. Wells Th. 22 Apr 1960 (Merry, Wellman, Meyer). A version of Sartre's *Huis Clos*.

SONG OF THE EARTH (*Das Lied von der Erde*), ballet, ch. MacMillan, m. Mahler, no décor, f.p. Stuttgart B., Stuttgart 7 Nov 1965 (Haydee, Madsen). Mounted for Royal B., C. Garden 19 May 1966 (Haydee, MacLeary, with Penney, Parkinson). The six Mahler songs, with the singers standing on each side of the stage. This music was also used by Tudor for his *Shadow of the Wind* (1948) and by Pauline Koner for her *Farewell* (1962).

SOPWITH, Noreen, b. Birmingham 1932. Eng. dancer. Studied S. Wells Sch. and became principal dancer of B. Rambert. Soloist of Royal Ballet from 1957. Now retired.

SOROKINA, Nina, b. 1942. Russ. dancer. Pupil of Bolshoi Sch. becoming soloist of Bolshoi B. 1961. Created rôles in *The Geologists* (the *Heroic Poem*) (1964) and young girl in *Rite of Spring* (1965). Varna Gold Medal 1966. Mar. Y. Vladimirov. Danced her first Aurora in *Sleeping Beauty*, Bolshoi Th. 1967.

SOUBRESAUT, lit. a sudden bound. A jump from both feet, in the fifth position, with the feet fully pointed so that one masks the other, giving a pencil-point impression.

SOURCE, LA, ballet 3 acts 4 sc., ch. Saint-Léon, m. Minkus (1st and 4th sc.) and Delibes (2nd and 3rd sc.), dec. Despléchin, Rube, Lavastre, Chaperon, f.p. Paris Opéra 12 Nov 1866 (Salvioni, Mérante). In this ballet Eugénie Fiocre made a great sensation in a secondary rôle and was painted in it by Degas. The chief rôle, Naila, was originally intended for Grantzow, but she was unable to assume it until the following year, when she completely eclipsed Salvioni's performances. Ballet on a Persian theme.

SOUS-SUS, see SUS-SOUS.

SOUTENU, lit. sustained or held. A turning movement on half or full point, during which the body describes a complete turn, e.g. the dancer, standing with feet in fifth position with the left foot back, extends the left foot to the fourth position back, describes a grand rond de jambe en dedans just above the ground, finishing in fifth position front on both half points, twists the body towards the right, at the same time reversing the position of the feet, and finishes facing in the same direction as at the beginning of the movement. The step may, of course, be performed on the other foot and also on full point. This is a soutenu en dedans and is the most commonly used, but it may be performed en dehors.

SOUTH AFRICA, BALLET IN, see under CAPAB BALLET (Cape Town), PACT BALLET (Johannesburg), PACOFS BALLET (Orange Free State) and NAPAC BALLET (Durban).

SOUTH AMERICA, BALLET IN, see under CUBAN NATIONAL BALLET, COLON, Teatro, and SAN MARTIN BALLET (both Buenos Aires) and CHILEAN NATIONAL BALLET.

SOUVENIRS, ballet, ch. Bolender, m. Barber, dec. Ter-Arutunian, f.p. N.Y. City B., City Center, N.Y. 15 Nov 1955 (Irene Larsson, Carolyn George). Nostalgic scenes in a pre-Great War hotel, ending with a chase. In the repertoire of several Cos. (Harkness B., f.p. Music Box Th., N.Y., f.p. 14 Jan 1969 (Cockerille, Duffy, Aiello).

SPAGNOLETTO, It. round dance, possibly of Sp. origin, in 3/4 or in common time, in which the male dancers make the rhythm by clapping their hands against those of the female dancers.

SPAIN, BALLET IN, there are no companies of classical ballet. The Liceo Th. in Barcelona has a ballet master who arranges dances for opera performances. There are many troupes of Spanish dancers.

SPAREMBLEK, Milko, b. Zagreb 1928. Yugoslav dancer and chor. Studied under Roje. Entered Zagreb Ballet 1947 becoming soloist 1953. Joined Charrat's Co. 1955, Miskovitch B. 1956. To Th. de la Monnaie, Brussels 1960 and was director of ballet 1963–64. To Lisbon 1970 to mount ballets for the Gulbenkian B. and was appointed director the same year, in succession to Gore. Among his ballets are *L'Echelle* (1957), *Les Amants de Teruel* (Tcherina's B. 1958), *Monumentum pro Gesualdo* (1971) etc.

SPARTACUS (Russ. *Spartak*), ballet 4 acts, ch. Jacobson, m. Khachaturian, dec. Khodasevich, f.p. Kirov B., Kirov Th., Leningrad 27 Dec 1956 (Makarov, Zubkovskaya, Shelest). Another version, ch. Moiseyev, was f.p. at Bolshoi Th., Moscow 11 Mar 1958, with less success. In

1968 Grigorovitch chor. a further version, f.p. Bolshoi B., Bolshoi Th., Moscow 9 Apr 1968 (Vassiliev, Maximova, Liepa, Timofeyeva), dec. Virsaladze. It was shown in London 1969. Jacobson's version was presented in a shortened form at the Bolshoi Th., Moscow in 1962 with Plisetskaya in the rôle of Phrygia. The story of the runaway slave who incites the Romans to revolt is ideologically very acceptable to the Russians. Another version, ch. Seregi, f.p. Hungarian Nat. B., Budapest 18 May 1968 (Zsuzsa Kun, Fulop, Havas) has had great success in Hungary. Performed at Edinburgh Festival 1973 (A. Orosz, V. Rona).

SPECTRE DE LA ROSE, LE, ballet 1 sc., ch. Fokine, m. Weber, dec. Bakst, f.p. Diaghileff's Co., Monte Carlo 19 Apr 1911 (Karsavina, Nijinsky). This romantic pas de deux was suggested by J.-L. Vaudoyer who had been inspired by a poem of Gautier. It was first danced in Russia by the Nat. B. of Cuba 1964. Then Maris Liepa of the Bolshoi B. decided to revive it and, with help from Karsavina, V. Koralli, A. Ozolin etc. he first danced it, with Bessmertnova in Havana, Cuba 12 Nov 1966. The music, *Invitation to the Dance* (a piano piece), was first used for a ballet 7 June 1841 when Berlioz orchestrated it for the first performance of *Der Freischütz* at the Paris Opéra, chor. Saint-Léon.

SPENCER, Penelope, b. London 1901. Eng. dancer and chor. Pupil Margaret Morris, soloist at C. Garden in the 1920s. The success of her *Funeral Dance of a Rich Aunt* (m. Berners) in the same programme as *A Tragedy of Fashion* (q.v.) did much to popularize the art of ballet in England at a critical time.

SPESSIVTSEVA, Olga (Spessiva), b. Rostov 1895. Russ. dancer. Graduated from Imp. Sch., St Petersburg 1913 and became ballerina 1918. She attracted the attention of Diaghileff in 1913 and he engaged her in 1915 to go to the U.S.A. in place of Karsavina. She rejoined him in 1921 as guest artist to dance *The Sleeping Princess* in London. In 1924 she was engaged by the Paris Opéra, dancing *Giselle* partnered by Aveline and Ricaux and remained there until 1932, also dancing for Diaghileff (cr. rôle of *La Chatte* 1927) in 1926–27. In 1932 danced *Giselle* in London (with Dolin) for the Camargo Society (recorded in a film in the possession of Marie Rambert). Mar. Boris Kniaseff. Étoile of the Paris Opéra 1931. Joined Fokine at Colon Th., Buenos Aires 1932. In 1934 ballerina of Dandré's Co. and went on Australian tour where she suffered fits of depression. To America 1939 and entered mental hospital 1943. In 1963 she was cured and with the help of Dale Fern, Dolin and Dubrovska she was discharged and now lives at Tolstoy Farm, the Russian settlement, N.Y. Many rank her the greatest of the classical dancers of the period.

SPIDER'S BANQUET, THE, see FESTIN DE L'ARAIGNÉE.

SPIES, Daisy, b. Moscow 1905. Ger. dancer. Pupil of Freeden, Gadeskov, Tels, Algo etc. Soloist Berlin Staatsoper 1924–31. In Weimar 1946, director of ballet Berlin Staatsoper 1951–55. Also ballet mistress in Linz. Taught at Wigman's School, Berlin 1962–65.

SPINAZIT, the 'petits rats' at the Scala, Milan.

SPIRA, Phyllis, b. Johannesburg 1943. S. African dancer. Pupil of Renée Solomon and Reina Berman. To Royal Ballet Sch. 1959 and joined Touring Royal B. 1960, becoming soloist 1962. Returned to S. Africa as ballerina of Johannesburg B. and in 1965 Cape Town B., generally partnered there and on tours by Gary Burne. Guest ballerina Canad. Nat. B. 1967.

SPLIT JETÉ, see JETÉ.

SPLITS, THE, an acrobatic feat of throwing oneself to the floor with the legs in a straight line, one in front, one behind. The term was introduced in 1861. Fr. *grand écart*. Ger. *Spagat*. It. *Spaccata*. Also see CISEAUX.

SPOHR, Arnold, b. Rhein, Saskatchewan. Canadian dancer and ballet master. Studied R.A.D. London and in N.Y. Joined Winnipeg B. 1947 and was a principal dancer until 1954. In 1955 chor. for Canadian television. Partnered Markova in *Where the Rainbow Ends*, Coliseum Th., London 1956–57. Appointed Director of R. Winnipeg B. 1958. Chor. *Intermède* 1951, *E Minor* 1959 etc.

SPOLETO FESTIVAL, the 'Festival of Two Worlds' for music and ballet, founded by Gian-Carlo Menotti 1958, taking place annually in July at Spoleto. At the first festival Robbins presented his Ballets: U.S.A. and premièred *N.Y. Export: Jazz*. Other Cos. appearing have been Butler's Chamber Ballets 1958 and 1959, B. Rambert 1963, Royal B. 1964, N.Y. City B. 1965 and Stuttgart B. 1965 and 1967, Harkness B. 1968, Am. Ballet Company (its première) 1969, Am. B. Th. 1970.

SPOTTING, a term used by dancers to describe the movements of the head during quick turns and fouettés, where the eyes fix to a spot in the auditorium or wings while the body is turned. The head is then turned quickly and the eyes return to the same spot, thus obviating giddiness. It. *fissare un punto*.

SPRING TALE, A, ballet 4 acts, ch. Jooss, m. Cohen, dec. Heckroth, f.p. B. Jooss, Stratford-on-Avon 2 Feb 1939 (Soderbaum, Zullig). An allegorical fairy tale.

SPRING WATERS, pas de deux, ch. Messerer, m. Rachmaninoff. A spectacular piece performed by the Russian dancers to show their extreme virtuosity. It contains a leap when the girl hurls herself across the stage and is caught horizontally by her partner and an exit when the man runs off the stage holding the girl aloft on one hand.

SQUARE DANCE, Am. folk dance in which an even number of couples take part, forming lines (a longway set) or a square facing inwards or a circle (a running set). The sequence of the figures is called out by a Caller. One occurs in *Rodeo* and in *Witch Boy*.

SQUARE DANCE, ballet, ch. Balanchine, m. Corelli and Vivaldi, f.p. N.Y. City B., City Center, N.Y. 21 Nov 1957 (Wilde, Magallanes). Also in repertoire of Joffrey B.

STAATS, Leo, b. Paris 1877, d. there 1952. Fr. dancer and chor. A pupil of Mérante, danced at the Opéra where he was maître de ballet 1909–36 and made numerous ballets there, notably *Cydalise et le Chèvre Pied* (1923). In 1933 the Royal Academy of Dancing (then the Operatic Association) commissioned him to make the dances in Berlioz's *Faust* at C. Garden. Opened his own school in Paris.

STAFF, Frank, b. Kimberley, S. Africa 1918, d. Bloemfontein 1971. S. African dancer and chor. Studied under Maude Lloyd and Rambert. Joined B. Rambert, and also danced in S. Wells B. 1934–35 and 1938–39. Danced for B. Rambert and London B. at other times. Chor. *Czernyana, Peter and the Wolf, Enigma Variations*—all for B. Rambert. *Fanciulla delle Rose* for Metropolitan B. etc. Returned to S. Africa to work for Cape Town Univ. B. Joined PACT (Transvaal) B. 1966. Director of Orange Free State B. 1970.

STAGES, entertainment in 2 stages, ch. Cohan, m. Nordheim and Downes, dec. Farmer, f.p. Contemporary Dance Th., The Place, London 22 Apr 1971 (Louther, Lapzeson). Dancing, films, gymnastics etc. on the tiers of seats, with the audience on stage.

STÅHLE, Anna Greta, b. Stockholm 1913. Swed. journalist and writer on the dance. Educ. Univ. of Stockholm. On staff of *Dagens Nyheter* 1954–66 (ballet critic from 1951). Scandinavian correspondent of *Dance News* from 1955, contributor to Chujoy's *Dance Encyclopedia* Now teaches history of dance at Choreographic Institute, Stockholm.

STANISLAVSKY AND NEMIROVITCH-DANTCHENKO THEATRE BAL-LET, Moscow, a troupe ranking high in Russia. In 1930 a well-known dancer, Victorina Kriger, formed a ballet company which sought to incorporate some of the theatrical principles of Stanislavsky. This company danced in Moscow and toured the provinces, and in 1939 it became a part of the Stanislavsky and Nemirovitch-Dantchenko Theatre (which already performed opera and opera-comique). From 1930 to 1971 the choreographer and maître de ballet was (with inter-missions) Vladimir Bourmeister (q.v.), who has choreographed most of its ballets. The repertoire has included *Esmeralda* (1950, ch. Bourmeister, m. Drigo, dec. Louchine), *Swan Lake* (1953, ch. Bourmeister— see under SWAN LAKE), *The Merry Wives of Windsor* (ch. Bourmeister and I. Kourilov, m. Oranski, dec. B. Volkov), *Les Rives du Bonheur* (ch. Bourmeister and I. Kourilov, m. Spadavekkia, dec. B. Volkov). The principal dancers in 1960 (girls) Violetta Bovt, Sofia Vinogradova, Ala Osipenko, (men) Alexis Tchitchinadze, Mikhail Salop, Sviatoslav Kouznetsov. The company appeared at the Châtelet Th., Paris in 1956. On Bourmeister's death in 1971, A. Tchitchinadze became director.

STARR, Helen, b. Beckenham 1940. Eng. dancer. Pupil of Joyce Booth, Royal B. Sch. and entered Royal B. 1958. Joined Festival B. as soloist, and principal 1967–70.

STARS AND STRIPES, ballet, ch. Balanchine, m. Sousa, dec. Hays, cost. Karinska, f.p. N.Y. City B., City Center, N.Y. 17 Jan 1958 (Allegra Kent, Hayden, Adams, d'Amboise). In military costume.

STATE THEATER, THE, New York, in Lincoln Center was opened 23 Apr 1964 by the N.Y. City B. whose home it now is. The architect was Philip Johnson and it seats 2,178. The stage is 80 ft wall to wall (proscenium arch 56 ft wide, 51 ft high) and 58 ft deep. There is a rehearsal room 47 ft by 55 ft. and a practice studio 35 ft by 36 ft. There are also other studios and rehearsal rooms.

STEARNS, Linda, b. Toronto 1937. Canad. dancer and teacher. Pupil of Byers, Bedells, Northcote, Am. Sch. of Ballet. Danced with Carl Rosa Op. and joined Les Grands B. Canadiens 1961, becoming soloist 1964, ballet mistress 1967. Worked with Pennsylvania B. Co. 1969 and 1970. Chor. for R.A.D. Production Club, and in Montreal.

STEPAN, Zlatica, b. Zagreb 1929. Yugoslav dancer. Pupil of Froman and studied in Paris with Preobrajenska and Peretti. Entered Zagreb National B. 1946, becoming ballerina 1950. Danced in London 1955.

STEPANOFF, Vladimir, b. 1866, d. St Petersburg 1896. Russ. dancer whose system of dance notation *Alphabet des Mouvements du Corps Humain*, the Stepanoff System, was published in Paris in 1892 and adopted at the Imperial Sch., St Petersburg in 1893, and at Moscow in 1895. It was with this system that Sergueeff (q.v.) brought the classics to Western Europe. The older living Russ. dancers (Karsavina, Massine etc.) know it and Massine has developed it and uses it in teaching choreography. As a result of his courses at the Royal Ballet Sch. (where it is used) 1968–73, the system is being taught in the Junior Sch. at White Lodge. See illustration to entry DANCE NOTATION.

STEVENSON, Ben, b. Portsmouth 1936. Eng. dancer and chor. Pupil of M. Tonkin and Cone-Ripman Sch. Won Genée Gold Medal 1955. Joined

Theatre Arts B. 1953, Royal B. 1956–60 and Festival B. 1960 and again 1964 (teaching in between). Also teaches in Portsmouth. In 1969 left Festival B. to become ballet master of Harkness Youth B. Chor. many works and in 1967 mounted *Sleeping Beauty* for Festival B. (with Beryl Grey). Chor. *Cinderella* (m. Prokofieff) for Washington Nat. B. 1970, and became assistant director 1971.

STEVENSON, Dorothy, b. Brisbane. Austral. dancer and chor. Studied under Pruzina. Joined de Basil's Co. 1939 and Borovansky Co. 1940, becoming ballerina until 1947. Rejoined Borovansky 1951 until 1952 when she retired and came to live in England. Chor. *Chiaroscuro* (m. Schumann) and *Sea Legend* (m. Rofe, dec. Bainbridge) 1945 for Borovansky Co., revived for International B., Granada Th., Clapham 24 Feb 1948 (Stevenson, de Lutry).

STEVENSON, Hugh, b. 1910, d. London 1956. Eng. designer. First décor *Unbowed* (1932) at Mercury Th. for Ballet Club. Designs include, for B. Rambert *The Planets, Jardin aux Lilas, Gala Performance, Giselle, The Fugitive*; for S. Wells B. *Swan Lake* (1934), *Gods Go A-begging, Promenade*; for S. Wells Th. B. *Mardi Gras, Pastorale*; for Festival B. *Giselle, Symphonic Impressions* (Lichine).

STILL POINT, THE, ballet, ch. Bolender, m. Debussy, f.p. N.Y. City B., City Center, N.Y. 13 Mar 1956 (Hayden, d'Amboise). A lonely girl who searches for understanding. Many companies dance it. Its first performance was at Jacob's Pillow 3 Aug 1955 by the Dance Drama Co. (Frankel, Ryder).

STONE, Bentley, b. Plankinton, S. Dakota. Cont. Am. dancer, chor. and teacher. With Ruth Page, founded Page-Stone Ballet 1938–41. Guest artist B. Rambert 1937. Teaches in Chicago.

STONE FLOWER, TALE OF THE, ballet, ch. Lavrovsky, m. Prokofieff, dec. Starzhentsky, f.p. Bolshoi Th., Moscow 12 Feb 1954 (Plisetskaya, Chorokhova, Yermolayeff, Koren, Preobrazhensky. Later Ulanova, Struchkova). A new version, ch. Grigorovitch, dec. Virsaladze, f.p. Kirov Th., Leningrad 27 Apr 1957 (Kolpakova, Osipenko, Gribov, Gridin). Lavrovsky produced this new version at the Bolshoi Th., Moscow 7 Mar 1959 (Plisetskaya, Vasiliev, Maximova, Levashov). The Mistress of the Copper Mountain helps a Stone Cutter to find his ideal of beauty.

STRATE, Grant, b. Cardston, Alberta 1927. Canadian dancer and chor. Pupil of Mets, Franca, Oliphant. Joined Nat. B. of Canada 1951, becoming soloist 1953 and in 1958 resident choreographer. Chor. *The Fisherman and his Soul, The Willow, House of Atreus* (1963) etc. Chor. for R. Flemish B. Antwerp 1966. From 1958–66 assistant to

471

director of Canadian Nat. B. and resident chor. from 1960. In 1970 appointed associate professor and director of the Programme in Dance, York University, Toronto.

STRATHSPEY, national dance of Scotland in a slow common time, said to derive its name from the Strath, the valley of the Spey. It was known well before the late eighteenth century.

STRAVINSKY, Igor, b. Oranienbaum 1882, d. N.Y. 1971. Russ. composer, son of an opera singer. Studied under Rimsky-Korsakov. Diaghileff heard his *Fantastic Scherzo* and *Fireworks* at a concert in 1909 and commissioned him to compose the music for *L'Oiseau de Feu*. He became one of Diaghileff's closest collaborators, and composed *Petrouchka* (1911), *Sacre du Printemps* (1913), *Le Rossignol* (1914), *Pulcinella* (1920), *Les Noces* (1923), and *Apollon-Musagète* (1928). He remained in the West and settled in America. Other ballets composed by him are *Baiser de la Fée* (1928), *Persephone* (1934), *Jeu de Cartes* (1937), *Orpheus* (1948), *Danses Concertantes* (1944), *Scènes de Ballet*, *Octet* (1958) and *Agon* (1957) etc. See NEW YORK CITY B. for the 1972 Stravinsky Festival, N.Y.

STREETCAR NAMED DESIRE, A, ballet, ch. Bettis, m. North, dec. Bolasni, f.p. Slavenska-Franklin Co., Her Majesty's Th., Montreal 9 Oct 1952 (Slavenska, Franklin). Version of Tennessee Williams's play. In repertoire of Am. Ballet Th.

STREET GAMES, ballet, ch. Gore, m. Ibert, dec. Wilson, f.p. New Ballet Co., Wimbledon Th. 11 Nov 1952 (Angela Bayley, Constance Garfield, Margaret Kovac, Shelagh Miller, Jack Skinner, Kenneth Smith, Nigel Burke). Children playing with hoops and skipping ropes. Often revived in other Cos.

STRIKE, Lois, b. Sydney 1948. Austral. dancer. Pupil of Scully-Borovansky Sch. To Royal B. Sch. 1965, joined Royal B. 1966 and became soloist 1972. Principal 1973.

STRIPLING, Jan, b. Essen 1941. Ger. dancer. Pupil of Jooss, Anne Woolliams, Tudor, Volkova. Danced in Ballet Jooss 1961–67. Soloist Stuttgart B. 1969.

STROBEL, Fredric, b. Chicago 1936. Am. dancer. Pupil of Berenice Holmes and Sch. of Am. B. Joined Birmingham (U.S.A.) Civic B. 1956, R. Winnipeg B. 1957, Chicago Opera B. 1959, returned to R. Winnipeg B. 1960 becoming a principal dancer. Joined Washington Nat. B. 1970.

STROGANOVA, Nina, b. Copenhagen. Danish dancer and teacher. Pupil of Moller and R. Danish B. Sch. and Preobrajenska. Ballerina Opéra Comique, Paris 1936, Mordkin B. 1937, B. Theatre 1940, Orig.

B. Russe 1942–47. Guest ballerina R. Danish B. 1950. Now teaches with her husband V. Dokoudovsky in N.Y.

STRUCHKOVA, Raisa, b. 1925. Russ. dancer. Entered Moscow Sch. 1935, pupil of E. Gerdt, graduating 1944. Now one of the prima ballerinas at Moscow. Honoured Artist of the R.S.F.R. Danced in England (where she is extremely popular) 1954, 1956, 1963, 1968, Stockholm 1955. Mar. Lapauri.

STUART, Muriel, b. London 1903. Eng. dancer and teacher. Pupil of Pavlova at Ivy Lodge, Cecchetti, Graham etc. Soloist of Pavlova Co. 1916–26. Opened School in San Francisco 1927, ballet mistress Chicago Civic Opera 1930. Taught in San Francisco 1931–34. From 1934 teacher at Sch. of Am. B. Author of *The Classic Ballet: Basic Technique and Terminology* (1952).

STUKOLKIN, Timofei, b. 1829, d. St Petersburg 1894. Russ. character dancer. Joined Maryinsky B. 1848 and excelled in comic and character rôles. To Moscow as guest artist 1851. He was the first Dr Coppélius in St Petersburg (1884), and created the rôles of Drosselmeyer in *Casse Noisette* (1892) and Catalabutte in *Sleeping Beauty* (1890). He died after the second act of *Coppélia* in which he was playing Dr Coppélius and in which Karsavina was making her first appearance on the Maryinsky stage (as one of the crowd).

STURMAN, Marjorie, b. London 1902. Eng. teacher. Pupil of Madame Ravodna (Ray Espinosa) in Johannesburg and also of Judith and Édouard Espinosa and Volkova in London. Began teaching in Pretoria 1922 and became Ravodna's assistant. Opened her own school in Johannesburg 1934. In 1926 passed her R.A.D. examinations and introduced the R.A.D. system to South Africa. Founded the Pretoria Ballet Club 1943 and in 1944 (with Ivy Conmee and Poppy Frames) formed the Festival Ballet Society which was the beginning of ballet productions in Johannesburg. It existed until 1956 (see PACT BALLET). In 1953 the Transvaal Education Authority established an Art Ballet and Music School in Johannesburg and she has been the principal ballet teacher there ever since, training most of the dancers who later joined PACT B. and the Royal B.

STUTTGART BALLET, THE. In 1759 the Duke Carl Eugene of Württemberg invited J. G. Noverre to Stuttgart to take control of the dancers who were already attached to his Court, and he remained there until 1767 when he went to Vienna. During those eight years in Stuttgart he was greatly respected for his work. But little more is heard of the ballet in the court or city, though it continued to support a ballet, until after the Second World War. At that time, and for the twenty years or so preceding, the style was 'Central European' in common with the rest of Germany, and in 1945 the Co. reopened with Anneliese Mörike as ballet mistress (she is still attached to the Co. as Assistant). She was followed by Bernhard Wosien, Oscar Lemanis and by Robert Mayer who, between 1950 and 1957 produced *Giselle, Swan Lake, Puppenfee, Scènes de Ballet, Les Noces, Cinderella* etc., all chor. by himself.

It was not until 1957, when Nicholas Beriozoff was appointed ballet master, that any significant change took place. His *Sleeping Beauty* in 1957 was a turning point. It was remarkably well received and he followed this with *Les Sylphides* and *Giselle* in 1958, *Nutcracker* in 1959 and *Swan Lake* in 1960. By this time the public had become lovers of classical ballet and his dancers of a high standard (he had Xenia Palley, Dulce Anaya, Georgette Tsinguirides, Hugo Delavalle, Donald Barclay).

On Beriozoff's leaving, the Intendant, Dr Erich Schäfer, invited John Cranko of the Royal Ballet to succeed him as ballet master in 1960. Cranko's first production was his *Prince of the Pagodas* (1961) which he had created for the Royal B. In it he presented his new prima ballerina, Marcia Haydee, who had been a soloist of the de Cuevas B. She has been his most distinguished artist ever since. He introduced several Royal B. ballets (*Solitaire* by MacMillan, *Antigone* and *Lady and the Fool* by himself) and in 1962 chor. his *Romeo and Juliet* which set the seal on his work and his company. He paid particular attention, during his early years, to his young students (Birgit Keil was among them) and sent them to train at the Royal Ballet School and engaged Anne Woolliams as his teacher. His enthusiasm and easy manners (so unlike those prevailing in the German opera houses) were infused into the whole company and made it unique in Germany for its discipline and atmosphere of creativity. Among his important ballets have been *Katalyse* 1961, *Swan Lake* 1963, *Onegin* 1965, *Opus 1* 1965, *Concerto for Flute and Harp* 1966, and above all *The Taming of the Shrew* 1969. He died returning from New York in 1973

Such is the excellence of the company that dancers from all over the world clamour to join it and among the dancers are Marcia Haydee (ballerina throughout Cranko's reign), Birgit Keil, Susanne Hanke, Judith Reyn, Jane Landon, Egon Madsen, Richard Cragun, Heinz Clauss, Bernd Berg, Jan Stripling. In 1971 Cranko opened a full-time residential ballet school on the lines of those in Paris, Moscow and London, with Anne Woolliams in charge, and also started a second company, the Noverre Ballet (q.v.). MacMillan has created some of his best ballets for Stuttgart—*Las Hermanas* 1963 and *Song of the Earth* 1965, and members of the troupe have distinguished themselves elsewhere—John

Neumeier as ballet master in Frankfurt and Hamburg, Ray Barra as a teacher etc.

The Stuttgart Ballet danced at the Edinburgh Festival in 1953, and have appeared in Vienna, Paris, Spoleto, Baalbek, Rio de Janeiro, and in 1969 made their first visit to New York followed by a tour of the U.S. arranged by Sol Hurok. In 1971 they toured Russia. Cranko continues to pour out a stream of new ballets and (backed by the Intendant Dr Schäfer) has made his company the best in Germany and one of the best in the world.

SUBLIGNY, Marie, b. 1666, d. c. 1736. Fr. dancer who succeeded Lafontaine at the Paris Opéra. She danced in London 1700–2 and was the first professional ballerina to be seen in England.

SUBRA, Julia, b. Paris 1866, d. 1908. Andalusian dancer. Pupil of Zina Mérante. Début at Opéra in *Hamlet* 1882 and was an étoile there 1882–98 at the time of Rosita Mauri. Cr. one of the leading rôles in *Namouna* 1882.

SUGAR PLUM VARIATION, the ballerina's solo (ch. Ivanov) in the last act of *Casse Noisette*, danced to the accompaniment of the celesta (the first music to be composed for this instrument). It was originally danced by Antonietta dell'Era.

SUITE DE DANSES, ballet, ch. Clustine, m. Chopin, f.p. Paris Opéra 23 June 1913. Inspired by *Les Sylphides*, it was remade by Aveline in 1931 (Spessivtseva, Lifar).

SUITE EN BLANC, ballet, ch. Lifar, m. Lalo (from the ballet *Namouna*), f.p. Paris Opéra B., Grand Th., Zürich 19 June 1943 (Darsonval, Schwarz, Chauviré, Bardin, Dynalix, Ivanov, Lifar, Fenonjois, Ritz). It was then presented at the Paris Opéra 23 July 1943 (same cast). This is a ballet blanc with no décor, and displays all the Company. A version, under the title *Noir et Blanc*, was danced by the Nouveau B. de Monte Carlo (1966) and by de Cuevas Co. Festival B. also dance *Noir et Blanc*, f.p. Festival Hall, London 15 Sept 1966 (Aldous, Samtsova, Miklosy, Gilpin). Also in repertoire of Dutch Nat. B. (reproduced by R. Cazenave).

SUITE NO. 3, ballet, ch. Balanchine, m. Tchaikovsky, dec. N. Benois, f.p. N.Y. City B., State Th., N.Y. 3 Dec 1970 (von Aroldingen, Mazzo, Morris, G. Kirkland, Blum, Ludlow, Clifford, Villella). The final section of this is his 1947 ballet *Theme and Variations*.

SUJET, see BALLERINA.

SULICH, Wassili, b. Puscice 1929. Yugoslav dancer. Studied under Anna Roje, de Vos, Kniaseff. Début 1946 in folklore troupe. Danced in Zagreb Ballet 1946–49, in Charrat's Co. 1956–59, Miskovitch's Co. and

Massine's Balletto Europeo in Nervi and Edinburgh 1960. Worked in Lyon, Geneva 1962 and 1964. From 1964 director of the Folies-Bergère troupe in Las Vegas.

SUMEN, Meric (Güventürk), b. Istanbul 1943. Turkish dancer. Trained under Molly Lake and Beatrice Appleyard in Istanbul and Ankara and Royal B. Sch. in London. Entered Turkish State Ballet and became prima ballerina in 1963. The first Turk to dance Aurora in *Sleeping Beauty* (Ankara 1963).

SUMMER INTERLUDE, ballet, ch. Michael Somes, m. Respighi's arrangement of Old It. Airs and Dances, dec. Fedorovitch, f.p. S. Wells Th. B., S. Wells Th. 28 Mar 1950 (Patricia Miller, Elaine Fifield, Trecu, Blair). Flirtations on a beach.

SUMNER, Carol, b. Brooklyn 1940. Am. dancer. Pupil of Sch. of Am. B. Joined N.Y. City B. becoming soloist 1963.

SUNAL, Husnu, b. Istanbul 1937. Turkish dancer. Studied in Turkey under Joy Newton, Beatrice Appleyard, Molly Lake, becoming principal dancer of Turkish National B. in 1957.

SUNDAY BALLET CLUB, organized by James Ranger and Francis Sitwell (both of the Oxford University Ballet Club) gave its first performance at Wyndham's Th., London 23 Mar 1958. It gave performances of new ballets by new chors., danced and produced professionally. Its most successful work was *One in Five* (q.v.) in 1960. Dissolved in 1966.

SUN MUSIC, ballet in 5 movements, ch. Helpmann, m. Sculthorpe, dec. and cost. K. Rowell, f.p. Australian B. at Her Majesty's Th., Sydney 2 Aug 1968 (Josephine Jason, Karl Welander). Differing scenes under the Australian sun.

SUNSHINE MATINÉES were founded in 1919 by Mrs Dorothy Claremont, organizer of the Sunshine Homes for Blind Babies, and P. J. S. Richardson (q.v.) to show the development in stage dancing in England each year. The first was at the Queen's Theatre, London 25 Nov 1919 in the presence of the Queen of Spain (in aid of the Sunshine Homes), the last in 1930. There were ten in all and among the dancers appearing were Mary Wigman, Camille Bos, Yvonne Daunt, Trefilova, Dolin, Bedells, Markova, de Valois, Astafieva etc., and Ashton's early ballet *Leda and the Swan*, danced by 'the Marie Rambert Dancers' and conducted by Constant Lambert (his first appearance as a conductor), was first presented in public at the Matinée at the Apollo Th., London 10 July 1928. The Matinées came to an end in 1930, by which time the Ballet Club and the Vic-Wells B. had been established. They played an important part in the history of ballet in England until the foundation of the Camargo Society which took over their functions. In 1965 Beryl Grey became president of the *All England Sunshine Dancing Competition* and she presented the first Sunshine Gala, Drury Lane Th. 13 July 1965. This competition started in 1924 at the suggestion of Lillie Cone (q.v.) and is also in aid of the Sunshine Homes. The early heats are held throughout England and the judges give their services free. It is for people of all ages up to 22 and includes most forms of dancing. The Beryl Grey Award is given to the best classical dancer.

SUPPORTING LEG, the leg supporting the body so as to leave the working leg free to execute a given movement.

SURINACH, Carlos, b. Barcelona 1915. Sp. composer. Studied in Barcelona, Düsseldorf, Cologne. Conducted in Paris 1947 and in 1951 went to N.Y. where he now lives and composes. His scores have been used for many modern ballets, notably *Ritmo Jondo* (ch. Humphrey 1952), *Embattled Garden* and *Acrobats of God* (ch. Graham), *A Place in the Desert* (ch. Morrice), *Hazana* (ch. Morrice), *La Sibla* (ch. Butler), *Feast of Ashes* (ch. Ailey) etc.

SURMEJAN, Hazaros, b. Skoplje 1943. Yugoslav dancer. Pupil of A. Dobrohotov in Skoplje and Hightower in Cannes. Joined Skoplje B. 1960 becoming soloist. Joined Mannheim B. 1962, Cologne B. 1963–66. Principal dancer Canad. Nat. B. 1966.

SUSANA AND JOSÉ, a pair of dancers who gave recitals of Spanish dancing and flamenco. Susana is Susana Audeoud (q.v.) and José is José Udaeta (q.v.). They began their recitals in 1948, in Geneva, and until 1970 they toured the world together.

SUS-SOUS, or SOUS-SUS, lit. over-under or under-over. A familiar name for a temps de cou-de-pied (q.v.). Probably from Fr. *dessus-dessous*, but it has also been suggested that it is from the It. *su e giù*, up and down.

SUTHERLAND, Paul, b. Louisville 1935. Am. dancer. Pupil of Hancock. Joined Am. Ballet Th., R. Winnipeg B. and in 1958 Joffrey B. creating many leading rôles. Joined Am. Ballet Th. 1964, becoming a principal dancer 1966, and Joffrey B. 1967. Mar. Brunilda Ruiz.

SUTOWSKI, Thor, b. New Jersey 1945. Am. dancer. Danced in San Francisco B. and later Washington Nat. B. Joined Norwegian B. as soloist 1966, principal 1968. To Hamburg 1970. Mar. Sonia Arova.

SVETLANA, ballet 3 acts, ch. Popko, Posspekhine, Radunsky, m. Klebanoff, f.p. Bolshoi Th., Moscow 20 Dec 1939 (Lepeshinskaya, Kondratov, Messerer). Spy story, set in a forest, introducing Kazakh, Ukrainian, etc., dances.

SVETLOVA, Marina (née von Hartmann), b. Paris 1922. Fr. dancer. Studied Trefilova, Egorova, Gsovsky. Soloist de Basil 1939, Ballet Th.

1942–43, ballerina Met. Op., N.Y. 1943–50. From 1953 had her own Co. touring Europe and U.S.A. Guest artist Festival B., R. Swed. B., Finnish B., Opéra-Comique, London Palladium. Director of Dallas Civic B. 1965. From 1970 chairman of the Dept. of Ballet, Indiana Univ., Bloomington, U.S.A.

SVETLOW, Valerien, b. 1860, d. Paris 1934. Russ. author and ballet critic whose *Le Ballet Contemporain* (1911, St Petersburg), decorated by Bakst and with many reproductions, drawings, and photographs, is one of the most comprehensive and beautiful books on ballet ever produced. Mar. Vera Trefilova. Left Russia 1917 and settled in Paris.

SWAN LAKE, THE (*Le Lac des Cygnes;* Russ. *Lebedinoe Ozero*), ballet in 4 acts, book Begitchev and Geltser, ch. Wenzel Reisinger (b. 1827, d. 1892), m. Tchaikovsky, dec. Shangin, Valts and Groppius, f.p. Bolshoi Th., Moscow 20 Feb 1877 (Pelageia Karpakova, b. 1845, d. 1920, as Odette-Odile, Gillert II as Siegfried). This version was a failure. The music seemed revolutionary to the semi-amateur conductor and was pronounced impossible of execution, with the result that cuts were made in the score and dances from other ballets interpolated; the dec. and cost. were poor and the choreography indifferent. Tchaikovsky seems to have attributed the failure in some measure to his score and said he would revise it, but died before he could do so. The ballet was revived in Moscow 13 Jan 1880 with ch. by J. Hansen (q.v.), but this also was unsuccessful. In 1893 the Imperial Theatres at St Petersburg sent to Moscow for the score and entrusted a revival to Petipa, who had already produced *The Sleeping Princess*. He sketched out the dances and left their completion to his assistant Ivanov. The difference in the characterization is accentuated by the lyrical tenderness of the 2nd and 4th acts due to Ivanov, opposed to the hard brilliance of Petipa's choreography in the 3rd act. The composer died in November 1893, and the 2nd act only was given at a memorial concert of Tchaikovsky's work at the Maryinsky Th. 1 Mar 1894, with Legnani as Odette.

The first performance of the complete ballet, dec. Botcharov and Levogt, was given at the same theatre on 27 Jan 1895, with Legnani as Odette-Odile, Gerdt as Siegfried. It was an immediate success and is the version seen in Western Europe and the U.S.

In 1901 Gorsky revived *Swan Lake* in Moscow, with his own revisions, and the version now in the Soviet repertoire is his new version of the first 3 acts with the 4th act by A. Messerer.

The 1st act is in the nature of a prologue in which great use is made of traditional mime. The 2nd act is complete in itself and is often given separately. It is almost pure dancing and introduces a number of variations of great beauty. The 3rd act (the ballroom scene, with Odile) contains a number of character dances and includes, in the coda of the Black Swan *pas de deux*, the famous thirty-two fouettés. The 4th act is short and contains some of the most moving music in the ballet. The rôles of Odette and Odile are usually interpreted by one ballerina, on whom it makes a heavy demand, both by reason of the high technical proficiency required and of the dual personality to be expressed. Occasionally two dancers take the two rôles. The ballet had its 1,000th performance at the Bolshoi Th. 20 Oct 1965 (Plisetskaya, Fadeyechev).

Swan Lake was first performed in England 16 May 1910 at the Hippodrome, London (Preobrajenska). In France by Diaghileff's Co. at Monte Carlo 13 Apr 1912 (Kschessinska). In America the first performance was 19 Dec 1911 (Geltzer) at the Met .Op. In Denmark on 8 Feb 1938 at the Royal Th., Copenhagen (Margot Lander). The Vic-Wells B. first performed the complete ballet, reproduced by Sergueeff, dec. Stevenson, at S. Wells Th. 20 Nov 1934 (Markova, Helpmann). A new production was given at the New Th., London, with dec. Hurry 7 Sept 1943 (Fonteyn, Helpmann), and another production, with new dec. by Hurry, at C. Garden 18 Dec 1952 (Grey, Field).

The International Ballet gave the full-length *Swan Lake* by Sergueeff, dec. Chappell, at Adelphi Th., London 18 Mar 1947 (Inglesby, Spurgeon). The R. Swedish B. gave its first full-length version, arranged by Mary Skeaping, in 1953 (Mariane Orlando, Teddy Rhodin). The N.Y. City B. danced Act II of *Swan Lake* in a new version by Balanchine, dec. Beaton, f.p. City Center, N.Y. 20 Nov 1951 (Maria Tallchief, Eglevsky). At the Stanislavsky and Nemirovitch-Dantchenko Th., Moscow, a new complete version was mounted by Bourmeister on 24 Apr 1953, using the original (and some hitherto unused) music of Tchaikovsky. Costumes were by Arkhangelskaia, dec. by Louchine, and Odile-Odette was danced by Bovt. The first full-length *Swan Lake* to be produced in Germany was in Munich 3 Dec 1959, mounted by Skeaping and Joan Harris (Anaya, Hallhuber). Bourmeister mounted his 1953 Moscow version at the Paris Opéra, dec. Bouchêne, f.p. 21 Dec 1960 (Amiel, Van Dijk) and for Festival B., dec. Delany, f.p. Festival Hall, London 31 July 1961 (Borowska, Briansky). At the Colon Th., Buenos Aires, a new version using the original 1877 score was chor. Jack Carter 28 May 1963 (Fontenla as Odette, Agoglia as Odile, Lommi as Siegfried). This version he mounted for Festival B., dec. Truscott, f.p. Fenice Th., Venice 12 Feb. 1966 (Maryon Lane as Odette, Aldous as Odile, Gilpin). Just previously Festival B. had had a version chor. Orlikowski (Act 2 was Bourmeister), f.p. Arena, Verona 1 Aug 1964 (Samtsova, Gilpin). Cranko chor. for Stuttgart B., dec. Rose, f.p. Stuttgart 14 Nov 1963 (Haydee, Barra). He mounted this for Munich B. 9 Apr 1970 (Vernon,

Bosl). The Royal B. mounted a new production, after Petipa-Ivanov but new chor. by Ashton (Nureyev and Fay) and produced by Helpmann, dec. Toms, f.p. C. Garden 12 Dec 1963 (Fonteyn, Blair). The Touring Royal B. had a new version, ch. Ashton, dec. Hurry, f.p. C. Garden 18 May 1965 (Nerina, Labis). For the Vienna Staatsoper B. Nureyev mounted his version, dec. Georgiadis 15 Oct 1964 (Wührer, Nureyev). For the Deutsche Oper B., W. Berlin, MacMillan chor. a version, dec. Georgiadis, f.p. 14 May 1969 (Seymour, Frey). R. Danish B., Copenhagen, ch. Flindt, dec. Bo, f.p. 14 May 1968 (Simone, Flindt). Bolshoi B., Moscow, ch. Grigorovitch, dec. Virsaladze, f.p. 25 Dec 1969 (Bessmertnova, Fadeyechev). Beryl Grey made a new version for Festival B. (dec. Truscott), f.p. Congress Th., Eastbourne 28 Feb 1972 (Samtsova, Dubreuil).

SWAY BACK, a description to describe a dancer's legs when, looked at from the side, they are not straight but curved with the knees lying behind the line joining the hips to the ankles. Technically called hyperextended knees, popularly 'banana legs'. Compare *arqué* and *jarreté*, the other two descriptions of the legs.

SWEDEN, BALLET IN, see under SWEDISH BALLET, ROYAL, SCANDINAVIAN BALLET and CRAMER BALLET. There are also municipal ballets at Gothenburg (directed by Elsa Marianne von Rosen) and at Malmö (directed by Conny Borg).

SWEDISH BALLET, THE ROYAL, was founded in 1773 by Gustavus III, the 'Theatre King'. There was already a good corps de ballet in Stockholm from troupes of Fr. dancers and actors. One of these Fr. dancers, Louis Gallodier (b. 1733, d. 1803), who arrived from the Paris Opéra in 1758, was appointed the first ballet master. In 1782, Antoine Bournonville, who married a Swede, became premier danseur and introduced the principles of his master Noverre, whose *Lettres sur la Danse* he published in Swedish. On the whole the R. Swed. B. has relied on its own good corps de ballet but with foreign maîtres de ballet and visiting ballerinas. From 1809–16 and 1818–20, Louis Delande was ballet master. A Fr. comic dancer, and a great eater and drinker, he had studied in Paris under Gardel: he was the last of the 'Gustavus III epoch'. F. Taglioni (who had also married a Swede in 1803 when he was premier danseur in Stockholm) was ballet master in 1818. In 1833 the first Swed. ballet master was appointed, Anders Selinder (q.v.). He reigned 1833–45 and 1851–56, and introduced the Romantic ballet to Sweden (*La Sylphide* was first danced there in 1841). August Bournonville made several visits to Stockholm, and it was to him at Copenhagen that the great Swedish dancer Christian Johansson went to study— only to make his reputation in Russia. Selinder was succeeded by

Sigurd Lund, a Dane, ballet master 1856–62 and 1890–94 (his wife, Hilda Lund, was principal dancer 1866–68). He presented many Bournonville ballets in Stockholm. A famous dancer at the time was Charlotte Norberg (q.v.). The ballet went into a decline at the end of the nineteenth and beginning of the twentieth centuries. In 1913 Fokine went to Stockholm, mounting his ballets and dancing in them with his wife, Vera Fokina, making a renaissance of the art in Sweden. He came again in 1914, 1917, 1918, 1919, and 1925, and in his later seasons his prima ballerina was the talented Jenny Hasselquist (q.v.). In 1920 Sven Tropp became ballet master and it was at this time the Ballets Suédois (q.v.) were formed. The Pole, Jan Cieplinsky (q.v.), ballet master in 1927, was succeeded in 1931 by Julian Algo (q.v.) who, with his ballet *Orpheus in Town* and others, introduced a modern element into the Opera. Dancers of that period were Carina Ari, Cissi Olsson, Elly Holmberg, Ebon Strandin, Brita Appelgren, C. G. Kruuse. In 1940 a Finnish musician, George Gé (Grönfeldt), was appointed, mounting classical works. The 'Central European' influence has always been strong in Sweden and the ballets of Birgit Cullberg and Åkesson (q.v.) have lately become successful features of the repertoire, whilst in 1953 Mary Skeaping (q.v.) was appointed ballet mistress, mounting full-length classics and bringing the R. Swed. B. into the great ballet revival which is now current. The Opera House (built on the site of the 1782 one) was opened in 1898, and seats 1,187 people. The stage measures 82 ft wide by 108 ft deep. In 1955 the principal dancers were von Rosen, Lindgren, Orlando, Holmgren, Rhodin, Mengarelli, and Beryl Grey made guest artist appearances in 1953 and 1955. In 1955 also Struchkova and Kondratov from the Bolshoi Th., Moscow, were guest artists. In 1960 Gerd Andersson and Caj Selling were added to the principal dancers. The Co. danced at the Edinburgh Festival 1957 and in America 1958. Skeaping retired in 1962 (but returned regularly to stage ballets for the Drottningholm Court Th.) and was succeeded by Tudor who revived several of his works and created *Echoing of Trumpets* for the Co. 1963. In 1964 Brian Macdonald took his place, presenting many of his ballets, taking the Co. to the International Ballet Festival in Paris and instituting the annual Ballet Festival in Stockholm in June 1965. He left 1966 and was succeeded by Erik Bruhn 1967, who mounted his *La Sylphide* and Nureyev his *Casse Noisette* 1968. In 1970 the principal dancers were Gerd Andersson, Yvonne Brosset, Mariane Orlando, Berit Skold, Annette av Paul, Maria Lang, Lillemor Arvidsson, Hervor Sjostrand, Nils-Ake Håggbom, Verner Klavsen, Nisse Winqvist, Jonas Kåge. In 1972 James Moore became director, succeeding Erik Bruhn.

SWEET DANCER, ballet, ch. Gore, m. F. Martin, dec. Cordwell, f.p.

B. Rambert, New Th., Oxford 17 June 1964 (Hinton, Chesworth). The Yeats poem on a mad girl.

SWINSON, Cyril, b. London 1910, d. St Albans 1963. Eng. publisher and writer on ballet. Director of publishers A. & C. Black, London and made them famous for their list of ballet books. Author of many books on ballet (under *nom de plume* Hugh Fisher or Joseph Sandon), notably *Ballet for Boys and Girls* (1952), *Story of the Sadler's Wells Ballet* (1954), *Guidebook to the Ballet* (1961) and fifteen books on famous contemporary dancers. On editorial board of *Ballet Annual*. He was also a writer and producer of pageants.

SWITZERLAND, BALLET IN, there are municipal companies in Zürich (directed by Geoffrey Cauley), Geneva (directed by Patricia Neary), Bern (directed by Anna Menge), Lucern (directed by Riccardo Duse), Biel, Basel (directed by Heinz Spoerli) and St Gallen.

SYLPHIDE, LA, ballet 2 acts, book A. Nourrit, ch. Filippo Taglioni, m. Schneitzhöffer, dec. Ciceri, cost. Lami, f.p. Paris Opéra 12 Mar 1832 (Marie Taglioni, Noblet, Mazilier, and Mme Elie as the Sorceress). This work, by its success, launched the Romantic era in ballet and altered the whole path of ballet, which hitherto had used classical themes for its stories. Gautier wrote: 'After *La Sylphide* it was not possible to present *Les Filets de Vulcan* or *Flore et Zéphire*: henceforth gnomes, undines, salamanders, elves, nixes, wilis, peris ... have taken over the Opéra.' On 21 Nov 1831 a ballet of nuns by Filippo Taglioni (in which his daughter appeared) in the opera *Robert the Devil* at the Opéra had caused a great sensation. The tenor in the opera, Adolphe Nourrit, suggested to Dr Véron, the Director of the Opéra, the scenario of a ballet, based on Nodier's story *Trilby ou le Lutin d'Argail*, called *La Sylphide*. The Scottish setting, with its theme of a supernatural being falling in love with a mortal, epitomized the Romantic movement in literature. The costume created for Taglioni, with its tight-fitting bodice, leaving neck and shoulders bare, and its white muslin bell-shaped skirt, coming midway between knee and ankle, rapidly became the accepted costume for the danseuse in the Romantic ballet. In this ballet also dancing on the points first fully established itself. The ballet was first performed (by Taglioni) in London 26 July 1832 (C. Garden), St Petersburg 18 Sept 1837 (Maryinsky Th.), Milan 29 May 1841 (La Scala). It has been revived for the Ballets des Ch. Élysées, ch. Gsovsky, dec. Serebriakoff, cost. Bérard, Th. des Ch. Élysées, Paris 15 June 1946 (Vyroubova, Petit). It has been in the repertoire of the Royal Danish B., ch. Bournonville after F. Taglioni, m. Lovenskjold, since 28 Nov 1836 (Lucile Grahn, Bournonville). Lander mounted a version of this for de Cuevas Co., Empire Th.,

Paris 9 Dec 1953 (Hightower, Golovine), dec. B. Daydé. A ballet *La Sylphide* was also produced by Henry (q.v.) at the Scala, Milan in 1827. The Danish (Bournonville) version was mounted for the Ballet Rambert by Elsa Marianne von Rosen, S. Wells Th. 20 July 1960, dec. R. &. C. Ironside (von Rosen, Flindt). At Scala, Milan, Lander mounted it (dec. Varesio) 18 Jan 1962 (Fracci, Pistoni). Bruhn also mounted it for Scala, Milan 24 Mar 1966 (Fracci, Nureyev) and for R. Swed. B., Stockholm 1 June 1968 (Andersson, Haggbom). Lander also mounted the Danish version for Am. Ballet Th., with additional music by Cosma, f.p. San Antonio, Texas 11 Nov 1964 (Toni Lander, Royes Fernandez). Bruhn mounted it for Nat. B. of Canada, Toronto, f.p. 31 Dec 1964 (Seymour, Bruhn). At Bremen, Adama chor. the Schneitzhöffer version, dec. Herrmann, f.p. 10 Dec 1964 (Elizabeth Paul, Zink). After making researches into the original (Paris Opéra) production of 1832, Pierre Lacotte mounted a version for French Television, embodying his discoveries 1 Jan 1972 (Ghislaine Thesmar, Michaël Denard). This version, cost. Michel Fresnay (after Lami), dec. Marie-Claire Musson (after Ciceri) was presented at the Paris Opéra 7 June 1972 (Noella Pontois, Cyril Atanassoff) and subsequently for a season at the Th. des Ch. Élysées, with numerous cast changes (Thesmar at the Opéra 14 June 1972).

SYLPHIDES, LES, ballet 1 act, ch. Fokine, m. Chopin, dec. Benois, f.p. outside Russia by Diaghileff's Co., Th. du Châtelet, Paris 2 June 1909 (Pavlova, pas de deux and mazurka; Karsavina, valse; Baldina, prelude; Nijinsky, pas de deux and mazurka). The first performance of *Chopiniana*, in the form subsequently renamed by Diaghileff *Les Sylphides* (probably to recall *La Sylphide*), was given at a charity performance at the Maryinsky Th., St Petersburg 8 Mar 1908 (Preobrajenska, Pavlova, Karsavina, Nijinsky). On 10 Feb 1907 Fokine had presented a ballet *Chopiniana* at a charity performance. This was set to a suite of Chopin pieces of that name, orchestrated by Glazounov, and was a series of scenes in national costumes. One of these scenes was a pas de deux to the valse, danced by Oboukhoff and Pavlova, who wore the long white tutu of *La Sylphide*. From this dance came the conception the following year of *Chopiniana* as a ballet blanc.

After the Prelude (Op. 28, No. 7) played as an overture, the curtain rises on a Nocturne (Op. 32, No. 2) danced by the entire company, followed by the Valse (Op. 70, No. 1) danced by a première danseuse, the Mazurka (Op. 33, No. 2) usually danced by the prima ballerina (although she is sometimes cast in another of the pas seuls), the Mazurka (Op. 76, No. 3) for the premier danseur, a repeat of the prelude danced by another première danseuse, the pas de deux danced by the two principals to the Valse (Op. 64, No. 2), and the final Grande Valse (Op. 18, No. 1) for the full company. *Les Sylphides* is a romantic composition, classical in form, but the four variations and the pas de deux, set between the ensemble dances with which the ballet opens and ends, merge into each other without the stilted choreographic joinery of the old classical ballets. It is a ballet of mood—there is no plot, but pure interpretation of the music into terms of movement, and to this extent it must be regarded as a forerunner of the symphonic ballet. The faultless technique and plasticity of movement, which it demands of soloists and corps de ballet alike, make *Les Sylphides* one of the hardest tests of a company and it is the ambition of every dancer to make a successful interpretation of one of the solos. Several other settings have been used for the ballet notably one inspired by a painting of Corot, but the original décor of Benois, with its ruined monastery, remains the best. The ballet is in the repertoire of many Cos., and Fokine himself revived it many times with slight changes in choreo- graphy (for Am. Ballet Theatre for example) but without enhancing the beauty of his original version. *Les Sylphides*, with various modifications, is given by some companies under its original title of *Chopiniana*— notably by the R. Danish B., by the Paris Opéra and by the Russian companies.

SYLVIA, or LA NYMPHE DE DIANE. (1) ballet, 3 acts, 4 sc., book Barbier and Reinach, ch. Mérante, m. Delibes, dec. Cheret, Rubé, Châperon, cost. Lacoste, f.p. Paris Opéra 14 June 1876 (Sangalli, Marquet, Sanlaville, Mérante). The ballet was revived at the Opéra in 1919 (by Staats), 1941 (Lifar), and 1946 (Aveline), and was then principally associated there with the dancer, Lycette Darsonval. At the Scala, Milan, it was first performed in 1895 with Carlotta Brianza in the title rôle. In London, a production at the Empire Th. was staged by C. Wilhelm and Fred Farren 18 May 1911 (Kyasht, P. Bedells, Unity More, Mossetti, Farren). (2) ballet, 3 acts, ch. Ashton, m. Delibes, dec. R. and C. Ironside, f.p. Royal B., C. Garden 3 Sept 1952 (Fonteyn, Somes, Hart, Grant, Farron). The story follows the original Paris version with slight alterations. He reduced it to a one-act version, f.p. C. Garden 18 Dec 1967 (Nerina, Sherwood). As a result of difficulties put in his way when he attempted to stage *Sylvia* at the Maryinsky Th., St Petersburg in 1900, Diaghileff resigned from the staff of the Imperial Theatres. Ivanov was working on a revival of the ballet when he died in 1901. See also FADETTA.

SYLWAN, Kari, b. Stockholm 1940. Swed. dancer. Pupil of Karina, Koslowski and Skeaping. Entered R. Swed. B. 1958 becoming a principal dancer.

SYMONS, Oliver, b. London 1936. Eng. dancer. Pupil of N. Robinson and S. Wells Sch. and entered S. Wells Th. B. 1954. Joined Western Th. B. 1957 when it was founded and cr. many rôles. Rejoined Royal B. and became ballet master of its Ballet for All group 1965.

SYMPHONIC BALLET, a ballet which uses a complete symphony for its music. Massine's *Les Présages* is usually taken to be the first in this genre, followed by his *Choreartium*, *Symphonie Fantastique*, and *Seventh Symphony*. At the time many musicians criticized his use of such music but his case was vigorously supported by Ernest Newman. Since then, 1933, many choreographers have made symphonic ballets, rarely with success. Much earlier examples exist, however, and Beethoven's Pastoral Symphony was danced in a dramatized version, ch. Deshayes, at King's Th., London 22 June 1829 (Pauline Leroux, Mlles Pean, Vaque-Moulin, MM Coulon, Gosselin, Frédéric), and again on 6 July 1835 at Drury Lane by the Misses Ryals, Thomasin, Mr and Mrs Payne, and Mr F. Sutton. It was also danced in *The White Fawn* (q.v.) in 1868 in N.Y. Isadora Duncan danced Beethoven's *Seventh Symphony*. N.Y. 1908.

SYMPHONIC VARIATIONS, ballet 1 act, ch. Ashton, m. César Franck, dec. Fedorovich, f.p. S. Wells B., C. Garden 24 Apr 1946 (Fonteyn, Shearer, May, Somes, Danton, Shaw). A purely abstract ballet for six dancers, one of Ashton's most successful.

SYMPHONIE CONCERTANTE, ballet 4 movements, ch. Balanchine, m. Mozart, f.p. by pupils of Sch. of American B., Carnegie Hall, N.Y. 5 Nov 1945. Taken into Ballet Society, City Center, N.Y., dec. J. S. Morcom 12 Nov 1947 (Maria Tallchief, LeClerq, Bolender) and then into N.Y. City B. Ballet of pure dancing.

SYMPHONIE FANTASTIQUE, ballet 5 sc., ch. Massine, m. Berlioz, dec. Bérard, f.p. de Basil's Co., C. Garden 24 July 1936 (Massine, Toumanova, Riabouchinska). The story is that of Berlioz's *Fantastic Symphony*.

SYMPHONIE POUR UN HOMME SEUL, ballet, ch. Béjart, m. Schaeffer and Henry, f.p. Ballets de l'Étoile, Th. de l'Étoile, Paris 3 Aug 1955 (Michèle Seigneuret, Béjart). The ballet is danced to *musique concrète*. M. Cunningham, also ch. *Collage* (1952) to a part of this score.

SYMPHONY, ballet, ch. MacMillan, m. Shostakovitch (*First Symphony*), dec. Sonnabend, f.p. Royal B., C. Garden 15 Feb 1963 (Sibley, Parkinson, Macleary, Doyle). Pure dancing.

SYMPHONY FOR FUN, ballet, ch. Charnley, m. Don Gillis, dec. Lingwood, f.p. Festival B., Festival Hall, London 1 Sept 1952 (Rossana, Landa, Gilpin). Gay inconsequential ballet in the modern idiom.

SYMPHONY IN C, see PALAIS DE CRISTAL.

SYMPHONIE PASTORALE, LA, ballet, ch. Cauley, m. Martinu, dec. Unsworth, f.p. Royal B. (Touring), C. Garden 13 May 1970 (Grater, Thorogood, Conley, Davel). After Gide. A pastor befriends a blind girl and falls in love with her. She recovers her sight, but kills herself.

SZALAJ, Karola, b. Budapest. Hungarian dancer and teacher. Ballerina of Nat. B. of Hungary, from 1954 teacher of the boys' class at Scala, Milan.

T

TACONEO, in Sp. flamenco dancing, the part played by the heel.

TAGLIONI CAKE, CUTTING THE, a traditional ceremony of the Royal Ballet originated by Cyril Beaumont. It takes place in the Green Room at Covent Garden usually on the last Saturday afternoon of the season and the cake is made according to a recipe found by Mr Beaumont in the notebook of a friend of Marie Taglioni, known to be liked by her. In the presence of the dancers, the cake is cut by a distinguished guest or by a retiring dancer. The ceremony was first performed in 1957 by Markova thereafter by Ashton, Philip Chatfield and Rowena Jackson, Nerina, Julia Farron, Rambert, Plisetskaya, Helpmann, Doreen Wells, de Valois, Ursula Moreton, Annette Page, Stanley Holden and in 1970 by John Hart, Stanislas Idzikowsky 1972 (not cut by a dancer in 1971).

TAGLIONI, Filippo, b. Milan 1778, d. Como 1871. It. dancer and chor. Father of Marie and Paul Taglioni. Début Pisa 1794. In 1799 he studied under Coulon and made his début at the Opéra. To Stockholm in 1893 as chief dancer, and maître de ballet 1818. He travelled all over Europe with his family, producing ballets. From 1837 to 1842 in St Petersburg. Retired to Como 1852. His chief ballets are *Le Dieu et la Bayadère* (1830), *La Sylphide* (1832), *Nathalie ou La Laitière Suisse* (1832), *La Révolte au Sérail* (1833), *La Fille du Danube* (1836), *La Gitana* (1838), *L'Ombre* (1940), *Aglaë* (1841).

TAGLIONI, Marie, b. Stockholm 1804, d. Marseilles 1884. It. dancer of a Swedish mother, daughter of Filippo Taglioni. Studied under her father and in Paris. Début at Hoftheater, Vienna, 1822 in *La Réception d'une Jeune Nymphe à la Cour de Terpsichore* (chor. by her father for her). Danced in Germany and Italy and Paris 1823. Début at Paris Opéra 1827. In 1832 she created the rôle of *La Sylphide*, the work which launched the Romantic era in ballet, and of which she was the greatest figure. In 1837 she went to St Petersburg for three years and then returned to Europe, dancing in all the capitals (appearing regularly in London 1830–47 and in the provinces). She retired in 1847, last dancing in London, to Venice, but she lost her fortune in a way which has never been explained, and returned to Paris and London to earn money by teaching dancing and deportment. In 1832 she had married Count Gilbert de Voisins and bore a son, but they were separated in 1835. She chor. *Le Papillon* (1861) for her favourite but ill-fated pupil Emma Livry. She also taught Mlle Salvioni. After the success of *La Sylphide*, Taglioni became a world-famous name, and no other dancer has had such an international reputation. From 1832 to her retirement her name on a bill could fill any theatre in Europe. She was one of the first to wear the now conventional 'ballet dress' (designed possibly by Lami in *La Sylphide*), and although others had danced on their points before her, it was she who made this style of dancing part of the dancer's normal technique. Her centre-parted hair has also become a convention of dancers to the present day. She was essentially a dancer of elevation, of extreme lightness and with a spirituality in her style which was new to the art (Gautier called her 'a Christian dancer'). She appeared to float over the stage, and lithographs showed her poised on a flower or resting on a cloud. Her greatest rôles, besides *La Sylphide*, were *La Fille du Danube*, *Le Pas de Quatre*, *La Gitana*, and *Le Dieu et la Bayadère*.

TAGLIONI, Marie, b. Berlin 1833, d. Neu-Aigen 1891. Daughter of Paul Taglioni and Amalia Galster and niece of the great Marie Taglioni. It. dancer who appeared in many of her father's ballets and danced in London 1847–58. In 1866 she retired and married the Prince Windisch-Grätz.

TAGLIONI, Paul, b. Vienna 1808, d. Berlin 1888. It. dancer and chor. Called 'Paul the Great', brother of Marie Taglioni. Studied under his father and under Coulon. Début Stuttgart 1825 and danced all over Europe, making a great success in Berlin, where his partner was Amalia Galster, whom he married. His chief ballets are *Coralia* (1847), *Thea* (1847), *Fiorita* (1848), *Electra* (1849, the first ballet in which electric light was used), *La Prima Ballerina* (1849), *Les Plaisirs de l'Hiver* (1849), *Les Métamorphoses* (1850) (all these were first performed in London), *Flick and Flock* (1858).

TAGLIONI, Salvatore, b. Palermo 1790, d. Naples 1868. It. dancer and chor. Brother of Filippo, he was principal dancer and ballet master at Naples in the 1830s, where he chor. some important ballets, notably *L'Eridita* (1834) and *Tolomeo Evergete* (1834). His daughter, LOUISE TAGLIONI (b. 1823, d. 1893), was a principal dancer at the Paris Opéra 1848–57, and in 1855 in America.

TALES OF HOFFMANN, ballet 3 acts, ch. Darrell, m. Offenbach, (arr.

Lanchbery), dec. Livingstone, f.p. Scottish Th. B., King's Th., Edin-burgh 6 Apr 1972 (McDonald, St Claire, Debden, Aitken, Cazalet).

TALLCHIEF, Maria, b. Fairfax, Oklahoma 1925, of Am. Indian descent. Am. dancer. Sister of Marjorie Tallchief. Studied with Belcher, Nijinska, Lichine. Joined B. Russe de Monte Carlo 1942, becoming soloist. Cr. Coquette in *Night Shadow*. Guest artist at Paris Opéra 1947 (*Apollo*, *Baiser de la Fée*, etc.). Joined Ballet Society as ballerina in 1947 and N.Y. City Ballet 1950, cr. rôle in *Orpheus* and many others in the ballets of Balanchine (to whom she was then married). In 1954 became chief dancer of the B. Russe de Monte Carlo, returning to N.Y. City B. 1955–65. She also danced with Am. Ballet Th. 1960–61 includ-ing its tour of Russia and was guest artist of Ruth Page B. 1961 and R. Danish B. 1961.

TALLCHIEF, Marjorie, b. Denver 1927, sister of Maria Tallchief. Am. dancer. Studied Nijinska, Lichine, joined Ballet Theatre (1944–46), Original Ballet Russe (1946–47), Grand Ballet de Monte Carlo—later Grand Ballet du Marquis de Cuevas—of which she became a ballerina. Étoile of Paris Opéra 1957–62. Danced classical and dramatic rôles, cr. rôles in *Annabel Lee*, *Idylle*, *Prisoner of the Caucasus*, etc. Joined Harkness B. 1964–66. Mar. Skibine in 1947. Now teaches in Dallas.

TALVO, Tyyne, b. Helsinki 1919. Finnish dancer and chor. Studied classical and modern techniques and danced in her husband's, Ivo Cramèr, companies. After studying at Choreographic Institute, Stock-holm 1964–67, chor. *The Hill of the Winds* and *Sauna* in 1968 for the Cramèr Ballet.

TAMBOURIN, old Provençal dance in 2/4 time, deriving its name from tambourin, the tabor of Provence, to which it was originally danced. It enjoyed a certain popularity in the eighteenth century and was intro-duced by Rameau into a number of his operas.

TAMING OF THE SHREW, THE (Der Widerspenstigen Zähmung), ballet 2 acts, ch. Cranko, m. Scarlatti-Stolze, dec. Eliz. Dalton, f.p. Stuttgart B., Stuttgart 16 Mar 1969 (Haydee, Cragun, Hanke, Madsen). Full-length comic ballet of the Shakespeare play.

TAMIRIS, Helen, b. N.Y. 1905, d. there 1966. Am. dancer and chor., who arranged the dances for a number of musicals, incl. *Showboat* (1946) and *Annie Get Your Gun* (1948).

TANCREDI, ballet, ch. Nureyev, m. Henze, dec. Kay, f.p. Vienna Staats-oper B., Vienna 18 May 1966 (Nureyev, Lisl Maar, Ully Wührer). Nureyev's first original ballet.

TANGO, dance in 2/4 time of cadenced rhythm. Originally brought to Central America by African slaves in the early nineteenth century and thence, when they migrated, to the dockland of the Argentine and Uruguay, where it merged with certain elements of the habanera and the bolero before assuming its present form. It began to be accepted as a ballroom dance about 1912. Ashton has introduced a tango into his *Façade*.

TANZARCHIV, DAS, German dance periodical published monthly in Hamburg. Founded 1953, editor Kurt Peters. In 1966 it moved to Cologne.

TANZ-FORUM, the name given to the ballet at the Cologne opera house from Sept 1971 when Helmut Baumann became ballet master and produced experimental works there. It also tours.

TAP DANCING, a type of dancing in which the toes and heels are rapidly tapped on the floor. It is derived from the clog dancing of Ireland and Lancashire, and is popular on the variety stage, especially in America. Among the great tap dancers are Bill Robinson, Eleanor Powell, Fred Astaire, Paul Draper, Ray Bolger, and Ann Miller. The dancer's shoes are hard and fitted with metal cleats. With soft shoes the style is known as 'soft shoe dancing'. Tap had a revival in the 1970s.

TAQUETÉ, from the Fr. *taquet*, a peg. Term first introduced about 1834 to indicate a pizzicato type of dancing on the points. Levinson said 'Taqueté is the intoxication of living on earth'.

TARAKANOVA, Nina, b. Moscow 1915. Russ. dancer. Studied under Kschessinska. Début in Pavlova's Co. 1930; in de Basil's Co. 1933–34, Blum's Co. 1936–39, International B. 1941–43. Cr. chief rôle in *Gaîté Parisienne*. Lives in London.

TARANTELLA, It. dance in a rapid 6/8 time. The origin of the name has been attributed to the town of Taranto in Southern Italy and to a spider common in that area, the *Tarantula*. There is a superstition that the bite of this spider caused a disease known as Tarantism, which produced in the victim a sort of delirium tremens, the cure for which was an energetic dance. This legend was made the subject of a ballet of the romantic period *La Tarentule*. There is a tarantella in the Ballroom Act of *Swan Lake*, in *Napoli* and in *La Boutique Fantasque*.

TARAS BULBA, ballet 3 acts 4 sc., ch. Lopokov, m. Soloviev-Sedoy, dec. Kaplan, f.p. Kirov Th., Leningrad 12 Dec 1940 (Dudinskaya, Chaboukiani). Based on Gogol's novel about medieval Ukraine and the Cossacks. Later versions have been ch. Zakharoff, Bolshoi Th., Moscow 26 Mar 1941 and ch. Fenster, Kirov Th., Leningrad 2 June 1955 (Shelest, Dudinskaya, Mikhailov, Makarov, Sergeyev).

TARAS, John, b. N.Y. 1919. Am. dancer and chor. Studied under Fokine, Vilzak, Sch. of Am. B. First appeared in musicals. Joined Am. B.

Caravan 1940, Littlefield B. 1940–41, Ballet Th. 1942–46, first in corps de ballet then soloist and ballet master. Successively ballet master to Markova-Dolin 1946, de Basil 1947, and Grand B. du Marquis de Cuevas 1948–53 and again 1955. Ballet master N.Y. City B. from 1959. Chor. *Graziana* (1945), *Camille* (1946), *The Minotaur* (1947), *Designs with Strings* (1948), *Tarasiana* (1951), *Cordelia* (1952), *Piège de Lumière* (1953), *La Guirlande de Campra* (1966), *Haydn Concerto* (1968) etc. He has mounted his ballets and Balanchine's all over the world. Appointed ballet master of Paris Opéra 1969–70, Berlin 1971–72. Returned to N.Y. City B. 1972. Chor. *Rite of Spring*, Scala 1972.

TARAS, Paul, b. Saskatchewan 1942. Canadian dancer. With Canada Council grant to study with Hightower in Cannes and at the Royal B. Sch. Joined Strasbourg B. and came to London 1967, touring with B. Minerva. Joined B. Rambert 1968.

TARENTULE, LA, ballet 2 acts 3 sc., ch. Coralli, m. Gide, f.p. Paris Opéra 24 June 1839 (Elssler, Mazilier). Romantic ballet set in Calabria. The hero is bitten by a tarantula spider.

TAUBERT, Manfred, b. Berlin 1935. Ger. dancer and chor. Pupil of T. Gsovsky, Kiss. Joined Berlin Städtische Oper B. 1952–63, ballet master Salzburg B. 1963–64 and Braunschweig B. from 1964.

TAVERNER, Sonia, b. Byfleet 1936. Eng. dancer. Studied at Elmhurst Sch. and Royal Ballet Sch. Joined S. Wells B. 1955, R. Winnipeg B. 1956 becoming the principal dancer.

TAXELL, Lisa, b. Helsinki 1931. Finnish dancer. Studied at ballet sch. of National Ballet of Finland and in Paris and London. Joined National Ballet of Finland 1947, becoming soloist 1953 and ballerina 1958.

TAYLOR, Jonathan, b. Manchester 1941. Pupil of Lloyd and Andrew Hardie. Joined Massine's Nervi Co. 1960, Amsterdam B. 1960–61, and B. Rambert 1961 becoming a principal dancer. Chor. *Diversities* (m. Badings 1966), *'Tis Goodly Sport* (sixteenth-century music 1970), *Listen to the Music* (m. Hymas 1972) and other ballets for B. Rambert.

TAYLOR, Paul, b. Alleghany County 1930. Am. dancer and chor. After leaving university studied dance under Tudor and Craske at Juilliard, and with Martha Graham. Danced with Merce Cunningham's Co. 1954, Pearl Lang's 1955 and in musicals. From 1954 he has had his own company which has appeared all over the world (Spoleto Festival 1960 and 1964, Mexico 1963, Europe 1964, London 1964 and 1970 etc.). Chor. many ballets incl. *Three Epitaphs* (1954), *The Tower* (1957), *Tablet* (1960), *Scuderama* (1963), *The Red Room* (1964), *Orbs* (1966) etc. From 1955–61 soloist in Graham's Co. also, and danced in Balanchine's

Episodes (1959) with N.Y. City B. Guest chor. Nederlands B. 1960. One of the leading figures in Am. modern dance.

TCHAIKOVSKY, Peter, b. Viatka 1840, d. St Petersburg 1893. Russ. composer whose music embellishes every ballet for which it is used. His ballets incl. *Swan Lake, Sleeping Beauty, Casse Noisette*, and his music has been used for many other masterpieces, *Serenade, Présages, Ballet Imperial, Designs with Strings* etc.

TCHAIKOVSKY MEMORIAL TOKYO BALLET, one of the many classical companies in Japan. The first school of classical ballet in Tokyo, the Tokyo Ballet Gakko, was founded in 1960 by Koichi Hyashi, and its pupils make up this company which was originally directed by Tadatsugu Sasaki. It toured Russia in 1966 and appeared at the Paris International Festival in 1970. The artistic director is Hideteru Kitahana. It has had many distinguished Russian teachers and guest stars. Also known as Tokyo B.

TCHELITCHEV, Pavel, b. Moscow 1898, d. Rome 1957. Russ. designer whose works incl. *Errante* (Balanchine 1933), *Ode* (Massine 1928), *Nobilissima Visione* (Massine 1938), *Balustrade* (Balanchine 1941).

TCHEREPNIN, Nicholas, b. St Petersburg 1873, d. Issy-les-Moulineaux 1945. Russ. composer and Diaghileff's first conductor, comp. *Le Pavillon d'Armide* (1907), *Narcisse* (1911) etc. His son Alexander (b. St Petersburg 1899, d. Paris 1969) comp. *Trepak* (Mordkin B. 1937), *Déjeuner sur l'Herbe* (Petit 1945), *Chota Roustavali* (Nouveau Ballet de Monte Carlo 1946), *La Femme et son Ombre* (Charrat, B. de Paris 1948).

TCHERINA, Ludmila, b. Paris 1924. Fr. dancer, pupil of Preobrajenska and Alessandri, who has danced in Nouveau Ballet de Monte Carlo, B. des Ch. Élysées, guest artist at Scala, Milan 1954, and in films incl. *The Red Shoes, Tales of Hoffman, Un Revenant*. Danced title-rôle in *Le Martyre de S. Sébastien*, Paris Opéra 1957. Formed her own company, Th. Ballet de Tcherina, 1959 which appeared in London that year. Mar. the late Edmond Audran. Legion d'Honneur 1969.

TCHERKAS, Constantin, b. St Petersburg 1908, d. Paris 1965. Russ. dancer and chor. Studied at Imp. Sch. and became member of Diaghileff's Co. Premier danseur and chor. of Opéra Comique 1934-36. Retired 1956.

TCHERNICHEVA, Lubov, b. St Petersburg 1890. Russ. dancer. Studied Imp. Sch. and graduated 1908. Joined Diaghileff 1911, becoming a principal dancer and in 1926 ballet mistress also of de Basil's Co. Mar. Serge Grigorieff 1909. In 1954 she and her husband mounted *Firebird* for Royal B. and at Milan, *Petrouchka*, for R. Ballet, 1957, and revised

491

Les Sylphides for S. Wells B. In 1955 she began giving regular classes to Royal B. Joined Festival B. 1956–57 with her husband. Now retired and lives in London.

TECHNIQUE, the ensemble of the mechanics of the art of dancing. A sound technique is a prerequisite of good artistic performance and should be automatic in the trained dancer.

TELFORD, Nona, b. Ottawa 1942. Eng. dancer. Pupil of Cone-Ripman Sch. Joined Festival B. 1960 becoming soloist.

TELLOLI, Bruno, b. 1937. Italian dancer. Entered Scala Sch., Milan, 1950, graduated in 1957 and became soloist 1958. Now ballerino.

TEMPS, (Fr.) lit. time. Is variously used to describe a movement in which there is no transfer of weight (e.g. temps levé) or the division of a step into a number of movements (e.g. balloné à trois temps). Blasis writes it as 'tems'.

TEMPS DE COU-DE-PIED, a relevé on to the half- or full-point in the fifth position, drawing the feet together. Usually a preparation for a big jumping step such as the male dancer's double turns, or the danseuse's entrechat six or a big supported lift. Also known as a SUS-SOUS.

TEMPS DE CUISSE (also Pas de Cuisse), lit. thigh step. A sissonne fermée, preceded by the snatching up of the working foot from fifth position and replacing it quickly in preparation for the sissonne fermée. It can be executed en avant, en arrière, dessus, and dessous.

TEMPS DE FLÈCHE, lit. arrow-step, a man's step in which the dancer jumps from the left leg and lands on the right which, though first thrown out in front, is bent and drawn back and the left foot thrown forward in landing.

TEMPS DE L'ANGE, lit. angel's step. Similar to a temps de poisson (q.v.) executed croisé, arms en couronne and the knees bent.

TEMPS DE POISSON, lit. fish's movement. A step in which the dancer, standing in the fifth position facing one of the down stage corners, with a demi-plié jumps diagonally forward, raising the arms to the fifth position en haut, leaning well back with the top part of the body whilst keeping the fully pointed feet in a tight fifth position, and then alighting on the front foot with the back leg in arabesque. It will be seen that whilst in the air the body assumes the outline of a leaping fish. It is the first step of the man's solo in the *Bluebird* variation from *The Sleeping Beauty*. See FISH DIVE and TEMPS DE L'ANGE.

TEMPS LEVÉ, lit. a raised movement, or more simply a hop with the raised foot in any required position, such as sur le cou-de-pied, or en arabesque. This latter step is used in the entry of the leading swans in the second act of *The Swan Lake*.

TEMPS LIÉ, (Fr.) connected movement, a series of exercises in the centre of the classroom, part of the adage, in which the arms and feet are simultaneously put through a variety of smooth, graceful movements.

TEMS, word used by Blasis for a movement of the leg, e.g. *tems de chaccone, tems de vigueur*. Presumably a corruption of *temps*.

TENNANT, Veronica, b. London 1946. Canadian dancer. Trained at Arts Educational Sch. London and Canad. Nat. B. Sch. Entered Canad. Nat. B. 1963 as soloist, becoming principal dancer.

TENDU, (Fr.) stretched out or held, e.g. *battement tendu*.

TERABUST, Elisabetta, b. Varese 1946. It. dancer. Studied at Rome Opera Sch. 1955–63, ballerina in Rome 1966, Festival B. 1973. Mar. Vantaggio.

TER-ARUTUNIAN, Rouben, b. Tiflis 1920. Armenian (American since 1957) artist. Studied in Berlin, Vienna and Paris. Designed for N.Y. City B., *Souvenirs* (1955), *Seven Deadly Sins* (1958), *Ballet Imperial* (dec. only, 1964), *Nutcracker* (1964). For Taylor, *Fibers* (1960). For Graham's Co., *Samson Agonistes* (dec. only 1961), Tetley's *Pierrot Lunaire* (1962), *Sargasso* (1965), *Ricercare* (1966) etc.

TERESA (Teresa Viera-Romero), b. N.Y. 1929. Am.-Spanish dancer. Pupil of Luisillo (whose wife she became). Danced in Carmen Amaya's Co. and in 1949 formed with her husband the Teresa and Luisillo Ballet Español. Toured the world and now has her own group.

TERMINAL, ballet 1 act, ch. Littlefield, m. Kingsley, dec. Pinto, f.p. Littlefield's Co., Th. des Ch. Élysées, Paris 1 June 1937 (Littlefield). Scenes at a railway station.

TERPIS, Max (Pfister), b. Zürich 1889, d. there 1958. Swiss dancer and teacher. From 1921 pupil of Wigman and became ballet master of Hanover B. 1923. Succeeded Kröller as ballet master of Staatsoper, Berlin 1924, but forced to leave by the Nazis in 1933. From 1941–43 ballet master in Basel. Author of *The Dance and the Dancer* 1946.

TERPSICHORE, Muse of Choral Dance and Song usually depicted with the lyre and the plectrum. Like all the Muses, she did not marry.

TERRE À TERRE, lit. ground to ground. Those steps in which the feet leave the ground only sufficiently to enable them to be pointed, in opposition to steps of elevation. Elssler was said to be a 'terre à terre' dancer in contradistinction to Taglioni who was a dancer of elevation.

TERRY, Walter, b. Brooklyn 1913. Am. writer on ballet and critic of *N.Y. Herald Tribune* 1936–39, 1939–42 and 1945–67. Author of *Star Performance* (1954), *Ballet in Action* (1954, photographs by Himmel),

Ballet (1958), *The Dance in America*, *The Ballet Companion* (1968), *Isadora Duncan* etc. Contrib. *Encyclopaedia Britannica*, *Dance Encyclopedia* etc. Also has television dance programmes. From 1967 ballet critic of *Saturday Review*. Director of Jacob's Pillow 1973

TERVAMAA, Mirja, b. Helsinki 1942. Finnish dancer. Pupil of Helsinki Nat. B. Sch. and studied with Anna Northcote and Kiss. Joined Finnish Nat. B. 1961 becoming soloist 1963. Joined Zürich B. 1965 becoming soloist, Düsseldorf 1972. Mar. M. Tikkanen.

TER WEEME, Mascha, b. Amsterdam. Dutch dancer and chor. Pupil of Wigman, Georgi, V. Gsovsky etc. Assistant to Y. Georgi 1936–44 and then gave recitals with Antony Raedt. Director of the Ballet der Lage Landen, Holland 1947–59 and of Amsterdam Opera B. 1959–61. She then worked for a time with Dutch Nat. B. Now teaches.

TESTA, Alberto, b. Turin 1922. Italian dancer, chor. teacher and writer. After his dancing career in Italy became chor. and teacher at the National Academy of Dancing. Contributor to Ricordi's *Dictionary of Music*. Wrote *La danza nel mondo* (1970). Organizer and artistic director of the dance recitals at Spoleto Festival of Two Worlds 1967 and 1969.

TETLEY, Glen, b. Cleveland, Ohio 1926. Am. dancer and chor. Pupil of Hanya Holm and member of her Co. 1946–51. From 1959 also studied with Craske and Tudor. From 1952–54 in N.Y. City Opera. A principal dancer of John Butler's Co. in 1955, guest dancer Joffrey B. 1956–57, Graham's Co. 1958. Joined Am. Ballet Th. 1960 and toured Europe and Russia, and Robbins's Ballets U.S.A. 1961. Joined Nederlands Dans Th. 1962 as guest, becoming their choreographer. In 1969 he became their Artistic Director (jointly with van Manen) until 1970. Among his many ballets, chor. *Birds of Sorrow* (m. Hartman 1962), *Pierrot Lunaire* (m. Schoenberg 1962), *Game of Noah* (1965), *Ricercare* (m. Seter 1966), *Mythical Hunters* (1966), *The Anatomy Lesson, Free Fall* (1967), *Ziggurat* (1967), *Mutations* (m. Stockhausen) (1970). His ballets have been a great influence in moulding the new Ballet Rambert. In 1969 he toured his own Co. in America and Europe. For Royal B., chor. *Field Figures* (m. Stockhausen) 1970, *Laborintus* (m. Berio) 1972. For Hamburg, *Threshold* (m. Berg) 1972. For Austral. B. *Gemini* (m. Henze) 1973.

THAMAR, ballet 1 act, ch. Fokine, m. Balakirev, dec. Bakst, f.p. Diaghileff's Co., Châtelet Th., Paris 20 May 1912 (Karsavina, Bolm). Dramatic ballet about the Queen of Georgia.

THAT IS THE SHOW, ballet, ch. Morrice, m. Berio, dec. N. Baylis, f.p, B. Rambert, Jeannetta Cochrane Th., London 6 May 1971 (Craig, Bruce), Berio's *Sinfonia* for 8 voices and orch.

494

THÉÂTRE D'ART DU BALLET, ballet company founded by Anna Galina (Evelyn Cournand) in 1957. It is based in Paris with herself as principal dancer and Tatiane Piankova as artistic director and teacher. It tours widely—to Japan, Middle East, America etc. It has some Fokine ballets in the repertoire, *Les Elfes*, *Carnaval* etc. and William Dollar has worked for them. Bogdan Bulder is principal male dancer.

THÉÂTRE FRANÇAIS DE LA DANSE, ballet company based on Paris and state supported. It was founded to present the talents of Joseph Lazzini, the choreographer, who was its director. It first appeared at the Baltard Pavilion, Paris 17 June 1969 (and for a six week season at the Odeon Th. from 10 Oct 1969) with Lazzini's ballets '+ —' (m. Varèse), *Two Movements* (m. Bartok), *Ecce Homo* (m. Berghmans) and *Lascaux* (m. Antill). Among the dancers were Sombert, Bruel, Vincent Warren, Denise Soulié, Pomsar. It came to an end in 1971.

THEILADE, Nini, b. Java 1916. Danish dancer and chor. Studied in Denmark and with Egorova. Soloist B. Russe de Monte Carlo. Cr. rôles in *Nobilissima Visione* and *Bacchanale* (Venus). Chor. ballets for R. Danish B. and received Order of Dannebrog. Opened school in Svendborg, Denmark 1970.

THEME AND VARIATIONS, ballet, ch. Balanchine, m. Tchaikovsky (Suite No. 3 in G), dec. Woodman Thompson, f.p. Am. B. Th., Richmond, Va. 27 Sept 1947 (Alonso, Youskevitch), f.p. in N.Y. City Center 26 Nov 1947. In classical tutus. See SUIT NO. 3.

THÉODORE, Mlle, b. Paris 1760, d. Audenge 1799. (Marie-Madeleine Crespé.) Fr. dancer. She was known as 'the backstage philosopher'. She was the wife of Dauberval, and in 1782 she was imprisoned and suspended from the Opéra for eighteen days for uttering witty epigrams directed against the administration of the Opéra. Cr. rôle of Lise in *La Fille Mal Gardée* (1789). Pupil of Lany.

THESMAR, Ghislaine, b. Peking 1943. Fr. dancer. Studied under Yves Brieux and Solange Schwarz at Conservatoire Nat. de Musique in Paris. Joined de Cuevas B. 1960 until 1962 when it ended. Toured with Skibine's group and joined in 1962 Lacotte's Ballet National des Jeunesses Musicales de France as principal dancer. In 1967 danced as guest artist of Ballet Rambert in London, and also toured Canada and Italy (1968) with the Ballet de Roland Petit. Guest artist of Strasbourg B. 1968. Mar. Pierre Lacotte. See *La Sylphide*. In 1972 étoile of Paris Op. B.

THIBON, Nanon, b. Paris 1944. Fr. dancer. Studied at Paris Opéra Sch. Joined the Co. and became première danseuse 1963, étoile 1965. Won Blum Prize 1960.

THOMPSON, Basil, b. Newcastle-upon-Tyne 1936. Eng. dancer and ballet master. Pupil of Nellie Potts and S. Wells Sch. Joined C. Garden Opera B. 1954 and Royal B. 1955. In 1955 taught in Loring's Sch. etc. in America. Joined Am. B. Th. 1960. Joined Joffrey B. becoming ballet master.

THOMSON, Norman, b. Vancouver 1920. Canad. dancer and chor. Pupil of Freda Shaw. In 1939 joined W. Christensen's San Francisco B. becoming soloist. War service 1942–46, and while stationed in Europe danced with B. Rambert and International B. 1944–46. Joined S. Wells Th. B. 1946 then S. Wells B. as soloist, partnering Beryl Grey. Turned to musicals 1947. Then to work in Europe and chor. many musicals in Vienna, Budapest etc.

THOROGOOD, Alfreda, b. Lambeth 1942. Eng. dancer. Pupil of Lady Eden's Sch. and Royal B. Sch. Joined Royal B. 1960 becoming soloist, and principal 1968. Mar. David Wall.

THREE CORNERED HAT, THE (*Le Tricorne*), ballet 1 act, ch. Massine, m. de Falla, dec. Picasso, f.p. Diaghileff's Co., Alhambra Th., London 22 July 1919 (Karsavina, Massine). One of Massine's greatest ballets and now in the repertoire of many companies. Revived for S. Wells B., C. Garden 6 Feb 1947 (Fonteyn, Massine) and Joffrey B. 1969 (Remington, Fuente), Festival B., Congress Th., Eastbourne 16 Mar 1973 (Nicol, Sanchez). See also FELIX.

THREE EPITAPHS, ballet, ch. Paul Taylor, m. Am. folk, cost. Rauschenberg, f.p. Paul Taylor Co. 1956. Comic ballet with grotesque, faceless figures in black.

THREE FAT MEN, THE, ballet 4 acts, ch. Moiseyev, m. Oransky, dec. Matrunin, f.p. Bolshoi Th., Moscow 1 Mar 1935 (Lepeshinskaya, Moiseyev, Yermoleyeff). A propaganda ballet in humorous, fantastic vein, in which the people overthrow the Three Fat Men (their oppressors).

THREE IVANS (Innocent Ivan and his Brothers), danced in the last act of *The Sleeping Beauty*. It was not in the original Petipa version, but was introduced into the Diaghileff 1921 version with ch. Nijinska. The music used is properly that written for the coda in the final Grand Pas de Deux. In the S. Wells version the ch. was by de Valois.

THREE MUSKETEERS, THE, ballet 2 acts, ch. Flindt, m. Delerue, dec. Daydé f.p. R. Danish B., Copenhagen 11 May 1966 (Kronstam, Ryberg, Martins, Madsen, Simone). Also mounted by Munich B. 8 June 1967.

TIC-TACK, ballet, ch. Chesworth, m. Kreisler, f.p. B. Rambert, Jeannetta Cochrane Th., London 14 Mar 1967 (Merry, Bruce, Reyneke). A sketch of an unhappy couple and an intruder, in the style of a cartoon by Ungerer.

TIGHTS (Fr. *maillot*, German *tricot*), the skin-tight stocking and knickers combined worn by dancers. Tights are often said to have been invented by Maillot, costumier at the Paris Opéra at the beginning of the nineteenth century, who has given his name to the garment in the Fr. vocabulary, but it seems certain that they were in use before that. It is probable that with the shortening of skirts and the use of transparent material a real or fancied dislike of naked flesh on the stage caused their general adoption. Stage tights are of silk, nylon, or cotton, whilst practice tights are usually of wool. Openwork tights ('fishnets') are also used, but not in classical ballets.

TIKHOMIRNOVA, Irina, b. Leningrad 1917. Russ. dancer. Studied at Bolshoi Sch., graduated 1936, soloist the same year and becoming prima ballerina at Bolshoi Th., Moscow. Stalin Prize 1947 and Honoured Artist of the U.S.S.R. Mar. A. Messerer. In 1968 became ballet mistress of Moiseyev's classical Co., Young Ballet.

TIKHOMIROFF, Vasili, b. 1876, d. Moscow 1956. Russ. dancer. Graduated Imp. Sch., St Petersburg 1893 and became principal dancer of Bolshoi Th., Moscow. Mar. Geltzer and danced with her in London 1911. Partnered Pavlova on 1914 tour. From 1896 to 1937 taught at Moscow Sch. Chor. one act of *The Red Poppy*.

TIKHONOV, Vladimir, b. Kischinev 1935. Russ. dancer. Studied in Leningrad, danced in Kischinev (Moldavia) but joined Bolshoi B., becoming soloist in 1960, Varna Gold Medal 1965.

TIKKANEN, Matti, b. Helsinki 1945. Finnish dancer. Pupil of Onkinen, Ahonen, Northcote. Joined Finnish Nat. B. 1961. Joined Zürich B. 1968 as soloist. Guest artist Festival B. 1969. Guest of San Francisco B. 1970, 1971. Düsseldorf B. 1972. Mar. Tervamaa.

TIL EULENSPIEGEL, ballet, ch. Babilée, m. R. Strauss, dec. Keogh, f.p. B. des Ch. Élysées, Th. des Ch. Élysées, Paris 9 Nov 1949 (Babilée, Vallée, Darmance). See also TYL EULENSPIEGEL.

TIME OUT OF MIND, ballet, ch. B. Macdonald, m. Creston (*Invocation and Dance*), dec. Ter-Arutunian, f.p. Joffrey B., Fashion Inst. of Technology, N.Y. 28 Sept 1962 (Helgi Tomasson, Eliz. Carroll, Lawrence Rhodes). Sexual yearnings between men and women. It was taken into the repertoire of the Harkness B. 1965, R. Swed. B. and Dutch Nat. B.

TIMOFEYEVA, Nina, b. 1935. Russ. dancer. Trained at Kirov Sch., Leningrad, graduated to Kirov B. 1953. Left in 1955 and joined Bolshoi B. 1956 as soloist. Created rôle of Asel in *Asel* 1967 and Aegina in Grigorovitch's *Spartacus* 1968. Mar. conductor Gennadi Rozhdestventsky. People's Artist R.S.F.S.R. 1969. First danced in London 1956, N.Y. 1959.

TIRE-BOUCHON, EN (Fr. like a corkscrew), a position of the leg in which the thigh is in the second position and the toe of the working leg touching the knee of the supporting leg (retiré or raccourci en tire-bouchon).

TIRESIAS, ballet 3 sc., ch. Ashton, m. Constant Lambert, dec. Isabel Lambert, f.p. S. Wells B., C. Garden 8 July 1951 (Fonteyn, Somes, Field). The legend of Tiresias who tastes love as a woman and as a man, and is struck blind.

TIROIRS, FAIRE LES (Fr. to move like a chest of drawers), a movement of the corps de ballet in which opposite lines of dancers cross the stage, passing each other, and move back again. It can be seen in *Giselle*, Act II.

'TIS GOODLY SPORT, ballet, ch. Jonathan Taylor, m. sixteenth-century court music, dec. Cazalet, f.p. B. Rambert, Jeannette Cochrane Th., London 30 Nov 1970 (Craig, Pietje Law, Avrahami, Curtis). A bawdy Tudor frolic.

TIVOLI PANTOMIME THEATRE, in Tivoli Garden, Copenhagen, was built in 1874 by the architect Dahlerup, who also built the Royal Danish Opera House. It is open from May to September (as are the Gardens) and each afternoon it performs little ballets and commedia dell'arte pantomimes for chidren, The principal actors in the commedia dell'arte are Pierrot, Pantalone (called Cassander in Denmark), Harlequin and Columbine (who wears a tutu). Performances all end with the children calling to Pierrot 'Speak!' and he talks to them.

TOE SHOES, Am. term for point shoes. German "spitzenschuhe".

TOMASSON, Helgi, b. Reykjavik 1942. Icelandic dancer. Pupil of Bidsted, Volkova, Bruhn. Joined Tivoli Th., Copenhagen 1957, Joffrey B. 1961, Harkness B. 1964 becoming a principal dancer. Mar. Marlene Rizzo. In 1970 joined N.Y. City B. Danced in London (with Verdy) 1973.

TOMBÉ, (Fr.) fallen, in which the dancer falls from one leg to the other, or from both feet to one, bending the knee as he lands.

TOMSKY, Alexander, b. Moscow 1905, d. Milan 1970. Russ. dancer and ballet master. Pupil of Mossolova and Messerer in Bolshoi Sch., Moscow. Joined Zimin Th., Moscow 1923 and other Cos. in Russia subsequently. Ballet master of Bolshoi 1948–51 and soloist, artistic director 1957–59. In 1960 appointed artistic director Stanislavsky Th., Moscow. Returned to Bolshoi B. 1969.

TONIN (TONIN-NIKIC), Boris, b. Nikinici 1933. Yugoslav dancer and chor. Studied in Belgrade and in London. Soloist in Salzburg, Amsterdam, Zürich and Wiesbaden. To Monte Carlo 1965 and founded his own touring group. In 1967 appeared at Montreal Expo Theatre and in Chicago, etc. In 1968 was chor. of B. de Wallonie and in 1973 formed in Zürich the touring group Festival-Ballet Nikic Monte Carlo which toured his *Swan Lake* in Switzerland, Germany etc.

TONNELET, (Fr.) the cask-shaped skirt, stretched over hoops, of the eighteenth-century danseuse.

TOOLEY, John, b. 1924. General Administrator of the Royal Opera House (opera and ballet), Covent Garden from 1970, succeeding Sir David Webster. Educ. Repton and Magdalene Coll., Cambridge. Secretary of Guildhall Sch. of Music 1952–55, assistant to General Administrator of C. Garden 1955–60, Assistant General Administrator 1960–70.

TORDION, third section of the Basse Danse.

TOTEM, ballet, ch., m. and lighting Alwin Nikolais, colour design by Constant, f.p. Henry St Playhouse, N.Y. 29 Jan 1960 (Louis, Bailin, Lamhut etc.). A series of rituals. Revised 1 Feb 1962 and in repertoire of Nikolais Co.

TOTH, Sandor, b. Budapest 1937. Hungarian dancer and chor. Pupil of National B. Sch. Joined Hungarian Nat. B. becoming soloist. In 1970 appointed director of B. Sopianae at Pecs. Chor. *Under your Hat* (m. Kincses 1967) and *Circus* (m. Ranki 1968).

TOUMANOVA, Tamara, b. in a railway train near Shanghai 1919 when her parents were leaving Russia. Russ. dancer. Début at Paris Opéra at age of 9 in *L'Éventail de Jeanne*. Studied with Preobrajenska in Paris, when in 1932 Balanchine saw her and engaged her for the B. Russe de Monte Carlo and chor. *Cotillon* and *La Concurrence* for her. Joined Balanchine's Les Ballets 1933 and rejoined B. Russes de Monte Carlo in 1934, of which she remained the ballerina until 1938. Danced in musical *Stars in your Eyes* and rejoined the B. Russe de Monte Carlo in Australia in 1939. In 1943 made film in Hollywood, *Days of Glory*, and in 1944 married its producer, Casey Robinson. Guest artist B. Theatre 1944–45, Paris Opéra 1947 and 1952, San Francisco Civic B. 1948, de Cuevas Co. 1949, La Scala, Milan 1951 and 1952, Festival B. 1952 and 1954. She was, with Riabouchinska and Baronova, one of the original 'baby-ballerinas' of the first de Basil seasons, the brilliance of whose dancing did much to revive the interest in ballet, which was in danger of declining after the death of Diaghileff. She has danced in many films *Tonight We Sing* (in which she was Pavlova), *The Torn Curtain* (1966), *The Private Life of Sherlock Holmes* (1970) etc.

TOUR DE REINS, lit. turn of the back. A coupé jeté (q.v.) but the jeté

499

is executed en tournant, finishing in an attitude croisée on landing. The coupé jeté is usually preceded, to give force to the turn, by a sissonne tombée to the fourth position or by a coupé-chassé en avant (which might also be en tournant). Often done in a series or en manège.

TOUR EN L'AIR, a turn in the air, usually executed by the male dancer only. Several turns may be made without touching the ground, double tour en l'air, triple tour, etc. Writing in 1895, Desrat (q.v.) condemns this step as acrobatic and says that it is 'newly introduced into theatrical dancing'. One can only assume that it had fallen into desuetude until that time, for it occurs in *Giselle* and in the Bournonville ballets and must have been a trick known to all male dancers from earliest times.

TOURING ROYAL BALLET, see ROYAL BALLET.

TOURS, PETITS, lit. small turns, usually executed on the point. A series of petits tours executed diagonally across the stage to a rapid tempo are sometimes referred to as petits tours chaînés or enchaînés, or simply as chaînés (lit. a chain of turns). When performed in a circle round the stage they are sometimes described as manège (from the custom of schooling horses on a circular track or *manège*). See DÉBOULÉS.

TOUTE LA DANSE, Fr. ballet journal published in Paris. The first number was May 1952.

TOYE, Wendy, b. London 1917. Eng. dancer, actress and chor. Danced in *Hiawatha* at Albert Hall, London, 1931, toured with Markova-Dolin 1934–35. Arranged the dances in numerous London shows and musicals, among them all George Black's productions from 1938 to 1944, *Hiawatha* 1939, *The Lisbon Story* 1943, *Gay Rosalinda* 1945, *Bless the Bride* 1947, and many pantomimes.

TRAGÉDIE À VERONE, ballet 1 act, ch. Skibine, m. Tchaikovsky, dec. Delfau, f.p. de Cuevas Co., Monte Carlo 4 May 1950 (Pagava, Skibine). This was Skibine's first ballet and tells the story of Romeo and Juliet.

TRAGÉDIE DE SALOMÉ, LA, ballet, m. F. Schmitt, (1) ch. Loïe Fuller, f.p. Th. des Arts, Paris 1907 (Fuller); (2) ch. Boris Romanoff, dec. Soudeikine, f.p. Diaghileff's Co., Th. des Ch. Élysées 12 June 1913 (Karsavina); (3) ch. N. Guerra, dec. Piot, f.p. Ida Rubinstein Co., Paris Opéra 1 Apr 1919 (Rubinstein); (4) ch. Aveline dec. Brayer, f.p. Paris Opéra 7 July 1944 (Lorcia), revived 15 Dec 1954 for Darsonval.

TRAGEDY OF FASHION, A, or THE SCARLET SCISSORS, the first ballet presented by Marie Rambert 15 June 1926, in Playfair's revue *Riverside Nights* at the Lyric Th., Hammersmith, ch. Ashton (his first ballet), m. E. Goossens, dec. F. E. D. (who was Sophie Fedorovitch). Among the dancers were Ashton and Rambert.

TRAILINE, Boris, b. Lemnos, Greece 1921. Fr. dancer. Studied under

Sedowa in Nice and Volinine in Paris. Soloist of Nouveau B. de Monte Carlo 1946 and danced in recitals and as partner to Chauviré, Toumanova etc. Now an impresario in Paris.

TRAILINE, Hélène, b. Bombas, Lorraine 1928. Fr. dancer, sister of Boris T. Début in de Cuevas Co. 1947, Ballerina of B. des Ch. Élysées 1950, of Charrat's Co. and guest artist of Ballet Rambert. Mar. J. Giuliano.

TRAIN BLEU, LE, ballet 1 act, by Cocteau, ch. Nijinska, m. Milhaud, dec. Laurens, curtain Picasso, f.p. Diaghileff's Co., Th. des Ch. Élysées, Paris 20 June 1924 (Nijinska, Sokolova, Dolin, Woizikovsky). This ballet was created to show off Dolin's acrobatic dancing and was never given again after he left the Co. Set on a Riviera beach.

TRAINING, term used in Germany for the daily class (given by the 'trainingsleiter').

TRAVELLERS, THE, ballet ch. Morrice, m. Salzedo, dec. Koltai, f.p. B. Rambert, Spoleto 27 June 1963 (J. Taylor, MacSween, Ariette Taylor, Curtis). Travellers held prisoner in an airport behind the Iron Curtain.

TRAVESTI, EN, term applied to a female dancer dressed as a man. The custom used to be widespread, but is now only found in pantomime. See PETIPA, Marie S., MALVINA CAVALAZZI and DANSEUSE TRAVESTIE.

TRECU, Pirmin (Aldabaldetrecu), b. Zaraus, Spain 1930. Sp. dancer. To England as a refugee during Civil War. Entered S. Wells Sch. 1946 and the S. Wells Th. B. in 1947, becoming one of the principal dancers. Transferred to S. Wells B. 1955. Left Royal B. 1961 and opened his own school in Oporto.

TREFILOVA, Vera, b. St Petersburg 1875, d. Paris 1943. Russ. dancer. Graduated from Imp. Sch. 1894, becoming prima ballerina 1906. In 1917 she moved to Paris and opened a school which became famous. In 1921 she shared the rôle of Aurora in Diaghileff's London production of *Sleeping Princess*. Her third husband was V. Svetlow (q.v.).

TREIZE DANSES, ballet, ch. Petit, m. Grétry, dec. Dior, f.p. B. des Ch. Élysées, Th. des Ch. Élysées, Paris 12 Nov 1947 (Vyroubova, Skorik, Petit). A disconnected suite of dances.

TREPAK, Russian dance in 2/4 time featured in the last scene of *Casse Noisette*.

TRES DIABOLOS, LOS, ballet 3 sc., ch. Grinwis, m. Offenbach, dec. Haxton, f.p. Borovansky B., Empire Th., Sydney, November 1954 (Sager, Trunoff).

TREVOR, Walter, b. Manchester 1931. Eng. dancer. Studied at Manchester B. Club. To S. Wells Sch. 1945, S. Wells Th. B. 1951, becoming soloist 1956. Returned to N. Zealand. From 1968 he and his wife, Sara Neil, have taught at the R. Ballet Sch., London.

TRIAD, ballet, ch. MacMillan, m. Prokofieff, dec. Unsworth, f.p. Royal B., C. Garden 19 Jan 1972 (Sibley, Dowell, Eagling). A girl who flirts with two affectionate brothers and chooses one of them.

TRICORNE, LE, see THREE CORNERED HAT.

TRIOMPHE DE L'AMOUR, LE, ballet in 25 entrées, dances arranged by Beauchamp (q.v.) and Pécour, m. Lully, dec. Berain, words by Benserade and Quinault, f.p. at the Fr. Court at St Germain-en-Laye 21 Jan 1681. On 16 May 1681 it was f.p. at the Paris Opéra (Palais Royal) and for the first time a professional woman dancer appeared (Mlle Lafontaine who was given the title 'Reine de la Danse'). Hitherto the Queen and her Ladies had taken the female rôles.

TRISLER, Joyce, b. Los Angeles 1934. Am. modern dancer. Pupil of Lester Horton, Tudor, Hanya Holm. Joined Lester Horton Co. 1951 and was in Juilliard Dance Theatre 1955–59. Now teaches.

TRIUMPH OF DEATH, THE, ballet, ch. Flindt, m. Koppel, dec. Breum and Thomsen, f.p. R. Danish B., Royal Th., Copenhagen 19 Feb 1972 (V. and F. Flindt, Poul Vessel, Englund, Weinreich and whole Co.). Based on the Ionesco play about a plague, with some nudity and the music recorded by a pop-group, The Savage Rose. Originally created for Danish Television and f.p. 23 May 1971 from the Copenhagen studio (same cast).

TRIUMPH OF NEPTUNE, THE, ballet 2 acts, by S. Sitwell, ch. Balanchine, m. Lord Berners, dec. from Pollock's toy theatres, f.p. Diaghileff's Co., Lyceum Th., London 3 Dec 1926 (Danilova, Lifar). Based on themes from traditional English pantomime.

TRNINIC, Dusan, b. Belgrade 1929. Yugoslav dancer. Pupil of Kirsanova, Royal Ballet Sch. and Preobrajenska. Entered Belgrade National B. 1946, becoming a principal dancer 1948. He has also danced in the Bayreuth and Edinburgh Festivals, Switzerland, etc.

TROFIMOVA, Natascha, b. Berlin 1924. German dancer. Studied under Edouardova and T. and V. Gsovsky. Début 1943 at the Scala Th., Berlin. Prima ballerina at Staatsoper, E. Berlin, 1946–51 and danced in Hamburg and Munich from 1951. In 1957 became prima ballerina at Staatsoper, Munich. Retired 1969.

TROUNSON, Marilyn, b. San Francisco 1947. Am. (now Eng.) dancer. Pupil of Merriem Lanova and, from 1964, Royal B. Sch. Changed nationality 1966 and joined Royal Ballet 1966. Ashton created the rôles in *Lament of the Waves* (1970) for her and Carl Myers. Danced chief rôle in *The Invitation* 1969.

TRUHANOVA, Natalia (Trukhanova), b. 1885, d. Moscow 1956. Russ. dancer. First danced in Russian variety theatres but went to Paris and made her career there under the name Truhanova. Joined Paris Opéra 1907, where her beauty attracted immediate attention. Much influenced by Isadora Duncan, she gave a series of recitals at the Th. des Arts, the Châtelet and the Opéra-Comique. She was a pioneer in using the music of modern Fr. composers and in 1912 there were created for her *Istar* (m. d'Indy, ch. Clustine), *La Péri* (m. Dukas, ch. Clustine), *La Tragédie de Salome* (m. Fl. Schmitt), *Adélaide* (m. Ravel). Left the stage on becoming the Countess Ignatieff.

TRUITTE, James, b. Chicago. Mod. Am. dancer. Pupil of Lester Horton, joined his troupe and took over his school on his death in 1953. Assistant to Ailey in Alvin Ailey's Dance Theatre and teaches in N.Y.

TRUMPET CONCERTO, ballet, ch. Balanchine, m. Haydn, déc. Kernot, f.p. S. Wells Th. B., Opera House, Manchester 14 Sept 1950 (Beriosova, Blair). Ballet of pure dancing, the only one Balanchine created for British ballet. It did not remain in the repertoire.

TRUNOFF, Vassilie, b. Melbourne 1929, Australian dancer and ballet master. Studied under Borovansky and became a soloist in his Co. Joined Festival B. as a principal dancer in 1950. Returned to Borovansky Co. 1953. Rejoined Festival B. 1959. From 1962 ballet master of Festival B. Mar. Joan Potter. Worked in Naples B. 1973.

TSCHAIKOVSKY FOUNDATION, THE, an archive in N.Y. founded 1945 to store and collect pre-Soviet Russian music. It publishes the complete scores, piano arrangements etc. of the Tchaikovsky ballets and others and is much used in research and by ballet companies. The director and editor is Peter March.

TSINGUIRIDES, Georgette, b. Stuttgart 1933. German dancer. Pupil of Morike, Lemanis, Egorova. Joined Stuttgart B. 1947 becoming soloist 1955. Took course of Benesh Notation at the Institute of Choreology and now notator of Stuttgart B. Mounted *Card Game*, Royal B. 1973.

TUDOR, Antony, b. London 1909. Eng. dancer and chor. Studied under Rambert and produced his first ballet *Cross-Gartered* 1931. Joined Vic-Wells B., 1933, as dancer. For the Ballet Club his ballets incl. *The Planets* (1934), *Descent of Hebe* (1935), *Jardin aux Lilas* (1936), *Dark Elegies* (1937), Formed his own Co., The London Ballet, 1938, for whom he chor. *Judgement of Paris, Soirée Musicale, Gala Performance*. To America in 1939 and joined Am. Ballet Theatre as chor. and Artistic Director, and ch. *Pillar of Fire* (considered to be his masterpiece), *Romeo and Juliet*, etc. In *Jardin aux Lilas* and his later work he developed the so-called psychological ballet in which human relationships and characters are portrayed in balletic movements. He mounted ballets for the R. Swedish Ballet where his brief stay in 1950 was a great inspiration to the Company. He has also worked in films. In 1962 he was appointed artistic director of the R. Swed. B. and in 1963 chor. *Echoing of Trumpets* for them. In 1964 he resigned and returned to America, mounting his ballets for companies and teaching in the Met. Op. B. Sch. (of which he has been director since 1950) and the Juilliard Sch. of Music Dance Department. In 1967 he mounted his first new ballet for Royal B. *Shadowplay* and in 1968 he created *Knight Errant* for the Touring Royal B. Chor. *The Divine Horsemen* for Australian B. 1969.

TUGAL, Dr Pierre, b. Russia 1883, d. Paris 1964. Fr. writer on ballet, and curator of the *Archives Internationales de la Danse* in Paris from its foundation in 1931 until it was dissolved in 1950. Delegate to U.N.E.S.C.O. and author of many books on the dance, including *Initiation à la Danse* (1947) and *La Danse Classique Sans Maître* (with Lucien Legrand 1956).

TULIP OF HARLEM, THE, ballet 3 acts 4 sc., ch. Ivanov, m. Schell, f.p. Maryinsky Th., St Petersburg 4 Oct 1887 (Bessone, Legat, Gerdt). In this ballet Bessone turned fourteen fouettés, but when Legnani danced the rôle in 1893 she turned thirty-two, the first time this feat had been performed in Russia.

TURANGALILA, ballet, ch. Petit, m. Messiaen, dec. Max Ernst, f.p. Paris Opéra 21 June 1968 (Motte, Rayet, Piletta, Thibon, Vlassi). It lasts 1½ hours. It was first choreographed by P. van Dijk with dec. Siercke for the Hamburg B., Hamburg 22 June 1960 (Kempf, Rayet, Lihn, Clauss, van Dijk).

TUNÇÇEKIC, Gülcan, b. Kirikkale 1942. Turkish dancer. Studied under B. Appleyard and Molly Lake in Turkey and at Royal B. Sch. Entered Turkish State B., becoming soloist.

TURFANDA, Oytun, b. Kirkagac 1947. Turkish dancer. Studied under Angela Bayley, Molly Lake in Turkey and at Royal B. School. Entered Turkish State B. becoming soloist.

TURKEY, Ballet in. In 1947 de Valois went to Turkey to advise about the formation of a national ballet school, which was duly founded at Istanbul the same year with Joy Newton as principal. In 1949 a demonstration of work was given in which the students were joined by Moira Shearer, Anne Heaton, Michael Somes, and Alexander Grant. In 1950 the school moved to Ankara, and in 1951 Beatrice Appleyard became principal. In 1953 Lorna Mossford and Robert Lunnon of the S. Wells B. went to Ankara to appear with the National Th. and assist at the school, in 1954 Molly Lake and Travis Kemp, and in 1960 Ailne Phillips. On 8 Nov 1963 *Sleeping Beauty* was f.p. in Ankara, dec. Howard, mounted by Mossford (Meric Sumen as Aurora). From 1965–69 R. Glasstone was director and mounted *Sylvia* and *Prince of the Pagodas* (1967). In 1970 Alan Carter became director of new state ballet school in Istanbul, where a new opera house opened in 1969. In Smyrna (Ismir) the state ballet school has been directed by Joan Turner 1968–70, and from 1970–72 by Jocelyn Mather. The Istanbul Opera House was destroyed by fire in 1970 and Carter left. In 1973 the Ankara Nat. B. was in the hands of Nevit Kodalli.

TURNER, Harold, b. Manchester 1909, d. Covent Garden 1962. Eng. dancer. Début 1927 in the Haines English Ballet. Studied under Rambert. Partnered Karsavina in 1930 and was a principal dancer of B. Rambert. Guest artist S. Wells B. 1930, later becoming a principal dancer. Cr. rôles in *Patineurs*, *Checkmate* (Red Knight), etc. Joined International B., but returned to S. Wells in 1945. Retired in 1950 and became ballet master of C. Garden Op. B. and taught at the Royal B. Sch. until his death. Mar. Gerd Larsen. He helped to establish a tradition of male dancing in Britain and was one of the greatest British male dancers.

TURNOUT (Fr. *Le en-dehors*). In the seventeenth and eighteenth centuries it was thought sufficient if each foot was turned out at 45° and possibly this was adequate for the limited range of steps performed by dancers in high-heeled shoes, but the great Italian teacher Carlo Blasis (1803–78), insisted on a fully turned out (90°) position, which has been held to be essential ever since. This turned-out position is not a mere convention, but is anatomically necessary to give the dancer freedom of movement in every direction by enabling the thigh bone fully to rotate in its socket. It also looks more pleasing and assists the dancer's line—it is an aesthetic necessity in dancing. This turned-out position is only acquired after a period of time varying according to the physical conformation of the individual and as a result of suitable exercises calculated to 'turn out' the leg from the hip without wrenching muscles or tearing ligaments. Noverre, in his *Lettres sur la Danse* published in 1760, condemned the use of artificial appliances such as the *tourne hanche* for achieving turnout and, with the spread of knowledge of anatomy and the raising of the standard of teaching, this harmful practice has disappeared.

TUTU, derived from the Fr. child's word *tutu* (i.e. *cul-cul*) 'bottom', and by extension the slang term used to describe the very short petticoat sewn together between the legs, sometimes still made and unmade at each performance, and worn by danseuses to conceal that part of

505

their anatomy. Today it designates the short classical ballet skirt, and is also sometimes used to describe the bell-shaped 'Sylphide' ballet skirt. Camargo in 1730 introduced the entrechat into the dance vocabulary of the danseuse, shortening the skirt to above the instep and wearing knickers, a wise precaution when performing steps of elevation as shown by the unfortunate experience of Mlle Mariette (in 1727) who, catching her dress on a piece of scenery, was obliged to do an impromptu pose in the nude for a full minute, after which a police regulation made it compulsory for all artists to add to their underwear a *caleçon de précaution*, or precautionary pants. Later the development of technique necessitating greater freedom for the legs, resulted in the skirt being progressively shortened until, with the dress designed by Lami for *La Sylphide* in 1832, it reached midway between knee and ankle, while the virtuosity of the Italian dancers in Russia in the eighties (notably Zucchi) caused it to be shortened to the brief classical tutu. The tutu is made of a pair of tarlatan knickers trimmed with four or five rows of superimposed tarlatan frills, each deeper than the previous one, and surmounted by two wider frills, the topmost being suitably ornamented with sequins or embroidery and usually strengthened by a wire hoop. The tutu proper is joined to a skin-tight basque surmounted by a low-cut bodice. At the Paris Opéra, the long tutu is called a *juponnage*. Russian dancers call it *patchka*.

TWELVE MONTHS, ballet, ch. Fenster, m. Bitov, dec. Bruni, f.p. Maly Th., Leningrad 16 May 1954 (Isaeva, Sheina, Stankevich, Mazun, Zimin, Khamzin).

TWO BROTHERS, ballet, ch. N. Morrice, m. Dohnányi, dec. Koltai, f.p. Ballet Rambert, Marlowe Th., Canterbury 14 Aug 1958 (Martlew, Chesworth, Morrice). Rivalry of two brothers in a back street. This was Morrice's first ballet.

TWO PIGEONS, THE, see DEUX PIGEONS, LES.

TYL EULENSPIEGEL, ballet (1) ch. Nijinsky, m. R. Strauss, dec. Jones, f.p. Met. Op., N.Y. 23 Oct 1916 (Nijinsky); (2) ch. Balanchine, dec. Frances, f.p. N.Y. City B., City Center, N.Y. 14 Nov 1951 (Robbins). See also TIL EULENSPIEGEL.

U

UBOLDI, Christian, b. Montevideo 1932. Uruguayan dancer and chor. Pupil of Chabelska, Kniaseff, Fenonjois. Joined ballet of Theatro Sodre 1949, Rio de Janeiro B. 1956, de Cuevas 1957–60, Massine's Co.

1960, Larrain's *Cendrillon* (Paris 1963), Béjart B., Marseille B. 1969. Chor. many ballets. Appointed ballet master at Limoges 1970. To Paris 1971.

UDAETA, José, b. Barcelona 1919. Spanish dancer. Trained in Madrid and was ballet master at the Liceo Th. in Barcelona. He met Susana Audeoud when she was ballerina in Madrid in 1947 and they gave their first recital together in Geneva in 1948—becoming the team *Susana and José* end engaged in concert tours of Spanish dancing and flamenco all over the world until 1970.

ULANOVA, Galina, b. St Petersburg 1910. Russ. dancer. Daughter of Sergei Ulanov (1881–1950) and Maria Romanova (1886–1954) both dancers at the Maryinsky Th. Graduated from Imp. Sch. 1928. Début in *Chopiniana*. Danced *Swan Lake* (1929), *Sleeping Beauty* (1930), *Giselle* (1932), *Fountain of Bakhchisarai* (1934, cr. rôle of Maria), *Romeo and Juliet* (1940, cr. rôle of Juliet), *La Bayadère* (1941)—all at the Kirov Th., Leningrad. Transferred to the Bolshoi Th., Moscow 1944 where she cr. the rôle in *Cinderella* (1945). Her first appearance in the West was at the Maggio Musicale, Florence 1951. First danced in London 1956 and N.Y. 1959. She retired as a member of the Bolshoi B. 1960 but remained as guest artist. Finally retired from the stage 1962 becoming principal ballet mistress and teacher in 1964. Her position in Russia is comparable only with Margot Fonteyn's in England. People's Artist of the R.S.F.S.R. 1951, Stalin Prize 1946, Lenin Prize 1957. Mar. (1) Y. Zavadsky, stage director, (2) V. F. Ryndin, stage designer. Chairman of Varna Competition since 1964.

UNDERTOW, ballet 1 act, ch. Tudor, m. W. Schuman, dec. Breinin, f.p. Ballet Th., Met. Op., N.Y. 10 Apr 1945 (Laing, Alonso, Adams). Symbolic ballet of the birth of man and his emotions.

UNICORN, THE GORGON AND THE MANTICORE, THE, ballet, ch. J. Butler, m. Menotti, cost. Fletcher, f.p. N.Y. City B., City Center, N.Y. 15 Jan 1957 (Magallanes, A. Mitchell, Janet Reed). An ironical fable. Also chor. Yvonne Georgi, Hanover 7 Sept 1959.

UNION PACIFIC, ballet 1 act, 4 sc., ch. Massine, m. Nabokov, dec. Johnson and Sharaff, f.p. de Basil, Forrest Th., Philadelphia 6 Apr 1934 (Massine, Delarova, Osato, Toumanova, Eglevsky). Witty ballet on the building of the Transcontinental Railroad in America.

URBAIN, James, b. Paris 1943. Fr. dancer. Pupil of Peretti at Paris Opéra, Hightower and Besobrasova. Joined Petit's B. de Paris 1959, de Cuevas 1960–62, B. Classique de France 1965, B. Russe de Monte Carlo 1967 (guest), Ballet-Théâtre Contemporain (Amiens) 1968, Festival B. 1969, Scala, Milan 1970. Dances much in Italy.

URSULIAK, Alexander, b. Edmonton (Canada) 1937. Canad. dancer and teacher. Pupil of Seychuk in Canada and Klavin and Zaytsev in Kieff. Joined Canad. Nat. B. 1961–63. In 1963–65 taught at Arts Educational Sch., London. Teacher at Vienna Staatsoper 1965–73. Teacher of Stuttgart B. from 1973. Mar. (1) Galina Samtsova whom he brought out of Russia (2) Christl Himmelbauer.

USHER, Graham, b. Beverley 1938. Eng. dancer. Entered S. Wells Sch. 1949 and joined S. Wells Ballet 1955, becoming soloist 1958. Danced Frantz in *Coppélia*, the first perf. of the Royal Ballet Sch. at C. Garden, in 1959. Retired 1970.

UTHOFF, Ernst, b. Duisburg 1904. Ger. dancer. Pupil of Jooss and Leeder. Joined B. Jooss 1927 becoming soloist and assistant ballet master. Left Co. in 1942 in Santiago and with his wife, Lola Botka, founded the Chilean Nat. B. Left the company in 1966. His son Michael U., b. Santiago 1943, is also a dancer, trained at Juilliard Sch. Joined Limon Co. 1964, Joffrey B. 1965. Mar. Lisa Bradley. DirectorHartford B. 1973.

V

VAGANOVA, Agrippina, b. St Petersburg 1879, d. Leningrad 1951. Russ. dancer and teacher. Trained Imp. Sch. and entered Co. 1897. Promoted to ballerina 1915 and retired 1917. Teacher at the Leningrad Sch. from 1919. Author of *Fundamentals of the Classic Dance* (1934, translated into Eng. by Anatole Chujoy 1937). Honoured Artist of the Republic and head of the Soviet Choreographic Technicum. She was one of the greatest teachers of this generation and, having been a pupil of Oblakhov, Ivanov, Vazem, Gerdt, and Legat, she was a direct link between the old Russ. Sch. and the present day, herself teaching Ulanova, Semyonova, and others, and also Volkova, who has transmitted her methods to the dancers of Western Europe and America. In 1957 the Leningrad Ballet Sch. was named after her (the Vaganova Institute). People's Artist 1936. Stalin Prize 1946.

VAILLAT, Léandre, b. Publier 1876, d. 1952, Fr. writer on ballet, critic, and author. Among his ballet works are *Histoire de la Danse* (1942), *La Taglioni* (1942), *Olga Spessivtseva* (1945), *Ballets de l'Opéra* (1943 and 1947), *La Danse à l'Opéra de Paris* (1951).

VAINONEN, Vasily I., b. St Petersburg 1898, d. Moscow 1964. Russ, dancer and chor. Graduated from Petrograd B. Sch. 1919. Until 1939 dancer and chor. at Kirov Th., Leningrad. Appointed chief of ballet at

Stanislavsky Th., Moscow 1939. In 1944 became chief of the ballet Co. at Minsk, and in 1946 returned to Moscow to become chor. and producer at Bolshoi Th. Chor. *Flames of Paris* (1932), *Partisan Days* (1937), *Gayané* (1957), and new versions of *Casse Noisette* (1934), *Raymonda* (1938). In 1949 he went to Budapest to revive the Hungarian Nat. B., staging *Flames of Paris* and *Casse Noisette* for them. He was also chief choreographer at Novosibirsk 1952–53. See MOSKOWSKY WALTZ.

VALBERG, Ivan, b. 1766, d. 1819. Russ. ballet master (possibly Swed. origin). Pupil of G. Angiolini and Canziani. Was the first Russ. dancer to gain real success and be paid a high salary. He was sent to Paris to study in 1802 and was protected by Empress Catherine II. Among his pupils was Eugenie Kolosova (q.v.) and his ballets included *Le Nouveau Werther* (m. S. Titov, f.p. St Petersburg 30 Jan 1799), which was inspired by Goethe. He chor. many patriotic ballets at the time of the Napoleonic Wars. He was made director of the St Petersburg B. Sch. 1794 and manager of the ballet Co. (then at the Bolshoi Th.).

VALSE, LA, ballet. (1) ch. Nijinska, dec. Benois, m. Ravel, f.p. Ida Rubinstein's Co., Monte Carlo 12 Jan 1929 (Rubinstein, Vilzak). In 1931 it was redone for Ida Rubinstein by Fokine (25 June 1931, Paris Opéra). (2) ch. Balanchine, dec. Karinska, f.p. N.Y. City B., City Center, N.Y. 20 Feb 1951 (LeClerq, Magallanes, Moncion). (3) ch. Ashton, m. Ravel, dec. Levasseur, f.p. Scala, Milan 1 Feb 1958. Taken into repertory of the Royal Ballet, C. Garden 10 Mar 1959 (Dixon, Beckley, Daryl, Burne, Farley, Rosson).

VALSE EXCENTRIQUE, divertimento for three dancers, ch. MacMillan, m. Ibert, f.p. Gala for Hungarian Refugees, S. Wells Th., London 10 Dec 1956 (Linden, Shaw, Grant). In old bathing dresses.

VALSES NOBLES ET SENTIMENTALES, ballet 1 act, ch. Ashton, m. Ravel, dec. Fedorovitch, f.p. S. Wells Th. B., S. Wells Th. 1 Oct 1947 (Heaton). Ballet of pure dancing.

VALTONEN, Martti, b. Uusikirkko 1937. Finnish dancer. Started ballet lessons in 1958 under Koskinen and Salin and joined National B. 1959. Became soloist 1966 and principal dancer 1968. Studied under Nora Kiss and Peretti, also at Royal B. Sch. and with Anna Northcote.

VAN BEERS, Sonja, b. Arnhem 1940. Dutch dancer. Member of the Nederlands B. and then a principal of the Dutch Nat. B.

VAN BOVEN, Arlette, b. Antwerp 1942. Belgian dancer. Pupil of Jeanne Brabants and Andelka Illitch in Paris. Joined R. Flemish B. 1958, Béjart's B. 1961–65. To England and joined Royal B. (Ballet for All)

1966, Western Th. B. 1967 as soloist. Soloist of Nederlands Dans Th. from 1969.

VANCE, Norma, b. N.Y. 1927, d. in air crash over Lake Erie 1956. Am. dancer. Pupil of Swoboda. With Slavenska 1943–44, Ballet Th. 1946, becoming one of their soloists. Was called Vaslavina until 1947.

VAN DAELE, Maria, b. Antwerp 1944. Belgian dancer. Studied under Brabants 1953–59, Royal B. Sch. 1957–58, André Leclair 1966–68. Entered R. Flemish B., Antwerp 1960, becoming soloist 1968.

VAN DANTZIG, Rudi, b. Amsterdam 1933. Dutch dancer and chor. Pupil of Sonia Gaskell, danced with her Ballet Recital group 1952–54. Joined Nederlands B. 1954 and chor. for them *Night Island* (1954), *Time and Tide* (1955), *Mozart Symphony* (1956), *The Family* (1957), *Spring Concerto* (1958). Joined Nederlands Dans Th. 1959–60 and chor. *Giovinezza* and *Looking Back* (1959). To the Dutch Nat. B. 1961 and chor. *Jungle* (1961), *Disgenoten* (1958), *Monument for a Dead Boy* (1965), *Moments* (1968), *Après Visage* (1972). In 1970 he chor. *Ropes of Time* for the Royal B. In 1969, on the resignation of Sonia Gaskell, he became joint director (with Robert Kaesen) of the Dutch Nat. B., and in 1971 sole director.

VAN DER SLOOT, Pieter, b. Amsterdam 1926. Dutch dancer and chor. Pupil of Schwezoff, Georgi, Volkova etc. Danced with Gaskell's Ballet Recital group, Nederlands B. 1943, Regent B., London 1948, Nice Opera B. 1952. In 1955 founded (with V. Rossi) Teatro Italiano de Balletto, a group which toured Italy. In 1969–70 was ballet master at Münster. Chor. many ballets.

VAN DIJK, Peter (also Van Dyk), b. Bremen 1929. Ger. dancer. Pupil of T. Gsovsky in Berlin. Début Berlin Opera B. 1950, soloist Wiesbaden 1952. Joined Charrat's Ballet de France 1952 and was principal male dancer in her *Les Algues* (1953). Appointed étoile of Paris Opéra 1955 and also danced as principal in Hamburg B. of which he became director 1963–70. Chor. *Pelléas and Melisande* (1952), *Peau de Chagrin* (Opéra Comique, Paris 1960), *Romeo and Juliet* etc. In 1972 director of Hanover B.

VAN GOETHEN, Louise, b. Paris 1870, d. there 1945. Fr. dancer. Pupil of Paris Opéra Sch., joined Co. and became *grand sujet* 1895. Became one of the teachers 1908 until 1933. In spite of her modest career, she has been immortalized by Degas who, when she was nine, modelled her in wax—his *Petit Rat* statues in the Louvre and in the Tate Gallery.

VANGSAA, Mona, b. Copenhagen 1920. Danish dancer. Pupil at Theatre Sch., Copenhagen, becoming solodancer 1942. Mar. Frank Schaufuss.

Retired 1962. Awarded Knight of the Order of Dannebrog. Peter Schaufuss is her son.

VAN HAMEL, Martine, b. Brussels 1945. Dutch dancer. Studied at Hague Conservatorium 1956–57 and under Henry Danton in Caracas 1957–59, Canad. Nat. B. Sch. 1959–63. Joined Canad. Nat. B. 1963 as soloist. Won a first prize at Varna 1966, partnered by Earl Kraul. In 1968 to R. Swed. B. as guest artist and of Joffrey B. 1970. Joined Am. Ballet Th. 1971.

VAN MANEN, Hans, b. Amsterdam 1932. Dutch dancer and chor. Pupil of Sonia Gaskell. Soloist Amsterdam Op. B. 1953–58, Petit's B. de Paris 1959–60. Joined Nederlands Dans Th. 1960, becoming director 1961–70. Chor. *Intermezzo* (m. Honegger), *Mouvements Symphoniques* (m. Haydn), *Moon in the Trapeze* (m. Britten), *Concertino* (m. Blacher), *Keep Going* (m. Berio), *Grosse Füge* (m. Beethoven) 1971, *Twilight* 1972.

VANINA VANINI, ballet, ch. Kasatkina and Vasiliov, m. Karetnikov, dec. Goncharov, f.p. Bolshoi Th., Moscow 25 May 1962 (E. Riabynkina, Tikhonov). The Stendahl story.

VAN PRAAGH, Dame Peggy, b. London 1910. Eng. dancer and teacher. Studied Aimée Phipps and Margaret Craske. Danced with Dolin 1929, opened school 1930. Joined B. Rambert 1933. In 1938 a principal dancer in Tudor's London B., and in 1941 joined S. Wells B., dancing solo rôles. On formation of S. Wells Th. B. in 1946, she became its ballet mistress and from 1952 to 1955 was its Assistant Director. She created rôles in *Jardin aux Lilas*, *Dark Elegies*, and *Gala Performance*. From 1955 mounted ballets in Canada, Munich, Copenhagen, etc. for Royal B. In 1960 to Australia as artistic director of Borovansky B. Guest teacher Cuevas B. 1961. In 1962 she was invited back to Australia to form the Australian Ballet of which she has been director since 1963 (from 1965 jointly with Helpmann). Appointed O.B.E. 1966 and D.B.E. 1970. A leading member and examiner of the Cecchetti Society since 1935. Author of *How I Became a Dancer* (1954) and, with Peter Brinson, *The Art of Choreography* (1963), *Ballet in Australia* (1965).

VAN SCHAYK, Toer, b. Amsterdam 1936. Dutch artist, dancer and chor. Joined Dutch Nat. B. 1967 and leading modern dancer of the Co. since 1968. Designed dec. and cost. of many of their ballets, including *De Disgenoten* and *Monument for a Dead Boy* (also creating the leading rôle). Formerly in the Nederlands B. Chor. *Post Imperfect* (m. Ligeti) 1971, *Before, During and After the Party* (m. Von Bergeyk) 1972.

VANTAGGIO, Giancarlo, b. Rome 1936. It. dancer. Studied at Rome Opera House Sch. 1947–57. Principal dancer in Rome 1959 and later danced in the ballets of Bordeaux and Bonn. Returned to Rome as primo ballerino 1966. Chor. many ballets. Mar. Terabust.

VARGAS, Manolo, b. Mexico. Sp. dancer. Danced in Argentinita's company in N.Y. Became first dancer of Pilar Lopez's company. In 1954 formed a new Co. with Ximenez.

VARIATION, a solo dance.

VARIATIONS, divertissement, ch. Lifar, m. Schubert, f.p. Paris Opéra 11 Mar 1953 for the six étoiles (Darsonval, Vaussard, Bardin, Lafon, Vyroubova, Daydé).

VARIATIONS FOR FOUR, ballet, ch. Dolin, m. Keogh, cost. Lingwood, f.p. Festival Ballet, Festival Hall, London 5 Sept 1957 (Gilpin, Flindt, Godfrey, Prokovsky). In repertoire of many companies.

VARIATIONS ON A THEME OF PURCELL, ballet 1 act, ch. Ashton, m. Britten (*Young Person's Guide to the Orchestra*), dec. Snow, f.p. S. Wells B., C. Garden, London 6 Jan 1955 (Nerina, Jackson, Fifield, Grant). See also *Fanfare* (Robbins).

VARNA, INTERNATIONAL BALLET COMPETITION, organized by the Bulgarian Ministry of Culture is held in July at Varna on the Black Sea. The first was in 1964, second in 1965, third in 1966, the fourth 1968 and thereafter every two years. There are senior and junior sections and competitors are housed and fed free on arrival. The jury has Ulanova as chairman and Haskell as vice-chairman (until 1973), with a number of international dancers and teachers. It awards gold, silver and bronze medals.

VARSAVIANA, dance similar to the polka, mazurka, and redowa, probably introduced to France by a dancing master, Desiré, in 1853. The music is in slow 3/4 time with strong accents on the first notes of the 2nd and 4th bar. Also varsovienne.

VASILIOV, Vladimir, b. Moscow 1931. Russ. dancer and chor. Joined Bolshoi B. 1953. With his wife, N. Kasatkina, chor. *Vanina Vanini* (1962), *The Geologists* (or *The Heroic Poem*) (1964) and new version of Stravinsky's *Sacre du Printemps* (1965), *Creation of the World* (1971).

VASLAVINA, see VANCE, Norma.

VASSILIEV, Vladimir, b. Moscow 1940. Russ. dancer. Trained at Bolshoi Sch. under Gabovitch and graduated to Bolshoi B. as soloist 1958. Created chief rôle in *Spartacus* (1968) and the Prince in *Nutcracker* (1965) both ch. Grigorovitch. Nijinsky Prize, Paris 1964, Varna Gold Medal 1964, Hon. Artist R.S.F.S.R. 1964, Lenin Prize 1970. Mar. E. Maximova.

VAUSSARD, Christiane, b. Neuilly 1923. Fr. dancer. Studied Paris Opéra under Zambelli, becoming première danseuse 1945 and étoile in 1947. Now retired but teaches at the Opéra.

VAZEM, Ekaterina O., b. Moscow 1848, d. Leningrad 1937. Russ. dancer. Entered Imp. Sch., St Petersburg 1857 and studied under Petipa and Ivanov (his junior class in 1858). Became ballerina, her reign lasting from 1864 to 1884. She had a faultless technique, and was cold and expressionless, but she was Petipa's favourite dancer and he created eight ballets for her (incl. *La Bayadère* and the *Grand Pas* in *Paquita*). She retired in 1884 at the height of her fame and taught, among others, Pavlova and Vaganova. Author of *Memoirs of a Ballerina of the St Petersburg Bolshoi Theatre* (1937).

VECHESLOVA, Tatiana, b. 1910. Russ. dancer. Graduated from Imp. Sch., St Petersburg 1928 (with Ulanova). She was ballerina at the Kirov Th. until 1953 when she retired. She was director of the Leningrad Sch. 1952–54 and is now one of the ballet-mistresses of the Kirov B. Author of *I am a Ballerina* (1964).

VEIGL, Eva Maria, b. Vienna 1724, d. London 1822. Austrian dancer, pupil of Hilferding, who attracted great attention at Hofoper, Vienna, under the name 'Mademoiselle Violette'. She came to London in 1746 under the protection of Lord and Lady Burlington and married the actor David Garrick in 1749. Although their marriage was resented by Mrs Cibber, Quin, Macklin and Barry, it was a supremely happy one (Garrick called her 'the best of women and wives') and lasted until his death thirty years later. She is buried in Westminster Abbey.

VENDRIG, Yvonne, b. Utrecht 1943. Dutch dancer. Joined Dutch Nat. B. 1961, becoming soloist 1967. Created leading rôle in *Monument for a Dead Boy* (1965) and Juliet in van Dantzig's *Romeo and Juliet* (1967).

VENEMA, Mea, b. Haarlem 1946. Dutch dancer. Studied in Haarlem and joined Nederlands Dans Th. 1963 becoming soloist 1970.

VENEZIANA, ballet 1 act, ch. Howard, m. Donizetti (arr. Ap Ivor), dec. Fedorovitch, f.p. S. Wells B., C. Garden 9 Apr 1953 (Elvin, Powell). Carnival in Venice.

VENTANA, LA (The Window), ballet, ch. Bournonville, m. Lumbye, f.p. by the Price family at the Casino, Copenhagen 19 June 1854, but later given by the R. Danish B. at the R. Opera House, Copenhagen 26 Dec 1854 (when the sisters Juliet and Sophie Price danced the Mirror Dance which is its most famous feature). Bournonville revised it 6 Oct 1856 and it has remained in the repertoire ever since, having its 100th performance there 6 Apr 1876 and its 200th 5 Sept 1945. It is Spanish in style. Taken into repertoire of Western Th. B., dec. Stoddard, f.p. S. Wells Th. 18 June 1968 (Mirror Dance by van Boven and Valerie Sanders). The Seguidilla in the ballet is 'after Paul Taglioni' (according to the 1854 programme).

VERCHININA, Nina, b. Moscow. Russ. dancer, sister of Olga Morosova. Pupil of Preobrajenska and Nijinska and later studied the Laban style. Début in Ida Rubinstein Co. 1929. Soloist of de Basil Co. 1933–37 and cr. rôles in *Les Présages* (Action), *Choreartium*, *Symphonie Fantastique* etc. Joined San Francisco B. 1937–38, Orig. B. Russe 1939–41, and since then settled in S. America, working in Buenos Aires and Rio de Janeiro, now teaching at her own school in Copacabana.

VERDE GAIO, Portuguese ballet company founded and controlled by the Ministry of Propaganda to dance national ballets based on national dances. Its first performance was in the Teatro da Trindade, Lisbon and its artistic director, chief dancer and chor. was Francis Graca. In 1941 it made its home the Teatro San Carlos, Lisbon. The Verde Gaio also presents ballets in the classical style having had Violette Quenolle, late of the Paris Opéra, as ballerina and ballet mistress. In 1960 F. Graca retired and was succeeded by Margarita de Abreu and Fernando Lima as directors. Ivo Cramèr, the Swedish chor. and dancer, has also worked with the Co., mounting his own works. The Co. has had a short season in Paris and in Madrid 1942. After 1968 the company no longer presented classical ballets but reverted to its original intention of performing national dances.

VERDY, Violette, b. Pont-l'Abbé 1933. Fr. dancer. Pupil of Rousanne and later of V. Gsovsky. As Nelly Guillerm (her real name) début in B. des Ch. Élysées 1945. Changed her name to star in film *Ballerina* 1949. Joined B. de Paris 1953 as principal dancer. Cr. rôle in *Le Loup* (1953). Also acted with J. L. Barrault at Marigny Th., Paris 1950–51. Joined Festival B. as principal dancer 1954, touring U.S. Ballerina at Scala, Milan 1955 and also principal dancer of Petit's Co. Guest star of Ballet Rambert 1957. To America 1957 as ballerina first of Am. Ballet Th. and since 1958 of N.Y. City B. Guest artist Royal B. 1964 and danced *Sleeping Beauty* etc. at C. Garden. Chor. *Sicilian Vespers* (m. Verdi) 1970 for Cincinatti B.

VERE, Diana (Fox), b. Trinidad 1942. Eng. dancer. Trained at Elmhurst Sch. and Royal B. Sch. Joined Royal B. 1962, becoming soloist 1968, principal 1970. Danced *Giselle* 1971. Mar. Gary Sherwood.

VEREDON, Grey, b. 1943. New Zealand dancer. Pupil of P. Gnatt and Royal B. Sch. Joined N. Zealand B. 1960, C. Garden Op. B. 1963, Stuttgart B. 1964–68. To Cologne 1968 and, with H. Baumann, founded the Tanz-Forum Co. Mar. S. Alexanders.

VERHAERT, Jacqueline, b. Antwerp 1936. Belgian dancer. Studied with Jeanne Brabants, Preobrajenska, Northcote. Ballerina Royal Flemish B., Antwerp 1957–70.

VERNON, Konstanze (Herzfeld), b. Berlin 1939. Ger. dancer. Pupil of T. Gsovsky, Kiss, Peretti. Joined Deutsche Oper B., Berlin 1956 becoming soloist. Soloist and principal of Munich B. from 1963. Also danced with T. Gsovsky's Berliner Ballet in 1959.

VÉRON, Dr L. D., b. Paris 1798, d. there 1867. Director of the Paris Opéra 1831–35, one of its greatest periods. During his régime were produced the opera *Robert the Devil* and *La Sylphide*, the ballet which launched Taglioni and the Romantic era in ballet (it was her dance in the opera which gave Nourrit the inspiration for the ballet). He made a fortune from a patent medicine, turned to journalism, and founded the *Revue de Paris* and revived *Le Constitutionnel*. He was a man of repulsive appearance, of great wit, and for a time Rachel was his mistress.

VERT-VERT, ballet 3 acts, ch. Mazilier, m. Deldevez and Tolbecque, dec. Cambon and Thierry, cost. Lormier, f.p. Paris Opéra 25 Nov 1851 (Plunkett, Priora). Ballet of the Fr. Court at Fontainebleau. 'Vert-Vert' is a boy, played by a danseuse travestie.

VESALII ICONES, solo dance, ch. Louther, m. Maxwell Davies, f.p. Queen Elizabeth Hall, London 9 Dec 1969 (Wm. Louther). A piece for 'cello and small group of instruments inspired by the illustrations from Vesalius's anatomical treatise *De Humani Corpus Fabrica*, 1543, with a near-nude dancer impersonating them. In repertoire of London Cont. Dance Th.

VESCO, Eleonore, b. Berlin 1925. Ger. dancer. Pupil of T. Gsovsky and Blank. Joined Staatsoper B., Berlin, becoming ballerina 1960, in Hamburg 1962 and Städt. Op. Berlin 1963–68. Retired 1969.

VESSEL, Anne Marie, b. Copenhagen 1949. Dan. dancer, daughter of Poul Vessel. Entered R. Dan. B. Sch. 1956 and the Co. 1967.

VESSEL, Poul, b. Copenhagen 1914. Danish dancer and régisseur. Entered R. Dan. Ballet Sch. 1923 and joined the Royal Danish B. 1933. Became régisseur of the Company 1944.

VESTRIS, Auguste, b. Paris 1760, d. there 1842. It. dancer, son of Gaetano Vestris and Marie Allard (the public called him Vestr'Allard). Début Paris Opéra 1772. He was premier danseur there for thirty-six years and was also maître de ballet at King's Th., London, for a time. He had remarkable elevation and technique, and, although short, he appears to have been one of the greatest male dancers of all time '. . . who on one leg could do what erst no mortal could achieve on two'. His last appearance was at the Opéra at the age of 75, partnering Taglioni, then 31. His great rival was Duport. His son, Armand

Vestris (1787–1825) made his début at Paris Opéra 1800 on the stage with his father and grandfather. Début in London 1809 and was chor. of King's Th. 1813–16. Mar. actress Lucia Elisabeth Bartolozzi, better known as Madame Vestris. He also worked in Naples and Vienna. August V.'s cousin, Charles Vestris (b. 1797), had début in Paris Opéra 1809 and was dancing there in the 1820s. He and his wife, Caroline Ronzi, danced with success in America 1828–29 (she was the mistress of 'Kangaroo' Cooke, *aide-de-camp* of the Duke of York in the Napoleonic Wars).

VESTRIS, Gaetano, b. Florence 1729, d. Paris 1808. It. dancer. Entered Paris Opéra 1748, studied under Dupré, whom he succeeded in 1751 as danseur seul, but was dismissed in 1754 for rushing at J. B. Lany, the maître de ballet, with a sword (on account of his sister, the dancer THÉRÈSE VESTRIS (1726–1808), who was Lany's mistress). Returned in 1756 (having produced his first ballet in 1755 in Turin) and became the idol of the public—greatly assisted by his brother Jean Baptiste, who called out during a performance, '*C'est le Diou de la Danse*', the title previously given to the great Dupré. Appointed assistant to Lany 1761, and in 1763 worked under Noverre at Stuttgart, with whom he was much in sympathy (his brother, ANGIOLO VESTRIS, was dancing there). Was instrumental in getting Noverre to Paris in 1765 to produce *Médée*, in which he danced with his mistress, Mlle Allard, who had born him a son, AUGUSTE VESTRIS, in 1760. From 1770 to 1775 he was maître de ballet at the Opéra. In 1781 he and his son were dancing in London and a sitting of Parliament was suspended to allow the Members to attend at the Opera House. He retired in 1782 and mar. Anne Heinel 1792. In 1772 he discarded his mask in the ballet *Castor et Pollux* and so ended the tradition of wearing masks in the theatre.

VIC-WELLS BALLET, see ROYAL BALLET.

VIENNA STAATSOPER BALLET, THE, The Vienna Opera House was built in 1869 but ballet played an important part in the Imperial Court long before at the Hoftheater and the Kärntnertor Th. Hilferding and Angiolini were Imperial ballet masters in the eighteenth century. Noverre worked there for seven years (1767–74) and Viganó chor. *The Creatures of Prometheus* composed for him by Beethoven in 1801. In the Romantic period Filippo Taglioni moved to Vienna with his family. His son Paul was born there in 1808 and his daughter Marie made her début at the Hoftheater in 1822. Her greatest rival, Fanny Elssler, was born in Vienna, worked and died there—Austria's greatest dancer. Paul Taglioni chor. *Sardanapal* (m. Hertel) which was the first ballet to be staged at the Opera House—a few weeks after it opened in 1869. In 1888 Josef Hassreiter's *Die Puppenfee* (m. Bayer) was first performed, and it is still in the repertoire. He was the first to engage all Viennese dancers instead of employing foreign artists as formerly. When Richard Strauss directed the Opera House he put on his *Legend of Joseph* (chor. by H. Kröller; originally it was by Fokine) in 1922 and his new *Schlagobers* (also chor. Kröller) in 1924. Other distinguished pre-Second World War ballet masters were Margarethe Wallman and Willy Fränzl.

The Opera House was destroyed in 1945 and between then and its reopening in 1955 the company performed in the Volksoper and the Theater an der Wien. After the War, Erika Hanka (q.v.) was ballet mistress and she recreated the company and revived the interest in ballet. Her notable ballets were *Der Mohr von Venedig* (m. Blacher) 1955, *Hotel Sacher* (m. Hellmesberger-Schonherr) 1957 and *Medusa* (m. Einem) 1957. She was a 'Central European style' dancer and in 1954 she brought in Gordon Hamilton of Sadler's Wells B. as her assistant. His production of *Giselle* was a turning point in the history of the company, restoring the classical style to the company. It was the first ballet to be presented in the new Opera House (29 Nov 1955, Bauer, Dirtl), sharing the programme with Hanka's *Mohr von Venedig*.

Hanka died in 1958 and was succeeded by Parlic and by Milloss. Orlikowski was ballet master 1966–71 (*Prince of the Pagodas* 1967) when Milloss returned and is again (1972) ballet master. Nureyev created his first ballet, *Tancredi* (m. Henze), there in 1956. The Staatsoper B. has 84 dancers and among its principals are Edeltraut Brexner, Christl Zimmerl, Gisela Cech, Susanne Kirnbauer, Ully Wührer, Erika Zlocha, Karl Musil, Michael Birkmeyer, Paul Vondrak. There is a large ballet school in the Opera House, directed by Alexander Ursuliak. The company toured America in 1972.

VIENNOISES, DANSEUSES, troupe of Viennese children founded by Josephine Weiss, ballet mistress at Josephstadt Th., Vienna. They were immensely popular in Europe, danced at the Paris Opéra 1845, at Her Majesty's Th., London, the same year, and at Drury Lane in 1846. This troupe was similar to, but founded later than, the Viennese Children's Ballet founded by Friedrich Horschelt, in which Heberle was trained.

VIGANÒ, Salvatore, b. Naples 1769, d. Milan 1821. It. dancer and chor. Nephew of Boccherini. Much influenced by Dauberval, whom he met in Madrid. Toured Europe with Maria Medina, his wife. In 1812 became maître de ballet at the Scala, Milan, where he devoted himself to choreography. Beethoven composed *Prometheus* for him in 1801. His ballets incl. *Gli Strelizzi* (1809), and *I Titani* (1819). Ballet in Italy had its greatest period under his influence and declined after his death. He was slow, unexcitable, and good-humoured.

VIKULOV, Sergei, b. Leningrad 1937. Russ. dancer. Graduated from Leningrad Sch. to Kirov B. 1956, becoming soloist. Varna Gold Medal 1964, Nijinsky Prize, Paris 1965. Hon. Artist R.S.F.S.R. 1966. Mar. Tatiana Udalenkova. Chor. two experimental ballets in Leningrad 1968. Grandson of A. Gorsky (q.v.). People's Artist R.S.F.S.R. 1970.

VILIA, ballet (story of *The Merry Widow*), ch. Ruth Page, m. Lehar, dec. Wakhevitch, f.p. Festival B., Palace Th., Manchester 30 Apr 1953 (Krassovska, Briansky, Dolin).

VILLELLA, Edward, b. Long Island, New York 1936. Am. dancer Studied at Sch. of Am. Ballet and at N.Y. High Sch. of Performing Arts. Joined N.Y. City B. 1957 and became a principal dancer 1959. First danced in London (with Violette Verdy) 1962 at R.A.D. Gala. Chor. *Narkissos* (1967).

VILZAK, Anatole, b. St Petersburg 1896. Russ. dancer and teacher. Graduated from St Petersburg Sch. 1915. Joined Diaghileff 1921 and later danced in de Basil and Rubinstein Cos. Since 1940 had a sch. in N.Y. with his wife, Ludmila Shollar. Joined San Francisco B. Sch. 1965.

VINCENT, René, b. Amsterdam 1938. Dutch dancer. Pupil of van Muyden 1955, S. Gaskell 1955, Harkarvy 1959. Joined Dutch Nat. Ballet 1955, danced in Nederlands Dans Theater 1959, Nice B. 1962, Geneva B. 1963 and returned to Dutch Nat. B. 1965 as principal dancer. From 1971 teacher of Scapino B.

VINOGRADOV, Oleg, b. Leningrad 1937. Russ. dancer and chor. Graduated from Kirov Sch. 1959 and joined Novosibirsk B. where he started his choreography. Chor. *Swan Lake* Act I, *Cinderella* 1963 (Okatova, Dolgushin), *Romeo and Juliet* 17 Apr 1965—all f.p. Novosibirsk. Chor. *Asel* 1967 for Bolshoi B., Moscow, and *Gorianka* (m. Kaglachev) 20 Mar 1968 for Kirov B., Leningrad. Appointed associate artistic director Kirov B. 1970. Chief chor. Maly Th. 1972.

VINOGRADOVA, Sofia, b. Staraiaroussa 1929. Russ. dancer. Entered Sch. of the Stanislavski and Nemirovitch-Dantchenko Th. 1939 and joined the Co. 1947, becoming ballerina.

VIOLETTE, Mlle, see VEIGL, Eva Maria.

VIOLON DU DIABLE, LE, ballet 2 acts 6 sc., ch. Saint-Léon, m. Pugni, dec. Despléchin and Thierry, cost. Lormier, f.p. Paris Opéra 19 Jan 1849 (Cerrito and Saint-Léon, who played the violin in it).

VIRGINIA SAMPLER, ballet 1 act, ch. Valerie Bettis, m. Smit, dec. Elson, f.p. de Basil Co., City Center, N.Y. 4 Mar 1947 (Bettis, Frank-

518

lin). This was the first ballet in the modern style to be commissioned by a classical company.

VISION OF MARGUERITE, ballet, ch. Ashton, m. Liszt, dec. Bailey, f.p. Festival B., Festival Hall, London 3 Apr 1952 (Wright, Gilpin, Briansky). The temptation of Marguerite by Faust. Liszt's Mephisto Valse had previously been used by Ashton for a ballet (see MEPHISTO VALSE).

VITALE, Adriano, b. Rome 1923. It. dancer. Became primo ballerino in Rome Opera House and now a teacher there.

VIVANDIÈRE, LA, ballet 1 act, ch. Saint-Léon, m. Pugni, dec. Grieve, f.p. Her Majesty's Th., London 23 May 1844 (Cerrito, Saint-Léon). Famous for its Redowa, danced by Cerrito and Saint-Léon.

VIVA VIVALDI!, ballet, ch. Arpino, m. Vivaldi, f.p. Robt. Joffrey Ballet, open-air Delacorte Th., Central Park, N.Y. 10 Sept 1965 (Trinette Singleton, Margo Sappington, Robt. Blankshine, Luis Fuente, Jon Cristofory).

VLAANDEREN, BALLET VAN (Ballet of Flanders), the State-supported company based in Antwerp serving the north, Flemish-speaking part of Belgium (whereas the B. de Wallonie serves the French-speaking part). It was founded in 1970 with Jeanne Brabants (q.v.) as Director and its first performance was on 10 Sept 1970 on television, *Prometheus* (ch. Leclair, m. Beethoven). The Co. replaces the long-established ballet of the Royal Flemish Opera in Antwerp. There were 40 dancers in first (1970–71) season, 48 in the second season and 54 in the third. André Leclair is the chief chor., Andrée Marlière the ballet mistress and among the soloists are M-L Wilderijckx, Kathleen Smith, Frieda Brijs, Winni Jacobs, Marleen Wouters, Aimé de Lignière, Stefan Schuller, Michel Rahn. In 1972 *The Rake's Progress* was added to the repertoire which includes *Ritus Paganus* (ch. Leclair, m. Glorieux), *Brandenburg Three* (ch. Czarny, m. Bach), *The Lesson* (ch. Flindt, m. Delerue), *Presto, Vivo et Lento* (ch. Brabants, m. Milhaud). The Co. danced at the Athens Festival 1971 and in Turkey 1972.

VLADIMIROFF, Pierre, b. St Petersburg 1893, d. N.Y. 1970. Russ. dancer. Graduated from Maryinsky Sch. 1911, and became a soloist 1915. Danced in Diaghileff's Co. 1912 and 1914. Left Russia 1918, danced the chief male rôle in Diaghileff's *Sleeping Princess* 1921. Partnered Pavlova 1928–31. When founding the Sch. of Am. B. in 1934 Balanchine invited him to be a teacher and he remained on the staff until 1969 when he retired. Mar. Doubrovska.

VLADIMIROV, Yuri, b. 1942. Graduated from Bolshoi Sch. to the Bolshoi B. 1961. Created leading rôle in *The Geologists* (1964). Varna Gold Medal 1966. Moscow 1969. Mar. Sorokina.

VLASSI, Christiane, b. Paris 1938. Fr. dancer. Studied at Paris Opéra Sch. entered Co. 1952 and became première danseuse 1960, étoile 1964. Mar. Labis.

VLASSOVA, Eleonora, b. 1931. Russ. dancer. Pupil of Bolshoi Sch., Moscow. Joined Stanislavsky-Nemirovitch-Dantchenko Th. 1949, becoming ballerina 1953. Hon. Artist R.S.F.S.R. 1957.

VODEHNAL, Andrea, b. Oak Park, Ill. 1938. Am. dancer. Pupil of Kotchetovsky and Am. Sch. of B., N.Y. Joined B. Russe de Monte Carlo 1957, becoming soloist 1961. Ballerina Am. Festival B. 1962 and ballerina of National B., Washington from 1962. Mar. Eugene Collins.

VOLÉ, lit. flown. Used to qualify a movement and indicate that it is aerial, e.g. Brisé volé.

VOLININE, Alexander, b. Moscow 1882, d. Paris 1955. Russ. dancer and teacher. Graduated from Imp. Sch., Moscow 1901, and became premier danseur at Moscow. Danced in Diaghileff's Co. 1910, and partnered Geltzer at Met. Op., N.Y., for two years. Became Genée's partner 1912–13 and Pavlova's 1914 and toured with her until 1927. Opened a school in Paris and taught the famous classical variations to the younger generation of dancers. Mounted *Giselle* for R. Danish B. in Copenhagen 1946. Author of articles *My Dance of Life* 1930.

VOLKOFF, Boris, b. Tula 1900. Russ. dancer and teacher. Studied at Moscow Sch. and toured Russia with various Cos. To Canada 1929 and opened a school in Toronto. From it he organized the Volkoff Canadian Ballet (first performing in 1939) and chor. many ballets for it.

VOLKONSKY, Prince Serge, b. 1860, d. Hot Springs, Va. 1937. Russ. director of the Imp. Theatres 1899–1901. He studied Dalcroze, and wrote a book on eurhythmics and others, on Delsarte and on the art of gesture. He encouraged Fokine in his efforts to become a choreographer and attempted reforms at the Maryinsky Sch. Following a quarrel with Kchessinska, who had great influence in St Petersburg, he had to resign his post and left Russia in 1917 after the Revolution, emigrating to America.

VOLKOVA, Vera, b. St Petersburg 1904. Russ. (now British) teacher. Studied at Sch. of Russ. Ballet (founded privately by Volinsky in 1920), under Maria Romanova (Ulanova's mother) and under Vaganova, whose style of teaching she brought to London in 1943 where she became the leading teacher of the contemporary classical style, with Margot Fonteyn among her pupils. In 1950 she went to the Scala, Milan, in charge of the ballet. In 1952 she went to Copenhagen as

Artistic Adviser to the Royal Danish Ballet. Awarded Order of Danne-brog 1956. In 1970 she was guest teacher of the Australian B.

VOLLMAR, Jocelyn, Am. dancer, b. San Francisco. Studied San Francisco Ballet Sch. Joined S. Francisco B. Co. 1943–48, Ballet Society, soloist de Cuevas Co. in Europe 1951–53. Joined Borovansky B. in Australia 1954. Since 1947 has been ballerina of San Francisco B. Retired 1972.

VOLTA, or VOLTE, or LAVOLTA. Dance, possibly evolved from the Galliard, in a rapid 3/4 time, of which a feature was the turning motion of the couples and the lifting into the air of the female dancer by her partner. It was beloved of Queen Elizabeth I.

VON AROLDINGEN, Karin, b. Thuringen 1941. Ger. dancer. Pupil of Sabineeress in Berlin. Joined Am. Festival B. 1958, Frankfurt B. 1961, N.Y. City B. 1962 becoming a principal in 1972.

VON BAHR, Margareta, b. Helsinki 1921. Finnish dancer. Studied at the ballet sch. of the National Ballet of Finland, joined the Company in 1938 becoming ballerina. Also studied in London with Nordi and Northcote. Danced as guest ballerina at Bolshoi Th., Moscow. Now retired.

VONDRAK, Paul, b. Vienna 1939. Austrian dancer. Studied under his father and at Staatsoper Sch. Entered Vienna Staatsoper Ballet 1953, became soloist 1957 and principal 1964. Mar. Gisela Cech.

VONDRUSKA, Petr, b. Hradec Kralove 1943. Czech dancer. Studied in Prague and joined Prague B. 1964 and 1967–69 the Nat. B. In 1969 joined Düsseldorf B. as principal.

VON LOGGENBURG, Dudley, b. Port Elizabeth 1945. S. African dancer. Pupil of Archbald in Rhodesia and Arts Educational Sch. Joined Festival B. 1962, soloist 1964, principal 1970.

VON ROSEN, Elsa Marianne, b. Stockholm 1927. Swed. dancer. Pupil Koslowski, Franchi, and guest pupil Royal Th., Copenhagen 1945–47. De Basil Co. 1947, at Oscar's Theatre in Stockholm, and ballerina of R. Swedish B. 1951–59. Soloist with the Swedish Ballet in London 1951. Cr. rôle of *Miss Julie* 1950. Formed the Scandinavian B. (q.v.) 1960. Mounted *La Sylphide* for B. Rambert 1960 and chor. works for R. Swedish B. Mar. Allan Fridericia, Danish ballet critic. In 1970 became director of Gothenburg B. Chor. *Don Juan* (m. Gluck) for R. Danish B. 15 Oct 1967 and mounted *Napoli* for Gothenburg B. 1971, *Swan Lake* 1972.

VON SWAINE, Alexander, b. Munich 1905. Ger. modern dancer. Pupil of Edouardova in Berlin, also of Margaret Craske in London. Worked with Reinhardt in Berlin and Salzburg and danced in his *Midsummer Night's Dream*. Soloist in Berlin and in 1936 Scala, Milan. Made tours

521

with Darja Collin and Rosalia Chladek, and in 1947 began his long partnership with Lisa Czobel. Their recitals became famous all over the world.

VOOS, Hanna, b. Houdeng-Goegnies 1916. Belgian dancer, chor. and director. Pupil of Cannes, Belowwa, Jooss at Dartington Hall 1937, de Valois in London 1953, 1957, 1958. Ballet mistress at Mons 1945–56, at Charleroi from 1956. In 1959 she founded the Ballet de Hainault based on the Palais des Beaux-Arts, Charleroi. In 1967 this became the state-supported Ballet de Wallonie (q.v.) (covering French-speaking Belgium) with herself as artistic director. Chor. many ballets, among them *Les Porcelaines de Tournay* (m. Grétry), *Bal des Ombres* (m. Bernier), *Symphoniette* (m. Bernier) etc.

VOYAGÉ, (lit. travelled) a movement across the stage during which the dancer holds a particular pose, usually an arabesque, and progresses in a series of hops or small jumps.

VSEVOLOJSKY, Ivan, b. 1835, d. 1909. Russ. diplomat, theatre director, author and painter. He was director of the Russ. Imperial Theatres 1881–1909, preceding Volkonsky, one of the greatest. He suggested the idea to Petipa that they should make *The Sleeping Beauty* ballet and he invited Tchaikovsky to write the music. Later he decided to mount *Swan Lake* again after its unsuccessful first version of 1877. He greatly influenced Petipa in his choice of subjects of ballets and in his work and his costume designs were used in 25 ballets, among them *Sleeping Beauty*, *Casse Noisette*, and *Raymonda*.

VTORUSHINA, Olga, b. Leningrad 1947. Russ. dancer. Graduated from Kirov Sch., Leningrad to Kirov B. 1966. Soloist 1969. Varna Gold Medal 1968. First danced in London 1970.

VUILLIER, Gaston, b. Gincla 1846. Fr. author of *La Danse*, a very complete history of the dance, Paris 1898, fully illustrated.

VYROUBOVA, Nina, b. Gurzof 1921. Russ. dancer. Studied under her mother, Trefilova, and Preobrajenska. Joined B. des Ch. Élysées 1944, and in 1946, cr. rôle of *La Sylphide* in their production. In 1949 was admitted directly to the Paris Opéra as an étoile. Ballerina de Cuevas B. 1957–61. Now teaches in France, at her own studio and at the Opéra, where she took the place of Madeleine Lafon (deceased). Her son, Yura Kniaseff, is soloist of the Nat. B. of Canada.

W

WACKER, STUDIO, in Paris—a building in the Rue de Douai (Place Clichy) in which, above a furniture store, there are a number of dance studios and a restaurant. Here Preobrajenska taught and also Rousanne, V. Gsovsky and Nora (Kiss). It is the centre for ballet dancers in Paris (resembling the much later Dance Centre in London), where they meet and exchange news. The large notice board at the top of the stairs displays advertisements for all the dancing jobs in France (ballet and show girls).

WADE, Kathryn, b. Bombay 1945. Scots dancer. Pupil of Madeline Watson, Royal Ballet School. Joined Royal B. 1965–70. Joined Festival B. as soloist 1970. Returned to Royal B. 1972.

WAKELYN, Virginia, b. Banff, Alberta 1941. Canadian dancer. Pupil of Gweneth Lloyd. Joined R. Winnipeg B. 1956, becoming soloist. Joined Royal B. 1961, becoming soloist 1967. In Ballet for All created *Cachucha* 1967.

WAKHEVITCH, Georges, b. Odessa 1907. Fr.–Russ. artist working in Paris who has designed many ballets, incl. *Le Jeune Homme et La Mort* 1946, *La Croqueuse de Diamants* 1950, *Le Combat* 1952, *Vilia* 1953, *Les Indes Galantes* (Le Généroux Turc scene) 1952, *Firebird* 1954, *Romeo and Juliet* (Lifar) 1955; for Vienna Staatsoper *Moor of Venice* (Hanka) 1955, *Giselle* (Hamilton) 1955, *Hotel Sacher* (Hanka) 1957 etc.

WALL, David, b. Chiswick 1946. Eng. dancer. Studied at Royal B. Sch. Joined Touring Royal B. 1963, becoming soloist 1964, a principal 1966. Mar. Alfreda Thorogood.

WALLMANN, Margarethe, b. Vienna 1904. Austrian dancer and opera producer. Studied at Vienna Staatsoper B. Sch. and under Edouardova and Wigman. Joined Wigman's Co. and in 1927 opened a branch of Wigman's School in Berlin. To America 1928 to teach Wigman style. Toured with her own group. In 1932 she turned her attention to opera and produced Gluck's *Orpheus* in Salzburg. From 1934–39 in charge of the Vienna Staatsoper B. and head of the school. She was director of the Colon B. Buenos Aires during the War and has produced operas at the Scala, Milan and at C. Garden since.

WALLONIE, BALLET DE, the Belgian company based on the Palais des Beaux Arts, Charleroi and serving the French speaking area of Belgium. It was formed in 1967 by Hanna Voos (who is the director) whose

523

Ballet de Hainault had existed in Charleroi since 1957. There was also a company attached to the Liège Opera—and these two combined to form the B. de Wallonie. It is supported by the three cities and by the state. Classical ballets are performed (about 30 performances a year) and guest artists and choreographers are invited. Among those closely associated with the company have been Boris Tonin, Jo Savino, Christian Hazera, Sonja Koeller, M.-L. Pruvot, George Skibine, Peter van Dijk, Vera Kirova. Tony Hulbert has been ballet master from 1970.

WALPURGIS NIGHT, the ballet in the last act of Gounod's *Faust*, was first chor. at the Paris Opéra by H. Justament 3 Mar 1869. The popular Russian divertissement was chor. by Lavrovski for the Bolshoi B. in 1941.

WALTER, Erich, b. Fürth 1927. Ger. dancer and chor. Pupil of Alperova. Joined Nuremberg B. 1946, Göttingen 1950, Wiesbaden 1951. In 1953 he was appointed ballet master of Wuppertal B. and by his chor. made it one of the important German Cos. In 1964 he became ballet master of the Deutsche Oper am Rhein, Düsseldorf, again making it into one of the important German ballets and in 1970 succeeded in making it independent of the operas (founding a small opera-ballet to perform in these). In all his career he has been greatly helped by the artist Heinrich Wendel (q.v.) who made his cost. and decs.

WALTZ, turning dance in 3/4 or 3/8 time, probably evolved from the Ländler which had been danced in Austrian and South German villages for centuries, and adopted into ballroom dancing about 1780. It would seem to have been first introduced on the stage in Martin Soler's opera *Una Cosa Rara*, produced at Vienna in 1776, whilst the first ballet to feature the waltz was Pierre Gardel's *La Dansomanie* in 1800.

WALTZ ACADEMY, ballet 1 act, ch. Balanchine, m. Rieti, dec. O. Smith, f.p. Ballet Th., Boston Opera House 5 Oct 1944 (Gollner, Petroff). About a ballet school.

WANDERER, THE, ballet 4 sc., ch. Ashton, m. Schubert, dec. Sutherland, f.p. S. Wells B., New Th., London 27 Jan 1941 (Fonteyn, Helpmann, May, Somes). A symbolical ballet.

WARD, Eileen, b. Camberley. Eng. dancer and teacher. Studied at Elmhurst Sch., Camberley and later at the Rambert Sch. and with Volkova. Joined International B. 1940 becoming soloist. B. Rambert 1946. Began teaching at Elmhurst Sch. 1951. To Rambert Sch. 1956 and also ballet mistress to B. Rambert. Opened own London studio 1960. Ballet mistress and teacher Festival B. 1962–63. Re-opened studio 1963 and has combined this with teaching at the Royal Ballet

Sch. since 1965. In 1970 she also became teacher to the Royal B. and from 1972 confined her teaching to the Royal B. and Royal B. Sch.

WARREN, Vincent, b. Jacksonville, Fl. 1938. Am. dancer. Pupil of Linton, Schwezoff, Tudor, Oboukhov, Chiriaeff. Joined Met. Op. B., N.Y. 1957, Les Grands B. Canadiens 1961–69 becoming soloist and principal. To Lazzini's Th. Française de la Danse 1969 Cologne 1970.

WASHINGTON, Donna-Day, b. Vancouver 1942. Canadian dancer. Pupil of Pratten, McBirney, G. Lloyd, and Royal B. Sch. Joined R. Winnipeg B. 1961, Western Th. B. 1964, becoming principal. Created many rôles for Western Th. B., notably *Beauty and the Beast* etc. Retired 1970.

WASHINGTON NATIONAL BALLET, directed by Frederic Franklin, opened its school in Washington D.C. in 1962 and gave its first performance at Lisner Auditorium 3 Jan 1963, with leading dancers Andrea Vodehnal and Eugene Collins. Appeared at Brooklyn Col., N.Y. same year and had first N.Y. season at City Center March–April 1967. Among its leading dancers have been Marilyn Burr, Ivan Nagy, and Fonteyn has been guest artist 1969 and 1970 partnered by Desmond Kelly. From 1971 Ben Stevenson has been assistant director. See DAY, Mary.

WATERMILL, ballet, ch. Robbins, m. Teiji Ito, cost. Zipprodt, dec. Robbins and Reppa, f.p. N.Y. City B., N.Y. State Th. 3 Feb 1972 (Villella, Dudlestone, Frohlich, Conde). A man reflecting on his past, present and future life. Influenced by Nō plays.

WATSON, Lynne, b. Krugersdorp 1949. S. African dancer. Pupil of Conmee and Sturman. Joined PACT B., Johannesburg 1967 becoming soloist.

WATTS, Jonathan, b. Cheyenne 1933. Am. dancer. Studied with Valentina Pereyaslavec and at N.Y. High Sch. of Performing Arts. Entered N.Y. City B. 1954, leading soloist 1959. Joined Joffrey B. 1962, Australian B. 1962–63, Cologne B. 1965–68 when he returned to America and directed the new Joffrey Junior B.

WEAVER, John, b. Shrewsbury 1673, d. there 1760. Eng. dancer, chor., and teacher. From 1702 to 1733 worked at Drury Lane and other London theatres producing ballets (called 'pantomimes'), sometimes dancing in them himself. His first pantomime-ballet was *The Tavern Bilkers* (1702). In 1717 produced a serious ballet, *The Loves of Mars and Venus* (the first ballet without words), in which Dupré and Hester Santlow were Mars and Venus. Also he wrote extensively on dancing and in 1706 published the first Eng. trans. of Feuillet's *Chorégraphie* under the title *Orchesography*, and in 1728 his *History of the Mimes and Pantomimes*.

WEB, THE, ballet, ch. Laverne Meyer, m. Webern, dec. Dewes, f.p. Western Th. B., Elmhurst School, Camberley 4 Sept 1962 (Gail Donaldson, S. Mottram). A man prevents a girl from committing suicide. Also performed by Nederlands Dans Th. 19 Feb 1963 and by Les Grands B. Canadiens.

WEBSTER, Clara Vestris, b. Bath 1821, d. London 1844. Eng. dancer. Début Th. Royal, Bath 1830, and first app. London 1836. During a performance of *The Revolt of the Harem* at Drury Lane (with Adeline Plunkett in the chief rôle) a fire occurred on the stage and Clara Webster received burns from which she died three days later. Her father Benjamin W., was a dancer, pupil of Vestris, with a ballet school in Bath.

WEBSTER, Sir David, b. Liverpool 1903, d. London 1971. Eng. director. General Administrator of the Royal Opera House 1946–1970. Educ. Holt Sch., Liverpool and Oxford. Chairman Liverpool Philharmonic Society 1940–45, Administrator of C. Garden Preliminary Committee 1944–46. Treasurer of Royal B. Sch. 1955–70. Governor of Royal Ballet from 1955. He built up the Royal Opera House to its present position as one of the greatest centres for opera and ballet in the world. Knighted 1960, Legion of Honour 1960 and created K.C.V.O. 1970. He was succeeded by John Tooley 1970.

WEDDING BOUQUET, A, ballet 1 act, ch. Ashton, m. and dec. Lord Berners, f.p. S. Wells B., S. Wells Th. 27 Apr 1937 (Honer, Fonteyn, Helpmann, Farron, de Valois). The ballet is accompanied by verses of Gertrude Stein: at first these were sung by a chorus, but later were spoken by Constant Lambert. Ninette de Valois (as Webster, the Maid) danced for the last time as a member of the Co. in this ballet, and in 1950, at the (so-called) 21st Birthday Performance of the Co., she danced the rôle again. It was revived 24 Nov 1964. Another version was given by the Ballet der Lage Landen, Holland, in 1947, ch. P. van der Sloot.

WEIDMAN, Charles, b. Nebraska 1901. Am. dancer and chor. Studied under St Denis and Shawn, and a leading figure in the Am. Modern Dance. Chor. *Fables of our Time* 1948 and many other ballets. Now teaches.

WELANDER, Karl, b. Antwerp 1943. Belgian dancer. Pupil of Brabants in Antwerp and at Royal B. Sch. Joined Harlequin B. 1959, de Cuevas B. 1960 and joined Australian B. as soloist 1962, becoming a principal 1964.

526

WELCH, Garth, b. Brisbane 1936. Australian dancer. Pupil of Danaber, V. Gsovsky, Northcote, van Praagh, Kellaway. Joined Borovansky B. 1952–58, Western Th. B. 1958–59, de Cuevas B. 1961–62. Returned to Australia 1962 as principal dancer of Australian B. on its formation. Chor. *Variations on a Theme* (1965), *Illyria* (1966), *Jeunesse* (1968), *Firebird* (1972) etc. Mar. Marilyn Jones. Partnered Fonteyn 1970.

WELLER, Dawn, b. Durban 1947. S. African dancer. Pupil of Manning Sutton, Spear. Joined NAPAC B., Durban 1964, PACT B., Johannesburg 1965, becoming soloist.

WELLS, Doreen (Marchioness of Londonderry), b. Walthamstow 1937. Eng. dancer. Studied at Bush-Davies Sch. and won R.A.D. Gold Medal 1954. Joined S. Wells Th. B. 1955 and the Royal B. 1956 becoming soloist. Promoted to ballerina of touring section of Royal Ballet in 1960. Cr. chief rôle in Nureyev's *Raymonda* (Spoleto 1964) and many others. Also dances with C. Garden section of Royal B. as ballerina.

WELLS, Kenn, b. Durban 1942. South African dancer. Pupil of D. McNair. Joined PACT B. 1964–67. Joined Western Th. B. 1968 becoming soloist (now of Scottish Th. B. and Festival B. 1972).

WENDEL, Heinrich, b. Bremen 1920. Ger. designer. His career was made with Erich Walter's (q.v.), having designed the dec. and cost. of most of his ballets at Wuppertal and Düsseldorf, contributing greatly to their success. He has also designed for many other European opera houses.

WENNERGREN, Lena, b. Karlstad 1947. Swed. dancer. Pupil of Lia Schubert, Holmgren, Bertram Ross. Joined Lia Schubert's Jazz Ballet 1965. To N.Y. 1966–67. Joined Cullberg B. 1967, becoming soloist.

WERNER, Margot, b. Salzburg 1937. Austrian dancer. Studied under Derra de Moroda and at Munich Staatsoper Sch. Joined the Staatsoper Ballet and also danced in the Edinburgh International B. in 1958. Became a soloist at Munich 1960. Retired 1973 and sings in cabaret.

WEST, Elizabeth, b. Alassio 1927, d. near the Matterhorn 1962. Eng. dancer and chor. Studied under E. Espinosa and at Bristol. Chor. for Bristol Old Vic Th. and the musical *Salad Days*. Co-founder (with Peter Darrell) and Artistic Director of the Western Theatre Ballet (q.v.) and chor. *Peter and the Wolf* and *Pulcinella* for them.

WESTERN SYMPHONY, ballet, ch. Balanchine, m. Kay, dec. Boyt, cost. Karinska, f.p. N.Y. City B., City Center, N.Y. 7 Sept 1954 (Adams, Reed, LeClerq, Eglevsky, d'Amboise). In cowboy costume.

WESTERN THEATRE BALLET, a small regional ballet company formed in Bristol, England, by Elizabeth West and Peter Darrell. Its first performance was at Dartington Hall, Devon 24 June 1957 and it danced in Italy, Holland, Belgium (Th. de la Monnaie, Brussels 1959–60) and Spain (1960). Its principal dancers were in 1960 Brenda Last, Anne Hyde, Hazel Merry, Oliver Symons, Laverne Meyer, Erling Sunde, Suzanne Musitz, Clover Roope. It received help from the Arts Council of Great Britain. In 1965 it was also the opera-ballet for the Sadler's Wells Opera. It gave its last performance at Th. Royal, Bath 15 Mar 1969 and became the Scottish Theatre Ballet (q.v.) based in Glasgow.

WEST SIDE STORY, Am. musical, libretto by Arthur Laurents, produced and chor. by Jerome Robbins, m. L. Bernstein, dec. Oliver Smith, cost. I Sharaff, f.p. Winter Garden Th., N.Y. 26 Sept 1957. A sung and danced music drama of gang warfare in New York. Its style of dancing epitomizes the American dance of that era. A film was made of it in 1960.

WHISTLER, Rex, b. London 1905, killed in action Caen 1944. Eng. artist and designer. Work includes dec. for *Rake's Progress*, *The Wise Virgins* (1940), and for International B. *Everyman* (1943).

WHITE FAWN, THE, ballet-extravaganza which followed *The Black Crook* (q.v.) at Niblo's Garden, N.Y., f.p. 20 Jan 1868. The dancers were Mlles Bonfanti, Billon, Sohiki, and a large corps de ballet. It was not a great success, but helped to familiarize the American public with ballet.

WHITE, Franklin, b. Shoreham 1924. Eng. dancer. Studied under Rambert, P. von Praagh, and Anna Northcote. Début B. Rambert 1939. Joined S. Wells B. 1942. Author of *Sadler's Wells Goes Abroad* (1951). In 1966 emigrated to Canada, staging operas and ballets in Vancouver and teaching in universities, later in America.

WHITLEY, Ann, b. Stirling 1945. Eng. dancer and choreologist. Pupil of Nesta Brooking and Royal B. Sch. Studied Benesh Notation at the Inst. of Choreology, graduated 1966 and stayed on as librarian. Joined B. Rambert 1967 as choreologist. In 1972 became director of the Co.'s Dance and Dancers Unit, small educational group for schools.

WHOOPS-DE-DOO, LES, ballet, chor. Macdonald, m. Don Gillies, dec. Korol, f.p. R. Winnipeg B., Community Centre, Flin Flon, Manitoba Oct. 1968 (Katronis, Shields, Wakelyn, Clouser). A Western story danced in classical style.

WIDERBERG, Tommy, b. Stockholm 1946. Swed. dancer. Pupil R. Swed. B. Sch. Joined R. Swed. B. 1964 becoming soloist 1967.

WIEDERSHEIM-PAUL, Annette, see AV PAUL.

WIEDMAN, Ilse, b. Buenos Aires 1933. Argentinian dancer. Pupil of Esmée Bulnes. Joined Colon Th. ballet 1955. In 1959 joined Stuttgart

B., becoming soloist 1962. Returned to Buenos Aires 1967 and appointed ballet mistress of San Martin B. 1968–73. To Hamburg 1973.

WIELAND, George, b. 1810, d. 1847. Eng. dancer and pantomimist. He danced in pantomimes and serious and comic ballets in England. He danced in all Taglioni's *Sylphides* in 1837, and in 1838 he put on a burlesque version of it with himself playing 'Taglioni'.

WIESENTHAL, Grete (b. Vienna 1885, d. there 1970), Elsa and Bertha. Austrian dancers, sisters. Grete and Elsa were trained at the Vienna State B. Sch., entered the Staatsoper B. and became coryphées. The three sisters gave recitals of waltzes and dances in the modern German style at the beginning of this century. Their distinctive style is still taught in Vienna.

WIGMAN, Mary, b. Hanover 1886, d. W. Berlin 1973. German dancer and teacher. Pupil of Dalcroze and von Laban (and his assistant in 1914). Became a solodancer, often dancing without music. Her own, non-classical, style of dancing has had great influence and she was one of the founders of the Modern European or Central European style, with its large following in U.S.A. Taught in Germany (Dresden) and Switzerland. Her first appearance in England was at a Sunshine Matinée. In 1957 she chor. *Sacre du Printemps* for the Berlin Festival.

WILDE, Patricia (White), b. Ottawa 1928. Canadian dancer. Studied Gwendolyn Osborne, School of Am. Ballet. Début Am. Concert Ballet 1943, Ballet International 1944, soloist B. Russe de Monte Carlo 1945. Cr. Hoop Dance in *Night Shadow*. Joined N.Y. City Ballet 1950, becoming a principal dancer. Resigned 1965. Principal of Harkness Sch. of B. 1965–67. In 1969 became teacher of Geneva Sch. of B. Teacher of Am. Ballet Th. from 1969.

WILDERIJCKX, Marie-Louise, b. Antwerp 1941. Belgian dancer. Pupil of Van de Beele, J. Brabants, Northcote, and Dudinskaya (in Leningrad). Joined Ghent B. 1957, soloist B. of R. Flemish Opera to 1968, Graz B. 1968–70. B. Van Vlaanderen 1970 as principal.

WILLARD, Helen, b. Chicago 1905. Am. museum curator. Educ. Univ. of Wisconsin. After working in the Fogg Museum, Harvard Univ. and in the Print Dept. of Museum of Fine Art, Boston, she became curator of the Harvard Theatre Collection 1960–70.

WILLIAMS, Marilyn, b. Wellington, N.Z. 1946. N.Z. dancer. Pupil of Daniels and Royal B. Sch. and joined B. Rambert 1965.

WILLIAMS, Peter, b. Burton Joyce, Notts 1914. Eng. writer on ballet and designer. Assistant editor of *Ballet* 1949–50. Editor of *Dance and Dancers* from its inception in 1950. Ballet critic of *Daily Mail* 1950–53.

Designed Taras's *Designs with Strings* 1948 (Metropolitan B.) and the setting for *Selina* (1948, also suggesting the story). Member of Advisory Panel (music and ballet) of Arts Council, and of the Theatre Advisory Panel of the British Council. Awarded O.B.E. 1971.

WILLIAMS, Stanley, b. Chappel, England 1925. Danish dancer. Studied at Royal Th. Sch., Copenhagen, becoming solodancer 1949, and since 1950 teacher at the school. Left R. Danish B. 1963. Guest artist and ballet master of Kirsta's Ballet Comique, London 1954. Guest teacher of N.Y. City B. 1960–61, 1961–62 and from 1964 has been a teacher at the Sch. of Am. B., N.Y.

WILLIS, Mary, b. Wimbledon 1945. Eng. dancer. Pupil of Letty Little-wood and Arts Educational Sch. Début as Clara in Festival B. *Casse Noisette* 1959. Danced in musicals and joined B. Rambert 1964. Mar. Peter Curtis. Retired 1971.

WILSON, G. B. L., b. Kew Gardens, Surrey. Eng. engineer, lexico-grapher, writer on and photographer of the ballet and Deputy Keeper of the Department of Civil and Mechanical Engineering at the Science Museum, London. Educated at St Paul's Sch. and Corpus Christi Col., Cambridge. Chartered Engineer, Fellow of the Institution of Gas Engineers. Member of Grand Council of Royal Academy of Dancing. Founder and chairman of the Association of Ballet Clubs since 1947, formerly vice-chairman of the R.A.D. Production Club (from 1946). Hon. Curator of the British Theatre Museum from its inception in 1957. Assistant editor of *The Ballet Annual* (1946–63). Member of Council of Newcomen Society. Photographer of the ballet since 1941. Author of *Off Stage* monthly feature of *The Dancing Times* since its inception in 1957. Contributor to *Encyclopaedia Britannica, Enciclo-pedia dello Spettacolo*, the U.N.E.S.C.O *History of the Cultural and Scientific Development of Mankind*. Author of *Dictionary of Ballet* (Penguin Press 1957), revised edition in Italian (1960), rewritten and published by Cassell (1961), and a new enlarged edition by A. & C. Black (1974). London correspondent of Am. *Dance News*, ballet critic of *Jewish Chronicle* from 1965, contributor on ballet to the *Annual Register of World Events* from 1965. Adviser on ballet careers to the Royal Ballet School from 1967 and librarian from 1971.

WILSON, Sallie, b. Fort Worth 1932. Am. dancer. Pupil of Craske, Tudor, Caton. Joined Ballet Th. 1949, Met. Op. B. 1950–55, returned to Ballet Th. 1955 becoming soloist 1957 and ballerina 1961. Between 1958 and 1960 she was a member of N.Y. City B. Since 1966 has inherited Nora Kaye's rôles in *Pillar of Fire* and *Fall River Legend*.

WILSON, Thomas, Eng. dancing master and teacher, who was Dancing Master of the King's Th., London, and published between 1800 and

1852 a number of books on dancing (country, national, ballroom, etc.).

WINNIPEG BALLET, ROYAL, is Canada's first ballet company and was an offshoot of the school and ballet club established in Winnipeg in 1938 by Gweneth Lloyd and Betty Farrally. Its first performance was in 1939. It became a professional company in 1949, danced a Command Performance before Princess Elizabeth on 16 Oct 1951 and was granted the title Royal Winnipeg Ballet in 1953 after performing before Queen Elizabeth II (hitherto it had been the Winnipeg B.). In 1954 a fire destroyed all its property and it did not perform again until 1956. It is the first British ballet to earn the title 'Royal'. In 1956 Ruthanna Boris was artistic director, until 1959. She was succeeded by B. Harkarvy 1959 for one season. Arnold Spohr was appointed Director in 1958 on G. Lloyd's resignation. Since 1957 the Co. receives a grant from the Canada Council. Brian Macdonald was appointed choreographer 1964–67. The Co. first danced in America (Boston) in 1964 and in England in 1965 (Commonwealth Arts Festival). It dances the classics and has its own repertoire of created ballets (some with a Canadian setting), among them *Shadow on the Prairie, Romance, Concerto* (all chor. G. Lloyd), *Les Whoops-de-Doo, Aimez-vous Bach?, Rose Latuluppe* (all chor. Macdonald—the last a full-length Canadian ballet), *The Rehearsal* and *Bitter Weird* (both chor. de Mille) etc. Among the leading dancers have been Arnold Spohr, Sonia Taverner, Carlu Carter, Marina Katronis, Richard Rutherford, Fredric Strobel, James Clouser, Bill McGrath, Eva von Gencsy, Eric Hyrst, Marylin Young, David Shields, Sheila Mackinnon, Bill Martin-Viscount. In recent years it has made some very big tours (in 1968 visited Paris and toured Russia and Czechoslovakia).

WINQVIST, Nisse, b. Gothenburg 1936. Swed. dancer. Pupil of Royal B. Sch., Bartholin, Skeaping, Schubert, Gardemeister. Joined Gothenburg B. 1954, Tivoli Th., Copenhagen 1957–59, R. Swed. B. 1959, becoming soloist 1964.

WINTER NIGHT, ballet, ch. Gore, m. Rachmaninoff (2nd piano concerto), dec. Rowell, f.p. B. Rambert, Princess Th., Melbourne 19 Nov 1948 (Gilmour, Hinton, Gore). Dramatic ballet of a man who discards his old love for a new.

WITCH BOY, THE, ballet, ch. Jack Carter, m. Salzedo, dec. McDowell, f.p. Ballet der Lage Landen, Amsterdam 24 May 1956 (Norman McDowell, Angela Bayley, Jack Carter). Taken into repertoire of Festival Ballet, Manchester 27 Nov 1957 (Gilpin, Landa, Sudell) and many other companies. The American Ballad of Barbara Allen.

WOIZIKOVSKY, Leon, b. Warsaw 1899. Polish dancer and ballet-master.

531

Member of Diaghileff's Co. 1915–29 and of de Basil's. In 1935–37 he had his own Co., Les Ballets de Leon Woizikovsky, in Paris. Returned to Warsaw 1937 as ballet master and was in Poland throughout the War. He was brought out by Dr Braunsweg to mount *Petrouchka* for Festival B. 1958 and *Schéhérazade* 1960 for Festival B. and has remained in the West ever since. Ballet master for Massine's Balleto Europeo 1959 and Festival B. 1961. Worked in Cologne with the Cologne B. and became Professor of Dancing at Bonn University. From 1968 has also been travelling to Antwerp teaching for the Royal Flemish B. and, from 1970, the Ballet van Vlaanderen, also mounting Fokine ballets. As a dancer he was famous in character rôles, notably as the Polovtsian Chief in *Prince Igor* and the Pickpocket in *Concurrence*.

WOOD, Michael, b. Sunderland 1912. Educ. Rugby and Heidelberg Univ. After war service in Grenadier Guards 1940–45, joined Royal Opera House, Covent Garden, as Public Relations Officer 1946–58. In 1958 appointed General Manager of Royal Ballet and in 1966 succeeded Arnold Haskell as Director of the Royal Ballet School.

WOOD, Roger, b. Madras 1920. Eng. action-photographer of the ballet, from 1944. Published many books of photographs, notably *Katherine Dunham, Her Singers, Dancers, and Musicians* (with Buckle) (1949), *Sadler's Wells Ballet at Royal Opera House, The New York City Ballet in Action*, etc. Now works principally as a photographer of archaeology.

WOODEN PRINCE, THE, ballet, ch. Otto Zöbisch and Ede Brada, m. Bartok, dec. Count Bánffy, f.p. Opera House, Budapest 12 May 1917 (Anna Pallai, Mariska Keresztes). A fairy tale. In 1939 Harangozó made a new version, with himself as the Prince. It has been choreographed by many others, incl. L. Seregi (Budapest 1970).

WOOLLIAMS, Anne, b. Folkestone 1926. Eng. dancer and teacher. Pupil of Judith Espinosa, Volkova. Joined Kyasht B. 1943, the Russian Opera B., St James's B. 1948, B. Jooss 1958–63. Teacher for St James's B. 1948, and Allegro Sch. of B., Chicago. Appointed chief classical teacher at Jooss's Folkwangschule, Essen 1948. From 1963 ballet mistress Stuttgart. Wrote *Ballettsaal* 1973.

WORKING LEG, the leg executing a given movement whilst the weight of the body is on the supporting leg.

WORTH, Faith, b. Scarborough 1938. Eng. dancer and choreographic notator. Pupil of Brownlie, Tweedy, Royal B. Sch. Studied Benesh Notation at Institute of Choreology and joined Royal B. 1960 as notator. Mounted ballets in Copenhagen, Budapest, Stuttgart etc. Chor. several ballets.

WOUTERS, Marleen, b. Antwerp 1944. Belgian dancer. Studied with

Jeanne Brabants 1955–60, Royal B. Sch. 1959–60, Grant Strate 1967. Entered Royal Flemish B., Antwerp 1961, becoming soloist 1965 and a principal of B. Van Vlaanderen from 1971.

WRIGHT, Belinda, b. Southport 1929. Eng. dancer. Studied Rambert School. Joined B. Rambert 1945, toured Australia with them. Joined Ballets de Paris 1951, Festival B. 1951, becoming one of their ballerinas. Left in 1954 and joined de Cuevas Co., but returned to Festival B. 1955. Danced with Gilpin in S. Africa 1960. Now dances as guest artist, partnered by her husband Yelko Yureska, making a world tour in 1967.

WRIGHT, Peter, b. London 1926. Eng. dancer and chor. Pupil of Jooss, Volkova, van Praagh. Joined B. Jooss 1945–46, Metropolitan B. 1947, St James's B. 1948, soloist S. Wells Th. B. 1949–51, returned to B. Jooss 1951–52. Rejoined S. Wells Th. B. 1952 becoming assistant ballet master 1955. Taught at Royal B. Sch. 1957–59. Assistant dance director of van Praagh's Edinburgh International B. 1958. To Stuttgart B. as assistant ballet master and has mounted his versions of *Giselle*, there 1966, in Cologne and for Touring Royal B. Mounted *Sleeping Beauty* in Cologne 1967 and for Royal B. 1968. Chor. *A Blue Rose* for Royal B. 1957, *Musical Chairs* for Western Th. B. 1959, *Namouna* for Stuttgart 1967 etc. Has worked much in television for B.B.C. Returned to Royal Ballet 1970 as Associate to the Director. Mar. Sonya Hana.

WRIGHT, Rebecca, b. Springfield, Ohio 1947. Am. dancer. Pupil of Fasting, Schwarz and became apprentice of Joffrey B. 1966. She joined the Co. the same year, dancing solo rôles from 1969.

WRIGHT HEPBURN GALLERY, the first gallery to be devoted solely to the theatre arts, was opened in London 14 Sept 1966. Its proprietors were Peter Wright and David Hepburn and it exhibited and sold the works of the designers of ballets, plays and operas. It opened a branch in New York. Finished in 1971.

WÜHRER, Ully, b. Vienna 1940. Austrian dancer. Pupil of Vienna Staatsoper Sch., Royal B. Sch., Pereyaslavec. Joined Vienna Staatsoper B. 1955 becoming soloist 1966 and creating rôle of Odile-Odette in Nureyev's *Swan Lake* 1964.

X

XIMENEZ, Roberto. Mexican dancer who took the place of José Greco in the Pilar Lopez Co. 1948–55. Formed, with Vargas, his own Co. in 1954, the Ximenez-Vargas Ballet Español, performing Mexican and S. American dances.

Y

YAKOBSON, Leonid, see JACOBSON.

YAVZINSKY, Jean, b. 1892. Russ. dancer. Graduated from Moscow Sch. 1910, and member of Diaghileff's and de Basil's Cos. Régisseur of B. Russe de Monte Carlo 1938–44 and taught in N.Y. until he retired in 1960.

YERMOLAYEFF, Alexei N., b. 1910. Russ. dancer and chor. Graduated from Leningrad Sch. 1926 and became member of Maryinsky Co. Transferred to Bolshoi Th., Moscow 1930 where he was a principal dancer. In 1939 chor. *The Nightingale* (m. Kroshner) in Odessa and later in Minsk. Stalin Prize 1946, 1947, 1950. People's Artist R.S.F.S.R. Retired from stage 1959 and in 1961 began teaching the boys' graduate class at the Bolshoi Sch.

YEVDOKIMOV, Gleb, b. Moscow 1923. Russ. dancer. Studied at Bolshoi Sch., Moscow, graduated 1941 and became soloist in 1944. Danced in London 1956 and 1960 and New York 1959. Retired 1962 and teaches at the Bolshoi Sch.

YMHA (Young Men's and Young Women's Hebrew Association), a social centre and theatre in N.Y., founded in 1937, where many soloists and groups and lecturers on the dance appear throughout the year.

YOUNG, Anita, b. London 1950. Eng. dancer. Pupil of Royal B. Sch. Joined Royal B. 1968.

YOUNG, Marilyn, b. Winnipeg 1936. Canadian dancer. Studied at Canad. Sch. of B. in Winnipeg, Joffrey and Sch. of Am. B. Début in R. Winnipeg B. 1951 in *Nutcracker* pas de deux, joined the Co. 1952 becoming a principal.

YOUNG BALLET (see MOISEYEV, Igor).

YOUSKEVITCH, Igor, b. Moscow 1912. Russ. dancer (Am. since 1944). Studied in Belgrade and in Paris under Preobrajenska. Member of Nijinska's Co. 1934, Woizikovski's 1935, B. Russe de Monte Carlo 1938–44 and 1956–57 and chief dancer in Ballet Th. from 1946 Danced with Alonso's Co. 1948, partnering her in *Giselle* etc. Now teaching in his own school. A great *danseur noble*, he was in his youth, in Belgrade, a member of the Yugoslav athletic group Sokol and took part in the Olympic Games.

YOUTH, ballet 4 acts, ch. Fenster, m. Chulaki, dec. Bruni, f.p. Maly Th., Leningrad 9 Dec 1949 (S. Sheina, Shishkin, Tulubiev, Isayeva).

An important work for it was the first really successful ballet about the Revolution and the civil war which followed.

YUGEN, ballet, ch. Helpmann, m. Toyama, dec. Heeley, f.p. Australian B., Her Majesty's Th., Adelaide 18 Feb 1965 (Gorham, Welch). In the style of a Nō play.

YUGOSLAVIA, BALLET IN. There are ten ballet troupes attached to opera houses, of which the most important are at Belgrade and at Zagreb. Others are Ljubljana, Novi Sad, Sarajevo Split, Maribor and Skoplje. The Belgrade Ballet started in 1921 with six dancers, one of whom, Natalia Boscovic, later became prima ballerina in Belgrade and then one of Pavlova's soloists. The ballet sch. was founded in 1922 and headed by Elena Poliakova (of Petrograd) and Claudia Issachenko. In 1924 the prima ballerina was Nina Kirsanova, formerly of Moscow. The first Yugoslav national ballet, *The Gingerbread Heart* (m. Baranovic) 1927 was chor. by Margaret Froman (q.v.) who was prima ballerina until 1930. In the 1930s the principal dancers were Ana Roje (q.v.) and Oskar Harmos, who later opened a school in Split. Kniaseff was in charge of the ballet 1934–36. The company was revived in 1945 and in 1947 the most popular ballet in the repertoire *The Legend of Ochrid* (q.v.) was chor. by Froman (m. Hristich), with Ruth Parnel as prima ballerina. The company danced at the Edinburgh Festival 1951, in Florence 1955 and Paris 1957. The Zagreb Ballet danced in London in 1955, with a repertoire and dancers similar to those of Belgrade (prima ballerina, Sonia Kastl). A feature of Yugoslav ballet is that nearly all its best dancers leave to dance elsewhere, but thereby bringing great credit to their country and their teachers. Among the well-known Yugoslav dancers are the Mlakars, Nenad Lhotka, Iovanka Biegovitch, Duska Sifnios, Miskovitch, Sulich, Markovic, Parlic, Trninic, Vera Kostic, Stevan Grebel, Mia Slavenska, Sparemblek.

YULE, Carole, b. Salisbury, Rhodesia 1940. Rhodesian dancer. Pupil of Joan Turner, Arts Educational Sch., Royal B. Sch. Joined Festival B. 1960, becoming soloist.

YURESHA, Yelko, b. Zagreb 1937. Trained by Ana Roje. Became soloist of Split Ballet 1958. Studied with Madame Legat in England and joined Festival Ballet as soloist 1960. Joined Royal B. 1962 and left to partner his wife, Belinda Wright, as guest artists.

YURIKO, b. San Jose, Calif. 1920. Am. modern dancer. Educ. in Japan, and toured with Konami Ishii Dance Co. 1930–37. Joined Martha Graham Co. 1944 and became a principal dancer, creating many important rôles in her ballets (Moon in *Canticle for Innocent Comedians*, Eve in *Embattled Garden*, Iphigenia in *Clytemnestra* etc.). Danced

Eliza in first production of Robbins's *The Small House of Uncle Thomas* in *The King and I* (1951–54) etc. Teaches at the Graham School and elsewhere.

Z

ZAKHALINSKY, Alexei, b. Moscow 1941. Russ. dancer. Pupil of Messerer, Tarasov. Entered Bolshoi B. 1960, becoming soloist. Mar. Adirkhaeva.

ZAKHAROFF, Rostislav V., b. Astrakhan 1907. Russ. chor. Graduated Leningrad B. Sch. 1925, and from Theatrical Technicum 1932. Appointed chor. of Maryinsky Th. 1932 and of Bolshoi Th., Moscow 1936. Chor. *Fountain of Bakhchisarai* (1934), *Prisoner of the Caucasus* (Moscow 1938), *Cinderella* (1945), *The Peasant Lady* (m. Asafiev, 1946), *The Bronze Horseman* (1949), *The Red Poppy* (new, Leningrad, 1949), *Under Italian Skies* (1952). Professor of Choreography at Lunacharski Institute of Theatrical Art, Moscow 1942–46. Stalin Prize 1942, 1945. People's Artist R.S.F.S.R. Author of *The Art of the Choreographer* (Moscow 1954). Teacher of the Choreographers' Faculty of the State Theatre Institute (GITIS), Moscow from 1946, professor from 1958.

ZAMBELLI, Carlotta, b. Milan 1875, d. there 1968. It. dancer and teacher. Studied at Milan Conservatoire, joined Paris Opéra 1894, becoming prima ballerina after Rosita Mauri retired. Cr. chief rôle in *Cydalise et le Chèvre Pied*. On retirement became senior teacher at the Opéra Sch. 1927. Awarded Legion of Honour 1956. Among her pupils were Darsonval, Chauviré, Dynalix, Jeanmaire, Vaussard, Motte and Vlassi.

ZAMBRA, a women's flamenco dance of Moorish origin.

ZANFRETTA, Francesca, b. Mantua 1862, d. London 1952. It. dancer and famous mime. Studied mime under Louis Rouffe of Marseilles. Prima ballerina of Deutsches Th. Prague 1878. First danced in England (C. Garden) 1880. Danced for many years at the Empire Th., London, in the Empire B. from 1895, and on retirement taught many of the great dancers of the younger generation. Ursula Moreton was sent to her to learn her It. mime, to transmit it to the S. Wells (Royal) B. and to the S. Wells (Royal) Sch.

ZANUZZI, Santina—see AUBRI.

ZAPATEADO, a flamenco dance in which stamping with the heels is predominant.

ZAPPOLINI, Walter, b. Florence 1930. It. dancer. Studied at Rome

Opera House Sch. 1939–46. Appointed primo ballerino Rome Opera 1947.

ZARASPE, Hector, b. Tucumán 1931. Argentinian dancer and teacher. Studied folk dance and later classical ballet under Esmée Bulnes in Buenos Aires. From 1949 to 1952 danced in the Teatro Colon B. and began teaching there in 1951. To Spain in 1954 and worked as teacher with the Cos. of Mariemma and Antonio. To New York in 1964 and taught at the Joffrey Sch. (Am. B. Center). Since then he has taught for the Vienna Staatsoper B. in 1966, the Dutch Nat. B. 1969–70, and the Cologne Summer Academy. In 1971 became director of Teatro Municipal B. in Rio de Janeiro, Brazil. Returned to N.Y. 1973.

ZÉPHIRE ET FLORE, ballet 1 act, ch. Massine, m. Dukelsky (Vernon Dukes), dec. Braque, f.p. Diaghileff's Co., Monte Carlo 28 Apr 1925 (Nikitina, Dolin, Lifar). This was Lifar's début as a soloist. See FLORE ET ZÉPHIRE, on which it was based.

ZHDANOV, Yuri, b. Moscow 1925. Russ. dancer. Graduated from Bolshoi Sch. 1944, later becoming a principal. From 1951 he became Ulanova's partner, in *Giselle, Romeo and Juliet, The Red Poppy* etc. Honoured Artist R.S.F.S.R. In 1972 he became director of Moiseyev's Classical Ballet Co.

ZIGGURAT, ballet, ch. Tetley, m. Stockhausen, dec. N. Baylis, f.p. B. Rambert, Jeannetta Cochrane Th., London 20 Nov 1967 (Chesworth, Curtis, Smith, Taylor, Sandra Craig). The overthrow of a god enthroned in a temple.

ZIMMERL, Christl, b. Vienna 1939. Austrian dancer. Studied at Vienna Staatsoper Sch. under Fränzl, Hanka and Hamilton and the Royal Ballet Sch., London. Entered Vienna Staatsoper Ballet 1953, became soloist 1955 and ballerina in 1957. Mar. Dr G. Brunner, ballet critic. Danced in London, Sunshine Matinée 2 July 1966.

ZIMMERMANN, Bernd Alois, b. Bliesheim, Cologne 1918, d. there 1970. German composer. Studied in the universities of Cologne, Berlin and Bonn. From 1957 taught music in the Cologne Musikhochschule becoming Professor in 1961. His scores have been much used in German ballet, e.g. *Alagoana* (ch. Bortoluzzi, Essen 1955 and Carter, Wuppertal 1967), *Kontraste* (ch. Roleff, Bielefeld 1954), *Befragung* (ch. Cranko, Stuttgart 1967), *Roi Ubu* (ch. Walter, Düsseldorf 1968), etc.

ZLOCHA, Erika, b. Vienna 1939. Austrian dancer. Studied under Fränzl and at Staatsoper Sch., Vienna. Entered Vienna Staatsoper Ballet in 1953 and became soloist 1957.

ZOLAN, Miro, b. Prague 1926. Czech dancer. Studied in Paris under

537

Preobrajenska and Egorova, and in London from 1946 under Volkova. Joined International B. 1947 (dancing under name of Zloch). To Australia with B. Rambert 1948. Joined Borovansky B. 1951–52 and returned to England 1953 as soloist of S. Wells Th. B. Ballet master of R. Winnipeg B. 1957–59. In 1960 to organize ballet in Teheran, with his wife Sandra Vane. Returned to London to become ballet master of Royal Opera B. at C. Garden. In 1970 to Mexican Nat. B. Staged *Cinderella* in Tokyo 1972.

ZOMOSA, Maximiliano, b. Santiago 1937, d. N.Y. 1969. Chilean dancer. Pupil of Hans Zullig. Joined Chilean Nat. B. 1960, Joffrey B. 1966. Created the chief male rôle in *Astarte* 1967.

ZORINA, Vera (Eva Birgitta Hartwig), b. Berlin 1917. German dancer (Am. since 1943). Studied under Edouardova, Gsovsky, Rambert and Legat. Début in Reinhardt's *Midsummer Night's Dream*. Soloist in de Basil's Co. 1934 and became a film-dancer in 1936, appearing in *On Your Toes*, *Goldwyn Follies*, etc. Formerly married to Balanchine. In 1967 staged *Cavalleria Rusticana* and *Pagliacci* at Met. Op., N.Y.

ZORITCH, George, b. Moscow 1919. Am. dancer. Studied Preobrajenska, Vilzak, Oboukhoff, Nijinska. Joined Ida Rubinstein Co. 1933, soloist de Basil Co. 1935–37, B. Russe de Monte Carlo 1938, then musicals. Soloist de Cuevas Co. 1951–54 and again in 1956. Rejoined B. Russe de Monte Carlo 1957. Opened school in Hollywood 1964 and teaches.

ZORN, Friedrich Albert, Ger. dancer and teacher of whom very little is known except that he was a teacher at the Richelieu Gymnasium in Odessa. In 1887 he published his *Grammatik der Tanzkunst* a textbook on dancing. To describe the steps he uses his own notation (very like Saint-Léon's method) and explains it. The book contains a few dances notated in this way, including a Cachucha (q.v.) which may have been (though not certain) that danced by Elssler.

ZUBKOVSKAYA, Inna, b. 1923. Russ. dancer. Joined Bolshoi B. 1941 but transferred to Kirov B., Leningrad same year, becoming a soloist. Stalin Prize and People's Artist R.S.F.S.R. 1957.

ZUCCHI, Virginia, b. Parma 1847, d. Monte Carlo 1930. It. ballerina. Studied under Blasis and became leading dancer in Padua, later dancing all over Europe. To St Petersburg 1885, dancing in an operetta, *Voyage dans le Lune*, at a *café-concert*, and later in *Brahma*, a ballet with m. Pugni. Here she attracted great attention and was commanded to dance before the Emperor. She was then engaged for the Imp. Theatres and made her début the same year in *La Fille du Pharaon* at the Bolshoi Th. She was altogether a remarkable dancer, dancing in an effortless manner with a brilliant Italian technique and powerful mime, which was a revelation to the Russian Schools, greatly influencing their subsequent teaching. Her genius revived interest in ballet in the capital at a time when it was waning. In taking curtain calls, instead of a simple curtsey, she acknowledged the applause with warm gestures to the audience, and she cut down the length of the Russian tutu, in the Italian fashion, gaining greater freedom for her legs. Possibly the greatest contribution to the ballet of the 'divine Virginia', however, was the enthusiasm she aroused in the young Benois (who never met her), sealing his fate as a lover and creator of ballet, with its far-reaching effects on Diaghileff and his circle. After leaving Russia in 1887 she danced in the European capitals, and finally opened a school in Monte Carlo, where she taught until her death.

ZULLIG, Hans, b. Rorschach, Switzerland 1914. Swiss dancer and chor. Studied under Jooss at Essen and Dartington, becoming member of the Co. and later a principal dancer. In 1948 joined S. Wells Th. B. as soloist. Rejoined Jooss in Essen 1950. To Chile 1956–61 as teacher. Chor. *Le Bosquet* for B. Jooss 1945. Succeeded Jooss as principal of the Folkwang Sch., Essen 1968.

ZUMBO, Francesca, b. Paris 1944. Fr. dancer. Pupil of Mona Pavia and Conservatoire Nat. de Paris. Joined de Cuevas B. 1961–62. Entered Paris Opéra Sch. 1962 and the Co. 1963 becoming première danseuse 1969. Won Gold Medal Moscow Internation Competition 1969 and danced as guest artist of Bolshoi B. Guest ballerina R. Winnipeg B. 1972.

ZVEREFF, Nicholas, b. Moscow c. 1897, d. St Raphael 1965. Russ. dancer and teacher. Joined Diaghileff's Co. 1912, becoming a soloist and remaining until 1926. From 1926 to 1936 toured in various companies with Nemchinova (whom he married), Dolin and Massine. In 1936 helped to reorganize the Ballets de Monte Carlo, dancing character rôles. Remained as ballet master until 1945 and worked with Lifar in mounting ballets at Scala, Milan. Then revived some Fokine ballets for the Paris Opéra—*Petrouchka* in 1948, *Prince Igor* in 1949, *Schéhérazade* in 1951 and *Spectre de la Rose* in 1954. Taught in Paris, Belgium and Switzerland, and ballet master Colon Th., Buenos Aires 1957–60.

ZVIAGINA, Suzanna, b. Moscow 1908. Russ. dancer. Studied at Bolshoi Sch., Moscow under E. Gerdt and P. Gusev. Graduated 1927 and entered Bolshoi Ballet, becoming a soloist 1937. A character dancer. Editor of the Bolshoi Ballet's journal *Soviet Artists*. Honoured Artist of the U.S.S.R. Danced in London 1956 and 1960 and New York 1959.